THE LIFE AND TIMES OF

MALCOLM McLAREN

THE LIFE AND TIMES OF

MALCOLM McLAREN

The Biography

PAUL GORMAN

Malcolm McLaren aged three, 1949. Malcolm McLaren Estate.

CONSTABLE

CONSTABLE

First published in Great Britain in 2020 by Constable

1 3 5 7 9 10 8 6 4 2

A CIP catalogue record for this book
is available from the British Library.

ISBN: 978-1-47212-108-0 (hardback)
ISBN: 978-1-47212-109-7 (trade paperback)

Typeset in Stempel Garamond by Hewer Text UK Ltd, Edinburgh
Printed and bound in Great Britain by Clays Ltd, Elcograf S.p.A.

Papers used by Constable are from well-managed
forests and other responsible sources.

Constable
An imprint of
Little, Brown Book Group
Carmelite House
50 Victoria Embankment
London EC4Y 0DZ

An Hachette UK Company
www.hachette.co.uk

www.littlebrown.co.uk

Endpapers: contact sheet of Malcolm McLaren and Vivienne
Westwood in various locations in London's West End, 31 March
1979. Photography by Barry Plummer. Stickers for Mayor of London
campaign, 2000. Designed by Scott King with Matthew Worley.

This book is dedicated to my love Caz Facey.

Contents

Contents

Foreword

It should be said right at the outset that I barely knew the man. Certainly not as well as the dozens of other voices cited in this riveting biography, nor for anywhere near as long: perhaps a half-a-dozen meetings in the legendary flesh and the same number of phone conversations mark the narrow boundaries of my relationship with the remarkable Malcolm McLaren. Then again, even the briefest of encounters with a genuinely phosphorescent being tends to burn their shape indelibly onto the retina, so that they're still there decades later if you shut your eyes.

With his fuse-wire physique and all that bubbling ginger foam erupting from his scalp, it didn't seem as if there was much more to him than essence; as if his whole personality had been distilled from an inflammable creative drive. It wasn't easy to imagine him boiling an egg without it being part of some ingenious agenda, such was the extraordinary focus that he brought to everything, the sense that every action was a project to which he'd commit his last subversive molecule. He was, I thought, a figure made entirely out of counterculture, someone who had flared inevitably into being from his tinder times, a petrol spirit without preamble or precedent.

While the above is obviously true, it cannot be more than a hasty dayglo cartoon of the man I met, viewed in a possibly infatuated lens and through the dazzle of his own mythology. There had to be a mortal being and a human story somewhere under all the zeitgeist, and Paul Gorman's thorough excavations here have finally exposed that narrative, along with the pre-torn and slogan-stencilled fabric of the century it mostly happened in.

And what a century, and what a narrative, both scarcely credible from our contemporary perspective and yet both inarguably real, fabulous glimpses of a world that's gone. The fertile post-war topsoil that Malcolm McLaren grew from, bombed and therefore rich in nitrates, was a medium of forgotten colours and Byzantine intricacy that to modern eyes cannot help but appear as an outrageous fiction, unbelievable and Gormenghastly. There's the anti-matter impresario's infancy and his redacted dad, his wayward mum out sugar-babying with Charlie Clore, his monstrous and sociopathic gran patiently sharpening the child into a poison dart to fling at the society she hated. There's the style explosion of McLaren's teenage years, safaris in the febrile city dark, Mandy Rice-Davies mopping down the bar and at the all-night café David Litvinoff, appraising culture with a knowing Chelsea smile. There's the young art student's discovery of psychogeography, transfusing London's streets and their intoxicating ghosts – Peter the painter, Blake in a red bonnet watching Newgate burn, Diana Dors – directly into his already-effervescing frontal lobe. This is his natal dirt, the neon nutrients that made him what he was, brandied in history and on fire with the future.

The trajectory charted here, from the flag-burning sixties radical in Grosvenor Square to the punk godfather and nemesis of hippies in the seventies, belies our neat perception of one movement born from only snarling opposition to the other, as if what emerged from that King's Road boutique could be reduced to no more than John Lydon's 'I Hate Pink Floyd' T-shirt. As if that incendiary period was nothing but a spat between antipathetic hairstyles. In Paul Gorman's reading of events we see instead a long, unbroken continuity of artistic dissent, the foetal punk scene fed from a placenta of Syd Barrett, Hawkwind and the *Oz* trials; swaddled in the *International Times* or the anarcho-psychedelic wraps of a majestic Jamie Reid. Just as Marxism has been called capitalism's most sophisticated method of talking about itself, so too can punk be seen as the late-sixties underground subjected to a vicious, necessary self-critique in order to transform itself to something new. One might think that there's only ever been a single counterculture, which, once in a while, changes its shoes.

When I met Malcolm he was at a juncture of his life and art that, given hindsight and this current volume, was most probably a haunted crossroads. His immaculate delinquent project of almost ten years before, the blackmail-lettered albatross that he knew would be dangling from the obituaries, had just gone down in litigation, flames and seven-figure settlements. Meanwhile, his second-act career in media and film remained in its uncertain early stages. Still, he gleefully rehearsed his new panto-mime role as Baron Hardup for the tabloid snappers with the same obvi-ous relish that had marked his previous performance as Aladdin's evil uncle – a persona then on prominent display in Alex Cox's *Sid and Nancy*. This Mephistophelian-if-not-actually-Satanic posture was at that point a default perception of McLaren, and from my perspective hard to square with the immensely likeable and charming man that I shook hands with. While I was, and still remain, in no position to refute the allegations made by those who knew him better and at earlier stages of his dragonfly development, my own experience was of someone else entirely. This discrepancy, between the warm and funny contra-intellectual and the moustache-twirling serial villain, was a disconnect that I'd return to now and then over the years, unresolved until the insights in this possibly definitive biography.

The late science-fiction revolutionary Harlan Ellison once floated the idea of 'one word' people; individuals whose behaviour cannot be under-stood until you're in possession of the single word or phrase that is the key to them. While Ellison enlisted both 'hooker' and 'junkie' as his judgemental examples, with relation to Malcolm McLaren there is a more sympathetic word suggested in the early chapters of *The Life & Times . . .*, that word being 'autistic'. Though this diagnosis will forever be unprov-able, it would explain a number of the man's apparent contradictions, not least the divide between his seeming lack of empathy and my impression of somebody who was by no means a stranger to compassion. If consid-ered in this light, McLaren's wilful lifelong drive towards outsider status is immediately understandable as an attempt to formalise and outwardly perform the alienation that was there inside. A place on the autism spec-trum can be seen as possibly resulting from – or else exacerbated by – the gothic Freudian nightmare of his childhood, as well as perhaps his only means of psychologically surviving that experience. Such an uncoupling of the intellect from the emotional responses is potentially also a point of origin for the ferocious drive and focus that fuelled all of his endeavours, heaving his brick telegrams proclaiming 'Magic's Back' through culture's stained-glass windows, something almost innocent in his appalling disregard for consequence.

Right from its title, this book recognises that Malcolm McLaren's life and times are indivisible; can only be regarded as a single thing. He was, without a doubt, a product of his era who went on to fashion much of that same era as a product of his own, as with the Escher image of hands drawing one another. It is from the sheer uniqueness of that life, those times, that there emerges an abiding flavour of the bittersweet: on one hand, this incredibly astute biography is an inspiring call to arms, a firebrand manifesto that will make its readers want to storm reality with nothing save for single-minded energy, velour and chicken-wire. And on the other, in its textured detailing of its unlikely subject's climb to agency and influence, like Mervyn Peake's ambitious and subversive Steerpike, it is a dispiriting reminder that the listing social scaffolding on which McLaren essayed his precarious ascent – the fanzines, underground press publications, music papers, pop charts, and reliable arrival of a new youth culture every four or five years without fail – does not exist anywhere in our present century, raising the question of where this world's necessary jolts of culture shock are going to come from. There's a sobering implication of what should have been apparent in the first place, that Malcolm McLaren was utterly unrepeatable.

In the conspicuous absence from the modern landscape of McLaren or of anyone remotely like him, the necessity for such upheaval artists is, now more than ever, thrown into unsettling relief. The ever-shifting teenage rampage that he represented has been missing and presumed dead since the early 1990s, since when we have come to understand that counterculture is not some aggressive pathogen attacking culture but, more accurately, is instead a vital organ in that culture's body, without which the body cannot function properly. Without dissident movements in the arts to criticise it and thus offer it new ways of moving forward, without fire-starters like Malcolm McLaren, culture will stagnate and atrophy into a listless retrospective orgy of recycled ideas and exhausted franchises, a stale morass of reboots, resurrections and limp re-imaginings. And here we are.

This masterful and painstaking biography opens its doorway to an era of fluorescent disenchantment and outlandish possibility through its robust investigation of that era's foremost architect; its careful mapping of a pyrotechnic world and worldview vanished so completely that, without this documented history, we might doubt that it was ever really there. Among these revelatory pages I was granted a more vivid understanding of this rag-trade polymath than I could ever have construed while in blinding proximity. I know Malcolm McLaren better now. Let this book take you on a one-chord ghost-train ride to a lost country, where you may discover that, in Paul Gorman's appraisal of the spit-flecked past, a bright potential future yet remains for England's dreaming.

Alan Moore
Northampton, 2 November 2019

Essay

Before the 'influencer', there was what some called the 'slasher'. Maybe the latter begat the former. The model-slash-DJ. The writer-slash-activist. The artist-slash-musician.

What was Malcolm McLaren? An artist/shop owner/designer/band manager/creative director? An eternal art student, forever renouncing traditional art practice? Within the slippery divides between disciplines and media – fashion, art, music, interiors, commerce – one finds McLaren, roaming and creating. His legacy is as much his ability to move across each field, and the invitation his existence provided for others to do the same, as it is any specific contribution within each discipline.

This book is about a way of working, about a mentality that sees that it is all for the taking, and that the categorisation that puts this or that in different aisles, different magazines, different archives or different rooms in a museum, is unhelpful at best and, at worst, boring, stifling even.

As Paul Gorman observes here, despite the above, McLaren's name has not become shorthand for boundary-blurring, genre-defying creativity, unlike, say, Andy Warhol. Ask a kid for an example today and they'd likely offer Donald Glover or Kanye West or Virgil Abloh – figures whose talents seem to flourish wherever they are applied, individuals who are denounced by many for being too much of a product of the zeitgeist, of youthful dissatisfaction, of the rabid way we consume, of the churn of the internet.

While not a direct influence, McLaren was in many ways their forebear. The reason his name isn't referenced more in this respect is in part due to his collaborative approach: his many circles and sets and the muddy nature of sharing credit. Issues of ownership, power balances and the legacy of authorship are important in considering the way McLaren has been viewed historically. Ironically, collaboration is now everywhere; though this has perhaps contributed to McLaren's lack of global regard it is one of his greatest legacies, for the creative landscape of today is dominated by cliques and partnerships. These many unions between creative directors and bands, stylists and icons, imagemakers and musicians are to a certain extent mandated by the success and impact of McLaren's ever-evolving shop-cum-ideas factory at 430 King's Road.

In the foreword to this book, Alan Moore writes, 'In the conspicuous absence from the modern landscape of McLaren or of anyone remotely like him, the necessity for such upheaval-artists is now more than ever thrown into unsettling relief.'

I politely disagree. If anything, there are more people than ever working to the McLaren model; more people thirsty for the new, questioning of the status quo, keen for something to stick but unsure how to categorise themselves, or whether they even need to. The mix of urgency and bubbling apathy that underpinned McLaren's life is in tune with the modern condition. Much of his work seems to predict the now: the boom in image, the visual literacy of the everyman, the desire to stand out while also being part of a tribe or community, the questioning of gender boundaries, the boredom that instantly occurs when an impulse has been satisfied.

It is not enough to say that counter-culture is dead and there can never be another McLaren. Maybe the counter-culture has so firmly penetrated the channels of power – the editors, the commissioners, the brand owners, the CEOs, the punks-turned-boomers – that the 'outsider' mentality is fully ingrained and, simultaneously, dampened, now little more than a line in the manifesto of a tech start-up, management shake up, new clothing label, magazine redesign. It has been devoured.

I'd say that McLaren would likely look at the conditions that pertain today and be disgusted by the march of commerce, confused by the banality of much pop, semi-perturbed and semi-ignited by the sheer global reach of things that pretend to be small, that sell themselves through a sense of 'authenticity' (whatever that means). Yet the loose philosophy that characterised most of his work is in tune with today's creative mood. He understood that a mix of existing elements can be as valid as a new product, that surface matters – dressing as an artist was almost as good as being one – that identity can, and must, be performed. That political ideas can be made fashionable or even commodified into something to buy – a required outfit, a readable badge of morality. That a revolutionary slogan packs its punch when rendered with design flair. That the wearing of certain shoes – in McLaren's case, blue suede ones – can be conceptualised as a political act. That a music star or celebrity can be engineered strategically from a style movement, rather than simply be a by-product of it. And that ideas are everything, and façade, not what's inside, is what reels us in.

McLaren also pre-empted the selective nostalgia fortifying contemporary creative output; as much as he campaigned against it, he drew constantly on the 'the mad, matriarchal, Jane Eyre, gothic Victorian world I came from [his words]'. He saw that what was once traditional can be made subversive – it was, after all, the restrictive corsets bought by his grandmother that inspired his notion that all fashion was really bondage, so we might as well explicitly reference it. He realised that a reference, a borrowed image, idea or clever name-check creates a guise of intimacy, pulling in those in the know and attracting those keen to be. He knew that little, if anything, will ever be truly original; McLaren himself was, of course, a by-product – one can trace it all back to Warhol, or the Situationist International, or Rauschenberg, or even the Bauhaus. And perhaps most importantly he came to realise that the delicate art of mixing – whether of the crass with the sincere, the familiar and the new, the grotesque and the beautiful, the high and the low – is where both discomfort and desire, and the hazy line between the two, can be found. We see that recipe today everywhere: in reality television, in streetwear, in hip hop, in memes, in the speeches of politicians, in a designer hoodie, in a Supreme x Louis Vuitton skateboard.

In a quote cited by Gorman, McLaren talks of, as a young man, looking to do 'something that would make us feel like gigantic poseurs, show-offs'. Where would the digital environment have taken him? McLaren's interest in the Situationist practices of *détournement* and the dérive suggests he would have had fun online. After all, *détournement* is basically Instagram and what is web browsing if not the *dérive*? Drifting aimlessly from link to link, page to page, occasionally recoiling in horror, though mostly entirely numb, we travel through worlds and contexts in a web of juxtaposition and confusion. McLaren liked to talk of himself as a Marco Polo or Walter Raleigh type, encountering new references everywhere, and bringing them home to share with others. Do we not all feel like that online? Locating an intriguing image or text and reposting it for others to see and acknowledge our coolness?

Of course, not all that McLaren expressed was modern. The 'boys will be boys' mentality, post-Me Too, seems synonymous with the blind eye-turning that allows for harassment and assault. But the anxious, stringy, interconnected nature of McLaren's creativity, if not some of his world-views, is relatable and pre-emptive of the agitation of the modern state.

We are, as he was, desperate to stand alone but enticed by popularity or fame, just as we are obsessed by the big city yet repelled by the spreading capitalism – the wealth, the cost, the generic new-builds, the banality of big shopping streets. Bored by middle class mediocrity in taste – the snooty undertones of a fur coat, the keeping-up of appearances – we are nevertheless fascinated by hierarchies as much as the need to break them. We are bristling to rebel, yet desirous of some kind of recognition from the 'system', be that the media, the art world, Fashion Week, the music industry, the shopper, the crowd.

Today, more than ever, McLaren's work is emblematic of the ever so delicate trade-off between success and opposition. Between making it and selling out. Between what disgusts us and what motivates us.

Lou Stoppard
February 2020

Author's Note

Malcolm McLaren brought us many things. During his lifetime, which was cut short at the age of sixty-four in 2010, McLaren's greatest gift was to consistently upset our expectations of what constitutes contemporary art and mass communication. In doing so, he set in train a series of surprising and exciting propositions that continue to ripple around the world.

Fashion design and popular music, where McLaren's activities gained most traction, were not alone in benefiting from his presence. From television advertising and film production to retail interiors and social activism, many spheres bear traces of McLaren's fingerprints.

The link between them lies in McLaren's formulation of a worldview predicated on self-determination and against-the-grain energy. Rising to the fore during the years of his association with the Sex Pistols, this punk attitude resides today as a byword for dissent. According to McLaren's art school friend Fred Vermorel, it 'resonates through innumerable PoMo lifestyles and subcultures, genres and media, through micro and macro politics, and still has the power to shock and stand as The Opposition, to confront, for example, the Kremlin and represent an internationally recognised rhetoric of rebellion'.

Ten years after his death, McLaren remains a spiky figure in the cultural landscape, unassimilated into the mainstream unlike such comparable luminaries as Andy Warhol, who similarly operated at the cross-hatches of art, celebrity, design, music, media and visual identity.

Wherever he be, McLaren must take a measure of the blame himself for misconceptions about his activities, since he was ceaseless in his dedication to breaking social mores. As you will see, this stemmed from an unwavering adherence to his grandmother's cantrip, 'To be bad is good, because to be good is to be boring', though it's ironic to note that several of McLaren's fellow travellers who once occupied the same troublemaking space are now ranked by the dubious social standing of 'national treasures'.

Then again, and unlike them, McLaren did not crave acceptability. In the words of Mel & Kim, he ain't never gonna be respectable.

As you will gather from this book, McLaren's chaotic upbringing and singular outlook sparked a determination to exist outside the norms of what was once quaintly termed 'straight society'. He started on this path in the early 1960s as a dynamic young art student, and the consistency in his oeuvre lies in the fact that it acted as both commentary on society at large and celebration of its outer limits, those discarded elements McLaren championed as 'the ruins' and 'the dispossessed'.

But McLaren was not interested in operating on the fringes. A child of one of the greatest diasporas of all time, his Jewishness was but one of the factors mitigating against the parochialism that has plagued many of his collaborators. McLaren was an enthusiastic internationalist intent on fast-tracking vanguard ideas to the heart of the world's mass media and entertainment industries, engaging along the way with major record companies, film studios, national broadcasters, the fashion trade and global ad agencies, and popping up in the public glare, whether at an Art Basel preview, a Beijing recording studio, on the front row of a Paris haute couture catwalk extravaganza or in a high-ratings British reality TV show.

Unlike many, these experiences did not blunt his capacity to cause and express outrage. That McLaren secured his position as the ultimate inside/outsider even unto the end of his days stands as a testament to the vigour and invention with which he applied himself to the task.

My book does not seek to shoehorn McLaren into the post-war pop-cultural pantheon nor elect him as a grand 'disrupter', for he was more interesting than that lazy epithet of the age suggests. As the late Australian curator Paul Taylor wrote in the 1980s, McLaren was in fact 'a new kind of visual artist', one who channelled his prodigious art education to ride waves of cultural and technological development and suggest a series of thrilling outcomes. Some took immediately – the attitudes, looks and sounds of punk, post-punk, New Romantic, world music and even hip-hop are unimaginable without McLaren – while others had to wait to find their time, among them his championing of the gender fluidity and identity politics at the core of the 1980s ballroom Voguing scene, his mid-1990s prophecies of the imminent free downloading of music, the populist approaches utilised during the 2000 campaign for the post of Mayor of London ('Don't give it to a politician'), all these and more spring to mind.

One way of understanding McLaren's life is to view his alignment with the Situationist International's aim of replacing the making of art with the creation of public interventions to transform the daily grind, in the words of the cultural theorist Thomas Levin, into 'a creative, continuously original, delirious, ecstatic experience'.

In my pursuit of the casting of new light over the life and work of Malcolm McLaren, I have not sought the input of those who have had their say about him multiple times down the years. These include his one-time partner Dame Vivienne Westwood, his brother Stuart Edwards and his son Joe Corré. This is not to diminish their importance to McLaren; in fact, I have done my utmost to ensure that these and others receive fair treatment in these pages. But their anecdotes and views, as well as those of several other associates of McLaren, have become familiar and can be found in the vast library of publications that include his activities over more than four decades.

It is my intention to provide a much more rounded portrait than has hitherto been available, one which incorporates previously untapped testimony. As a counterbalance, you will find here many exclusive contributions, from McLaren's stepmother Barbara Nicola and his 1960s art school teacher Keith Albarn to lifelong intimates, including friends of several decades, such as the television director/producer Andy Harries and Hollywood scriptwriter Menno Meyjes, McLaren's partner Eugenia Melián, who collaborated with him on an array of projects from Los

Angeles to Paris in the 1990s, London mayoral campaign manager Peter Culshaw, ad commercials and musical adviser Leigh Gorman (no relation) and digital expert Graham Brown-Martin. The information from these and many others has been enhanced by previously unpublished material from the archive of the Malcolm McLaren Estate, including the notes he and those he worked with maintained for articles, lectures, radio documentaries and other projects.

Crucial to negotiating a new path through McLaren's life has been the cache of papers left by Peter McLaren, the father from whom Malcolm McLaren was estranged from the age of two until his early forties. These proved critical in addressing many secrets, myths and legends, some propagated by McLaren himself, and advanced insights into his son's personality.

It is a fact that McLaren's hyper self-promotion as 'The Embezzler' during the punk years rebounded on him, creating a mediagenic and one-dimensional caricature defined in the popular press and elsewhere as mercurial and mercenary. While these were personality traits at certain times in McLaren's life, this public image was exploited by others not just to their gain but also antithetical to the views held by those in the concentric social circles of his life.

There is no doubt McLaren was flawed – which of us isn't? – and that his anti-sentimental streak, particularly as a younger man, was sometimes expressed with a distinct lack of empathy; years later there are people who nurse the wounds of association. But there are many, many more whose lives were enriched directly or indirectly, including myself.

I wouldn't say that I knew McLaren well but we were friendly enough and I benefited from his encouragement on occasion. I first encountered him as a fast-talking provocateur in mid-1970s London, later as a phlegmatic wit in Los Angeles at the turn of the 1990s and then as a generous and inspiring raconteur in his final decade, but trust that you will find that this book does not amount to a hagiography. I have not shrunk from cataloguing McLaren's imperfections and mistakes, but simultaneously I have sought to celebrate the unique outlook and boundless imagination revealed to me through conversations and interviews.

For an appreciation of McLaren, it is important to avoid defining him solely in terms of the association with the Sex Pistols. Consequently, I have approached the group's brief existence and its repercussions through the experiences of my subject, who, after all, gathered the musicians together, named them, provided the building blocks of a left-field outlook, directed musical content and visual image, and managed – he would claim misman-aged – his charges so that the group now occupies a position of great promi-nence in popular music even though they recorded just one album.

And so the chapters here regarding the Pistols do not represent a blow-by-blow account of their history, which was but one explosive episode in a life devoted to testing the limits of artistic endeavour.

There is poignancy in the fact that McLaren had to wait until the final years of his life to be formally recognised as a visual artist. The latter-day film installations *Shallow 1–21* and *Paris, Capital of the XXIst Century* were greeted as considerable works by the international fine arts commu-nity, but he was to enjoy this acclaim fleetingly.

I happened to be within the grounds of an art school once attended by McLaren when the news of his death hit London on 8 April 2010. In the company was the musician Mick Jones, whose life and career, like those of so many, was improved by connection with McLaren.

Naturally, Jones expressed sorrow, and his immediate response to the news of McLaren's passing struck me hard. 'We'll never hear Malcolm's latest thoughts again,' said Jones. 'All those brilliant, wild ideas which seemed to pour out of him on a daily basis, that's over. And that's really sad.'

I have sought to alleviate the loss in this book and show how one unusual individual from a troubled and unprepossessing background not only demanded but achieved the impossible; Malcolm McLaren shaped his times and left a legacy of genuinely alternative thinking that will be tapped by generations to come.

Paul Gorman
London

Prologue

Lydd Road, Old Romney, Kent, England

Peter McLaren, a wiry fellow approaching seventy with craggy features and longish hair for his age, is dapper in an emerald green shirt and white jeans.

An Alsatian at his side, Peter sips whisky and waits with his partner Barbara Nicola. It is gone three o'clock on a Monday afternoon in the first week of August 1989, and they are in the sitting room of the small flat above the Oasis Café, the roadside diner they run on Romney Marsh, the windswept 'sixth continent', as it is described by Kentish natives.

But Peter is not a local; Peter and Barbara installed themselves at the Oasis a few years earlier, having met a few miles along the south coast in Winchelsea in the mid-1970s. At that time he was bringing up two children from his second marriage, their mother having died young from cancer a decade previously.

Although he has never owned a passport or left Britain, Peter has seen a lot. By the time he first met Barbara, he was running a caravan park, having survived on his wits for decades. Another relationship was on its last legs, and a son from that union was to die tragically young in a motorbike accident.

In time, this taciturn man opened up to Barbara about his first marriage, a wartime affair that produced his first-born offspring, both boys.

He spoke of his first wife, Emily, and her flightiness, and also of his feelings of being overwhelmed by her quarrelsome family, whose figurehead was Peter's redoubtable mother-in-law Rose Corré Isaacs. Home on leave after the war, Peter's suspicions that Emily was not only promiscuous but serially slept with other men for money were confirmed over

1

a matter of months, and he walked out of the family home, leaving the toddlers Stuart, four years old, and Malcolm, just twenty-two months, in the Isaacs's care. In a curious arrangement, which could only have occurred in those confused post-war years when family structures were breaking down across the battered nation, Peter agreed to a Dickensian stricture imposed by the Isaacs: that he would never make contact with the two boys during Emily's lifetime.

Over the decades, Peter has abided by the agreement, even when his second son emerged as a public figure, first as manager of the Sex Pistols and then later as an all-round controversialist. Peter has proudly kept clippings of reports of Malcolm's exploits and constantly scans the newspapers for fresh information, discussing them with Barbara at every turn.

In fact, a few days before their wait in the sitting room above the Oasis, the pair read an interview with Malcolm in which he not only announced that his mother, Emily, was dead, but that he was now intent on finding his father. A contact number was provided with the article.

Peter and Barbara had talked it over. Might Malcolm hit his father in the mouth for deserting him? Would he be angry? Or sad? Glad? Pleased? They even wondered whether he would be snobbish and dismissive of his father's circumstances.

But Barbara called the journalist who wrote the article. Their number was taken and passed to Malcolm. The phone rang five minutes later. For the first time since the winter of 1947, father and son conversed. In Peter's own words, 'the die was cast'.

And so Peter sits and waits, his nerves fraying on this hot August day, while Barbara stands guard at the window, keeping her eye on local traffic. Four o'clock comes and goes and still no sign of a car bearing his sons on the A259 trunk road running alongside the café.

Peter wonders whether they have chickened out; maybe the anxiety and eternal discussions of 'should we, shouldn't we?' have all been a waste of time.

Then, at six o'clock, a chauffeur-driven Daimler pulls into the offroad. Peter composes himself and drops down to meet his sons. He notes that Stuart is correctly attired in slacks and shirt while Malcolm looks strange in checkered three-quarter length trousers and a blue oversized cotton shirt, the cuffs hanging loose below his wrists.

Upstairs in the flat, Stuart is suspicious, peppering Peter with questions, some of which, such as enquiries about the nineteen-year age difference between him and Barbara, Peter finds impertinent.

Malcolm, meanwhile, refuses refreshments and sits motionless, facing Peter, studying his face. He answers when questioned, but for the most part appears to his father to have been struck rigid with fear.

Then the spell is broken when he is asked if he has any questions to further establish Peter's identity.

'No,' replies Malcolm. 'I'm quite satisfied he is who he says he is.'

PART I

Boys Will Be Boys

Chapter 1

Malcolm Robert Andrew McLaren was born on Tuesday 22 January, 1946, at 47 Carysfort Road in north-east London's inner-city locale Stoke Newington.

Attending to the mother, Emily, was her own mother, Rose Isaacs, who lived in the house next door with her husband Mick, a tailor's cutter. Also present was Emily's husband, Peter. He had been given compassionate leave from his duties as a private with a company of the Royal Engineers retained on deferred service outside of London in the months after the cessation of the Second World War.

Meanwhile, in a cot in the same room, was the couple's first-born, two-and-a-half-year-old Stuart. The young boy slept throughout the birth, though this was an occasion infused with high drama, like many in Malcolm McLaren's life.

The voluble Rose had alerted the midwife supplied by the local hospital by phone when Emily's waters broke but London was suffering a cold snap – the temperatures did not rise above 0.5 °C that night – and the wintry fog and severe frost glazing the streets impeded the midwife's journey by bicycle to Carysfort Road. Time passed and the atmosphere grew tense, particularly after a second telephone call failed to summon her presence. 'Rose, who was supposed to be helping, spent the entire time having hysterics,' recalled Peter McLaren. 'She was a nuisance.'

And so it fell to the father to effect the delivery, wrapping 'the child, the placenta and umbilicus in a blanket until the midwife arrived and cleaned everything up', as he noted clinically in papers dictated in the late 1990s towards the end of his life. Peter maintained the matter-of-fact tone as he concluded his report on his second son's birth: 'The marriage, already strained, now deteriorated very fast.'[1]

As was also to occur throughout his life, Malcolm McLaren's arrival had a catalysing effect. Of course, the new-born could not be made directly responsible for the deepening strains on his parents' marital status. These may be traced back not only through the half-decade they had known each other but also to the psychological and emotional fault-lines that ran through Emily's family.

Britain had been at war with Germany for two years when Peter McLaren, twenty-two, met Emily Isaacs at a dance at the Tottenham Royal (later to become a popular haunt of London's mods in the 1960s).

During the wartime years, the dancehalls of Britain became sites of 'considerable independence for women, one of the few places they could venture on their own or with friends'.[2] This suited Emily Isaacs, a spirited dreamer who worked as a window dresser at a local department store.

Peter McLaren immediately took a fancy to the eighteen-year-old, who, unusually for the time, wore corrective braces on her teeth. He asked permission to walk her the mile-and-a-half south to her family home in Carysfort Road. Emily told him that, as a young single Jewish woman, she couldn't risk being seen alone with a gentile male, particularly at night. This would be frowned upon in her tight-knit community, and anyway, an uncle would soon arrive to escort her through the neighbourhoods, which had been strafed during the Blitz. In fact, in January 1941, in an attack on the area which killed ten people and rendered hundreds of locals homeless, a V-2 rocket had landed at the eastern end of Carysfort Road, damaging beyond repair eight houses in the terrace opposite the Isaacs's home while the Royal itself was closed intermittently due to war damage.[3]

McLaren, who lived with his mother and older sister Ivy a couple of miles west in Islington, was keen, and accompanied Emily and her uncle. As they strolled down Green Lanes and skirted Clissold Park, Peter managed to fix an assignation for the following week.

And so a courtship began, despite the fact that when Emily's mother Rose found out, she made her disapproval known in her usual forthright manner. A car mechanic of no rank, social standing or means, McLaren was viewed by the matriarch with great suspicion as an outsider lacking her family's exoticism. Though his son Stuart came to believe he was raised in Cuba,[4] the wiry, sandy-haired Peter James Philip McLaren was actually born in Islington in 1919 and never left the British Isles. Peter's father Alexander Cullis McLaren (who died in 1940) had spent time in Havana, the son of a roaming Scot who had returned to London before the First World War.

Rose Isaacs's background was, by the standards of England of the day, more colourful. She was born Roza Corré, a twin with her sister Abigail, in Mildmay Grove on the Dalston/Stoke Newington borders in 1893 to Abraham and Miriam Corré. In later life Rose, who insisted on keeping her surname as her middle name after marriage, would boast that the Corrés were not only descended from Portuguese aristocracy (the surname is a corruption of Corréia, that of one of the sixteen families that formed Portugal's nobility from the twelfth century onwards) but also diamond traders, though Abraham Corré was described in official documents as a 'general dealer'. He was born in Whitechapel in the 1860s not long after his own parents Solomon and Rozetta Corré arrived in London from the Sephardic community then operating diamond-processing ateliers in Amsterdam, though Solomon became a cigar-maker. After undertaking an apprenticeship in his father's business, Abraham became first a diamond polisher and then a jeweller. Abraham's relative wealth afforded his family a comfortable lifestyle; at the turn of the century they moved to a three-storey, nine-bedroom house with a live-in maid in Albion Road, south of Clissold Park.

Rose, Abigail and their younger sisters Emily and Lilian grew up in the early years of the twentieth century in a social caste removed from the hardscrabble immigrant milieu that occupied their area of the capital, described by the author Emmanuel Litvinoff as 'an extraordinary enclave, a kind of East European ghetto stuck in the middle of London. The languages that were spoken, the food that was eaten, the songs that were sung, everything was related to cities like Odessa, Kiev, Warsaw and Kishinev'.[5] This was the locus of such extraordinary events as the Siege of Sidney Street, which occurred when Rose was seventeen years old in January 1911. Latvian radicals who had attempted a jewel heist, as the last in a series of criminal acts which were interpreted as funding politically subversive activities, became involved in a gunfight with armed police.

Abraham Corré despised such people purely on the basis that they were from Eastern Europe, and instilled in his daughters a snobbish hauteur based on their family's perceived social standing. Through her teens the extrovert Rose harboured ambitions as an actress in the theatre or, failing that, the music hall, but these were thwarted by her father.

Such were Rose's dramatic abilities that as a young woman, she later claimed, Abraham Corré used her as a front, tapping into her ability to tell convincing sob stories to sell blemished and flawed diamonds to the jewellers of Whitechapel's Black Lion Yard. 'Her father would say: "That's my girl" when she came back with the money,' said his great-grandson, Malcolm McLaren.

By the age of seventeen, Rose was described in a census as a teacher. She later claimed to have also worked as one of Sir Thomas Lipton's secretaries at the tea magnate's offices in Bath Street in Clerkenwell. And she said her plans to wed an actor were quashed when Abraham pressed her into marrying twenty-nine-year-old tailor Michael Isaacs in the summer of 1915, almost a year into the hostilities of the First World War. Even though he was an Ashkenazi of Ukrainian heritage, he was accepted by Abraham as a better bet than a lowly theatrical trouper. Known as 'Mick', Isaacs cut his teeth at his family's popular Brick Lane cloth shop, Julius Isaacs, where 'all the club boys, the gamblers and the villains used to go to have their suits made because he had the best stuff'.[6]

'Her family forced my grandmother to marry him even though she hated him,' said Malcolm McLaren. 'She was married off to a man she had no interest in, and was full of anger the rest of her life because of it.'

Mick had joined up, so the couple lived for a time at barracks in

Grantham in Lincolnshire where, Rose later claimed, she conducted affairs with officers while her husband was on active service overseas. One liaison resulted in a pregnancy, which Rose claimed to have terminated at some risk to her health.

Perversely, Rose's resentment grew with the arrival of their first and only child, Emily, in 1923. 'She was living a life she didn't want and then had a child she didn't like,' according to her grandson.

Around this time Mick, Rose and their daughter moved to a home a few hundred yards along Albion Road at 49 Carysfort Road. With its fine nineteenth-century villas and terraces, Stoke Newington was still a cut above neighbouring parts of the borough of Hackney, and a decade away from the shift which commenced with the wholesale replacement of private Victorian stock with social housing blocks around Clissold Park and in Stamford Hill.

There were also many local amenities such as the local Adath Yisroel Synagogue for the Jewish and in particular Hassidic communities, which had settled there in waves to escape the pogroms of central and Eastern Europe over the preceding fifty years.

The Isaacs were not particularly observant. And Rose and her sisters – who often visited with their husbands and families – ruled the roost. Mick kept himself to himself, while their daughter Emily grew flighty, disliked by her own mother as the embodiment of frustrated ambition.

Rose thought Emily could do no right, and dubbed her 'man-mad', relating tales to her grandson Malcolm of Emily's constant risk of losing her window-dressing job 'because she spent all day staring at men passing by the window'. That this was projection on the part of Rose passed without comment from the somnolent Mick and the despised Emily.

Meanwhile more distant relatives – such as the family of the future *Daily Express* agony aunt Marjorie Proops (born Rebecca Israel and educated in nearby Dalston) – were entertained, and Rose and Emily both told the young Malcolm McLaren that they were also related to the American entertainer Danny Kaye via Mick Isaacs's family.

Rose claimed to be so friendly with Agatha Christie that she employed Christie's maid Mary after the thriller writer left London for her estate in Devon at the outbreak of the Second World War.

She was also visited by a local friend, Frances Pinter, mother of the British dramatist Harold, who grew up believing that his family was descended from Portuguese Sephardim (although his forebears in fact came from Poland and the Ukraine, which made him Ashkenazic). This ancestral tale had been related to his mother by an unspecified 'aunt' – could she have been the fabulist Rose? This is likely. As a young man Pinter was so persuaded by the story that he used the Portuguese-style surnames 'Pinta' and 'da Pinto' for authorship of poems. In Malcolm McLaren's notes on his childhood from 2000, he recorded that his grandmother had claimed that Pinter was actually 'Harold Dapinta'. Pinter himself confirmed to McLaren that he had accompanied his mother on trips to Carysfort Road.

Pinter later evoked his north-east London stamping ground of the period: 'It brimmed over with milk bars, Italian cafes, Fifty Shilling tailors and barber shops. Prams and busy ramshackle stalls clogged up the main street – street violinists, trumpeters, matchsellers. Many Jews lived in the district, noisy but candid; mostly taxi drivers and pressers, machinists and cutters who steamed all day in their workshop ovens. Up the hill lived the richer, the better-class Jews, strutting with their mink coats and American suits and ties.'[7]

This was the milieu into which Peter McLaren was drawn after his first encounter with Emily Isaacs in 1941. From the get-go he was sceptical of Rose's grandiosity, later describing her as 'short, fattish with short dark hair, always dressed in black. She had projecting teeth and wasn't well educated.'

Meanwhile her husband cut a morose figure: 'A gambler, Mick dressed smartly for his job but after work was very scruffy indeed, hanging about in trousers too dirty to bed a cat in. Medium height, thin grey hair, nearly bald.' Mick, when not at work, spent a lot of time staring into the fireplace muttering about his experiences during the First World War. Peter McLaren's doubt that he had served was counterbalanced by speculation that his mental condition was sufficiently damaged: 'he was in fact suffering from shell-shock'.

Peter's sister Ivy McLaren described Mick as 'an inveterate gambler' and 'a womaniser' though this did not square with Malcolm McLaren's recollection of his grandfather as 'a dark dismal creature' who largely kept to a den on the ground floor of the house working on clothing orders. 'He was a good tailor, especially for the local wrestlers and boxers whose sizes kept changing – he crafted good suits for them. They were pleased with the results.'

As for their daughter, despite Rose's view that Emily was 'man-mad', she and Peter McLaren courted without a physical relationship developing. 'That was normal for the times,' says Peter's third wife Barbara Nicola. 'He told me he liked her as a companion and they would often go dancing together but when it seemed to be going nowhere he started to think about ending it.'[8]

Whether Emily intuited this is not clear, but late one night in the early autumn of 1942 she appeared on the doorstep of the McLaren family's home in Crane Grove, Islington. Clutching a suitcase she begged Peter to marry her; she was convinced she was pregnant, even though she and McLaren had not had sex.

That this went against all logic did not stop what Peter McLaren later described to Nicola as 'a fracas developing. Rose turned up at the house as well, and his mother – who liked Emily – and his sister Ivy joined in, arguing about whether she should stay or go. Peter looked on as all four of them shouted and yelled at each other.'

Eventually, it was agreed that, for the sake of peace and quiet, Rose would return to Carysfort Road and Emily would stay the night, chaperoned by Peter's mother. The following morning, backed by his mother and sister, Emily continued in her insistence that they marry, and McLaren relented. 'He knew from the very start it wasn't going to work because her family was so against him,' says Nicola. 'It wasn't that he was a pushover. He was an honourable man and here was a young woman beseeching him. What else could he do?'

By the time Emily Isaacs revealed that she wasn't after all pregnant, the wedding arrangements had been made, though Peter McLaren retained to his final days the suspicion that she had genuinely believed she was pregnant by another and prevailed upon his naivety.

This was not an auspicious start. The wedding took place on 17 October 1942, at the register office in Liverpool Road, not far from the McLarens' home. A photograph portrays a smiling, stylish couple, Emily in a fashionable wide-shouldered coat with leopard skin detailing and matching pillbox hat, and Peter, his wavy hair smoothed by Brilliantine, in a sharp double-breasted suit which cost £12, three times the average price of a man's suit at the time.

In recognition of McLaren's roots, a Scottish piper played an air outside the register office as the couple emerged with the wedding party, which gathered at a reception at The Castle, a large Victorian pub in the major thoroughfare Holloway Road.

Emily's parents, who had not attended the register office, arrived with the gift of 'a lot of very nice silverware', per Peter's description. In wartime Britain this was extravagant; the only other present of note was an eiderdown from friends of Peter's parents.

Without a honeymoon, the newlyweds moved directly into a second-floor flat above Peter's brother Alec and his wife in Crane Grove. This was furnished with tables, chairs and a bed bought by Peter on hire purchase; his new father-in-law stood as guarantor for the payments.

Their marriage, like many others of the period, was marred by Peter's frequent service absences.[9] Money was tight since financial support was now withheld by the Isaacs as an expression of their distaste for the union. At every opportunity Rose gave voice to wild allegations that Peter was not actively serving in the army when he was away from home, but instead a deserter running a car-theft operation.

In the decades before he met his father as an adult, Malcolm McLaren was forced to rely on the whispers and lies of his childhood. In 1982, seven years before their reunion, he described his father to journalist Johnny Black as 'a petty but kind of glamorous burglar, one of the first guys that got involved in car stealing, [going] down country lanes and bringing them back to London, spraying them, re-number plating them and selling them. He was a bit of an artist, a sign writer for the GPO and a few other odds and sods. My grandparents bought him a second hand line of Humber Super Snipes, sort of Pullman-type cars for taking rich Rabbis to the train station. My father was a lazy guy and would never appear on time.'[10]

If Peter McLaren was involved in criminal activities, none of the cash made it back to Crane Grove. When his and Emily's son Stuart was born in the flat in the summer of 1943, the couple settled for a second-hand pram to transport him. Peter and his friend Bobby Johnston refurbished the pram in the make-do-and-mend ethos of the time, providing a fresh coat of paint, a fancy new mohair hood and re-chromed wheels.

Stuart's arrival failed to alleviate the tension between the couple. Left alone with the newborn for extended periods, Emily felt disconnected from her family and little empathy with the McLarens. Increasingly she prevailed upon Ivy to babysit so that she could resume her pre-marital social life, venturing to dances and the like.

On one such occasion Peter McLaren returned unannounced to find his wife absent and Stuart with Ivy. Asking after Emily locally, McLaren was told she had fallen in with a group of bookmakers (off-course betting was illegal at the time and attracted all manner of spivs and shady characters). He found Emily at the greyhound racing track in neighbouring Walthamstow in the company of these undesirables and persuaded her to accompany him home.

Another time McLaren blandishments were less successful. As he arrived at the flat, Emily brushed past him, dressed to the nines, refusing to stay, even for his first night at home on leave in some time.

In time Peter McLaren gave in to his wife's demands that they move closer to her family, and accepted the Isaacs's offer of the four-room apartment at 47 Carysfort Road. The move emboldened Emily, who spent more and more time dancing at the Mozart social club in Albion Road, less than fifty yards away. The Mozart, known locally as Jazz's, was a popular pick-up joint. According to Peter, on a night out at Jazz's with Emily he overheard a group of men whispering to each other: 'Better watch out, she's got her old man with her.'

The birth of their second son Malcolm did not restrain Emily from her gadabout ways, stoking the atmosphere of mistrust and secrecy.

Peter McLaren was discovering to his cost that family norms of loyalty had been corrupted by the Isaacs with boastfulness, derision, divisiveness, indulgence, infidelity and even neglect. Such was the emotional universe into which his son Malcolm McLaren was thrust.

The slow pace of demobilisation of the five million who had served in the British armed forces during the war resulted in Peter McLaren enduring an extra two years in the services before returning to civvy street.

While there were good times – Stuart treasured into adulthood a fancy tricycle his father had obtained for him as a birthday present off the back of a lorry – each visit home by Peter brought a new and unsettling revelation.

'Suddenly, she had a lot of cash which she kept in her handbag,' said Peter. 'This caused comment among our friends, particularly when I wanted to buy something but couldn't afford it. Later, one friend told me, "It wasn't right, her with all those fivers in her handbag."'

Since Emily was popular with local blades, some of them pretty sketchy, and also had money for which she would not account, Peter McLaren's concerns that his wife was accepting payment for sexual favours escalated when Emily arranged for a friend of ill-repute to take the spare room at their flat on the basis that she would provide company during his stints away.

'The girl had been a waitress at a local café but had been sacked for unsuitable behaviour which remained unspecified,' said Peter. 'She was stunning-looking . . . but known as "The Local Old Bag". I was very suspicious of her real occupation.'

Ivy McLaren continued to babysit the two boys when Emily and the Local Old Bag painted the town red, while grandmother Rose began to take an interest in Malcolm, one that she had not shown in Stuart, whose features and sandy hair resembled those of his father. Even as an infant, Malcolm was blessed with a curly mop of auburn hair, which Rose saw as providing evidence of direct lineage to the all-important Portuguese Sephardic nobility. She decreed that it should never be cut.

Meanwhile Peter reached breaking point when he realised that Rose was complicit in her daughter's deceptions. Late one evening in 1947 he waited for Emily in their apartment with the lights out: 'As she returned, I clearly heard Rose rush out of her house and warn Emily: "Be careful! He's home." '

According to his wife Barbara Nicola, 'Peter decided he could no longer carry on like this. Emily refused to explain the money or where she was going in the evening, so he was now forced to accept that she was on the game.'

Clearly overwhelmed, Peter McLaren confronted his sister, since she was most likely to have spotted the comings and goings during his absences. Ivy confirmed Peter's suspicions, saying that she'd kept her counsel because she was fond of the children and didn't want to intervene in his marriage. Around this time Peter encountered a local who had been a guest at their wedding five years before; this person told him that he should check for the silverware given by the Isaacs. McLaren discovered it was gone; piece-by-piece Emily had pawned it.

Thus it was, on finally receiving his demobilisation papers in November 1947, McLaren moved his possessions out of Carysfort Road back to his mother's house in Islington.

Mick Isaacs appears to have been expecting this, and promptly instituted a legal claim against Peter McLaren for the outstanding HP payments on the wedding furniture. The magistrate refused to grant the request on the grounds that this was no longer in Peter's possession.

Over the weeks following his departure, Peter made prearranged visits to Carysfort Road and took Stuart out for walks; the infant Malcolm was declared by Emily to be too young to spend time with his father. Peter was never again allowed to set foot inside his former home. Instead Stuart was brought to the door and often the Local Old Bag would accompany father and son to ensure the five-year-old's return. On one occasion Stuart told Peter that he had started Hebrew classes. This led Peter to surmise that Emily was by then seeing one Martin Levy, an observant East End Jewish gown manufacturer she had met on a trip to Brighton.

The marriage breakdown was irrevocable. Divorce proceedings were brought by Emily on the grounds of Peter McLaren's desertion (it would not have done for him to raise the issue of his wife's adultery). According to Malcolm McLaren, Mick and Rose Isaacs gave 'a pot of gold' to Peter on the basis that he relinquished all access to his own children.

Peter's account was that her family met the costs of the divorce. In return he agreed not to make contact with Stuart or Malcolm during Emily's lifetime. In 1998, he told Barbara Nicola that he 'truly believed Emily would make a good mother in spite of her lifestyle and that she would have all the necessary backing of her family'.

The dissolution of Emily and Peter's marriage was but one more statistic of the post-war fallout. Legal separation was steadily losing its stigma; in fact, by 1947 British divorces had increased by 1200 per cent from the pre-war annual total, spiking at 60,000-plus that year. Adoption and fostering numbers similarly increased as tens of thousands of children were orphaned or abandoned by at least one parent in those tumultuous years. Nevertheless, Peter McLaren's accession to the specific demand that he distance himself from his children for the duration of his ex-wife's life is remarkable. The most likely explanation was that this unworldly young man from a humble Islington background was no match for the emotional pitch at which the Isaacs thrived.

The turmoil experienced by Peter McLaren was as nothing to that which was about to be inflicted upon his two-year-old son. With the field clear, Rose Corré Isaacs made her move.

Chapter 2

Peter McLaren's exit from the Isaacs's world opened wide the floodgates of dysfunction at 47–49 Carysfort Road.

Many British families struggled with the harsh realities of the immediate post-war period, but the Isaacs's money at least provided a bulwark against the blight of austerity. However, the family's adults – prone to over-reaction and hysteria – became, if anything, needier and more emotionally unscrupulous, dwelling on the slightest of slights, indulging in feuds and bitter quarrels that sometimes escalated into estrangements.[1]

With the newly single Emily Isaacs off gallivanting, her father Mick – ostensibly the paterfamilias – was also often absent; for a time, as Malcolm and Stuart later told their father, their grandfather was 'thrown out of the house by Rose and went to live with some male colleagues in a flat where he spent his time playing cards'.

'I grew up in a household that had no real structure, no sense of family unity and no sense of order,' Malcolm McLaren said in adulthood. 'My mother and grandmother hated each other. My mother had tried to escape by marrying an unsuitable man only to be left with two small children when the marriage was over, but had no real desire to act as a parent to us, so the responsibility fell to my grandmother, who set up a triangle between herself, my mother and me. She created a constant friction between us all. My grandmother favoured me and told me to look upon my mother as an older sister who had gone mad – man-mad.'

McLaren said that he understood what this meant from an early age. He cited the times he was taken by his mother for tea at the posh Dorchester Hotel in London's West End. According to McLaren, he was left on his own in the lobby, while she visited male friends in their hotel rooms. It seems that these were usually married, wealthy and Jewish.

One, so McLaren later claimed, was the clothing entrepreneur Isaac Wolfson, owner of the hugely successful catalogue and retail business Great Universal Stores, which was worth £16 million in 1948.

The boy was informed by Rose that another was the businessman and philanthropist Charles Clore, whose holdings included the British carmaker Jowett. Clore was later to own Selfridges, the Oxford Street department store, which became of special interest to McLaren when he was taken there as a small boy by his grandmother at Christmas time. 'I'd gaze with astonishment at the Christmas lights and at all the shops filled with toys,' said McLaren. 'She would tell me fabulous tales of the scoundrels and rogues that once dwelled here. This street became part of our private kingdom, a world of fantasy and anarchy inhabited by the two of us.'

Once the divorce was made absolute, Emily, by now twenty-five, took a job as a travelling saleswoman for a local clothing company, entailing trips away from home around the country. Ivy McLaren ceased babysitting the boys, though she had already observed Emily Isaacs – having reverted to her maiden name – disappear into the night or entertain male visitors, among them Martin Levy, in the ground-floor flat.

Ivy saw that Emily's neglect of her children had a more visible impact on Stuart than Malcolm; at least the younger child enjoyed the physical comfort of staying with his grandmother in number 49. Ivy recalled in later life stories among the neighbours that Stuart was 'sometimes locked in 47 Carysfort Road alone, and that on at least one occasion, the NSPCC [National Society for the Prevention of Cruelty to Children] were called, but no action was taken'.

Malcolm, on the other hand, was mollycoddled. 'My grandmother became my legal guardian and told me that my mother wasn't fit to be a mother. I did everything with my grandmother,' he wrote. Occasionally Rose would take the boy out for drives in her car, another Humber Super Snipe driven by an employee called Charlie, around the neighbourhood and into the West End. 'My brother was left to play in the street, or if he was in her house, was sent upstairs. I wasn't allowed out onto the streets.'

This isolation, brought about first by the disappearance of his father and soon thereafter by Emily's disinterest, had a serious impact on McLaren's personality. 'He never really understood people and always had a sense that they would abandon him, disappoint him,' said Young Kim, McLaren's partner for the final decade of his life. 'That was very hard for him to deal with.'[2]

And so the years of McLaren's early childhood passed in unusual proximity to Rose, who was in her mid-fifties. He spent all his waking time and ate his meals in 49 Carysfort Road before hopping over the dividing garden wall to sleep in the flat at number 47.

Soon, Rose's affection had a smothering effect. At night, the boy and Rose shared beds together, and would do so intermittently until his late teens. There was no sexual aspect to this arrangement, but this breach into physical intimacy was to wreak psychic havoc.

Later, in his early teens, so McLaren claimed as an adult to friends and lovers, Rose even threaded embroidered silk ribbons into his pubic hair to ward off sexual encounters. 'According to Malcolm this was to ensure he was too embarrassed to do anything other than remain chaste,' says filmmaker Rebecca Frayn, who worked with McLaren in the 1990s.[3]

At the time, the boy was unaware of Rose's transgressive nature. In fact, he was enchanted by her tales of bravado and borderline criminal behaviour delivered in the theatrical and conspiratorial tones to become familiar to McLaren's acquaintances and interviewers as an adult. In this way Rose's penchant for often salacious self-mythologising had a profound impact on the child who was her sole audience.

'Because she'd been an elocution teacher I had this upbringing where you had to throw your voice out, and always look terribly confident,' he said during a documentary about his life.[4]

By Peter McLaren's account, it is unlikely that Rose had given elocution lessons, since she spoke in 'common, broken English'. This is unfair. Recordings made by McLaren later in Rose's life show that she possessed clarity of enunciation and sounds as though she had been on the receiving end of elocution lessons (as had many people of working- and middle-class origins in the period), though it's hard to accept McLaren's claim that she taught elocution during the war at London's leading conservatoire, the Guildhall School of Music & Drama.

'Music hall was a big influence on his grandmother,' said Fred Vermorel, who came to know McLaren in the 1960s and met Rose several times. 'That was transmitted to Malcolm. He just loved that – [it was] a tradition now lost, sanitized by the BBC – very raucous and vindictive Max Miller-type of stuff, grotesquely suggestive and overtly sexual.'[5]

The boy delighted in accompanying his grandmother on excursions: the local corset-maker's was a favourite. Here he would watch Rose undergo the detailed measuring process as he waited with female customers. 'I sat and observed, fascinated by the multiple measurements and the skill with which a new and elaborate garment was produced,' he said.

The experience was to feed into McLaren's singular approach to clothing design, which blossomed in partnership with Vivienne Westwood in the 1970s and 1980s. 'When I visited the corset-maker's with my grandmother I saw clothing as bondage – she was undressed and measured and squeezed into a corset. You didn't dress, you were incarcerated, like putting yourself in a cage. The shape of the person changed.'

Meantime at 49 Carysfort Road, the child Malcolm loved to fall asleep to the sound of Rose, his aunts and their pals sharing gossip and talking about their lives and loves. At other times, she regaled him with inappropriate stories of sexual impropriety. For example, Rose related how, during her employment with Sir Thomas Lipton, it fell to her to procure handsome young men to masturbate the tea magnate to issue in his locked office during lunch breaks. This was strong stuff; Lipton was a public figure who carefully cultivated an image as a ladies' man to cover the fact he was a closeted homosexual.

Whether Rose's tale was true or not (it is worth noting that this was decades before the fact of Lipton's sexuality became public), McLaren later recognised the impact such stories had on him, describing his grandmother as 'the demon – my mother thought she was the most evil person that ever walked the planet. She was a harsh woman and, although I respected her, she had no regard for morals or principles.' Of course, McLaren himself became the target of similar accusations in later life.

'For some time Rose's parents had resided in a house five doors along from the home were she had grown up. Number 175 Albion Road was an imposing property which also housed her married sisters Abigail and Emily and their respective families.'

McLaren told his partner Young Kim that his great-grandparents objected to his and Stuart's presence on the grounds that they were 'not Jewish enough' so visits were rare. Meeting Rose's parents, who were then in their eighties, clued him to the weirdness that permeated his background. 'I remember this grand house and the awful brown wallpaper that hadn't been changed in years,' McLaren wrote. 'Outside there were stacks and stacks of wood. I asked: "Nana, why does he have all this wood?" She told me he was preparing for winter but this wasn't true. He said he intended to burn the houses down around him because there were too many Eastern European Jews in the neighbourhood. He was insane.'

Such were Abraham Corré's mental health issues that, a year after the death of his wife Miriam, he died at the age of 83 in 1950 at the Tooting Bec asylum in south London.

In Carysfort Road the boy Malcolm's confusion as to where familial loyalties lay was amplified by his mother's insistence that they share baths, even though she otherwise left him to Rose's care. Exposure at close quarters to twenty-something Emily's naked body filled him with mixed emotions of awe and dread.

It fell to Rose to organise his attendance at a local nursery school. The child, already unusual, was prepared to enter the world with instructions in amorality from the central figure of his formative years.

'From a young age my grandmother told me "To be bad is good, because to be good is simply boring. And who wants to be boring?"' And so the young Malcolm caused a commotion at the school not only by cutting the tails off the rocking horses but also attempting to stick them back with jam. He was scolded by the staff but Rose 'seemed to approve', according to McLaren.

As a contemporary photograph attests, the boy's appearance set him apart: his lustrous locks had by now grown long. 'My hair isolated me from the other children,' said McLaren. 'My grandmother pinned it back with clips and on my first day at school – aged five – the clips fell out and my long hair was revealed for everyone to see.'

This occurred in autumn 1951 at William Patten Primary School, close to the Isaacs's homes, in Stoke Newington High Street. McLaren maintained throughout his life that he lasted a single day before his grandmother determined that he should receive tuition at home, from herself and occasionally a Rabbi Angel, who performed the duties of a private tutor.

'In addition to the strange family upbringing, he also failed to learn some of the social skills that kids learn in the playground, and therefore made up his own rules,' McLaren's son Joe Corré observed soon after his father's death in 2010.[6]

McLaren retold minor variations of the story of his single day at William Patten throughout his life; the version he recounted for *The South Bank Show* in 1984 contains the major elements: 'I couldn't understand why school was so full of rules and laws. On the first day I climbed under the table and wanted to look at all the girls' knickers, not necessarily out of interest for what was inside but [more because] I found it a better place to be than watching this awful woman who was trying to tell us how to read and write.'

Rose was then summoned by the head teacher. It was on this occasion that McLaren's grandmother uttered the line he was to use when the Sex Pistols were accused of infractions in the 1970s: 'Boys will be boys.' As McLaren announced on *The South Bank Show*: 'I always wanted to challenge convention and, just as my grandmother said, when I got wicked at school, and wicked at work, and wicked with my mother, "Boys will be boys".'

There is another explanation for McLaren's misbehaviour. In September 1951 – the same month as McLaren's short-lived attendance at William Patten – the gown manufacturer Martin Levy married McLaren's mother at Stoke Newington registrer office. The clerk noted that the groom had changed his name by deed poll. He was now the gentile-sounding Martin Edwards, who gave his age as twenty-nine.

Meanwhile a note was added to the bride's entry in the register: 'Formerly the wife of Peter James Philip McLaren, from whom she obtained a divorce'.

Now Emily – who was described as a 'dress presser' since she operated a dry-cleaning outlet – insisted on being addressed as Eve. And, in a move that compounded Malcolm and Stuart's confusion over their identities – were they Scottish? Jewish? Gentile? Who was their father? – Edwards insisted that they take his new surname.

After the wedding Edwards moved out of his home in Stepney to take up permanent residence with his wife, Stuart and, notionally, Malcolm in the ground-floor apartment at 47 Carysfort Road.

Though he was estranged from his mother the intensity of McLaren's dislike of Edwards was matched by Rose's. Nevertheless, in her contradictory manner, she was a witness at the couple's nuptials with Ivor Brooks, a colleague of Edwards.

Rose and Mick had also provided the funds for the dry-cleaning business, which produced profits that enabled Martin Edwards to take over the low two-storey commercial premises at 117 Whitechapel High Street on the eastern fringes of the City of London. The triple-fronted site had originally been built as a stationer's and then wholly reconstructed after a fire in 1952.[7] Here McLaren's parents installed their new manufacturing business Eve Edwards (London) Ltd, distributing and wholesaling smart and casual separates ('cocktail dresses and other cheap knock-offs of the latest Paris fashions', according to McLaren) to post-austerity womenswear retailers around the country.

Far from bringing stability into Malcolm and Stuart's life, the marriage further complicated matters. Eve/Emily continued to see other men, for which she was openly derided by their grandmother.

In addition their cuckolded stepfather insisted that the dysfunctional family become more observant. This entailed circumcision for the boys. McLaren even suffered a nightmare much later in life about the traumatic experience at the hands of the local *mohel* Dr Oster, according to Young Kim. In this, McLaren's foreskin was flung from a window only to be picked up by a dog in the street outside. In the dream, the boy Malcolm gave chase and became involved in a tug-of-war with the dog in an unsuccessful attempt to reattach it.

There are signs that McLaren attended William Patten for more than one day. He recalled in later life being pressed into performing a Scottish sword dance at the age of six at an end-of-term assembly at the school. For this, Rose arranged for a kilt to be made for the boy at Eve Edwards. 'This was unusual because most of my clothes were bought for me from shops, unlike most other children who had homemade clothes at the time,' said McLaren.

It is clear, however, there was a lengthy period of home-schooling, which consisted of laboriously reading 'classic' books by the likes of the Brontës, Conan Doyle and Dickens. 'It was very difficult for me at such an age – I think it was a whole year before I got through *Jane Eyre*,' said McLaren. 'The story of *Oliver Twist* had a huge influence over me, mainly because my grandmother adored Fagin.'

Rose told the boy that Dickens had based Fagin on a real person. 'She said it was codswallop for Dickens to pretend he was hanged,' McLaren reminisced. ' "No man as intelligent as Fagin would have hanged. He escaped and lived a rich life in Australia, building half of Sydney. That's the truth, Malcolm. Tell any teacher that that is the fact." '

McLaren also claimed that Rose insisted he read original manuscripts by Dickens, complete with printer's corrections. Their source is not recorded. 'I was forced to see all of the mistakes,' he wrote. 'Perhaps this instilled a love of mistakes in me, the sense that it was OK to get things wrong, indeed, that errors created a sense of a work in progress that was more interesting than a final statement, a love of the process of creation.'

For the child with little contact beyond Rose, loneliness was a huge factor. 'I didn't have any friends. The thought of playing with anybody was completely alien,' recalled McLaren. 'The height of my week was the laundry man arriving in a horse-drawn cart; I loved the way everything would come back clean and pressed in big boxes. I would go and get Mary the old maid, who was eighty, so the laundry man could take clothes back with him.'

There were trips together to the local 'bug-hutches', the Albion and the Vogue cinemas, and plays and pantomimes in the West End. 'My grandmother never paid for anything because she knew all the people on the door,' said McLaren.

Occasional summer outings to south coastal resorts such as Eastbourne brought out Rose's protective nature. In the 1980s McLaren told his lover Lauren Hutton that his grandmother forbade him from even paddling in the water. 'Rose didn't allow him to swim in the sea because fish pee in the sea,' recalled Hutton. 'She would take him to the beach for a day out but she'd cover his legs with blankets against the sun and put wet seaweed on his hair because she thought it was good for him. Crazy.'[8]

The boy and his grandmother particularly enjoyed reading plays together, indulging her long-dormant theatrical ambitions. This high level of literacy is another facet of Rose's character disputed by Peter McLaren. He later said that in the five years he knew Rose, he 'never saw her pick up or refer to a book or any other reading matter'.

Whatever the truth, there is no doubt that by the time the seven-year-old Malcolm re-entered the educational system at the Avigdor School, a private Jewish institution near Clissold Park, a short walk from Carysfort Road, he was a well-read and highly articulate, if troubled, child. 'I was really antagonistic toward any sense of authority, because it seemed as if I had read the whole of English Classical literature and [other pupils] were still trying to work out [Richmal Crompton's] *Just William* books,' said McLaren.

The return to formal schooling had also necessitated a haircut. According to Young Kim, McLaren remained so traumatised by the loss of his red curls in later life that he insisted on being accompanied whenever he visited a barber, and kept his eyes closed throughout.

Avigdor, where Stuart was also a pupil, was named after Rabbi Avigdor Schonfeld, whose son Solomon worked tirelessly to bring German children to London before, during and after the Second World War. It was a sober institution, where students wore yarmulkes and Hebrew classes were granted primacy, so not at all suited to the confident little troublemaker in its midst.

'The only interesting thing was that one teacher gave prizes at the end of each day and I never won any, so was totally pissed off,' said McLaren. 'So I decided to be first to get out of the class and scrambled over the other kids' tables and chairs like a wild animal to get out of there.'[9]

McLaren certainly did his best to shake up Avigdor, creating a shelter he called the Scarecrow Club in which he encouraged other children to dodge classes after lunch.

He was regularly reprimanded for such 'wild behaviour' and Rose was required to trot out her standard line to irate teachers. 'I was really at odds with the place and my grandmother, being one of those tyrannical creatures, gave me cotton wool and said: "If you don't like what they're saying put this in your ears," ' said McLaren.

'I was an obstreperous little shit,' he later admitted. 'I must have done it too many times and was brought up in front of the principal and was on the verge of being sent to what they called in England "Approved School", where you're lucky to get out alive.'

According to McLaren, Rose attended the meeting with an outsize Hermès-style 'Kelly' leather handbag. 'She declared that all he had had to do was beat me with such a bag: "Then he'll shut up and do as he's told." ' It is not known whether the teacher took this advice.

The unspectacular student regularly played truant in Clissold Park with his older brother. Meanwhile at home, life followed its path of warped indulgence. Rose threw a party for the boy's seventh birthday that included performances by a conjuror and the present of a tie featuring Dan Dare from the *Eagle* comic strip. 'I spent most of the afternoon in the bathroom learning how to tie it,' said McLaren.

This was the beginning of a lifelong obsession not just with clothes but also the signs and signifiers of visual identity. An incident at another child's home illuminates his unusual take on the importance of garments.

'I became conscious of clothing as more than just a means of keeping warm when I was staying at my friend's house one weekend and his mother asked me to bring some fresh towels to the bathroom,' he explained in the 1990s. 'On delivering them to her I was confronted by her standing in the bath completely naked. "So, what do you think, Malcolm?" she asked. I replied: "I can't tell, you haven't got any clothes on."'

At home, he ferreted through his mother's wardrobe: 'I used to search my mother's drawers to find her bras and make-up as I was fascinated by the idea of identity and what clothes meant.'

Relations in Stoke Newington were further complicated by the arrival of a half-brother, Colin, in the autumn of 1953. According to McLaren, Rose was furious with her daughter for bearing a child with Martin Edwards, and many rows ensued. The isolated McLaren later admitted to feeling no affection for his half-brother. There is a family portrait with Rose and Mick Isaacs when Colin was an infant; he and Stuart are wearing the Avigdor school uniform of open-neck shirts, matching socks, shorts and sleeveless jumpers. While Stuart leans fondly on Colin's pushchair, McLaren stares slyly into the camera lens and his grandmother is stern-faced.

At Avigdor, McLaren was constantly in hot water. 'Whatever school I went to I found myself searching for a surrogate mother, a gang I could call my own,' he said. 'These actions caused me untold problems – I was forever in trouble.'

In 1957, towards the end of his final year at Avigdor, Malcolm scraped through the eleven-plus exams which determined pupils' paths in secondary education; entry to the much-vaunted grammar schools was the aim of parents keen for their children to receive the best post-war educational opportunities outside the public school system.

Not that McLaren's parents appeared to have cared, but it was to his benefit that the problem-solving element of the eleven-plus was based on both verbal and non-verbal reasoning. With a gift of the gab already established, this was sufficient to gain the boy a place at Davenant Foundation School at 179 Whitechapel Road, just fifty yards from the Eve Edwards premises.

Known locally as Whitechapel Foundation, in the 1950s the institution was housed in a set of imposing buildings in red brick with terracotta flourishes constructed in both the neo-Georgian and so-called 'neo-Jacobean' styles with a grand assembly hall, ornate covered staircases and even a covered playground.

Since the late nineteenth century a large percentage of the school attendees had been Jewish, though the school itself was Church of England. McLaren later maintained this was a rough-house, with many tough kids displaying the emerging street fashions of early rock 'n' roll. 'In secondary school I tried to get the tightest trousers possible,' recalled McLaren. 'They made me feel dangerous and were a sign of rebellion.'

The Foundation School's end-of-term concert to celebrate Christmas in 1957 provided the eleven-year-old with what he would later describe as 'an epiphanic moment'. Among those selected to provide entertainment was a young male teacher who performed an enthusiastic rendition of Jerry Lee Lewis's rollicking 'Great Balls of Fire'.

McLaren was flabbergasted by the rawness of live rock 'n' roll. 'I'd never seen anything like it. I thought his head was going to come off.'[10]

Chapter 3

After leaving school in the late 1950s, Stuart Edwards became a stylistic and musical influence over his younger sibling. Malcolm McLaren recounted in later life that the 'Great Balls of Fire' revelation at the Foundation School was soon followed by attendance at a Buddy Holly & the Crickets performance in the company of his brother.

Given McLaren's later fascination for rock 'n' roll's first wave and the response to it from Britain's first mass youth cult, the Teddy boys, it is interesting to note that his entry point for popular music was – outside of Buddy Holly – the post-Ted, late 1950s saccharine pop from America.

'As well as "Rock Around the Clock" I heard Perry Como's "Magic Moments", which our mother had bought,' he said. 'The sound became interesting to me, because it seemed to be a language that everybody emotionally felt in some way. They responded. It could have been absolutely inane if you sat down and thought about it, but that didn't matter because it was a train people wanted to get on. They all thought it sexy, and so did I.'

As the writer Nik Cohn recorded, Ted style had peaked in 1956: 'Around the same time, the draped Ted jacket also began to fade out, to be replaced by the short, box-like Italian look, and from then on the signals were plain; by 1958, the full Teddy Boy regalia had become hopelessly outmoded and those that wore it were deliberately archaic.'[1]

McLaren's interest in the emerging male street styles was encouraged by Stuart, who frequented the livelier youth centres in neighbouring Stamford Hill, the area dubbed 'the Jewish playground'. A major draw was the amusement arcade known as the Schtip (apparently Yiddish for a waste of money). This was next to the E&A salt beef bar, a haunt of David Litvinoff and other young, gay Jewish gangsters.

According to a local, the late music writer Peter Simons who published under the pseudonym Penny Reel, the Schtip housed 'rows and rows of gleaming pinball machines, one-arm bandits and a jukebox containing some 50 rhythm and blues records'.[2]

'Stuart would tell me tales of the Schtip and people like Litvinoff, which I found very exciting,' said McLaren. 'These were glamorous, tough young guys in bespoke mohair suits. I was fascinated.'

McLaren himself visited the locale's Stamford Hill Boys and Girls Club along with other 'Modernists' – the forerunners of British mods – such as Mark Feld (later to transform himself into Marc Bolan).

Simons characterised the area's denizens as 'working-class rough Jews; sporting men, gamblers, card-players, boxing men, football men, the Schmutter-trade people, the rag-trade people. They were kind of comedy Jews really, they spoke a sort of Yiddish. The first mods I saw were Jewish tailors' sons. The thing that separated the Jews and the gentiles was that the Jews had bar mitzvahs at the age of thirteen, when they were required to get a suit. Their fathers being tailors, they had the pick of the new materials – the Nylon, the Rayon, the Mohair, so these kids were dressed in these.'[3]

So it was that, when Malcolm Edwards came of age in 1959, the thirteen-year-old wore a sharp double-breasted suit especially cut for him by his grandfather for his bar-mitzvah party held at central London's Cumberland Hotel in Mayfair.

McLaren's academic progress continued its downward path at the Foundation School, though he later claimed that the one area of school life where he excelled was football. Not only was he captain of the school team, he said, but he was also spotted by a scout for the local team Arsenal FC while playing in a game in Highbury Fields.

'He invited me to train with the juniors,' McLaren said in 2006. 'On the first day, I found myself running up and down the concrete terraces with a giant sand bag tied to my back. When I made it clear that I had no interest in this form of activity, I was accused of being an agent provocateur and given my marching orders.'[4]

McLaren wasn't to see out his secondary education in Whitechapel.

By the time of his bar mitzvah, the Eve Edwards business had become successful enough for McLaren's parents to move up in the world, from 47 Carysfort Road to 31 Cheyne Walk, a substantial five-bedroom detached house with mock-Tudor exterior décor in a quiet street in the north-west London suburb of Hendon.

Not wanting to be separated from her grandson, Rose – by now nearing sixty – insisted that she, Mick and Malcolm occupied the upper floor of the house, further driving the wedge between him and the rest of his family.

Malcolm became a pupil at the local boys' grammar school Orange Hill, 'an unwelcoming pile of red-brick and prefab'[5] a mile or so bus ride along the Watford Way in unprepossessing Burnt Oak.

He was horrified. While the move to Cheyne Walk had presaged a more traditional way for a family unit to live – parents and sons with grandparents at least under the same roof – McLaren felt the loss of his cultural bearings across the distance of eight miles to the place where he was born.

Cheyne Walk – also home to the light entertainer, gag-writer and film star Bob Monkhouse – was in another predominantly Jewish neighbourhood within walking distance of a synagogue, but this part of Hendon where it merged into Golders Green lacked the inner-city, cheek-by-jowl earthiness of Carysfort Road.

McLaren mischievously mischaracterised Hendon in notes in his later life as Edgware, an even more suburban and Jewish locale three miles north. 'Perhaps this sense of being an outsider struck me when I moved from a working-class culture to a middle-class one,' he wrote. 'There was an intimacy and genuine humanity in Stoke Newington that was sorely lacking in the coldness of Edgware. There was an alienating effect in middle-class culture compared to the sense of participation in working-class culture (even though I wasn't working class). If one is unable to reconcile one's class one is forced to create a world or anti-world.'

McLaren compared the Stoke Newington experiences of 'standing outside the music hall [and] interaction with neighbours' with the blandness of Cheyne Walk. This cultivated an 'ultimate hatred of bourgeois values which craved harmony and which bred a resentment of society'.

To the boy, his mother's insistence on wearing fur coats represented the worst of these tendencies. 'Her mink stole was an icon of the middle class,' he said.

And he later claimed that Emily Edwards, by then in her mid-thirties, had begun to openly flaunt her relationship with the tycoon Charles Clore (who had by now acquired Selfridges). According to McLaren, the wealthy entrepreneur would roll up to 31 Cheyne Walk in an impressive car and take his mother for nights out and even weekends away while her husband Martin put in the hours overseeing the Whitechapel manufacturing business.

Despite the misery McLaren felt at being transplanted to Hendon, he retrospectively recognised the oppressiveness of suburban existence in fact stimulated his visual expression: 'There was a sense that clothes defined identity in the suburbs and could be manipulated to express what one wanted to be.'

As McLaren said in 2000: 'By the 1950s, London and other British cities had become less community-based, more anonymous. This made us teenagers feel disconnected and alienated, and meant that we had to search for our own identity.'[6]

As evinced by his mother's behaviour, the move to Hendon had not alleviated familial tensions. In later life McLaren talked about how his childhood informed his adult choices because it was 'based on never knowing how to live in a family, how to treat family members. It was safest for me to live in chaos – my life at home was in constant turmoil and that was what I felt comfortable with, so I chose to recreate it in later life. My grandmother continued to create animosity in the household to force everyone apart. [Later] I made people uneasy all the time in my shops. This appealed to the young because they wanted to create chaos themselves.'

Photographs from the era show that McLaren didn't attempt to fit in; in one taken in the garden at Cheyne Walk, Stuart playfully wrestles with his youngest brother Colin while the early teenage McLaren is lankily hunched to one side in a smart scout uniform complete with beret.

In Hendon, the sole spot of solace was the Fiesta 'froffy' coffee bar, housed at the end of Cheyne Walk in Hendon Central station, next to the hulking Gaumont cinema and decorated in quasi-beat style with lobster pots in netting on the walls. 'It was another world,' McLaren would sigh. 'I had such a miserable time at home I'd escape there, nurse an espresso and watch the beatnik girls with their mascara-ed eyes and black Sloppy Joes.'

Around this time there was a fashion among adolescents to carry LPs as signifiers and badges of honour. 'People would sit on the bus or hang around in coffee bars with an album on display to show everyone what type of music they were into, that they were members of a secret society,' recalled McLaren. 'But that wasn't enough for me, because I had to have my feelings realised and represented, and, as you looked like a peacock, you became a member of a surrogate club of outsiders and rebels. I scoured every shop on the way home from school, studying details of scarves, shoes and socks in window displays.

'I had shifted my feelings and sense of being able to know your neighbours to a place where you were literally shut off; the only thing that brought life to me in the suburbs was the constant desire to go to the West End.'[7]

Initially trailing in his older brother's wake and later on his own or with a select group of friends, McLaren was lured by the boutiques that had sprung up in Soho and its surrounds: Vince Man's Shop in Newburgh Street, the theatrical shoemakers Anello & Davide in Charing Cross Road, John Stephen's outlets – particularly His Clothes – in Carnaby Street and John Michael Ingram's Sportique in Old Compton Street.

Many of the retailers, and a proportion of their clientele, were openly gay or at least overtly camp in their behaviour. This served to stimulate

McLaren's interest, since the liberalisation of the British laws regarding homosexuality was a good half-decade away. Vince's – run by the former muscle-boy photographer Bill Green – was regarded by his more conventional friends as a no-go zone, and had become the butt of jokes. (The critic and jazz singer George Melly claimed that he had his inside leg measured there when he dropped in to purchase a tie.) Yet the brazen McLaren bowled in and bought a pair of tight trousers with a low rise which accentuated the groin.

McLaren was one of a number of style-obsessed London youths – many of them also Jewish – flooding into Soho in this period. Celebrity photographer Richard Young recounts how, as a thirteen-year-old, he visited with his Hackney schoolmate, Marc Bolan-in-waiting Mark Feld. 'We'd play truant from school and catch the 73 bus into Soho. I'd never seen anything like the clothes at Sportique. There were amazing shirts in Swiss voile with a fly front, penny-round collars and detailed stitching for four guineas.' On leaving school, Young became an assistant at the shop.[8]

'The department stores were so desperate seeing these boutiques opening up in the back streets of Regent Street,' McLaren noted. 'It was originally the home of the gay fraternity but was now considered hip by the young and the sexually ambivalent. Why? Because it was part of something underground. If you purchased a pair of trousers in Carnaby Street you had to be prepared for the sales assistant to feel your balls!'

He was encouraged and financially indulged in these expeditions by Rose, who took pleasure at her grandson's increasingly wild appearance – by now comprising 'purple polka-dot shirts and bright-green hipster pin cords' – since it served to upset his mother and stepfather's fashion conservativism.[9]

When McLaren acquired a pair of winklepickers with money given to him by Rose, his parents and brothers expressed 'disgust; they hated that type of shoe because they were considered lewd, gauche, not respectable'.

Now McLaren relied on Rose for a weekly stipend 'for something new to wear, whether Madras cotton ties, embroidered handkerchiefs, bright blue Italian wool blazers, fly-fronted shirts with round collars – I wanted everything that was in fashion'.

His obsession reached such a pitch that McLaren's parents banned their son from purchasing any more clothing. He later claimed Rose resorted to buying him the fashions he desired and secreting them in the front garden.

'She would leave me packages filled with clothes in our hedge, and I would change into pointed shoes, brightly coloured jumpers and tight trousers and then go off to a club,' he said. 'My grandmother liked the idea of going against my mother's wishes ... she always wanted my allegiance.'

During the school holidays, McLaren's knowledge of the mechanics of clothing manufacture was expanded by stints at his parents' factory. He also persuaded Mick Isaacs to make him a woollen military-style overcoat, grey and double-breasted.

Simultaneously, the teen explored the music scene then coalescing around the fascination for black American blues and R&B which would power the oncoming British beat boom. His tastes had moved on from those of his first vinyl acquisition: Jan & Dean's upbeat cover of Hoagy Carmichael's 'Heart and Soul', bought in a Hendon record shop in 1961.[10]

'Many young teenagers drifted through the back streets of Soho looking for the blues,' he wrote. 'They listened to Muddy Waters and various other black musicians. At the same time sticking out of their pockets as they walked around on a Saturday morning in seedy old Soho would be certain books such as Thomas De Quincey's *Confessions of an English Opium-Eater*, a novel by Albert Camus such as *The Stranger* or, if they were very hip, the darker, more liberated novels like William Burroughs's *The Naked Lunch* or *The Story of O*, books that were banned here but published in Paris.'

McLaren connected this to the fact that there was a strong French presence among the owners and habitués of Soho's nightlife venues. 'They all wore the anti-fashion style of the existentialist: the ubiquitous black polo neck,' he wrote. 'These coffee bars and clubs were called La Bastille, Les Enfants Terrible, La Poubelle, Le Macabre, La Discotheque, the Saint-Germain-des-Prés . . . There you'd see the young Mick Jagger, the young Jeff Beck, the young Rod Stewart. It was here in these clubs that I picked up the style and sense of rebellion and combined that with a discovery of the blues.'

In Wardour Street, La Discotheque was notable for being owned by the notorious slum landlord Peter Rachman, and McLaren began visiting what is now recognised as Britain's first disco. 'Mandy Rice-Davies served behind the bar,' he recalled in the 1980s. 'Around the walls of this huge room were bare boards, a tiny little juke box, French-style, screwed into the wall, and all round were huge, bare-mattress beds with girls frolicking. It was the most incredible scene I've ever witnessed. My friend told me they were lesbians, in a whisper. I was staggered and taken up by the imagery.

'Within a few weeks the beds were gone and it became a straight discotheque with a little band playing called the Night Sounds Combo, of which Rachman was the saxophonist. Upstairs was a gambling room, the Mississippi Room, where you could bet on a huge roulette table for 2/6d. If you were really plucky, you would go over and, with this really dodgy looking bird, you played blackjack [and] chemin de fer.'[11]

McLaren's nocturnal forays into Soho became the stuff of legend at his school. One fellow Orange Hill pupil, David Edwards (no relation), later recalled: 'Before registration, he would regale us with stories of his visits to London clubs the night before. I remember one night he had heard the record 'The Lion Sleeps Tonight' which he urged me to buy.'[12]

In the summer of 1962, the sixteen-year-old McLaren left Orange Hill with scant qualifications: three O-level exam passes at a time a minimum of five was needed not just for further education but also for professional and skilled occupations.

What was to become of this unusual, barely educated but hugely literate dandy boy, totally estranged from his mother, stepfather and siblings, and spoiled into truculence and arrogance by his eccentric and overbearing grandmother?

Towards the end of the summer of 1962, with the express purpose of gaining her son a job, Emily Edwards ushered McLaren into the Labour Exchange in Hendon's main drag, Brent Street.

There appears to have been no desire on either side for the teenager to enter the family clothing business full-time. And there was no option of further education due to McLaren's dreadful exam results. In this immediate pre-Beatles era, unqualified fifteen- and sixteen-year-old school leavers were expected to accept whatever job was presented to them and then set about the joyless business of 'settling down'.

In a cubbyhole inside the cavernous Labour Exchange, a clerk reeled off that week's list of available jobs, including machine operator in a pen factory, assistant to a linen salesman and booking clerk for the shipping division of Fyffes, the fruit importer best known for its bananas – still an exotic foodstuff in post-austerity Britain – which ran passenger-carrying 'banana boats' to and from the West Indies.

One position attracted Mrs Edwards's attention: junior trainee taster at Geo. G. Sandeman Sons & Co. Ltd, the wine merchants to HRH The Queen, which produced popular sherries and ports from extensive vineyards in Spain and Portugal.

'My mother in her mink stole thought that this was an illustrious job from which she could benefit, by talking about it at cocktail parties,' said McLaren.

With offices in the City of London and Edinburgh, Sandeman's tasting rooms were in the cinema and theatre district in London's West End, and a few days later the sixteen-year-old presented himself at the company for one of the scant periods of formal employment in his life.

'I climbed a narrow staircase to a Dickensian garret,' he wrote. 'Room after bomb-struck room was filled with dusty ledgers and bottles. The six other trainees were boys from Eton and Harrow. The permanent staff was made up almost entirely of retired colonels and generals who had been stationed in Asia, back when it was referred to as "the Orient". Our red-faced, blustery boss was a former army general who had spent too many years in Burma – killing villagers, rumour had it.'[13]

As well as trainee taster, the quick-witted McLaren was earmarked as a potential salesman. To master this craft he was inducted into a thorough education of French wines. Up until this point, the only wine McLaren had tasted was the sweet sherry served on family occasions. Now he was required to learn the value and properties of individual varieties by age and quality. To achieve this, he was taught to recognise wines by taste and provenance; each day he and other trainees were blindfolded by senior staff and led to a spittoon. 'Here we were given test tubes of wine and asked to taste but not swallow,' wrote McLaren. 'Blueface (as the general came to be known by us for the blue veins that ran across his face, like a gorgonzola) would then lecture us about the qualities each wine possessed, followed by the inevitable question: What did we think of it?'[14]

To the embarrassment of the teenage trainees, the general used sexual-ised language to describe wine varieties. 'He talked about wine as virginal, needing to spread its legs, or over-ripe, or sexless, or homosexual,' McLaren told an interviewer in the 1980s.[15]

'While we young virgins stood frozen and blushing from learning about the facts of life this way, he talked about wines for men and wines for women. Wine that tastes like a man, and wine that tastes like a woman. Wine that was friendly, frilly, silly or simply handsome; heroic or cowardly and foolish. And wines that defied discussion – these were apparently homosexual.'

A lecture on a Sauternes pointed out the Roman influence in the making of this sweet Bordeaux wine. According to the general, it had 'a lot of fat under the arm'.

This impressed McLaren: 'Indeed, the wine felt heavy. Oily. Fatty. Perhaps, I thought, he is not entirely insane.'

As the weeks passed the wily boy adopted his teacher's tone. 'I'd say of one: "Virginal, sir. Not seen a man." And with cheap Bordeaux,

I'd mimic: "That's right, sir. Sharp, bitter, not much discipline in this wine."

' "Male?" Blueface would ask. "Female?"

' "Definitely female. Needs to be put in her place, doesn't she?" '

' "Well done!" he'd say. I was actually good at this. The general had begun talking about sending us to Oporto.'[16]

During weekday lunch hours over the autumn of 1962, McLaren escaped the stultifying atmosphere of the tasting rooms to wander the West End streets, in the main browsing racks of clothes in his favourite boutiques. 'One lunchtime after spotted dick at the café' in Soho's eastern border, Charing Cross Road, McLaren experienced a life-changing encounter . . . with a building.[17]

This 1930s quasi-modernist block, entered via a Portland stone entrance with distinctive carved mouldings and reliefs, was home to Saint Martin's School of Art. The large double doors were open wide, and the pavement outside teemed with apparently carefree young students. Later McLaren said his enchantment began when he followed a group of attractive girls dressed in beatnik style: oversize mohair jumpers and fishnet stockings.

'I thought: "What on earth is an art school?". Venturing in, I smelt something completely different from wine: oil paint. Down the corridors I looked through crevices and windows at various studios and discovered all sorts of things, including nude women being sketched. It was fantastic. People were smoking. I saw a kind of sexiness and wanted immediately to be part of it. This was a place far removed from the mad, matriarchal, *Jane Eyre*, gothic Victorian world I came from.'

His curiosity piqued, McLaren began to haunt Saint Martin's during his lunch hour. And he had not given up on his night-time visits to central London clubs and music venues, catching an early performance by the Rolling Stones at the former jazz club Studio 51 in Great Newport Street. 'I remember Mick Jagger wore a matelot top and the others had on dirty white shirts, scruffy long hair, an unshaven and unwashed look, but with the air of a dandy,' he said.

This was the period when the British Invasion and Carnaby Street, the twin music and fashion phenomena that set the sixties swinging, were emerging into public consciousness.

In October 1962, EMI Parlophone released the first single by the Beatles, 'Love Me Do'. The song acted as pre-ignition for the imminent explosion of their popularity. Within a matter of weeks, the quartet's second single, 'Please Please Me', went straight to the top, and Beatlemania was born. London style – and in particular that of Carnaby Street – was exported around the world by the waves of British groups who followed the trail blazed by the Fab Four: the Rolling Stones, The Who, the Animals, the Kinks et al.

A few weeks before 'Love Me Do' was released, *Town* magazine published a story about teen fashion mores, and interviewed Mark Feld (aka Marc Bolan). The article, with its insight into the network of clubs and a host of new groups, and photographs by Don McCullin, was a mod blueprint. The fourteen-year-old Feld opined: 'You've got to be different from the other kids. I mean, you've got to be two steps ahead. The stuff that half the haddocks are wearing I was wearing years ago.'[18] One of the few London clothiers rated by Feld and his gang was John Stephen, who now had five outlets on Carnaby Street. McLaren was, of course, also a Stephen customer and it was not lost on him that Sandeman's intention to install him in its Oporto vineyards would remove him from the Youthquake now brewing in central London.

He engineered a means of dismissal by staying alone in the tasting rooms one lunch hour and smoking as many strong-flavoured Gitanes as he could. At two o'clock, through the fug, which would have put paid to the afternoon's tasting session, he heard the general's voice booming: 'What filthy Turk has been in here?'

'I announced myself. "Sir, it's me."

' "What are you smoking?"

' "Gitanes," I said, trying to sound provocative.'[19]

According to McLaren, he was fired on the spot, and given a letter to present to his mother explaining that his presence was no longer required, on the grounds that he had deliberately sabotaged the tasting rooms and so prevented the other trainees from continuing their work that day.

In a 1984 interview, McLaren declared: 'So I gave up wine tasting and gave myself to art. Everything began and changed then. But still I'll think: "Virginal? Homosexual?" when passed a glass.'[20]

Chapter 4

The transformation of young Malcolm Edwards from apprentice wine taster to art student was not smooth.

Having taken a more active role in her son's affairs, Emily Edwards was enraged at his failure to stick at the job at Sandeman's, not least because acceptance of the offer of the transfer to Oporto would have removed his disruptive presence from the family home. So the boy was taken back to Hendon Labour Exchange where he took, first, the clerking job at the banana-boat operator Fyffes in Piccadilly and, subsequently, a similar post at an accountancy correspondence school in Marylebone. These lasted a few weeks each; he was fired for laziness and incompetence from both. At the latter – before it was discovered that, Billy Liar-style, he had thrown away documents it was his job to file – McLaren claimed to have encountered the neighbouring Dr Stephen Ward, the society fixer at the centre of the Profumo affair, which blew up at the beginning of 1963.[1]

Encouraged by his grandmother, McLaren enrolled for night classes at Saint Martin's. Here he was expected to produce life studies, some of nudes. When his mother discovered the drawings in the boy's bedroom, she called the school and had his name struck from the list of pupils.

But, in the spring of 1963, by now aged seventeen, McLaren returned to Saint Martin's and registered for a course in three-dimensional design, sketching functional and aesthetic objects. Although this was one removed from his ambition to become a painter, his application to the tasks set for the pupils was recognised by the tutor, the British painter and printmaker Ian Tyson, who was impressed by McLaren's inquisitive drive and suggested the teenager undertake a pre-diploma course at the school.

Hendon was out of Saint Martin's catchment area so McLaren was told to try Harrow Technical College & School of Art in the next borough to the Edwards' home.

To gain entry to the foundation course, which would allow McLaren to go on to study for the newly introduced three-year Dip AD (Diploma in Art & Design), five O levels were required, and – again funded by Rose – he passed the additional two exams at a crammer in the early summer of 1963. Armed with these and drawings from the three-dimensional classes, McLaren was accepted by Harrow.

At this time grants for students under the age of eighteen were paid to parents, who disbursed the money as they saw fit. Resentful of her unruly son's choice, Emily Edwards announced that, come the autumn, his access to funds would be limited by a number of conditions, including the stricture that he was not to stay away from home all night.

In the weeks before he started at Harrow, McLaren was sent by his mother to a summer school in the south of France; he told Young Kim that this was an internship with the painter André Masson. Whiling away the time on the beach at Cannes provided the boy with an opportunity to boast about his first-hand knowledge of Stephen Ward and the by-now notorious Profumo scandal. McLaren also visited the Riviera's casinos, in one of which he witnessed a performance by Dionne Warwick.[2]

On his return, McLaren prepared for the life of an art student with a sartorial rethink. 'At art school you wanted to look like a painter even if you couldn't paint,' he wrote in the 1990s. 'The thought of posing as an artist was a very romantic notion for anyone coming from a middle-class background.'

McLaren gave up frequenting Soho nightspots and backed away from the mod insistence on clean lines and neat edges by roughly customising his clothes, including the grey wool military overcoat Mick Isaacs had made, shortening it with a pair of his grandfather's cutting shears so that the fraying ends were displayed.

This was, McLaren later wrote, 'a style no one could touch. It couldn't be bought, you had to be it, know it, wear it as an attitude. Frayed coats, torn sweaters were outside of traditional modes of fashion. Wearing a sweater under a coat without a shirt was considered weird in those days, but you could do that at art school.'

The savage customising of the coat made for him by his grandfather was 'the first indication of manipulating ordinary clothes into a style you liked,' wrote McLaren. 'Opposite types of clothes you put together to create something else. A utility tweed overcoat worn with a pair of shiny trousers, a tight-fitting pink turtleneck and Chelsea boots. The juxtaposition of these would create another look, one that wasn't mainstream.'

As the British artists/academics John Beck and Matthew Cornford have pointed out, in the post-war period there were 180 art schools in towns across Britain, compared to just 28 universities: 'The idea of art school as culture, as a way of life, is why "Art School" as signifier in the UK has come to mean much more than the often prosaic day-to-day experience of being at art school suggests.'[3]

British art schools offered 'Bohemia as a viable career option,' according to writers Simon Frith and Howard Horne. '[This was] a time when shabby college buildings catered for fun and discovery, when artists were trained to be entertainers.'[4] Consequently, local art schools nurtured the talents of many of the young performers and designers to make an impact in the worlds of music and fashion, from John Lennon, Jimmy Page and Keith Richards to Mary Quant, Biba's Barbara Hulanicki and Ossie Clark.

Much later, McLaren claimed to have recognised from the outset that 'the idea was not to have a career, but to do the opposite really. The idea was not to become a painter but to express your individual concerns. The place where you could have these ideas supported was at art school. It was a haven in that respect [because] it wasn't directly involved in academia or career.

'One felt that this creativity was supported by an overground pop culture. It was really an open door to anyone who had any kind of talent that needed to be expressed. Everybody was prepared to listen and watch and join in – we were fuelling a new fire. It was the first time the pop culture was looking like it was seriously going to dominate the world and it afforded a desire by everyone to stretch themselves as far as possible. The limits were boundless.'

With entry ages from thirteen, technical college and art school pupils were drawn from a widely cast net, with promise and enthusiasm valued as much as educational qualifications; at Harrow, general studies were taught along with specialist subjects such as commercial art, illustration, painting, sculpture, three-dimensional design and silverwork. The faculty was headed by Ken Illingworth and the foundation course was run by the notable realist painter Ivor Fox. Teachers included Royal Academician Ken Howard, *Private Eye* cartoonist Barry Fantoni, architect Sir Hugh Casson and Peter Blake. On one occasion in his first term, McLaren encountered Blake playing a saxophone in a classroom. The pop artist responded to the student's enquiry as to what he was up to by saying, 'I'm painting'.

A student of McLaren's age, Patricia Whorwood, recalled: 'We were allowed to develop our skills at an age before we were too restricted. There was no uniform and there were students up to the age of 20; you couldn't tell the difference between the tutors and the students.'[5] In the area's main thoroughfare Station Road, Harrow Art School was housed in a separate building from the technical school. This, according to McLaren's fellow student Fred Vermorel, was 'a white stone Victorian building fronted by wrought-iron railings . . . the interior was multi-layered and ad hoc, with all kinds of unexpected passages and stairwells and dead ends, and strangely-positioned rooms and studios. Some studios were only accessible from the outside, making the building even more confusing, and were used for drug-taking and snogging, or dossing by itinerant beatniks.'[6]

The first term of the foundation course was dedicated to education across the range of practices. From the second term, students were expected to focus on fine art or an aspect of design, having formally applied to the diploma course of their choice.

McLaren later admitted to having been apprehensive on entering the school, claiming that one of the principals, either Illingworth or Fox, 'explained what a difficult task it would be for me to keep up. He believed I had no special talent or facility.'[7]

In his later years, McLaren often recounted the words he heard in his first lecture. Like many of the Harrow teachers, the tutor was evidently aligned with the Arts and Crafts Movement pioneered by the great Victorian artist, designer and thinker William Morris. And his attitude to creative endeavour was to leave a greater mark on the young student.

'A grisly, bearded professor with a distinct Northern accent looked down on us, the new arrivals, and bellowed: "None of you would bloody be here if it weren't for ol' Bill Morris."

'I wondered, "Who's ol' Bill Morris?"

'Without further ado he hung up a large piece of embroidered cloth. It had flowers on it and looked old and scruffy and reminded me of grandma's closet. Why, I thought, would anyone care about someone who was responsible for this?

'The lecturer continued, pointing, I believed, in my direction, and said: "If you want success, there's the bloody door. If you're going to be artists, you had better learn now that you're all going to fail. Don't think success will make you better artists."'

At this point, McLaren later admitted, he felt confused. But then the tutor announced: 'Failure's not such a bad thing you know, because it makes you struggle and that's the one thing that will get you up in the morning.'[8]

The diatribe embodied one of the abiding Arts and Crafts principles: acceptance of mistakes in the creative process as expressed in the Victorian church architect J. D. Sedding's aphorism, 'There is hope in honest error, none in the icy perfections of the mere stylist.' This became the mantra of one of the movement's supreme exponents, the Scottish architect and designer Charles Rennie Mackintosh.

The philosophy also chimed with McLaren's memories of reading the Dickens manuscripts in his childhood, where editorial corrections to the text were evident on the page.

'The men who taught us were the last gasp of that generation,' said McLaren. 'Things were changing; the introduction of the Dip AD was looking to a future of professionalism in the arts they weren't going to be a part of. They were glorious amateurs, the "art for art's sake" crowd which was on the verge of disappearing.'

The impact of the statement on McLaren was immediate and profound. 'I realised that by understanding failure you were going to be able to improve your condition as an artist. Because you were not going to fear failure you were going to embrace it and, in doing so, maybe break the rules and by doing that, change the culture and, possibly by doing that, change life itself.'

In his fifties, McLaren wrote about the tutor's speech: 'My lack of skill at drawing and painting no longer mattered. It was the struggle that counted. I took the tutor's words as gospel and my suburban world at home suddenly became alien. All its middle class rules went out the window.

'I had a different cause in life. Not a career, but an adventure.'[9]

At Harrow, McLaren supplemented his classes – where he was surprised to find that fellow pupils included thirteen-year-olds in short trousers from the Harrow Tech junior school – with weekend visits to London's art institutions. At these he worked on his draughtsmanship.

One Saturday morning McLaren sat on his sketching stool at the British Museum in front of the Elgin Marbles and elected to render the sculpture of the head of a horse from the chariot of the moon goddess Selene. 'For the first time I drew someone else's art,' wrote McLaren. 'I didn't know who the artist was nor how this head came to be, but the life that poured out of it seemed to be something I could worship. The flatness of the piece was very difficult to translate onto paper, but sitting as it did on a plinth with its jaw open, it made me constantly want to stroke it, touch it and feel it.

'Perspective and a knowledge of form had always eluded me and the horror of trying to render the life force of the head was something else.

The head, although carved from white marble, was turned black by my pencil and graphite lines into a whirling ball of intense matter. The paper was virtually worn through. By late afternoon I realised that my black head pushed forward off the white page and that was not normal. Black meant substance and came forward, white went back. This was my revelation and how I began to draw for the first time.

'I went back regularly, never tiring of drawing this horse, never worried about failing in my attempts. No one around me mattered, the floor would be filled with wood shavings from my pencils. All my thoughts now were lines on paper and their very failure to make sense proved that the struggle was all.'[10]

As he refined this peculiar technique, the student attempted to render life models convincingly during school hours and at other times visited the Victoria and Albert Museum, where he researched the life and work of William Morris.

Like the other students, McLaren took his pad and utensils onto the streets around the art school to capture everyday life. He also visited the cemetery of St Mary's church at the summit of Harrow-on-the-Hill where he sketched the tombstones, aware that the graveyard had been visited by Lord Byron (a memorial stone is erected there in the memory of Byron and Claire Clairmont's doomed daughter Allegra).

'It was painfully obvious how difficult drawing was,' he wrote. 'How to make sense of it all? I read biographies of artists. I looked at their pictures. I wanted to belong to the struggle.'[11]

McLaren's voracious search for knowledge took him to the large group exhibition *The Popular Image* at central London's Institute of Contemporary Art in autumn 1963. This was organised by the Parisian New York-based gallerist Ileana Sonnabend, then on a mission to promote the new American pop art in Europe. And so British art-lovers were granted exposure to eleven contemporary practitioners. Included with contributions by Jasper Johns, Robert Rauschenberg and Roy Lichtenstein were works by twenty-three-year-old Andy Warhol, including his *Marilyn Diptych*, a multiple portrait of Marilyn Monroe constituting fifty silkscreened images. This was roundly mocked by the popular press and Britain's art gatekeepers but the boy student from Hendon was bowled over. 'Warhol's works left a deep and indelible impression upon me,' McLaren said later. 'They confirmed what I had discovered, that art school was a sanctuary, a world apart from the norm.'

McLaren's confidence, already prodigious, blossomed as he began to prise himself from the emotional clutches of his grandmother and carve a life outside of his unhappy home, where his sullen demeanour and dress-down appearance came under increasing attack from his mother and stepfather.

'In art school no one would think you were out of sync,' he wrote. 'It made you feel that you had freedom to be true to yourself. You felt very special, and that made you think that you could do special things: smoke drugs, have weird hairdos and act as eccentric as possible. The point was you never wanted to return to "normality" again.'

McLaren's outgoing nature and quirky appearance soon attracted other students, among them a young London Irishman, Patrick Casey. 'There was an aura about Patrick,' said McLaren in later life. 'I really looked up to him. He was six feet tall, handsome with a ruddy complexion and black silky hair and came from a fairly middle-class family. His father, a building contractor, hated Patrick's girliness. Patrick was self-obsessed and extremely arrogant but really very insecure and a bit shy, the perfect companion for me.'

As singular as his acquaintance, Casey insisted on using coloured ballpoint pens rather than pencils in classes; his life drawings and still lifes were 'like gyroscopes – they had a kind of fake sense of form, extraordinary', according to McLaren.

Casey was also up on the latest musical developments and tried to persuade McLaren to the charms of Bob Dylan's eponymous debut LP released the previous year. 'I couldn't understand what he saw in him,' said McLaren, referring to the cover portrait of the puppy-faced Dylan. 'I didn't get the music either. There was no beat – it wasn't like Elvis. I was very naive to this folk-driven music. You had to listen to the lyrics not just the pop tune, so it fascinated me.'

Similarly, McLaren was confused by Casey's Leadbelly and Big Bill Broonzy records. 'I thought, what is all this? This was a world I had no idea of. I didn't understand,' said McLaren.

Casey led a mysterious, unconventional life. On an occasion when he and McLaren were sketching at a museum, two friends of Casey's arrived with a pram that contained not a baby but a packet of biscuits, some photographs and a sketch pad. McLaren described one of the pair as 'a man with a weird hairstyle, wearing mascara', while the other was 'a tiny girl – they had an intense conversation with Patrick, as if they were both in love with him, or maybe she was girlfriend to both men'. After the couple left, Casey revealed that the girl had once been his partner and that he had impregnated her.

That he was also partial to drugs – in particular marijuana and speed – added to Casey's allure for McLaren, whose experience of mind-altering substances was non-existent while his sexual encounters had been restricted to teenage fumblings at Jewish youth clubs and house parties.

'Patrick became my very close friend and was the one person that I felt was really "art school",' said McLaren. 'He was always chuckling to himself, I never knew what about. He gave me confidence, assuming an air of authority though he was never really in authority. I always had an air of awkwardness about me.'

And Casey was also something of a dandy. For these strange young men, the pose was as important as their creative output. 'The role that you played was as much an act as it was an action,' said McLaren. 'Coffee breaks and teatime were as relevant as anything else because of where you sat, who you sat with and how you looked when you were sitting.'

Satisfyingly, the effort the pair put into public displays was observed by another new entrant, Fred Vermorel. He noticed the

intriguing young man with a shock of auburn hair, who always wore a tartan scarf knotted rakishly around his scrawny neck. He went around with a tall and morose student, darkly handsome and fetchingly sinister. These two always sat together in the canteen, at a table nearest the entrance, and made a great show of being haughty and secretive – consumed in intimate derisions and chuckling disconcertingly at passers-by, throwing out trails of insults as people came and went. No one was safe from this pair – not the sternest tutor, the prettiest girls. Everyone ran a muttered gauntlet.[12]

Vermorel himself was sardonic and intense, self-consciously cultivating the air of the *poète maudit*. After acceptance on the same foundation course as Casey and McLaren, he had quickly dismissed the majority of art students at Harrow as 'a disappointingly respectable bunch'.

This led him one lunchtime to brave Casey and McLaren's withering looks by daring to introduce himself and join them at their table, 'gradually insinuating my observations into their caustic commentaries'.

They in turn accepted him into their clique. Casey, Vermorel concluded after this first encounter, was a man of outré tastes. 'Precociously, he lived with a woman who he claimed liked to be tied up and whipped with his belt. This was a new one on me,' Vermorel later wrote. 'Malcolm was much more interesting. His dominating characteristic was his way of laughing, of dissolving and directing, and thereby manipulating, every situation in explosions of contagious laughter.'[13]

As they came to know each other better, Vermorel also saw that McLaren's 'cosmopolitan Jewishness enabled him to absorb a lot of influences, and be a bit more creative than most kids would have been at that age; self-confident anyway. He had a certain kind of self-aggrandizing chutzpah, which he got from his background and from his grandmother.'[14]

Vermorel believes that the mutual attraction felt by McLaren and Casey was 'because they were both renegades. Unafraid to be surly and both against the system.'[15]

Certainly McLaren relished standing up to authority. Vermorel has related that, among his many disputes with Harrow staff, the most memorable was when a tutor snapped at McLaren, 'You think you know everything,' and was rendered speechless by the student's response: 'There's nothing to know!'

According to Vermorel, McLaren's bravado extended to his view of himself as an artist. 'This is what marked Malcolm out, even as a seventeen-year-old; he was preposterously convinced that he would "do it" and that he was as good as the best. That attitude enabled him to produce some remarkable work. A seventeen-year-old doesn't usually attempt to outdo Jackson Pollock. There was no middle ground with him – he wasn't "trying to be", he was certain he was "going to be".

'Sometimes he would fall flat on his face. But at other times, the ferocity of his work – I'm thinking of some self-portraits he gave me which I subsequently lost – was extraordinary. He would draw and overdraw and overdraw with intensity until the work was thick with graphite and sometimes the paper was torn by the effort.'

In Vermorel's view, McLaren 'wasn't any good at representation, as you had to be in those days. There was no way he would have got into the Slade, which was the prize.'

McLaren's experience with the Parthenon horse's head had confirmed that he did not have a conventional take, even as a student. 'As an artist I was certainly off-centre and odd,' he wrote. 'When I drew heads they ended up like giant pieces of granite. I was different.'

In Vermorel's view, McLaren was already betraying talents as a graphic artist. 'As well as making those self-portraits, Malcolm was good with shapes, use of colour and abstract geometrical patterns. I noticed that there was the same effect in the clothes that he wore; it was the unusual combination and the patterns. He had a flair, which was another thing which attracted him to me.'

Such were McLaren's innate sensibilities in regard to visual style. 'He wore clothes as a model does,' wrote Vermorel in the 1990s. 'They hung on him transiently, the statement, the cut or cloth louder than the wearer, clearly semiological. Thus his tartan scarf cocking a snook, with its ruffian knot and proletarian connotations, at the earnest Carnaby Street fashions sported by other students. He was the complete dandy, in and out.'

Baked into this visual flair was a predisposition to the fabulism of his forebears. 'He was the biggest liar I have ever known,' Vermorel wrote of

McLaren. 'He told fibs and his self-fantasising bordered on delusion. Every event in his life became aggrandized, every step of his life heroic. And very soon we were all implicated. Because, of course, he would tell lies about everyone else, soon nobody knew what was true or false anymore; speculations flew and confusion was rife.'[16]

Vermorel came to know the youthful McLaren's unusual verbal tics and behaviour well and diagnosed them much later, in 1987, after research into forms of autism were first disseminated outside clinical academia.

Reflecting on the young student he first encountered in the Harrow Art School canteen in the 1960s, Vermorel claimed McLaren suffered from Gilles de la Tourette's syndrome 'distinguished by manic bursts of energy, muscular inco-ordination and the compulsive copying of other people's behaviour . . . he gave the impression his grotesque mannerisms and physical gaffs were deliberate. In this way he was able to create a legendary aura around himself – fairly easy in the art college/fine arts context where the idea of genius as behaviour has been accepted at least since Marcel Duchamp.'[17]

Certainly, McLaren's personality was difficult to decode. That he displayed signs of being on the spectrum (as underlined by his elfin wit, unusual and expressive use of language and apparent lack of empathy) did not deter admiration from Vermorel, who promptly introduced McLaren to his own circle.

'There was me, a friend called Tony Gibney and Gordon Swire,' says Vermorel. 'We'd met at the Catholic youth club at Ruislip Manor and formed the core of a loose gang; Gordon was the coolest of us – he always had money, slept with women and drove a car.'

Swire, who was nineteen and studying for his A levels at Harrow Technical School, had two older sisters, one of whom, Vivienne, was a married trainee teacher leading the respectable existence of a young suburban housewife living with her Hoover factory apprentice husband, Derek Westwood, and their infant son in Harrow's Station Road, not far from the art school.

By now a raconteur as voluble as his grandmother, McLaren regaled his new friends with his theories on art, music and fashion and tales of his strange upbringing, weird relatives and colourful experiences in Cannes. He also joined them on night-time jaunts to gigs, parties and clubs.

Swire drove the gang to watch live music at the Railway Tavern in Wealdstone and the Marquee in Soho, and at house parties the youths would misbehave. 'We might pretend to dance, caricaturing the moves of the day with absurdist variations,' wrote Vermorel. 'Or we'd take over the record player. At one party, given by a Christian poetess in Chiswick, I began playing Édith Piaf instead of the Beatles. Malcolm warded off the protests. Drawing himself up into a Shakespearean posture, he bellowed: "Piaf . . . and Elvis! ARE LIKE THAT!", entwining his two forefingers and glaring maniacally. The inanity of the remark was compensated by its ferocity. The protesters sloped away.'[18]

McLaren, Casey and Vermorel bonded over a shared fascination for the brooding British rocker Billy Fury whose star was waning as the Beat Boom took hold. They enjoyed imitating the lanky Fury's trademark stoop and sulky demeanour, and were so excited when they heard Fury was drinking with an entourage in the art school local, the Havelock Arms, that they crossed the road and 'made a pilgrimage to gawp at him'.

Vermorel recognised that his new friend was more dedicated to schoolwork than most. 'He wasn't a skiver,' wrote Vermorel. 'He was in it for the art, for the culture. No dilettante, his studies were assiduous and deep, sometimes fanatically so. He burned to be a "Great Artist" and take his place in the pantheon. This reverence for the art game and traditional artistic values gave him an edge when he later turned to pop culture – a knack for mis-quoting (and abusing and mashing up and détourning) cultural signs from connoisseurship.'[19]

The young students were befriended by their art history tutor, the Spanish-born painter and Royal Academician Theodore Ramos.

'I enjoyed meeting that curious suburban generation,' said Ramos in the late 1980s. 'Malcolm was one of the odd ones; one couldn't tell whether he was going to go far in any direction. He was far more angry and intense than most of the students, an entirely different calibre.'[20]

Ramos, whose portraits of the royal family were popular with the public, invited the trio to his King's Road home in the area of Chelsea in west London known as World's End. On the walls hung a painting by Jackson Pollock, which impressed the boys mightily.[21]

McLaren recalled regularly visiting Ramos at the Royal Academy with Casey, and Vermorel later claimed that McLaren adopted Ramos's 'perverse suavity' so that it 'shaped Malcolm's own cynical charm'. Indeed, McLaren also absorbed Ramos's view that musicians were not real artists. 'Theo said they lacked the intelligence and only imbeciles spent time practising,' said Vermorel.

Influences were flooding in. An expedition in the early spring of 1964 to an exhibition of works by Robert Rauschenberg at Whitechapel Art Gallery – just a hundred yards along the road from the Eve Edwards factory – proved inspiring, not least for McLaren's later use of bricolage in fashion, film and music.

'He was absolutely blown away,' recalled Vermorel of McLaren. 'Rauschenberg put disparate and different elements in collages. Collage was definitely a thing for Malcolm.'[22]

For the first time in his life, McLaren felt secure in his relationships. 'At art school I met similar people like Patrick; everyone had problems,' he wrote in notes in the 1990s. 'I wanted to create an anti-world – being disenfranchised became glamorous – [we had] a common bond. I saw that I could succeed in art school – it became my new family. Art school made me feel important and desirable – especially to girls. Learnt to have a style that cannot be bought – have to be it, know it and wear it as an attitude.'

In the second term, in 1964, McLaren chose to study the history of art and become a painter. A mildly curious aspect of his adolescent behaviour was that sexual activity was not a factor; this pretentious young man forswore female company to friends and family in favour of his pursuit of artistic purity.

'I announced that I was remaining celibate and worked, worked, worked, determined to become the best draughtsman,' said McLaren.

'I took my cue from Malcolm – women got in the way and genius was manacled by foolish things,' says Vermorel. 'I was impressed by his calculated disdain for girls.'

Now McLaren needed an A level pass by the end of the foundation course so that he could proceed to the Dip AD. But his outspokenness sparked regular contretemps with teachers.

'He was constantly in and out of trouble; the tutors loved and hated him at the same time,' says Fred Vermorel. 'Then, at one point, and I can't remember what caused it, but he disappeared. We knew where he was but nobody else had seen him at home or at college. His mother rang the head, Illingworth, asking after her son. Then a farce ensued when Illingworth and our tutor Ivor Fox toured around Harrow in a car expecting to find him strolling down a street.'

McLaren had in fact set up camp in the secluded Harrow-on-the-Hill cemetery, and Vermorel and other friends surreptitiously ferried him food and cash for cigarettes. This lasted a few days before McLaren returned to Cheyne Walk, where tensions continued to simmer. Even the pungent herbal cigarettes he smoked, purchased from the Heath & Heather health store in Harrow, infuriated his mother.

'I had created an image which transformed me from a suburban boy into an artist, and I hated my parents for dismissing the idea,' he wrote.

Not long afterwards, on a Saturday evening McLaren and some pals pitched up at the all-night Busy Bee café in North Harrow's Honeypot Lane. This also constituted a dual-lane stretch known as the Watford Bypass, so the venue was a magnet for 'Ton-up' boys and nocturnal ne'er-do-wells. He then moved on to a house party in the area where he drank himself incapable. After sleeping it off, McLaren returned to Hendon the next morning for the inevitable showdown with his mother.

'She said she'd had enough,' he later recalled. 'My hair was too long, my clothes were shabby, I had become a Bohemian, not respectable. I was growing beards and smoking cigarettes that smelt awful; she was terrified they were drugs.'

An almighty row ensued after which McLaren fled upstairs to Rose. Ever divisive, his grandmother opted not to attempt to smooth relations between mother and son and instead gave McLaren enough money to enable his exit. Dramatically, the eighteen-year-old flounced out of the house for a destination unknown; twenty-five years unfolded before he spoke to his mother again. The woman he had known as Emily McLaren, Emily Isaacs and then Eve Edwards was effectively out of his life for good.

Chapter 5

On leaving 31 Cheyne Walk that Sunday afternoon, eighteen-year-old Malcolm Edwards determined, like many another suburban beatnik of the period, to take to the road.

With a satchel he had retained from his time in the boy scouts containing a change of clothes and a blanket, McLaren journeyed down the Northern Line from Hendon Central to Charing Cross, where he caught a train to the southern edge of London as it merges into the Kent countryside. Here, he thought, fruit-picking work might be available.

'I got on this road that if you put your thumb out, you could hitch into the wilderness of England,' he recalled in the 1990s. 'I'd heard that south of Sidcup there were apple orchards where you could make money.'

Intermittently grabbing lifts from passing cars, the boy travelled through Kentish towns and villages and then along the verge of the A21, one of the main roads to the south coast. En route he joined forces with an 'extraordinary tramp', an older black man named Charlie.

As night fell the odd couple approached Eastbourne, an Edwardian resort McLaren had visited on day trips with his family. Charlie advised against heading into town. Instead, he suggested, they should camp in the woodland where the tip of the South Downs, the expanse of rolling hills along this part of the UK's south-eastern coast, met Eastbourne's town limits.

'Being a middle-class brat I'd never actually been in a forest,' said McLaren. 'My grandmother told me they were polluted places where you'd be bitten by snakes; they weren't places for humankind, not the sort I was made of anyway.

'Here I was terrified, but not wanting to show my fear. There I was in the middle of a forest at night with a black tramp having left my middle-class home six hours before.'

When McLaren expressed his fears about snakes, Charlie fashioned protection for his legs using secured polythene bags.

'When he tied the twine around my knee caps he said, "It's OK now, no snake can get in." I believed him and collapsed down and fell asleep.'

The next day they visited Eastbourne's pebbled beach where Charlie taught Malcolm how to scavenge loose change that had fallen underneath the pier from the trouser pockets of basking holidaymakers, then they journeyed west to a town where they found shelter in a monastery. 'We stayed there for a week, earning our keep by helping the monks sweep and tidy the place,' said McLaren. 'Then Charlie left, going God knows where. And I hitched to Cornwall.'

This was a considerable distance of at least a couple of hundred miles, but the country's westernmost county, with its distinctive Celtic character and myths and legends, was a destination for young creatives; the Cornish town of St Ives had been home to Britain's artistic community since before the Second World War, attracting the likes of sculptor Barbara Hepworth and the painters Ben Nicholson (Hepworth's husband), Keith Vaughan and Patrick Heron.

According to McLaren, he was among a group of young assistants recruited to help out at Hepworth's Trewyn Studio in the centre of St Ives. Thus he was occupied for a period before returning to London and seeking out Fred Vermorel and Gordon Swire.

After Dora and Gordon Swire Sr protested their son's offer to McLaren to sleep on the couch at his parents' home above the post office and general store they ran in Station Road, an alternative was found: the back seat of the younger Gordon's Morris Cowley parked outside.

From the warmth of the car over the next few days, McLaren pondered his next move: first he registered back at Harrow using the Swires' address and continued his pre-Dip studies.

'At eighteen you could apply for a grant yourself, using the address in whatever borough you were living in,' explains Vermorel. 'There was no checking, not only on the address but also whether you had received a grant in another borough. Malcolm cottoned onto this.'

It is at this stage that Gordon Swire's older sister, the housewife Vivienne Westwood, entered McLaren's life for the first time.

The twenty-three-year-old had married Derek Westwood in 1962 and spent her days looking after their son Ben, who was born the following year. But the marriage had soured early as the imaginative introvert balked at the humdrum suburban existence which bore no comparison with bucolic Tintwistle in Snake Pass, near Glossop in Derbyshire's picturesque Peak District, where she was born and raised.

'Vivienne was intrigued by Gordon's guest, having seen the wild-looking redhead asleep in the car several times; Malcolm would sleep late quite often, on display to the residents and an added embarrassment to Gordon's parents,' says Vermorel.

Every day, once the older Swires had started work at the post office downstairs, Gordon entertained McLaren and Vermorel to breakfast in the flat before they set off to college.

The trio were sometimes visited by Gordon's sister, her husband already at work.

'One morning we were sitting around when Vivienne turned up with Ben,' says Vermorel. 'I remember her trying to make conversation with Malcolm, but he was particularly anti-social. We all lit up and left for Harrow thinking nothing of it. But Vivienne had fallen in love.'

McLaren described Westwood as being 'very shy because of her accent. She was also scared of London's unfriendliness. She came from a tiny village where everyone knew each other. London, I think, seemed very impersonal to her. She was taken away from her closed, small village life to a huge unfriendly city and she felt insecure in it. I remember she had problems using the phone, particularly talking to strangers.'

According to Westwood's biographer Jane Mulvagh, 'Vivienne admired this camp dandy in his makeshift home, and he was amused by her Sunday school ways. [She] believed that McLaren could provide access to a fascinating world: "I felt there were so many doors to open, and he had the keys to all of them." '[1]

But the unlocking of those doors would have to wait; it was to take another two years for Westwood to disentangle herself from her marriage, and anyway, McLaren was not in the least interested. Of immediate concern was bed and board. Then, he believed, he could devote all his energies to creative quests. McLaren made contact with his grandmother and wangled an invite to Cheyne Walk when his mother and stepfather were out. Even without his parents present, the interaction in the household took a typically fractious turn. McLaren arrived to find his brother Stuart, now twenty-one, and Mick Isaacs at home. Since his hair had grown long and he had announced that he had forsworn female company in pursuit of his calling as an artist, they surmised that he was a homosexual.

'I was, I suppose, asexual and introverted, quite narcissistic,' said McLaren. 'If I was interested in men, it was more often than not because they were my lecturers and consequently my mentors. I was attracted to boys if they looked good, but never in a sexual way.'

He responded to what he saw as this challenge to his sexual nature by exploding into characteristic anger. 'I smashed all the cups in the kitchen, throwing them against the walls and cupboards. My grandfather called the police and when they arrived I said: "You can't do shit to me" and walked out, forever.'

McLaren then turned to one of his mentors, Theo Ramos, who took pity on the boy and allowed him to stay at his studio for a brief period.

'He saw himself as the creator, the thinker,' Ramos said of McLaren. 'This is what he learnt at art school, to draw quickly, to think on paper and having thought something out, to discard it and pick up something else.'[2]

The student also resided at a series of sleazy digs. First above a Greek shoemaker in Berwick Street, Soho, where McLaren was apparently evicted because the screams which came from his room as he experienced nightmares upset the landlord, and then at a rooming house in Notting Hill Gate which, it soon became apparent, was in fact a brothel where the kitchen cutlery had been used to effect an abortion.

McLaren also claimed that, for a spell, Rose paid for him to stay in a residential hotel in St Martin's Lane in the West End, not far from where he had worked at Sandeman's just a couple of years previously.

At the start of the second year at Harrow, McLaren was among students addressed by the 'grisly Northern professor' whose statement about the need to embrace failure had resonated so strongly.

'There weren't so many of us as the year before,' McLaren said. 'He looked at the few of us left, shabbier and poorly dressed, not so fresh-faced, looking a little more decadent I guess. "So you have understood about failure, you've learnt a little," he said. "Well, don't think you can just fail. That's not good enough. You have to learn how to be a magnificent failure, the most brilliant failure, the most flamboyant failure. For it is better to be a flamboyant failure than any kind of benign success." '

McLaren said that it took a while for him to take on board the professor's point. 'Those words rang in my ears,' said McLaren in the 2000s. 'They were prophetic but difficult for an eighteen-year-old to understand. Eventually I saw that he was saying the only way you were going to change life, by changing the culture, was learning to become fearless. You had to learn how to never listen to the rules and to create your own world, or anti-world. This was to be a very different and far less cosy life than the one I had in the suburbs of north London.'

The art student was absorbing this information without his closest friends. Patrick Casey had dropped out, later to surface on a fine art degree course at Chelsea College of Art. Vermorel also left around the same time. 'Like it is now, the foundation course was a means of collecting a portfolio so that you could do the rounds of art colleges for a degree,' says Vermorel. 'I went to Brighton and Malcolm embarrassed me by telling everyone I'd been accepted when I hadn't. Ivor Fox congratulated me on something that hadn't happened, so I felt a right mug. But anyway I was like Patrick and Malcolm, a troublemaker, so like them I didn't last the two years.'

Vermorel began studying for extra A levels at home in order to enter university and become a writer. 'I was also taking various jobs, on building sites or at a Lyons Corner House,' says Vermorel. 'You could do that then, pitch up somewhere and pick up a job immediately. Malcolm worked with me at Lyons for a very brief while, washing up, laying the tables, menial stuff.'

Rose intervened in her grandson's life once more by securing him a bedsitting room at the house of a Mrs Gold, one of her elderly friends who lived in Finchley Lane, Hendon, some distance from the Edwards family home in Cheyne Walk.

Gordon Swire drove Vermorel to the Edwards' house to pick up McLaren's belongings and delivered them to his new abode, a bedsit with a sink; the lavatory and bathroom were along the hall.

Soon, due to his permanently precarious position with the teaching staff, McLaren exited Harrow and enrolled at South East Essex School of Art in Walthamstow, north-east London.

The school – like many others around the country – had rich pop-culture associations. In the late 1950s Vivian Stanshall, the songwriter and singer best associated with the Bonzo Dog Doo-Dah Band, studied there alongside Ian Dury, the polio-stricken pub-rock performer whom McLaren was to know in later life. One of Dury and Stanshall's fellow students was the British avant-garde filmmaker and composer Peter Greenaway.

At Walthamstow, McLaren was taken under the wing of the artist Keith Albarn, who was a part-time teacher at the school while working with his wife Hazel Dring on environmental structures and the early public interventions becoming known as 'happenings'. The father of Blur and Gorillaz frontman Damon and his artist sister Jessica, Albarn was six years older than McLaren and something of a public figure – he was soon a regular contributor to the BBC TV arts strand *Late Night Line Up*.

'I remember Malcolm as a bit of a pain in the arse, actually,' says Albarn, smiling. 'He could be very charming but very spiky with it and was quite a challenging student. I always liked that, because it was an indication that there was something going on.

'Though I saw him fairly regularly over this period, I could never work him out. He was very good on ideas but to my mind short on application. There wasn't a great deal of focus, except in his head, so he seemed to be playing at abstraction. But the work was developing. Malcolm was really finding his way, I knew that even then.'[3]

At Mrs Gold's and now beyond all parental control, McLaren's behaviour verged on the extreme. He spent a lot of time behind the locked door of his room staying up late into the night, treating it as his studio.

'Malcolm did some of his best work to date in that bedsit,' averred Vermorel.

It was there he remarked it was more interesting to tackle a small problem intensively than a large one slackly. I was particularly struck by a series of Klee-like experimentations in gouache.

I was spending my days in reference libraries and in the evenings I would report on my researches. Then we would review his day's work. Nescafé and cigarettes were consumed.

I recall the roughness of these associations – the sour taste of tobacco and coffee, the painterly mess and unkemptness of his room, dirty cups and spilled clothes (we both used to piss in the sink rather than go down the corridor), the astringency of our conversations and an energy to break the artistic pain barrier.[4]

In channelling this energy, the student fast became a nightmare tenant for Mrs Gold. His room, paint-spattered and littered with unfinished gouaches and sketches, also contained environmental structures built in the style of Robert Rauschenberg's 'combines' with materials raided from local building sites.

'Art school had made me interested in ruins, and it was ruins I believed in rather than culture,' he said later. 'I adored the thought of living in debris.'

Never a straight arrow, the teenage McLaren's oddness at this stage in his life may be attributed in part to his grandmother's reassertion of her grip over him. She and husband Mick had fallen out with the Edwards and moved from Cheyne Walk to a sizeable apartment in Westbury Court, the sprawling mansion block which houses Clapham South tube station in south London. According to jottings made by McLaren in the 1990s after he had undergone therapy, Rose – then seventy-two – would occasionally stay the night with her grandson at Mrs Gold's rather than take the long tube journey to her new home: 'My grandmother was always wanting to bond with me; she tried to do this through the two of us having secrets together. She would come and visit me and if it got late she would stay the night in my bed. I didn't feel anything sexually towards her. I also didn't understand the notion of caring about myself or having self-worth. If my grandmother wanted to sleep in my bed then of course I would let her.

'I didn't have any boundaries [and] was so submissive and passive about such things. I didn't think it was my right to refuse. I thought it was her right to do as she wanted. And whenever I came into contact with girls I didn't feel anything other than fear I wouldn't know what to do.'

McLaren increasingly channelled the emotional turmoil and confusion wrought by such transgressions into his work, with no regard for Mrs Gold's possessions. A chair was broken into its constituent parts, which were then used to create a combine with boards torn from the floor. Then a visit by McLaren's horrified landlady to his unlocked room resulted in him being given his marching orders.

The boy fled to his grandparents' Clapham flat and deputed Fred Vermorel to accompany Rose to pick up his possessions from Mrs Gold.

'Rose and I packed up his belongings and took them to him on the tube,' said Vermorel. 'She cackled all the way about "the bloody state" of Mrs Gold and "the bloody state" of Malcolm's room.'

Vermorel described Rose Isaacs as 'five foot two and stick thin. She had a shrill Cockney manner and an unnerving laugh, doting on Malcolm and relishing his scrapes, greeting each revelation with a whinnying rasp of hilarity.'

Vermorel was aghast when he witnessed the brusqueness with which the members of the Isaacs clan expressed themselves. 'My first thought was that they all hated each other,' he said. 'An explosive malice punctuated every exchange. Everything was shouted at a market trader's pitch, with that rhythmic aggression.'

And he noted their exaggerated, playfully injured, Pinteresque speech patterns.

Malcolm habitually addressed his grandmother with contempt: 'What's that you're fucking saying? Speak up girl! God Christ all fucking mighty! What's she on about now?!', waving his hands in mock disbelief.

Rose might suddenly yell at me about my mother: 'How is she? Still in France is she?' Malcolm would shout: 'For fuck's sake! You asked him last time!'

Ignoring this, Rose would look slyly to see if I was sharing the joke before asking me like a sweet old lady: 'Fancy a spot of toast dear?'

Malcolm: 'He don't want no fucking toast! Can't you see that? Toast? What's he want toast for?!'

Me (anything for a quiet life): 'Yes. Toast.'

Rose, triumphantly to Malcolm: 'See!'

Malcolm, laughing in mock exasperation: 'Oh, all right, Jesus fucking Christ almighty, make him some fucking toast then! Jesus!'[5]

Just as Peter McLaren had believed McLaren's grandfather to be suffering from a form of PTSD in the 1940s, Vermorel observed Mick Isaacs's damaged personality twenty years later. 'My thought was that he was senile, suffering from Alzheimer's. He'd be sat in his armchair glowering at everyone, not saying a word. Suddenly and with no warning he would rear up and bellow: "WHERE'S ME FUCKING TEA?" then he would sink back. Rose would laugh like a hyena, then say: "Oh, he wants his tea does he? Silly bugger. He'll get his tea all right!", winking at me. Then we'd all forget about Mick and his tea.'

Soon McLaren left Walthamstow; one story has it that he was expelled. In this period, Theo Ramos found McLaren work, making props for the designer Barry Kay, then producing sets for the staging of a play called *Kindly Monkeys* by the American dramatist Milton Hood Ward, which ran at the New Arts Theatre in central London's Great Newport Street in spring 1965. This was an alternative venue where, as the Arts Theatre, Sir Peter Hall had directed the English-language debut of Samuel Beckett's *Waiting for Godot* in the 1950s. It had later built on its reputation for championing daring new work by premiering Joe Orton's *Entertaining Mr Sloane* in 1964.

One of the *Kindly Monkeys* sets was the interior of a Himalayan hill temple, and McLaren was contracted to make the fluted columns from papier-mâché. 'The producer thought they were so bad he kicked them off the stage and barred Malcolm from making anything else,' says Vermorel.

The chronology of this chaotic time is difficult to order, not least because the waters have been muddied by McLaren's serial and sometimes multiple applications to art colleges in various London boroughs under different surnames, including that of his birth and also Corré. 'I was this extraordinary creature who could keep reapplying to different art schools on the periphery of London,' he said. 'They were under different councils and, of course, one council didn't speak to the other so I'd plot where I'd go next.'

McLaren followed his time at Walthamstow with a spell on a music, mime and theatre course at Chiswick Polytechnic in west London. 'He had this Wagnerian idea of doing all the arts combined, multi-media stuff, which was very trendy in those days,' says Vermorel. 'I remember him trying to learn the piano with disastrous results.'

McLaren meanwhile maintained contact with Keith Albarn, who became the latest in the series of older male guides for the troubled twenty-year-old. 'You could see he was going to do something,' said Albarn. 'He was one of those students you just knew was going to be a misfit whatever he did, in the best sense of the word.'

In the spring of 1966 Albarn provided McLaren with a return to work as a prop-maker. 'I was part of a small group making sets for various venues in the West End and so gave Malcolm bits and pieces to do,' says Albarn. 'He needed the work and we needed the help because we were often quite stretched.'

Among Albarn's commissions was the Easter 1966 production of *Der Rosenkavalier* directed by Luchino Visconti at the Royal Opera House. The film director also designed the sets, which were constructed by Albarn and his team. According to McLaren, a birdcage he made out of balsa wood collapsed, releasing the lovebirds it contained into the audience.

There are indications McLaren took drawing and painting classes at City & Guilds London Art School in Kennington, south London, and also stories that he travelled far south to study at Reigate & Redhill School of Arts and Crafts in Surrey for a while.

And, for a period, McLaren tried again to complete his foundation course, this time at Chelsea College of Art, where Patrick Casey had also pitched up.

'We had always kept in touch,' said McLaren of Casey, whose fellow fine-art students included the British pop artist Duggie Fields, who lived in room-shares with groups of students including Casey, first in Queen's Gate Terrace, Kensington, and then Edith Grove in World's End (notable for the grotty apartment shared by members of the fledgling Rolling Stones a couple of years earlier).

'I don't remember Malcolm at Chelsea so assume he was there fleetingly,' says Fields, who concurs with the views of others that 'Patrick was tall, handsome and flamboyant – he looked cool'.[6]

Fields is correct about McLaren's tenure at Chelsea; but during his time there the young artist shifted direction and produced a number of large-scale constructs using the by-now trademark concentrations of black. Their size was influenced by the forty-foot canvases that had recently been exhibited by the British artist Stan Peskett. To further complicate matters, Peskett later claimed to have known McLaren from a course at the Royal College of Art.

Match held under Stars and Stripes

Said to have unfolded a large Stars and Stripes flag and to have held a match under it outside the United States Embassy on Independence Day, Henry Adler, aged 23, student, of Lindfield Gardens, Hampstead, N.W., and Malcolm Robert Edwards, aged 20, sculptor, of Finchley Lane, Hendon, N.W., were found Guilty at Marlborough Street Magistrates' Court yesterday of insulting behaviour contrary to the Public Order Act.

Adler, who lit the match, said it was a symbolic act of protest against American policy in Vietnam and there was no intent to burn the flag.

Mr. Edward Robey, the Magistrate, said the act was guaranteed to insult American national pride and was enough to inflame anybody.

He added: " I am indeed more than surprised—and I suppose it is because of the quick action of the police—that some American did not go up and start trouble with these two rash young men."

He fined Adler £30 with three guineas costs and Edwards £20 with three guineas costs and bound both over, each in the sum

First media appearance: *The Times*, 29 July 1966.

Another Stan, a fellow student whose surname is lost to memory, was an influence at Chelsea. 'He was a Trotskyist who played a mean jazz saxophone and politicised Malcolm,' says Vermorel. For McLaren, radical politics opened up a world of possibilities when entwined with his investigations into art. Encouraged and initially accompanied by Stan, McLaren began attending rallies and demonstrations protesting on behalf of the causes célèbres of the day: against the war in Vietnam and South Africa's apartheid regime.

Long gone were the polite CND parades peopled by earnest chaplains and fresh-faced Home Counties youth in duffel coats chanting 'Kumbaya'. Taking their cue from the US uprisings such as that among the African American community on Chicago's West Side, the British protestors of 1966 brought activism to new heights in direct confrontation with the authorities. A turning point was the July central London rally calling for the British government to disassociate itself from US military policy in south-east Asia.

McLaren was among the 4,000 who amassed in Trafalgar Square before marching on 10 Downing Street and then to the US Embassy in Grosvenor Square. Once there, pitched battles were fought with the police, stoked by such acts as McLaren joining a faction setting fire to the American flag in full view of the US Embassy.

With thirty demonstrators, McLaren was arrested for insulting behaviour contrary to the Public Order Act. His court appearance a few weeks later featured in *The Times*'s Law Report, which noted that twenty-year-old Malcolm Edwards, who described himself as a sculptor and gave as his address Mrs Gold's house in Finchley Lane, was fined £20 and bound over to keep the peace for twelve months along with another protestor, a South African named Henry Adler.[7]

'There was so much activity in those days, you couldn't help but jump in,' said McLaren. 'It wasn't my idea to burn the flag; I was just there and ended up holding it as it was set alight. After we were arrested we spent eight hours at West End Central police station before we were bailed. Then I was whisked off to Drayton Gardens in Kensington with a load of Libyan diplomats who were going on about being anti-Vietnam and anti-American.'

Adler was among those who shared a cell with McLaren; in fact his lawyer paid McLaren's bail. Three years older than McLaren, Adler was a moneyed exile who had been lured by tales of Swinging London and set about spending his monthly allowance on enjoying the cultural activities the British capital offered.

McLaren was impressed with Adler's sangfroid and promptly introduced him to his circle. 'We gathered that Henry was the misfit of his family,' recalls Vermorel. 'He told us that they had insisted he receive treatment for what they saw as his odd behaviour.'

Adler chose analysis under a fellow South African, the radical psychiatrist David Cooper, who was aligned with R. D. Laing's experiments in 'anti-psychiatry' at the former's Kingsley Hall community in east London. Fired by his sessions with Cooper, whom Laing claimed to have been trained by the KGB as an anti-apartheid revolutionary, Adler turned his new friends on to the range of alternative experiences and conjoined them in petitions of politicians, adding McLaren to a group which visited the House of Commons and lobbied the MPs Eric Heffer and Tony Benn to change the Labour government's stance on Vietnam.

A cinephile, Adler encouraged his younger friends to investigate film in all its varieties. 'His idea of a good time, a day virtuously employed, was to watch one movie through successive showings in the same cinema – something OAPs also did, only they nodded off while Henry was rapt and intense and took notes,' says Vermorel. 'These movies didn't have to be *Citizen Kane*. Henry was fascinated for example, by the Marx Brothers as exemplars of anti-authoritarian alienation.'[8]

Accompanying Adler, McLaren and Vermorel on such expeditions to London's alternative movie theatres was Gordon Swire, who, by the autumn of 1966 was bent on working in cinema and studying at the London College of Film Technique (now the London Film School) in Covent Garden. Swire had moved out of the family home in Harrow to a house-share with two American film students in Kings Avenue in Clapham, not far from Rose and Mick Isaacs's home. Soon they were joined by McLaren, who took a room there.

One of his new housemates, the American John Broderick, who had come to London after a stint with the San Francisco Mime Troupe, described McLaren's appearance as 'very thin and emaciated in a long coat. He almost looked like one of the Jewish guys that were led out of the ghetto by the Nazis during World War II. I had the feeling he was a persecuted fellow, that he was from a lower middle-class family that he had been forced out of or left, but in any event was kind of estranged from. But I figured he was the kind of fellow who would have been estranged anyway.'[9]

With his artistic work developing and his political consciousness expanding, 31 Kings Avenue provided a safe haven for the 'puny aggressive flâneur'[10] after years of domestic insecurity. McLaren's later claim that the terraced house sheltered US draft dodgers and drug dealers was rooted in the residence of another American film student, Chuck Coryn.

Coryn's jailing in Britain over importation of illegal substances from the Lebanon had in fact freed up the room for McLaren. And another room became available on Coryn's arrest, that of his girlfriend, who was deported, according to Broderick.[11]

Within a month this was occupied by a new tenant: Gordon Swire's sister Vivienne, who arrived with her three-year-old son Ben, having divorced her husband.

Chapter 6

Vivienne Westwood capped her separation from her husband by enrolment on a two-year teacher-training course at St Gabriel's College in Camberwell, a short bus ride from her new home in Kings Avenue.

Having left school without O levels, Westwood's previous stint of further education had consisted of a few weeks of the foundation term at Harrow Art School in the early 1960s, where she had toyed with the idea of becoming a jewellery-maker before leaving to accept a variety of mundane jobs and then settling on teacher training.

Westwood didn't last long at St Gabriel's, so spent more time at her new home with her young son Ben. Since her brother Gordon and his fellow student John Broderick were committed to their film studies and attending college during the day, the only other adult company was Malcolm McLaren, then twenty and five years her junior. When he wasn't joining Henry Adler on escapades around town, McLaren worked hard on his practice and planned his next move in arts education.

Unlike Westwood's ex-husband, McLaren says he 'was not a typical guy in a typical job. I was someone who seemed to be on a much bigger adventure. I was on a bigger trip and interested in the world from a perspective that fascinated her.'

Ignobly, McLaren's initial response to Westwood and her son's arrival at Kings Avenue was one of 'shock and horror, because I hated the idea that girls should come and inhabit this house. It was boys only, as far as I was concerned . . . I brought her to tears and she had this little kid who I hated and loathed, and I brought him to tears as well.'[1]

McLaren observed that Westwood's life at that stage 'was based around looking after Ben, knitting jumpers, seeing her teacher training friends and going to church on Sundays. She'd had a very parochial lifestyle.'

He, on the other hand, was 'a serious loner, regardless of the world I worked in. Maybe that's why it all came together. I never really understood what I had in common with her. I did find her very attractive in lots of ways.'

And so, according to Westwood's biographer Jane Mulvagh, the pair passed the hours 'hunched over an inadequate bar-heater, sharing beans on toast and tea or smoking Woodbines and downing whiskies late into the night'.[2]

Such intimacy panicked the virgin McLaren, still in thrall to the overbearing Rose Isaacs and, conversely, experiencing vivid and dramatic nightmares about the mother he professed not to care about.

'Malcolm began complaining to me,' wrote Fred Vermorel. 'Vivienne was pestering him. Fucking woman! What should he do? The pestering involved attentions which, according to him, had got to the point of lewd absurdity. Whenever they were alone in the house she would walk around in states of undress. And one night he claimed she had walked into his room naked and climbed into bed with him.'[3]

Westwood remembers it differently, claiming she was at first indifferent to McLaren's charms, but then boredom gained the upper hand.[4]

'He was physically so curious-looking,' recalled Westwood of McLaren in the Kings Avenue days. '[He had] very, very short hair, about half an inch long, though he wasn't a skinhead or anything. He had this very, very pale face and very red mouth, and he was just so intense that his voice would suddenly break into something like a shout. Really, he was so neurotic.'[5]

In another of McLaren's versions of the story, their intimacy proceeded after he feigned sickness and asked to sleep in her bed. Whatever occurred between them initially, the pair became lovers. Her suburban parents were distraught and, when McLaren introduced Westwood to his grandparents, Mick was silent while Rose was disapproving. Soon Westwood was drawn into his group of friends and McLaren helped her make the costume jewellery she occasionally sold in west London's Portobello Market.

'It became very inventive,' said McLaren in the 1990s. 'I used radio parts and turned them into jewellery and packaged them in tube maps. I tried to make them something that tourists might buy and tried to sell them to Carnaby Street but people preferred the simple commercial silver that Vivienne made.

'My ideas were far too eccentric but I wasn't deterred. I just thought it was an idea that didn't work. I guess those were the first things we ever did together. It set up a relationship between us.'

And the creative exchange shaded into clothes making; Westwood sewed a series of 'proletarian boiler suits in primary colours' McLaren devised for himself. 'Vivienne was always brilliant at making things – a mask for fun, a piece of jewellery, a knitted sweater, a curtain, whatever, she could make it,' said McLaren. 'I loved that about her because it was much more difficult for me. I was too much about ideas and just didn't have the patience to sit down and carry them out, and, really, I didn't have the skill. I was a messy person and a messy painter, I didn't know my left from my right. Vivienne was far more articulate in a way that allowed her to carry out my ideas with her sense of craft. This was to become a terrific partnership I thought.'

Spurred on by Henry Adler, McLaren and his friends were by now regulars at such haunts as the Tolmer Cinema, a fleapit in Euston, which specialised in bizarre, low-rent double bills.

'We also went to the Academy in Oxford Street for Italian cult movies, the Cameo-Poly in Regent Street and the Paris Pullman in Chelsea, but the Tolmer was the weirdest, showing totally forgotten films, Norman Wisdom comedies or fifties sci-fi,' says Vermorel. 'Malcolm and I got to know the projectionist. He used to make random edits to the films that made no sense; we found out it was because he wanted to leave work early so chopped entire sections out. The spare footage was chucked in the bin outside.'

No longer was Westwood the outsider, but part of the gang. However, since this was the 1960s, she remained not quite an equal. Vermorel recalls her washing clothes for the selfish McLaren, who stoutly refused to express affection towards Ben, even banishing the three-year-old from crawling into bed with them.

It's not a surprise, given his complicated relationship with his mother, that McLaren actively enjoyed the fact that he was markedly younger than Westwood. Soon he advised her on adjusting to a *soigné* look to magnify the age gap.

'She was into fashion but she didn't have a grip on it like I did,' he said. 'At first I can only remember her wearing a red tartan mini kilt with a grey charcoal jumper she had knitted herself. I had an aversion to home knitting – the idea used to freak me out.'

And so, as an expression of disgust with the domesticity that this suggested, McLaren urged Westwood to buy from the West End high-end shops, which had been a fascination since his childhood forays with Rose, who now funded these shopping expeditions.

'I loved Vivienne to look even older than me at times, persuading her to buy clothes from the more refined shops in Old Bond Street, clothes that made her look mature and sophisticated, all things that I didn't look,' said McLaren.

While they didn't share everything – 'She had no interest in going on any demonstrations, and I never took her to one,' he recalled – there existed passion between them.

Early in the relationship, McLaren failed to return to Kings Avenue after a night out. The next day a confrontation occurred in a warped echo of his final encounter with his mother a couple of years previously.

'I remember Vivienne coming in to art school and being really angry with me,' he said. 'Out of the blue she turned up in the canteen. I was very impressed and proud, as she had a Ferragamo bag, Charles Jourdan shoes and an elegant mac she'd purchased in Piccadilly. Her hair had been cut by Leonard [Lewis, a prominent Mayfair hairdresser]. There I was, all scruffed-up, sitting with tea everywhere, roll-ups, charcoal-covered students. She swung the bag across my face and screamed and went quite mad at me. The students were all smitten that I was with a woman that was so severe and serious and at the same time, from her appearance, important.

'Getting on the train with her home and hearing the students the following day, I was really chuffed and thrilled that she came across as this tough creature who was completely outside of any other art school girlfriend. I adored that about Vivienne.'

In the early spring of 1967 Westwood announced that she was pregnant. McLaren was shell-shocked and claimed that he had been tricked since Westwood had told him she was taking contraception.[6] Immediately he ran to Rose Isaacs, who, characteristically, was beside herself at the news and decreed that she would arrange and pay for a termination, then illegal in Britain.

A booking was made at a clinic in the centre of London's private medical community, Harley Street. Given Dame Vivienne's international celebrity these days, the story of her abandonment of the plan is fairly well known: on the steps of the doctor's practice, accompanied by McLaren with the cash from Rose, Westwood walked away from the appointment, heading south to the fashion retail district around Bond Street. Here they purchased an expensive and stylish garment, later described as either a fancy coat or a blue cashmere twinset.

'There was some connection between loving Malcolm and not wanting to have an abortion,' Westwood said in the 1980s. 'I suddenly realized I had this wonderful treasure in front of me. It was like my life had been the front of the coin and I suddenly flipped it and could see the other side. There it was. I realized I could get up and go with this thing.'[7]

But their shared delight was short-lived. Westwood has described how McLaren almost immediately withdrew from her, abnegating his responsibilities on the basis that, since she had decided to abandon the termination, she would have to deal with the consequences, betraying the harsh and emotionally immature aspects of his nature. Later, it emerged that McLaren's feelings about the event were more complex. He told

Westwood's biographer Jane Mulvagh in the 1990s: 'When she was pregnant I never saw her looking so beautiful . . . it was the time I'd seen her look the most kind, the most open, the most centred and somehow as though she belonged . . . it was meant to be.'[8]

Around the time of Westwood's decision to keep their child, McLaren had again been picking up work assisting Keith Albarn who, with some partners, had attracted a backer to fund a gallery and live event space in the ground floor and basement premises of a former restaurant in Kingly Street, Soho, beneath the offices of the pop star Cat Stevens.

The 26 Kingly Street Environmental Co-operative – which had previously been known as Artists' Own Gallery – was dedicated to the new environmental art in all its forms, from performative to structural. The fact that the basement fish pool from the restaurant had been left intact was a bonus, since this added a dimension to the light shows and happenings that occurred there. 'We put it to good use at the evening events,' Albarn told artist Lucy Harrison in 2013. 'That involved things poking up through the gelatin in the pool, lots of foam, smoke machines, experimental music and so on – without the fish I hasten to add.'

Heather Albarn staged a show at the gallery in May 1967 that required visitors to don masks and costumes she had made, so that 'the exhibition moved around; on the night of the opening we all went out onto the street'.[9]

Twenty-six Kingly Street was in one of the London epicentres of the 'Summer of Love', which had superseded the capital's 'Swinging' manifestation. Along the road at number nine was the Bag O'Nails, the nighterie favoured by pop stars such as The Who and Jimi Hendrix, and next door to that was Kleptomania, a psychedelic boutique operated by Tommy Roberts, who was to befriend McLaren within a few years.

While McLaren was notionally opposed to psychedelic excesses, he had made the leap from creating work about his environment to making environments of his own, a move aligned with the Albarns' practice, which declared: 'Experiment Towards Interplay: A new form to enjoy, return, reuse this arena of discovery.'

The Kingly Street group put the word around that they welcomed artistic contributions from others. 'Malcolm had helped set a few things up,' says Keith Albarn. 'He was one of the students who pitched in occasionally. We'd built a big environment with sensory pads and lights and one day he asked whether he could do something.'

No longer satisfied with painting huge black constructs, McLaren proposed a melange of artistic disciplines: appropriation, film, installation, intervention and performance.

'One of the things that was a pleasure to us all was that we were able to open the doors to lots of different activities and very different people to have access to a space in central London,' says Albarn, who, for a weekend, gave over the Kingly Street gallery for McLaren's first public exhibition.

For this, McLaren acquired several giant rolls of industrial corrugated paper, six feet in height, and constructed a labyrinth which he wove through the basement and ground floor levels of the gallery (in the event, taking his cue from Heather Albarn's show, this extended onto the narrow street outside).

The labyrinth included several deliberate dead-ends and a few false floors stretched over empty spaces. A drunken attendee at the Friday-night launch party – apparently an on-leave soldier who had wandered into the event on a night out in Soho – is said by Vermorel to have suffered considerable injuries when he fell through a false cardboard floor down a flight of stairs.

'I'd also picked up odds and ends, fragments of an Audie Murphy war movie from the projectionist's bin at the Tolmer Street cinema,' McLaren recalled in 2009, by which time he had returned to visual art with a series of formal film installations.

'I borrowed a couple of projectors and beamed the fragments onto the walls of the labyrinth with flashing lights and snippets of music. It was very much a piece of its time; Keith's place was always having such events. In the end we all ended up drinking too much cheap gallery wine and smashed up the labyrinth. The police were called, so it ended in chaos, which was rather satisfying.'

Prominent among fallacies about Malcolm McLaren is that his disavowal of the cultural products of Western society in the 1960s – as expressed by his derision of hippies, championing of Teddy boys and his role as the architect of punk – was based on a disengagement from culture during the decade.

As we have seen, nothing could be further from the truth. And, as Britain's underground gathered steam, so McLaren gained front-seat exposure to the variety of alternative experiences on offer. His guide to this brave new world continued to be the super-connected Henry Adler.

For example, at Adler's behest, McLaren attended one of the key countercultural events of the summer of 1967, the two-week conference at the north London arts centre, the Roundhouse. It was entitled 'The Dialectics of Liberation: Towards a Demystification of Violence' and organised by the American radical educationalist Joe Berke and his colleagues in the Institute of Phenomenological Studies as an attempt to 'demystify human violence in all its forms, and the social systems from which it emanates, and to explore new forms of action'.

Adler's association with such South African contributors as the anti-apartheid activist Myrtle Berman and R. D. Laing's fellow traveller David Cooper enabled his friends McLaren and Fred Vermorel to have free tickets and full access. Here they appreciated an eclectic array of speakers, including the US Black Power leader Stokely Carmichael, beat poet Allen Ginsberg (who was accompanied by William Burroughs), Tariq Ali, soon to found politico underground paper *Black Dwarf*, and radical artists Gustav Metzger and Carolee Schneeman. The musical highlight of the conference was provided by the abrasive, garage-punk Social Deviants, led by Britain's leading, and possibly only, White Panther, Mick Farren.

Adler also turned McLaren and Vermorel on to the country's first Arts Lab, opened by the expat American mover and shaker Jim Haynes in Covent Garden's Drury Lane in September 1967. There they joined a crowd described by critic Kenneth Tynan as 'classless youth, buying avant-garde magazines at the bookstall, sampling cheap and pleasantly experimental food in the cafeteria, and looking at two exhibitions of work by new painters'.[10]

It was at Haynes's Arts Lab that McLaren witnessed the first UK screenings of Andy Warhol's split-screen *Chelsea Girls* and Kenneth Anger's *Inauguration of the Pleasure Dome*, both of which made an impact.

In these ways, Adler acted as 'the conduit, the medium'.[11] And for the former Harrow art students, there was no more significant introduction conducted by Adler than that to the ideas of the Situationist International (SI), the continental European radical arts group that had been in existence for around a decade and was at that stage coming into its own in the exploitation of actions and events to progress political subversion on university campuses across France.

Led by the philosopher Guy Debord, the SI believed that traditional modes of artistic expression were inadequate in the face of the dehumanising ravages of twentieth-century consumer society. Characterised as 'the spectacle', this, they suggested, made everyday existence banal and promoted passivity on the part of the populace. The SI's aim was to replace the making of art with the creation of disruptive public interventions to transform daily life into 'a creative, continuously original, delirious, ecstatic experience'.[12]

Of particular appeal to McLaren were the SI practices of *détournement* (the provocative juxtaposition of pre-existing elements such as the insertion of political sloganeering in ephemeral cartoon strips) and psychogeography (the mapping of the emotional and cultural undercurrents of a territory), as well as the *dérive* (literally 'drift', where Baudelarian individuals become flâneurs, allowing themselves to wander urban landscapes and become bored, repelled or enchanted by what they encounter).

'When I heard about the Situationists I was looking for a cause, like every other rebel without one,' McLaren told documentarists in the

1980s. 'We looked to do something that would make us feel like gigantic poseurs, show-offs. We felt dreadfully unfashionable as people.'[13]

But direct action of the sort promulgated by the SI would have to wait; Vivienne Westwood was by the autumn of 1967 coming to the full term of her pregnancy, having spent a lot of it living with her parents.

With support again from his grandmother, McLaren found a new home for himself, Westwood, her son Ben and their soon-to-be-born offspring in a double-fronted flat in Aigburth Mansions, Mowll Street, a mile or so east of Clapham in the shabby genteel Kennington hinterlands.

Fred Vermorel recalled a visit that revealed to him McLaren's lack of affection for six-year-old Ben. 'I found him weeping in the street, several streets from home, looking distraught, almost traumatised,' Vermorel said after McLaren's death.

It was raining and he was soaked. I took his hand and led him home. I mentioned to McLaren that his plimsolls were wet through and maybe in this weather he needed proper shoes. McLaren bellowed, mock paterfamilias, 'Plimsolls are good enough!'

Later Vivienne was apologetic. She confided that Ben had been unhappy of late. It was McLaren's fault. He was hard on the boy. I later took Ben to the park; he told me he hated McLaren and wished him dead, and that McLaren was horrible and used to deliberately stand on his foot and pinch his arms in punishment.[14]

The move from Kings Avenue coincided with a wider splintering of the group of friends who had come to know each other at Harrow Art School. With Gordon Swire remaining in Clapham, Vermorel left for the Sorbonne in Paris and the course 'Civilisation Français', which enabled onward progress to university, where he aimed to study philosophy. McLaren used his new residence to enrol on a vocational painting course and study for the all-important A level in art history eight miles due south at Croydon College of Art.

Before he left for France, Vermorel warned his friend of the perils of succumbing to domesticity, though his efforts did nothing to dampen Westwood's ardour.

'I noticed that Malcolm had become more settled, dangerously – as I advised him – patrician,' wrote Vermorel in the 1990s. 'I had dabbled in sociology and told him that being a father was just a social definition. Society was a sham, a hoax, a series of floating "roles" and "representations". Malcolm thought all this over and abandoned his responsibilities. Not that Vivienne minded. Like many women of that time, she was prepared to take it all on. Their poverty, his fecklessness, my outrageous advice.'[15]

So swayed was McLaren by Vermorel's words that he absented himself from the birth of his son in November 1967. When he arrived at the hospital a day or so later, one of nurses remonstrated with him, though Westwood later recalled his appearance fondly, remarking how handsome he looked in a newly purchased tweed overcoat.

Ungallantly, McLaren disputed paternity at the bedside. Contradictory to the last, he also announced that the boy's name would be Joseph Ferdinand Corré in tribute to his Sephardic heritage and a favourite painting, the Velázquez portrait of Archbishop Fernando de Valdés y Llano.

While McLaren was never to fulfil the conventional role of a father, he did, as Vermorel had surmised, start to lead a routine existence for the first time since leaving Hendon five years previously. New friends from Croydon – where he had enrolled in October 1967 – were entertained at Aigburth Mansions at dinner parties, where Westwood cooked and washed up.

At Croydon, McLaren's artistic direction and theoretical approach were refined not just as a result of his political awakening but also – though he was actively fighting against shouldering his load in the relationship – the maturing effect of fatherhood. In an essay from this time, McLaren reconciled his consistent application of black to his artworks by quoting Goya's view that it was 'the most exciting colour. Black when used in different ways appears the most infinite and mysterious, the most spatial and loose.'[16]

The radicalism he had absorbed over the previous year now manifested itself in his work, inspired by the urban development of the satellite town in semi-rural Surrey.

This had been initiated by the Croydon Corporation Act of the early 1960s masterminded by an autocratic local Conservative Party alderman, James Marshall. Blocks of Victorian and Edwardian streets were flattened to make way for a brutalist landscape of roadways, tower blocks, flyovers, shopping centres and car parks. Since skyscrapers were proscribed in central London, no less than forty-nine were constructed in Croydon during this period and, by the time of McLaren's arrival at the art college in its centre, the locale had become a byword for the excesses of desensitising urbanism.

Tower block sketch drawn at Croydon College of Art,
October 1967. Malcolm McLaren Estate.

'I used to spend hours looking out of Croydon's art school windows observing and then struggling to come to terms with these giant triffids of buildings that rose up and spread themselves all along East Croydon's path,' McLaren said towards the end of his life.

'Using charcoal, pen and anything else that came to hand, I drew and drew and drew. Croydon will always be remembered as a rite of passage. The constant roaming at night through its market streets and thereafter navigating those deep leafy suburbs into the countryside beyond.'[17]

One sketch, made on his arrival in October 1967, depicted a teetering concrete tower in the town centre and accompanied notes that demonstrate the intensity of the young student's engagement: 'Stimulated by my environmental experiences, shop windows, museums, the kitchen, I find myself working with these associations. Shoe shops as opposed to grocery shops as opposed to meat shops as opposed to jewellers' shops.'[18]

Not long after his son's birth, McLaren produced a collection of 2D and 3D works, some using his ferocious application of black and one clearly influenced by Warhol in its repetition of a graphic flower shape.

Building on the constructs created at Chelsea, McLaren also made a series of slab-like sculptures in abstract shapes, which he placed as public interventions on the walls of an underpass in Croydon.

These denoted McLaren's artistic progression since the tentative forays on the Harrow foundation course three years previously. 'Malcolm was really dedicated when he was at Croydon,' says fellow student and musician Robin Scott. 'He was forever rushing between history of art lectures and paying attention at every one of them.'[19]

Scott and McLaren became friendly; the former later said their relationship was 'a mixture of fantasy and fanaticism. What Malcolm applied to the whole punk thing wasn't dissimilar to his period in college. To me it was just a foregone conclusion that he might put it into entertainment channels and make use of the fashionable aspects of the left.'[20]

It wasn't until April 1968 that McLaren encountered another Croydon student who was to make a greater impression. Jamie MacGregor Reid was born and raised locally, the son of a political editor of the national newspaper the *Daily Sketch*, and in his fourth and final year at Croydon.

Reid was also preoccupied with the urbanisation of his hometown, and, enamoured of McLaren from the get-go, he promptly painted a portrait of his new friend entitled *Up They Rise: A Playground for the Juggler*. McLaren was drawn naked and cross-legged against a backdrop of tower blocks and a dark giant juggling the planets. Reid described the work as 'very prophetic, a gouache of a real imp . . . an inspired guess at things to come'.[21] The British academic Vicki Maguire interprets the portrait as a depiction of McLaren as 'manipulator of the new urban environment'.[22]

The timing of McLaren and Reid's first meeting was to inform their first collaboration; that month, across town, trouble was brewing at one of the capital's leading centres of further arts education, Hornsey College of Art. Vocational students at one of the schools (Hornsey was an organisational mish-mash spread across nine north London locations) had long been protesting about poor conditions and lobbying for improved resources, and the students were demanding control of union funds as well as participation in the institution's governing body. When this wasn't forthcoming, they set about occupying the college premises with a series of mass discussions and performances by visiting bands, which brought them into open and sometimes physical conflict with the college authorities.[23]

Similarly, at the London School of Economics, faculty grumblings were spilling over into direct action. The year 1968, said the author Tom Bower, an LSE student at the time, had become 'a seminal moment in Britain's social history. It created students who were cynics: dissatisfied and non-conformist.'[24]

Among the most dissatisfied and non-conformist was McLaren, who was receiving first-hand reports from Fred Vermorel of the student-led public dissent then breaking out in Paris as the events of May unfolded and striking workers raged against the Gaullist government.

'I made excited calls to Malcolm and Vivienne's flat from phone booths in the Latin Quarter,' said Vermorel. 'During one of these a riot was raging in the background with CRS lobbing tear gas grenades and blast bombs. I wrote to Malcolm he should come over. Malcolm wrote back, "Fred coming over Saturday or Friday, that is 17th or 16th May . . ." Malcolm was convinced. But by then it was too late. Rail and air strikes had paralyzed France.'[25]

Frustrated at the hurdles to active participation in Paris and within weeks of their first encounter, McLaren and Reid, abetted by Scott, decided to stage an occupation of their own. McLaren, adopting the nomenclature 'Malcolm the Red' in emulation of the various titles declared by the leaders of the Paris Uprising such as Daniel Cohn-Bendit's 'Dany le Rouge', was energised by the fact that the Paris rioters were influenced by Guy Debord and the Situationist International.

'When those students in Paris took his ideas, turned them into a reality, made the streets their own, and virtually brought down the Government de Gaulle, it excited us over here no end,' he said. 'So we tried to pay homage by ransacking and sitting in and taking over our own art school.'[26]

Scott later dismissed the act as 'just a continual gripe about anything associated with the establishment; we homed in on typical sort of art student problems, like no free expression and all that rubbish.'[27]

But McLaren was serious. 'In 1968 students suffered an enormous crisis, the realisation that we hated the world which suggested we should pursue careers,' he said. 'We decided we didn't want that straitjacket and believed we were the generation that would change things and that the culture was a ball at our feet we could kick in any direction we chose.'

Reid meanwhile noted the difference between Croydon and the more academically noteworthy colleges. 'You had a young, enthusiastic student body at Croydon which wasn't interested in formal education. Our solution to all the talk about network structures and changing years and departments was to tear the dividing walls down. So we did. Suddenly what had been the head of fine art's little room with fitted carpets, secretaries and sherry glasses was now part of the life class studio, naked and exposed.'[28]

This occurred in early June when McLaren, Reid, Scott and others used the occupation to demand greater rights for the student body and even an end to examinations and abolition of the students union. Similar actions were also taking place at colleges across the country, from Rugby in the Midlands to Brighton on the south coast.

During a particularly raucous debate at Croydon, McLaren claimed, 'a young sculptor shouted at the top of his lungs: "Why can't we make our sculptures in . . . gold?!" The outrage of such a suggestion in our context thrilled me.'[29]

McLaren later made wild claims of orgiastic night-time behaviour on the part of the occupying students, though these were not substantiated by others who took part in the protest. After a few days, McLaren, Reid and Scott were inveigled into meeting staff at the main college faculty on the pretext of resolving the situation. On their return they discovered the art annexe was locked. The occupation was over.

By now much media attention was focused on Croydon. Reid was interviewed by the local BBC TV programme *Town Around*[30] and a report in *The Times* included quotes from Scott, who announced himself Robin the Fair-Haired and complained: 'We have been tricked. We were given no warning about this. It was all done behind our backs. The authorities have created a situation which could become ugly and violent.'[31]

Outgunned by the college authorities, the activists were summoned to negotiate further, but with their leverage lost and the summer term over, the students' passions dissipated. McLaren was no longer interested in continuing the fight. As one of the ringleaders, he had come under direct pressure from college staff including the head of the painting course, Peter Cresswell. According to Reid, the Croydon governors threatened to have McLaren committed to a mental institution. This, of course, would have kyboshed his chances of pursuing the Dip AD.

Nevertheless, Scott fumed. 'When it came to the crunch, he had nothing to say,' he said of McLaren decades later. 'When the opportunity arose to change the system, or do anything about Croydon School of Art, he fucked off. It was the other Malcolm coming out.'[32]

The May letter McLaren had sent to Vermorel also expressed his artistic interests. As well as his wish to join the workers and students who had taken to the Paris streets, he announced that he intended to visit the Louvre to view *L'Europe Gothique XII XIV Siècles*, a large exhibition of gothic art in the recently redesigned Pavillon de Flore, which ultimately was not mounted due to the rioting. And he informed Vermorel of his increasing appreciation for the masters: 'Beginning to feel for the greats: MASSACCIO! . . . I have begun to see and BEGIN to understand Cezanne! (Bernini is marvellous). The Renaissance was fantastic.'

Simultaneously, McLaren displayed a paternal aspect to his personality hitherto unrevealed to Vermorel, writing of his six-month-old son: 'Joe is so sensitive, his movements are something that reveal his specialness.'

With the Paris protests having ended in late June after President de Gaulle called for new parliamentary elections (which, in the event, provided a mandate for his own party), McLaren made the trip to the French capital where he met up with Vermorel. 'We toured the scenes of devastation,' says Vermorel. 'But the Louvre was closed.'

McLaren marvelled at the sights, particularly the facade of the august École des Beaux-Arts – which had been one of the centres of dissent – obscured by radical posters and graffiti.

Then he travelled south and met Vivienne Westwood and Henry Adler. With the infant Joe and five-year-old Ben in the care of Westwood's parents, the couple and their friend explored all that cultural Provence had to offer, including an arts festival in Avignon, which included performances by the free-form, audience-participatory Living Theatre, a ballet directed by the choreographer Maurice Béjart and a screening of Chittaranjan Mittra's 1950 film *Shri Jagannatha*, apparently highly recommended by Adler.

They also visited Nice, where they saw Jean-Luc Godard's masterpiece *Le Mépris* (starring Brigitte Bardot, a lifetime obsession of McLaren's), and visited Arles, Aix-en-Provence and the Camargue.

Using a Primus stove acquired by Adler, the trio often camped and cooked outdoors. And in a letter to Vermorel, McLaren's references were all to artists. According to him, the sea in the Mediterranean light compared to the colour planes employed by the Danish/German painter Emil Nolde, while the countryside around Mount Saint-Victoire reminded him of the series made in the area by Paul Cézanne.[33]

On their return to London, McLaren received good news. He had passed the A level art history exam taken at Croydon before the occupation. This secured him an interview for a place on the third-year painting course at the art school of Goldsmiths College in Lewisham, south-east London.

Chapter 7

One of the first people McLaren encountered when he attended Goldsmiths for the admission interview in the autumn of 1968 was his Croydon foe Peter Cresswell, who had transferred to the college to assume a post in the fine art department. According to McLaren, Cresswell promptly warned the twenty-two-year-old that he would face immediate expulsion if he did not keep his nose clean.[1]

'He arrived from under a cloud of some sort,' said Cresswell in the 1980s. 'The one thing you can say about him was that McLaren was aggressive, unusually aggressive. It was not physical aggression, it was just his style. Malcolm developed a trick early on of not behaving the way you think he would – it was ever so slightly disturbing. And he would stimulate a confrontation just to see how people behaved.'[2]

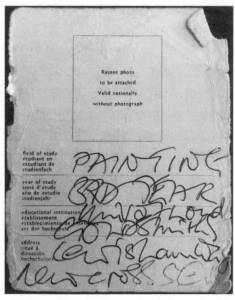

Goldsmiths student card, October 1968. Paul Burgess Archive.

Having inspected the scenes of the Paris riots and immersed himself in the artistic and sensual delights of the south of France, McLaren's dander was up. 'By the autumn of 1968 we were thinking about how we were going to redesign our lives and it led us ultimately to try and create a lifestyle in which we, in turn, could turn the tables and we, in turn, could do things which would shift the intelligence,' he said.[3]

Having been accepted by the college, McLaren set about making his mark. Russell Profitt, then a sociology student and the first black president of Goldsmiths student union (and latterly an equal opportunities champion in British public life), recalled McLaren lobbing tomatoes at union committee members when they were in session, while the artist Malcolm Poynter claimed that he was pushed to the verge of knocking McLaren out by his allegations that Poynter had embezzled college funds.[4]

McLaren's confrontational tendencies were stoked by the literature of the Situationist International, introduced to him by Fred Vermorel, who had returned from Paris and was sharing a house with Westwood's brother Gordon Swire in Anerley, a south London suburb not far from Goldsmiths.

One afternoon, while waiting with McLaren for a bus outside the college, Vermorel showed his friend two issues of the SI's 'accomplished, disdainful, dangerous and suave' journal *Internationale Situationniste*.[5]

McLaren was enchanted not only by their elevated production values – on quality paper stock, the second issue from 1958 was encased in a mirrored silver book jacket and number nine from August 1964 was in a vivid mauve – but also the content: images of black-clad cowboys holding smoking guns, détourned 1950s space-age comic strips, bikini-clad South African beauty queens, psychogeographic maps and cool monochrome portraits of besuited SI members. These were displayed with intriguing chapter headings using stark slogans such as *Le Monde Dont Nous Parlons* ('The World We Are Talking About'), *Les Loisirs Travaillant* ('Working Leisure') and *L'urbanisme comme volonté et comme representation* ('Urbanism as will and representation').

One article in issue nine, *Reflections on Violence*, included contemporaneous reports on the mod riots at UK seaside resorts in the early 1960s alongside revolts and insurgency from Algeria to Bulgaria (where, apparently three *hooligan sadiques* had indulged in mindless mayhem in 1964).

'Without knowing much French, Malcolm grasped their import from the style and illustrations,' said Vermorel. 'As the SI slogan read: "Our ideas are already in everyone's heads." What had previously been art school posturing was crystallized and argued with philosophical and sociological sophistication in theses as pithily as the most potent advertising slogans. And with a design panache to match.'[6]

The unlikelihood of McLaren abiding by Cresswell's command that he kept his nose clean was further intensified when Henry Adler introduced him and Vermorel to the members of the SI's mischief-making British offshoot King Mob.

This group took its name from the title of Christopher Hibbert's book about London's violent anti-Catholic Gordon Riots of June 1780 during which 12,000 troops were mobilised and 700 people killed.[7] With ambitions to provoke similar widespread public disorder, King Mob was led by the writer Christopher Gray with writer/translator Don Nicholson-Smith, art historian T. J. Clark and the Notting Hill-based builder brothers Dave and Stuart Wise, and constituted a group of around thirty activists interested in 'the transcendence of art into a rejuvenated everyday life'.[8]

King Mob engaged in such activities as interrupting art events, the weekly smashing of the window of the Wises' local Wimpy Bar as a protest against the banality of consumerism, and peppering the streets of the west London neighbourhood with erudite graffiti interventions, including Blake's 'The road to excess leads to the palace of wisdom'. King Mob's most successful critique of the numbing effect of contemporary existence was visible to commuters on trains shuttling along the Metropolitan and City line between Westbourne Park and Ladbroke Grove: 'SAME THING DAY AFTER DAY – TUBE – WORK – DINER (sic) – WORK – ARMCHAIR TV – SLEEP – TUBE – WORK

– HOW MUCH MORE CAN YOU TAKE – ONE IN TEN GO MAD – ONE IN FIVE CRACKS UP'.

King Mob had earned Debord's derision when the Situationist king-pin sprung a surprise visit on Dave Wise, after he impulsively claimed there was an army of hundreds of British activists who would take to the streets when given the word. Debord arrived unannounced at Wise's home to find his fellow radical watching *Match of the Day* from the comfort of his sofa. Debord is said to have turned on his heel and left. Soon King Mob was expelled from the SI for siding with the US agitator Ben Morea's anarchist organisations Black Mask and Up Against the Wall, Motherfucker.

King Mob's coruscating newsletter *King Mob Echo* mightily impressed McLaren, as did such crude poster artworks such as that of a woman's vagina headed 'Keep the Dialectic Open'. He was also swayed by their pamphlet *Art Schools Are Dead*, which encouraged dissent from within, reading in part: 'Revolution against the art school trick must be seen as revolt against the status quo – against its duplicity and ever increasing hypocrisy.'[9]

McLaren's first meeting with the members of King Mob took place not long after he started at Goldsmiths, in late October 1968 during the so-called 'Vietnam Occupation' of the LSE, one of a series at the trouble-spot institution in Holborn over that autumn and winter.

Vermorel recalls that King Mob had congregated at the George V pub in Portugal Street, not far from the LSE campus.

The discussion was about how to escalate the 'situation'. I'd rung Malcolm to get him to this meeting. In the middle of our earnest discussion he rushed in. He was breathless, wild-eyed, his curly red hair in a shock, fizzing with enthusiasm.

But this was not for the revolution. He told everyone that he'd just come from the National Gallery, where he'd been checking out Van Gogh's *Sunflowers* and had a revelation. Van Gogh's images were incandescent. Transcendent. Fucking amazing, man.

This did not go down well with the King Mob apparatchiks. Several frowned. Some became surly. Others looked astonished at Malcolm's bravura innocence. Did this man not know that culture was not to be consumed: that art was dead? And that this death was one of the most sacred tenets of Situationism, and any truck with culture in any form was a heinous banality and political crime?

But in the end such was the force of Malcolm's enthusiasm that they gave him the benefit of the doubt, thinking that, although dubious, he was too mad to be a police spy.[10]

The Wises have acknowledged McLaren's participation in their most notorious escapade: a Christmas-time invasion of the toy department of Selfridges, the store which had figured prominently in his childhood, not only because of the fondly remembered visits with his grandmother but also the lurid association between his mother and the owner Charles Clore.

McLaren later depicted the King Mob intervention, notably in his 1991 British TV film *The Ghosts Of Oxford Street*. 'Oxford Street became my battleground,' he intoned in the voiceover of a scene in which several people dressed as Father Christmas handed out wrapped toys and presents to gleeful kids. In this version, McLaren was one of the Santas being chased by security guards and simultaneously represented by a ringleted 1940s child in a sailor-suit firing a toy machine gun. ' "Boy oh boy, Christmas", I and my friends sang. "Let's smash the great deception." For on Oxford Street I saw that modern life had been reduced to the spectacle of the commodity.'

In fact, there was only one member of the King Mob crew dressed as Santa Claus when the gang of fifteen or so invaded the department store in December 1968. They did hand out toys as presents and chant, per McLaren, citing lines from the copies of the leaflet with which they littered the scene: 'Christmas: It's meant to be great but it's horrible. Let's smash the great deception. Light up Oxford Street, dance around the fire.'

Dave Wise has confirmed that McLaren was an enthusiastic participant even if he was not the person dressed in Christmas costume.
'McLaren had dash and audacity and proved to be very plucky and imaginative, darting here, there and everywhere during the battle for
Selfridges,' Wise wrote in 2008.[11]

By this time, McLaren had become friendly with a Goldsmiths student
he met while waiting to be interviewed on his enrolment day at the college.
Helen Mininberg was, like Henry Adler, a moneyed Jewish South African.
Of restricted growth, she lived in a posh apartment in the terrace above the
Western Jewry Synagogue in Marylebone, central London.

'While we were in the queue Helen asked me: "What are you going to
do if you don't get in?" and I replied: "Start a revolution",' recalled
McLaren. 'She thought that was really funny so we shared the same
painting class studios. I got to know her very well.'

Unlike McLaren, Mininberg favoured marijuana and associated with
such street-rock groups as the Pretty Things and the musicians who
would later form London's outrageous outfit the Pink Fairies. McLaren
took to visiting Mininberg's home near Marble Arch, which he described
as 'quite a little drug den. It was very central so everyone stayed there,
though I was pretty innocent compared with some of them.'

A couple of years younger than McLaren, Mininberg painted a portrait
of her new friend and asked him to accompany her on an acid trip. 'She
wanted me to walk around with her but she needed a safe spot, so we
decided on Hyde Park,' said McLaren. 'There we could just wander
through the trees, so we took LSD and bounced around. It was a strange
thing. We spent virtually all night there.'

In his first year at Goldsmiths, one of McLaren's tutors was Barry
Martin, a twenty-five-year-old who had graduated from the college a
couple of years previously and also attended Saint Martin's. A practising
artist (showing such experimental work as large-scale kinetic sculptures),
he had more in common with the students than many on the staff.

'Each student had a personal tutor who would talk to them about their
work on a one-to-one basis; I was given Malcolm and a couple of others

by the head of fine art Andrew Forge,' said Martin. 'Because I was only a couple of years older than some of them it was felt I could handle the youthful rebellion that was going on. The climate was one of insecurity on the campuses. One didn't know whether there might be a resurgence of what had happened earlier that year.'[12]

Doubtless with Cresswell's input, the Goldsmiths administrators had agreed that, as a difficult student, McLaren required special handling. 'He was argumentative,' concurs Martin. 'He liked trouble and causing a disturbance, constantly questioning what we were all doing. I think he saw himself as a Che Guevara figure, rousing the troops to storm the barricade.'

Meanwhile, McLaren was careful to cover his tracks in terms of the development of his practice at other schools and colleges. For example, Martin did not know until decades later that McLaren had created environmental installations such as the Kingly Street labyrinth, the Chelsea structures or the public interventions in Croydon.

This information would have been valuable when, over a two-week period, Martin and another Goldsmiths teacher Bill Tucker organised a mixed-media project for students including McLaren and Mininberg in a hut at the back of the college. 'We brought in lots of materials you wouldn't necessarily include in paintings: chicken wire, plaster, sand and wood, and gave them the entire space to see what they might come up with, either working as a group or individually. Malcolm never said anything to me about the fact that he'd done this sort of work before. Since he was shifting around between art schools under different names, he would not have wanted me to know he had created environments elsewhere.'

Arriving early one morning Martin found McLaren laying out chicken wire across the Goldsmiths' hut floor and unsuccessfully trying to hook it up directly to the mains. McLaren told Martin that, once electrified, his idea was to encourage a chicken to walk across the wire, a variation of the music hall routine of making hens dance on biscuit tins by placing lit candles inside them.

Pointing out that this was extremely dangerous for McLaren, let alone the chicken, Martin persuaded the student to abandon the plan and saved him from electrocuting himself.

The group nature of the mixed media project brought to the fore McLaren's manipulative side. 'Often, while we were considering work in the studio, he would throw in asides which were nothing to do with what we were talking about,' said Martin. 'That would draw in the others and we'd spend a lot of time pursuing his line of inquiry.

'For example, when we came to what his group had produced on the mixed-media project, he constantly challenged Bill Tucker and I to justify our views, and repeatedly asked why we had even embarked on the exercise. This would get some of the other students riled up.'

Martin said that he was always able to persuade McLaren to back off, but not without some effort. 'There were sixteen in the group – it was definitely his aim to corral all of them to support his view that the exercise wasn't worthwhile,' said Martin, who proved a doughty opponent. 'He didn't get away with it. I thought his attempts to manipulate the other students just wasn't on.'

Try as he might, Martin failed to identify the reason for McLaren's disruptiveness. 'It wasn't as though he was saying "I'm a Marxist and this is all bourgeois activity" or "We should be talking about what's going on in Vietnam". I could never get to the bottom of it. He was never clear in his intent beyond apparently wanting to stir things up.'

To those who knew McLaren, it was obvious he was in his element at Goldsmiths. As his painting style matured, he made a name for himself among other rebellious students; as well as Mininberg, McLaren became tight with Niall Martin, a colourful south Londoner with a witty line in repartee.

'Niall was one of the most ferocious of the Goldsmiths crowd,' says Fred Vermorel, who describes him as 'a spindly youth, explosive with ribald spleen'.

And so McLaren thrived creatively with like-minded rebels amid the chaos he found so comfortable. This explosive atmosphere extended to his home life, where the relationship with Westwood was 'on-and-off. We were so different and opposite, lost in our own particular worlds. It was difficult to think how on earth we had any kind of common ground other than a child. But we did, in as far as to say that she was always very interested, almost over-awed by the word "culture". It meant more to her than anything else.'

In the face of their considerable financial insecurity (Rose Isaacs had for the time being ceased providing funds), the couple did not renew the lease on the apartment at Aigburth Mansions and, cut adrift by McLaren's inability to commit to her and the children, Westwood was left with no option but to take Ben and Joe to live with her parents in the house in Oxfordshire they had bought on their retirement from the Harrow post office.

McLaren moved back to his grandparents in Westbury Court above Clapham South tube station, and occasionally visited his partner, though he was not made to feel welcome by the Swires.

By now McLaren had lost contact with Patrick Casey, whose role as McLaren's confidant was increasingly filled by Mininberg. But this was complicated by a brief love affair with a girl he met in a local library. For the time being, his relationship with Mininberg was platonic, but she was fiercely protective of him and her turf.

'Helen wasn't happy about the girl in the library. She also got a lodger to help pay the rent who turned out to be a mad sex fiend,' said McLaren. 'She'd have it off with all the art lecturers who'd come round, one of whom Helen liked. This made Helen angry; the two girls were constantly arguing but I think they both slept with one of the lecturers together.'

With Mininberg, Fred Vermorel and Henry Adler, McLaren maintained a presence at protest rallies and demonstrations, returning with them to the LSE in January 1969 when 'students ran riot inside with pickaxes and crowbars', according to the *Daily Telegraph*, and the gates were torn down, allowing the protestors to storm the college.

According to Paul Hoch and Vic Schoenbach, two overseas students who were eventually expelled from the college for their roles in the riot, 'two wild-looking, bearded anarchists who nobody had ever seen before had somehow appeared for the occasion, and were flailing away with sledgehammers with all their might. Students looked on in amazement, shock and approval [at] that wild desire to smash the domination of our lives by things, by smashing the things themselves . . .'[13]

It is likely that the wild-looking pair were the Wise brothers, though McLaren later indicated he was one of them.[14] What is certain is that he came to know Hoch and was also present and willing to get stuck in at another college occupation in this period.

The British writer Dick Pountain has recalled the tensions when a large crowd gathered in support of the LSE rioters at the University of London Union. 'The whole thing was very fraught because you'd got this mass of students, the New Left people telling them to be serious and responsible, and King Mob telling them to get their rocks off, let it hang out,' said Pountain in the late 1980s. 'It was very iffy, because the great mass in the middle were swaying both ways. Only a minority supported us; the majority wanted to be quiet and respectable, but these two guys came out of the crowd and joined in with us and said 'We're with you' . . . One was called Fred Vermorel and the other was Malcolm Edwards.'[15]

Alongside his activism, McLaren voraciously consumed the alternative media of the day, in particular the underground and workers' presses. He was a regular customer of the radical bookshop Compendium in north London's Camden Town, where he bought countercultural literature including the works of William Burroughs and the erotic paperback *Helen & Desire*, written by Burroughs's fellow traveller, the Scottish junkie beat writer Alexander Trocchi, who had been expelled from the Situationist International in the mid-1960s.

Through Vermorel and such bookshops as Compendium, McLaren learned about the Lettriste International, the French group which preceded the SI, included in its membership Trocchi and Debord and aimed to transcend art by 'an international of direct communication' and making 'poetry out of everything'.[16]

As well as using words as images, the Lettrists originated the concepts of *dérive* and *détournement*, and not only applied, as their name indicates, text to public spaces – one 1953 graffito in Paris proclaimed 'Never Work' – but also adorned their clothing with Dada and Surrealist statements and revolutionary messages. For such a visually aware and verbally dextrous creature as McLaren, this was extremely alluring.

It fell to Henry Adler to effect an introduction to the heavily addicted Trocchi, who by then was reduced to selling second-hand books and manuscripts and living in a shabby flat on the Kensington and Chelsea borders. The invitation to McLaren was extended because Trocchi was eager to meet radical students to help him work on his utopian Project Sigma texts, though McLaren was more impressed with the Scotsman's background and the banned pornography such as *Helen & Desire* he had written for the Olympia Press in Paris in the 1950s.

At the end of his first year at Goldsmiths, McLaren was required to show examples of his work. He chose seven gestural paintings, mainly oils on canvas. Some integrated text statements and others were outcomes of the mixed media experimentation, incorporating the aforementioned chicken wire, hammered wood planks and, in one case, an inverted paper envelope against depictions of leaf forms.

A work entitled *14 Pink Figures on Moving Sea of Green* presented a number of stickmen both vertically and horizontally. 'All the people holding hands are happy because all the people on the ground are dead,' McLaren solemnly told Barry Martin.[17]

Another, *I Will Be So Bad*, detailed a still black silhouette against the inverted and repeated lines of the title, as though written during detention, and paraphrasing his grandmother Rose's mantra, while the chicken wire was used to cover a text statement: 'The Intangible Manipulation of Our Minds'. This wasn't the last time McLaren would apply the wire netting, for which he appeared to have developed something of an obsession.

Martin, who interpreted the latter artwork as 'a cry for help', conducted a ninety-minute end-of-year critical review with McLaren, during which the student declared his opposition to the limitations imposed by traditional art forms, in particular painting.

'He told me he was done with it, that it was outmoded, that he was driven to investigate new ways of expressing himself,' said Martin. 'I was quite sad; Malcolm was a troublesome student but a talented painter who could have made a name for himself in the art world.'

McLaren subsequently destroyed all but one of the first-year works. In a symbolic statement, the exception, the largest canvas – the seven-foot-tall *Map of British Isles with Yellow Star and Hole*, in which he had already kicked a sizeable tear 'because he didn't like the symmetry', according to Martin – was left to rot in the summer rain in the yard at the back of the college. Eventually it was torn apart and taken away by binmen.

In repudiating traditional art practice, McLaren was joining other art students of the period and inserting himself into the lineage that included such figures as the Danish artist and SI fellow traveller Asger Jorn, who had produced psychogeographic maps with Guy Debord and proclaimed 'Painting is dead' in 1958. In particular, McLaren's determination for a new direction was aligned with his hero Andy Warhol, who explained his sponsorship of the Velvet Underground in 1967 by saying: 'Since I don't really believe in painting anymore we have a chance to combine music and art.'

With Warholian multi-media experiences on his mind, McLaren had by the time of his final crit from Martin eagerly helped organise an event that became known as the Goldsmiths Arts Festival. In contributing, he hoped to draw upon the happenings in which he had been involved at 26 Kingly Street a couple of years previously as well as 'The Dialectics of Liberation' conference he attended at the Roundhouse.

Incorporating film screenings, panel discussions and live performances, McLaren worked on the planning of the festival with a student feminist activist named Liz Martin and his friend Niall Martin (no relation), and used the connections he had made via Henry Adler to book appearances by R. D. Laing, Alexander Trocchi, the firebrand communist trade unionist Jack Dash, Michael X, the Black Power radical who had become a countercultural figurehead, and Paul Hoch, one of the organisers of the LSE occupation.

The poster produced by the college trailed the event with the tagline 'Everything will be free – absolutely free' and also promised the Living Theatre (who McLaren had witnessed in France the previous year), the actor David Hemmings (star of *Barbarella* and *Blow Up*), the US artist Jim Dine, R&B band the Pretty Things and the poetry collective the Liverpool Scene, as well as electronic music, drama and mime.

'They were very politically aware times, and I wanted to fill the college with these people and see what happened,' said McLaren in the 1990s. Advertised in the listings of the *International Times* and trailed on DJ John Peel's late hours *Night Ride* national radio show, the festival was due to run all week from Monday 30 June but in the event was held over the Thursday and Friday of the first week of July 1969.

Ever ambitious, McLaren described the festival as 'a mammoth event' telling the *International Times* that even the barbecued food was free of charge, and that films would include footage from the Paris protests in May 1968 and a performance by Lindsay Kemp's experimental dance troupe. He also gave his and Niall Martin's names as contacts, with the Goldsmiths' student union phone number.[18]

On the first day, proceedings commenced sedately enough with the local group the Action Theatre's staging of *The Lover*, the 1963 play by McLaren's favourite dramatist Harold Pinter, followed by poetry readings by the singer-songwriter Michael Chapman and others as well as screenings of Luis Buñuel's surrealist classic *Un Chien Andalou* and Ken Loach's gritty *vérité* masterpiece *Cathy Come Home*. The surreal Bonzo Dog Doo-Dah Band, whose line-up include Goldsmiths alumni, were also bannered to perform.

The second day, a Friday, was twenty-four hours before a much-touted free performance by the Rolling Stones in Hyde Park. Many of the students intended to attend that gig, so used the Goldsmiths festival to get in the mood.

McLaren had inserted into the programme a talk by Fred Vermorel entitled 'All in a Day's Work' in the college lecture theatre. 'It was never intended to take place; the title was concocted by Malcolm as a joke because I was on the dole at the time,' says Vermorel. 'A lot of the "events" and "appearances" were there to give semblance of a proper, rounded festival/conference. Quite a lot was fake and not all of the advertised participants were even contacted, let alone responded. As far as I know, no-one had a clue how to get hold of Burroughs. The only candidate was probably Trocchi, who was ultra unreliable.'[19]

The aim of a discussion set up by McLaren was to consider 'The Revolution, anti-public relations and formation of resistance groups'. Student Dave Walton, meanwhile, referred to McLaren's panel as 'a motley crowd of male star rebels, many of them media hate figures . . . [it was] little more than a radical version of a chat show'.

Incensed at the non-representation of women, Liz Martin and fellow feminists staged a disruption and, according to Walton, 'were treated in a blatantly patronising manner. We felt we had to support the women, though, quite honestly, I remember feeling that everyone was a bit on show, including the women.'

The police were called to calm the mood of the crowd. Vermorel later claimed that the feminist intervention caused a mini-riot, but the police were treated with indifference rather than physical reaction.[20] 'McLaren was furious, rightly, that none of us did anything to attack them – well, no one got arrested, despite the hash-smoking,' said Walton.[21]

Meanwhile, the musicians McLaren had booked were well received. There are some reports that Slade played; Robert Fripp has confirmed that his inventive prog-rock ensemble King Crimson performed (the next day they made their mark nationally in Hyde Park, supporting the Stones).

The event made a splash in the local paper, which reported the presence of 'dolly birds and girls that seemed to strut about with an "I'm holier than thou" expression' and sets by local folkies Gordon Giltrap and the Strawbs.[22]

'In fact there was some damn good stuff,' said attendee Paul Thompson. 'It wasn't like Malcolm advertising a non-existent festival with non-existent guests. Pre-publicity did make too much of people with whom the organisers were negotiating, right up to the last minute, so some names went out who eventually didn't perform.

'Of course Malcolm was there with a grin on his face having a great time. But then he often had a grin on his face in those days.'[23]

Chapter 8

Over the summer of 1969 McLaren visited Westwood, Joe and Ben in Oxfordshire; despite his fecklessness, Westwood remained dedicated to their reunion but was bristling at the lack of space at her parents' home.

With McLaren's encouragement, she found new digs: a caravan owned by Westwood's aunt in a park in the seaside resort Prestatyn, in north Wales, not far from Liverpool.

This was a difficult time for Westwood and the children. Living close to the breadline, without work and little or no support from McLaren, she used all her resources to feed and clothe the family. There was one comfort: with the disapproving Swires safely in Oxfordshire, McLaren felt more inclined to journey from London and spend time with them in the Welsh countryside.

When in London, McLaren escaped his elderly grandparents by staying at Helen Mininberg's apartment. Briefly, they conducted a sexual relationship. 'Vivienne was away and I don't think she ever knew,' said McLaren later. 'I did it out of friendship more than anything else. I felt that was what Helen wanted and I couldn't deny her such things.'

The location of Mininberg's Marylebone flat was key to McLaren's creative direction. Wallenberg Place is two streets from Marble Arch, the ornate John Nash-designed structure marking the western end of London's main shopping thoroughfare, Oxford Street.

The tall arch stands on the site of the Tyburn Tree, the triple gallows where hundreds of executions were staged in London up until the late eighteenth century. As a means of maintaining public order, the authorities paraded prisoners from Newgate Gaol in the east past the jeering mob along Oxford Street to their doom at Tyburn.

Through his King Mob connections, McLaren already knew that the Gordon Riots of 1780 had precipitated a redesign of Oxford Street into a straight roadway, bottle-necked at one end to contain public insurrection and enable an army, if it so wished, to march on the City of London.

As a Situationist, McLaren recognised that the subsequent commercialisation of Oxford Street in the nineteenth and twentieth centuries exercised a more peaceful, if insidious, means of control through zoning and signage.

Set to return to Goldsmiths for his second year, McLaren envisioned a film about the street, its rich history and present status. He later said that his intention was to approach the subject matter 'from a crowd-gathering and social, political point of view to watch how crowds and people are manipulated, and the whole consumer aspect of society'.[1]

The idea was that the film would also enable him to slip the bonds of painting and environmental sculpture and enable the incorporation of psychogeography, the *dérive* and *détournement*, as well as the SI's over-arching themes of alienation and commodification. And McLaren planned to inject himself into the narrative, drawing on his childhood trips to the street's vast department stores with his grandmother and his more recent participation in direct action in and around central London.

'By this stage I had no interest whatsoever in making any kind of art,' declared McLaren in the 1990s. 'I was only interested in devising a point of view about Oxford Street and the rise of the facade. Streets were very much part of my life, having been on various demonstrations and controlling the streets and colleges and talking about how laws and architecture control the movement of people.'

McLaren quickly prepared a proposal to switch the direction of his fine art degree to film. The introduction read:

From Tyburn at the gallows to the Gordon Riots and *Barnaby Rudge* to Nash and the rebuilding of the street from its dangerous curves to a wide and perfectly straight highway so an army could swiftly move down it without fear of ambush. For a new bourgeois to parade down it to the invention of the cul-de-sac and the door-man to trap and catch thieves in it. The coming of the department store and crowd control. The politics of boredom and the fact that more Mars bars are sold on Oxford Street than anywhere else in the world. This is a journey in 24 hours of a life on Oxford Street.

Despite his qualms about McLaren as a person, Goldsmiths' Peter Cresswell approved ('he seemed much more suitable to film than paint-ing'[2]) and provided the college's Bolex camera for McLaren's use.

Then the twenty-two-year-old embarked on a period of research. 'George Cruikshank did tremendous etchings at the time, *Barnaby Rudge* has it as a background, but there are very few reference books,' said McLaren in the early 1980s.

I found stuff in the London Library. It was Nash who decided to move the poor out to Shepherd's Bush, keep the centre for the rich and bourgeois, create these avenues with large stores, the cul-de-sacs, like Stratford Place off Oxford Street. The doorman was invented at that time to look out for rough types, and thieves were caught easier because they couldn't get off [Oxford] Street.

Seven Dials was a hell-hole where the criminals were safe, but it couldn't happen on Oxford Street. It was straight so the army was in no fear of ambush, 'cause when it was a higgledy-piggledy street people could lie in wait. It was the first straight street in the world. New York was based on it, Paris was rebuilt.

I was trying to show how London was, how the street was ruled by the people, but now the street rules the people [which] by virtue of its architecture, governs your movement.[3]

Over the next two years, with input from fellow students including Mininberg, as well as Jamie Reid, Fred Vermorel, Niall Martin and others, McLaren wrestled with the film, shooting interiors and street scenes, and interviewing a variety of contributors.

'I was concerned with its history,' he said later. 'It was really a search for identity, the root, where the magic was. I was concerned with what Oxford Street had to sell and whether what it had to sell was what anyone truly wanted.'

McLaren was keen to include such figures as the tragic nineteenth-century writer Thomas De Quincey, whose memoir *Confessions of an English Opium-Eater* (which McLaren had encountered as a Soho-obsessed beatnik just a few years previously) recounted the search for the mysterious prostitute 'Ann of Oxford Street'. This underlined the influence of King Mob; the group's Stuart Wise credited De Quincey as 'the originator of the *dérive*'.[4]

'I wanted to relate the stories of people considered outlaws, those who had a romantic outlook on life,' said McLaren. 'I hunted for the address of the apothecary where De Quincey bought his first bottle of laudanum and was constantly looking for signs in the literal sense: shop signs, old signs, signs indelible in the brick work, markings, graffiti and bits of old architecture left over from a time that had passed.'

McLaren also discovered the subterranean street of abandoned Victorian shops underneath Selfridges, which was still accessible in the 1960s via the Lilley & Skinner shoe store at 360 Oxford Street.

'In creating the movie, I became totally fascinated by the facades of shops, and how they could change so quickly and thereafter change your entire point of view,' he said later. 'One facade covered another, and then another. The more you peeled away, the more would be revealed, to the point where, when you wandered into the basement of this particular shop, you found an entire street.'

In the summer of 1970, McLaren persuaded his grandmother to find a new home for himself, Westwood and the boys. She located an apartment in Thurleigh Court, a small 1930s block 500 yards from her home along Nightingale Road, which runs along the southern edge of Clapham Common.

The rent was £6.50 a week, a considerable amount for a penniless student and his partner. Westwood took up teaching again, in Brixton, and she and McLaren decorated the flat with pale blue lino ('which looked like the sea') and lanterns from London's Chinatown. 'We spread across the walls stencils of little figures and made them textured,' recalled McLaren.

The move to Thurleigh Court was as much for his son Joe. Mininberg told Westwood's biographer Jane Mulvagh: '[McLaren] was concerned to be around for the kid, so he wouldn't be brought up in a narrow, working-class way like her family.'[5]

In writing about McLaren accompanying Westwood and her pupils on school trips to the countryside, Mulvagh summons the storytelling capabilities he inherited from his grandmother:

> Gathered round the campfire, the two adults would tell magic tales for the children. Leaping through the long grass like a demonic wizard, McLaren warned his spellbound audience that if they did not keep the fire burning, snakes – poisonous of course – would attack. He was a mesmerising performer. His oratory could provoke mayhem as he built up the children's natural restlessness, with his flaying arms and fire-bright eyes, into a conflagration of mischievous adventure. Here was an adult who thought like a naughty child. It was a trait he would trade on for many years.[6]

At Thurleigh Court, McLaren drafted in Vermorel to work on *The Story of Oxford Street*. Using a professional Uher reel-to-reel recorder, Vermorel taped attempts at a voiceover from a couple of unusual narrators.

'Malcolm had two ideas he wanted to try out,' says Vermorel. 'One was a ten-year-old black kid who was one of Vivienne's students reading the script, but that didn't work so then he persuaded his grandmother to have a go. In a way that could have been incredible because she had such a funny voice but it turned out terribly. She kept on breaking up and cackling. She thought it was hilarious, though of course he didn't.'

In a recording made by Vermorel, Rose struggled with the script's ornate sentence structures and references to James Wyatt, the proprietor of the eighteenth-century place of public entertainment, the Pantheon. As she mispronounced the painter Raphael's surname as well as the words 'loggia' and 'stucco', there were constant interruptions and prompts from McLaren and the tape concluded with much tittering from his grandmother.

As the months wore on, McLaren accumulated footage without a semblance of narrative thrust. 'We didn't have the techniques or skills to pull it off,' admitted Jamie Reid later. 'But it was potentially a very interesting project and gave us our first taste of an idea we later developed with the Sex Pistols.'[7]

In December 1970, eighty-four-year-old Mick Isaacs was in a geriatric hospital back in Hendon. McLaren accompanied his grandmother on a visit. 'He was on his death bed,' recalled McLaren in 2000. 'He looked up at me and said to her: "What the hell have you brought him here for?" Maybe, because I had been dragged about everywhere by my grandmother, I had got in the way of any relationship he thought he might have had with his wife. I was sort of sad, really, and a bit shocked. I didn't know what to say.'

As McLaren's interest in the Oxford Street project waxed and waned he engaged in various diversions. At grant time – he received £75 at the beginning of each term – McLaren persuaded a couple of his fellow Goldsmiths students to accompany him on day trips to the provinces, where they'd pick up rare books and then resell them in central London.

'We'd find Victorian era books with illustrations by Gustave Doré in places like Warwick and Leamington Spa and then sell them on,' said McLaren. 'Sometimes I was tripling my grant. But then I got more outrageous and stole rare books from the Goldsmiths library and steamed off the labels.'

Among McLaren's customers for this contraband was Albert Jackson, in the rare booksellers' strip in Charing Cross Road. 'He never shaved, with long hairs coming out of his nose and always wore a dressing gown,' remembered McLaren. 'He'd always give us £5 for twenty books because he knew full well what we were doing.'

Incredibly, McLaren claimed that he and two unnamed college friends caused a huge fire at the library when the college authorities called the police in to investigate the thefts. 'I was so concerned. They were getting close to nabbing me,' said McLaren. 'And like lunatics we decided the best thing to do is to burn the library down so there would be no fingerprints. We thought . . . let's burn it down. And that's what we did. We burnt down the Goldsmiths College library.'[8]

According to his story, there were no repercussions. The fact is that there was a severe fire at the college's library in 1971, which destroyed many precious books.[9] It is now impossible to confirm whether McLaren was telling the truth and was responsible for this crime, particularly since he never named his accomplices.

There is, of course, a chance that the arsonist was someone else, and that, at a safe distance, McLaren laid claim to amplify his image as a dangerous subversive. He certainly delighted in telling Goldsmiths alums, including the British artist Damien Hirst, who observed that McLaren had likely impaired his education at the institution in the 1980s as a result.

Simultaneously, McLaren later claimed he indulged in other destructive acts. These centred on a peculiar artistic and pagan activity. 'I spent a lot of time making *petit cadeaux* out of bricks,' he said. 'I decorated each one with ribbons to which I attached a little tag reading: "Magic's Back". Then I'd go out at night and hurl them through the church windows in Lewisham in the hope that a priest would pick one up and read the message. I did that with different friends and sometimes on my own but not with Helen. She knew about it though. It was my little conceptual art gesture.'

As well as his excursions into the provinces, McLaren had taken to scouring London's junk shops and street markets. Ever the forward adopter, he was among the first of the post-hippy cognoscenti to evaluate the then-unfashionable decorative arts objects and ephemera from the 1950s and 1960s.

It was Patrick Casey who introduced him to this new world of retromania. They reconnected when Casey spotted McLaren in

Tottenham Court Road from the laundry van he was driving. McLaren said, 'Soon after he sent me a wonderful postcard with a photograph of Billy Fury on the front. It stuck in my mind as one of the most fashionable desires I had ever had, desiring the look and the feeling to be as close as possible to Fury, who represented to me the English Elvis Presley and the era of glamorous, romantic, lean, desperate, hungry, glittered cool dudes which the Afghan coats and ethnic clothes of the time did not represent at all.'

Soon McLaren joined Casey in combing the stalls in the huge market held in west London's Portobello Road each weekend. 'I loved going there, searching for old records, for artefacts that conjured up that lifestyle of times forgotten,' said McLaren. 'I felt that within pop's cultural past there was undeniably a sense of design and attitude that was greater than what was going on at the present. The past conjured up something far more magical. This was just ten or fifteen years previously, something that had just gone out of style, a little niche, a moment that seemed so out of fashion yet for me seemed so in fashion.'

While at art school McLaren had consistently kept his eye on stylistic developments, devouring fashion magazines and talking to Westwood about her choice in clothes and presentation. 'This would often lead me to Bond Street and sometimes even those parts of Oxford Street that seemed more interesting and chic,' he said. 'I remember buying a pair of green patent leather sandals with a giant brass buckle for myself. They were astonishing looking and seemed to have come from another time, strange fake versions of eighteenth-century slippers. I liked them, but they looked rather odd with my utility second-hand tweed overcoat and drew criticism from the Maoist group whose meetings I occasionally attended at Goldsmiths.'

McLaren's visual sensibilities also drew him to the King's Road in Chelsea. This was out of step with mainstream fashion, which by this time was split in Britain between the regionally manufactured high-street rag trade and the upper echelon retailers and labels emulating Paris styles in London's West End.

The King's Road was now past its heyday. From Mary Quant opening the country's first boutique, Bazaar, there in 1955 through the psychedelic-influenced stores of the mid-to-late 1960s such as Hung On You, Granny Takes a Trip and Dandie Fashions – and one-offs such as Just Men and Quorum, which was home to the brilliant Ossie Clark – the conversation had moved on.

Granny's, at number 488, was bought in 1969 by a former Dandie manager, Freddie Hornik, who had trained as a tailor. He installed two American partners in the shop – Marty Breslau and Gene Krell – and they sharpened the offer, producing a new, stylised peacock look in appliqued velvet and silks favoured by the likes of Rod Stewart, Anita Pallenberg and Keith Richards.

Around the same time, the twenty-year-old north Londoner John Lloyd had opened Alkasura towards the World's End area, offering a similar deal in satins and sequins which stoked the look of glam and was worn by such emerging glitter rock artists as Marc Bolan (McLaren's peer from the Stamford Hill youth club days).

Yet, inhabited as it was by eccentrics, outsiders, bohemians, louche aristos and working-class movers and shakers on the make, the King's Road remained shabby and edgy, which explains its attraction to McLaren.

In particular he was drawn to the audacious pop art boutique Mr Freedom, which had been opened at 430 King's Road in World's End in September 1969 by young fashion entrepreneurs Trevor Myles and Tommy Roberts.

'We wanted to be comic-land, totally different, not a bunch of barrow-boys selling knock-off kaftans,' said the ebullient Roberts, who was four years older than McLaren and had studied at Goldsmiths.[10] He was what the Italians understand as a 'design editor': while Roberts rarely designed himself, his in-depth knowledge and understanding of the field enabled him to bring out the best in a team working across a range of disciplines. This explains Roberts's appetite for fresh talent emerging from London's art schools, including textile specialist Jane Wealleans and wacky menswear designer Jim O'Connor (who had both emerged from the Royal College of Art).

The fascia, fittings and interior design of Mr Freedom were commissioned by Roberts and Myles from Electric Colour Company (ECC), which had recently been formed by four sculptors and painters operating from a studio in Hackney, east London. With the practice of interior design only just coming into focus, ECC's adventurous and experimental environments were not executed within proscribed boundaries of taste and design, and their endeavours would in turn inspire and encourage McLaren.

For Mr Freedom, ECC produced an unusual design bursting with energy and replete with references to Americana and comic book culture, incorporating images of Dick Tracy and the Lone Ranger on the back of his rearing steed Silver. The sales counter comprised an oblong unit into which were cut apertures displaying television screens behind panes of tinted plastic film. Roberts explored his taste for the absurd by installing large wooden facsimiles of 78-rpm vinyl discs from the 1950s at the end of the clothing rails. From design duo Sue and Simon Haynes, also recent products of London's art school system, Roberts commissioned a series of odd display pieces including an eight-foot-tall blue fun fur representation of King Kong and a balsa wood plate of egg and chips of twelve-foot circumference.

Mr Freedom clothes, meanwhile, were more than a match for Roberts and Myles's stage-set; the pair became the first fashion label to incorporate Disney characters in their designs, while Roberts resolved to create a garment for the 1970s that would rival the mini-skirt of the 1960s. Experimentation with designer Pamla Motown led to the production of a prototype pair of short shorts. These became known as hot pants when eagerly displayed in the national press the day after the first samples had arrived at the shop, thus setting in train one of the biggest womenswear trends of the decade. Mr Freedom was sexy and sassy: suede dungarees featured a heart-shaped cut-out in the rear to expose the wearer's buttocks, and tops flashed absurd slogans: 'Pow!' and 'Omo 6d off'.

'I loved Mr Freedom,' declared McLaren. 'In art school, we'd already come to the conclusion that art was no longer holy or sacred. In fact art had become a commodity that could be designed, marketed and sold like any other product on the high street. Rock 'n' roll seemed to have a far more credible hold on all of us which is why only Andy Warhol seemed exciting, since he was associated with bands doing their record covers, starting newspapers and making films.

'Warhol had created a more glamorous lifestyle than what we had expected from the lecturers and artists we came into daily contact with. This gave purpose to my thinking that dressing up and engaging in fashion suddenly seemed as artistic as anything else that you might do.'

Westwood was similarly impressed with Roberts and his shop and purchased a number of items, including a long green jersey dress printed with stars, a frilled 1950s skirt appliqued with musical notes ('I persuaded her to buy it because the references were close to music hall,' said McLaren) and a pair of leopard-print velvet trousers. Ever resourceful, she was soon making her own clothes in brassy fabrics from vintage patterns.

'I clearly remember Vivienne pushing her pram around Mr Freedom; she made an impression even then,' said Roberts. 'There was something about her; the way she held herself and wore her clothes. We didn't talk much then but she stuck in my mind.'[11]

McLaren wanted to incorporate Roberts and his shop in the Oxford Street film. One treatment he wrote with Jamie Reid homed in on a broadcast about the business of fashion from one of the TV screens set in the Mr Freedom sales counter. This treatment, from May 1970, also contained a brief, biting manifesto of McLaren's: 'Be childish. Be irresponsible. Be disrespectful. Be everything this society hates.'

When Tommy Roberts found a backer to fund Mr Freedom's ambitious move to larger premises in neighbouring Kensington at the end of 1970, McLaren and Westwood were among the customers who followed him. In the spring of 1971 McLaren bought a pair of Mr Freedom's quilt-topped creepers with D-rings. In blue suede, these were designed to the original lasts and manufactured by the originators of the thick crepe-soled footwear, George Cox and Son.

Creepers had long gone out of fashion as 1970s street style lurched towards the ungainly silhouette defined by feather-cut hair, the ubiquitous flared loon pants, stack-heeled boots, platform shoes and velvet suits. In fact, Mr Freedom was the only fashion outlet to stock the shoes at this time; the creepers made by Cox and its imitators had otherwise been consigned to the so-called 'Ted's Corner' displays in dusty provincial gentlemen's outfitters.

These blue suede shoes, McLaren later declared with eyes a-glitter, were 'probably the most important things I ever bought. To wear them at that time made a statement about what everyone else was wearing and thinking. It was a symbolic act to put them on. Those blue shoes had a history that I cared about, a magical association that seemed authentic. They represented an age of revolt – of desperate romantic revolt – to change your life. I proudly wore them around art school.'[12]

McLaren was increasingly frustrated with the Oxford Street film, which remained an incoherent jumble of footage. Required to show it to Goldsmiths' examiners as part of his finals at the end of the summer term in 1971, McLaren was 'utterly obstreperous in my attitude towards them and somewhat embarrassed by not being able to articulate what it was I was trying to do'.

The degree review ended in disaster. McLaren was firmly instructed to focus on rescuing the film over the summer and to return to Goldsmiths in the autumn. If they deemed what he presented worthwhile, the Goldsmiths board was prepared to invest in a grant for another year, 'at which point they would then supposedly give me my degree, but I was as disorganised as anyone else on that street. I couldn't seem to make a complete story of the film. And I was bored with the idea of my future.'

Rather than applying himself to *The Story of Oxford Street*, McLaren spent the following weeks carousing with Patrick Casey, who, according to McLaren, 'was part of a world that I was fascinated by, but couldn't

seemingly be part of, part artistic and part fashion. I desperately wanted
to join. And so, wearing my new blue suede shoes, I hung out with him.'

The pair became inseparable as they searched increasingly out-of-the-
way sources of original rock 'n' roll records and garments. 'Patrick led
me to strange places where the clothes that he sometimes wore could be
purchased, in the outer reaches of London, such as Limehouse and the
Isle of Dogs,' said McLaren. 'Some were even closer to town. We went to
the Strand where there were many army surplus stores then. If you knew
what you were looking for, you would find fabulous 1930s and 1940s
leather jackets. Patrick also knew where you could get beautiful early
Teddy boy checked sports jackets.'

Casey was by now a heavy-duty speed freak and encouraged McLaren
– who had previously avoided mind-altering substances apart from the
LSD escapade with Mininberg – to join him in his regular bouts of amphetamine consumption. In this way, Casey, according to McLaren, became
something of a muse and encouraged visits to Soho gay clubs such as Le
Duce in D'Arblay Street and the Stud Club in Poland Street. Just four
years after the liberalisation of the British laws restricting homosexuality,
with an age of consent for gay people much higher than that for hetero-
sexuals, these visits were charged with the forbidden and added an apparently unfulfilled homoerotic flavour to McLaren and Casey's friendship.

'Patrick would inspire me to dress up,' said McLaren. 'He brought it
out of me since he was a poseur and thought I too had a great sense of
clothes. I spent many nights going out with him, though I never ever
went out with Vivienne socially in this way.

'I guess I may have been a little gay or maybe that I just preferred the
company of my friends who I didn't want to know I had a girlfriend.
That made me seem less interesting. I couldn't be close or private with
them if they knew that. I used to stay out all night with Patrick and he
made me take speed. Once I got alarmingly sick and paranoid and I
thought "What an awful time I am having in these seedy gay clubs."'

Bob Chait, a tailoring specialist who met Casey and McLaren on the
club scene, recalls the duo as having 'an air of bisexuality about them.

Patrick was terribly good-looking and Malcolm was certainly quite girlish.'[13]

And Casey was evidently a connector of out-there types; he was also friendly with a fellow collector of ephemera, a founding member of the UK Gay Liberation Front who gloried in the name Neon Edsel. Casey had met him through his girlfriend, who was a petrol pump attendant in a garage in the King's Road; as his assumed surname suggested, Edsel was interested in classic cars and ran a rare early 1950s Austin Atlantic four-seater convertible at the time, so was a regular customer of Casey's girlfriend.

In turn, Casey had introduced Chait to Neon Edsel at the Yours or Mine, the Kensington gay basement *boîte*, where David and Angie Bowie and their circle were also habitués. It was also known as the Sombrero because of the street-level sign for the adjoining Mexican restaurant.

Importantly for McLaren, Edsel operated a stall within Kensington Market, selling reconditioned radios and kitsch gewgaws from the 1940s and 1950s as well as art deco pieces. Here was a retail operation making waves in the culture. 'Geoffrey [Neon Edsel's birth name] was brilliant, gifted,' said Chait. 'He perceived fashion years in advance not just in clothing but also bric-a-brac. He also single-handedly began the art deco revival.'

So this was the social swim into which McLaren dived headlong. He was led further into his 1950s investigations by the publication of *Today There Are No Gentlemen*, a volume of essays on post-war menswear by the cultural commentator Nik Cohn, who was the same age as McLaren.

This was recommended to McLaren by Helen Mininberg, and provided a celebratory social history of the development of youth cults from the cosh-boy of the early 1950s to the skinhead and the hippy, and even included references to Mr Freedom.

Cohn's infectious prose resonated deeply with McLaren, the deserted offspring of a doomed wartime marriage:

With the Teds, the effects of the war became apparent. It had destroyed the sense of family and tradition, of one generation handing on to the next. For the first time kids didn't want to look like their fathers. Essentially their clothes said just three things: *I am different*; *I am tough*; *I fuck*. In the place of heritage, the Teddy Boys began a new culture: Pop. The essence of this was that the past was irrelevant. In Pop, it was the moment that counted, and the immediate future, and everything was made instant.[14]

As he assimilated the powerful messages in Cohn's book, McLaren made another attempt to re-engage with the Oxford Street film by conjuring a device informed by his newfound fascination with the music, films, visual styles and ephemera of the 1950s.

Now McLaren planned to persuade a performer of the original rock 'n' roll generation to become the documentary's roving reporter, appearing in links and reading voiceover parts from the script, all to give the film narrative thrust.

The final shooting script for the Oxford Street film had incorporated footage of Billy Fury in performance and the fashions worn by his fans as well as an interview with the secretary of the star's fan club. On the basis that Fury was an avowed animal lover, this was intercut with footage of performing dolphins with scantily clad 'aquamaids' shot at the Pleasurama Leisure Group's London Dolphinarium, which had been opened in Oxford Street with much publicity in April 1971.

And so McLaren decided to approach Fury himself to provide the voiceover. The Liverpool-born singer, whose real name was Ronald Wycherley, had been a member of the scheming manager Larry Parnes's early 1960s stable of young male stars to whom he gave exuberant surnames – Vince Eager, Marty Wilde, Georgie Fame et al. – and scored a number of hits in that period, including 'Wondrous Place' and 'Halfway to Paradise'. Although a wooden actor, Fury's vulnerability and photogenic glamour lent lustre to such films as 1962's *Play It Cool*.

But the Fury fan-club secretary told McLaren that the singer had given up on performing; a five-year contract with EMI Parlophone had recently ended without any hits and his health was shot (Fury had suffered problems since a childhood bout of rheumatic fever and was soon to undergo the first of two open heart surgeries).

As a result, as McLaren was informed when he tracked down Fury's manager Hal Carter, the performer was now quietly dedicating his time to animal rescue, particularly birds at the wildlife sanctuary he had established on a Welsh farm acquired for him by his partner, the daughter of the London property developer Cecil Rosen.

Thinking on his feet, McLaren proposed Fury be filmed in the bird sanctuary at London Zoo. The resultant interview could be cut into the existing footage, he said. Unsurprisingly, Carter declined the offer.

In late September 1971, McLaren made one last bid to rescue *The Story of Oxford Street*. Spying an advert for a low-key midweek appearance at Soho music club the Marquee by Gene Vincent, he figured the US rocker could be an intriguing provider of the film's voiceover elements and linking shots.

But times were tough for Vincent. At just thirty-six, the soft-spoken Virginian was in serious physical decline brought on by the combination of alcoholism and addiction to prescription drugs taken to dull the constant pain in his left leg. This was the result of a crippling motorbike accident in his youth and the lingering effects of having been in the 1960 Wiltshire car crash which killed Eddie Cochran.

And Vincent's troubles were multiplying. Come the autumn 1971 UK visit – his second that year – Vincent's backing vocalist partner Marcia Avron had elected to stay home in their apartment in California's Simi Valley. Unbeknown to the singer, on his departure she stripped it of their belongings and disappeared from his life without a word.

On arrival in the UK, Vincent was served with High Court maintenance documents by lawyers representing his British ex-wife Margaret Griffith, with whom he had a daughter. Meanwhile Vincent's fourth wife Jackie Fusco had instituted divorce proceedings in the US.

Vincent's two most recent albums – now judged cult classics for their weird, psych-pastoral flourishes – had been flops and he was a much reduced figure, playing residencies at down-at-heel venues.

So the Marquee gig, a guest appearance at a 'special rock revival disco dance night', had been scraped together as a quick earner in between those dates.[15] That night, prior to Vincent's appearance, McLaren made his way through the desultory crowd and, gaining access to the backstage area at the Marquee, was horrified by Vincent's debilitated condition.

It was clear Vincent was in no condition to contribute to McLaren's film. As confirmed by the British musician Chas Hodges, who had been a member of Vincent's support group in the early 1960s, the Marquee guest appearance was cancelled. Hodges dropped by the club to see his friend on the night of McLaren's visit to find a sign positioned outside: 'Owing to circumstances beyond our control Gene Vincent will not be appearing here tonight.'[16]

In early October Vincent fulfilled two bookings at Liverpool's Wooky Hollow Club before returning to the US. A week later, the singer died from a perforated ulcer after collapsing in the forecourt of his parents' mobile home in Saugus, California. His last words were: 'Momma you can phone the ambulance now.'[17]

By the time of Vincent's final utterance, McLaren's frustration with his film had boiled over.

'I couldn't finish my degree,' he wrote later. 'I didn't have anything to show them at Goldsmiths.'

Up before the board again in the autumn of 1971, McLaren brought along the largely unedited film reels he had compiled, but rather than hook them up to a projector he opted to make an elliptical statement using a set of simplistic chalk drawings of the topography of Oxford Street on a blackboard.

This did not go down well, particularly since the college had been indulgent of McLaren and his antics, providing him with resources and funds over the preceding two years. 'I truly felt it was a waste of time and walked out, leaving the film there,' said McLaren. 'I don't know what happened to it.'

The Story of Oxford Street was dead in the water and McLaren's time at Goldsmiths was over. This exit from the safety net of the art school system after eight years had serious psychic repercussions for the hyper-sensitive McLaren, precipitating a personal crisis. Soon after the final Goldsmiths meeting, McLaren was arrested for shoplifting a roll of linoleum from the branch of Woolworths in Clapham High Street, for which he was fined the then-punitive £25.

. Clearly overwhelmed, McLaren returned to Thurleigh Court and insisted on painting black the hallway of the apartment he shared with Westwood and the boys. This mildly unbalanced behaviour was followed by a period of introspection. 'He was like a bird circling for direction,' says his friend Fred Vermorel.[18]

The dilemma experienced by McLaren reflected the wider unease among those who had contributed to but also paid the costs of the 1960s era of protest and liberation. That this was at an end had been clarified in the election the previous year of the Conservative government under Edward Heath, which introduced free-market policies and began the dismantlement of the welfare state, setting the scene for the brutal Thatcher years of privatisation ahead.

'We never anticipated a time when we may have to have a career,' said McLaren. 'The culture that had belonged to you, as we felt in the 1960s, was now being organised by corporations.'

McLaren and his peers were struggling to reconcile the fact that the counterculture had to a large extent become popular culture. Everywhere rang cries of 'Sell out!' Marc Bolan, the ur-mod turned psychedelic pixie who had warbled cross-legged at the Roundhouse where McLaren had witnessed 'The Dialectics of Liberation' was now topping the charts with teen-friendly glam rockers T. Rex. Bolan's friend David Bowie, who had performed as part of the experimental trio Feathers at another of McLaren's haunts, the Drury Lane Arts Lab, was laying the building blocks for superstardom; Andy Warhol was not the preserve of the hip few but the subject of a major exhibition at London's Tate Gallery; and the Rolling Stones were heading for tax exile.

McLaren, like many who had been cosseted by grant aid and indulged by family, friends and college teachers, was distinctly underprepared for the real world.

'When I left art school it didn't bode well because I knew very little about life or business,' said McLaren. 'I wasn't equipped to truly survive in this world. And Vivienne wasn't any more equipped than me, except that she had a job.'

This wasn't true; as she had shown handling the erratic McLaren and bringing up her children over the previous four years, Westwood was capable and stoic, though her tolerance was tested when he installed Patrick Casey in the spare room at Thurleigh Court.

'Vivienne didn't know what I was intending to do but she knew that I adored Patrick,' said McLaren. 'And so Patrick came to live with us. He would never get up until late in the afternoon; it was so difficult to rouse him. Of course it was due to the fact that he took all those drugs. He lived such a weird lifestyle while I got up at 7.30 in the morning and would wait hours for him to wake up, desperate to play with him. Desperate for him to suggest what to do next.'

Still, Westwood and McLaren had become simpatico, though he continued to dominate the relationship. 'Vivienne's need to have an understanding of culture led her to be very governed by my world, by all my thoughts and attitudes,' he said. 'I liked to destroy things to create better things. This fascinated Vivienne. At times it definitely replaced sex, so at times our relationship became platonic. However, there was a great sense of camaraderie. We did feel very much in sync. I guess you could say she was following me rather than the other way round. I had original ideas and references, in her mind.'

PART II

Let It Rock

Chapter 9

It didn't take long for Malcolm McLaren to rouse himself from his reflections following the debacle at Goldsmiths.

In a move that both erased uncomfortable connections to his past, particularly the alienated teenage years in Hendon, and the unsatisfactory end to his academic career, he declared he would no longer be known as Malcolm Edwards and reclaimed the surname of his birth (though was not to formalise this legally for some time). Although she had been thoroughly disapproving of his father, his grandmother Rose welcomed the slight against her daughter and son-in-law.

McLaren also organised for Fred Vermorel to sell the Goldsmiths Bolex camera at Westminster Polytechnic as part of a fundraising effort for a new venture crystallising in his mind.

The Mr Freedom brothel creepers, Patrick Casey's postcard of Billy Fury, the original rock 'n' roll records, fashions and ephemera he had bought at street markets and out-of-the-way shops, and the glamour he detected among the World's End rock 'n' roll fashion milieu; all of these elements propelled him forward.

The influence of Nik Cohn's book *Today There Are No Gentlemen* must not be underestimated. This was but one of a series of texts providing wellsprings for bursts of creativity in McLaren's life and work, but it was arguably the most important. Cohn not only detailed the progression of the visual identity of youth in Britain over the post-war decades, but also celebrated the London locations and addresses where music and fashion had come together, providing the basis for a psychogeographic mapping of the style undulations across the capital and uncovering, in the process, the significance of the outlets McLaren had frequented in his teenage years such as Vince Man's Shop and John Michael Ingram's Sportique.

Importantly, Cohn dedicated a chapter to the King's Road and provided insights into two of the outlets that had operated from the ground-floor retail space of number 430 and made their mark through uptake by celebrities and rock musicians: Hung On You, which was at the address in 1967–9, and Mr Freedom from 1969–70.

'The King's Road was like having a bridge between art school and the street,' said McLaren in the 2000s. 'Art school was a very disenfranchised place in which we disenfranchised creatures could separate ourselves from the world and be snobbish about it. It was a safety valve, a hermetic environment. But when we were thrown out into the real world, what the hell were we going to do? That was the most astonishing revelation.'[1]

The youth group that made the greatest impact on McLaren was the country's first mass cult, the Teddy boys. In his book, Nik Cohn detailed how working-class youths had adapted their look from a flash-in-the-pan trend for neo-Edwardian tailoring among Savile Row tailors in the late 1940s: long drape jackets, high-waisted, narrow-cuffed guardsman-cut trousers, thick-soled shoes, fancy waistcoats and Slim Jim ties worn with long, society-defying hair slicked back into so-called 'ducks' arses'.

'Because Teddy boys were associated with teenage violence, the idea of fashionable clothes as a threat to society was born,' explains fashion historian Colin Woodhead.[2]

'I was fascinated because they were just out of the reach of my experience,' said McLaren. 'The Teds were something of a childhood memory to me; I remember being aware of how powerful-looking they were on the streets of north-east London, but by the time I came to enter fashion as a teenager they had retreated, which I think made them all the more alluring.'

How McLaren came to not only join but eventually embody the culture expressed by, in his phrase, 'the look of music and the sound of fashion' constitutes the creation myth of his life. Burnished until it assumed an epic quality, this was the tale of a glittering promenade which resulted in a chance but life-altering encounter.

McLaren related many times the yarn of 'The Boy in the Blue Lamé Suit'. It started in November 1971 when he sketched a design for a pair of 1950s-style trousers and matching jacket, copied from the cover of an Elvis Presley record. In one of their early fashion collaborations, according to the story, this clothing was run up for him by Westwood on her domestic sewing machine.

The fact that the fabric was lamé was key for McLaren. 'I was obsessed with this cloth made of gold or silver thread woven through a woollen or cloth backing,' he said. 'It was part of me wanting to create new worlds. I had recently bought for our apartment a rather dreary utility wardrobe that I adorned with little pins each holding a tiny sequined leaf that I purchased in bags from a theatrical costumier. That made it magical. It was as if I were dressing the wardrobe in a star-spangled frock. I loved anything glittery, and lamé assumed a world that had disappeared or could only be seen on the covers of records by Elvis.'

McLaren related that, dressed in the suit, the Mr Freedom creepers and a matching ice-blue satin shirt, he ventured forth from Thurleigh Court to the King's Road, catching a bus to Sloane Square, at the eastern end of the two-and-a-half mile thoroughfare.

'I decided it would be really cool to be like Elvis, to be a Teddy boy in a kind of defiant anti-world and anti-fashion gesture,' said McLaren. 'I thought by looking confrontational, a chance rendezvous would occur; someone would confront me or say that I looked terrific or surprise me and take me to a place or guide me. After all, I came from the background of the *dérive*, of Thomas De Quincey, that world of inhabiting the streets and changing your life by doing so.'

According to McLaren, the skies turned grey, the rain fell and he became dispirited by the time he arrived to the western end of the King's Road as it curved into World's End. There hadn't been so much as a glance of acknowledgement from fellow pedestrians. 'Nobody noticed me at all; I was expecting to be confronted because I felt like a fantastic traffic light, but no bloody person even bothered to say "hi",' he told Sex Pistols guitarist Steve Jones in 2006.

McLaren found himself standing opposite 430 King's Road, at that time home to Mr Freedom's successor at the address, a boutique called Paradise Garage. According to McLaren, he had never previously visited this fashion outlet.

'I got to the end and thought I had better jump into a phone kiosk and make a call to Vivienne and tell her that nothing had happened. Just as that thought crossed my mind a Mephistophelean creature crossed my path; this guy spun across the street completely dressed in black with a big fifties pompadour haircut. He spoke in a deep Brooklyn accent: "So, what are you doing round here?"

'I looked up at him and said: "I got stuff man! I got stuff, man, stuff to sell!"

'He pointed across the road and said: "Go on, do it in there." I crossed the road and entered through this black hole in the wall and right at the back was a gleaming jukebox blaring out all these 1950s jewels. He pointed to this makeshift dancefloor and said: "Behind that jukebox, on that floor, put your stuff. Add on 25 per cent to whatever you're gonna charge and that's mine!"

'I looked around the shop and thought, "Wow this is a real scene," and ran out. I couldn't wait to get home and tell my friends I'd found this place.'[3]

As dramatic as this story became in the retelling, it is a fact that McLaren had already checked out opportunities in the King's Road, and had homed in on Paradise Garage in particular, knowing the premises as he did from his shopping trips with Westwood to Mr Freedom the previous year.

To understand the importance of the timing of the Boy in the Blue Lamé Suit's promenade, it is necessary to cut back six months to May 1971, when Paradise Garage was opened by the handsome and rakish Trevor Myles.

Prior to that, Myles had briefly joined his partner Tommy Roberts in the 'department store' version of Mr Freedom in Kensington before terminating the relationship. To fund a new business, Myles and his

American flatmate Marty Fromer smuggled large quantities of heavy-duty metal biker studs, unavailable in England, from New York and – selling them to fashion contacts under the business title of Mr Stud 'Em in a deliberate attempt to provoke Roberts – raised some cash to reopen 430 King's Road, which had lain empty in the months since Mr Freedom's move.

With an additional £5,000 from investors including local retail/property businessman Tom Salter and Roberts's former partner Charlie Simpson, the lease was purchased and Myles came up with the concept of Paradise Garage. He visualised an exotic location filled with authentic and what would now be called vintage American clothing but was then dead stock and second hand. 'The inspiration came out of nowhere,' said Myles. 'I just woke up one day and thought: that's it!'[4]

Salter and Simpson took over the lease to 430 King's Road on Myles's behalf as he organised the importation of a huge bale of used clothing from the US. In this way Myles pioneered the sale of utilitarian overalls, faded denim, ticking dungarees, souvenir jackets, Hawaiian, bowling and baseball shirts and worker's T-shirts in this country. Garments of the highest quality, such as straight-legged Levi's 501s which were against the flared grain of the time, were cherry-picked and sold alongside new retro-style items including striped and animal print jeans.

In keeping with Paradise Garage's Americana/Hawaiian stock, the frontage and interior of 430 King's Road was again realised by the art collective Electric Colour Company, this time at Myles's direction to blend South Seas charm with American grit. Tiki-style signage was erected onto the green-painted corrugated iron facade, a 1950s petrol pump was placed outside (sometimes with Myles's tiger-stripe flocked 1968 Mustang parked nearby), while inside there were lovebirds in a bamboo cage, a *trompe l'œil* rustic farmyard scene rendered onto an interior door, straw matting over the surfaces and painted oil drums supporting the wooden sales counter.

And the shop was an immediate hit with Britain's fashion set, at the forefront of the faded denim fad to which the rag trade responded by creating such national retail chains as Jean Machine and Jean Junction. Even top-notch fashion magazine *Harpers & Queen* gave its thumbs-up with a portrait of Myles and his crew lounging outside Paradise Garage: 'Suddenly this summer it's all been happening for the garage mechanic's boiler suit manufacturers. People who've never seen a spanner in their lives have leapt cheerfully in blue jeans and dungarees, in what looks like a valiant attempt to get back to the horny-handed sons of toil image after all those frills and effeminacies.'[5]

As the months passed the restless Myles became bored. The best of the used stock ran out and, in keeping with the fast-changing retail identities associated with the King's Road (Granny Takes a Trip had set the pace by changing the facade at least half a dozen times in its first three years), he opted for a tougher, rock 'n' roll proposition. The shop's interior was painted black and Myles installed a late 1950s BAL-AMi jukebox. In the back of the 400-square-foot oblong space Myles constructed the raised 6 foot x 10 foot dancefloor where customers were encouraged to jive to the 45s blaring through the shop.

Gone was Paradise Garage's dustbowl hick vibe; now studded denim and appliqued jersey tops were displayed with figure-hugging 1950s dresses and flared skirts pinned to the black walls, and piped, satin trousers hanging from the racks. With the design team of Chris Snow and Diana Crawshaw (themselves also refugees from Mr Freedom), Myles attracted contributions from the talented, doomed young designer Dinah Adams (soon to make her mark at Granny's but dead from an overdose within a couple of years) and the husband and wife duo John and Molly Dove.

Another member of Chelsea's hard-partying crowd, Bradley Mendelson became involved as shop manager. In the late 1960s Mendelson had gravitated to the British capital and World's End in particular with such fellow New Yorkers as Granny's Marty Breslau and Gene Krell.

'I can't remember exactly how I met Trevor but it was by hanging out in Chelsea; it was natural that I started working with him at the shop,' said Mendelson. 'We had a very interesting clientele there, they all used to come and hang out before they were famous.'

Mendelson describes the arrangement he had with Myles as 'pretty loose. The roles were never defined; we assumed the positions we wanted. I became the manager by default because somebody had to do it.'[6]

Myles was soon distracted by a love affair with a Swede named Lisa Petersson, and his enthusiasm for the business had drained away in the autumn of 1971 when he was visited by McLaren soon after the ex-student had abandoned *The Story of Oxford Street*. With Patrick Casey in tow, McLaren discussed with Myles the possibility of selling their stock of rock 'n' roll records, refurbished valve radios and dead-stock clothing from the by-now disused dancefloor at the back of the shop. Myles was disinterested. 'I was so off-the-planet in those days I didn't really care,' said Myles. 'We only had one chat about it, really casually. I'd never met Malcolm before. I always say that all I remember about that occasion is that he was such a fast talker.'

After Myles and Petersson married, at Chelsea Town Hall in November 1971, they disappeared with a third party on an extended honeymoon in the Caribbean.

As a wedding present, 'I was bought tickets to Jamaica,' says Myles. 'Around this time I knew a very wealthy girl who had split from her man. She ended up coming along and the three of us had a scene in Jamaica. It was only on the way back that I found the tickets had been bought on a stolen credit card.'

While the trio cavorted in Jamaica, Paradise Garage was left in the hands of Mendelson, the black-clad 'Mephistophelean creature' of McLaren's creation myth. 'I guess I talked to Malcolm because his look was so great; I was intrigued,' accepts Mendelson, these days a prominent New York real estate broker. 'I was also on my own and probably bored, wanting to while away the afternoon before shutting up shop. Paradise Garage was winding down by then.'

Mendelson confirms that he had recently had his hair cut in the 50s style recalled by McLaren, and that the young man had told him his suit had been made to his design by his girlfriend. And he did agree for McLaren to occupy the dancefloor in exchange for a cut of his sales.

So there are many crucial elements of the story of the Boy in the Blue Lamé Suit that are true. McLaren's *dérive* along the King's Road may have been more calculated than he later spun it; nevertheless what would have appeared to the casual observer as nothing more than a polite exchange between two eccentrically dressed young men on that rainy November day was to change not only the trajectory of the lives of McLaren and his partner Vivienne Westwood, but also the course of music, fashion and pop culture history.

Chelsea chose Malcolm McLaren, just as he plumped for it.

For the twenty-five-year-old ex-student, the King's Road opened up the vistas, presenting a range of options antithetical to the crowded, ghettoised east of the city of his childhood, the mealy-mouthed blandness of that part of north London where he spent his teens, and the down-at-heel scruffiness of the southern suburbs of Clapham, Croydon, Lewisham and Kennington of his art school years.

Unlike those in his circle such as Adler, Casey, Mininberg, Vermorel and Westwood, McLaren wasn't a blow-in or the offspring of immigrants. He was a proud fourth-generation Londoner with forebears who had arrived in the capital more than 100 years before his encounter with Bradley Mendelson. By this time, of course, the young man had not only been inculcated in London's treasures by his grandmother Rose but also discovered many of its delights himself.

An aerial map of the first quarter century of McLaren's London life would present a spaghetti junction of wanderings across the metropolis, but it is in Chelsea and specifically World's End that he found a place to pause and construct a creative base where he could draw together a new gang, just as he had built the Scarecrow Club off-limits to Avigdor School and provoked the authorities at the age of seven.

World's End runs west along the King's Road for a mile or so from Beaufort Street and is bordered to the north by transient Earl's Court and to the south by the Thames, the riverside location offering a diffuse light and gentler microclimate, particularly in autumn. A mile-and-a-half from bustling, upmarket Sloane Square, World's End marks the point where the road's commerce tails into residential conformity and former semi-industrial torpor.

By the time of McLaren's arrival, the neighbourhood had assumed an air of gentility, though the brooding presence of the brutalist red-bricked World's End Estate – construction of which began in the late 1960s – and the towering chimneys of the Lots Road Power Station ensure that gentrification will never be fully achieved.

And this is somehow fitting. For the very notion is at odds with the history of this locale, where a marginal status is combined with one of ill-repute, as first proclaimed by Charles II in 1680. When an axle broke on a coach carrying him to meet the 'pert, vivacious' Nell Gwyn at a house of entertainment among the muddy fields and sand banks running down to the Thames, the King sighed: 'Odd's blood. It would have to happen at the world's end.'

And so the local highway tavern was granted the name that was then bestowed upon the district as a byword for licentiousness that has never quite been shaken. In the 1840s the twelve-acre Cremorne Pleasure Gardens – bordered by Lots Road in the south-west and the World's End pub (by now a gin palace) to the north-east – were opened to the populace of London by entrepreneur Thomas Bartlett Simpson. Every night this entertainment playground, with fire-eaters, tight-rope walkers, balloonists, a theatre, a dancing area, supper alcoves and a maze, attracted 4,000-visitors to the heart of World's End.

Soon, however, the gardens were overrun by rowdier elements who settled in the quarter, and in 1877 Cremorne Gardens was forced into closure upon refusal of a liquor licence, such was the scale of public drunkenness and disorder. Property development moved apace along the King's Road with the construction of four new terraces west from 428 to Edith Grove. Number 430 was built as a four-storey private residence housing three families who lived amid the dowdy environs of a neighbourhood now rife with bankside prostitution and all manner of low life.

'It is shabbier than Oxford Street with its straggling dirty stucco mid-century houses and shops,' wrote the painter William Rothenstein,[7] while other writers and artists who colonised the area in the Victorian era included the Pre-Raphaelite Brotherhood, Oscar Wilde, Turner and Whistler. Their presence later led to the foundation of Chelsea School of Art in nearby Manresa Street and the Chelsea Arts Club around the corner.

Such bohemian types lived cheek-by-jowl with the poor souls toiling at the factories and wharves lining World's End's dismal stretch of riverside. 'By the beginning of the 20th century the area was quite the opposite of a pleasure ground, full of terraces of houses without bathrooms, with noisome industries fronting a filthy river,' writes local historian John Richardson.[8] The clamour increased in 1902 with the erection of the massive power station for London's Underground over the artesian well in Lots Road.

At the end of the First World War, 430 King's Road underwent a significant transformation; the resident, Joseph Thorne, refurbished the ground floor as commercial premises in which he opened a pawnbroker's business in 1919.

The chief elements of this cheap conversion completed a century ago remain to this day. The iron pillar in the centre of the floor space supports the roof three storeys above; the only natural light emanates from the front window; and the three-metre span widens at the back into a dogleg of an extra half-a-metre in front of the small stockroom. Until the 1990s there was no lavatory.

In 1937 Pamela Hansford Johnson, poetess, author, girlfriend of Dylan Thomas and later wife of C. P. Snow, took the area's apocryphal name for her novel about moral responsibility amid political and financial unrest. In his review of *World's End*, Evelyn Waugh took the opportunity to memorably characterise the area's shabby milieu: 'They are people economically, politically, socially, theologically, in a mess.'[9]

During the Blitz the power station attracted heavy bombing to the neighbourhood. German bombers failed to knock out the target but destroyed much surrounding property, including the Guinness Trust buildings, which were redeveloped in the 1950s into the vast Cremorne council estate.

At the beginning of that decade, World's End's most prominent resident was Diana 'Swingin'' Dors, Britain's sex-kitten blonde bombshell who provoked public comment not only by living publicly with her lover, the jewel thief Michael Caborn-Waterfield (known as Dandy Kim), but also insisting he flaunt her along the King's Road in his open-topped powder-blue Cadillac.

In 1951, 430 became a lively caff run by Ida Docker (the door arch it shares with 430a remained as the entrance to a series of adjoining restaurants until 2016). After Docker's departure in the late 1950s, it was occupied by yacht agents who used the proximity to the river to service the post-war leisure boom in sailing.

Then, for a spell, the site was a motor-scooter dealership run by Stanley G. Raper, who conducted a sideline in much sought-after Levi's bought from US merchant seamen at the dockside. The blue jeans became such hot potatoes that Raper resorted to piling them on the pavement outside 430 on fine days; the stock would disappear within minutes.

'I remember going down to the end of the King's Road at Worlds End where you could get jeans,' recalled the interior designer David 'Monster' Mlinaric. 'All the stuff was out on the pavement like a greengrocers, rows and rows and rows of Levi's.'[10]

In the early 1960s the premises became the site of one of the first Swinging London clothing outlets outside Britain's style epicentre Carnaby Street. With the street number emblazoned in giant numerals above the front window, Stanley Raper's scooter shop was transformed into the 430 Boutique by the couple who bought the lease from him: former deb Carol Derry (daughter of flying ace John Derry, the first British pilot of a plane to exceed the speed of sound) and her older lover Bill Fuller.

'They were an odd couple, kind of mismatched,' says Paul Gardner, a musician who occupied the attic room at 430 from the spring of 1964 to autumn 1966. 'I arrived on a Saturday. There was a group playing inside with a party going on in the street; 430 was a proper dolly-bird shop, with Carol running the show and Bill in the shadows. I'd nip downstairs to pay the rent every week, and Carol was always very welcoming while Bill glowered, the scruffiest guy I think I've ever met.'[11] The 430 Boutique was an oasis of cool in the locale; the era's more feted Granny Takes a Trip didn't open until February 1966, a couple of blocks to the west at 488 King's Road.

By the time Granny's was grabbing the headlines, the ambitious young Beaverbrook scion Jonathan Aitken had included the 430 Boutique in *The Young Meteors*, his book about the Youthquake generation of movers and shakers: 'At 430 King's Road ex-naval officer Bill Fuller, aged 33, and his girlfriend Carol Derry, 26, sell "the cheapest clothes in London this side of Biba's", and have an unusual line in imported French style.'[12]

Even then a lightning rod for shifts in pop culture, taste and demand, 430's lease was relinquished by the pair when the continental mod attire of Swinging London went mainstream. The 'young man of unconventional religious persuasion'[13] who stepped into their shoes in the spring of 1967 was twenty-six-year-old Michael Rainey, son of the socialite Marion Wrottesley.

For the previous eighteen months Rainey and his wife Jane Ormsby-Gore, daughter of the British ambassador to Washington Lord Harlech, had run the proto-hippy tailoring business Hung On You from an outlet a mile or so east in Cale Street, Chelsea Green.

The Hung On You set ran fast, led by Tara Browne, the doomed Guinness heir whose death in a car-crash inspired the Beatles' 'A Day in the Life', while Ormsby-Gore's family was beset by tragedy on every side. Her brother Julian's suicide by shotgun in 1974 plunged his friend Nick Drake into a final depression (the cult folk singer took his own life less than three weeks later), and her youngest sister, Alice, conducted a five-year relationship with rock god Eric Clapton before her death by overdose, alone in a Bournemouth bedsit.

Back in 1967, when Hung On You shifted to 430, Rainey was a face about town, having been depicted in his louche glory on the cover of the Beatles' first greatest hits compilation, *A Collection of Beatles Oldies*. He and Ormsby-Gore set about transforming the premises to match the growing interest in ethnic exotica (Brian Jones draped himself in Hung On You's goatskin waistcoats and Moroccan suede boots for his addled appearance at that year's music festival in southern California's Monterey).

On the exterior, the new manifestation was announced by a single poster of Kali designed by the Summer of Love's graphics team Hapshash and the Coloured Coat, while the inside of 430 was now draped in kilims and tapestries brought back from India by Ormsby-Gore.

'Michael would find lovely materials, all made in London in the East End by proper old-fashioned tailors,' says Ormsby-Gore. 'He was a great stickler. The Stones and Beatles would come in and say, "We want four of those . . ."'[14] With a kaleidoscopic range of pink harem pants, Afghan jackets, snakeskin boots and Nehru-collared silk suits attracting custom from Jimi Hendrix, George Harrison, Keith Richards and Syd Barrett, 430 was now dubbed 'a dipsomaniac's nightmare' by the *Evening Standard*.

Hung On You's aesthetic was appropriated by other boutiques of the period such as Dandie Fashions, run by Rainey's former employee John Crittle. Rainey, who died in 2014, was forever regretful about situating his business at 430. 'Looking back, I think my biggest mistake was moving to the King's Road,' he said. 'It was too off-the-beaten track in World's End. People stopped coming because all these other places opened up down the road and ripped us off.'[15]

Early in 1969, the Raineys upped sticks, gave away all their possessions and moved to the island of Gozo. 'London times and everything were over,' said Jane Ormsby-Gore.[16]

It is at this point that Trevor Myles and Tommy Roberts stepped into the frame and opened the first Mr Freedom at 430 King's Road, intent on upsetting the hippy apple cart with their pop art take on fashion and a penchant for glitter and rock 'n' roll, which, when fine-tuned by Myles as Paradise Garage, opened the door for Malcolm McLaren.

'I was feeling barren, having lived in a world that was anti-career and, having failed, I decided I wanted to enclose, encase and wrap myself inside somebody's bosom in the King's Road,' said McLaren of his encounter with Paradise Garage manager Bradley Mendelson. 'I wanted to be part of it somehow – I wanted to find myself in there. That was a domain I wanted to be in. The King's Road was where you felt the cutting edge of that culture was.'

Chapter 10

Thrilled as he was to have been offered a niche in the King's Road, Malcolm McLaren later admitted that after the encounter with Bradley Mendelson he 'wasn't certain. I didn't know if that's what I was looking for or not.'

Similarly, while she was delighted that there was a prospect of income from the 1950s and 1960s remnants her partner had accumulated, years of penury led Vivienne Westwood to be quite reasonably pessimistic about the prospects for a tiny floor space at the back of a failing shop at the wrong end of the King's Road.

'Vivienne was very concerned with making a living; she hadn't been to art school so it was a different philosophy for her,' said McLaren. 'She wasn't getting on with Patrick [Casey] and thought we were all a bunch of good-for-nothings. But for me, engaging in fashion seemed as artistic as anything else you might do.'

Immediately after he met Mendelson, McLaren sought the advice of the only person he knew who was involved in the mainstream fashion business, Bob Chait, the expat American he had come to know with Casey on Soho's gay club circuit.

Chait was an alterations hand, a highly trained tailoring specialist in repair, modification and fit whose services were called upon by many leading designers. 'At the time I was operating the alterations business for a lot of London's boutiques to build up enough money to get residency here and start my own menswear line,' says Chait. 'Malcolm was never the most generous of people so it's nice to hear that he gave other people credit, particularly Patrick.'

McLaren later admitted he was in awe of Chait. 'Bob was part of Patrick's world, fashionable and artistic. I thought he was close to the inner sanctum,' said McLaren. 'Bob seemed so glamorous to me, very fashionable-looking and living in a very posh part of London. I sat down with him and Patrick at his flat in Kensington and explained what had happened to me on the King's Road. Should I do it or not?

'They were as excited as me by the possibilities. I remember Bob was taking in a pair of trousers when he told us he thought it was a good idea. Of course, he already had a job so wasn't going to be directly involved but said to Patrick: "You can work with Malcolm, why not?"'

The next afternoon McLaren and Casey caught the 49 bus from Clapham to meet Mendelson at 430 King's Road, taking with them boxes of the 1950s artefacts, which they laid out meticulously on the Paradise Garage dancefloor. Reconditioned radiograms and 1950s records were set out in labelled wooden boxes and the walls were decorated with sports jackets on hangers, framed photographs of their favourite artist, Billy Fury, and stills of James Dean from such movies as Elia Kazan's *East of Eden*.

'We spent lots of time rearranging things,' said McLaren. 'It was our domain and had to be perfect. Patrick often wouldn't get up until 5 p.m., so in the evenings we'd go there and put up fifties wallpaper we'd bought in shops in the back streets of Brixton and Streatham. Patrick was very concerned with detail. We would open at about 8 p.m. for an hour and that would be it.'

There wasn't much custom over the first weeks but soon important additions to the stock arrived. Although Vivienne Westwood had retained her teaching job in Brixton, as November 1971 turned to December she was called upon to produce new sales items in the evenings. Among these were oversize mohair jumpers in vivid colours, to be worn with trousers or as dresses with tights.

From a closing down sale at Whiteleys department store in Queensway, west London, Bob Chait sourced twenty pairs of original peg trousers, pinstriped with metallic gold. 'They were wonderful,' said Chait. 'In bright blue or the deepest black with a gold belt which went with the pinstripe. They looked really good with the sweaters which Vivienne was making.'

It is likely that stock was obtained from Casey's friend Neon Edsel. 'Geoffrey had a really good eye and avant-garde taste for the time,' says the artist and fellow 1950s aficionado Duggie Fields, who was Casey's former flatmate and also a friend of Edsel. 'Some of the things he collected would have fitted in very well with what Patrick and Malcolm were up to.'

With Mendelson still running the main part of 430 King's Road, Casey and McLaren applied a cottage-industry ethic to their tiny business, which they called In the Back of Paradise Garage, as advertised on a chalkboard erected onto the street outside the shop. Using a John Bull stamping kit, McLaren printed the name on brown paper bags acquired from a local greengrocery for the packaging of sales. The stamp was also applied to white cotton labels, which Westwood stitched into the garments she was repairing in her spare time.

After a fortnight or so, Mendelson changed the arrangement at the shop, not least because Casey and McLaren were arriving just as he was preparing to knock off for the day. 'Trevor had left with a kind of "see you later",' says Mendelson. 'I didn't really know whether he was going to come back or not and here were these people who were really enthusiastic about doing something while my mind was elsewhere.'

One day Mendelson gave McLaren the keys to the premises. 'He told us he'd see us the next day and that was it. He didn't turn up and I never saw him again,' said McLaren. 'We waited for him for a while and held over the money from customers who were buying the old Paradise Garage stock until it became obvious that there was no one coming back.'

In fact Mendelson had left the UK for Marbella in the south of Spain before hooking up with another Chelsea scenester, Mim Scala, in Tangiers and driving around looking for adventure in North Africa in a Land Rover.

'Eventually I got very sick, contracting hepatitis in Morocco, so came back to the States,' says Mendelson. 'I was done with my London excursions.'

And so Casey and McLaren took over occupation of the entire store, and drafted in former art school pals to help out, among them Helen Mininberg and Niall Martin from Goldsmiths. For McLaren, being at 430 King's Road, 'was an extension of my studio, like jumping into the musical end of painting'.[1] He and his friends now filled the shop with odd appliances; McLaren was returning to his environmental installation past and even to using chicken wire, this time in sheets against a wall against which shoes were hung by their heels.

Then came a visit from Trevor Myles, back from Jamaica and in a bad way: he was not only broke from the trip but his new bride had left him as soon as they arrived home. Finding squatters occupying his premises was the final straw.

'I went into the shop and Bradley was gone,' says Myles. 'There was no money for me, but there were all these people. In the back was an old metal hospital bed with rubber sheets on it. It had T-shirts hanging from it and looked like an art piece. I asked them what was going on and they said they had taken the place over. I stormed out, went home and hid.'

McLaren claimed that Myles told him that he and Casey had to leave. 'I immediately reacted by demanding squatters' rights,' said McLaren. 'My sixties upbringing on demonstrations qualified me to make such remarks.'

Rather than engage with McLaren, Myles ploughed his energies into obsessing over the whereabouts of his wife (even going so far as so hire the Mr Freedom assistant Harold the Ted to spy on her at various central London nightspots). This became all-consuming. 'I realised everything at Paradise Garage had ground to a halt anyway so I went back in one day and told them they could have it,' says Myles. 'I just walked away from it all.'

Over the Christmas holiday of 1971, McLaren picked up the baton from the immediate predecessors at the address, and with no prior experience of interior design, he and Casey undertook a thoroughgoing overhaul of 430 King's Road which he had decided was to be called Let It Rock, taken from a Chuck Berry A-side on the BAL-AMi jukebox.

In his mind McLaren was creating a salute to the brutal sensuality of English Teds as identified by Nik Cohn: 'Style was their only value and about that they were fanatic. The Teds made clothes sexual again. After a hundred and fifty years of concealment, it was Teddy Boys who brought back flamboyance and preening. The baroque complexities of their costume, the tightness in the thigh and crotch and their rituals of attraction, like the hair-combing in front of women – all of this was in the classic peacock tradition: direct sexual display.'[2]

At first, menswear comprised the clothes chosen by McLaren and Casey. 'All could have been worn in a typical fifties teen rock movie,' said McLaren, who visited the clothing wholesaler Kornbluth's in Aldgate High Street, not far from his mother and stepfather's factory Eve Edwards.

This sold fluorescent nylon socks, bootlace ties, gold lamé waistcoats and blue-black and red-black striped corduroy caps. 'These became wonderful accessories for our installation,' said McLaren. 'Women's clothes were far more difficult to obtain.'

In the window of Frederick Freed's theatrical dance shoe and ballet slipper store in St Martin's Lane, McLaren spied a pair of 'Puss in Boots' stiletto shoes decorated with a fluted top in black patent leather with pink pearlised leather linings. 'They were stunning. I decided to buy them for Vivienne,' said McLaren. 'It so happened the display was one of the only pair they had and was in six and a half, Vivienne's size.'

And he styled Westwood, persuading her to add pads to the shoulder line of the hand-knitted mohair sweaters to create a more powerful silhouette. With this sweater and fishnet stockings – also from Freed's – the boots clinched the female counterpart to Let It Rock's men's clothing range.

The boxes of records were of particular interest to London's leading hotshot young advertising executive Charles Saatchi, who had heard about McLaren and Casey's strange outlet and, intent on adding to his already huge collection of original 1950s vinyl and shellac, arrived after working hours in his Rolls-Royce.

'Of course he was interested, because this was a shop that purported to sell relics, the remnants of an authentic past,' said McLaren. 'We'd be inside, not caring if we sold anything and he'd be banging and banging on the shop door, acting like a lunatic. We'd be thinking "Who is this guy? He's not a Teddy Boy or a King's Road person" and told him we were closed, but eventually let him in. The first time he tried to buy the jukebox, but when we told him it wasn't for sale he started to buy records. We sold him a hell of a lot of them. It got to the stage where we knew at six o'clock every night this guy in the Roller would be coming.'

Another visitor to 430 King's Road in this transitional phase was the young British photographer David Parkinson, also a collector of ephemera and memorabilia. Parkinson had documented the changes at the address when it was Mr Freedom and Paradise Garage via his friendship with members of the Electric Colour Company and encouraged a fellow collector and dealer to accompany him. Stephane Raynor had been a schoolmate of Parkinson's in their native Leicester. 'Malcolm was in the middle of working out what to do with the place,' said Raynor. 'I know the favourite thing he had at that time – which he wouldn't sell – was a black "Rock Around the Clock" shirt with alarm clocks all over it. I told him I could get some bits and pieces, and we had a working relationship. I'd drive a VW van to London and he'd be upside-down in the back, arse sticking in the air, rooting through things.

'Then, when we went back a few weeks later, it was up-and-running. Entering the shop feels like entering the set of a fifties B-movie. There were old Teds, dwarfs and generally disfigured people just hanging around. There was a little sign outside, Bakelite radios on the street and Lurex trousers on the wall.'[3]

By the New Year the transformation was complete. Gone were any hints of Paradise Garage's romantic Americana or the cheery pop-art vibrancy of the Mr Freedom phase which preceded it. McLaren was delighted: 'After art school I had created another world for myself where I could run wild, where there were no rules, only the ones I made up and where similar people would congregate.'

To Westwood's relief, Casey had by now moved out of Thurleigh Court to a flat to the south-west of London in Richmond. Often he failed to make the last bus home, and slept on the shop floor at night. 'The shop became a squat of sorts, but at the same time a place we both felt was magical,' said McLaren, who later confessed: 'I loved Patrick in a way. He was an incredible person.'

Inside, Let It Rock was split into two sections. The front part was dedicated to sales; here Trevor Myles's black-painted walls were the remaining vestige of his residency. Against them were pinned pairs of the gold pinstriped peg trousers found by Bob Chait, juxtaposed with Kornbluth's dayglo socks and 1950s lobby cards. A large display hanger showed red rockabilly shirts made by West End designer Frederick Starke in the early 1960s, Slim Jim ties and the broad-check sports coats located by Casey. There were also velvet collared Ted jackets and new drape coats made by the East End tailor Sid Green, to whom McLaren had been introduced by David Sutch (the novelty horror-rocker Screaming Lord Sutch). McLaren had come to know him on his rounds of the Ted and rocker revival circuit.

One section was dedicated to posters and publicity stills of Sutch, which were placed above an upright piano draped with original Empire brand denim rocker jeans. Also on the walls were posters for continental European versions of the big 1950s rocksploitation movies, acquired via the Paris branch of the Elvis Presley fan club: *Vive le Rock!* (for 1958's *Let's Rock*), *Place Au Twist* (Chubby Checker vehicle *Don't Knock the Twist*), *Le Cavalier du Crepuscule* and *L'Amour Frénétique* (Presley's *Love Me Tender* and *Loving You*), *Jeunesse Droguée* (MGM's *High School Confidential!*) and *De Blonde En Ik* (the Dutch release of the Jayne Mansfield-fronted *The Girl Can't Help It*).

The reconditioned 1950s and early 1960s valve radios were of appeal to the retro clientele; McLaren employed a local pensioner enthusiast to clean them up so that he could issue a three-month guarantee with each sale.

On the floor 78s and 45s tumbled out of wooden boxes next to dead-stock creepers and elasticated sided winklepicker boots by the big British 1960s brand Denson's. These caught the eye of the Godfather of Punk Iggy Pop, who arrived in London in the spring of 1972, courtesy of David Bowie's management company Mainman, to record what would become the Bowie-produced album *Raw Power*.

For the duration, Pop, guitarist James Williamson and Ron and Scott Asheton of the Stooges resided at a house rented by Mainman from the writer Frederic Raphael in Seymour Walk in South Kensington, and the singer, when not recording, occupied himself by roaming the London streets. Given that World's End is a five-minute stroll from Seymour Walk, it was perhaps inevitable that Pop would happen upon Let It Rock. There, he recalled in 2014, McLaren's deliberately casual display of winklepickers was 'the most punk thing I ever saw in my life'.

'Two hundred yards up the King's Road was Granny Takes a Trip, where they sold proper rock-star clothes like scarves, velvet jackets, and snakeskin platform boots,' said Pop. 'Malcolm's obviously worthless box of shit was like a bomb against the status quo because it was saying that these violent shoes have the right idea and they are worth more than your fashion, which serves a false value. This is right out of the French Enlightenment.'[4]

McLaren was less generous in return. 'I remember when Iggy Pop and James Williamson used to come in all the time asking for such-and-such a record,' he told the *New Musical Express* a few years later. 'I'd tell 'em to get out. I thought they were a couple of bleedin' hippies then.'[5]

It's not recorded what Pop thought of the back section of Let It Rock, which was by contrast a surreal and postmodern space, the summation of McLaren and Casey's plans for In the Back of Paradise Garage.

Visitors were confronted with a weirdly domestic non-retail scenario, an imagined Teddy boy's sitting room as it would have been had the occupant lived in one of London's northern suburbs such as Willesden, said McLaren.

This was a proletarian vision, expressing the faded glamour of the mundanity of 1950s post-austerity Britain. The out-of-date wallpaper acquired in south London now extended across the three back walls, where a blue Formica-panelled lounger was arranged next to a stick-legged coffee table containing piles of vintage trash magazines, mainly American: girlie mags such as *Glamour Revue*, celebrity sheet *Picturegoer* and fanzines including *Teen Scene* and *16*.

The area was designated for relaxation, and consequently contained a blue fabric-covered fridge, a radiogram, an original Bakelite single-reel tape player and the jukebox, which McLaren described as the shop's centre of gravity – it pulled people in'. A modernist rug lay on post-war linoleum flooring, which extended onto a raised platform at the centre back of the shop, and on which was placed the *pièce de résistance*: an ornate glass cabinet decorated with roses containing silk scarves in blue, black, white and orange, flick-knife combs, love-heart necklaces and jars of Brylcreem.

On top of the cabinet were pink nylon flounces around the displays: a plate depicting a wild-haired Sutch and the pair of the kinky black patent leather, stiletto-heeled, flute-topped boots McLaren had found in the window of Frederick Freed. Above them, around the air vent in a side door, was a hyper-colourised scene from the Lake District.

Casey and McLaren were surfing the zeitgeist; not far away in Earls Court, Casey's former room-mate, the British painter Duggie Fields, had converted the mansion flat he had previously shared with the Pink Floyd founder Syd Barrett into a veritable tribute to the decorative style of the 1940s and 1950s, influenced by *Modern Art in Your Life*, the 1949 catalogue for a show at New York's Museum of Modern Art which traced the influence of such artists as Miro and Mondrian on post-war design.[6] But Fields's apartment – with original 1950s curtains, linoleum floors, coffee tables and a lounge suite – proposed a softer, more affectionate environment than that realised by Casey and McLaren.

'We were very happy with the look and feel of the shop,' said McLaren. 'But Patrick was worrying me. If he was around he would get annoyed if anybody touched anything or moved the magazines or records. And I started to think that we'd never open as he couldn't get up or be constructive. We argued and I knew Vivienne didn't like him. Not that that mattered but somehow it came to pass that Patrick couldn't get it together. I never knew where he'd be. Probably buying drugs I suppose.'

In January 1972 the completed refurbishment of 430 King's Road was captured by photographer David Parkinson. Casey was inevitably absent, so McLaren and Westwood were Parkinson's subjects in a variety of settings. McLaren wore the Mr Freedom creepers with which he matched blue silk socks, black drainpipes, a black spread-collared shirt, skinny gold tie, brocade waistcoat and a brand new dove-grey fingertip drape with pink lining. His tumbling locks swept away from his forehead, McLaren appeared intense in the shots, biting into an apple, caught mid-flight with *The Buddy Holly Story* in his hands and proudly presenting a pair of black and red winged Denson boots as worn by the 'Shakin' All Over' hit-makers Johnny Kidd and the Pirates.

Westwood, meanwhile, exuded serene beauty, her eye make-up simple and effectively catlike, hair cropped in spiky blonde to match the yellow of her mohair jumper dress, with black tights and black suede shoes, lounging in one of the chairs at the front, gazing at McLaren or addressing the camera with an unwavering gaze.

Within days of the Parkinson shots being taken, McLaren arrived at his new shop to find a scene of devastation. The locks had been changed and, peering inside, McLaren could see that the lino had been ripped up, the displays turned over and the mini-platform constructed to hold the glass cabinet smashed. The stock was gone.

Out of loyalty to Trevor Myles and resentful at the invasion of the non-rent paying McLaren, one of the leaseholders, Charlie Simpson, had taken it upon himself to intervene and assert his rights as the de facto landlord.

McLaren had pitched himself against a faction of London's rag trade. Simpson had once been in league with McLaren and Westwood's friend Tommy Roberts; until a falling out, they had been partners in the mid-1960s in the off-Carnaby Street boutique Kleptomania (in Kingly Street, scene of McLaren's labyrinth installation). Simpson's co-leaseholder in

430 King's Road was Tom Salter, who had scored great success with his Carnabetian furniture shop Gear and, most recently, the clothing market Great Gear Trading Company halfway down the King's Road.

The gentlemanly Salter was horrified at Simpson's action. 'That wasn't my style at all,' says Salter. 'I took a back seat on that lease because I was busy doing other stuff. Charlie got too heavy and put us in the wrong. I was embarrassed by it and had words with him. You just can't do that.'[7]

To resolve the situation, McLaren called upon Tommy Roberts for advice. Roberts was planning a new boutique, City Lights Studio, with a new partner, Willy Daly; they told McLaren to defend his rights of occupation.

'Malcolm was beside himself,' says Daly. 'We suggested he talk to our lawyer Charles Humphreys.'[8]

Humphreys sued Simpson on McLaren's behalf and a court hearing was scheduled. McLaren and Westwood arrived in their Let It Rock gear, her in stiletto-heeled boots and miniskirt. 'Charles got all hot and bothered when Vivienne turned up,' laughed Roberts. '"Ooh Mr Roberts," he said, "I had to walk to court with Mrs Westwood dressed like that!" He loved every minute of it!'

In the event, Humphreys's representations were not impaired by his clients' appearance; because of Simpson's heavy-handed actions, the court ruled against him, ordering the handover of the keys, return of the stock and transfer of the lease to McLaren, who was established as the rightful occupant.

Now, money was needed not only to settle the legal bill but also to start paying for the lease. In his last year at Goldsmiths, McLaren had come to know French Turkish art student Jocelyn Hakim, who was seeking UK residency. In exchange for £50 (around two months' shop rent), McLaren married Hakim at Lewisham register office on 25 February 1972.

Described as a 'shop manager', he had still not officially reverted to his birth name and was registered as 'Malcolm Edwards, formerly known as

Malcolm McLaren'. Although McLaren depicted this to be a purely financial transaction, he later claimed that there was an emotional attachment, at least on Hakim's part.

In notes he made in the late 1990s, McLaren mentioned that Hakim was keen that they live together and that there was a subsequent altercation with Westwood, but this blew over and the couple went their separate ways, divorcing a few years later. In the interim, Hakim took Edwards as her surname and bestowed it upon her daughter, who became the actress Jodhi May, when she was born in 1975.

In later life McLaren dated the wedding to Hakim to at least a year earlier, when he was still struggling to complete *The Story of Oxford Street* at Goldsmiths. He claimed that the £50 was actually to pay for costs for the film, and there may have been a grain of truth in that.

The same month that he married Hakim, local Chelsea newspaper reporter Vivien Goldsmith's report on Let It Rock's opening mentioned that McLaren wanted 'to earn enough money from Let It Rock to be able to finish his film, which he had to give up for lack of funds'.[9] Evidently, McLaren had not forsworn the venture, which he now said had turned into a tribute to Billy Fury.

By the time this article was published, Patrick Casey had again disappeared from McLaren's life. He was to encounter his friend and muse only once more, a few years later, by which time, according to McLaren, Casey was in reduced circumstances.[10]

But McLaren wasn't alone for long. At the end of the school spring term in 1972, Westwood was persuaded that Let It Rock had a future and gave up her teaching job. Working from Thurleigh Court so that she could care for Joe, now four, and Ben, eight, she focused on the tasks of cleaning, pressing and repairing dead stock and producing short runs of replica clothing and designs to which they added twists of their own.

McLaren confessed that the generic white thick cotton T-shirts from Kornbluth's gave him 'the horrors because they seemed so boring', yet he knew that the tee was a key factor in the 1950s wardrobe. 'Up to this point in my life, I had never worn a T-shirt,' said McLaren. 'I was so freaked out by the dull cut and horrible, thick, nasty quality, I had Vivienne tailor and customise one on my body.

'I knew that to resell the batch of T-shirts we had to change them somehow, so I tried to create a James Dean-style effect with little capped sleeves. The only way to do it was to cut the T-shirt sleeve and sew it so that it just came over the top part of the shoulder muscle. Vivienne carried out that task on her sewing machine. We worked long and hard to get it right.'

But Westwood's small domestic machine wasn't fit for purpose, so an investment was made in a professional seamstress's apparatus. To finance this McLaren decreed that the Thurleigh Court phone was cut off, leading to tensions at home but at last the couple were united in creative pursuit.

'We finally partnered up and began to support my idea to create a shop in line with the philosophy in art school,' said McLaren. 'It was never about making things successful or commercial or having a career in fashion. It was about creating a scene.'

Chapter 11

In Let It Rock's earliest media coverage Malcolm McLaren stressed his principal aim that the shop become a 'centre for people to meet and talk', like Keith Albarn's gallery and the art school canteens he had frequented where the exchange of ideas was given primacy.

In fact, McLaren shared his doubts about even running a retail outlet, informing local paper journalist Vivien Goldsmith that 'capitalism stinks'. She noted that he appeased his conscience by buying fizzy drinks and cakes for visitors while they sat and listened to the jukebox.[1]

Nevertheless, after Patrick Casey's disappearance and the necessity to repurpose the interior as a result of the invasion directed by Charlie Simpson, McLaren needed cash for the final stages of the refurbishment as well as for investment in stock. The money from the marriage to Jocelyn Hakim was a start, and grandmother Rose – who he was visiting decreasingly – added to the pot. Since she was now involved more directly in the business, Vivienne Westwood persuaded her retired parents to make a loan.

The wallpapered living-room set-up remained in the back, and racks were positioned towards the front to display menswear and womenswear. And the facade was converted: Paradise Garage's bamboo lettering was removed and the green corrugated iron sheets painted black. For the shop's new name, McLaren cut out giant musical letters in pink paper in the jaunty style of the font used on a poster for the 1950s film *Mister Rock 'n' Roll*, a biopic of the American DJ Alan Freed who had coined the phrase and promoted it into the mainstream. Freed was also of interest to McLaren because his career crashed and burned after he became mired in a payola scandal. The criminality that infused the music business of the period added to the atmosphere of outsider-dom.

The letters were pasted onto the corrugated iron with the assistance of David Sutch, who – when he was not caked in pan-stick trying to scare the bejesus out of his audiences – ran a window-cleaning business on his home turf in north London, so was able to provide both the head for heights and the ladders for the job in exchange for being featured in the shop displays. Sutch later recalled McLaren and Westwood as 'very arty and wild, so we suited each other'.[2]

Underneath the name, the entrance was a key part of the experience of visiting Let It Rock at this time. McLaren retained the flexible frontage that had been installed by Tommy Roberts and Trevor Myles when they opened Mr Freedom at 430 King's Road a couple of years earlier. This comprised three foldback glass-fronted doors that gave the option of presenting no threshold between the interior and the pavement.

This had been Roberts's nod to the pre-war 'in-and-out' drapery store run by an uncle in south London, but now served McLaren's aim of making the space more communal. Teddy boys usually ran in packs, so began to congregate outside smoking, eating takeaways from the local fish-and-chip shop and jiving on the pavement to the tunes blasting from the BAL-AMi.

Curious about the changes being rung at these premises so close to his outlet Granny Takes a Trip at 488 King's Road, Gene Krell visited 430 within a few days of Let It Rock opening.

'My whole background was in rock and roll,' says Krell, who had acquired a 50 per cent share in Granny's with his business partner Marty Breslau from the owner Freddie Hornik a year or so before. 'I was brought up in Brooklyn where you either fought or danced, or sometimes did both at the same time. I'd been in doo-wop groups in the fifties so could give Malcolm and Vivienne a direct line to what they were interested in. And we got on. I remember one of the first things Vivienne said to me was: "I don't like your shop but I like you." '[3]

The pixie-like Krell was a dazzling presence. Invariably dressed in velvet suits and stack-heeled patchwork boots, with long black ringleted hair, Krell whitened his hook-nosed visage with make-up and allowed his black-painted fingernails to grow into talons, three inches in length.

'In a sense I was in the enemy camp,' Krell recalled in the late 1990s. 'I seemed to have little to do with their reality. Malcolm was such a character, portraying himself as this street-smart Ted while discussing Dadaist art. I have never encountered a more diverse mentality, or such a Walter Mittyish existence.'[4]

Krell's commitment to unusual visual expression intrigued McLaren and Westwood, and their friendship was cemented one night when Krell invited the couple – who didn't own a television – to his place to watch a broadcast of *Blackboard Jungle*.

Krell believes the pair were on a mission from the outset. 'It's not a word you'd associate with them, but they were idealists,' he says. 'Everything was black or white. They truly believed that it was the dawning of a new age and a new attitude, where all the crap had to be discarded. That was something we hadn't witnessed before.'

Cannily recruiting prominent London Ted Bill Hegarty as his first sales assistant, McLaren further put the word about in the British rock 'n' roll community by designing a handbill. Headed 'TEDDY BOYS FOR EVER! The Rock era is our business', this was rendered by McLaren with Letraset rub-on lettering and decorated with crudely drawn musical notes and simple illustrations.

The handbill detailed a fully rounded collection, from drape jackets for men and women (£25), black straight-legged jeans (£2.50), creepers (£7) and caps in leopard print (£1.25) to fringed rocker dresses (£6) and the Frederick Freed stiletto ankle boots for which McLaren had found a manufacturer (£12.50). Much of the stock came from the wholesaler Kornbluth's, but some items were now being made in-house, such as the mohair mini-rocker dress (£10).

The flyer was distributed by McLaren, Westwood and Hegarty at venues that hosted 1950s events, in particular the City of London pub the Black Raven where McLaren would wisely take a backseat (Teds weren't known for their polite acceptance of interlopers, particularly ex-art school students posing as the real deal) while the bold Westwood prowled the floor, chatting to likely looking customers and talking up Let It Rock.

The Black Raven had been attracting the rocking community since 1967, and was packed to the gills at weekends, inspiring other pubs across London, such as the Castle in Tooting and the Fishmongers Arms in Wood Green, to throw Saturday night dances. In fact, the Ted revival had been bubbling under for some time; in 1968 a reissue of Bill Haley's 'Rock Around the Clock' was a surprise UK hit. Grassroots interest in neo-Edwardian style was spurred by second-generation Teds, characters such as London's lugubrious Sunglasses Ron and dwarfish Tongue-Tied Danny, who became avid Let It Rock customers.

Once the word was out, Teds came from far and wide. In February 1972, within weeks of the shop opening, a coachload arrived from Wakefield, Yorkshire, 200 miles from London. 'They came bolderin' in 'ere, all dressed up in their gear, their drapes and everything, they spent three hours playing the records, buying glow-in-the-dark socks, pants and magazines,' McLaren told American journalist Jerry Hopkins, his street vowels drawing on his north-east London roots before switching to art school speak. 'It was quite dynamic, really.'

The spiel worked. Hopkins promptly filed a front-page report on the British rock 'n' roll revival for *Rolling Stone*. Referred to as co-owner of the shop with his art-college pal Niall Martin, McLaren – in powder blue sports jacket and 'luminescent peggers' – told Hopkins that he and Martin still hoped to complete the Billy Fury film and 'revive the rock 'n' roll'.[5]

McLaren treated the ground floor of 430 King's Road in the same way as he had the rooms and studios where he made art, constantly tinkering with the presentation and elements on display. The big sales day was Saturday and regular customers became frustrated if the shop wasn't open by 10.30 a.m.

'It became a cult for Teddy boys,' wrote McLaren in the 1990s. 'Each Friday Vivienne was up all night detailing clothes while I spent the same time perfecting the environment, like creating the setting for a performance. By one o'clock it still wouldn't be finished and everyone outside would be going crazy. The Teds were creating their own scene on the pavement and local residents and the other shopkeepers started complaining.'

There was a tale of McLaren being physically attacked in local pub the Roebuck by a retailer angered by the mob scene he was intent on creating. And, around this time, McLaren's former Goldsmiths tutor Barry Martin encountered McLaren and his gang in the King's Road. 'I was walking along the pavement when I saw this crowd of people dressed as Teds striding towards me in a V formation, with Malcolm at the back,' said Martin. 'They were barging pedestrians out of the way but I stood my ground in the centre of the pavement and they simply flowed around me. I caught Malcolm's eye but he didn't look back.'

The Let It Rock crew soon had a new member, an ethereal young American named Addie Isman, whose pale, doll-like appearance, feather-cut black hair and slim physique made her a bookend to the bottle-blonde Westwood and added an extra dimension to the shop.

'The shop's club-like atmosphere attracted a range of different characters,' said McLaren. 'Addie turned up every day and eventually became a fixture.'

Obsessed with fashion, Isman was offered Hegarty's job by McLaren, as ever fascinated by Americans. Isman was another moneyed Jewish expat drawn into McLaren's orbit, and had a familial background in retail; her father was a franchisee of the US discount chain Two Guys, selling everything from electrical appliances to clothing and toys from a 190,000-square-foot space in a vast mall in the East Coast's Jersey City.

That this was a far cry from the tiny ground floor of 430 King's Road made working at Let It Rock all the more appealing. 'Addie was beautiful, a very gentle person, and made quite a contrast for the shop,' said McLaren. 'I always made sure she appeared in photographs, particularly in tough clothes, studded tops and jeans. She looked wonderful when posed with me, or some of the Teds or Vivienne, though she wasn't sure about Addie. For me it was great because I had been on my own most of the time at the shop since Patrick had left.'

Isman – who appeared with McLaren in photographs taken by the *Daily Mirror* in March 1972 dressed head to toe in Let it Rock's cleavage-exposing V-neck top, skin-tight Lurex jeans and a pair of the flute-topped patent leather stilettos – became friendly with one of Let It Rock's youngest customers, Yvonne Gold, a fifteen-year-old Londoner who spent her time haunting Chelsea's boutiques.

'I wasn't particularly into rock 'n' roll but loved Let It Rock because it was another of those great King's Road places where you went as much for the theatrical experience as the clothes, and meeting people like Addie was very much part of that,' says Gold, who went on to become a prominent make-up artist working on the catwalk shows staged by McLaren and Westwood in the early 1980s.

'That's when I first met Vivienne. She was intimidating for me as a young person; Vivienne had that schoolteacher vibe, because she had been one. Malcolm was much easier going, a bit of a lad, some bravado there. You got the impression he had reinvented himself. He was acting out the Teddy boy entrepreneur role, always looking for the angle, where to make a buck or finding out what was going on. Malcolm was always great at spotting a trend. He approached things in an integrated, current way.'[6]

Interest from forward adopters such as Gold was an indicator that the mainstream fashion industry was paying attention. Almost as soon as it had opened, Let It Rock received valuable media coverage when the influential stylist Caroline Baker selected a pair of Let It Rock Lurex trousers and a wide leather belt to appear on a model in a double-page spread in *Nova* magazine[7] and that spring the *Sunday Times Magazine* dedicated four pages to the shop, proclaiming 'there are now an estimated 20,000 revivalist Teddy Boys in England, and the drainpipe-trouser trade is booming'.

The publication put its best talents onto the story. German photographer Hans Feurer staged a fashion shoot at the Fishmongers Arms, with models wearing Let It Rock clothes while they danced in the venue or posed onstage with Screaming Lord Sutch and the pub's house band the Houseshakers.[8]

At least one of the dresses was from leftover stock designed by Diana Crawshaw for Paradise Garage, but never mind. All the glory went to Let It Rock, announced as 'new and influential' by fashion writer Valerie Wade, who noted that the business was attracting fashionistas as much as it was purist revivalists: 'The phenomenon of Let It Rock is that it is situated in Chelsea, which Teds regard as "enemy territory"; now they're selling to the natives.'

McLaren told Wade that the shop drew female customers interested in 'shaggy mohair sweater-dresses and winklepicker boots', the styles relating to rockers, the motorbike-riding greasers who supplanted the Teds as the major British youth cult in the late 1950s and early 1960s.

Yet Wade was unconvinced as to the aesthetic value of the clothes McLaren was promoting. 'Fashion can thank the Fifties for some of the most unglamorous and unflattering clothes we ever knew,' ran the pay-off to her piece. 'That is what makes their unmodified rebirth so difficult to understand.'

This incomprehension on the part of British fashion's gatekeepers delighted McLaren, particularly since the wider media was recognising the visual appeal and dynamism radiating from 430 King's Road. Not long after the *Sunday Times* piece he was championing the Teds as youth culture's first and truest rebels in the national daily press: 'Today's kids don't know how much they owe Teddy Boys. Teds started the youth revolution. They were the first kids to break away from their mums and dads. They did their own thing in spite of parental opposition. They wore what they liked. They did what they liked.'[9]

Such coverage alerted one Let It Rock customer to the marketing potential of the 1950s revival. The advertising pacesetter Charles Saatchi had noted the shop sold dead-stock pairs of jeans made by Lybro, the Liverpool brand which had been popular in the early 1960s and advertised by the Beatles. Lybro was among the clients of Saatchi & Saatchi, the company Charles had launched a couple of years earlier with his brother Maurice. Sniffing the pop-culture winds blasting from 430 King's Road, Saatchi promptly produced a television ad for Lybro in 1972, cut to Little Richard's rambunctious 'Good Golly, Miss Molly'. Doubtless this derived from the impressive collection of original rock 'n' roll records Saatchi had amassed from Let It Rock.

The buzz around the 1950s revival really started to build when record company UA embarked on a huge reissue campaign for a series of LPs featuring the best tracks by the most prominent American performers. The music business was starting to seriously reappraise its back catalogues; hitherto records from the past had languished in the vaults or been knocked out on cheapo compilations. 'This was the first era of post-modernism in pop,' said the music journalist Iain MacDonald. 'Music started to be conscious of itself and look back, beginning to make syntheses and style references and be ironic.'[10]

That McLaren was applying such practice at Let It Rock was evinced by the T-shirts he designed for sale at 'The London Rock 'n' Roll Show' staged in early August 1972 by promoters Ray and Ron Foulks. Fresh from organising mass musical events on the Isle of Wight starring contemporary artists such as Jimi Hendrix, Bob Dylan and Joni Mitchell, the Foulks's rock 'n' roll show was the first music festival to be held at the 100,000 capacity Wembley Stadium in north-west London.

An all-dayer, the London Rock 'n' Roll Show lined up most of the surviving American greats apart from Elvis Presley – so Chuck Berry, Bo Diddley, Bill Haley, Little Richard and Jerry Lee Lewis – with home-grown talent such as Billy Fury and Screaming Lord Sutch and appearances by contemporary acts who plugged into primal rock: the MC5 from Detroit, Britain's ludicrous and as it turned out thoroughly unsavoury Gary Glitter, and Roy Wood of the Move's new outfit Wizzard.

As the only boutique in Britain selling 1950s fashions, Let It Rock was a shoo-in; McLaren booked a large stall near the main entrance to the stadium and with Westwood set about designing new clothing to sell there. This represented their first fashion collection, a coherent and complementary mix of designs for which McLaren drew upon his knowledge of such processes as appropriation, collage and juxtaposition. Meanwhile Westwood conveyed serious powers of invention alongside sensitive use of fabrics and an innovative approach to garment construction.

The collection also marked a shift away from the original intent of Let It Rock, which McLaren later said 'was digging in the ruins of past cultures that you cared about. It was giving them another brief moment in the sun. It wasn't about doing anything new. It was an homage. It was nostalgia.'[11]

And so the London Rock 'n' Roll Show pointed to a new direction. After just six months, he and Westwood had become dispirited by the stick-in-the-mud ways of the Teds whose right-wing political beliefs were based on a bedrock of homophobia, ignorance, misogyny and racism. The satisfaction at shocking the denizens of Chelsea's boutique strip by encouraging these beer-swilling characters to hang out there had been supplanted by their unremitting tiresomeness.

'Get increasingly discouraged – feel that what began as a search for the authentic has been reduced to mere nostalgia,' wrote McLaren in notes in the 1990s. 'Got bored with the Teddy Boys who appear to stand for revolt but who turn out to be just glamorous trainspotters.'

The collection unveiled on the Let It Rock stall at Wembley looked in harmony with the Teds' simplistic worldview. Five silk-screened T-shirts celebrated the biggest names at the show. One each was dedicated to Berry, Lewis, Little Richard and Sutch. 'We printed these reversed-out in white on black to make them more mythic,' said McLaren. The fifth was a white T-shirt designed as an immediate memento for the event, emblazoned with 'Rock 'n' Roll Lives', Let It Rock's address and signatures of a dozen or so rock 'n' roll greats.

McLaren sourced the images and titles of the T-shirts from ephemeral materials at the shop: foreign-language film posters, record sleeves, promotional stills, lobby cards, theatrical half-sheets (also used for display in cinema foyers), all were up for grabs as McLaren meshed them into fresh composites that explored the links between untamed rock 'n' rollers and the troublemaking political movements that had bewitched him in the late 1960s.

Not only was McLaren adopting *détournement* but he was also plugging into the legacy of a literary hero, the German philosopher Walter Benjamin, who believed that coherent views of culture emerge from the accumulation and arrangement of fragments and detritus.

Benjamin's political commitment led him to 'focus on the everyday, the "refuse" of a rapidly expanding mass culture which was tied to industrialism. He often focused on the discarded fashions, seeing them as an emblem of an acceleration of everyday experience associated with industrial capitalism.'[12]

And so the T-shirt image of the knock-kneed Berry was taken from an Italian poster for the release of Alan Freed's 1956 musical *Rock! Rock! Rock!*, Sutch's wild-haired pose (in glitter green on black) came from the same promo handout that inspired the plate in the display at In the Back of Paradise Garage, and Jerry Lee Lewis hammering away at his piano (underneath McLaren's cartoon lettering from the title of a Lewis LP that year, 'The "Killer" Rocks On!') was an isolated image from a lobby card for 1958's *High School Confidential!*

The most successful and, as it turned out, enduring of these T-shirts paid tribute to Little Richard by showing the flamboyant black performer striking an outstretched pose taken on the set of the 1956 film *Don't Knock the Rock*. This was juxtaposed with script declaring 'Vive le Rock!' screen-printed from a Belgian poster for Harry Foster's jubilant 1958 flick *Let's Rock!* The choice of statement was crucial. 'Vive la Commune!' a Chinese Communist Party pamphlet had declared when marking the one-hundred-year anniversary of the 1871 French socialist government the Paris Commune the year before Let It Rock opened. McLaren hoped that his usage of the urgent title on the Belgian poster would act similarly as a clarion call, a condensation of the political energy he dreamed of fusing with the insurrectionary power of wild 1950s sounds.

Using leftover stock of black jersey tops printed with glitter lettering from the Paradise Garage era as prototypes, McLaren and Westwood cracked the code of how they had been produced and created a series that used bold characters to spell out the names of various other 1950s stars – 'Eddie', 'Buddy', 'Elvis' and 'Gene Vincent & His Blue Caps'.

For the latter, Westwood gave clues to her willingness to manipulate the form of garments by removing the shoulders from T-shirts so that the necklines were left and the bodies of the tops were suspended by tiny chains.

The others were printed in blue, green and red glitter onto cap-sleeved and sleeveless shirts with broad midriff seams taken from an original design for summer shirts sold in Vince Man's Shop, the men's boutique McLaren had haunted as a teenager.

Some of the glitter tops were emblazoned with motorcycle patches and others were threaded with the linked metal chains bought from hardware stores; their practical use was for lavatory cisterns.

'I felt we needed to create something new,' said McLaren. 'So I put a chain around the shoulders of some of the shirts. Toilet chains were the inspiration. This is the beginning of an exploration of the possibilities open to the bricoleur. I threw together the fragments which were close at hand, setting up the essence of all my work to follow.'

By this time McLaren was investigating the long-established British motorcycle-wear manufacturer D. Lewis and Co, famed for the zip-laden jackets produced under the Lewis Leathers brand. 'As well as the heavyweight, thug-like black jackets they sold wonderful packets of biker studs and enamel and woven cloth badges of famous bike names – Norton Dominator, Indian Brave, Triumph,' said McLaren. 'Dominator in particular was a great name. It had a rhythm to it and held all sorts of sexual connotations. Triumph too. With these materials, we started to invent a contemporary world of biker fashion.'

And so black jersey tops were decorated with patches, chains and heavy, leftover Paradise Garage studs, which spelt out slogans such as

'Rock N Roll Ruby' and 'Triumph T120' (the first model of the rocker's favourite bike, the Bonneville).

From one of the vintage pieces he and Casey had located for In the Back of Paradise Garage – a strange fringe-fronted jerkin in blue, brown and white from the early 1960s – McLaren and Westwood took the rubberised shoulder panels and applied them to tops to which they added more studs and fringes in various materials including strips of black or white suede.

And a group of leather miniskirts and waistcoats were overloaded with materials, images and slogans – motorbike patches, phrases such as 'Rock 'n' Roll' and 'Rebel' in white or red paint and 'Elvis', pyramids and peace symbols in studs with adornments of multiple chains and fringes.

Ahead of the Wembley show, London's daily paper the *Evening Standard* published a special edition. Along with profiles of Sutch, Fury and the MC5 and colour posters of Berry, Lewis et al. was an article by fashion journalist Geoffrey Aquilina Ross on Let It Rock, complete with photographs of Addie Isman and Bill Hegarty.

The media puzzlement at McLaren's decision to place a celebration of working-class pop culture in this part of west London was foregrounded in the introduction: 'Here it is, London's first ever rock 'n' roll shop, sited of all places in the middle of Chelsea's boutique strip,' wrote Aquilina Ross, who garnered McLaren's advice on sartorial matters. 'You wear your creepers with your drapes and you wear your winkies with your drainpipes,' pronounced McLaren, who cited as evidence of the 1950s revival gathering pace the first British production of *Grease* being planned for the autumn. 'Meanwhile, back in Fulham Road is Small's Café, a trendy 50s-oriented joint, its walls smothered with pictures of the singing stars of the period, serving workmen's café food to deafening rock music,' reported Aquilina Ross.

Despite such pointers to the fact that Let It Rock was riding the zeit-geist, McLaren continued to tout the unfinished Goldsmiths film, nine months after installing himself at 430 King's Road and nearly a year after he had given up on it. 'He ran out of money at the time, but he is deter-mined to get the film finished,' wrote Aquilina Ross. 'McLaren calls Billy Fury "Britain's only rock 'n' roll singer of note".'[13]

For Wembley, McLaren recruited a team of helpers to join Westwood, Isman and himself. These included Fred Vermorel and Yvonne Gold.

'Maybe Malcolm liked my look,' says Gold. 'I'd dyed my hair shock-ing pink with cochineal and had it cut short and spiky. Also the fact that I wasn't an old Ted probably helped. We got there late and there was a kerfuffle about setting up. It was quiet at first, until the word got around and then we were overwhelmingly busy. The T-shirts just flew; we took a lot of money.'

Gold was captured in director Peter Clifton's film of the event – which was attended by, among others, Mick Jagger – dealing with customer demand with McLaren on the Let It Rock stand. He played the market huckster, barking 'Large Jerry Lee!' at Gold in leopard-print cap, 1950s sports coat and 'Rock 'n' Roll Lives' T-shirt. She later confirmed McLaren's intention to use the London Rock 'n' Roll Show to drive a new direction: 'The decorated leatherwear came about because Malcolm really had his finger on the pulse; the rocker thing was so much sexier than the Teds.'

McLaren agreed to Vermorel's proposal that he and nine-year-old Ben Westwood set up another stall at the entrance at the opposite end of the stadium to pick up more custom. 'I added a third to the takings that day,' said Vermorel. 'But when I said that they should build on the popularity by licensing Let It Rock clothing to other, bigger retailers, Malcolm and Vivienne refused to consider it.' Such a move – which Vermorel inter-preted as small-minded 'boutique mentality' – would have tainted the purity of McLaren's vision for the shop.

Participation in the London Rock 'n' Roll Show paid dividends, though McLaren had over-ordered the T-shirts, some of which, in the first instance, were converted into underpants and knickers with frills added by Westwood.

The event in fact failed to attract the tens of thousands anticipated by the promoters, but there were still enough attendees to provide a physically aggressive response to the newer acts on the bill. 'Hardcore Teds are lobbing the cans everywhere,' wrote Douglas Gordon in the underground magazine *Frendz*. 'Gary Glitter: present day rocker rep in the Top Ten . . . fatal after MC5 . . . brown ale's flying everywhere'.[14]

Although McLaren felt no sympathy with Glitter or even the MC5, such displays of conservatism confirmed McLaren's decision to complete the move out of pure replication. David Sutch later recalled McLaren's demeanour at Wembley to author Johnny Rogan:

> His air seemed more confident, as though he had stumbled on a secret formula that could make him a fortune. As he packed away his collection of unsold T-shirts, Malcolm announced that the next major movement in pop music would not merely be linked with a fashion, but created by that fashion. He cited Brian Epstein's manipulation of the Beatles' dress style as an example, but indicated that a more radical approach would be necessary for the decadent 70s. It was clear that McLaren regarded the under-15 market as his target group.[15]

Over the autumn of 1972 McLaren discussed new directions with Westwood as popular culture caught up with their activities at 430 King's Road. The writer Marit Allen, who showcased new talent in British *Vogue*'s 'Young Idea' section and was also a clever costume designer for film, called upon McLaren and Westwood to contribute authentic-looking clothing to 1950s Britrock movie *That'll Be the Day*, which was co-produced by her husband Sandy Lieberson with David (now Lord) Puttnam.

Allen's connection to the fashion magazine did not hold much sway with McLaren, whose stance was determinedly against the fashion establishment. '*Vogue* journalists were thrown out of the shop,' he later said. 'Anything in *Vogue* was a disease we didn't want to catch.'

But McLaren saw that *That'll Be the Day* enabled him to circumvent the fashion press and present Let It Rock clothing in as unmediated a way as possible.

McLaren and Westwood worked with the film's costume consultant Ruth Myers and wardrobe supervisor Ray Beck, and invited the lead actors to visit their premises at 430 King's Road for fittings.

But the groups of Teds outside the shop proved off-putting for Ringo Starr, who played the main supporting role. One day, just as the film was about to go into production, McLaren was visited by a staff member at Ricci Burns' Chelsea hair salon requesting a size 36 drape jacket for Starr, who was unwilling to risk the phalanx of Teds.

'Poor old Ringo was hanging about at the other end of the King's Road waiting for his jacket,' wrote McLaren. 'So this guy, who was the same size, tried on a few until he came across a blue woman's drape with pink velvet collar.

' "This will do fine," he said.

' "But it's got bust darts," I told him.

' "Don't worry. He'll like this." '

And so, in *That'll Be the Day*, Starr's period Let It Rock costume of high-collared light blue shirt with darker blue trimmings, ice-blue Lybro jeans and white quilt-topped brothel creepers was matched with a women's jacket, bust darts and all.

Such was McLaren and Westwood's dedication to the shop that it consumed their home life and informed a decision to dispatch the boys Ben, then nine, and Joe, aged five, to a series of boarding schools. 'My dad gee-ed me up, saying it was going to be a great adventure,' Joe Corré recalled in his early forties. 'Then suddenly the gates closed and I was in this Victorian workhouse in Wales, straight out of a child's worst nightmares: little kids bawling all night, wetting the beds and shitting themselves with fear. They used to beat you with wire coat-hangers. I ain't exaggerating, it was unimaginably awful. Traumatic. I withdrew into myself. When my parents came to visit, they couldn't get me to talk. Not a word. They got the message and took me out of there.'[16]

Still, Corré was also dispatched to Hawkhurst Court in West Sussex and later Summerhill, the co-educational 'free' school in Suffolk established by the Scottish writer A. S. Neill.

This choice of educational path for the young children confirms McLaren's disinterest in assuming a paternal role as well as his lack of appreciation for familial ties.

'I always had the impression that me and Ben drove my dad mad,' said Corré in 2009. 'I was forever taking bikes apart in the living room and he had to step through all my mess, huffing and puffing. He didn't have the patience to be a traditional parent.'[17]

According to Westwood's biographer Jane Mulvagh, she was so much in McLaren's thrall she agreed with his announcements that such experiences would imbue the boys with a spirit of independence.

During his days behind the counter at Let It Rock, McLaren was encouraged by visits from Gerry Goldstein, a highly literate Jewish East-Ender who was friendly with *That'll Be the Day* producer Sandy Lieberson and recalled McLaren as a fellow teenage habitué of Soho and the youth clubs of Hackney and Stoke Newington. Goldstein had also knocked around with such fellow modernists as Mark Feld and the tailor John Pearse of Granny Takes a Trip. Subsequently he had led a life on the edge and had acquired a heroin habit, which he repeatedly attempted to kick, most recently before he started to appear at Let It Rock.

A sensitive and entertaining autodidact, Goldstein was on the road to becoming a bibliophile of some standing and his luck had come in a couple of years previously when he won a year's wages in the form of £1000 on the Premium Bonds. As well as using his winnings to acquire a valuable Martin acoustic guitar from Eric Clapton, who threw in a few lessons, Goldstein also indulged his passion for rare books.

As a result he provided more intellectually stimulating company for McLaren than the Teds who refused to expand their horizons beyond Charlie Feathers's B-sides and the correct adjustment of a Slim Jim tie.

'Gerry arrived out of the blue one day claiming to remember all sorts of things about me,' said McLaren. 'He was an original mod from Stamford Hill who, having won the Premium Bonds, went to the King's Road and never looked back. He took all the junk available to him, became a complete freaked-out kid, totally dressed up in Granny Takes a

Trip or whatever was happening at that time and became part of that whole King's Road scene: Marianne Faithfull, Mick Jagger, Keith Richards, David Litvinoff, Donald Cammell.

'They'd all be fucking these horny girls in the back of rock star limos which were permanently parked outside Granny's. I liked Gerry; we used to bounce ideas off each other. The fact that he knew that whole set around people like Marianne added a bit of danger to the mix.'

A more stylistically directional customer was eighteen-year-old East-Ender David Harrison, these days an eminent British painter and sculptor. At the time Harrison worked in the post room of magazine publisher IPC, whose titles targeting young style-conscious women included *Honey*, *Petticoat* and *19*. A leading IPC fashion editor was Norma Moriceau, an Australian admirer of McLaren and Westwood's who regularly featured their clothing in her fashion shoots (and went on to realise the apocalyptic punk look as the costume designer of the Mad Max films).

'I'd moved on from being a skinhead and Roxy Music were gods to me, but I was also into Gong because they were wild and quite Dada,' says Harrison. 'It was a weird transitional period, the early seventies. Then I adopted a rock 'n' roll look, mainly through second-hand and dead stock in the East End. The problem with original fifties creepers was that the crepe had usually dried, so that when you wore them, the soles cracked. Then a girl working on *Petticoat* told me I had better check out this new shop.'[18]

On his first visit, Harrison ran the gauntlet of the jeering Teds outside Let It Rock and chatted to Addie Isman. 'They were waiting on a delivery of creepers and were very friendly; she did this kind of ditsy act about loving Teddy boys when I mentioned them,' says Harrison. 'I left my number and she called me a couple of days later to tell me they'd arrived.'

On his return, Harrison's eye was caught not by creepers but by a pair of purple suede Beatle boots. 'I tried them on and even though they hurt I thought I'd take them. Then I heard a voice behind me say: "Ooh love, you don't want to get them if they don't fit you, they'll cripple your feet,"' recalled Harrison. 'That was the first time I met Vivienne Westwood. She had blonde hair with black roots showing, purple lipstick and purple lines to accentuate her eyes and ripped fishnet tights. She looked incredible.

'I became friendly with her and pretty soon afterwards if I dropped by she would invite me for a drink with her and whoever else was around, though I always felt Malcolm was a bit of a snob. He'd be in the background talking to other people. I felt he didn't talk to me very much because of my accent.'

When Harrison confessed to Westwood that he was scared of the threatening Teds, she told him: 'Take no notice, they're idiots.'

Another keen customer was Ben Kelly, a student on the Royal College of Art's new interior design course, which had been introduced in recognition of the practice now rapidly developing outside of old-fashioned 'interior decorating'. Wearing a Let It Rock-acquired outfit of creepers, fluorescent socks in pink or green, tight black jeans and a satin jacket embroidered with the letters 'RCA' (as in the record company but applicable to the educational institution), Kelly turned himself into a living sculpture, 'The Photo Kid', whose presence at various locations, including 430 King's Road, he integrated into his degree course.

In December 1972, US journalist Jerry Hopkins returned to Let It Rock for a *Rolling Stone* piece on the growing market for rock collectibles, or, as he described it 'Leftover Teenage Crud becomes, at the flick of greasy quiff, Precious Anthropological Artefact'. Among the precious items he noted at the shop were a framed photograph of Little Anthony & the Imperials for a then-outrageous £4.50 and a programme for the remembrance service for James Dean marked 'Not for Sale'.

Hopkins asked McLaren why, beyond commercial concerns, he framed other Dean memorabilia – such as studio stills and news cuttings of the film star's tragic death – for display in the store.

'Somebody's got to keep track of these things,' McLaren said. Hopkins noted that he sounded 'a proper historian'.[19]

McLaren's near-obsessional focus on the world he and Westwood were creating at 430 King's Road distracted him from paying attention to the person who had until relatively recently been the single most important figure in his life: his grandmother. Rose had grown frail since the death of her husband Mick two years previously and died at the age of seventy-eight in early December 1972.

One story had it that she was found dead at home when police were called to her apartment in Clapham, and McLaren was subsequently informed that the cause was malnutrition. Fred Vermorel has written that it was in fact McLaren who found his grandmother's body sitting bolt upright in bed and naked, after he was forced to break down her front door when he hadn't heard from her for some time.

And McLaren told a third version, that her hospitalisation forced him into visiting her. 'She said to me, "I don't know why you're coming to see me now, you're not getting any of my money." Two days later she was dead.'

Whatever the circumstances of Rose's demise, this once all-powerful patron was gone. Yet McLaren didn't attend the funeral for fear of encountering his mother who, he heard from a relative, was the sole beneficiary of the substantial will.

Chapter 12

Malcolm McLaren may not have betrayed much emotion over the death of his grandmother, but he was to pay homage to her for the rest of his life.

He started soon after her demise with a project that sprang from the catechism Rose had dinned into him as a child: 'To be bad is good because to be good is simply boring.' Let It Rock's championing of the brutishness of the Teddy boys, their music and fashion may be seen as his first exploration of that ethos in terms of street style, but in the early weeks of 1973 McLaren embarked on a more demonstrative celebration of this amoral code when he made the potentially commercially reckless decision to abandon Let It Rock's backward-looking stance in favour of a direction 'less pretty, more dangerous, even offensive'.

Despite what he had told Jerry Hopkins, McLaren was shrugging off the role of 1950s rock-culture historian.

Ennui had set in. 'I was bored with it all,' he wrote thirty years later. 'Bored with the same surrogate suburban Teddy boys that drifted in from God knows where. Bored with the hippies and refugees of Chelsea's swinging 60s looking for charity and kindness. Bored with the demands of the BBC wardrobe department and their dreadful revivalist TV shows. I felt like *Steptoe and Son*. I was lost in dead tissue. I wanted something new.'[1]

In later life McLaren related that the final nail in Let It Rock's retro-revivalism was hammered home by no less a figure than Lionel Blair, the bouffant-haired, snake-hipped British light entertainer who arrived at 430 King's Road one day demanding costumes for a rock 'n' roll routine to be performed by the dance troupe he led on his early evening Saturday show on BBC TV.

For McLaren, approaching the contemporary was encapsulated in a nihilistic phrase: 'Too Fast to Live Too Young to Die'. He had clocked this on the back of a biker's jacket, the words surrounding the image of a dead pigeon, dripping with blood, its wings outstretched. After some thought McLaren decided to use the slogan as the name of the recast 430 King's Road. That it had been adopted by James Dean fans after the film star's tragic death added to the fatalistic purpose of the new enterprise, which was dedicated to the Ton-up boys who had defied British decorum in the early 1960s just as the Hells Angels had done in the US in the immediate post-war years.

The fetishistic aspects of the greasers' garb – tight leather and oily denim jeans, torso-accentuating T-shirts, heavy boots, white scarves and studded black leather motorcycle jackets with peaked caps – provided a satisfyingly provocative homoerotic overlay, as communicated by such movies as the British B-feature *The Leather Boys* and Kenneth Anger's underground classic *Scorpio Rising*. 'The shop was to be the embodiment of speed, danger and death,' said McLaren.

No. 430 King's Road was closed while an overhaul of the facade took place. The pink Let It Rock lettering was stripped away; in its place, against the black corrugated iron, McLaren oversaw the painting of the slogan in white. 'The shop sign looked like a huge eye with "Too Fast to Live" as the upper lid and "Too Young to Die" as the lower, and a skull-and-crossbones as the pupil. A biker's jacket, studded with "Let It Rock" in light bulbs, hung in the window as a memory of the last incarnation. The shop was darker and tougher than before. I brought in fake lampposts and painted murals of an industrial wasteland on the walls [and] created the "outside" "inside". The home became the street.'

McLaren later related that his fascination for changing the environment at 430 King's Road was rooted in his discomfort with commercial and critical acclaim. 'If the shop became successful, one would immediately close it down, one never thought it cool,' he said in the 1990s. 'It was a strange, ironic perverse thing that I did [but] none of it would have remotely occurred had I not been in art school throughout the sixties.'

An under-acknowledged influence on Too Fast to Live was the atmospheric City Lights Studio, the proto-Goth boutique which had been opened in London's Covent Garden – then the locus of a bustling wholesale fruit, vegetable and flower market rather than a tourist and fashion destination – by McLaren's friends Tommy Roberts and Willy Daly a couple of months earlier in November 1972.

City Lights marked Roberts's rejection of the primary-coloured pop art of his by-now failed Mr Freedom venture. In the top floor of a warehouse he described as 'an atelier', the new venture was decorated in macabre style by Andrew Greaves and Jeff Pine of Electric Colour Company.

The grey walls were spattered Jackson Pollock-style with black paint and the wooden floors varnished with gold flake that glittered when sunlight filtered through the heavy blinds. A sarcophagus served as a counter for accessories, an upright stage coffin housed a mannequin in a minstrel's gallery and high-backed Victorian chairs sourced from a theatrical prop shop lent 'melodrama', according to Roberts. Pine created an astonishing display piece: a low glass-topped table cantilevered by T-section metal supports with, at each of the four corners, a plastic replica of a human skull acquired from a medical supplies specialist.

With national media coverage, City Lights was initially a great success: the young model Jerry Hall made her first forays into nightlife in London and Paris in a gold City Lights two-piece, Twiggy was featured in an outfit from the store in a British *Vogue* cover story and David Bowie wore a suit by in-house menswear specialist Derek Morton on the sleeve of his *Pin Ups* LP.

McLaren attended the opening party and was very impressed, so took to visiting Roberts and Daly at the close of the day's trading. 'After hours he would come by so we could go for a drink; he was intrigued,' said Roberts. Daly added: 'Malcolm loved City Lights. You could tell he was warming to the idea of doing something a bit darker than selling to Teddy Boys.'[2]

Given City Lights' out-of-the-way location, Daly and Roberts printed maps so that fashionistas could find their way through the fruit, veg and flower market. These were distributed to fellow fashion retailers for inquisitive customers. 'We heard that Malcolm was charging 50p each for the maps or even just to give directions,' said Roberts. 'There was always a bit of rivalry there.'

At 430 King's Road, McLaren's ideas for Too Fast to Live were distilled in a new voodoo-style design, which he had been contemplating since the interview given to local paper reporter Vivien Goldsmith a year previously. Then McLaren had talked about producing a line in 'chicken-bone jackets . . . leather or suedette jackets with a pattern of real chicken bones on the outside'.[3]

By the time Let It Rock was visited by American shock-rocker Alice Cooper and his band in the summer of 1972, this notion was taking shape. The American singer asked McLaren whether he could provide an exclusive, one-off top for the group's showcase performance at the major London venue Wembley Empire Pool and, in the event, wore a black vest studded with his first name in capitals on the front. Guitarist Glen Buxton meanwhile sported a sleeveless Let It Rock shirt studded with 'Rock & Roll Music'.

But Cooper's request had set McLaren thinking. 'I decided I needed to do something more nasty than I had so far, something less "product" looking. I was consciously moving into an area of anti-fashion.'

He talked through with Westwood the technical aspects of creating a design using blanched chicken bones, and sourced these from Rick Szymanski, a waiter at a World's End Polish restaurant who was later to become a British tabloid entertainment gossip writer.

Westwood drew upon her jewellery-making skills and drilled tiny holes into the bones, inserting chain links to studs on the front of a heavyweight jersey top. 'I tried and tried to write something, a word in bones,' said McLaren. 'The one which worked best was "R-O-C-K".'

To support the bones, Westwood designed a soft leather yoke around the shoulders and armholes in black with contrasting red lining. The result reminded McLaren of an object 'out of a New Orleans black magic ceremony, a much darker place than we had inhabited before'.

These strange designs were hanging in 430 King's Road when the young French aristocrat artist/designer Jean-Charles de Castelbajac stopped by early in 1973.

A pop-culture fiend and motorbike enthusiast who had haunted London in the mid-1960s as a fan of the R&B outfit the Yardbirds, de Castelbajac had taken over his mother's ready-to-wear line and gained attention from the Paris fashion crowd for his experimental collections of clothing made from household materials such as blankets, floor cloths and bandages.

'I was always fascinated in the electricity coming from London, so went there often to check out curious and experimental work,' said de Castelbajac. 'And I was drawn to the store because I was constantly looking for an encounter of the third kind with other creative people.'[4]

Bowled over by the audacity of the chicken-bones tops, de Castelbajac asked the female running the shop – who he now believes to have been Westwood – the name of the designer. 'She told me it was Malcolm and about getting the bones from the local restaurant,' said de Castelbajac. 'I was already using trash materials and thought: "Wow, this is an idea I could have had or would have loved to have had." But my concept of recycling didn't go as far out as incorporating bones. I had to know who made them.'

De Castelbajac left a note on a card with his address. 'I wrote that we were of the same family, with the same thoughts, me on one side of the English Channel and him on the other,' said de Castelbajac. 'I invited him to visit me in Paris so we could talk about our ideas together.'

A couple of months later, to de Castelbajac's astonishment, McLaren appeared unannounced at his apartment in the rue de Trévise close to the Folies Bergère in the ninth arrondissement.

'It was a huge space, 200 square metres on the fourth floor; I shared it with a cool artist friend Robert Manabal and the crime writer Jean-Patrick Manchette,' said de Castelbajac. 'Around ten o'clock one night we heard the doorbell ring and there was this guy standing on the doorstep, his hair as red as the label on the magnum of Johnnie Walker he held in his hands.'

McLaren was welcomed in, and stayed with de Castelbajac for five days, exploring the city he hadn't visited since the aftermath of the events of May 1968. 'He was obsessed with Paris, with the café culture, with the flâneurs,' said de Castelbajac. 'I introduced him to my friends and he taught me to "flân", so we walked around the city and talked about everything from Eddie Cochran to my fascination for genealogy. He loved that I could put together the genealogy of the electric guitar.'

McLaren maintained a friendship with de Castelbajac in later life, and recalled the flat in rue de Trévise in the CD sleevenotes of the soundtrack he composed for the French designer's 1993 collection:

I have known Jean-Charles for over 20 years.

I drunk whisky, he drunk wine.

He liked the Yardbirds and English Rock, I liked Little Richard and rock 'n' roll.

He lived at the back of the Folies Bergère. His apartment was haunted by the ghost of the mistress of the old duke of Trévise.

I wore Teddy boy clothes, he wore Perfecto.

He had a red Harley, he rode up the Boulevard Montmartre.

He played pinbull [sic] all night, he was very good, I wasn't.[5]

The trip to Paris also provided McLaren with a breather from a fraught situation that had developed in London; around the time of the switch to Too Fast to Live, an affair McLaren had been conducting with Addie Isman came to light. Westwood's instinct that the young American spelled trouble had been on the money.

The fact is that Isman and McLaren's romance went beyond the bounds of a workplace fling. 'I forced myself to fall in love with Addie,' was McLaren's unusual take years later.

In the 1990s McLaren reflected not on his foolhardiness and infidelity but on his inability to control his compulsion to create complicated relationship dynamics that brought all parties into conflict.

'When I met Vivienne I saw in her a mother figure, a figure I never had,' he wrote. 'I had my life with my friends and I went home to Vivienne like you would to your mother. I then set out unwittingly to recreate the pattern of the triangle of my childhood, with Vivienne taking the place of my mother and soon friction arose between her and my grandmother. And then I did this with Addie and Vivienne, recreating the triangle again.'

Isman fled home to New Jersey, and she and McLaren remained in contact by post. Unhappy, Westwood nevertheless took the dalliance in her stride, not least because the creative relationship with McLaren was blossoming now they had introduced the Let It Rock label, the undulating characters printed in black capitals on pink or white. Despite the Too Fast to Live slogan, it was by this name that their business continued to be known.

To complement the bones tops, the pair produced a range of détourned T-shirts from unsold stock from the London Rock 'n' Roll Show. Deliberately distressing a number of the black shirts depicting Chuck Berry, Jerry Lee Lewis and Little Richard, they washed them until they faded, and dyed the white 'Rock 'n' Roll Lives' top until it was grey.

'We trampled on them and shredded them; I wanted those frankly boring shirts to look as if they were old oil rags left under a Bonneville in a repair store,' said McLaren. 'I thought no one would want to buy them; a sale would be impossible.'

Westwood laboriously hand-sewed holes and tears into the fabric of the shirts, sometimes removing a sleeve or the neckline. On the front, on top of the now faded rock 'n' roll lettering and portraits of 1950s rockers, were collaged images of naked, big-breasted women cut from the vintage porn magazines scattered around the shop, presented in small panels made from stitched coloured lighting gels. Short zips were placed to reveal nipples or lower the neckline and, in a *coup de grâce*, the pair dipped the wheels of their son Joe's bicycle in black ink and skidded the tyres over the surfaces of the tops, as though the garments had survived road accidents.

Black sleeveless jersey tops were also used as the basis for another design which developed on the Gene Vincent shirts debuted at Wembley the previous year. These were studded with the words 'Venus' or 'Dominator' and decorated with link chains and biker decals and badges. The tyres of children's bicycles again came into play. These were cut into semicircles and placed around the armhole seams and studded with horsehair attachments, providing a warrior-like appearance for the wearer.

The bones, détourned and studded T-shirts mark the formalisation of McLaren and Westwood design relationship. From this point onwards, he, the partnership's conceptualist and art director, generated ideas, graphics, text slogans and content, styling and detail. McLaren also led the sourcing of materials and location of suppliers of readymade clothing and was responsible for the naming and design of the successive shop environments. Westwood, meanwhile, was his match in terms of innovation, acting as design partner and sounding board, as well as technician and production head, supervising manufacture via tailors, shoemakers, knitters and other outworkers.

For the next decade, the potency of their design work was achieved through McLaren's ability to draw on his extensive art education and development as a visual artist while Westwood's contributed her intuitive and daring technical skills.

The new Too Fast to Live tops also contained the aspects that distinguished the collaboration: balance in the proportions; deft use of juxtaposition; confidence in realisation; surprising use of colour; wit in the application of motifs; and acute sense of framing, particularly of text and visual imagery.

'Making those tops changed the way Vivienne and I thought,' McLaren said. 'Reconstructing and reclaiming history in this way almost turned our T-shirts into an art form. They didn't fit the role of fashion as a commodity. This was fashion as an idea.'

In fact, McLaren was channelling not just Situationist techniques and Walter Benjamin's theories about detritus, he was also utilising the approaches of his art heroes, in particular Robert Rauschenberg. The British academic Amanda Knight has explained how Rauschenberg 'saw infinite creative potential in mundane materials (a sensitivity honed by his former Bauhaus tutor Josef Albers to whom he paid great credit). He was also acutely aware of the material excesses of modern living, another ethos handed down from post-war Bauhaus. He enjoyed the "gifts from the street" – stuff he found on the pavement – and used them in a celebratory rather than scolding way.'⁶

McLaren's recasting of the shop achieved his aim of opening up 430 King's Road to inquisitive young Londoners beyond the suburban Teds who had begun to bore him. One such was seventeen-year-old south Londoner Don Letts, a first generation Afro-Caribbean British sales assistant at the King's Road outlet of Jean Machine, the most successful of the denim-boom shops.

'Back in the day Jean Machine was pretty cool,' said Letts. 'There were all sorts of freaky and hip people working there: gays, dykes, drug addicts. We used to have a right laugh, going to all the parties and hanging out with the people from Alkasura and Paradise Garage.'

Letts struck up an acquaintanceship with McLaren, and benefited from his knowledge of, and participation in, alternative political and art movements.

'I was hankering after knowledge,' said Letts. 'For me, Malcolm joined the countercultural dots, helping me understand that the cultural developments which interested me didn't happen in isolation but were part of a legacy and a tradition.'⁷

Too Fast to Live's mordant worldview was very much of a piece with a new sensation gripping London's alternative theatregoers in the summer of 1973. *The Rocky Horror Show* was conceived by Australian actor Richard O'Brien, a Let It Rock customer who shared with McLaren a taste for the bizarre and a love of trash culture.

They moved in the same social circles and O'Brien invited McLaren to the opening of the musical – the cast of which included another fan of

McLaren and Westwood's clothes, O'Brien's fellow Australian actor, Nell Campbell – at the Royal Court Theatre in Sloane Square in June 1973.

The gender-bending show was an immediate hit, transferring along the King's Road first to the Chelsea Classic Cinema and then taking up a long residency at the King's Road Theatre.

Costume designer Sue Blane's mix of sexiness and shock and awe incorporated Too Fast to Live clothing in the production, including Campbell's candy-stripe pedal pushers and glitter socks, Paddy O'Hagan's leopard-print waistcoat (as later worn by Sex Pistol Sid Vicious) and, for lead actor Tim Curry in the role of the transvestite monster Frank-N-Furter in the film version, a badge-laden, chain-decorated leather jacket.

Never one to align himself with camp, McLaren wasn't a *Rocky Horror* fan. 'I liked Richard as a person, he was always very witty,' said McLaren. 'But I couldn't see what it had to do with us. We were much more serious in our intent.'

To McLaren's chagrin, the intention of making an anti-fashion statement by creating Too Fast to Live Too Young to Die backfired. The changeover was promptly noted by Catherine Tennant in a survey of World's End outlets in British *Vogue*, sending fresh waves of custom to the shop: 'At Let It Rock, which now has "Too Fast to Live, Too Young to Die" written above it, you can buy old rare rock records, black studded leather and glittery t-shirts commemorating such all-time greats as Chuck Berry and Elvis Presley – not to mention their beautiful Lurex socks.'

As well as mentioning the glam Nudie the Rodeo Tailor stylings on sale at Granny Takes a Trip, Tennant also praised local vegetarian restaurant the Chelsea Nuthouse, just 100 yards or so west at the King's Road end of Langton Street: 'Open for long hours, it's a good place to go for something that'll do you good.'[8]

McLaren and Westwood agreed, for it had become a regular after-work haunt for the couple. Here they became acquainted with Roberta

Bayley, a young American waitress biding her time in London after a trip around continental Europe.

'I had a little flat in World's End and they were customers; we got to talking about this and that,' says Bayley, whose photography was later to define punk and in particular its roots in New York's mid-1970s demimonde. 'Because I was in the neighbourhood I used to drop by the shop. I didn't think about the clothes very much, though I liked the drape suits and the socks. That was a cool look since, as an American, I'd never encountered Teddy boys.'[9]

Bayley was also friendly with the members of the Flamin' Groovies, fellow San Franciscans then recording in London and buying Let It Rock clothing as stagewear.

At the same time as she was waitressing, Bayley was earning pin money in stints at the box office at the Paris Pullman arthouse cinema in Chelsea's Drayton Gardens; here she had separately come to know Gerry Goldstein. By a coincidence, on Addie Isman's return to the US, McLaren had asked Goldstein to fill in at Too Fast to Live at the increasingly busy weekends.

'Gerry couldn't do it, so Malcolm asked me whether I was interested. I said yes and maybe worked there six days in all over that period. One time Marianne Faithfull dropped by to buy something for a weekend in the country with her boyfriend Oliver Musker. I can't remember what she bought, but it had kind of kinky connotations, and that's when I realised that there was something else going on there in terms of the content of the clothes.'

Bayley also accompanied McLaren and Westwood to gigs by Fats Domino and pub-rock ensemble Kilburn & the High Roads, where she was introduced to the lead singer Ian Dury, with whom she conducted an on-off romance. One day in April 1973, while Bayley was serving a customer, Gene Krell dropped by with news: Picasso had died. 'Malcolm said: "Oh good." I'd never heard anyone talk like that before. For a girl from San Francisco that was quite a revelation.'

As a counterpoint to the Too Fast to Live rocker designs, McLaren brought in a range of 1940s-style men's suits which were sold with pinhole-collared shirts and gaudy ties produced at the neckwear factory of Tommy Roberts's father and featuring saucy scenarios such as 'What the Butler Saw'. Once again McLaren's fashion direction had been inspired by Nik Cohn's menswear history *Today There Are No Gentlemen*, and in particular the chapter on the so-called 'American Look', the prevalent pre-Teddy boy British style modelled on the clothes worn by gangsters in Hollywood movies.

As detailed by Cohn, the trend had been promulgated by Cecil Gee, the Lithuanian Jewish entrepreneur whose Charing Cross Road store was a street-style mecca in the post-war era: 'The American Look was based on double-breasted, wide shouldered jackets, often pinstriped with wide lapels and big drapes. Gee was essentially a seller of ready-mades, the first Pop designer.' Cohn explained that this gave rise to the popularity of the zoot suit in Britain; like its US counterpart, this exaggerated Gee's silhouette 'with jackets halfway to the kneecap and shoulders padded like American football pros. It became the standard uniform of the spiv. By 1950, the whole American Look had grown delinquent implications. Gee's styles may have been ambivalent; his imitators were absolutely blatant. The ties had nudes on them and there were champagne-bottle tiepins'.[10]

Cohn's words prompted McLaren to research the Zoot Suit Riots, the uprising among young Mexican American swing-dancing soldiers during the Second World War after racial attacks triggered by their 'un-American' preference for excessive amounts of fabric in their civilian suits at a time of austerity.

This enabled McLaren to draw parallels between the zoot suiters, Teds and rockers – all railed against conformity in their choice of clothing and music.

The suits as signifiers of delinquency also tapped into McLaren's personal history, and in particular his experiences as a child observing Mick Isaacs carefully tailor clothing for the men of the Jewish community of Hackney in the 1940s and 1950s. And his grandfather would likely have broken bread with the customers and staff of Gee's pre-war shop in Whitechapel Road.

McLaren sketched two variants from old photographs: the so-called 'Alan Ladd' double-breasted version and the 'Jazz' single-breasted zoot. He worked with the tailor Sid Green on realising these, as well as sports jackets and peg trousers, in fabrics such as city stripe and gabardine from the Brick Lane cloth merchants Levy's.

Around this time Marco Pirroni, then a north London schoolboy and later Adam Ant's musical collaborator, became a customer and appreciated McLaren's understanding of garment construction. 'One time Malcolm fitted me for a powder blue drape suit with black velvet collar,' said Pirroni. 'He had the tailor's lingo and even the tape measure around his neck. He knew every detail and advised me on the exact proportions of the cut. Malcolm knew what he was talking about.'[11]

The photographer David Parkinson captured the Too Fast to Live collection of the summer of 1973 in a seven-page fashion spread in men's magazine *Club International*.[12] In collaboration with his partner Valerie Allam, who was then head of art and design at London's East Ham College of Technology, Parkinson prefigured the digital age stylist-cum-photographer, driving around town in his silver-blue Messerschmitt bubble car picking out strange props from rag markets, selecting non-professional models and scouting street-level locations.

For his Too Fast to Live feature, Parkinson photographed a leather-jacketed grease-monkey model in a peaked leather cap striking an Anger-esque pose with a bike in a repair shop. A spread showed a lounging fishnet-stockinged female partially obscured by a guitar-shaped mirror Parkinson had acquired from 430 King's Road, and a Brixton photoshoot incorporated a male model in sports coat, pegs and plain cap shoes being overlooked by a housewife figure in pink pedal pushers with a poodle on a chain. Across two pages, a glowering McLaren peered over the rear lights of a 1959 Cadillac while two men – one white, one black – posed against a billboard in an Alan Ladd and Jazz suit apiece with leery ties and overlong watch chains.

Since seeing *The Rocky Horror Show*, McLaren had mused about staging a musical based on Colin MacInnes's 1958 novel *Absolute*

Beginners, which centred on the race riots caused by Teddy boy aggression towards Caribbean immigrants. By the 1970s, *Absolute Beginners* had been long out of print; McLaren picked up a second-hand copy during his researches into London life in the 1950s. The 'outside insider' MacInnes – a middle-aged South African homosexual – was an acute observer of youth trends, and so *Absolute Beginners* and the writer's other London novels *City of Spades* and *Mr Love and Justice* were gifts for McLaren in terms of detailing the era's underclass street style and sociopolitical atmosphere. And, as if as a prompt, the *Absolute Beginners* narrator is given the line: 'My Lord, one thing is certain, and that's that they'll make musicals one day about the glamour-studded 1950s.'

McLaren's friend David Parkinson was also a fan; the *Club International* photoshoot, which was notable for using a black model, can be seen as a tribute to the stylised, street-smart world evoked by MacInnes.

Late one Saturday morning in August, just a few weeks after the publication of Parkinson's fashion story, a seventeen-year-old schoolboy dropped into the shop. Glen Matlock, a west Londoner, hadn't seen the *Club International* article, but was on the hunt for a pair of brothel creepers.

'It was one of the first times I'd been down the King's Road,' he said. 'I was looking for some creepers because, for a time, they became the thing for people who had been skinheads to wear, I don't know why. Then I noticed a pair in the window of this shop which seemed to have two names.'[13]

The Willesden Ted's space created by McLaren with Patrick Casey was still in place. 'It looked like my granny's sitting room,' said Matlock, who was scouting for part-time work since losing a Saturday job at Whiteleys, the Bayswater department store where Bob Chait had sourced the Lurex threaded trousers for Let It Rock eighteen months before. Matlock asked Gerry Goldsmith, who was behind the counter, whether any employment was available, and was told to wait for McLaren.

When he arrived, Matlock was perplexed by both McLaren's garb and behaviour. 'He was wearing some kind of rock 'n' roll suit, the sort of thing Jerry Lee Lewis would have worn – or more likely the duds you'd see on a young country buck in one of those dreadful 50s US musicals like *Carousel* or *Country Fair*,' Matlock recalled in his memoir *I Was a Teenage Sex Pistol*.

It was flecked cloth with zips down the side of the jacket – which looked absolutely horrible – and peg trousers. At that time no-one was wearing peg trousers. He was selling Teddy Boy gear but what he was wearing – drecky as it was – had moved on beyond that into something new.

Even before I had a chance to talk to him he was all round the shop talking to everyone. The strange thing was that he spoke to everybody with a different accent. Sometimes posh, sometimes American. What's up with this bloke? I thought. He can't seem to make up his mind who he is. By the time he got to me his accent was thick Cockney, all 'cor blimey'. He sounded like my granddad actually.

'Ere, what you been doin' then boy?' he said.

Working at Whiteleys.

'Whiteleys eh? That's where Brian Jones worked. What else do you do?'

I'm at school.

'Why do you want to work here?'

Well I need a job. And as soon as I'd said that I realised it was the wrong thing to have said.

'What do you mean?' he asked suspiciously.

Forget it, I said. For a moment I thought he was going to tell me to sling my hook. Then he must have changed his mind. 'Well, we do need someone,' he said.

And that was that. I was Malcolm McLaren's Saturday lad.[14]

Matlock was told to start in a couple of weeks, and left happy at the prospect of receiving £3.50 a day – £1 more than he had received at Whiteleys – working at a shop which opened at a leisurely 11 a.m.

When he appeared for work on his first Saturday, Matlock wore his best clothes: a three-piece corduroy suit with flared trousers from the high street chain Take Six. It was immediately obvious that this would not fit in with his new environment. 'I started wearing their gear: straight trousers, a mohair sweater and those shirts which were copied from a Vince's catalogue.'

But, on that first day, McLaren wasn't present. He was in New York promoting Let It Rock with Westwood and Goldstein. Just as Matlock's life was altering course, so McLaren's destiny was being sent into a spin by exposure to the dynamic city and its outré citizens.

Chapter 13

It was fellow King's Road boutique owner John Lloyd who turned Malcolm McLaren on to the idea of taking a stand at New York's rag-trade fair the National Fashion & Boutique Show in the late summer of 1973.

Lloyd had operated the glam-rock clothing store Alkasura from a King's Road site 100 yards east of Let It Rock since 1969, retailing a look based around separates in luscious fabrics – cherry-print satin jackets, shot silk waistcoats, velvet trousers – worn by such stars of the era as Rod Stewart, fellow member of the Faces Ronnie Wood and, in particular, Marc Bolan, to whom Lloyd was close.

Alkasura was a success, but Lloyd was troubled. He had fallen victim to drugs and become a religious obsessive, filling his shop with plaster cast saints and even installing a working font and doors taken from a church. For a period Lloyd became involved with a fanatical cult, which did not aid his already fragile mental state. (He committed suicide in 1975.)

'John would often be seen creeping around the lower end of the King's Road dressed in a monk's habit,' said McLaren. 'I liked John. He told me he was going to the Boutique Show with a few others from the King's Road; they had tales of getting big orders. It was also an opportunity to experience New York, so that's how Vivienne [Westwood], Gerry [Goldstein] and I ended up taking a room at the Hotel McAlpin to showcase Let It Rock.'

The trade fair had been flourishing in recent years; towns and cities across America were now dotted with unusually titled retail outlets selling flamboyant glam fashions. Tommy Hilfiger built his casualwear empire from running one such, the People's Place, in Elmira in upstate

New York, and the appetite for 'English' styles across America was huge. Those who flocked to the Boutique Show included staff from such places as A Long Time Comin' in San Anselmo, the Bead Experience in Baltimore, the Great Linoleum Clothing Experiment in LA, Bouncing Bertha's Banana Blanket and Jenny Waterbags in New York, and Mom's Apple Grave in San Francisco.

With Ben and Joe staying with Westwood's parents – as they did most summers – McLaren was extremely excited about spreading the Too Fast to Live anti-fashion aesthetic around the US. But, on arrival at the twenty-five-storey McAlpin, which occupied an entire block at the corner of Broadway and 34th Street in midtown Manhattan and was abuzz with hustlers, he discovered that the booking he had made was for a small single bedroom. 'In my naivety I assumed that we would have a suite of rooms,' said McLaren. 'But John came to our rescue and we joined him and the others from the King's Road at a Holiday Inn nearby.'

At the McAlpin, the trio decorated the sixth-floor room with nude photographs from vintage magazines *Spick* and *Span* and set out displays of the Jazz suits, ties, Capri-collared shirts, Vive le Rock panties and the détourned tops, to which had been added burn holes made by cigarettes.

McLaren dressed in his Let It Rock finery and attempted to engage with passers-by. Around the show were distributed copies of a flyer showing McLaren and Goldstein in front of the Too Fast to Live front-age and the line: 'Clothes by Let It Rock' with their shop and home phone numbers.

Interest from trade-show visitors in their odd wares was slow, though orders were taken from some retailers, including a Philadelphia store called Up on Cripple Creek and Ian's People, a Greenwich Village outlet which, when it moved to St Mark's Place on the Bowery, became Ian's and sold Let It Rock clothing to such customers as Lou Reed.

Ian's was owned by Frankie Pisaro and his wife Mariann Marlowe; they had been importing clothes from 430 King's Road since they came across Let It Rock on a visit to London the previous year.

Among the visitors to the fair was New York Dolls' guitarist Sylvain Sylvain.[1] Together with the group's late drummer Billy Murcia – who had died from an overdose in London the previous December – Sylvain (birthname Sylvain Mizrahi) had a background in the fashion business, having worked with Murcia's family for the Truth & Soul knitwear label. He had also hung out in London earlier in the decade and remembered 430 King's Road in its Paradise Garage phase.

The Dolls had recently released their eponymous debut LP and gained a reputation for drugged-out debauchery to back up their wild music, which drew on girl group passion as much as garage rock. At the time of Murcia's death, they had been touted as the next big thing, and supported the Faces at Wembley.

In August 1973, the Dolls were in their hometown for the duration of the trade fair, playing a week-long residency at New York's leading nightspot, Max's Kansas City, haunt of the Warhol set and visiting rock 'n' roll royalty.

'I always went to the fair if I was in town, so dropped by and saw this fellow dressed from head-to-toe as a Teddy Boy,' said Sylvain. 'Vivienne looked amazing as well and they were both very friendly, though when I said something was nice, he would go: "Ah go on, you can have it" while she would grumble at him for being unbusiness-like. We really got on well and then it clicked – I remember having gone to their store.'[2]

McLaren invited Sylvain back for the closing day of the fair; he brought with him the rest of the group: lead guitarist Johnny Thunders, singer David Johansen, drummer Jerry Nolan, bassist Arthur Kane and their associate Peter Jordan, who sometimes depped for Kane. 'They had some great things: Jerry Lee Lewis underpants and English-style 50s shirts, like Billy Fury and Adam Faith would have worn,' said Jordan.[3]

McLaren hadn't heard of the New York Dolls; in fact, he had been deliberately isolating himself from developments in contemporary pop and rock music since the early 1960s, having subscribed to his art teacher Theo Ramos's notion that musicians weren't authentic artists since they dedicated most of their lives to rehearsing and practising rather than committing to the spontaneous act of creation.

And McLaren was bemused when Johansen played him and Westwood tracks from the Dolls' raucous album. This put him in mind of another art teacher, Harrow's Ivor Fox, who was given to condemning student work by saying: 'Anything this bad has to be good.'

In this way, McLaren connected the Dolls to his grandmother's dictum. Confused as he was by the cacophony he heard, they certainly weren't boring.

'I was shocked by how bad they were,' said McLaren. 'How much it hurt my ears! And then I started to laugh – laugh at how stupid I was. By the fourth or fifth track, I thought they were so, so bad, they were brilliant. I was smitten – like my first real desire, first kiss, first everything. I had seen the Beatles, the Rolling Stones, the Yardbirds, the High Numbers, John Lee Hooker, Muddy Waters and Screamin' Jay Hawkins, but this was the first time I had fallen in love with a group.'[4]

On Sylvain's advice, Goldstein, McLaren and Westwood moved out of the 26th Street Holiday Inn to the more suitable Hotel Chelsea, long the haunt of bohemians, artists and weirdos. They hosted a party in their room attended by the Dolls and their entourage, which included the socialite Patti D'Arbanville, Bob Colacello, editor of Andy Warhol's *Interview*, transsexual superstar Candy Darling, actor Michael J. Pollard and Eric Emerson, the Warholite who had appeared in *Chelsea Girls* and *Heat* and fronted the similarly glam-punk the Magic Tramps.

'Our entertainment was our rack of clothes from Too Fast to Live Too Young to Die (we wanted everyone to try them on), a punch bowl, some Hula Hoops and the reggae soundtrack of the Jimmy Cliff film, *The Harder They Come*,' said McLaren. 'Guests screamed from the balcony of the hotel down to the streets below, welcoming everyone up. Some peed out of the window.'[5]

Nights were spent attending the Dolls gigs at Max's Kansas City and connecting with the city's demi-monde including punk poet Patti Smith and the face-tattooed 'Witch of Positano' Vali Myers. 'We had a very wild time,' said McLaren. 'This was the first time I did cocaine and also my first exposure to all sorts of sexual deviancy, voyeurs filming people being whipped, that sort of thing.'

Colacello invited the trio to the Factory, Warhol's centre of operations then close to Union Square Park. The great artist wasn't around but McLaren and Westwood were placed on two seats and videotaped answering questions. This was not one of Warhol's famed screen tests, but standard procedure for interesting-looking visitors. Westwood was shyly quiet-spoken in her answers; McLaren on the other hand was confident, though unusually downbeat.

This resulted in a plug for Let It Rock in Warhol's monthly newspaper *Interview*: 'Vivienne, a teased-out platinum blonde who favors blue mesh gloves, black ruffled skirts and "Vivid Violet by Elizabeth Arden" lipstick, wanted to know: "Who's this Halston chap I'm always reading about?" When told he represented the height of good taste in American fashion, she said, "I can't understand good taste. We like vulgarity." '[6]

At the end of the month the Dolls departed for Los Angeles and the Brits returned to London, McLaren infused with New York's street energy and ambitious to up the stakes at 430 King's Road. He also reflected on the city's sexual permissiveness in contrast to London's grinding staidness. 'When I was in New York I met many people who told me stories about people in the fashion business . . . of one photographer who had himself strapped to a chair and beaten to death,' said McLaren a couple of years later. 'That happens an awful lot in New York. There are many more cases. They are very big on S&M in New York, and it is mainly young people in their mid-20s. If you talk to them you realise they are prepared to go to enormous lengths to get what they want.'[7]

Soon after their return, McLaren arranged for partnership deeds to be drawn up. These formalised the creative and business relationship with Westwood and shared equal authorship in their designs.

Ever restless, he began to formulate a new direction for the outlet. Too Fast to Live had popularised their clothing, now worn as stage costume by countless rock acts and featured in fashion spreads and on record covers. But he felt that Too Fast to Live's reliance on suits and tailoring had taken them in too formal a stylistic direction.

'It was probably the worst mistake I could have made,' said McLaren. 'I just got involved in style, line and cut.' He complained that being too faithful to the past wasn't what had attracted him to the Teds and rockers. 'You know, the leather jackets, studded belts and leather studded skirts. It didn't have any of that raunchiness. It was clothing to pose in but not clothing to inspire action on behalf of the people.'[8]

Westwood had been just as affected by New York, and with McLaren produced a fresh range that took its cue from a book of the designs from the legendary LA lingerie outlet Frederick's of Hollywood. This was appropriated from a friend, the London-based American scenester/performer/writer Judy Nylon.

'They came to visit me and were absolutely enthralled by it,' said Nylon. 'That Frederick's book was pretty precious to me but I lent it to them and, of course, never saw it again.'[9]

The results were such suggestive garments as pink satin jeans overlaid with black lace and vinyl studded cuffs, as well as black mohair tops with swooping cleavages and pink marabou feathers that spelt out the word 'Doll'.

McLaren meanwhile was filling his notebooks with the names and addresses of traditional manufacturers he gleaned from telephone and trade directories. These aided him when he came to contact them direct and comb through archives for items to complement the new designs. This way of reactivating the old and forgotten – which was unheard of in the clothing business at the time but has since become standard practice – demonstrated McLaren's approach to fashion through historical research, even of the relatively recent past.

In November 1973 McLaren arrived at George Cox & Sons shoe factory in Northampton, about 100 miles north of London, and ordered samples for six styles of brothel creeper, including grey suede footwear with black interlacing and buckles.

'My dad told me that Malcolm turned up with an original pair of our creepers from the fifties asking if we could remake them,' says Cox's fourth-generation owner Adam Waterfield. 'In fact we were still actively producing them for the network of shoe shops around the country who had little dedicated Cox selections for their Ted customers, so it was a matter of showing Malcolm the range and letting him pick which ones he preferred.'[10]

The addition of new creepers to the shop's range was a great success. 'On Saturday mornings, you'd turn up pretty late and there'd be this queue of people wanting to buy the creepers which had been delivered from Cox's the night before,' said Glen Matlock. 'They'd all be gone by the middle of the afternoon.'

Matlock has related how McLaren once again returned to his fascination for wire netting for a window display. 'We made a waste-paper basket out of chicken wire and hung shoes from it,' wrote Matlock in the early 1990s. 'I had a day off and when I came back there was a big trophy sitting there in the shop. "Where did that come from?" I asked. "These people came in yesterday judging a competition for the best window displays in the King's Road and I won," he said.

'Not we won, you notice, but "I won". Thank you Malcolm.'[11]

McLaren and Westwood's visibility received a serious leg-up after a visit by the costume designer Shirley Russell, scouting for a dream sequence in her husband Ken's film of the life of Gustav Mahler. In the director's trademark overwrought style, the composer was to be presented as part rock-star figure/part victim of his overbearing wife.

'A visit to Too Fast to Live Too Young to Die – the rocker's shop in World's End, Chelsea – provided the perfect outfit for Cosima Wagner,' wrote Shirley Russell. 'Worked on a little and teamed with a German helmet and a pair of my old boots it had the perfect anti-Semitic feeling.'[12]

Russell chose a studded black tyre-sleeved shirt and a black mock crocodile skirt decorated with chains to be worn by the actress Antonia Ellis, who sported make-up – purple lipstick and accentuated eyebrows – akin to Westwood's in this period. As well as the Nazi helmet decorated with a flying 'W', Russell directed the film's costume department to add a large silver cross to the front of the top and studded a swastika onto the rear of the skirt. This made for an eye-popping combination. Summarised by *Variety* on opening as 'another maddening meeting of Russellian extremes, brilliant and irritating, inventive and banal, tasteful and tasteless, exciting and disappointing', *Mahler* provided powerful international exposure for McLaren and Westwood's design work.[13]

Meanwhile there was cause for great excitement at 430 King's Road; the New York Dolls were returning to the UK for a series of gigs before departing for continental Europe.

'When we arrived in London, Malcolm and Vivienne were there to greet us,' said Sylvain Sylvain. 'They were at Brown's Hotel when we got in from the airport. We hung out with them as much as possible. They gave us a bunch of clothes – I really liked the little black Too Fast to Live top with the zips and nude photos in plastic pockets.'

The group played provincial university dates before taping a performance on the late-night BBC rock show *The Old Grey Whistle Test* and a showcase gig at the ornate Rainbow Room atop Biba, Barbara Hulanicki's six-storey outlet in Kensington.

And they visited McLaren at his shop.

On a typically rainy, grimy London day, I stood by the jukebox glumly listening to the antique rock 'n' roll music, occasionally falling asleep to the whining semi-literate, pimply, racist wannabes debating whether to buy pink or yellow fluorescent socks.

Suddenly, a force-10 gale blew open the doors of my pathetic sartorial oasis, and in burst this gang of girly-looking boys looking like girls dressed like boys. Tiny Lurex tops, bumfreezer leggings and high heels, this gang with red-painted lips and rouged cheeks and hair coiffed high ran riot. They crawled all over the jukebox, destroying the neat racks of Teddy boy drapes in their wake. The Uxbridge Teddy boys were stunned into silence by this alien invasion.[14]

Le tout Londres was in attendance at the Rainbow Room shows, including Paul McCartney, and Sylvain wore McLaren and Westwood's lace-covered pink satin jeans and marabou-feather top, though Biba was enemy territory for McLaren and Westwood. Hulanicki's aesthetic was post-hippy deluxe, diametrically opposed to their street-tough take on fashion, and the Biba designer Kasia Charko noticed at the show

> some people there who got up and danced frantically and were really into them. They were not a Biba crowd at all, very different with a rocker-ish edge to them. Needless to say the place was getting a bit dishevelled as the set went on with a lot of chairs tipped and drinks spilled. The Dolls were very impaired that night and I heard later that they had insisted on a stash of forty bottles of champagne. I think they had indulged in other substances as well. They had also been on a rampage through the store apparently helping themselves to clothes. The head of Biba security had caught them but they were reluctantly let go.[15]

During *The Old Grey Whistle Test* taping, the low-voiced host 'Whispering' Bob Harris set the tone by introducing them dismissively: 'They are to the Rolling Stones what the Monkees were to the Beatles – a pale and amusing derivative', and later sniggered that the music made by the Dolls was 'mock rock'.

Not that the Dolls or McLaren and Westwood cared; derision from such establishment characters confirmed their direction. The Chelsea designer couple left for Paris with the group the next day, staying in the same hotel, the Ambassador in L'Opéra, and travelling with them to dates in Lyons and Lille as well as performances in the French capital's L'Olympia and Bataclan.

As recorded by Nick Kent, high-profile journalist for Britain's *New Musical Express*, the Dolls made an impact immediately upon arrival at the terminal at Orly.

Five minutes off the plane in Paris, walking up towards the airport entrance, and Johnny Thunder throws up. Bl-a-a-a-a-g-g-h-h!

God knows how many photographers are there: *Paris Match*, *Stern* magazine – all the European rock press and the nationals. The record company folks have arranged a special little welcome. Bl a-a-a-a-g-g-h-h!

The members of the band look stone-faced and wasted, wondering if he's maybe going to fall into his vomit.

David Johansen, who's always one to inject a little humour into any given situation, pulls out his best German officer impersonation: 'Vee did not co-operate viv de Naz-ees'. David finds this very funny. The massed media minions look just a little more nervous. Bla-a-a-a-g-g-h-h![16]

Such excessive antics delighted the un-embarrassable McLaren, as did Johansen's response during the subsequent press conference, as reported by Kent: 'The conversation turns to the Olympia gig. "I can't wait. I mean, when I think of all the great artists who have performed there . . ."

'Like James Brown?

' "No, like Édith Piaf." '[17]

During the trip there was much carousing at Jean-Charles de Castelbajac's huge apartment in rue de Trévise where the Dolls spent more time than at the Ambassador.

'The Dolls were already legendary in Paris at the time,' says de Castelbajac. 'My place wasn't prepared for such an invasion but we had many parties and a great time with the transvestite, glam-rock people who visited. I remember Malcolm told me before the Olympia show that David had announced he wanted to be Mao-Tse Tung, Marlene Dietrich and Maurice Chevalier at the same time. We worked on his outfit and did his hair together. He looked amazing when he went on stage.'

McLaren was regarded as an interfering irritant by the Dolls' managers Steve Leber and Marty Thau, who wreaked revenge when the Londoner organised a shindig for the Americans to celebrate de

Castelbajac's twenty-third birthday at the legendary Montparnasse brasserie La Coupole.

The Dolls sang 'Happy Birthday' to the young designer, and McLaren arranged for a birthday cake while a group of twenty sat down for dinner and revelry, but Leber and Thau quietly absented themselves during dessert. 'I suppose their managers thought that us Europhiles had money to burn, being foolish entrepreneurial shopkeepers who were running around after the Dolls, but of course I couldn't pay the bill,' McLaren told the Dolls biographer Nina Antonia. 'It was a banquet for twenty people, including all these various hangers-on. We had to run for it and these two young French journos got collared by the staff and slung back into the restaurant, where they had to find a way to pay the bill.'[18]

In early December the Dolls left for Germany and the Netherlands, wreaking more chaos. McLaren and Westwood returned to London exhausted by the excesses in which they had partaken but even more resolved to intensify the project at 430 King's Road.

Some indications of the new direction were evident in Westwood's participation in a feature in the London giveaway magazine *West One*. The magazine's editor Janet Street-Porter used the article to celebrate the capital's womanhood at a time of great financial strife. By the early winter of 1973 Britain was suffering the economic repercussions of the global oil crisis and political instability caused by the so-called 'Yom Kippur War' that October between Israel, Egypt and Syria. As a result, the UK was preparing for the introduction in the New Year of the three-day week (the government imperative restricting the supply of power and energy to commerce and industry).

West One's fashion team Pru Walters and Jane Merer chose eight females who expressed 'individuality and freedom. Women like these now make up their own minds about what they are and what they wear. Perhaps the rest of us should get the message and start being living fashion.'[19]

Captured in a series of portraits by fashion photographer John Bishop, among these so-called 'London Belles' were the milliner Diane Logan (sister of the artist Andrew) and a former Let It Rock assistant Shelley Martin, who both wore designs from City Lights Studio, and rocker Suzi Quatro. Westwood appeared in a Let It Rock pinstriped wool suit, ankle boots, tasselled stockings and a détourned Too Fast to Live Chuck Berry top.

Each was subjected to a questionnaire. While the rest of the responses were entertaining and informative, Westwood's were radical. She chose as her favourite book *Summerhill* by A. S. Neill, the rebel educator whose school of the same name her son Joe attended. Asked to describe her perfect day, Westwood – in contrast to Logan, who chose walking in the Tuileries, and Quatro, who plumped for 'flying around the world' – announced that her twenty-four hours would be spent with Valerie Solanas, the incarcerated radical feminist author of the SCUM (Society for Cutting Up Men) manifesto who had nearly succeeded in assassinating Andy Warhol in 1968.

Chapter 14

On a quiet afternoon early in 1974, a downbeat David Bowie strolled into 430 King's Road in the final weeks of its manifestation as Too Fast to Live Too Young to Die.

Occupying a house in neighbouring Oakley Street with his wife Angie, son Zowie and their entourage, Bowie had become an occasional visitor to the boutique over the preceding months; on one occasion Malcolm McLaren politely declined Bowie's request that he produce a T-shirt featuring the image of James Dean from the 1956 movie *Giant* adopting a Christ-like pose with a rifle slung across his shoulders.[1]

In this period Bowie was recording tracks for what would become his solo album *Diamond Dogs* at Olympic Studios, not far from Chelsea in the south-western suburb of Barnes. The LP marked a departure for Bowie, not only from the Ziggy Stardust character he had killed off the previous summer but also from working with his backing band the Spiders, who had supported him through the previous two years of stratospheric success.

A few days before Bowie's latest and, as it turned out, last visit to 430 King's Road, a bohemian character had arrived at Let It Rock with a large painting depicting the broken body of a rocker who had been thrown from his bike. The artist told McLaren he had been inspired to paint it by Too Fast to Live, and asked if he could prop it against the back wall while he made a trip to the countryside. If it sold, then McLaren could take a cut. If not, the individual promised to collect the artwork a few weeks later.

'Then David Bowie wandered in,' said McLaren. 'He looked utterly alone and miserable. I was on my own minding the till. Bowie browsed the leather jackets and studded tops, looked around the shop and ended up at the back, studying the painting.

'After a few minutes he said wistfully and to himself, with his back to me: "You know, a year ago, I would have bought that."

'And then he wandered out. I didn't see him again until we met in the 1980s in LA.'

This encounter was suggestive of Bowie's mood in that period of transition. As soon as he completed *Diamond Dogs*, the superstar left for America, ending his residency in England.

Similarly, McLaren was cogitating on his future in the wake of the sensory overload he had experienced with the New York Dolls in their native city and in Paris.

New York had made a particular impact. On a desultory day like the one of David Bowie's final visit, McLaren had doodled sketches of ties and braces on the shop ledger, interspersed with musings on Manhattan's lure: 'In NY more people ... bump into each other more often ... London – people trying to find a lot of interesting [crossed-out] people in one place. But if there's only a couple they feel they're wasting themselves ... people feel their own potential by way of a diffuse? excitement but they don't use it they just keep up the brightness until they feel tired ...'[2]

Now twenty-eight, McLaren was, on the face of it, running a successful boutique and conducting an extremely fruitful design collaboration with Vivienne Westwood. The legal ratification of their partnership the previous autumn appeared to have brought some equilibrium to their home life, with Ben often staying with his father or grandparents and Joe spending term times at boarding schools. Westwood's transition from suburban housewife to radical fashionista was complete, and she seemed in many ways to be the ideal partner for McLaren. After years of financial struggle and reliance on relatives, the couple enjoyed regular and secure income from the retail business. An indicator was the purchase of a car, a green Mini, driven by Westwood (McLaren didn't pass his driving test until the 1980s).

But McLaren's innate distrust of domestic harmony and inability to commit was marked by continuing airmail correspondence with Addie

Isman – to whom he had confessed his love – and also to friends such as Roberta Bayley, whom he was excited to find out had settled in New York.

With Let It Rock's popularity had come coverage in the national media, custom from some of the best-known names in the entertainment business and orders for clothing from such hip American outlets as Ian's in New York and the Los Angeles branch of Granny Takes a Trip, opened by the British owner Freddie Hornik.

McLaren and Westwood were now members of a hedonistic sub-stratum of London's glitterati, hanging out with the likes of Gene Krell and Marty Breslau, who co-owned the Granny's outlet in London. Both drug fiends whose shop was as famous for its pharmaceutical indulgence as it was for fashion – Keith Richards had become a close friend and Black Sabbath singer Ozzy Osbourne was such a frequent visitor that he bestowed upon cocaine the codename 'Krell' – they would barrel around town in the boutique's delivery car, which was adorned with a back-window sticker that read: 'Granny Takes A Trip – Clothes To Fuck Your Best Friend's Wife In'.

Also in McLaren and Westwood's swim were Gerry Goldstein, who remained as on/off shop manager, the former Granny's acolyte and street demagogue Bernard Rhodes, photographer/stylist David Parkinson, guitarist and customer Chris Spedding, and Tommy Roberts and Willy Daly of City Lights Studio.

McLaren and Westwood were also spending time with the *NME* journalists Nick Kent and Chrissie Hynde, who lived not far from their home in Thurleigh Court.

McLaren had met Kent on the New York Dolls trip to Paris and was impressed by the epicene journalist's March 1974 article on sexual ambiguity in rock. This described the Dolls as 'the only home-grown self-styled androgyny band left with any real chance of making the grand connection popularity-wise . . . their popularity has reached such proportions in their home town that the only way it appears one can get laid in New York these days is to be part of their entourage'.[3]

Conversations with Kent stimulated McLaren's renewed interest in contemporary pop music. 'He wanted to know about everything that had happened between 1963 and 1974,' Kent told Jon Savage. 'For him Billy Fury was the archetype. Malcolm was obsessed with Larry Parnes; he adored him. He claims he saw the Rolling Stones at Eel Pie and then stopped, was not interested. So I told him about the Doors and Jimi Hendrix. He started going out to gigs and clubs all the time, and he really researched.'[4]

McLaren sometimes accompanied Kent, Krell and co. on their nightly visits to West End rock hangout the Speakeasy. 'Then we would carouse at somebody's flat in Chelsea,' said McLaren. 'I remember this was around the only time I tried heroin. I snorted it and was as sick as a dog. I remember lying with my head in Vivienne's lap all night. She took care of me.'

Among Let It Rock's regular customers was a group of young west London teenage tearaways including best friends and former school-mates Paul Cook, Steve Jones and Wally Nightingale.

Jones in particular gravitated to McLaren. An illiterate kleptomaniac and music obsessive, the eighteen-year-old had similarly never known his father, and was brought up in an abusive home environment by his mother and stepfather. Aware of McLaren's music connections via the shop's customers, Jones – who had been visiting Let It Rock for a couple of years – was keen to forge a relationship.

'It was easy to see that he'd had a very confused upbringing,' Jones said of McLaren in his memoir *Lonely Boy*. 'I never found out exactly what it was, but some weird shit definitely went on with his mum and gran, and he left home really young, like I did.'[5]

McLaren later related that the first time he encountered Jones was when he chased him along the King's Road in an attempt to retrieve a garment the teenager had stolen. Yet he was attracted to the tough-talk-ing Jones's evident vulnerability, while the boy's tales of thievery and roguishness in regard to the opposite sex appealed to the older man's amoral streak.

'There was a generosity about Malcolm at that time,' said Jones. 'He had his fucking issues, same as we all do, but I couldn't help but like him, and I got a lot out of our friendship – probably more than he knew.'

Even though he didn't have a licence, Jones was a competent driver by dint of his serial car thefts, so took to ferrying McLaren around London's tailors and shoemakers in the Mini.

'Sometimes when Ben was away I'd tag along home with his mum and stepdad after the shop had closed to get something to eat and stay over in the spare bunk bed,' said Jones. 'Joe and I got along well. He seemed like a normal kid and we'd have a laugh together.'[6]

One of Jones's peculiarities was that he enjoyed stealing from his favourite musical artists: a coat from a house belonging to Ronnie Wood of the Faces; microphones from the set-up for Bowie's last stand as Ziggy Stardust at the Hammersmith Odeon; a guitar tuner and gold disc of Bryan Ferry's, all were added to his haul. In time Jones had amassed enough equipment for him, Cook and their mates to mess around rehearsing as a group.

Meantime ideas for transforming 430 King's Road flooded McLaren's brain. These were informed in part by his readings of the early twentieth-century German psychoanalyst Wilhelm Reich, who believed that societal problems were caused at root by sexual repression. Reich's 1933 book *The Mass Psychology of Fascism* had been subjected to reappraisal in countercultural circles in the late 1960s, and provided McLaren with a theoretical basis for a head-on confrontation with the repressive attitudes baked into British life.

This, he thought, would be a way of uniting his gift for visual expression with the radical views of his protest years. 'I wanted to extend the concept of Too Fast to Live into the sensual, the erotic, making sex the point of fashion,' he said. 'I explained to Vivienne that I couldn't bear the shop to be just another successful boutique. And I wanted to stretch the limits so thought about combining sex and politics.'

The three-day week hit British retailers hard in the first quarter of 1974. In February, McLaren took the opportunity to close his shop for a period of refurbishment. Matlock wasn't pleased, since the break in his Saturday earnings was extended over several weeks. And Westwood was quite reasonably furious. Finally, at the age of thirty-three, she had made a breakthrough in her career as underlined by her inclusion as one of *West One*'s 'London Belles', which validated her audacious contributions to the 430 project.

'I hadn't worked out exactly what I was going to do and that worried Vivienne,' said McLaren. 'She said: "For God's sake, why do you have to keep changing the shop? It was successful before! There's nothing to sell any more. You've got to go and get all those brothel creepers back in the shop, open it normally and just sell them, it doesn't matter!"

'I told her "The sign's gone now, everything's taken down, we're in the process, don't worry."'

McLaren had a notion to convert the ground floor of 430 King's Road into an environment inspired by the underground clubs he had visited in New York. 'I wanted wall-bars because I was trying to make the place look like a sex gymnasium, but had no money and didn't know how to employ builders,' said McLaren. 'I was scared that they would charge me a fortune and I wouldn't be able to pay them.'

He discussed his plans with the artist Andrew Greaves, who had modelled Let It Rock clothes for David Parkinson photo sessions in *Club International* and been a member of the now-disbanded interiors studio Electric Colour Company.

'We didn't get very far but I produced some sketches including an exterior which spelt out the name "GYM" in large capital letters over the facade,' says Greaves.[7]

McLaren also considered a much more convoluted title for the new retail experiment, from a sentence he'd read in a porn magazine: 'The dirty stripper who left her UNDIES on the railings to go hitchhiking said you don't THINK I have stripped all these years just for MONEY do you?' This, McLaren decided, would be written onto sponge sheeting in the style of the spray-can graffiti he had seen in Manhattan's Lower East Side. And his proposal for a window display was no less bizarre: the juxtaposition of a single thigh-high patent leather stiletto boot, white mice in cages and a caption reading 'Modernity Killed Every Night', a quote taken from the Situationist-friendly Surrealist Jacques Vaché, which McLaren had come across in the 1968 King Mob pamphlet *Art Schools Are Dead*.

While McLaren dithered and Westwood complained, many of their fashion retail competitors were investigating alternative streams of income as the recession bit hard.

Some, like Lloyd Johnson of Kensington Market's Johnson & Johnson, survived by pulling out of manufacturing new designs altogether and instead sold dead-stock styles from the 1950s and 1960s. Others, such as David Parkinson's friend, the clothing dealer Steph Raynor – who had hooked up with the jukebox dealer John Krivine to launch Acme Attractions from a stall in the King's Road antiques market Antiquarius – followed Let It Rock's path and presented cult clothing: double-breasted spiv suits, pin-collared shirts, exotic ties, Beatle boots, mod apparel and soul-boy plastic sandals.

Others turned to music. City Lights Studio partners Willy Daly and Tommy Roberts settled on talent management as a means of supplementing their income, since the record industry – though affected by the downturn – continued to enjoy impressive revenues from sales and live performance fees.

Initially the pair hot-housed a concept that achieved commercial viability within a couple of years: the boyband. Daly and Roberts determined to create such an outfit by recruiting the group via ads in the theatrical press. 'We had this idea for three or four handsome young blokes performing songs in singlets and shorts, throwing a medicine ball about the stage or skipping with ropes inside a boxing ring,' guffawed Roberts.

'We would do the image, the packaging, the clothes, and the rest would take care of itself if we got the right people,' says Daly. 'This was at a time when there was a wave of boutique rock. John Lloyd [of Alkasura] had a similar plan to manage musicians, I recall.'

Roberts concurred: 'A few months earlier I'd been down to the Speakeasy to see Alice Pollock [of another Chelsea fashion outlet,

Quorum] try and launch her own rock band and Malcolm was talking about how the fashion trade had lost its sparkle.'

In this period McLaren toyed with the idea of becoming a music manager himself after an encounter with fellow Croydon art school student turned musician Robin Scott at north London American-style diner Maxwell's, which he visited with Roberts and Bernard Rhodes in tow.

'They were trying to get into the music business,' said Scott a few years later. 'They saw it as another fashionable medium, and they were trying to find somebody to fit the bill. I wasn't for it.'[8]

For a while McLaren had thought about titling his shop 'Craft must have clothes but truth loves to go naked', one of the adages of the eighteenth-century proverb compiler Thomas Fuller (which McLaren misattributed to Jean-Jacques Rousseau), testing it out by spray-painting the slogan in gold on the lintel over the shopfront.

The Fuller quotation came from one of a series of missives sent to him by Fred Vermorel. 'I didn't think that Malcolm being a shopkeeper was revolutionary so decided to embark on an anonymous critique,' says Vermorel. 'I went to Westminster Reference Library and looked up various quotes about fashion and sent them to him on a number of cards. On each I wrote a sentence I had discovered. I didn't sign them. The "craft" motto was among them, as was the question "Must passion end in fashion?"'

In April 1974, McLaren expressed his growing disgruntlement with fashion retailing in an *NME* feature on designers and retailers providing clothing to pop stars of the period. Filed by Nick Kent, this included Granny's Breslau and Krell, Jean Seel of Alkasura and Antony Price, who designed for Roxy Music and their solo star Bryan Ferry.

Headlined 'The Politics of Flash', the article captured McLaren entering a transitionary phase. With Fuller's aphorism sprayed over the front in place of the now dismantled Too Fast to Live sign, the clothing continued to carry the Let It Rock labels for several more months. The chicken bones T-shirts were still in stock, but there were also rubber skirts ('pure S&M' according to Kent).

'Basically we're all artists and I felt it was time to get a more personal angle in the way of designing what the spirit of the 50s represented,' McLaren told Kent, before revealing that he had contacted R. D. Laing, the radical psychiatrist he had known in the 1960s, to design a range of suits suitable for both sexes.

'I noticed people like Alice Cooper and the New York Dolls coming in and buying clothes that I'd made for women, and that gave me an idea which germinated into a more transsexual approach,' said McLaren.

He revealed that he had given up on the 'Dirty Stripper' rebrand ('it was four lines long and people wouldn't have remembered it') and, in condemning Bryan Ferry's visual style, echoed what Westwood had told *Interview* the previous summer about her love of vulgarity: 'I think Ferry's stuff is too reserved, too "English" – I dislike how he puts it all together. I hate anything "chic" – that's terrible!'[9]

McLaren's attitude impressed Kent's partner Chrissie Hynde; later that summer she left the *NME* to work as a sales assistant at 430 King's Road. 'It felt more progressive to be in the orbit of two genuine eccentrics than churning out reviews,' Hynde wrote of McLaren and Westwood in her memoir *Reckless*:

They saw things differently from everyone I'd ever met. They had 50s stuff on the jukebox and 'Tell It Like It Is' by Aaron Neville. I doubt they'd even heard of the Buffalo Springfield and surely had never bought a Led Zeppelin album. I was intrigued. And they looked great, especially Viv, with spiky platinum-blonde hair, drainpipe trousers, winklepicker shoes and 50s rocker shirts.

Malcolm too had his own look, totally original and subtle, but you noticed: curly ginger hair, pale and sensitive looking, with an inquisitive, almost pervy expression of wonder. You knew this guy didn't play sports. It was all about the clothes; the clothes did the talking. If you saw Malcolm in any police line-up in the world, you would say, "Nope, I'd definitely remember him."[10]

Hynde's spell of employment at 430 King's Road was short-lived and ended in tears when Kent, suspecting her of infidelity, physically attacked Hynde on the premises, whipping her with his belt. McLaren was among those who witnessed the assault and after the elegantly wasted rock scribe was floored by a punch from an assistant named Adrian, Hynde was told her presence was no longer required.

'The Politics of Flash' prompted Steve Jones to increase his lobbying of McLaren to become involved in his group. But his tea-leafing proclivities sparked problems for McLaren's friendly rivals at City Lights Studio.

In the month Kent's article was published, City Lights went to the wall. Their music management plans having faltered, Daly and Roberts had reached a deal with bailiffs regarding a huge debt by offering all the remaining stock as payment. In this way they would have been able to walk away from City Lights scot free. But the settlement was scuppered when the shop was mysteriously burgled the night before the handover. Without any assets to his name, Roberts was forced into bankruptcy.

Roberts learned many years later that the burglary had been carried out – of course – by Steve Jones, abetted by his pal Wally Nightingale. 'We turned Roberts over, took every single bit of clothing that he had in the shop, shoes and everything,' said the unrepentant Nightingale a decade or so later.[11]

In the 1990s Jones confessed the crime to Roberts as an 'amend', to use the terminology of addiction recovery. Jones was under the impression that Roberts was forgiving, but this was not the case. 'I told him "It's too late old son, it's history,"' snorted Roberts, who never quite disabused himself of the belief that McLaren had approved of the crime. 'I won't go into it. There was a reason for all that. They wanted us out of the way. As it happens I'd had enough of it all anyway. I'd made my statement.'

In fact, as they were licking their wounds over the failure of City Lights, Daly and Roberts had joined McLaren for a drink in World's End local the Roebuck, a hundred yards from 430 King's Road.

In tow were Jones, Nightingale and Paul Cook. The budding musicians were now calling themselves the Strand. All knew what had happened in regard to the City Lights job, but not a word was said as Daly and Roberts discussed their financial problems and mentioned in passing they had given up on the boyband idea after holding a series of unsuccessful auditions in a large spare room at the Furniture Cave, a vast complex of antique and second-hand homewares stalls not far from Let It Rock.

According to Willy Daly, McLaren offered to take the Furniture Cave room booking off their hands. This was small solace for Daly and Roberts but an important staging post in the early development of the Sex Pistols, as the Strand became.

Undaunted, Roberts and Daly continued to pursue their management ambitions and represented in turn the demented performer Arthur Brown, who had scored a considerable hit in the 1960s with the track 'Fire', and, when that fizzled out, Ian Dury's more on-point ensemble Kilburn & the High Roads.

Soon, Jones's light-fingered ways caught up with him and an arrest for another burglary threatened to curtail his rock-star ambitions. Given Jones's serious form, the court would have doubtless taken an extremely dim view of his recidivism had not McLaren intervened on his behalf after the boy spent time awaiting trial in the youth remand centre in Ashford, Kent.

Latterly Jones has suffered from memory loss to the particular crime he committed and even the circumstances of his court hearing have been blanked out, though he believes it took place at Marylebone Magistrates' Court. What Jones does recall is McLaren's act of kindness in winning him a probationary rather than custodial sentence.

'Malcolm was the first person who'd ever cared enough about me to get involved in my life on this level,' said Jones in 2016. 'He gave the judge such a brilliant line of bullshit about what a bright future I had in front of me and what a great contribution I was going to make to British society that the guy in the wig let me off with a final warning.'[12]

McLaren's reference for the delinquent kid was a manifestation of his generosity towards younger people. Glen Matlock recalls trips around

London with his employer. 'Malcolm once took me to the West End restaurant run by Bill Green, who'd had Vince Man's Shop, where we talked about the history of fashion and music in the fifties and sixties,' says Matlock. 'He also took me to Le Macabre in Meard Street. It still had the coffin-lid table tops that had been there when Malcolm was going to Soho as a teenager.'

Matlock has also cast McLaren in the role of an older brother. 'Malcolm was impressive,' he said in the late 1980s.

You'd find yourself copying him and his mannerisms, as did everyone else. We'd hang out with him all the time. He liked being with Steve and Paul because they were like his bit of rough. He was a middle-class radical who fancied the idea of being around two real street kids. We'd drink in The Roebuck every Saturday straight after work. We'd sit around chatting then go on to gigs or to parties or out to eat. One time we went to the Last Resort in Fulham Road. Malcolm was pissed and agreed to pay for everyone's meal. He was never tight-fisted but it wasn't often he was that generous.[13]

McLaren had grown frustrated with the task of physically realising the ambitious plans he had for his shop and, by May 1974, was actively contemplating selling the lease. In a letter to Roberta Bayley, he stated his intention to return to New York for a longer period and revealed that he had written the lyrics to two songs 'one called Too Fast to Live Too Young to Die. I have the idea of the singer looking like Hitler using those gestures, arm shapes, etc and talking about his Mum in incestuous phrases.'[14]

It is not known for whom these lyrics were intended, but McLaren did reveal that he was 'still fuckin trying to sell' the shop, though he'd had 'no luck so far'. Not long after he sent the letter to Bayley, McLaren entertained an offer for the shop's lease from a Pakistani retailer who intended to install a sari fabrics shop at 430 King's Road.

The future of street style and popular music could have been fundamentally altered had not McLaren pulled back from the brink after a chance encounter with a neighbour in Clapham. 'This guy called Vic Mead lived in a tiny one-room apartment down the end of my street in Clapham; I walked past it every day on my way to get the 49 bus to Chelsea,' said McLaren. 'One day I happened to bump into him outside his place. He had handfuls of old film magazines. I immediately made a deal to buy them and told him if he had any more he should visit me at the shop.'

Not long after, Mead arrived with more magazines to find the shop once again closed and McLaren inside tinkering with the fittings. 'He asked me what was going on and I told him I didn't know what to do. I was thinking of having wall-bars installed like I remembered from PT in the school assembly room,' said McLaren. 'When I said I didn't know any builders he revealed that he was a trained wheelwright, a first-fuck-ing-rate carpenter. It was unbelievable!'

Importantly, Mead noticed that the dancefloor erected by Trevor Myles during the days of Paradise Garage was made of hardwood, so perfect for the wall-bars McLaren envisaged.

'Vic ripped it up and cut the planks into exactly the kind of bars I wanted,' recalled McLaren. 'We drove over to the East End where he had them bevelled. It was clear he understood how to make things. Vic in many ways saved me.'

While he toiled, Mead informed McLaren he had once harboured an ambition to be a racing driver. This was handy. McLaren was preparing to visit a number of fetish-wear suppliers he had located around the country through the discreetly worded classified advertisements that littered the back pages of various national newspapers.

McLaren's vision for the new outlet was that it would continue to serve a cult audience with bespoke garments handcrafted in limited runs by specialists. The difference between this clothing and that which had been presented for Teds and rockers in the shop's previous incarnations was that it would be overtly sexually oriented.

'I avidly studied those adverts in the *Observer* but the contact details were invariably PO boxes,' said McLaren. 'I would write to them for their phone numbers but that got me nowhere. They insisted on being visited, so you had to go there.'

The unlicensed Steve Jones was too much a risk as a chauffeur outside London, so Mead was given the job of transporting McLaren in the Mini. 'Vic became my driver,' confirmed McLaren. 'I would put together a list and Vic and I would go all over the place with a road map of England, hunting down these fetishistic characters. I was uncovering a secret world where preposterous architects would open their doors and in the back rooms they were making rubber masks, the most beautiful things with pumps to blow up and expand them like the Michelin Man.

'There were places where you would come across girls in white vinyl with short miniskirts sitting by sewing machines in the middle of wind-mills making rubberwear. Only in England will you find this. It was unique and, I thought, culturally significant.'

McLaren related how he visited one rich couple who had set up a small factory in the grounds of their farmhouse producing lingerie in rubber, and another in Dorset who were obsessed with oilskins.

On an occasion when Mead wasn't available, McLaren caught a train to a town in the north of England to follow up on a conversation with what he thought was a modest rubberwear supplier. 'At the train station I was met by a man in a Rolls-Royce, smoking a pipe, a typical, normal English guy,' said McLaren. 'I jumped into the car and thought: "Wow. He must be making a fortune out of rubber knickers." But he told me that this was just his hobby, he'd been head of a big betting company but they had fired him for turning up at work in women's clothing. And, as he changed gear, I looked down and realised he was wearing a negligee and carpet slippers.'[15]

McLaren also discovered a loose network of fetishists who banded together as the Rubber Duck Club when they met up and admired each other in their latest designs. 'And we ordered from John Sutcliffe who had AtomAge in Covent Garden, though their latex clothing was very expensive because it was so labour intensive,' said McLaren. 'A catsuit could cost £450.'

When McLaren discovered that his friends David Parkinson and Valerie Allam were visiting New York he persuaded them to purchase for him a number of black leather hoods he had seen at an underground sex shop on his trip there the previous year. These were added to the shop display, as were a set of rubber mackintoshes popular among fetishists, sourced from the north of England manufacturer David Marsh. McLaren and Westwood's visit to Marsh's Manchester factory is recalled not just for their unusual appearance but also for the fact that they paid for a selection in cash kept by Westwood inside her bra.

This journey was the only occasion when McLaren visited Tintwistle, the Derbyshire village where Westwood had been born and raised. 'It was tiny, a place with just a handful of houses,' said McLaren. 'Going there made me truly understand Vivienne.'

Around this time, a rainwear dress, which doubled as a belted mac and was made from ultra-thin ciré, was put into production at the shop from a design sketched out by McLaren. This was soon imitated by the main-stream fashion business. 'A woman's firm totally ripped it off for one of the mid-market youth fashion houses and made a mint out of it,' said Glen Matlock. 'Without paying a penny to Malcolm and Vivienne, whose idea it was. Well, sort of. They probably ripped it off themselves from a Hollywood still [in fact, it came from a catalogue reproduction in Judy Nylon's Frederick's of Hollywood book]. But that's not the point really. Theirs was a fully-developed idea and garment.'[16]

With the interior bars complete and latex, vinyl, nylon and leatherwear skirts, trousers, stockings and T-shirts providing the basis for the stock, McLaren and Westwood worked together in the summer of 1974 on a new range of complementary tops containing sexually charged text and images.

McLaren later said that along with Mead, Bernard Rhodes was an important contributor to realising his vision during this period of transition. Given to gnomic utterances on a range of subjects from reggae to radical politics, Rhodes was cut from similar cloth, though cagey to the point of paranoia whereas McLaren was an open book, whether about his dysfunctional past or the politics of sexual deviancy.

Rhodes too had never known his father and was born in the latter days of the Second World War in Stepney, east London, to a German Jewish evacuee. In the late 1950s and early 1960s he experienced the same pop-cultural wash as McLaren, making the most of Soho's night-life and boutique culture. Rhodes was a technically proficient autodidact, lacking McLaren's formal art education, and had been forced to survive on his considerable wits. By the time he was introduced to McLaren and Westwood by their mutual friend Gerry Goldstein in the mid-1970s, Rhodes was operating a Renault repair shop in north London and selling jackets and other clothing in and around the King's Road.

Importantly, Rhodes had recently acquired a state-of-the-art screen-printing press. When told about the new collection of T-shirts being planned, Rhodes offered his services. 'I brought the means of printing photographic imagery on T-shirts to Malcolm,' said Rhodes. 'Half-tones had only just become possible with silk-screen printing.'[17]

In the East End McLaren acquired from the Brick Lane cloth merchant Halstuck cheap rolls of plain cotton jersey in pink, peppermint green, lemon and light blue, and Westwood set to work devising the simplest of designs: she cut two squares from one of the rolls and stitched them together, leaving apertures for the neck and arms.

'This was absolutely super: two squares with the seam showing outside, not tucked inside,' declared McLaren. 'One size fitted all. It was sexy, subversive, the perfect frame to make bold statements.'

The stomach-revealing garment was used as the base for the new T-shirt designs printed by Rhodes and introduced over the summer of 1974 at the still-unnamed outlet.

The first carried a paragraph of text from Alexander Trocchi's novel *Helen & Desire* starting with the words 'I groaned with pain . . .' McLaren hand-lettered the words in italics in tribute to the cut-up method disseminated by another alternative literary lion, William Burroughs. 'Burroughs was a pop cultural icon if ever there was one,' said McLaren. 'In true Burroughs style I cut out paragraphs from Trocchi's dirty books and then appropriated one, brazenly copying it in my own handwriting across the chest of one of those square shirts.'

The Trocchi shirt represented the first formal annexation of text in the sphere of fashion. This had been occurring in fine art circles for decades. McLaren was of course familiar with that process, having integrated words into his artworks on the Goldsmiths fine art course in 1969.

Prior to McLaren, the usage of words in clothing design was the preserve of novelty, as in Mr Freedom's shirts appliqued with such deliberately banal statements as 'Pop!' and 'Wow'. By drawing on the work of the Lettrists of the early 1950s, McLaren transformed the T-shirt from humble undergarment into a powerful means of communicating social and political commentary.

And he didn't stop there. To further endow the 'I Groaned with Pain' tops, McLaren ordered that tears were made in the fronts so the wearer's nipples were exposed. He also had Westwood stitch ball and chain zips at breast level in others 'to add a sense of open lust. I finally felt I had arrived at the spirit of the outlaw in these clothes that clearly were anti-fashion.'

This opposition extended to the fashion establishment. 'The last thing we ever wanted was to be in *Vogue* or any other of those magazines,' said McLaren in the 2000s. 'I mean you'd lose all credibility. No way would you ever consider putting yourself beside Yves St Laurent et al.'

Michael Roberts, talented photographer and fashion editor of the *Sunday Times*, did not escape McLaren's abhorrence for the field's gate-keepers, even though he was the first to feature 'I Groaned with Pain' in national media, placing it on a square-jawed male model and pairing it with a gold hard hat from Biba. Soon after the photograph appeared in Britain's most prestigious weekend newspaper, Roberts was rudely expelled from the shop's premises and ordered never to return for crimes unstated.

Such was the contentious atmosphere of the shop. Meanwhile McLaren followed 'I Groaned with Pain' with another outsider design using found material, this time playing on the deep-rooted and racist fears within white society. 'A big, bruising, handsome, naked black foot-baller, would, I thought, if hung in the window, terrify the locals!' exclaimed McLaren. 'That is exactly what I wanted to do. This thought provoked me to do just that: print one on a T-shirt.'

This presented a stark portrait of the NFL footballer Maurice Spencer taken from an issue of a male physique magazine called *Bob Anthony's Beefcake*, which McLaren had obtained in a gay book store in Christopher Street during his New York trip the previous summer.

Spencer's large flaccid penis dominated the image, which, when his body was isolated on a T-shirt in lurid green or dark blue, made for unsettling viewing. Satisfyingly for McLaren, local residents complained when these T-shirts were displayed in the shop window.

However predictable the reaction, it persuaded McLaren of the appro-priate name for the shop: Sex. 'That is the one thing that scares the English,' he said. 'They are all afraid of that word.'

Later in life, McLaren rationalised the central preoccupation of the outlet he unveiled in the early autumn of 1974. 'As a child my mother had numerous lovers and picked up men at the Dorchester with me in tow; I was aware of this from the age of nine or ten,' he said. 'From the age of six I listened as my grandmother reminisced with her sister about the First World War and how fantastic it was because her husband was away and she could run wild and sleep with as many men as she wanted. She also used to tell me about procuring those young boys for Sir Thomas Lipton. Being aware of the notion of sex in this regard I became some-what fascinated with it from a fetishist point of view. In Sex I created the largest family with the most disorder and chaos.'

PART III

Sex, Style & Subversion

Chapter 15

Leaving 'Craft must have clothes but truth loves to go naked' on the lintel of the facade of 430 King's Road, McLaren sketched out a design for the letters S-E-X to be erected in front of it. The planks were cut at a local woodyard under Vic Mead's direction, pieced together, covered in sponge and wrapped in pink vinyl, recalling a Claes Oldenburg assemblage or typographer Herb Lubalin's early 1970s cladded signage for the New York flagship store of jewellery chain Georg Jensen.

McLaren co-opted Steve Jones, Glen Matlock and Wally Nightingale to assist him and Mead in the sign installation, which proposed a more surprising intervention into the public realm than the 2D black sculptures he had hung in Croydon underpasses as an art student six years before.

Beneath the sign, the three glass doors were no longer opened but fixed in position, their frames painted pink and the central access hidden behind a curtain. Each side displayed items in front of more curtains; sometimes the latest T-shirts, other times jumbled mannequin torsos. To the central door was affixed a metal handle sculpted to resemble a folded handkerchief with 'SEX 430' embroidered in pink enamel. This was designed by Electric Colour Company's Andrew Greaves and opened the doorway into a cloying environment where visitors encountered creepy, flesh-like latex curtains draped from the ceiling to the floor, the gym bars racked with sexual paraphernalia and walls lined in pinkish foam rubber to suggest a padded cell in homage to R. D. Laing's view that insanity is 'perfectly rational adjustment to an insane world'.[1]

Glen Matlock was by now studying on the foundation course at Saint Martin's School of Art. 'I'd asked Vivienne if Malcolm would be up for providing me with a reference as my employer, and she'd said that was a terrible idea because he'd been thrown out of more art schools than she could count.'

Due to his developing graphic skills, McLaren chose Matlock to assist him in decorating the interior walls of Sex with New York-style spray-can graffiti in orange, purple and yellow. McLaren selected these from Trocchi's porn literature – including the 'I groaned with pain . . .' paragraph from *Helen & Desire* – and statements from Valerie Solanas's Society for Cutting Up Men manifesto such as: 'Men cannot cooperate to achieve common ends because each man's end is all the pussy for himself.'

There were also slogans from May 1968, including '*Sous les pavés, le plage*' (Under the paving stones, the beach) and '*Prends ce que tu désires pour la réalité*' (Take what you want for reality).

The use of these exhortations was made timely by the 1974 publication of Situationist International images and text translated by the former King Mob kingpin Christopher Gray. These were gathered together in the compendium *Leaving the 20th Century*. Assistance in the form of graphics was provided by Jamie Reid, who had spent the previous half-decade operating the Croydon community printer Suburban Press (which also distributed his Situ-styled underground magazine of the same name).

The graffiti texts moved Sex beyond pastiche into more uncomfortable territory. 'Conceived as a parody of a conventional sex shop, its appearance mimicked the sleazy look of authentic sex shops, the kind secreted in red-light districts,' wrote cultural commentator Jane Withers. 'The central doorway was curtained to conceal the interior from public inquisition. It was deliberately intimidating.'[2]

Glen Matlock understood Sex to be an expression of McLaren's interest in what he described as 'secret worlds'.

'Malcolm saw rubber fetishism as one of the few remaining genuine underground cultures,' said Matlock. 'And he always wanted to be in on any underground culture going. He was like a kid making a camp under the dining table with some blankets and pillows. Everybody would be sitting there around the table having their Sunday dinner while down below the kid would think he had the only important world to himself. I always thought Malcolm was a bit like that kid.'

According to Matlock, McLaren delighted in joining clubs and secret societies, taking his sales assistant and friends to venues such as the Candy Box, the nightclub for Soho workers which opened at 3 a.m. that he had frequented with Patrick Casey during the speed-fuelled summer of 1971. 'A real den of iniquity, it was divided into several little catacombs. It was absolutely horrible but Malcolm would insist on taking you there because it made him feel part of some secret society.'[3]

McLaren's vision for Sex was that it was an assault on the mainstream. 'Fashion is only a cult that has been prettified and taken over by the big names,' he told the sex-education magazine *Curious*. 'Now the cults are the sex people. The leather people, rubber freaks, transvestites, shoe fetishists. The shop is about these people, it's for them and to cater to their needs.'

And his aim was that the appeal of the clothing would extend beyond the cultists. 'Why should it stick there?' he asked. 'I'm just taking the clothes further. In fact we're probably stopping making so much of the more "regular" gear and concentrating on the leather and rubber more. As I said, the shop is about real people. The shoes, for example, you can stand up in them, which you can't in some kinky shoes. It's all to do with the strength of the last.'[4]

This emphasis on quality was one of the hallmarks of the clothes produced for sale in Sex. Both McLaren and Westwood were sticklers for detail and finish, and he in particular delighted in tracking down skilled workers. 'To make the fetish women's shoes I found an excellent Italian shoemaker who used to be the maker for Regent Shoes, the store downstairs from the original Whisky a Go Go in the sixties; I remembered it as a thirteen-year-old,' said McLaren. 'This was a bespoke business in a workshop up towards Wood Green in a tiny strip of stores. He had a collection of old heels and lasts, so was the perfect person. You didn't have to purchase lasts, but could choose a stiletto, a club heel, a Little Louis heel, anything you wanted.'

McLaren also commissioned work from Dimitri, a repair outlet in Camden Town which produced custom-made shoes to order, and for leatherwear, Mintos in Caledonian Road.

'He had a little sweatshop, two people, him and an assistant,' said McLaren. 'I spotted some leather jackets in the window and thought maybe we could do something together.'

McLaren's fascination for the crafts and skills underpinning the fashion business was matched by his political purpose, as acknowledged in an interview with David May about the influence of Wilhelm Reich's theories on sexual repression and fear of the orgasm causing political suppression and fascism. 'If ideas like his became more significant then what I am doing here would appear to be very ordinary,' said McLaren.[5]

As an environmental installation, Sex was sensational; it literally assaulted the senses. The hectoring tone of the scrawls on the 'soft' madhouse walls, the heavy jersey of the T-shirts showing severe images and text in queasy colours, the lack of natural light which produced a dull shine on the clinical black rubber garments and the powdery-looking drapes, the clammy atmosphere, the 1960s garage-punk blasting from the BAL-AMi, all combined to make the experience unsettling, commanding commitment – a big Sex word – on the part of the visitor. When the door was closed, one felt less like a customer than a client entering a well-appointed dungeon, particularly when coolly appraised by the stern-faced Westwood.

By contrast McLaren was affable, ready to laugh and engage, evidently proud of the achievement. He would have cut a Mr Polly-like figure were it not for the weird setting and the fact that he was black-clad in transparent nylon top, leather jeans and dainty Granny-style high-heeled, lace-up, calf-leather ankle boots.

'Sex became a magical place,' wrote McLaren in 2009. 'People spent hours there; no one wanted to leave. In it, I created a feeling that was both euphoric and hysterical. You felt an enormous range of possibilities – that whatever was happening couldn't be predicted, but it was a movement towards a place unknown.'[6]

With the shop renamed, the exterior and interior recast and the clothing ranges replete with new designs – supplemented by such accessories as cock rings, tit clamps, body harnesses, leather hoods and studded wristbands – McLaren added a final flourish with the choice of labelling which announced each item of clothing as a 'SEX Original'.

'I ordered them to be made from an agent I found in Streatham, south London,' said McLaren. 'The ribboning was manufactured in Austria to the highest quality, beautifully woven in dark blue letters on a pink cloth background.'

Such detail acknowledged McLaren's rag-trade background. By some irony, at the same time as he was overseeing the realisation of arguably the world's most radical fashion venture, McLaren's stepfather and mother were exiting the business after twenty years, having sold their Whitechapel premises to a children's and women's wear manufacturer.

While Sex obeyed certain business conventions, and the most regular complaint among customers was over the premium pricing, McLaren's vision for the store was absolutely aligned with artistic practice, and the outcome not so much a commercial retail experience but a high-concept environment containing clothing as 'multiples', limited editions of original artworks.

Among these were 'flasher's macs' in light-blue gabardine and leather T-shirts with zippered necks. The predominant colour of the clothing was black, consistent with the anti-colour schemes of McLaren's early student artworks. 'Black expressed the denunciation of the frill. Nihilism. Boredom. Emptiness,' wrote McLaren in the foreword to my book *The Look* in 2001.[7]

McLaren's intention was that the new collection of designs would be as socially disruptive as the shop itself. 'Malcolm had always wanted to make a political statement,' said Westwood in the 1980s. 'The idea was that it was "rubber wear for the office", that to walk down the street in this stuff was subversive.'[8]

Although complementary ranges cherry-picked from previous decades were reintroduced – suede creepers, peg trousers, straight-legged Levi's and rocker-style leatherwear commissioned from the south London gay fetish emporium the London Leatherman – Sex represented McLaren's rejection of the historicism that had so far powered the retail business at 430 King's Road under his jurisdiction. Rather than take another leaf out of his touchstone, Cohn's *Today There Are No Gentlemen*, the new concept made a giant leap forward, distilling the elements of post-war street style and mixing them with new designs projecting provocation. In doing so, Sex adhered to the British designer Peter Saville's proposition that postmodern practice is a composition of 'the past, the present and the possible'.[9]

Every artistic vision requires a manifesto, and Sex's was realised in October 1974 just as the changeover was complete. One day, Bernard Rhodes arrived excitedly at the new shop. He informed McLaren and Goldstein of his wish to create a 'them and us' statement on a T-shirt, two opposing lists of cultural positives and negatives communicating the best and worst of English cultural and political life.

'Bernard was so incredibly earnest, always pushing the idea of every-body becoming a gang,' said McLaren, ignoring the fact that he had spent the years since leaving home gathering groups of people around him. 'He came in with this testimony where we publicly named people who were out and people who were in, people who were horrible and people who were cool, but his slogan didn't quite work, so we talked about it and added to the lists.'

A new headline was agreed: 'You're Gonna Wake Up One Morning and Know What Side of the Bed You've Been Lying On!' This was hand-lettered by Rhodes above two diagonally opposing typewritten lists, which had been expanded from his originals with additions made by Goldstein and McLaren.

'This was our first T-shirt for Sex; our manifesto,' said McLaren. 'The way it was printed was down to Bernie. He said: "If you put two colours into the screen it won't look flat, it'll have dimension," and he was right.

The effect was kind of wonderful. Blue on one side and pink on the other. As you screened them, each one would be different, so every time we would be making an object that was unique.'

Characteristically, Rhodes has been less generous about McLaren and Goldstein's involvement, despite the presence of content contributed by them. 'I created it, put it together, presented it and printed it,' he said bluntly in 2007.[10]

From this distance, 'You're Gonna Wake Up' can be seen as not only a multi-layered slice of invective but also a portrait of a divided country and fragmented culture. The recession sparked by the oil crisis had resulted in widespread industrial turmoil and an explosive political climate across the UK. Further, the general election of October 1974 – the second that year – resulted in an extremely narrow victory for the Labour Party, which had promised a referendum on membership of the European Economic Community (the forerunner of the European Union).

'You're Gonna Wake Up' adopted a Situationist literary style, in particular that of the UK's King Mob and specifically a panel on the inside cover of the 1967 issue of the short-lived and 'often confusedly anti-art' magazine *Icteric*, which was created by associates of the group and nominated heroes such as the artists André Breton, Giorgio de Chirico and Marcel Duchamp, the jazz musician Charlie Parker and the filmmaker Sergei Eisenstein.

As in the *Icteric* list, the declamatory tone, aggressive punctuation, satirical bite and use of basic typographical emphases such as the repeated forward slash and random capitalised text of 'You're Gonna Wake Up' combined to detonate a densely packed cultural device.

Hence the references to artists David Holmes, Mel Ramos and Patrick Heron (and his campaign against the Tate Gallery's promotion of the New York school of painters), the literature of such radical writers as Alfred Bester, David Cooper, George Dangerfield, Konstantin Paustovsky and Bernard Wolfe, the reportage of left-wing journalists Alexander Cockburn and Mervyn Jones, and the political activism of peace campaigner Pat Arrowsmith and IRA hunger strikers Marian and Dolours Price.

Such content shows that the compilers were looking to the contemporary: the *Guardian* published Heron's 14,000-word Tate critique over consecutive days between 12 and 14 October 1974, the Mervyn Jones article appeared in the *New Statesman* on 4 October and an Elton John quote regarding his birthday expenditure came from an interview published in the *NME* the previous week.

In the latter regard, pop culture dominated the content of 'You're Gonna Wake Up'. The 'wrong' side of the bed majored on such figures as Granny Takes a Trip founder Nigel Waymouth and his wife Nicky, the fashion editor Chelita Secunda, socialite journalist Anthony Haden-Guest, the girl-about-town Anne Lambton (daughter of a disgraced Tory peer) and the Chelsea-based artist Pauline Fordham (who had run a Carnaby-era boutique called Palisades). To these were added sacred cows of the old school from various areas: music – as well as Elton John, Bryan Ferry, Leo Sayer, David Essex, Yes, Rod Stewart ('Oh for money and an audience') and the BBC TV weekly chart show *Top of the Pops*; media – *Honey*, *Vogue*, *Harpers & Queen*; and fashion – Stirling Cooper, Jean Junction, Browns, Take Six, C&A and Biba ('Old clothes, old ideas and all this resting-in-the-country business').

There were no fashion references among the 'Loves' but a strong contingent of black musicians, as well as rock 'n' rollers, cults and a few contemporary acts. This category includes Eddie Cochran, 'Jamaican rude boys', Archie Shepp, Bob Marley, Jimi Hendrix, Sam Cooke, King Tubby's Sound System, dreadlocks and zoot suits, Jim Morrison, Guy Stevens records, Iggy Pop, 'Spunky James Brown', Marianne Faithfull, Gene Vincent and 'Kutie Jones and his own Sex Pistols'.

This was the first mention of the group, inserted onto the T-shirt by McLaren, who had by this time suggested that Paul Cook, who was a drummer, Steve Jones, then lead vocalist, and Wally Nightingale, a guitarist, recruit Glen Matlock as their bass player. McLaren also scored them rehearsal time at a community centre run by the residents of Covent

Garden, and made proposals as to what songs the youngsters should cover.

Then he advised them to abandon the Strand in favour of the new name on 'You're Gonna Wake Up' (according to Jones, only Nightingale liked it). Sex was of course a reference to his shop and other elements were inspired by tacky 1960s glamour mags strewn around it: 'Kutie' was a variant of the magazine title *QT* and the rest of the name was prompted by a publication called *Continental Keyholes*. 'I thought, "What goes into a continental keyhole?" and that's how I came up with the name Sex Pistols,' said McLaren in the 2000s. 'I saw them as sexy young assassins. The idea of "pistols" since they were only eighteen their privates were probably very small, so the idea of a little pistol was perfect. I thought that, yeah, they are going to go out and kill all the other pop stars.'[11]

In regard to the lists on the T-shirt, the plan was that 'You're Gonna Wake Up' would perform several functions: it would score points, settle scores (however petty, such as alleging that Fordham suffered from halitosis, or including David Essex because the pop singer's offhand attitude had once provoked Goldstein into flinging a pair of hefty brothel creepers at him), celebrate outsiders and generally create embarrassment and controversy among those who inhabited the London art, design, fashion, media and music scenes.

'None of that happened, of course,' said McLaren. 'It didn't matter what side of the bed you were lying on, as long as you were lying on it. Everybody was flattered, from Anne Lambton to Kutie Jones to Anthony Haden-Guest. It just goes to show how everyone loves to have their moment whether good, bad or indifferent.'

Now 430 King's Road was becoming a hive not just for fetishists but also for eccentrics and outsiders, the customers including the exotic likes of male model and art deco collector David 'Piggy' Worth and his friend the New Yorker Judy Nylon, the French tightrope walker Hermine Demoriane and Philip Sallon, a theatre dresser with a viperish tongue.

Chelsea's artistic loners also gravitated to the shop. 'One time a guy appeared with a set of gouache illustrations by Tabou[12] which he wanted me to sell, offering me a cut,' recalled McLaren. 'They were scenes of beatnik existentialists in fifties Paris nightclubs. One had graffiti on the walls with "Vive Sartre et le Coca-Cola" crossed out and "Vendu aux USA" (Sold to the USA) in its place. I loved them, so emptied the till and bought them all on the spot, hanging them in the window. They seemed to me to make sense in the context of Sex.'

Around this time, Cook, Jones and Matlock accompanied McLaren and guitarist Chris Spedding to a midnight showcase gig by Kilburn & the High Roads at the King's Road Theatre (home at the time to *The Rocky Horror Show*).

For the performance, the Kilburns' managers Tommy Roberts and Willy Daly had kitted Dury with clothes from Sex: a tailored 1940s-style double-breasted Alan Ladd suit, a pin-collared shirt and a tie made from peacock feathers. The gig was organised to promote the group's debut single 'Rough Kids', the B-side of which was a sing-song list of little-celebrated London locations entitled 'Billy Bentley (Promenades Himself in London)'.

In addition to the suit, McLaren and Westwood also provided Dury with a silk boxer's gown inscribed with 'Billy Bentley', as well as a matching brown Derby hat and a boxer's jumpsuit, to be worn during the performance of the song.

McLaren was impressed. 'Ian and Kilburn & the High Roads summed up the whole London arena of fashion, music and art at that time,' he said later. 'Tommy was expert in communicating that.'[13]

But, for the time being at least, McLaren was less interested in the London music scene – whether it be following Kilburn & the High Roads' trajectory or aiding the musical development of Kutie Jones and his Sex Pistols – than achieving his desire to return to Manhattan.

Now that every aspect of the refurbishment at 430 King's Road was complete, he saw no reason to stay. His ardour for former Let It Rock assistant Addie Isman had reached such a pitch that he resolved to travel to her in New Jersey with a view to renting an NYC apartment for them both, though this plan was kept secret from Westwood, as was his mention to Isman of the possibility of an engagement.

Ahead of his trip McLaren set up a series of meetings to negotiate wholesale and distribution deals for his and Westwood's clothing business, since the name change on the label from 'Let It Rock' to 'SEX Original' had caused no little confusion, not to say consternation, among some US fashion buyers.

There was yet another attraction. Acquaintances such as *NME* writer Nick Kent had kept McLaren up to speed on the exciting musical developments across the water. At home overblown prog, sappy pop and unpretentious pub rock dominated, but the British music press was now alert to the new raft of exciting groups emerging from the Bowery dive CBGB. McLaren's friend Roberta Bayley was soon to start working the door on Sunday nights when one of the most prominent of the new groups, Television, had a residency.

The trip would also provide an opportunity for McLaren to reacquaint himself with the New York Dolls who, he had heard, were not faring well. The chaos they generated with such ease had not abated and the Dolls' managers, already discouraged by the poor critical and commercial reception to second album *Too Much Too Soon*, were thoroughly exhausted by the band members' drink- and drug-addled antics.

Without regard for Westwood or their son Joe and her son Ben, McLaren booked a one-way ticket and informed them and his social circle that he was leaving.

'I said to Bernie: "Look mate. I'm off,"' recalled McLaren. 'I told him: "You look after this group while I'm away and check in with Vivienne if she needs anything." And the shop was all ready for Vivienne. I said to her: "You've got all the names, Bernie's gonna help you, everything's fine, see ya."'

And, like that, McLaren was gone.

Chapter 16

Malcolm McLaren arrived in Manhattan at the beginning of 1975 with a wedge of cash and luggage bursting with the latest designs from Sex.

'After all, I had been inspired by New York, so felt it fitting that I delivered those strange T-shirts and the other clothes Vivienne and I had made back to the source,' said McLaren. 'I was bringing coals to Newcastle.'

Staying with Marty Fromer, Trevor Myles's partner from the days of Mr Stud 'Em who was by now operating a thrift store near Washington Square Park, McLaren was unprepared for the drastic changes that had been rung in the social and music scenes since his visit with Westwood and Gerry Goldstein.

Sixteen months before, they had experienced the scratchy end of the 1960s Warhol era; Max's Kansas City was then the key nexus of activity and the New York Dolls were in their pomp. Now the Dolls were no longer the kingpins. Both guitarist Johnny Thunders and drummer Jerry Nolan had become seriously addicted to heroin and bass player Arthur 'Killer' Kane was way down the road to being a hopeless alcoholic (peppermint schnapps being his favourite tipple, drunk straight from the bottle on waking every day). Consequently guitarist Sylvain Sylvain and singer David Johansen were at their wits' end. The excess that lent a glamorous edge had curdled into grim reality as their presciently titled second LP *Too Much Too Soon* scraped to 161 in the Billboard Top 200.

'Being dropped by their managers meant they weren't getting $200 a week any more, which was a big deal to them for various reasons,' said photographer and Dolls comrade Bob Gruen, who met McLaren for the first time at the beginning of 1975 and was to remain a lifelong friend.

'The record company didn't know what to do with the band, and, on top of the album not doing well the promoters stopped booking them even though the tickets would sell. Johnny and Jerry were off copping dope and Arthur was on another planet, so they'd show up on stage two hours late and there would be a riot with doors smashed and seats torn up.'[1]

Most prominent among the groups that had supplanted the Dolls as media darlings were Television, led by the charismatic twin frontmen Richard Hell and Tom Verlaine, one handsome and heavy-lidded with spiky hair and torn clothing, the other sensitive and introspective.

They had kicked off the scene by being the first new group of note to play CBGB. After Television came the deluge, notably the Ramones, Talking Heads, Patti Smith, and Debbie Harry and Chris Stein's Blondie. When they weren't playing, these performers made up the audience, where they mingled with curious members of the previous generation of rockers, including David Bowie, John Cale, Brian Eno, Bryan Ferry and Lou Reed.

Meanwhile young music fans and camp followers Legs McNeil and John Holmstrom were launching a fanzine dedicated to this blossoming of talent.

Its title?

Punk.

Having visited Bayley at CBGB and checked out some of the new groups, McLaren made as his next port of call the New Jersey home of Addie Isman. As batty (and conventional) as it may sound, he intended to ask her parents for her hand in marriage, even though the couple hadn't seen each other in eighteen months.

'I caught the train and then a taxi way out to this mansion,' recalled McLaren. 'I was dressed in my clothes from the shop, but didn't care about the strange looks I received. I walked down a long drive and rang the bell, and was greeted by her father, who invited me in. He seemed a nice man, though cautious. Then I realised why. When Addie came down the stairs I didn't recognise her. She had had so much plastic surgery I thought it was someone else.'

McLaren had received no hint of this in their correspondence, nor the fact that the young woman appeared to have fallen victim to mental illness. 'I just couldn't handle it and when I started to make my excuses, her father asked me to stay, indicating that he would be happy for us to marry,' said McLaren. 'It was clear he was trying to get her off the family's hands, because she was so troubled and had obviously become a burden. I felt terrible for him, and sad to see her in such a way. We had written to each other about setting up in an apartment together in New York, but those dreams were all dashed.'

McLaren retreated to Manhattan, obtained a sublet on 20th Street and threw himself into the downtown scene, clubbing and socialising. He became a regular at the Hotel Chelsea, which was close to his apartment, and one day there he met Sylvain Sylvain, who brought him up to speed on the Dolls' travails.

'Malcolm told me that although he liked some of the new bands, none of them were a patch on the Dolls and, in fact, they wouldn't even exist if it wasn't for us,' said Sylvain.

The pair began meeting daily at Marty Fromer's shop in Greenwich Village to mull the group's prospects. 'I was introduced to Malcolm around that point and got the impression he had expected that the band would wear his clothes while someone else handled the business side, but that had all gone; they had no bookings,' said Bob Gruen.

Not according to Frome. 'He was just beginning to work out the kinks in the idea of the rock band as outlaws,' said Fromer in the 1980s. 'I remember late nights staying up talking with him. He would tell me incredible plans for something he called the new wave of rock 'n' roll. Instead of toning the Dolls down he wanted to make it more outrageous. I say he planned it, the whole thing.'[2]

Possibly as a diversion after the disastrous end to his relationship with Addie Isman, but more likely because his notions on the intertwining of popular music and visual style were beginning to coalesce, McLaren offered his services and threw himself enthusiastically into the task of revitalising the Dolls.

First, he sat them down for a session to clear the air of the gripes that were tearing them apart. 'Arthur [Kane], Jerry [Nolan] and Johnny [Thunders] promised to clean up their acts,' said Sylvain. 'David [Johansen] agreed to stop acting as though he was our boss, though we all took his point that we had to stop giving him reason to believe this. It did us some good.'

Next McLaren drew on the money he had set aside for himself and Isman, and paid for Thunders and Nolan to visit a doctor specialising in heroin addiction. And, again at his own expense, McLaren found a place for Kane in the Smithers Alcoholism Center of the Roosevelt Hospital, uptown near Columbia University.

This had opened two years before as the first residential rehab facility associated with a New York teaching hospital and was based in a forty-room, five-storey townhouse on E. 93rd Street previously owned by the US showman Billy Rose. Long before it became usual for every common-or-garden rock star to endure at least one spell in rehab, this was forward-thinking, not to say generous. Kane's weeks-long recuperation cost $800.

'I remember visiting Arthur there with Malcolm,' said Gruen. 'It did Arthur some good for a while. Malcolm was a great organiser, intelligent and very capable.'

There was no management contract between McLaren and the Dolls, and group members ever after resisted suggestions that this was his role. Johansen's line is that McLaren was his 'favourite haberdasher'. This may have been true and his association with the group was relatively short-lived. Nevertheless, in that time the Londoner fulfilled the creative and administrative duties that have enabled others to assume the title of manager.

Certainly McLaren's involvement has been downplayed, though he was a key factor in their career over a number of months, during which time Sylvain and Johansen wrote several new songs – many more than had been recorded for their second album – and the group as a whole accepted a radical new visual identity, playing around thirty concerts, including some which fans have said were career bests.[3]

'I thought Malcolm was a genius from the moment I met him,' said Bob Gruen. 'He was such an inspired and inspiring person. The first thing we did together were pictures of the band which he organised to be transferred into colour Xeroxes. That was the first time I'd even seen those. He'd met someone who had the capability to do it and I was impressed that Malcolm understood this was a new way of presenting the band, and also that he had the money to pay for it, because the prints were $3 apiece at a time when you could get a hundred for £20.'

As Thunders, Nolan and Kane emerged from their collective torpor, McLaren rented a loft on 23rd Street for the group to rehearse new songs and cover versions, among them the 430 King's Road jukebox favourite, Clarence 'Frogman' Henry's novelty 1950s hit 'Ain't Got a Home'.

'It had been wired and set up as a practice room by a group called Mandrill and was perfect for us, on an upper floor with high ceilings and huge windows which Malcolm washed down himself with a squeegee and a bucket of water and soap,' said Sylvian. 'Me and our roadie Frenchie held onto his legs as he hung from the ledge, cleaning the outside. Malcolm was like a man possessed.'

McLaren also applied his powers of persuasion to overcome promoter and venue-operator resistance by booking a handful of gigs in and around New York at such venues as Coventry and My Father's Place in Long Island.

These were tough places for a Limey music business ingénue. Sometimes placed in physically perilous situations, McLaren soon learned the wisdom of obtaining payment before the group delivered its set.

The 23rd Street loft meanwhile became a hive of activity. 'All manner of schemes were dreamed up there,' wrote Sylvain. 'All kinds of crazy ideas and wacky notions that we could sit up all night discussing, and it didn't matter that a lot of them would be forgotten by morning. We were communicating again, we were brothers, we were alive.

'Malcolm was in on these conversations, but for the most part he kept quiet. He might add a thought or two on occasion, but he was happy just to see the band become a band again, and it was only later I realised *that* was perhaps his most impressive talent.'[4]

Sylvain confirms that McLaren didn't charge commission – industry practice would have dictated between 10 and 20 per cent – or seek any return on his considerable investment, which included hiring a lawyer to ringfence the group from claims made by their previous management.

Among the new songs produced by Johansen and Sylvain was a loping, harmonica-refrained rocker entitled 'Red Patent Leather'. From this kernel, McLaren later related, he grew a full-blown concept, proposing the Dolls take a sensationalist new tack: in the spirit of reviving the Red Menace scares at the height of the Cold War, they should adopt the attitudes of card-carrying Communists. This political edge would wind up the media, help regain momentum and, he believed, make them relevant. The group's members accepted, some more eagerly than others.

'I decided to make them look not like girls, but worse, like Communist dolls,' said McLaren.

Red, patent leather Communist dolls. I had a fondness for all that Chinese stuff. Drugs and alcohol had seeped into their lifestyle and they were already past their shelf life. The music industry paid no attention to anyone who liked the New York Dolls, dismissing them mistakenly as homosexuals. It now continued to deteriorate even further.

The Vietnam war was just about to end and for me, red was the colour and I thought it needed to be their colour. Their lyrics, I felt, should have the word 'red' in them at least six times.[5]

Sylvain has disputed this, claiming that the idea grew from band members' simple requests for red clothing. 'Malcolm fired off a telegram letting Vivienne know what we all wanted, basically, a wardrobe full of bright red and shiny stuff, and then David said to Malcolm, "Hey, why don't we just hang up the red flag?"' recalled Sylvain.

'Malcolm and David were never especially close; it was rare for them to really connect. But at that moment they did. They were both silent, just looking at one another, and you knew they were both having the same idea at precisely the same time.'[6]

McLaren's order to Westwood included such Sex designs as vinyl trousers and tops, the 'Granny' patent leather laced ankle boots, leather and ciré T-shirts and gabardine trousers, waistcoats and jackets, heavy *Clockwork Orange*-style braces and trilby hats all, of course, in pillar-box red.

'The day the clothes arrived was like Christmas, two huge boxes with every garment conscientiously labeled with the intended recipient's name,' wrote Sylvain. 'She needn't have bothered. We piled in and pulled out whatever we could, then traded back and forth until we all had what we wanted.'[7]

In a press release headed 'What are the politics of boredom? Better Red Than Dead', McLaren announced a weekend of shows in late February 1975 at the Little Hippodrome Theatre, a midtown drag and comedy club.

The reference to boredom was straight out of the Situationists' play-book in regard to the alienating effects of commodity culture, and the rest of communiqué adopted the language of the hard left. The group's former managers were condemned as 'paper tigers', Mao Zedong's phrase for rivals he viewed as ineffectual, and McLaren made the tongue-in-cheek claim that the performances were 'co-ordinated with the People's Republic of China'.

'The New York Dolls,' McLaren announced, 'have, in fact, assumed the role of the "People's Information Collective" in direct association with the Red Guard.'

The release – which credited the production of the shows to 'Sex Originals of London c/o Malcolm McLaren' – mentioned that the Dolls had recently completed a film called *Trash*, 'the first Red, 3D rock 'n' roll movie'.

The short – actually a mimed band performance of new song 'Teenage News' – was the result of a hook-up with a Canadian film unit experimenting with a 3D filming process. Their request to film the Dolls as a demo test was accepted and a set was built on an abandoned film lot in Astoria, Queens. 'It dated back to the twenties or maybe even the teens, when Charlie Chaplin had apparently been filmed there. It was a vast room and freezing cold,' said Gruen. 'Malcolm, me and the rest of the band huddled around the arc lights trying to get warm while Arthur lay on the floor in the foetal position.'

The group was shot against fake brick walls decorated with such graffiti as 'Heavy Mental Kids' (a riff of Johansen's on the William Burroughs phrase). The group, dressed head to toe in the red Sex outfits, lip-synched and paraded amid an array of dustbins.

The new songs and visual identity, the satirical political edge and adventurous photography and footage, together with the presumptuous announcement of the Little Hippodrome performances, all these elements underlined McLaren's integrated and serious approach to the band's relaunch – even the tablecloths at the Hippodrome were red. And he revelled in the collaborative aspects of this effort, just as he had in taking part in street protests, in the organisation of the Goldsmiths Free Festival, the Oxford Street film and the realisation of the manifestations of the unusual fashion business at 430 King's Road.

'I think, you know, it's very hard on your own. You need a gang,' McLaren said in the 2000s. 'The gang gives you strength. I feel that the gang element is absolutely vital. For me, I can only work within a team, I have to work within a team, I can't work just on my own.'[8]

By early 1975 McLaren had recognised a fellow traveller in Richard Hell, and so made an ingenious choice in booking Television as support when a second weekend of gigs was added by the Little Hippodrome promoters. Television's presence, as well as those of African-American punk band Pure Hell and Jayne County – then Wayne – as DJ, helpfully connected the Dolls to the new wave of performers, but the support slot was as much a result of McLaren's admiration for Hell, who wore his ennui on the sleeve of his shredded shirts and ripped suit jackets.

'When I saw Richard Hell at CBGB he had on a perfectly groomed torn, holed T-shirt,' McLaren recalled to performer Nick Currie in the

2000s. 'His head was down, he never looked up, he sang this song "Blank Generation", his hair was spiked, he had a kind of nihilistic air, he looked contemporary to me, he looked everything that rock and roll wasn't. He had a poetry about him. He, for me, was very, very creative, he really was art, and I thought "That's exactly who I want to sell in my store, that icon!" That's what I was already selling, it was uncanny that I was tearing holes in T-shirts, making pulled-down clothes, deconstructing, and here was a guy who had done that with his own T-shirt.'[9]

In his memoir *I Dreamed I Was a Very Clean Tramp*, Hell wrote:

Malcolm was interested in the possibilities of rock and roll for affecting the culture. He was an artist and intellectual. I probably wouldn't have described him exactly that way at the time, but most of it was apparent at some level.

Malcolm saw that Television represented an authentic shift in purpose and style, and the part that interested him was what I brought. The Dolls had been a culmination of hippie communal values, of classic blues-based rock and roll, of quasi-effeminate glam, while Television were the beginning of the rejection of hippie values and the rejection of star worship (even ironically), replaced by a furious, if icy at times – and somewhat poetic – alienation and disgust and anger, expressed in the way we looked and behaved and in songs like '(I Belong To The) Blank Generation' and 'Love Comes In Spurts' (as opposed to 'All You Need Is Love').[10]

For the first three performances by the Dolls at the Little Hippodrome, McLaren chose support from Eyeshow, a performance trio fronted by another fashion designer involved in music, Steve Lyons. He had operated a boutique called Zoo in partnership with the pop star Peter Noone of Herman's Hermits in the 1960s.

But the *coup de grâce* of the residency was a red backdrop with a huge star containing a hammer and sickle logo sewn by Johansen's partner Cyrinda Foxe. This was hoisted during the Dolls performances. McLaren also involved himself in the Dolls' stagecraft, urging Johansen to brandish a copy of Mao Zedong's *Little Red Book*, housed in its distinctive red vinyl jacket and once championed by the Black Panthers.

Such flourishes overegged the presentation, and stodgy US rock critics, not known for their appreciation of visual flair let alone radical politics, were wary.

'The Red Guard hype seemed to be a put-on,' declared Alan Betrock in the monthly *Phonograph Record*. 'Almost all their new songs lack the lyrical wit and musical power of their predecessors. By comparison to most other bands, the Dolls are still an eye opener. The new Dolls are certainly better than no Dolls at all.'[11]

On the night of the first Little Hippodrome gig, Manhattan's rock-crit doyenne Lisa Robinson expressed her horror at McLaren's transformation of her favourite group. McLaren, however, delighted in Johnny Thunders's insouciant riposte to a Robinson query as to whether the guitarist was now a communist. 'What's it to ya?' sneered Thunders.

'When he relaunched the band like a rent boy regiment of the Red Guard, McLaren saw only the aesthetics and not the context,' opined the group's biographer Nina Antonia. 'The Vietnam War was still raging [in fact, the conflict was in its final throes]. The New York Dolls had already assailed the senses of the moral majority and suffered for it, but taking the Commie route was suicidal.'[12]

Despite the critics' qualms, the repurposing of the group was agreed to have been a success, with some fans, notably Chris Stein of Blondie, expressing the belief that these shows were among their best ever.

One of the Little Hippodrome nights coincided with the staging of the Grammy Awards, which were broadcast live from the Uris Theatre on Broadway. Attendees included John Lennon and Yoko Ono and a very strung-out David Bowie. Photographer Bob Gruen was there in an official capacity, and wore a Sex white raw silk double-breasted Alan Ladd jacket loaned by McLaren. 'I later read Malcolm say that when he met John Lennon at Max's one night, John had asked him for the jacket, and that I acted as intermediary and asked him to take it off,' said Gruen. 'In usual dramatic style, the story was that Malcolm gave me his keys so I could go to his apartment and get him something else to wear. That was all a dream of Malcolm's. I don't remember introducing John to Malcolm at any point and if they ever met I wasn't there. But it's true I did borrow Malcolm's jacket that night and there is a picture of me in it with John and Yoko.'

Staging the Dolls residency at the midtown theatre, however, hadn't been without its problems. One night Pure Hell's drummer was enlisted to deputise for the incapacitated Jerry Nolan, and the group's associate Peter Jordan was drafted in to play bass when Arthur Kane also fell off the wagon.

After the relative success of the Hippodrome dates, Kane emerged briefly from rehab for a concert at a disco in Malaga, New Jersey, but Nolan again failed to make it. Paul 'Ziggy' Goldberg, a Dolls fan who had attended forty of their performances, noted backstage that the band members were 'cranky and upset. In less than two years they'd gone from a sold out Felt Forum (in Madison Square Garden) supporting Mott The Hoople to playing before 50 disco fans at a bar'.[13]

After all McLaren's efforts, the Dolls were again in danger of imploding due to addiction, over-indulged egos and indolence. Just as he was to do in a similar situation with the Sex Pistols three years' hence, McLaren's plan to re-energise the musicians was to propose a mini-tour of the southern states of the US. This was to culminate in a triumphant return to New York for a weekend residency at the prestigious 4000-seater Academy of Music near Union Square Park in early May.

His thinking was that the trip would remove the musicians from the druggy miasma suffocating Nolan and Thunders and from the gaze of the hypercritical Big Apple rock hacks who presumed ownership over the group. 'By going to Florida, Malcolm believed this was a way of presenting the Dolls to a bunch of people who had no preconceptions and would either take to them or start throwing things,' said Gruen.

When McLaren discovered that Jerry Nolan's mother owned a trailer park in Tampa, Florida, he persuaded the group to use it as their base for the series of dates. On the group's acceptance, McLaren arranged the hire of an eight-seater Plymouth Fury 3 station wagon to be driven by roadie Roger Mansour, and the party headed south in late March 1975.

The journey was broken by a three-night residency at a small club called the Left Guard in Columbia, South Carolina, supported by NY glam-rockers Sniper, whose lead singer had been Joey Ramone and keyboard-player was Frank Infante, later of Blondie. At the Left Guard the Dolls put a brave face on proceedings by sticking to the Red Patent Leather set, wearing full red vinyl outfits, but bassist Arthur Kane was a mess – his alcoholism having returned in full force. Consequently, McLaren organised for Mansour to drive Kane to the town's airport, where he caught a flight back to New York and his incoming replacement, once again Peter Jordan, was collected.

McLaren's booking policy betrayed his inexperience and he relied in part on Mansour. After arriving in Florida, the Dolls played such cheesy joints as Dante's Den in Palm Beach and the Flying Machine in Fort Lauderdale, where the entrance was made from an ancient seaplane.

Nolan and Thunders were by now openly sniping at McLaren, whose goofiness the New Yorkers mocked. 'We went to the beach one time and seeing Malcolm there was hilarious!' exclaimed Peter Jordan. 'He was all peachy, all dressed up in these fucking clothes! I said: "Malcolm, you're wearing shoes and socks? We're in Florida, on the beach!"'[14]

There was also a residency in Tampa, and the group even delivered a set in the double-wide trailer which functioned as the lunchroom cafeteria of the Crystal Springs trailer park of Nolan's mother.

'We sat around night after night discussing the band's future, our future,' recalled McLaren.

The roadies told tales of their past adventures with the Dolls in Louisiana. Stories of them dressed in schoolgirls' clothes, feather boas, and spandex, paddled by the roadies in canoes through the swamps. The locals, Cajun rednecks, didn't understand. They thought the Dolls were still wearing their clothes from childhood and were too poor to buy new clothes that fit. Taking pity upon them, they offered Sylvain Sylvain and Johnny Thunders clothes fit for men – lumberjack shirts.[15]

After less than a fortnight on the road, Nolan and Thunders had had it. None of the drugs they had obtained fulfilled their craving for New York-strength heroin, and they were both contemptuous of McLaren. 'Malcolm's just a parasite,' said Nolan in the 1980s.[16]

Over dinner in the trailer of Nolan's mother during a row about the direction instituted by McLaren, the pair announced their intention of returning home, promising to come back after they had scored.

Johansen would have none of it, and announced that if drugs were more important than the group, it was over. He soon received a response; the drummer and guitarist packed their belongings, took their cut of whatever earnings had been made and high-tailed it to the nearest airport. 'Roger drove them, and I went with him,' recalled Sylvain. 'I'll never forget, as I was helping them take their bags out of the trunk I said to Jerry: "But what about the Dolls?" And he said, "Fuck the Dolls."'

The remaining members of the group played two more club bookings with a local kid, Steve Duren, filling in for Thunders on guitar; he would later become known as Blackie Lawless of 1980s metallists W.A.S.P.

Then Johansen, Jordan and Mansour followed suit and headed back to New York.

'So there we were, Malcolm and I, left with the Fury 3,' said Sylvain. 'We basically thought: "Fuck those guys" and, since Malcolm had never been to New Orleans, headed to Louisiana. He wanted to experience it all, particularly the music.'

There was an issue, however; Sylvain, like his fellow McLaren chauffeur Steve Jones, didn't have a licence. 'I'd never passed my test – you didn't do that sort of thing in New York,' said Sylvain. 'So we met a couple of girls who were hitchhiking and one of them had a licence. She got us so far to New Orleans and when they moved on Malcolm gave me the cash to take a test in a parking lot. We were shit-scared of being pulled over.'

In fact, the pair had toned down their appearance; it wasn't wise to wear red vinyl trousers, ciré tops and cute ankle boots in Cajun country. 'Those clothes could have got us shot,' said Sylvain. 'We stuck out like sore thumbs so hit up an army surplus store and bought khakis and T-shirts.'

In New Orleans, McLaren and Sylvain roomed at the Cornstalk Garden Hotel in the heart of the Latin Quarter and spent their days visiting record shops, music clubs and bars.

On seedy Bourbon Street the culture vulture McLaren acquired an unusual T-shirt: this displayed the print of a pair of pert female breasts on the front at chest height. 'I remember the shop where I bought it clearly. It was opposite a house in which, on the second-floor window, there was an open curtain,' he recalled. 'Every ten seconds a girl on a swing traversed the street in midair, her legs wide to an open crotch, and then back through the window and the curtain closed. It was a knocking shop and she was advertising the wares.'

McLaren was struck by the T-shirt's gender-challenging qualities, 'the way in which it transformed the wearer, man or woman'.

This was no accident. The so-called 'Tits tee' was originated as an art school project in the late 1960s by Janusz and Laura Gottwald, students at Rhode Island School of Design. Subsequently the Gottwalds scored commercial success when they put it into distribution via San Francisco-based label Jizz Inc.

The shirt was sold through a variety of outlets across the US and was worn by such performers as Alice Cooper, Iggy Pop and Rolling Stones drummer Charlie Watts. By the time McLaren bought his version, it had become a novelty item. Nevertheless, for the curious Englishman, its provocative impact was aligned with designs he and Westwood were creating at Sex.

While in New Orleans, McLaren tracked down a musical hero, the singer/songwriter/producer Allen Toussaint (who wrote among other classics the 430 jukebox staple 'Tell It Like It Is'). 'Malcolm found his studio phone number and called him up,' said Sylvain. 'He invited us to drop by and Malcolm told him I was going to form a new group with these guys he was working with in London. Allen was really gracious and said that if we ever needed a studio when we were in town we could use his.'

McLaren was horrified to discover he had contracted an STD from a sexual liaison, and the pair then made their way back to New York in the Plymouth, breaking their 1300-mile journey to stay at cheap motels. 'We had a fine time, bought great records, smoked some pot, partied with girls we met.'

On the road they talked about their respective futures and – as indicated by McLaren's conversation with Toussaint – the ways in which they might combine. The music management bug had bitten. After all, how difficult could handling a group be in the wake of the destruction wreaked by the Dolls? McLaren declared his intention to return to the UK and start working in earnest with the young musicians he had encountered through his shop. Maybe, as he had suggested, there would be a way to fit Sylvain's New York flair and sass into the line-up.

On their return, McLaren stayed in Manhattan for a few weeks, raising cash for his ticket home by selling the rest of the Sex clothes he had held over in a lock up during the trip south.

Cyrinda Foxe made an introduction to the hotshot guitarist Rick Derringer and his wife Liz, and they allowed McLaren to hold a sample sale in their brownstone on 12th Street. Bob Gruen bought a leather T-shirt with a zip at the shoulder ('David had come back from England with one of those which I really liked') and a blue gabardine overcoat.

'We kept hold of the station wagon and I drove him around various people I knew,' said Sylvain. 'We would park on the street and open up the trunk. That's where Debbie Harry bought some spike heels and black zippered tops.'

Harry had recently split from girl group the Stilettos and was in the early stages of putting together Blondie with her partner Chris Stein. British art director Steve Ridgeway was in town for the launch of men's magazine *Club* with McLaren's photographer friend David Parkinson, and recalled meeting McLaren with Harry and Sylvain at McSorley's on East 7th Street.

'Malcolm was pitching to manage her and take her back to England to join the others,' says Ridgeway. 'I got the impression that she wasn't too taken with the idea, but that he was obviously someone worth seeing since he had worked so closely with the Dolls.'[17]

In this period, McLaren also touted his services to Richard Hell, who had departed Television and was in the early stages of forming a new group, the Heartbreakers, with his drug buddies, the now determinedly ex-Dolls Jerry Nolan and Johnny Thunders.

The Londoner had been on Hell's case even while he was in Television. 'He told me that if I left the band he'd do anything to help me,' said Hell. 'I appreciated that, but I knew I didn't want anyone looking over my shoulder. Malcolm was obviously a strong personality and I wanted to be on my own.'[18]

Similarly McLaren failed to persuade Sylvain to join him on the return trip to London. 'I couldn't just up and leave; I was flat broke and David and I were still talking about our plans for the Dolls,' says Sylvain. 'But I gave him my guitar and Fender Rhodes keyboard. We agreed to stay in touch and if something came up, then I would come over. He promised me a ticket.'

On 11 May 1975, McLaren joined Sylvain, Bob Gruen and 50,000 others in the Sheep Meadow in Central Park for the festival celebrating the end of the Vietnam War. With performances by such protest singers as Phil Ochs and speeches from the likes of New York Democrat Congresswoman Bella Abzug, the event brought McLaren full circle from the anti-war demonstrations in which he had participated in the 1960s. A portrait taken by Gruen that Sunday captured him in a carefree, blissed-out mood, curly-locked in the white Alan Ladd jacket and holding a joint.

The next day, with a ticket bought from the funds raised from the clothing sales, McLaren caught a flight home. The word in certain NYC circles was that McLaren had to leave town quickly after stiffing the

Dolls' tough Vietnam vet road manager Frenchie over the 20th Street sublet. That's as maybe, but foremost in McLaren's mind was returning home on an evangelising high, loaded with the first-hand evidence of the scene that had so invigorated him. In later life McLaren compared himself to 'Marco Polo or Walter Raleigh'.[19]

Having checked the keyboard and a bag full of flyers and underground literature, his hand luggage consisted of Sylvain's white Gibson Les Paul Custom guitar, a totem of the lessons learned from his experiences with the Dolls.

'They gave me a fundamental belief in the strength and purity of the amateur over the slickness of the professional and the eternal devotion to an uncontrollable youthful urge to behave irresponsibly and be everything this society hates,' he wrote of the Dolls thirty years later, echoing the 'be childish' sentiment from a draft of his Goldsmiths Oxford Street film script. 'That became the legacy of the New York Dolls. It remains the war cry of the outlaw spirit of anything new in pop culture today.'[20]

Chapter 17

During Malcolm McLaren's absence from London in the first third of 1975, Vivienne Westwood forged a life for herself.

At thirty-four, she cut a stunning figure stalking the streets of west and central London, with her shock of blonde hair complemented by such Sex designs as rubber knickers and stockings and a porn T-shirt or a studded Venus top. In a photo session with photographer David Parkinson's protégé William English at the beginning of the year, Westwood proudly posed inside 430 King's Road in the so-called 'French letter suit', a head-to-toe catsuit in clear latex revealing every aspect of her body. Yet Westwood did not project sensuality or even the faintest hint of eroticism. Rather, English's photographs showed Westwood as a fashion antagonist against the backdrop of the gloomy drapes and a bizarre display item: a life-size sculpture of a human leg bloodily severed at the thigh created by a customer, Larry Daniels.

The photo-shoot took place at the request of English, who had frequented 430 since it housed Paradise Garage, for the photographic portfolio that formed part of his application for film studies courses at a couple of London colleges.

'Vivienne was friendly and happy to be photographed,' recalls English, who shot a single roll of film on a Nikon borrowed from Parkinson. 'After taking a few pictures I asked her to pose like a mannequin, to become stiff and awkward rather than the usual "relax and look natural".'

In the event the photographs proved a hindrance to English achieving his ambition. 'I was turned down by both colleges,' he says. 'During the interviews they just blanked the photographs, wouldn't even discuss them. In retrospect they may have thought I was aiming to get involved in making porn films.'[1]

With gathering confidence and a ready line in countercultural dialectic, Westwood was stepping out of McLaren's shadow, a reality confirmed by romantic flings with suitors including the young playwright Jonathan Gems. The son of a dramatist, Pam Gems, he introduced Westwood to theatregoing as well as to his friend Jean Seel, who had been interviewed by Nick Kent for 'The Politics of Flash' article in the *NME* and showed her how to cut patterns.

Jonathan Gems told Westwood's biographer Jane Mulvagh of her penchant for 'tough types' but Westwood also had a dalliance around this time with the skinny young art student Nils Stevenson, who worked on a stall in neighbouring Beaufort Market.

And by the time of McLaren's return, Westwood had recruited another effete young man, Michael Collins, as shop manager. Collins was a camp pretty boy with blonde corkscrew curls, who, in turn, hired a female sales assistant as traffic-stopping as Westwood herself. Pamela Rooke went by the uncompromisingly asexual name Jordan, and had been alerted to the existence of the peculiar boutique at 430 King's Road by mentions the previous autumn in *Honey* magazine. Behind a mask of dramatic jet-black eye make-up with hair whipped up into an exaggerated peroxide candy-floss beehive, Jordan adorned her buxom figure with flamboyant home-customised and Sex designs. Jordan was forthright and funny, delighting in teasing and remonstrating with customers (there are tales of visitors being overcome by excitement when in contact with the sensual materials in the changing room, and the staff having to clean up after them).

Jordan and Westwood bonded over their encounters with the perverts, fetishists and voyeurs frequenting the store, as recounted by Mulvagh: 'Once a customer trying on a rubber mask began crying for help. "You go, Jordan," said Vivienne. "No, you go." Eventually Vivienne went to the man's assistance, and from behind the screen came whimpers and slapping noises as he tried to unzip his face. When Vivienne emerged, flustered and sweating, the two dominatrixes lost their icy pose and burst into giggles.'[2]

Jordan became a King's Road celebrity, a Warholian sales assistant superstar who was feted with a mixture of terror and admiration by those who visited the shop. These included the national TV network newsreader Reginald Bosanquet. A Chelsea resident, Bosanquet regaled Jordan with gifts of flowers, and told her that his winks to camera while reading the *News at Ten* were signals that under his suit trousers he was wearing the black rubber knickers he purchased from Sex.

The shop drew a wider crowd than fetishists. In the US thrift bible *Cheap Chic*, artist Duggie Fields declared it to be his favourite store. Photographed in his pop-art/1950s/kitsch apartment, Fields described Sex's stock as 'porno embroidered t-shirts and humorous clothes. My idea of wearing clothes is to make myself smile. I like that in others. I don't think clothes should be serious.'[3]

Over the months of their employment, the sarky, sparky Collins and Jordan had emboldened Westwood; now she had her own gang, although this quickly became subsumed into the dominating McLaren's world as he returned to live at their flat in Clapham.

McLaren admitted that he was much changed by his experiences in debauched New York. 'I'd had very many sexual adventures; I mean I'd been like a kid in a candy store,' he confirmed. 'You were open to all these places which didn't exist in London, these gay strips like Christopher Street. Anyway, I came back much more enlightened, if you like.'

Meanwhile, Westwood's relationship with McLaren remained tempestuous. Ben Westwood and Joe Corré have recollected in adulthood that stormy arguments between the adults would sometimes escalate into physical altercations. 'I did used to get angry,' related Westwood. 'I used to hit Malcolm. One day he hit me back. That's the last time I hit him.'[4]

Nils Stevenson told Jane Mulvagh: 'Vivienne would boast that she'd given him a big slap over something the night before. And she'd lock him in a cupboard. But Malcolm loved that reputation. He got a kick out of it.'[5]

Curiously for such an intense person, McLaren was not given to displays of temper outside of the home. Throughout his life, socially frustrating or unsatisfactory situations were met by a sanguine phrase or two and manic gales of laughter suppressing the anger within.

For the first time in at least a decade, McLaren was at the cutting edge of rock music, and the shop was used to communicate this. On his first day back at 430 King's Road he dedicated space on a wall to posters, handbills and clippings he had collected in the US.

'It was like I'd seen the light,' said McLaren. 'I had all this material under my arms: "Hey! I've got the CBGB Television poster, I got the New York Dolls poster. Hey! I got this stuff, it would be great for the shop . . . what are you all looking so miserable about?" '

Collins and Westwood informed McLaren of a visit recently paid by Scotland Yard detectives investigating vicious sexual assaults on young women carried out over recent months by an individual dubbed in the media the Cambridge Rapist (the attacks had all occurred in the university city sixty or so miles north-east of London).

The culprit was notable for his leather-hood disguise. Since Sex stocked such masks – those brought back from New York the previous year had been replicated by the London Leatherman – Michael Collins was swept up by public hysteria over the case and had contacted the authorities and the press, convinced that he had identified the criminal. In turn, the police demanded the names and addresses of clientele living in the vicinity of Cambridge but were prepared to wait for McLaren's return since he was the leaseholder and Westwood, disapproving of Collins's actions, was not willing to engage with them.

Simultaneously, Collins had gleefully appeared in a newspaper photograph holding one of the hoods, proclaiming that he had solved the case (in fact, the innocent customer Collins had in mind was based in Yorkshire, 160 miles north of the location of the attacks).

McLaren confirmed much later that this wouldn't have happened on his watch. 'I didn't employ Collins and was bemused as to his reasons for becoming embroiled. My view was: "Why would anyone want to collaborate with the police?"' said McLaren. 'It showed Collins to not really understand what my shop was about. I told the police: "We're not at liberty to reveal this sort of thing." Just like the Hippocratic oath; there must be some kind of haberdashers' vow that says we are not allowed to reveal the privacy of our clients.'

The callousness of this position should not be underestimated. Stoked by intense press speculation, the Cambridge Rapist had assumed sensational proportions in the national popular imagination, and his attacks at knifepoint were reported in lurid detail.

The nocturnal attacker, a forty-six-year-old delivery driver named Peter Cook, was arrested within weeks of McLaren's return from America and, as it turned out, fashioned his hood from a leather bag, but by this time McLaren had created one of his most controversial artworks.

Speculating on the power of the garments now being sold at 430 King's Road, he organised the printing on the front of a dozen or so white T-shirts a stark monochrome photograph of one of the Sex shop's hoods.

McLaren's intent was not to celebrate the rapist's activities but to comment on the way Cook had made front-page news in the manner usually reserved for celebrities, pop stars and politicians. The artwork resembled the menacing image of a masked man taken from the cover of an issue of *King Mob Echo*,[6] the publication that aimed to stir up public emotions by praising the likes of Jack the Ripper and the child murderer Mary Bell.

Soon McLaren embellished the design with stylistic and satiric elements. Above the hood he added in decorative script with musical notation the first line from the Beatles' song: 'It's been a hard day's night ...' Given the ordeals suffered at the hands of the Cambridge Rapist's victims, this was brutal. Across the mask, in 'marquee' lettering with graphic stars picked out in hot pink and fluorescent green, McLaren emblazoned the name 'Cambridge Rapist' as though it were a pop star's pseudonym.

At bottom left he placed a professional portrait of the Beatles' manager Brian Epstein, who had died from an overdose in 1967. Next to that he positioned a pastiche newswire report suggesting Epstein's death had resulted from sado-masochistic practices. This stemmed from gossip McLaren had been told by the gallerist Robert Fraser, who had known Epstein well. Fraser was a prominent 1960s art dealer who made the connections between American pop art and the British rock scene, and was jailed for possession of heroin during the notorious police raid on his friend Keith Richards's country house Redlands in 1967.

As a student McLaren had visited shows staged by Fraser at his Duke Street gallery for such artists as Jim Dine, Clive Barker and Richard Hamilton (who depicted 'Groovy Bob' handcuffed to Mick Jagger in his painting on the Redlands affair, *Swingeing Britain*).

'Robert was right there, right in the centre of it, always wearing those ubiquitous sunglasses and he looked spookily cool,' McLaren told Fraser's biographer Harriet Vyner. 'He looked sometimes like a Hollywood film producer, sometimes like a very high-society drug dealer and sometimes like an art dealer, I guess. But an art dealer of a certain type – vaguely mysterious and cooler than cool. All that made you look at him in some way in awe and with a certain sense of trepidation and almost intimidation.'

By the mid-1970s Fraser was a fallen angel. One of his haunts was the Roebuck, the characterful local frequented by rock stars, gangsters and drug dealers fifty yards from Sex, where McLaren was thrilled to be introduced to Fraser by their mutual friend Gerry Goldstein. 'He was a major icon,' said McLaren. 'You were very conscious of what he represented. I certainly felt when Robert was around the presence of someone who was important.'[7]

And Fraser's knowledge of, and participation in, London's subterranean gay scene proved informative for McLaren when he added the Beatles-baiting elements to the Cambridge Rapist shirt. 'I wrote the press-wire report because I'd heard from Robert that Brian Epstein would visit Holland Park and liked to be beaten up in the bushes,' said

McLaren. 'Sometimes Robert would turn up at Charles Street in Belgravia at his house for a drink and Brian would have stitches which had been put in at a Harley Street clinic he frequented.'

In McLaren's mind, the Cambridge Rapist collage, which was double-printed, with one screen slightly off register to providing a newspaper-style shadow outline, was both a response to the media's obsession with Cook and a fine-art approach to a grim subject, in the manner of, say, Warhol tackling capital punishment in his *Electric Chair* series of the early 1960s.

Later, McLaren defended the design to the former underground journalist David May, who accused Sex's owner of exploiting the terrorising of innocent victims.

'Look, why treat [Cook] as an individual?' snapped McLaren. 'Why not treat him as a symbol of what is happening to everybody . . . I'm saying that if everyone did wear these clothes then this particular island, and all the violence that has been pushed down, would fucking explode!'[8]

In McLaren's absence another King's Road retailer had upped its game. The former Let It Rock supplier Steph Raynor and his partner John Krivine moved their second-hand outlet Acme Attractions from a ground-floor stall in Antiquarius to new premises in the basement of the antiques market.

This had been announced in a David Parkinson fashion shoot in *Club International* featuring Raynor, manager Don Letts and others in sharply tailored menswear.[9] The suits followed the trail blazed by the experiments McLaren had instigated two years previously with his Jazz and Alan Ladd suits. In this way Acme was post-Let It Rock, but offered a more inclusive and welcoming retail experience than that at the oft-times cliquey Sex.

Flagged by a neon sign at the top of the stairwell, Acme made the most of its new location. Letts sported dreadlocks – one of the first Britons to do so – and boomed out dub reggae while the scent of weed pervaded all manner of new and pristine second-hand clothes. The most popular lines were the winklepickers and peg trousers available in a range of materials, from pearl grey to electric blue and shocking pink, cut by Tony Daniels, one of the tailors used by McLaren and Westwood.

Many who entered via the dangerously steep staircase would become stars in their own right, including Chrissie Hynde, members of The Clash, Patti Smith and Bob Marley.

Acme's shift to the new premises marked the return of the King's Road as a destination for younger people – students, clubbers, weekenders – seeking cutting-edge fashions, and a parade between Raynor and Krivine's outlet and McLaren and Westwood's half a mile west became a regular occurrence.

A couple of weeks after his return from New York, McLaren was given a national platform to champion the foregrounding of sexual freedom at 430 King's Road in the pages of the *Guardian* newspaper. 'Young people are moving into enjoying fabric: the feel, the effect,' he told fashion editor Angela Neustatter.

> Nowadays people are far more sexually liberated than they were and this means they are prepared to show it overtly by dressing in a fabric which is very sexy and they can get a kick out of wearing.
>
> Certainly this will be called a kink's shop, but it is not entirely true. Certainly some of the fabrics used are identified in that way, but the fact that I have them made up into normal clothes, in colours hanging on rails out in the open is quite different to the idea of mail order and brown wrappers. I simply see rubber as a thing of the future – I guess it won't be too long before Yves St Laurent is using it too.'[10]

Stimulated as he was by his return to the fashion business at 430 King's Road, McLaren's dedication to involving himself in representing musicians was manifested in an approach to Ian Dury, whose group Kilburn & the High Roads had disintegrated on the departure of managers Tommy Roberts and Willy Daly and the lukewarm reception to their only LP, *Handsome*, released just before his return from New York.

'Malcolm's back in London and did I want to see him about management?' Dury wrote to Roberta Bayley in May 1975. 'I said I'd love to see him but certainly not about management or boxer's robes.'[11]

The return to England hadn't reduced McLaren's ardour for what remained of the New York Dolls. At a garden party held by the Chelsea fashion doyenne Ulla Larson-Styles, he bumped into the record producer Chris Thomas, a customer at Sex along with his wife Mika Fukui of the rock group Sadistic Mika Band.

Thomas had worked with such top-flight acts as the Beatles, Pink Floyd and Roxy Music, and McLaren also knew Thomas from his association with Chris Spedding's quintet Sharks, but it was the rawer, more street-edged sound achieved for the Kilburn & the High Roads single 'Rough Kids' that impressed him most.

'I walked in, and it was like everybody I had ever met in my life was there,' Thomas told journalists Stuart Grundy and John Tobler in the 1980s. 'Nico, Bryan Ferry, John Cale, even an actor from the Royal Shakespeare Company who I'd met in Japan, but who I hadn't seen for years. A really weird day, and that was where Malcolm McLaren asked me whether I'd be interested in recording the New York Dolls.'[12]

McLaren's sojourn in America had severed many of the ties to his 1960s life; the countercultural connector Henry Adler was out of his swim, Patrick Casey was long disappeared and, for the time being, he socialised with Fred Vermorel intermittently, though had incorporated the line 'Must passion end in fashion?' – from one of the postcards sent by his Harrow Art School friend the previous year – among the graffiti on the walls inside Sex.

It was, after all, a pertinent inquiry.

Meanwhile Jamie Reid had given up publishing the agitating underground paper *Suburban Press* and moved off-grid to the Outer Hebrides. Robin Scott remained in sporadic contact and Helen Mininberg – by this time Helen Wellington Lloyd, having married to obtain British citizenship, like her fellow Goldsmiths student Jocelyn Hakim before her – had only recently returned from a stay in South Africa.

Now Sex was attracting more and more younger customers, some of whom were as interested in the display about new music from New York as the unusual fashions hanging from the racks. McLaren's dream from the earliest days of his occupation of 430 King's Road of creating a place for the exchange of exciting ideas – 'a centre where people can meet and talk' – was reaching fruition.

'Suddenly the shop was like a sort of information centre,' boasted McLaren. 'It had a kind of magic because it was different from all those other King's Road shops. This bomb of fashion and music that I brought back would set alight London, reigniting the energy and excitement of what I had experienced with the Dolls in America.'[13]

Among the fresh set of visitors that summer was the nineteen-year-old Islington Anglo-Irish youth John Lydon, who favoured the store 'because it was so fucking different. I thought it was good gear. It says something good about someone who'll wear that kind of gear and fucking fight back if someone laughs at them.'[14]

Lydon was a member of a gang of north-east London youths who had met at various colleges of further education and shared the first name: the others were Lydon's friend John Gray, John Ritchie (later Sid Vicious) and John Wardle.

The latter – who became the prominent bass player and performer Jah Wobble – had already been made aware of Sex by a girlfriend. 'Margaux was very stylish and had been going there since it was Let It Rock,' says Wardle. 'The shop was confrontational but very interesting, heavy with references.'[15]

Other visitors included Susan Ballion (later Siouxsie Sioux). Then eighteen, she bought such lines as stilettos in transparent pink and also commissioned Westwood to make for her a pair of fishnet tights adorned with gold tassels. Her friend Steven Bailey (later Severin, the guitarist in their group the Banshees) believed that the shop's prices spurred on punk's coming DIY ethic. 'Only those with rich parents could afford Sex clothes,' he opined later. 'That's when all the home-made thing started. There were plenty of jumble sales around where you could pick up bits and transform them into something else.'[16]

Boy George – then fourteen-year-old George O'Dowd – agrees: 'The clothes were expensive so we used to sequin, bead, stitch, dye, print and alter Oxfam clothes. Then we'd parade down the King's Road, and dare each other to go into Sex.'[17]

Many years later, McLaren sought to explain why Sex was attracting this new crowd: 'Sex translated in fashion becomes fetish, and fetishism is the very embodiment of youth. Youth has to behave irreverently – it has to take drugs because of its fundamental belief in its immortality, which it needs to assert over and over again. Fashion and music are the natural expressions of youth's need for confrontation and rebellion, and fetishism in both is its necessary razor's edge, the exhilarating border between life and death.'[18]

Certain clientele was not so welcome. The story was put about that Mick Jagger had tried to enter the shop but the door was slammed in his face in a gesture of defiance to the old order. 'Now, this is all total fantasy,' Jagger told the *NME*. 'I don't even know where the Sex shop is . . . Hold on, I vaguely recall where Let It Rock used to be. But there's a lot of clothes shops in the King's Road, dear, and I've seen 'em all come and go. No one ever slams the door on me in the King's Road. They all know I'm the only one who's got any money to spend on their crappy clothes. Though even I would draw the line on spending money on torn T-shirts.'[19]

Soon after McLaren's return in the spring of 1975, members of the rabble-rousing Scottish rock group the Sensational Alex Harvey Band, a favourite act of Glen Matlock's, arrived to browse the stock. 'I was chuffed when they came in, and was serving away when Malcolm started getting really edgy,' said Matlock. 'He told me to get rid of them, so I had to tell them we were closing early. Once they were gone, he insisted that they were tax inspectors on the snoop. I kept telling him they were a big rock band, but he wouldn't have it.'

A few weeks later, Matlock coerced McLaren and Bernard Rhodes into accompanying him to a Sensational Alex Harvey Band performance at major London venue the Hammersmith Odeon. 'It was absolutely packed with kids going mad; that's when I think the penny dropped with Malcolm,' said Matlock. 'It coincided with us getting the band together and being more on the case.'

In McLaren's absence, Matlock, Paul Cook, Steve Jones and Wally Nightingale had developed musically with Rhodes's encouragement, performing live at a birthday party at the Chelsea wine bar owned by Tom Salter, the previous leaseholder of 430 King's Road. They also benefited from an arrangement engineered by Nightingale's father that enabled a permanent rehearsal space on a sound stage in a disused part of BBC-owned studios in Hammersmith.

The collapse of the Dolls had whetted McLaren's appetite; in his view, packaging and managing a provocative new group would be as valid a means of making artistic statements as the disciplines he had experimented with earlier, from painting and 3D objects to environments and fashion.

'I didn't think that if I wanted to be a sculptor I necessarily needed clay,' said McLaren many years later. 'I suddenly thought, "You can use people." And it's people that I used like an artist. I manipulated. So creating something called the Sex Pistols was my painting, my sculpture.'[20]

Customer Ben Kelly, who had graduated from the Royal College and was starting his journey to becoming one of the UK's most prominent interior designers, recalls McLaren's enthusiasm.

'One day when I dropped by, Malcolm was crouched down fixing one of the front doors,' says Kelly. 'I clearly remember him looking up at me and saying: "I've got this band, they're called the Sex Pistols." I was astounded: "They're called what??!!" I could barely believe what I'd heard. The juxtaposition of those two words was incredible.'[21]

McLaren took to visiting the youngsters regularly, encouraging them to write new songs and pitching ideas for covers to practise. They came up with a couple of compositions and worked up versions of such 1960s tracks as the Foundations' 'Build Me Up Buttercup', Love Affair's 'A Day Without Love', Marianne Faithfull's Jagger/Richards classic 'As Tears Go By' and songs by The Who and the Small Faces.

But McLaren wasn't interested in the quartet graduating into just another rock band. Driven by his grandmother's twin tenets 'To be bad is good, because to be good is simply boring' and 'Boys will be boys', his ambition was that Kutie Jones and the Sex Pistols should aim for mass appeal by becoming the street's alternative to the manufactured Bay City Rollers, the Scottish boyband that had stormed the charts during his absence in New York.

It was the popular response to that group's visual presentation that intrigued McLaren. Masterminded by the calculating – and later disgraced – music business maverick Tam Paton, the Rollers wore tartan-customised outfits which were emulated by thousands of teenage, and predominantly female, fans across Britain. It helped that the Rollers' costume designer Bambi Ballard was an acquaintance of McLaren's. She introduced him to the group's bass player Stuart 'Woody' Wood at a party at her north London house around this time.

'He asked me about the fans, our look and the tartan and even how Tam Paton was managing us and how he got us a deal,' said Wood in 2018. 'It was pretty obvious he was wanting to put a Rollers together – but a different type of Rollers.'[22]

McLaren insisted the nascent Pistols embrace the attitudes of not only the New York Dolls – not a stretch since all were enthusiasts having witnessed the 1972 Wembley support slot for the Faces – but more importantly the newer NYC acts, showing them Roberta Bayley's striking portrait of the first line-up of the Heartbreakers wearing white shirts smeared with ketchup to resemble gunshot wounds.

And McLaren maintained correspondence with Richard Hell and Sylvain Sylvain, urging them to visit London and throw their respective lots in with him and the rehearsal group, but to no avail. In July 1975 Sylvain joined David Johansen and others in reforming the Dolls for a lucrative concert tour of Japan. 'I hooked them up with a promoter friend of mine and went along for the ride,' said Bob Gruen. 'Malcolm wasn't happy about that. He thought I had become their manager but that wasn't true. I was simply introducing friends. The guys earned $10,000 each out of it which was a considerable sum, enabling them to settle months of back-rent and get back on an even keel.'

In terms of the new group in London, McLaren was most concerned about the bespectacled and charisma-free Wally Nightingale, a workmanlike musician without much spark and, more importantly, a visual liability. He lobbied for Nightingale's dismissal and for Jones, who was never completely comfortable as the frontman, to take up the guitar so that a new singer could be found. But this manoeuvre would prove tricky, since Nightingale's father had enabled access to the Hammersmith rehearsal space.

'That boy was big and dopey,' says Sex customer David Harrison. 'The others kind of used him because he had the practice room and some of the equipment. They were never very nice about him behind his back.'

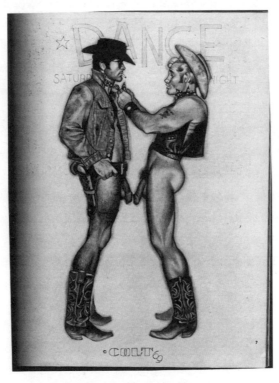

Jim French drawing (credited to Colt '69) which appeared in *Manpower!* magazine acquired by McLaren in New York in 1975. Jim French.

Emily Isaacs and Peter McLaren, Liverpool Road register office, Islington, London, 17 October 1942. (© *Malcolm McLaren Estate*)

With (from left) step-brother Colin, unidentified and brother Stuart, Eastbourne, 1953.

With (clockwise from top left) Mick Isaacs, Emily Edwards, Rose Isaacs, Stuart Edwards and Colin Edwards, 1954.

In scout's uniform with Stuart and Colin, Hendon, 1959.

(above) *Up They Rise: A Playground for The Juggler*, Jamie Reid's portrait of McLaren in Croydon, 1968. *(Jamie Reid/John Marchant Gallery/ © Jamie Reid. All Rights Reserved, DACS 2020)*

(left) *I Will Be So Bad*, 1969.
(© Barry Martin/Malcolm McLaren Estate)

Portrait of McLaren by Helen Mininberg, 1969.
(Paul Burgess Collection)

With Addie Isman outside 430 King's Road after the erection of the Let It Rock sign, March 1972.
(© Trinity Mirror/Mirrorpix/Alamy Stock Photo)

With Denson's winged boot in front of poster display, Let It Rock, January 1972.
(© David Parkinson)

With Vivienne
Westwood and
display cabinet in
the 'Willesden Teddy
Boy's sitting room'
installation, 430 King's
Road, January 1972.
(© David Parkinson)

Those Were The
Days fashion
story for Club
International,
Acre Lane,
Brixton, London,
summer 1973.
(© David Parkinson)

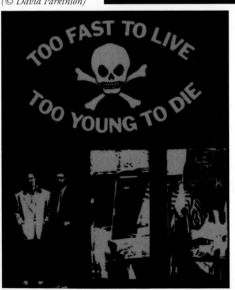

With Gerry Goldstein, 430 King's Road, summer 1973.
(Malcolm McLaren Estate)

Posing for 'The Politics of Flash' article in *New Musical Express*, April 1974. *(© Pennie Smith)*

Ben Kelly as 'The Photo Kid', 430 King's Road, autumn 1974. *(© Ben Kelly)*

David Harrison in customized Sex t-shirt, 1975. *(© David Harrison)*

The New York Dolls on the set of the *Trash* short film in Sex attire, January 1975. *(© Bob Gruen)*

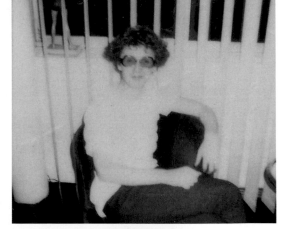

At a summer party at Valerie Allam's apartment, St John's Wood, London, summer 1975. *(© David Parkinson)*

With Sylvain Sylvain at the War Is Over! rally, Sheep Meadow, Central Park, New York, 11 May 1975. *(© Bob Gruen)*

'The Colonel Tom Parker of the Blank Generation' in Anarchy shirt at the Glitterbest offices, central London, November 1976. *(© Pennie Smith)*

Façade for Seditionaries at 430 King's Road on completion, December 1976. *(© Ben Kelly)*

With Sex Pistols 'signing' A&M record contract outside Buckingham Palace, 10 March 1977. *(© PA/PA Archive/PA Images)*

In Paris, spring 1979. *(© Adrian Boot)*

For the meantime, McLaren gave Jones Sylvain's white Gibson guitar, on which the teenager started to teach himself to play. But all plans for the group were interrupted by a bona-fide controversy. To McLaren's pleasure, Sex made the front pages of the national press and became the subject of questions in the House of Commons over yet another of his T-shirt designs, this one incorporating a homoerotic illustration he had brought back with him from New York.

Longhorns – Dance was a male physique study drawn by American artist Jim French in 1969 and circulated as one of a set of six 5 x 7 inch prints published by his company Colt Studio.

Signed by 'Colt '69'and distributed around the US via secretive mail order ads and a network of underground bookshops, the charcoal and ink drawing depicted two handsome cowboys facing each other in side profile against a sign reading 'Dance Tonight', pants-less in boots, Stetsons and neckerchiefs, one wearing a denim jacket, the other a leather waistcoat. The cowpoke on the right leans back and reaches to adjust the other's scarf with a tattooed, muscular arm. Their semi-flaccid penises, prominently on display, are close to touching.

Such charged intimacy was a trademark of French's erotica, which he had rendered since the Second World War and sold increasingly widely over the following decades. In the years before the decriminalisation of homosexuality in states across the union, this was a fraught occupation and French – a trained commercial artist and fashion illustrator – ran the gauntlet, using small independent print presses and repro houses whose activities were targeted by the authorities on the grounds of obscenity.

'There were relatively few people doing what I was trying to do: celebrate the magnificence of the naked male body,' said French.[23] Although hyper, his masculine archetypes – soldiers, cowboys, bikers – were truer to life than those produced by the better-known Tom of Finland and drew an equally eager audience. In 1967 French founded the Colt Studio imprint to produce these highly detailed works for self-published books, calendars and magazines.

Longhorns – Dance was reproduced in the Colt Studio publication *Manpower!*, a copy of which Malcolm McLaren acquired at a bookshop in New York's gay quarter, Christopher Street, and brought to London in the spring of 1975.

For McLaren, the drawing exuded ennui, chiming with the disillusionment he experienced on returning to Britain after his American adventures. 'Those cowboys summed up the frustration and boredom I felt at the time,' said McLaren. 'It was as though they were waiting for something to happen, just like everyone I knew in London.'

McLaren also understood the image contained considerable potential to shock when made the centrepiece of a new artwork for a Sex T-shirt. He appropriated French's drawing and juxtaposed it with an imagined laconic exchange between the two figures, as if uttered on a quiet Saturday night:

''ello Joe been anywhere lately'
'Nah its all played aht Bill'
'Gettin too straight'

Like 'You're Gonna Wake Up' before it, the 'Cowboys' shirt can be seen as a response to the apathy McLaren detected during the mid-1970s cultural low into which Britain had sunk: critical commentary remained in the hands of the media voices who had dominated since the 1960s, fine art had run out of steam when conceptual and performance art failed to gain traction, and the decorative arts, including fashion, languished.

'Because of the economic crisis that is prevailing throughout the Western world, people are trying to consume as much as possible,' McLaren told journalist David May. 'Ideas are very dead. There aren't any to express this mood. People in the fashion world cannot come up with a new design. It's just not relevant.'[24]

The counterculture McLaren had enjoyed was long splintered, protest was factionalised and, in popular music, rock had been co-opted by the major entertainment combines, which stifled grassroots youth movements.

The production of the Cowboys design applied the same technique used for McLaren's previous T-shirt artworks 'I Groaned with Pain' and the 'Naked Footballer', in that it was achieved by *détournement*.

In repurposing such hijacked material, McLaren aligned himself generally with the Situationists' aim of challenging the passivity and doubt of everyday life with acts of playful affirmation, and in particular with a panel in *Le Retour de la Colonne Durruti*, a four-page SI 'comic' circulated by André Bertrand at Strasbourg University in October 1966.[25]

In this, Bertrand imposed speech bubbles (using dialogue from a novel by the SI fellow traveller Michelle Bernstein) on a photo-strip of two cowboys on horseback. The exchange provided the basis for McLaren's 1975 reflection:

'What's your scene, man?'

'Realisation.'

'Yeah? I guess that means pretty hard work with big books and piles of paper on a big table.'

'Nope. I drift. Mostly I just drift.'

Not only was the *dérive* mentioned, but there was also the reference to realisation: Guy Debord believed art should be 'realised' so that creative acts became part of daily life.

And McLaren's hope that the Cowboys artwork would lead to such a realisation was fulfilled almost as soon as it had been printed by Bernard Rhodes on soft jersey tops and first displayed for sale in Sex on Monday 28 July, 1975.

That day, Alan Jones, a member of the shop's coterie, purchased two T-shirts: the Cambridge Rapist and the Cowboys. He changed into the latter before setting off on foot to central London. Soon Jones's *dérive* led to an encounter with a couple of policemen while he was walking through Piccadilly.

The location was important. The thoroughfare was at that stage the locus of social tensions over its rent-boy population; just a few days earlier the national broadcast network ITV had shown *Johnny Go Home*, a documentary about male sexual predators and teenage runaways. This had caused a nationwide moral panic and thrown the spotlight on the Dilly Boys' trade. Like the Cambridge Rapist episode, McLaren had effectively barged his way into an existing media furore.

It was in this atmosphere that the policemen decided that the brazenly worn Cowboys T-shirt (Jones claimed not to have noticed the consternation it was causing) was too much so took Jones into custody. There he was charged with 'showing an obscene print in a public place' under the Vagrancy Act of 1824 and ordered to appear a few weeks later at Vine Street Magistrates' Court in central London.

According to Jones, the arresting officers specifically referred to the broadcast of *Johnny Go Home*. When he asked them if the shirt would be considered indecent 'if it carried the image of a famous naked statue which could be seen in London' they told him that wouldn't have led to his arrest.

MP attacks T-shirt charge

A charge against a man for wearing a T-shirt with a picture of two naked men on, it was described as "preposterous" by Dr Colin Phipps, the Labour MP for Dudley West, yesterday. He said the charge seemed part of 'a concerted attack on liberal views of sex and nakedness."

In a letter to Mr Roy Jenkins, the Home Secretary, Dr Phipps urged a review of laws which allowed prosecutions for what many people regarded as accepted behaviour.

"It would appear to me to be more logical for a prosecutor to have to demonstrate a specific public hurt in matters of taste rather than being able to rely on antique laws."

Report on Cowboys t-shirt arrest of Alan Jones, *The Guardian*, 2 August 1975.

The exchanges between Jones and the arresting officers – as reported in national media – were worthy of Joe Orton (the sexually charged and caustic dramatist who had died at his lover's hand eight years earlier was one of McLaren's heroes):

'Mr Jones says the tee-shirt was then taken from him and it was a big laugh for all the police officers. Then one of them said, "It's a very nice tee-shirt but the reason you are wearing it is that you're sexually inadequate." Mr Jones says that he was asked when he had last seen his parents and told them two weeks ago. He said: "They asked me what kind of reaction I'd had from people." He had said there had been very little.'[26]

The police raid on 430 King's Road took place the following day. The remaining stock of eighteen Cowboys T-shirts was seized, and McLaren and Westwood's arrest on indecency charges escalated the affair into a free-speech cause célèbre when Labour MP Colin Phipps called on Home Secretary Roy Jenkins to review the outmoded law.

'It would appear to me to be more logical for a prosecutor to have to demonstrate a specific public hurt in matters of taste rather than being able to rely on antique laws,' Phipps wrote to Jenkins.[27]

Despite the outcry, guilty verdicts and fines were handed down to Jones and McLaren and Westwood, who had been accused at Vine Street 'of exposing to public view an indecent exhibition on a display rack at the shop, Sex, in the King's Road, Chelsea'.[28]

As well as the Cowboys shirt, police also pulled from the racks the Naked Footballer and a design featuring a typewritten extract from Alexander Trocchi's 1967 porn novel *School for Wives*: 'She felt the seed stir at the pit of her belly in response to the strong tongue movements _____ Glady's [*sic*] hand now pushed forward on Doreen's superb buttocks so that she could drink deeper at the well of her desire.'

This paragraph was repeated above and below a red stencil reading: SCUM, the acronym for the would-be Warhol assassin Valerie Solanas's Society for Cutting Up Men.

In the event, the authorities decided against including the Naked Footballer T-shirt in the charges, as sex education magazine *Curious* reported: 'The police have had a rethink about one particular design – the one showing a super-muscular black man, complete with all he's got (and how!) hanging down between his legs.'[29]

McLaren hoped that the court hearing would continue the process of 'decensorship' of British life that had begun with the 1960 victory to publish D. H. Lawrence's *Lady Chatterley's Lover*, thus aligning Sex with such cases as those that surrounded Trocchi's *Cain's Book* and William Burroughs's *The Naked Lunch*, which both occurred in 1964, and the obscenity trial of underground magazine *Oz* in 1971.

British academic John Sutherland has identified how 'manifest and unfair "political" persecution on spurious grounds of obscenity had the effect of keeping liberals, who might otherwise have hung up their guns in 1968, in a state of militant opposition to censorship'.[30]

In their defence, McLaren and Westwood called upon expert witnesses to attest to the artistic value of the artworks. Among them were McLaren's Harrow Art School teacher Theo Ramos and Ted Polhemus, an anthropologist and curator at the Institute of Contemporary Art.

Rather than the hoped-for confrontation with the rule of law, the hearing descended into farce. 'I'd been angling to get Malcolm, Jordan and Vivienne to participate in a fashion forum I was organising at the ICA, but they refused point-blank until the "Cowboys" shirt business happened,' said Polhemus. 'Then they said they would take part if I gave testimony in the trial. It was totally bizarre. The judge was at least eighty and completely horrified, particularly when he received the explanation as to what SCUM meant.'[31]

The prosecution relied in part on whether the cowboys' penises were touching in French's artwork. This would have made it a sexually explicit design and so arguably indecent when publicly displayed. 'Of course, everyone knew that the tension from the image stems from the fact that though they are close, the large members are not actually in contact with each other,' said Polhemus. 'Eventually the judge asked for a ruler so that the distance between the cocks could be measured, and then the courtroom was consumed by a debate about fractions of inches.'

Although the defence successfully established sufficient distance between the penises, the judge ruled against McLaren and Westwood and imposed upon them a hefty fine. McLaren's hopes for igniting a media furore were dashed when the case received scant coverage.

Alan Jones later claimed that McLaren and Westwood reneged on their offer to reimburse him for his own £30 fine, but, for McLaren, the police and court reaction had at least fulfilled the promise of an engagement with the authorities he had been hell bent on provoking.

'Kids today don't look at two men undressed as something that is sexually disgusting,' McLaren said in the aftermath of the trial. 'It's still regarded as taboo for someone in the street wearing a T-shirt with a picture of a man in the nude. If you keep it in a book, that's alright. We are just going a little bit further.'[32]

Chapter 18

Throughout the Cowboys court case, McLaren continued to stock the T-shirts in his shop. In fact their notoriety powered popularity among such hardcore Sex customers as David Harrison, then sporting a distinctive look combining a bleached James Dean haircut with second-hand clothes and the latest McLaren/Westwood designs, some of which he customised.

Westwood liked Harrison's svelte appearance and had occasionally given him clothing, including a pair of red vinyl trousers as worn by the New York Dolls. This was a habit of McLaren and Westwood's. While it is natural for fashion designers to take pleasure in attractive people wearing their clothes, the couple believed that providing their eye-popping designs to select youngsters would communicate their message of liberation more widely.

Both were in agreement that Harrison had potential as the frontman for the group. Naturally stylish, he was nineteen and working class from a tough background ('we were brought up in slums, it was rough, I tell you'). He was also bright, with a catty sense of humour and of a creative bent, though Westwood appreciated this more than McLaren. Harrison was at that time developing as a visual artist but his attempts to engage the former art student on the subject of painting were unsuccessful, particularly when McLaren reconnected with Helen Wellington Lloyd. 'I stayed over at her place in Bell Street sometimes with the rest of them,' says Harrison. 'They'd be talking about art and I'd try to interject but was met with a pretty condescending attitude from Malcolm: "Yeah, whatever." He definitely thought he was on a higher intellectual plane than me, maybe because of the way I spoke.'

Still, McLaren saw that there was something about Harrison that might spark when combined with Steve Jones et al. His approach to Harrison coincided with a regular occurrence at Sex: a theft.

'I wanted a "Cowboys" shirt, but they were pretty expensive, so one day I took an orange one off the rails, rolled it up, put it in my pocket and wandered out,' says Harrison.

The following afternoon Harrison received a visit from McLaren and Jones at his workplace, the post room of IPC magazines in central London. 'I got a call from reception that they were waiting for me,' says Harrison. 'I was wearing the shirt I'd pinched, and thought they had come to retrieve it so was pretty sheepish when I met them outside the building but Malcolm said: "Oh you've got one of our T-shirts, that's great."

'Then they started appraising me. Malcolm asked the other one: "Do you think he'd be any good?" Steve kind of grunted and Malcolm said to me: "Do you want to be the singer in our band?"

'I said: "Not really. I can't sing."

'Malcolm said: "That doesn't matter." So when I asked him what the band was like he said: "A dirty version of the Bay City Rollers. We're called Kutie Jones and the Sex Pistols but we're probably going to change that."'

Within a couple of days Harrison met up with the duo and Cook, Matlock and Nightingale for the first of half-a-dozen rehearsals, initially at the studio in Hammersmith.

'We'd sit around and they'd occasionally play and I'd try and sing,' says Harrison. 'They were pretty bad but I liked the musical direction. It reminded me of the Pretty Things, sixties English pop, music I was brought up on. I sang some Small Faces songs, including "All or Nothing", and the Monkees' "Stepping Stone".'

McLaren and Westwood often dropped by with friends including Nick Kent, Bernard Rhodes, Gene Krell from Granny's and Andrew Greaves of Electric Colour Company.

'I remember when I first turned up in my adapted T-shirts and glitter drainpipes, Malcolm and Vivienne said to Paul and Steve:

"Look at what he's wearing. We want you to dress like him." And they'd look at each other and say: "I ain't wearing that. I'd look like a right poof." '

Harrison was shy and by no means a natural performer, but his sharp visual presence threw into relief Wally Nightingale's lack of appeal.

Backed by Rhodes and Westwood, McLaren decreed that Nightingale had to go and fired him one afternoon in the presence of the rest of the group and Nick Kent.

'McLaren coldly told him he didn't fit into the group and that he should basically fuck off and never darken their towels again,' Kent wrote in the 2000s. 'While Nightingale was balefully packing his guitar case, McLaren told everyone I was to be their new guitarist. It was news to me too. Suddenly I was a Sex Pistol.'[1]

Kent rehearsed with the group for a brief period[2] during which time they dropped the more lightweight covers and added two from the 1960s suggested by McLaren from the 430 jukebox: 'Do You Really Love Me Too (Fools Errand)', a yearning song by his hero Billy Fury, and Dave Berry's aggressive 'Don't Give Me No Lip Child'.

'Malcolm used to court [Kent],' wrote Matlock in the late 1980s. 'As he was the *NME*'s star writer I guess Malcolm realised that once the band really started to get going Nick would be able to help us out. Mind you, Malcolm did take the piss out of him as well, calling him "Troy Tempest in a leather jacket".'[3]

Although Nightingale appeared to accept the dismissal, even joining the rest for a drink that night, he subsequently severed all links, ordering them to remove their share of the equipment in the Hammersmith rehearsal room and took the keys.

All was not lost. At the suggestion of Sex customer Peter 'Sleazy' Christopherson,[4] who worked at the design studio Hipgnosis, McLaren secured the budding musicians a new practice space in workshops housed in a largely derelict dockside granary warehouse in Rotherhithe in east London occupied by a community centre and the film animation company Crunchy Frog.

'I spent most of my time running around exploring,' says Harrison. 'I was already a closet birdwatcher, so my saying "Oh look, there's a cormorant!" didn't go down very well.'

McLaren believed enough in Harrison's potential to arrange for fellow Chelsea fashion retailer and keen amateur photographer Manolo Blahnik, whose shoe shop Zapata was in neighbouring Old Church Street, to take portraits. 'They were head-and-shoulders shots,' says Harrison. 'He came by the shop one day and took them there. I guess Malcolm was testing my look and how I fitted in visually with the others.'

This wasn't enough to calm Harrison's qualms. 'I just didn't feel comfortable standing upfront without anything to do with my hands,' he admits. 'So I asked whether I could play the saxophone but Malcolm was really against that. He suggested Steve should teach me the guitar. I thought: "He can barely play himself!"'

Jones was deputed by McLaren to visit Harrison at his family home in Stratford, east London, and walk him through the rudiments of the instrument. 'My parents were away for a week so I said he should come and stay over,' says Harrison. 'We did that all the time in the days before night buses. We couldn't afford cabs. I remember once we stayed at Bernie's place in Camden Town after a practice. What a tip! And I went to see Glen with Vivienne and Malcolm in Greenford, which is really suburban. Glen told me that, despite what they looked like, his mother said to him after we had gone: "I don't want you to ever bring a boy like that here again."'

Jones's trip to Stratford is memorable to Harrison for reasons unrelated to guitar tuition. 'What a pig! As soon as he arrived he asked if there was any food and then ate everything my parents had left for me for the week,' exclaims Harrison. 'Then he asked me what kind of music I was into, so I showed him all my records, reggae, soul, T. Rex and Gong. I played him Daevid Allen's *Banana Moon* and he said: "Fucking hell! Don't let Malcolm know you listen to that shit! He hates fucking hippies."'

Jones left with a haul of the albums, including *Banana Moon*, 'so we can look at them and copy the riffs', according to Harrison. 'I never got them back; he basically nicked them.'

Thereafter Harrison's association with the band fizzled out. 'Malcolm called every day but I didn't answer the phone and when my parents got back I told them to tell him I was out,' says Harrison, who had left IPC to work at the Holborn vintage-clothing store Nostalgia and hang out with the art/fashion crowd that included the stylist and photographer Johnny Rosza and the artist Andrew Logan. 'I met Malcolm at the shop and told him it wasn't really my cup of tea, but the final nail in the coffin was probably when he realised I was gay,' believes Harrison.

By this time he had become friendly with the Sex sales assistants Michael Collins and Jordan, socialising with them on London's gay club scene. When at the shop, the trio shared camp gossip, shrieking and queenily infuriating the stoutly heterosexual likes of Cook and Jones by imitating the gibberish language of TV puppets the Woodentops.

'One day Jordan asked me out of the blue in a kind of teasing way: "Have you been fucked hard recently?" I said: "Yes, as it happens I have, just last week." Malcolm looked at me curiously, so Jordan and Michael started going on about how I was a pervert because I liked older men. I knew that Malcolm didn't have anything against people being gay – after all, he liked to mince around – but saw that it was wrong for the image of the frontman he had in mind.'

With Rhodes, McLaren continued the search for a singer, having entertained and then dismissed the notion that he could fulfil the role. McLaren went so far as to take a few lessons from celebrity vocal coach Tona de Brett – who later said he had 'a lovely singing voice' – before accepting that he was too old.

A half-hearted approach was made to New Yorker Mike Spenser, frontman of pub-rock group the Count Bishops, who declined. The Bishops were leather-jacketed R&B merchants whose set included a hard-driving version of the Strangeloves' 1965 hit 'I Want Candy', which was on the 430 jukebox.

Over a couple of days in the summer of 1975 McLaren and Rhodes undertook a money-raising expedition through the north of England to Scotland to offload the stolen musical equipment accumulated by Steve

Jones. Outside a Glasgow music shop they encountered the young musician James 'Midge' Ure, the guitarist/singer in the 1950s-style Slik, which performed songs by the writers for the Bay City Rollers.

'I was approached by Bernie Rhodes, who said: "Would you speak to my mate around the corner?" In this beaten-up Cortina was the most effeminate man I'd ever met in my life, with his curly hair and mohair jumper,' Ure told Steve Jones in 2018. 'I sat in the car with these two strangers and Malcolm started telling me about Sex, the clothes that he made and the New York Dolls. About half an hour in he told me he was putting a band together, [and asked] "Would you be interested in joining?" I thought, "He hasn't asked me about my music and what I do," so I said, "Thanks but no thanks." I never knew what role they wanted me to play.

'It seems they had travelled up from London stopping off at various cities selling slightly hot equipment they had in the back of the car. So they opened up the boot and I turned down the chance of being in the Pistols but bought a Fender amp head.'[5]

Chapter 19

In late August 1975, as London sweltered and preparations were underway for the extended bank holiday weekend marking the end of summer, the Sex customer John Lydon entered 430 King's Road on a shopping trip.

Like David Harrison, Lydon was a working class nineteen-year-old from a rough-and-tumble background (in the latter's case, the housing estates of Finsbury Park, north London). But Harrison's good-natured sauciness was tempered by a tendency to diffidence, whereas Lydon was openly confrontational, his belligerent, wide-eyed stare – a consequence of childhood meningitis – backing up the withering articulacy of the literate Irish.

The course of Lydon's life, and those of many others, not least McLaren's, was about to change forever.

To get to the truth of what happened over the course of this particular day – Friday 22 August, 1975 – one must parse many different accounts, sometimes conflicting even when from the same source (including, but not restricted to, McLaren).

The facts are these. At the time Lydon – who had been employed over the summer as a playground teacher for children with educational difficulties – cut a remarkable figure visually, even in the context of the adventurous habitués of Sex. That year he had cropped and dyed his spiky fair hair, giving it the appearance of being green, and wore distressed and customised clothing, most notably a torn Pink Floyd merchandise T-shirt portraying the group's members; above the logo Lydon had scrawled 'I HATE'. He also defaced the musicians' faces with scrawls and cigarette burn holes. This was a DIY composition aligning itself with the Sex design 'You're Gonna Wake Up', though Pink Floyd didn't appear on that T-shirt, and McLaren was an admirer of the group's tragic founder Syd Barrett.

Several in the Sex set had clocked the extraordinary-looking youth parading the King's Road in his quasi-Lettrist garb, among them McLaren's sidekick Bernard Rhodes and younger friend Steve Jones.

'I'm from the street and know better,' said Rhodes in the 2000s. 'That's why I was able to pick Johnny Rotten; I found him on the street and recognised he was something special.'

But in 1977 Jones claimed that he'd noticed Lydon as early as the spring of 1975. 'I thought he looked pretty good and said to Malcolm to look out for this bloke, he's got green hair and that,' said Jones.[1]

According to McLaren, Westwood had already identified a Sex customer named John as a potential frontman. This was Lydon's friend John Ritchie, who became Sid Vicious. 'She said, "He's ever so good looking and wears clothes really well. You've got to watch out for him Malcolm,"' McLaren said Westwood had told him. 'Then in came this John, a very, very obstreperous creature looking for a pair of brothel creepers in white suede. I thought this must be the one who Vivienne had mentioned. I didn't have the shoes in his size but told him I could get them the following week.

'And I asked him, as I was asking anyone who came in the shop at that time, "Do you sing?" and he said, "Nah – only out of tune."

'I thought, "All right, we'll test you." I told him, "If you want these shoes, I may even give them to you if you promise to head down tonight to this pub around the corner called the Roebuck where you can meet the rest of the band."'[2]

Lydon brought along a college friend, John Gray. 'Fuck this, it sounded like a setup to me,' said Lydon. 'I thought they must be joking . . . that really pissed off Steve [Jones]. He was a bit thick, and couldn't make out what I was talking about. He didn't seem to understand me.'[3]

Jones has confirmed his growing annoyance with Lydon's clever-clever attitude, though memory loss has eradicated the details of the encounter. When they met on the guitarist's LA radio show, McLaren reminded Jones that he had become so irritated that he was on the verge of physically attacking the potential singer.

'I was sitting at the bar talking to a couple of guys, the typical fashion and drug victims you got on the King's Road, and let you get on with it,' McLaren told Jones in 2005. 'You came up to me and said you were going to beat the shit out of him because he was playing up, and suggested taking him to the shop. We dragged him there and I became very officious. I grabbed a broken shower attachment – I don't know why we had it – and asked him to stand at the end of the shop and behave as if he was on stage otherwise you were going to beat the living daylights out of him.'

From the jukebox, Lydon chose 'I'm Eighteen', the 1971 track by Alice Cooper, and mimed to it, 'gyrating like a belly dancer'.[4] The pop-eyed contortions and hair-raising shapes thrown by Lydon bewildered some of the handful of people who had gathered inside Sex, but mightily impressed McLaren.

'He was somewhat embarrassed and strange,' said McLaren. 'I laughed. I thought it was funny and brilliant.'[5]

As with David Harrison, Lydon was invited by McLaren to try out with the group at Crunchy Frog. He accepted and a few days later made the arduous journey to the building in London's post-industrial waste-lands. Accompanied again by John Gray, Lydon was extremely annoyed when the others failed to turn up.

Cook, Matlock and Jones hadn't been sufficiently impressed by the jukebox audition to make the trip; the latter had in fact decided that he wasn't keen on this new band member in the slightest.

But McLaren was insistent on Lydon joining the group, not just because of his resemblance to Richard Hell, though of course this helped. 'There was a vulnerability about him which was very persuasive,' said McLaren. 'I could see from the start that he would bring enormous charisma.'

When McLaren found out about the trio's no-show at Crunchy Frog, he prevailed upon Matlock to call Lydon and apologise. '"I'll kill you," said John in his best whine,' recalled Matlock, who persuaded him to return to Rotherhithe the following weekend.

'"This guy is the one," Malcolm said, and we went along with him,' said Matlock. 'Who knows why? It certainly took us a while to understand John's plus points. All we could think was that he couldn't sing. "Malcolm's got us this singer," we kept saying to each other, "and he can't sing. What is this all about?"'[6]

McLaren understood what this raw, bizarre youth brought to the group even if his charges didn't. He pressed them into continuing rehearsals and encouraging them to write their own songs, first at Crunchy Frog and then in practice rooms in Wandsworth and Camden. Lydon soon proved himself a unique frontman and also a clever wordsmith, readily providing lyrics that immeasurably improved a song the others had composed with Nightingale.

Lydon was also a knowledgeable music fan with a taste for the avant-garde and the obscure, so suggested cover versions that further elevated the ensemble's range.

Now they rehearsed 'Shake Appeal' by Iggy & the Stooges and 'Psychotic Reaction' by 1960s garage greats the Seeds, as well as British mod tunes such as 'Substitute' by The Who, 'Through My Eyes' by the Creation and 'Understanding' by pint-sized quartet the Small Faces, whose rousing 1965 hit 'Whatcha Gonna Do About It' was modified by Lydon. He sang the first line as 'I want you to know that I *hate* you baby' rather than 'love you baby', and inserted a negative into the second line so that it came out as: 'I want you to know I *don't* care'.

Lydon's aggressive delivery and lyrical dexterity meshed with Matlock's melodic sensibilities, Cook's rhythmic crunch and Jones's muscular chord progressions to produce such autumn 1975 group compositions as 'Seventeen (I'm a Lazy Sod)', 'Pretty Vacant' and 'Submission', all of which appeared on the Pistols' debut LP two years later. The latter had been written at McLaren's instigation; he announced the title and asked Lydon and Matlock to explore themes of dominance and submission. In this way, thought McLaren, the group's music would lock directly into the sexual practices promoted by Sex. The two younger men thought this seedy, and instead created a pulsating track equating a submarine mission with pursuit of a love affair.

In fact, many of the group's early songs resulted from, or reacted against, McLaren's directives. With 'Pretty Vacant', Matlock took his cue from the manager's proposal that the group write an anthem along the lines of Richard Hell's '(I Belong to the) Blank Generation', while another lesser track, which was abandoned early, was entitled 'Kill Me Today', after the 'Please Kill Me' slogan worn on a shirt by Hell in a photograph shown to the group by McLaren.

Apart from a brief honeymoon period when the group first assembled, a reciprocal antagonism soon developed between the middle-class, art school-educated McLaren and the proudly proletarian Lydon; the first lyrics written by the latter sneeringly addressed McLaren's age in the opening lines of 'Seventeen': 'You're only 29, Got a lot to learn . . .'

Their antipathy was established from the off, claims Lydon. 'I never really got on with him, never knew much about him,' said Lydon in the 2000s. 'He was some weird little bloke in lace. Black lace. Ooh, how kinky. Just repulsive.'[7]

It wasn't always thus. Matlock has recalled that Lydon was discreetly impressed by the manager, and unwittingly adopted some of McLaren's peculiar vocal mannerisms, stretching out vowels and elongating sentences to comic effect. In this way Lydon channelled the idiosyncratic locution McLaren had learned on his grandmother's knee.

For the time being, the singer and McLaren rubbed along, though the manager's established friendship with Cook and Jones and Lydon's irritation with Matlock's easy-going nature were to exacerbate his feelings of isolation throughout the group's existence.

'We always knew the one thing, that John came from north London, the rest of the band came from west London,' said McLaren. 'John didn't really have a relationship with the rest of his band and felt constantly insecure and believed he had to show another side to himself. He did that by constantly bringing his crew, his crowd, with him.

'John's persona, his sense of being a singer, a pop singer by default, whichever way you want to describe it, didn't sit comfortably with the rest of the group. Glen didn't like it, Jones put up with him because he thought, "Better keep Malcolm happy otherwise it's all going to collapse." So Jones took care of Paul, and that's how it worked.

'But it was very, very difficult to have a relationship with John. He had references and ideas that no one else was interested in. He was interested in Captain Beefheart but that just washed over everybody, it didn't relate. These kids were into the Beatles, Small Faces, Rod Stewart, New York Dolls, rock 'n' roll. This was not John Lydon. He actually hated that music.'

This, according to McLaren, was to the Pistols' advantage. 'The fact that they disliked each other created a necessary friction which set them apart and produced great work,' he said.[8]

With distinctive short haircuts and accoutred in clothes from Sex, the Sex Pistols had finally taken shape. Lydon's uncompromising demeanour, dishevelled appearance and indifferent dentistry inspired a nickname from the mickey-taking Jones, one that stuck: Johnny Rotten. McLaren had his British version of Richard Hell and punk's inversion of the adoption of romantic nomenclature by Larry Parnes's previous generation of music stars – Billy Fury, Marty Wilde, Georgie Fame – gathered pace.

Four years after Lydon joined the Pistols, music journalist Michael Watts captured his appeal, particularly to McLaren in 1975:

A livid-faced hobgoblin with undernourished, prole features, he exceeded the rock 'n' roll tradition of anti-heroes. Mick Jagger, the Sixties *bête noir*, had disturbed prevalent notions of attractiveness with his bulbous-lipped sexuality. Rotten wasn't sexy at all, but then the new shibboleth was violence; and, with his bad skin and demented glare, he had an ugly theatricality all his own.

Rotten was like the teenage characters of Colin MacInnes' London novels: small, perky and street-wise, very aware of the figure he cut, but with a chip on his shoulder, always suspicious and alert to the moves going on around him. In at least one respect he was very like McLaren: he insisted on having his own way.[9]

When Westwood discovered that McLaren had mistaken Lydon for her recommendation of the future Sid Vicious, there was hell to pay. 'She came up to Chelsea to meet him in the pub and said: "He's not the bloody John I told you about. It's another John. You've got the wrong guy!"

'I said: "It's OK Vivienne, he'll be fine, there's something about him."

'But she said: "He's not the John I told you about. You're going to have a lot of trouble with him. You're never going to hear the last of it. Well, now you've done it. You've made your bed you're going to have to bloody lie in it." And she walked out.'[10]

Domestically, tensions were running high between Westwood and McLaren, and in October he moved out of Thurleigh Court, once again leaving his partner with Ben, now thirteen, and seven-year-old Joe. His new London base was a two-bedroom apartment rented by Helen Wellington Lloyd in Bell Street, Marylebone, much closer than Clapham to the centre of town and its clubs, venues and record company offices.

'I was angry with Vivienne, I can't remember what about,' said McLaren decades later. 'Bell Street provided me with a place where I could concentrate on the new group and ensure that they would take a path like none other before them.'

The rapid development of the group and the seriousness of McLaren's intent were underscored when he paid £1000 less than four weeks after Lydon's 'audition' for the lease on a two-room rehearsal space behind a bookshop in central London's Denmark Street, the music-publishing strip otherwise known as Tin Pan Alley. The space at no. 6 was christened by McLaren the QT Rooms in honour of its new resident: the itinerant Steve Jones was to live there rent-free for two years, and it became a stopover point for the others, particularly Cook and Matlock. The money for the lease purchase came out of McLaren's pocket and included earnings from the sale of the Fender Rhodes keyboard entrusted to him by Sylvain Sylvain.

Housed in an early Victorian building, the neglected interior was gloomy and mice-ridden. Ever-resourceful, McLaren bought a cat and called upon the services of interior designer Ben Kelly to make good the rotting walls.

'We were at a tea party at Duggie Fields's, who was serving Battenberg cake, which went perfectly with his paintings,' says Kelly. 'Malcolm told me about the Denmark Street rooms. "It's a right fucking mess," he said. "Can you sort it out for me?"'

Kelly proposed lining the walls with MDF fibreboard and arranged a visit. 'As I banged on the door I noticed a sign next to it which said: "Throbbing Gristle",[11] which gave me pause. Anyway, there was no answer and I walked off, to be chased down Denmark Street by Paul Cook in his underpants. He'd obviously just woken up, so ushered me in. They were living on the first floor and the ground floor was set up with equipment, including a fantastic old mic like Elvis would have used. The gear they had was phenomenal.'

Having measured up, Kelly contracted a builder to carry out the task. The MDF wasn't painted and, in between rehearsals, Lydon decorated the walls with caricatures lampooning the other band members and McLaren.[12]

Now there was a problem. Paul Cook – the only Pistol holding down a regular job as an apprentice at a brewery – voiced serious misgivings about the enterprise after McLaren bought the lease on the QT Rooms.

'He rang and said that I shouldn't waste my money, and that he was going to quit,' said McLaren. 'He came up with a variety of reasons: Jones wasn't good enough, Rotten's voice was awful, but maybe it was because his apprenticeship was nearing its end and he was being told by somebody that he shouldn't throw away his career, however mundane.'

McLaren craftily came up with a way to mollify Cook. His plan from the start of the summer had been that the group should replicate the New York Dolls' line-up and feature two guitarists. Sylvain Sylvain, recently returned from the lucrative Japan dates, continued to stall on flying to

London, so McLaren proposed placing a want ad for another guitarist. That might further professionalise the outfit.

Cook agreed to stay on that basis and McLaren's *Melody Maker* advert ('Whizz kid guitarist – Not older than 20 – Not worse looking than Johnny Thunders – Auditioning Tin Pan Alley') attracted a few respondents, including Mick Jones, future member of The Clash. The social scene surrounding interesting new music in London was minuscule at this point: a month earlier he had encountered Bernard Rhodes at a gig; Jones was wearing a 'You're Gonna Wake Up' T-shirt.

Rhodes instantly offered his services as manager, but that held no sway at the October auditions, where Jones failed to make the cut. A fifteen-year-old named Steve New, who would later play with Matlock's post-Pistols group the Rich Kids, was also put through his paces but it was decided that his mastery of lead guitar added too many frills to the mix.

The sessions made plain the fact that there was no one sympathetic in terms of attitude and ability for this unusual new group. Since Steve Jones's prowess was rapidly developing, Cook's nerves were calmed. He didn't give up his job but the drummer was happy to proceed. McLaren's intervention having steadied the ship, the new group was introduced to several people in his circle.

Fred Vermorel recorded his response in a book in the 1990s:

The phone rings. It's Malcolm. He's at a party above the Swanky Modes boutique in Camden Town. He says I must come. When I arrive I notice several bored louts among the fashion-conscious guests. This is my first exposure to the Sex Pistols. Steve Jones is slumped in an armchair, his arms dangling, a beer bottle in one hand, a fag in the other. The others ostentatiously 'lurk' in corners of the flat.

Malcolm is excited. He explains these yobs are something to do with 'something' he is 'starting'. This 'something' is connected to the fact that, according to Malcolm, the lads have just stolen some jewellery from a bedroom cupboard. Malcolm seems very chuffed about this and proud of his boys. They nick stuff all the time. He boasts they recently broke into Pete Townshend's house and stole some guitars.[1]

The try-out David Harrison first met Lydon one night in the Speakeasy. 'I could see immediately that he had that X factor, that something I didn't have,' said Harrison. 'I bumped into Malcolm, who said I should go over and say hello, which I did. He was sat at a table practising snarling, looked me in the eye and said, "I *hate* you." So that was a conversation stopper. I went back to Malcolm and told him, and he said, "I know, he says that to everybody. He hates everything." '

The name of the new group was among Lydon's objections. 'He told me he wanted to call the group "Sex", just that,' said McLaren in the 2000s. 'I said: "You don't get it, boy." The point was that the name had to be active, that they were young pistols ready to shoot down the established order.'

Privately, McLaren continued to lobby Sylvain hard, which indicates he retained qualms about the Sex Pistols as a quartet. On 22 October 1975, a little more than two weeks ahead of their first live performance, he dashed off a letter marked 'Urgent' by airmail to New York.

Addressed to the guitarist's mother with the note 'Please give to Sylvain as quickly as possible, his friend Malcolm McLaren', the missive was prompted by a visit to Scx by the super-groupie Sable Starr. She had brought McLaren up to date on her ex-boyfriend Johnny Thunders's involvement with Richard Hell in the Heartbreakers and also news that the Dolls' attempts at recording new songs had been unsuccessful.

McLaren's seven-page letter amounted to a powerful pitch, though he took the opportunity to vent about Bob Gruen, whom he perceived as having attempted to assume his role as Dolls manager: 'I'll get this over with once and for all. Bob Gruen I can't stand. He is so spineless he gives me the creeps . . .'

The main thrust of the communication was to wrangle Sylvain into joining the Sex Pistols: '*Look* pack a suitcase, grab your guitar and come here immediately . . . I trust you. Let me hear from you *again*. Right now. Okay, Toledo. Always sexy. Malcolm.'

Included in the package were photographs of Lydon – captioned 'John Rotten' – and photo booth shots of the other musicians. Notably, Jones was designated 'rhythm' guitarist.

'Malcolm said the Sex Pistols were going to be my band,' says Sylvain. 'On the back of the Johnny Rotten photo he wrote: "He can't sing, but he's definitely better than Johansen."'

This was all to no avail. Flush with the cash from Japan and the promise of a solo record deal, Sylvain stayed put.

Meanwhile, with McLaren's blessing, Glen Matlock had arranged the debut appearance of the Sex Pistols. The venue? The common room of Saint Martin's School of Art, the building in Charing Cross Road not far from the Sandeman's wine-tasting rooms where, thirteen years previously, the callow sixteen-year-old McLaren had 'given myself to art'.

Life, for the time being, had come full circle. Soon it was to spin out of control again, bringing with it waves of chaos and disorder even Malcolm McLaren would have difficulty embracing.

PART IV

I'm a Sex Pistol Baby Oh Yeah

Chapter 20

In the late summer of 1982, Malcolm McLaren spent a few weeks in South Africa recording tracks for his *Duck Rock* album.

During downtime, inhaling blasts of sweet South African grass in Soweto township shebeens and Johannesburg recording studios, McLaren regaled his audience of Zulu musicians and singers with the 'greatest story ever told': the tale of the Sex Pistols.

'They couldn't believe when I told them about causing chaos across the land, taking hundreds of thousands of pounds from gullible record companies and sticking a safety pin through the Queen's lips,' said McLaren. 'By the end of the story the Zulus were laughing and cheering the group on.'

For the promo video of the *Duck Rock* single 'Zulus on a Time Bomb', McLaren organised for dancers to wear T-shirts with the track's title on the front. And the back of the shirts bore another slogan: 'I'm a Sex Pistol Baby Oh Yeah'.

Four years after the group's demise, McLaren was turning over the whirlwind twenty-nine months of the Pistols' existence, just as he was to the end of his life in public lectures and private conversations.

Unlike others involved in the group's tumult, however, McLaren refused to allow his central role to define him at the expense of all else.

Rather, he drew a line from their triumphant pop-culture subversion back to the lessons in social divisiveness learned from his troublemaking grandmother – he regularly referred to Rose Corré Isaacs as 'the first Sex Pistol' – and forward to such adventures as his quixotic end-of-the-millennium bid for the role of Mayor of London ('Everybody can be a Sex Pistol' ran the campaign motto).

Nevertheless, in rueful moments, McLaren accepted that the group's name would appear in the first sentence of his obituaries.

As, of course, it did.

Great things have been claimed of the primacy of McLaren's role in the Sex Pistols. Here's Fred Vermorel: 'Considered as an artwork, a two-and-a half-year project and in its own terms, McLaren's Sex Pistols was as seminal and resonant as Picasso's *Guernica*. Only this was a master-piece made not of paint and canvas but of headlines and scandal, scams and factoids, rumour and fashion, slogans, fantasies and images and (I almost forgot) songs – all in a headlong scramble to auto-destruction.'

Vermorel relates the group's existence to McLaren's processing of the radical politics he had absorbed in the 1960s, and detects links to the copies of *Internationale Situationniste* he showed his friend at a bus stop outside Goldsmiths art school in south London seven years before the group's formation.

'Their attention to detail and austere and snarling stylishness is evident in McLaren's creation of the Sex Pistols,' says Vermorel. 'The Pistols, and Punk as received through the Pistols, was Malcolm McLaren's moment. He drove and guided it and to a large extent invented it. Everyone else was a walk-on part. Without McLaren, no Sex Pistols and no Punk as we have come to know it.'

He continues:

The Sex Pistols project was equally a Situationist treatise-by-example, its unremitting and obdurate core being McLaren's grasp of the theory of situations, as proposed by the SI. Indeed, the story of the Pistols is a Situationist textbook of how to create situations *from which there is no return*. You refuse to negotiate, to compromise, to be co-opted, you exacerbate every crisis and recklessly play loser wins, and then you blow up all the bridges so then there is no way back.

We are then forced to invent another future. Or maybe simply relish the mess, 'the ecstasy of making things worse'.[1]

Further, Vermorel associates the group's visually disruptive presence with McLaren's art school education. 'The Pistols was a new form of post-art anti-art,' he declares. 'As a multimedia phenomenon it drew visually on eclectic sources derived from McLaren's love affair with the history of art, from Matthias Grünewald's austerely macabre altar pieces, to the carnivalesque bawdy of Hogarth's *Rake's Progress* and the dense nightmares of Gustave Doré's *London Illustrations*, to Robert Rauschenberg's chaotic assemblages.'[2]

As defined by the critic Greil Marcus, the Sex Pistols' pared-to-the-bone reconfiguration of previous musical and visual styles resulted from the application of one of the main SI techniques. '*Détournement* was cut-up, collage, juxtaposition, the refusal of original creation and the belief that everything that needed to be said was already there waiting to be picked up and put together in new ways,' said Marcus in the late 1980s.

'When it came time to change pop music in the mid-seventies and pop fans such as Malcolm McLaren were bored and disgusted with pop life, Situationist notions of change, of outrage, of excess were a lot of what drove him to create the Sex Pistols.'[3]

It is difficult to reconcile such elevated determinations with the humdrum circumstances of the first live appearance by the Sex Pistols, yet the elements that defined punk for McLaren and would guarantee the group's notoriety were present: aggressively presented non-conformity, an expressive DIY stance and a chaotic outcome.

'From the outset I was determined that they shouldn't play the same old places,' said McLaren. 'When Glen Matlock came up with Saint Martin's it was perfect. Having been at so many, I understood art schools as hotbeds of the dispossessed, and saw that these would be the launch-pad for a different type of group, one which didn't rely on rock 'n' roll venues or clichés.'

On the evening of Thursday 6 November Matlock organised for the Pistols to provide support for a performance by the retro-revivalist outfit

Bazooka Joe, whose drummer Mark Tanner – later a notable sculptor whose life was tragically cut short by illness – was a fellow student.

Bazooka Joe's ranks included bass player Stuart Goddard, then studying graphics at Hornsey College of Art and later to transform himself into Adam Ant. Not much older than the Pistols, he and his fellow musicians had created a band antithetical to the group McLaren and the Pistols envisaged, having carved a name around town as junior members of the pub-rock fraternity, paying their dues by performing enthusiastic versions of original rock 'n' roll songs, dressed in the clothes of 430 King's Road in its Let It Rock phase – creepers, Levi's, black T-shirts – and followed by young Teds, rockers and stylistically aware students. Disregarding the facts that they included in their set the rambunctious Fleetwood Mac cover 'Somebody's Gonna Get Their Head Kicked in Tonite' and their concerts were occasionally marred by outbreaks of crowd trouble, Bazooka Joe were essentially good time guys lacking the Pistols' soon-to-be trademark sulphate-fuelled street suss.

The audience on the night of their live debut included McLaren, Westwood, their accountant Andrew Czezowski and his partner Susan Carrington, Helen Wellington Lloyd, Jordan, Michael Collins, David Harrison and Central School of Art and Design attendees Sebastian Conran, scion of the Habitat design empire launched in the 1960s by his father Terence, and his friend Alex McDowell, now a leading Hollywood set designer. The latter pair had agreed with Matlock for the Pistols to play their college in Holborn the following night, and were eager to witness the strangely named new group in action.

The Pistols arrived without equipment beyond Steve Jones's guitar and Glen Matlock's bass, and McLaren persuaded the headliners to allow them to use their PA and drumkit by claiming the group's non-existent van had broken down on the way to the venue.

'We said sure, OK,' says Bazooka Joe frontman and future film director Danny Kleinman. 'We'd put all the money we'd earned into buying our own gear – 150 watt amps, the works, and were still paying for it on HP, in that we'd put some money down and every week our gig money would go towards the van hire and paying off the loan. There wasn't a lift so we sweated the huge cabinets with concrete bases up six flights of stairs and set it all up.'[4]

During a soundcheck Jones discovered the guitar amp he was assigned was not to his taste. He remembers wheeling a sizeable 100-watt Marshall amp, stolen from Hammersmith Odeon a few months before, from the QT Rooms to Saint Martin's – a distance of 150 yards or so – to use in the performance, for which Lydon wore his adapted Pink Floyd T-shirt, gold-threaded pinstripe 1940s trousers given to him by McLaren, and braces.

'They came in as a gang; they looked like they couldn't give a fuck about anybody,' said Adam Ant. 'Jonesy was tiny, he looked like a young Pete Townshend. Matlock had paint-spattered trousers and a woman's pink leather top. Paul Cook looked like Rod Stewart, like a little Mod really. I watched them play; Malcolm was at the front, orchestrating them, telling them where to stand.'[5]

According to Kleinman, it was Lydon's use – and abuse – of his band's PA that led to their performance descending into disarray.

In front of the crowd of around forty people and stoked by the vodka with which McLaren had primed them, the group played a short set which included covers of the Monkees' '(I'm Not Your) Steppin' Stone', Dave Berry's 'Don't Give Me No Lip Child' and The Who's 'Substitute' as well as the new composition 'Seventeen'.

'They were good but Johnny seemed really embarrassed to be there and kept on turning his back on us,' says David Harrison of his successor.

During a rendition of new song 'Did You No Wrong' the set was abruptly terminated ... by Bazooka Joe. 'I wasn't overly impressed,' admits Kleinman. 'They did cover versions, and by that time we were concentrating on our own material, and there was some not-too-competent playing. They seemed OK until they started smashing up our equipment. Johnny Rotten was kicking one of the speaker cabinets that we hadn't finished paying for and had lumbered up all those stairs.

'I thought, "What's going on? You're not Pete Townshend, mate." I got irate and jumped in and manhandled him so it all stopped. It wasn't my finest hour. I'm probably too dull to have picked up on the fact that this was a game-changing event. Perhaps it set the tone for their later infamy.'

Lydon doesn't recall any applause from audience members during the performance. 'The college audience had never seen anything like it,' he said during a conversation with Paul Cook in the 1990s. 'They couldn't connect with where we were coming from because our stance was so anti-pop, so anti-everything that had gone before.'

Cook responded by neatly summarising the Pistols' attitude as compared with that of groups such as Bazooka Joe: 'We weren't being nice. That was the main difference between us and them.'[6]

Matlock's main memory of the night was Alex McDowell's response. 'He roared with laughter all the way through the set – well, what we managed to do of it. I really thought we'd blown it when I saw him cracking up. But in fact he really liked us.'[7] As did Stuart Goddard, who soon announced his departure from Bazooka Joe.

For McLaren, the group's first public outing confirmed his lifelong dedication to involvement in events that upset the status quo. 'We were angry and determined that we would make something really count in the culture, something really new and something that was not going to be processed,' McLaren said in the 2000s. 'It was something that denied respectability.'

Working from the Bell Street flat, McLaren hustled the Pistols into a series of appearances by working contacts at art schools and colleges in and around London.

Five weeks after the Saint Martin's show, the group attracted a particularly avid young fan, Simon Barker. He attended their sixth live performance, which took place at Ravensbourne College in Chislehurst, Kent, and encouraged friends from his home in a neighbouring suburb to follow him to successive gigs; they became the Pistols' (and punk's) first hardcore fanbase, the so-called Bromley Contingent.

In late November 1975, McLaren gave a wide-ranging interview about Sex and sexual politics to journalist David May for New English Library's recently founded adult magazine *Gallery International*.

'It's unlikely that cities will shake or nations start to rock under the impact of Malcolm McLaren's sexual revolution. A few people might die though,' wrote the prescient May. 'McLaren is a mixture of entrepreneurial cultist, sexual evangelist, businessman, artist, fetishist and political philosopher; a psychotic visionary in the ephemeral subculture of the fashion world.'[8]

Curiously, there was no mention in the piece of the Sex Pistols. This may have been an indicator that McLaren was as yet undecided as to the group's longevity, though after the interview was completed he invited May to attend the appearance at Ravensbourne College.

May was an experienced journalist who extracted thought-provoking material from McLaren. Having emerged from the underground press to build a reputation for fearless reporting for *Time Out* and *Sunday Times*, May had been arrested and cautioned for a series of stories and was heading for hot water in a high-profile court case over an article on the kidnapping of a French banker by Spanish anarchists.

In response to a request from *Gallery International*'s editor Jo Buckley for 'edgy' ideas, May proposed covering Sex after his girlfriend became a customer. 'I'd been in Let It Rock, but one night in 1975 my girlfriend wore a beautiful black calf-length thin latex mac from Sex,' says May. 'She looked stunning; wherever we went that night people were amazed because her dramatic look was in stark contrast to the velvet jackets and the hippy, floaty silks that so many people on the King's Road were dressed in.'[9]

May was aware of the consternation caused by the Cowboys T-shirt prosecution, and impressed not only by the boldness of the Sex project but in particular McLaren's discourse.

'The entire enterprise seemed loaded with danger; these were difficult and controversial ideas McLaren was pushing into the open,' says May, who wrote in the article: 'The shop is an apparently heterogeneous collection of images that, nevertheless, form in McLaren's mind a definite artistic statement.'

May also detailed Sex's customers ('young working class or middle class girls, the fad-seeking rich and the Saturday shopper'), prices (£5 to £50), décor and stock, including the French Letter Suit and the bestselling lines, the shoes ('In clear plastic with peep-toes and pillar-box red soles. Red patent stilettos. Green patent stilettos. Gold iridescent stilettos') and T-shirts ('Not the sort you would buy in boutique land ... little more than two scraps of material sewn together with holes left for the arms and neck').

During their exchange May challenged McLaren on his indifference to the victims of the Cambridge Rapist ('Oh come on . . .'), and also lured him into discussing territory beyond the purview of regular fashion retailers.

McLaren said that he was particularly interested in the social impact of the lingering aftershocks of the global recession that had been caused by the oil crisis of two years previously. In 1975, Britain's economy continued to rest on shaky ground as unemployment rose above the one-million mark.

Without mentioning the Sex Pistols or his fast-hatching plans to use the music business as a gateway to creating controversy and dissent, McLaren told May: 'What I am primarily concerned with is showing young people, eighteen, nineteen years of age, who need to find expression in what they are doing. There are always moods, but it takes someone to articulate them. If it happens to be me, then it's me.'

May closed out the final passage of his interview with McLaren by pondering 'whether he will be able to continue with his extraordinary combination of perversion, decadence and commercial high fashion', and characterised his interviewee's mood as 'suitably apocalyptic' about the outcome.

McLaren's November 1975 prediction on future judgement of his role in the forthcoming – and still unnamed – social experiment must be considered in the light of subsequent events.

'They can only condemn me,' McLaren told May. 'If they do, or have to run me out of town, they have to do it . . . If I take my fantasies to the extreme it is because extremity is where it's at. Anything that is extreme has to be far more important, and I must go to those ends to find out exactly what it means.'

To which May added the coda: 'Assuming, that is, he lives to tell the tale.'

With every appearance, the word-of-mouth about the Sex Pistols among London's cognoscenti grew louder. For example, in the small audience for a concert a month after Saint Martin's – at Chelsea School of Art in early December 1975 – were artist Duggie Fields, Viv Albertine, later of the Slits, and her boyfriend and try-out as second Pistols guitarist Mick Jones.

Albertine and Jones were accompanied by Rory Johnston, a fellow Hammersmith College of Art student who was already acquainted with McLaren. 'I worked at nights behind the bar of the Portobello Hotel, which was one of the few places in town at that time which opened late,' says Johnston, who was to become an important figure in McLaren's life.[10] In shabby Notting Hill, the hotel was a colourful establishment frequented by visiting rock bands, film people and oddballs and the night-desk was run by Sex customer/assistant Alan Jones, who had been at the centre of the Cowboys T-shirt furore the previous year.

'I'd been in the shop in the Teddy boy days and got to know Malcolm when he started turning up at the bar, often with other people from Sex and sometimes the Pistols in tow,' says Johnston, who was studying mural design at Hammersmith. 'Malcolm came off a little bit affected, a bit of a Flash Harry. I liked him. Being on the periphery of the arts world myself, we shared common ground. I could see that the Pistols were coming from an intriguing direction.'

The interest in the Pistols from the likes of Johnston was the result of the steady drumbeat being maintained by McLaren. His notebooks from the period are crowded with addresses and details for colleges, venues and music business contacts. At Chelsea he secured potent live photos of the group by alerting Mick Rock; David Bowie's favourite photographer captured the wild-eyed Lydon in a Cambridge Rapist top, Steve Jones striking guitar-hero poses with Sylvain Sylvain's Gibson in a Cowboys T-shirt and Matlock sporting a suedehead hooligan crop. The group looked as they sounded: like none other.

Meantime, McLaren tested promotional possibilities with a series of portraits taken by photographer Peter Christopherson, who had recommended Crunchy Frog the year before and worked at Hipgnosis across the courtyard in 6 Denmark Street.

Shot at the local YMCA and in the dank surrounds of the Denmark Street cloisters, the band members were presented as passive dead-end kid archetypes: Cook comatose in his bed, his torso adorned with bullet holes, Matlock cast as a rent boy, leaning over a sink, swathing his bare chest with a towel, Lydon a grinning lunatic in a straitjacket and Jones a felon in prison pyjamas and handcuffs. In the event, they weren't considered usable by McLaren, who thought them too downbeat.

It wasn't long before the Pistols received their first national media mention, in a review of an all-night end-of-term party at posh Queen Elizabeth College in Kensington. McLaren had wangled them onto the bill with such live stalwarts as Georgie Fame & the Blue Flames by accepting payment for expenses only.

'The Sex Pistols were huddled against a far wall of the dance floor,' wrote *New Musical Express* staffer Kate Phillips. 'They are all about 12 years old. Or maybe about 19, but you could be fooled.' Pointing out that McLaren was the manager, Phillips predicted: 'They're going to be the Next Big Thing. Or maybe the Next Big Thing After That.'[11]

Meanwhile McLaren amplified the Pistols' outsider qualities in the dedication of a new artwork to them. 'This was my first attempt at making a Sex Pistols T-shirt,' said McLaren in the 2000s. 'I wanted to create something of a stir.'

The design centred on a repeat monochrome print of a prepubescent boy holding a cigarette dangerously close to his flaccid penis. The photograph came from a copy of the paedophilic magazine *Boys Express* acquired by McLaren in a backstreet shop in Brixton.

Once again, McLaren was heading for Lost Boys/*Johnny Go Home* territory (the outrage over the documentary had not abated), but the absence of prurience in the design was magnified by the other elements. Over the multiple boy images was an outline of Matlock's bass screened in red, around which McLaren lettered the group name in capitals containing musical notations referencing the Let It Rock era.

Working with sidekick and screen-printer Bernard Rhodes, McLaren created a series of variants, continuing the Sex approach of producing T-shirts as multiples. 'Bernie was a bit frightened by the nude-boy print,' McLaren recalled. 'It was too much for him. He used to perspire as he printed at the kitchen table, as if somebody was about to break down the door, arrest him and charge him with being a paedophile, and haul him off to prison. That would have been all my fault.'

Unappreciative that the 'Smoking Boy' was but the latest manifestation of McLaren's campaign to make public the seamy sexual underbelly of Britain's repressive society, Rhodes remained furious decades later at McLaren for having involved him in the escapade. 'Look, I'm saying this only once,' asserted Rhodes in 2007. 'I worked on a few of those shirts but wasn't interested in naked little boys, not because I'm square, but because it's dull. Vivienne and Malcolm come from repressed, Victorian, middle-class backgrounds so they get a kick out of that stuff.'

The design precipitated a split with Rhodes, who was disappointed that his demands to co-manage the Pistols had been rejected by McLaren. From this point Rhodes set about gathering the component members for what he envisaged as a rival group, The Clash.

McLaren was undeterred by Rhodes's unwillingness to continue printing the T-shirts. 'All I needed was to announce the group's name and draw a guitar,' said McLaren. 'We didn't make very many, forty or fifty at most, and they were in quite small sizes. They were supposed to be sold in the store but at first I gave them away to people who looked cool.'

Among recipients were Caroline Coon, the radical activist who became an early champion of the Pistols during a spell as a *Melody Maker* journalist, as well as Chrissie Hynde and her compatriot the photographer Kate Simon, who lived in west London with another US camera-wielder, McLaren's friend Joe Stevens.

'Malcolm dropped the shirts off at my Finborough Road studio; they were freshly silk-screened,' says Stevens, who was up for provocation, having cut his teeth on underground press titles such as *IT* and *Friends*. 'Chrissie was living in a squat and cleaning offices for a living. She'd drop by the pad to take showers. I'd hear her singing in there and realised she had a wonderful voice. The shirts were supposed to be for me but the ladies kept them.'[12]

ICA curator Ted Polhemus was also given a Smoking Boy shirt, and on 4 February 1976, McLaren and Westwood acquiesced to his request that they participate in the institution's fashion forum. This placed Sex in the context of such contemporaries as Rae Spencer-Cullen, whose retro-kitsch label Miss Mouse featured similar synthetic materials and directional designs, as did Esme Young and Willie Walters's Swanky Modes. Also participating were Alice Pollock's label and shop Quorum, which had been around for a decade and showcased the designs of Ossie Clark and the textiles of his wife Celia Birtwell, Shelagh Brown, who had been at Harrow Art School with McLaren, and Paul Howie, the Australian fashion designer who ran a boutique in Fulham with his wife, the uber-PR (and model for *Absolutely Fabulous*'s Edina) Lynne Franks.

McLaren opted out of participating publicly, so Westwood and Jordan were interviewed about fetish design by the *Guardian*'s Angela Neustatter, who had talked to McLaren for her piece on futuristic fashion the previous spring.

'Malcolm was lurking in the audience with the members of the Sex Pistols who were generally being rowdy and causing a commotion,' says Polhemus. 'The conversation had just got into the ways in which rubber could be used in fashion when two firemen burst in and announced that we were OK, the building wasn't on fire. I found out much later that while they were talking Malcolm had encouraged the Pistols to set off the fire alarm as an act of Situationist disruption.'

Delighted at the turn of events, the game Polhemus promptly booked the group to perform at the arts institution, but was soon blocked on the grounds that the ICA didn't then have a live music licence.

Just three months into their career, the Pistols found themselves at the centre of fast-accelerating interest, stoked by their manager but mainly due to their unique musical stance and uncompromising attitude, particularly towards fellow groups, audience members and even each other.

At one 100 Club performance an onstage contretemps with Matlock led to Lydon storming offstage and out of the venue onto Oxford Street, where McLaren found him waiting at a bus stop and informed him that if he did not return to the performance he was out of the group. Lydon acquiesced, but the incident served to advance his dislike of both the manager and his bass-playing bandmate.

On the heels of the ICA event came the first substantial recognition of the group's existence, again in a live review in the *New Musical Express*.

The music paper's features editor Neil Spencer had been alerted to the Pistols by Kate Phillips and her partner Tony Tyler, the assistant editor who had also been at the Queen Elizabeth College all-nighter a few weeks before. Spencer and Tyler seized their opportunity when McLaren informed the paper the Pistols were supporting Essex R&B group Eddie & the Hot Rods at Soho rock venue the Marquee.

'When we arrived the doorman said: "You'd better get in there quick, they're busting the place up,"' Spencer said years later. 'I opened the door and a chair sailed across the room and crash-landed. There were only about twenty people there, but it was immediately obvious that something fantastic was going on.'[13]

Enlivened by a Mick Rock close-up of the spiky-haired Lydon, Spencer's review – headed 'Don't look over your shoulder but the Sex Pistols are coming' – provided exciting copy which challenged the rest of the content of that week's issue. Aside from the cover star Patti Smith, who was granted reverential treatment by McLaren's NYC *bête noire*

Lisa Robinson, and articles on reggae stars U-Roy and Toots Hibbert, the rest of the editorial was dedicated to such plain fare as Genesis sans Peter Gabriel, Manfred Eicher of jazz label ECM and fast-fading pop star David Cassidy.

Crucially, Spencer's review ended with an inflammatory exchange with Steve Jones:

'"Actually we're not into music," one of the Pistols confided afterwards.

'Wot then?

'"We're into chaos."'[14]

From this point, McLaren's energetic PR input ensured that the Pistols would become as much a media as a musical phenomenon. For example, the 'Thrills' gossip column in the following week's issue of the *NME* noted that they had been sacked from the series of support spots for Eddie & the Hot Rods over their antics at the Marquee (from which they were also barred).

But the paper was not to keep tabs on the group's progress for several months, allowing such rivals as *Melody Maker* and *Sounds* to pick up the baton on championing the group. This was due to McLaren and the Pistols' revised attitude towards former fellow traveller and *NME* star writer Nick Kent; the assault on Chrissie Hynde in Sex and attempts to co-opt the younger musicians before Lydon's entry the previous summer had not been forgotten.

When McLaren was photographed by Kate Simon embroiled in a fight in front of the stage at west London pub venue the Nashville Rooms while the Pistols played – triggered by Westwood slapping another audience member – the other music papers made hay, with journalists such as *Melody Maker*'s Caroline Coon and *Sounds*' Jonh Ingham gaining access to the Pistols via McLaren.

Ingham, a sharp-witted Australian who had grown up in the US and worked for the music press there before migrating to Britain, was looking to make a name for himself among the crowded rock-crit ranks.

His early encounters with the group enlightened him to the odd dynamic imposed by McLaren. There had been pushy managers and agents in popular music before, but never one as willing to assume the role of public-facing conceptualist and spokesperson.

Having seen the group after reading Spencer's *NME* review, Ingham requested an interview. McLaren insisted they meet in a central London café. 'It was kind of an audition,' says Ingham. 'I was impressed with his articulacy and grasp of the social impact he was convinced the group was going to have, but more than that I was amazed by the audacity of his look: he was wearing black leather jeans and jacket and a pink nylon polo neck. It was March, so quite cool outside, but inside the café was stuffy, yet he showed no sign of the discomfort he must have felt. I realised then that the group's music and the clothes that he and they wore required conviction.'[15]

Even though Ingham's request was accepted, he was given the runaround. The group failed to turn up for the first assignation, and when they finally met, Lydon was initially absent, so concerned was McLaren about the singer's ability to alienate outsiders. When he arrived, Lydon provided electrifying quotes, which Ingham incorporated into an article that lit the fuse to wider music press and industry interest.

Meanwhile the group blazed a trail of wreckage around the live circuit, as exemplified by Lydon again provoking an aggressive audience response when he smashed monitors belonging to McLaren's one-time Let It Rock compadre Screaming Lord Sutch.

'The effect it had on you was to think about it all the time,' said Sutch of the Pistols' performance. 'My band said, "What an amateur bunch of bastards they are." I said, "But look at all the bands that have supported us. How many of them do you remember?" They created something that night. The crowd reacted against them.'[16]

Similar mayhem proceeded when McLaren leveraged his art-world contacts to book the Pistols to play a St Valentine's party held by the British artist Andrew Logan at his New York-style warehouse loft on the banks of the Thames in Bermondsey. The tone of the evening was set when Lydon – in the full embrace of an acid trip – gained entry after a misunderstanding at the door and punched Westwood in the face as a form of misguided retribution.

During the final of three sets that night, McLaren encouraged Jordan to strip her clothes off and wrestle with Lydon. In the audience was the group's erstwhile guitarist Nick Kent who viewed the event as a stand-off between two subsects of London's counterculture. 'Logan's premises were somehow instantly transformed into a highly amusing tentative baiting-ground for a kind of aesthetic gang-warfare,' reported Kent several months later.

> On one side was the by now long established Logan Set – a sprawl-ing array of stagnating lounge-lizard males and predatory-looking females all of whom having so earnestly cultivated an air of heavy-duty ennui that they looked like they spend the majority of their waking hours ensconced in an opium den even though drugs are so irrevocably passé.
>
> And then there was the Sex shop faction. They were quite easy to tell because of their chosen uniform: all tarty jet-black dyed hair plus an abundance of leather, ripped T-shirts and a particular twist to the features which broke open the old ennui death mask of Logan's well-seasoned poseur bunch with a sort of insular 'don't mess with me' sense of tough.
>
> They looked slightly diseased, morose in a way that was soon to stand as a visual prototype for the standard hard-core brutal thug-gish-ness of the Sex Pistols' most select aficionados; safety-pins in the left nostril, missing earlobes, the works . . . The strange thing was, though, that it still looked to be a pose – pretty impressive but a pose nonetheless, and as such it was just as sexless and desperate as Logan's washed-up crew.[17]

McLaren fed off such exercises. 'The Sex Pistols were the epitome of chaos and disorder, which is just what I wanted,' said McLaren in the 1990s. 'This was where I had been most at home since I was a child with no structure in my life. The Sex shop and the Sex Pistols were a continu-ation of that family, a world I could manipulate that had no rules, that was about the destruction of anything ordered – this was something I had learned as a child.'

This perversity was acknowledged in McLaren's continuing denial of the family unit to which he could justifiably have laid claim: Westwood, Joe and Ben. Although he socialised with his partner and worked with her on designs for the shop, he was still spending most of his time at Wellington Lloyd's Bell Street flat, using it as an office to book gigs and generate promotional material with the group's newly employed road manager Nils Stevenson.

'That's where we came up with the Sex Pistols ransom-note lettering,' said McLaren. 'I knew from our days at Goldsmiths that Helen was great with found materials, and she simply cut up newspaper pages to create a new visual language.'

Using the same approach taken with the New York Dolls twelve months previously, McLaren issued a distinctive press statement.

It began, 'Teenagers from London's Shepherds Bush and Finsbury Park. "We hate everything" . . .', and proceeded to set out their biography as creation myth, with McLaren dead centre: 'The boys met at the shop Sex in Chelsea's World's End in October '75. Enthused and spurred on by the shop owner, Malcolm McLaren, they became the Sex Pistols. November found them gatecrashing college gigs throughout London and its suburbs, causing furore wherever they went . . . The Sex Pistols' spontaneity and honesty threatens all the highly packaged pop of the past.'

In regard to the Pistols, McLaren believed that, even more than himself, the boutique was integral to extending the group's music into the realm of art/fashion conceptualism. In the early 2000s, he wrote: 'The Sex Pistols could only really exist in the context of the store – created energy and focus – they had failure programmed into them. The SEX PISTOLS as a product does not exist – There was only ever the Sex Pistols as an idea.'

In early 1976 McLaren created a new design for Sex by using his son Joe's stencil kit to emblazon the SI's slogan 'Be Reasonable Demand the Impossible' in black across the front of a few white shirts, and wore one for a portrait by Joe Stevens that appeared in an interview about Sex in the short-lived lifestyle magazine *Street Life* in the spring of 1976, by which time the Pistols were in full swing.

Headed 'Would You Buy a Rubber T-shirt from This Man?', the feature is striking on two fronts. Firstly, McLaren was sharpening his take on contemporary pop culture to such an extent that it was jam-packed with quotable lines predicting the oncoming punk phenomenon.

'I think now that kids have a hankering to be part of a movement, like Teddy boys in the 50s and mods in the 60s,' said McLaren. 'They want to be the same, to associate with a movement that's hard and tough and in the open, like the clothes we're selling here.'[18]

Secondly, and inexplicably, McLaren does not mention his involvement in the Sex Pistols or the role played by the shop in their formation, and there is no reference to them; odd when one considers the majority of *Street Life*'s content was dedicated to music.

The same goes for an interview Westwood gave to adult magazine *Forum* a month or so later. Like McLaren, she was keen to discuss sexual politics and the foregrounding of fetishism as a means of challenging established values, but even though the photographs taken by David Dagley included Steve Jones, nowhere in the piece by American staff writer Len Richmond was there an allusion to the Pistols.

Richmond had been drawn to 430 King's Road by the pink vinyl Sex sign. 'The leather gear interested me,' says Richmond. 'As a gay guy from San Francisco I was into leather, though I thought the rubber stuff was curious. I hadn't really hooked into the British love of rubber, the cutting-off of the air, the really constrictive clothing. It kind of horrified me, to be honest, as liberal as I was. But I saw that the t-shirts with the porn extracts were part of the overall act of rebellion. Whatever they could do to piss off people, they would.'[19]

Richmond suspected that the rubberwear was part of the arsenal of provocation. 'It was another way to say: "Nothing bothers us. We're going to throw this in your face and get a reaction from you." I suppose the Sex Pistols were a natural progression of that attitude.'

During Richmond's visit McLaren took a backseat; Westwood had complained to him that she was not receiving the media coverage that she thought was her due. And so she gave the journalist a tour and history of their residence at 430 King's Road, laced with McLaren-style polemic.

'We're here to convert, liberate and educate,' Westwood told Richmond. 'We want to inspire people to have the confidence to live out their fantasies and change. What we're really making is a political statement with our shop by attempting to attack the system.'[20]

On Richmond's return for the photoshoot with Dagley a couple of days later, the atmosphere was very different, with Jones, Chrissie Hynde, Alan Jones, Jordan and equally buxom customer Danielle Lewis in attendance.

'It was like a party,' says Richmond. 'Everyone was so wild; I don't know whether it was drugs or what to put it down to, but they didn't have any of that British fear of sex. Look, I got laid a lot in England; that's one of the reasons I stayed eighteen years. I found the British were so inhibited about picking each other up that when I went into gay bars and was assertive, I frequently got what I wanted.

'So, to me, everyone in England seemed ashamed of the fact that they had sexual needs. But at the photoshoot I was in an environment which actually embarrassed me, quite a feat at the time. When the women painted the letters S, E, and X on their buttocks and started sticking their arses into the photographer's face I thought: "This is too hot for *Forum*! These people are on another planet."'

Dagley was phlegmatic. 'I could see that this was ground-breaking stuff, but for me it was just another job,' says the photographer. 'It was my idea that they write the shop name on their buttocks. I thought it would add another fun element to the session, and they were certainly up for it.'

So up for it, in fact, that Richmond fled. 'I had to get the hell out of there once we were through,' says Richmond. 'It was too much for me, very heterosexually threatening. They were basically saying: "Fuck me, fuck me, fuck me", very into touching and seducing. I don't know that they would have gone through with it but I could tell they rather enjoyed my fear.

'When I reflect on that day I realise it was a turning point in my life. I was very smug about being so sexually liberated but these people taught me I was still inhibited, a bit behind the times. That was sobering and I was never quite so smug again.'

Chapter 21

The atmosphere of abandon propagated by Malcolm McLaren spilled over into Pistols concerts, where Lydon's bullyboy friend Sid Vicious sparked brawls by starting the trend of crashing into other audience attendees when he created the bounding, vertical dance which became known as the 'Pogo'.

As 1976 progressed, the young filmmaker Julien Temple snuck into performances to capture the group playing live. Captivated by 'the stunning, Antonin Artaud-like theatricality' of the *mise en scène*, Temple abandoned a student mod film he was developing in favour of a project about the Pistols and their audience. 'Malcolm was very strict about people filming the band,' says Temple. 'The first time me and the sound guy were discovered, he threw us out. The next time he let us stay after I explained we were students using college equipment, not shooting for commercial gain.'

Soon, Temple fell under McLaren's spell. 'I found him intriguing, charismatic and constantly surprising, particularly when he was explaining to me his need to patrol access to the group,' says Temple. 'He was already very clear that they were going to be huge and that the ideas around the Pistols were more important than the group itself. That wasn't a normal thing for a manager to say. He was more of a propagandist.'[1]

The young film student started taping the group in earnest during a spring residency at Oxford Street's 100 Club. Early fan David Harrison had by now witnessed several performances, which culminated in an altercation into which he was drawn at the central London venue.

Harrison believes this was instigated by Lydon. 'I was sitting at a table with some friends when I noticed Johnny Rotten point straight at me while he was singing,' says Harrison. 'The next thing I knew an entire tray of glasses was emptied over me by this horrible bloke standing behind me.

'At that point the East End came out. I told my friend to get round the back of him and pin his arms while I booted him in the bollocks with my winklepickers, all the while thinking to myself: "He may dress like a queen, but can kick like a mule."

'He started screaming: "Don't hurt me, don't hurt me!" Of course it was Sid Vicious, an absolute plank. He was on the verge of tears.'

Unbothered by Lydon's dislike for Harrison, McLaren remained interested in exploring his potential and drew the twenty-year-old into plans he was hatching for a stable of performers under his management auspices, in the manner of the early 1960s independent music business entrepreneur Larry Parnes.

Notebook suggestions for names for group with proposed line-up including
Chrissie Hynde on bass and Richard Hell as vocalist, 1976. Paul Burgess Archive.

McLaren's 1976 notebooks reveal potential band names for new acts, including Teenage Novels, Le Bomb, The Beyond, The Subterraneans and The Damned. One line-up, the Loveboys or Lover Boy, was to include Richard Hell on guitar and Chrissie Hynde – with short hair and men's clothes – on bass.[2]

But Hell remained unwilling to make the Atlantic crossing, particularly since his new group the Voidoids was taking shape, so – in a repetition of the approach he made to Harrison the previous year – McLaren, with Hynde in tow, tackled Harrison about joining a new group at his workplace at the Covent Garden vintage store Nostalgia.

'I wasn't really up for it, particularly after what had happened with the Pistols,' says Harrison. 'Not that I was sore about that, but more because I didn't think I could sing. But Malcolm was insistent, and said I would be up front with another guy called Dave.'

This was twenty-year-old David Lett, who had adopted the surname Zero and was to change it to Vanian. McLaren enlisted Chris Millar as the drummer, having approached him at a Pink Fairies gig at Dingwall's dancehall by the canal in shabby Camden Town.

'Malcolm had heard that I could drum and asked whether I'd be interested,' says Millar, who became better known by the punk soubriquet Rat Scabies. 'I didn't have a phone where I lived in Notting Hill so wrote my address on a piece of paper. The next morning he turned up at my front door with Chrissie and they got me into the group. It seemed to me to be a genius idea to have the two Daves fronting it.'[3]

McLaren gave the new ensemble the absurd name Masters of the Backside and booked them rehearsal time in a studio. 'I thought it would be funny to do it with someone else,' says Harrison. 'Maybe I could camp it up a bit. The other David was very nice but a bit strange. He was in love with Jordan, forever going on about whether we thought she loved him or not.'

Masters of the Backside covered Harrison favourites such as the Troggs' 1960s hit 'Wild Thing'. 'Chrissie came round to my house and looked through what records I had left which Steve Jones hadn't stolen,' says Harrison. 'She saw I had King Floyd's "Groove Me" so we also did that.'

Somewhere along the way, Scabies's Croydon pal Ray Burns – who became known as Captain Sensible – was drafted in as bass player. After a few rehearsals McLaren and Westwood arrived to check on developments, and the musicians performed a short set, though Harrison was irritated that Vanian adopted a Johnny Rotten-style approach to his vocals. 'Vivienne and Malcolm said that they thought what we were doing was OK, and after they left Chrissie took over and sang a song,' recalls Harrison. 'I remember saying, "For fuck's sake you've got such a good voice, what's the point of us doing it?" And that was it for me.'

Hynde remembers Harrison as being as reticent as he was when he was tested for the Sex Pistols. 'It was a complete madhouse, of course, because this shy Dave didn't want to do live gigs,' said Hynde in the late 1970s. 'McLaren was too busy dealing with the Pistols, and the rest of the boys really wanted to gig. So they went off and formed The Damned and I was on my own again.'[4]

New groups were launching at every turn, with McLaren often playing a part. Joe Strummer had joined The Clash after the Pistols had supported his pub-rockers the 101'ers. 'I walked onstage while they were doing their sound-check and heard Malcolm going to John "Do you want those kind of shoes that Steve's got or the kind that Paul's got? What sort of sweater do you want?" And I thought, "Blimey they've got a manager and he's offering them clothes!"'[5]

Meanwhile Mancunians Howard Devoto and Pete Shelley formed Buzzcocks when McLaren not only gave them the go-ahead to arrange appearances by the Pistols in their city but also paid for the venue hire. Famously, at these gigs, many audience members were inspired to become musicians and performers, including Steven Morrissey (the Smiths) and Mark E. Smith (The Fall). At the first, poorly attended performance at the city's Lesser Free Trade Hall, Peter Hook, who became the bass player in Joy Division and New Order, articulated the galvanising effect McLaren had hoped the Sex Pistols would have on Britain's youth.

Malcolm McLaren sold me my ticket, dressed in leather. There really was a feeling that the aliens had landed. When you went in, there was hardly anybody there. The Sex Pistols, their attitude and the noise was horrendous. I've since heard a bootleg and they actually played quite well. There were a lot of cover versions and it was mostly rock 'n' roll, but on that night you felt as though you were party to something unique, something revolutionary. I wanted to tell the world to fuck off, just like Johnny Rotten. Bernard [Sumner of Joy Division and New Order] and I formed a group on the spot and walked out as musicians.[6]

At an appearance by visiting Americans the Ramones and Talking Heads at the Camden venue the Roundhouse McLaren made an approach to the nineteen-year-old south Londoner Vic Napper, who was part of a gang of friends that dressed in an unusual style.

'McLaren said, "You look like you are in a band," ' recalled Napper, who changed his surname to Godard and became the frontman of Subway Sect. 'We were wearing Oxfam clothes dyed all dark grey to make us look really drab. [It was] McLaren who told us to form a group.'[7]

Once again, McLaren paid for rehearsal time, telling Godard and the other members of Subway Sect that he intended to add them to the bill of a two-day punk festival he was arranging at the 100 Club as a means of consolidating record company attention.

Similarly, while on a visit to Paris in the summer of 1976 to organise an appearance by the Sex Pistols in the French capital, McLaren spied an interesting-looking young woman in a flea market. 'I was wearing my usual attire at the time, which included completely destroyed jeans held together with safety pins,' says Elli Medeiros, then twenty years old.

I had on a ragged old sweater full of holes plus a pink coat from the 40s with stuff glued onto it, playing cards, plastic eggs, spiders, that kind of thing.

This guy walks up to me and starts asking about my clothes. I tell him I think they're beautiful and I don't feel that anybody should dictate what is or isn't beautiful. He asks what I do, and I realize he maybe wants to hire me, so I tell him I sing in a band. He says, 'I'm organising a punk festival in London, do you want to come?'[8]

And so, in late September, Medeiros and the other members of her group Stinky Toys made their debut appearance at the 100 Club alongside the Pistols, Subway Sect, The Clash, The Damned, Chris Spedding and the Vibrators, and the early line-up of Siouxsie & the Banshees, another group which had formed at McLaren's suggestion.

A couple of weeks prior to this event were the Pistols' clutch of performances in Paris for the reopening of the venerable Bois de Vincennes dancehall Chalet du Lac, which had been refurbished by young designer Philippe Starck. McLaren had been angling to take the group to the city since its inception, and the visit provided an opportunity to showcase the collection of new designs he had worked up with Westwood for sale in Sex in the capital of haute couture.

Among these was a so-called 'Peter Pan' shirt repeat-printed with a Peeping Tom-style nudie playing card. The shirt's distinctive rounded collar was based on a sample acquired from a supplier of uniforms for Britain's elite boarding schools.

'I was always interested in uniforms, particularly school uniforms which were part of the repressive society,' said McLaren. 'To have this shirt from the manufacturer for those schools was interesting. We also did sleeveless versions with leatherette or vinyl panelling over the shoulders.'

Lydon and McLaren were too similar to forge a profound relationship, but the younger man was open to new and radical ideas and absorbed the social and political commentary espoused by McLaren, Vivienne Westwood and Jamie Reid, who had returned from the Outer Hebrides at McLaren's insistence to handle the group's graphics.

Among the results was a song that had been worked up over the summer and became the Pistols' clarion call and soon-to-be debut single 'Anarchy in the UK'.

Against a fiery backdrop Lydon uttered a series of declamations. The lyrics were entirely his composition – there is no basis in Westwood's 2014 claim that she came up with the song title – but some of the content may be traced back to conversations around McLaren and Reid's engagement with the Situationist International, King Mob and Suburban Press.

'One of the central images of "Anarchy in the UK" is the idea of all of England as a single, lifeless, ugly, empty block of public housing,' said critic Greil Marcus. 'England: "Another council tenancy" – that is the Situationist critique of architecture and society boiled down to a couple of lines.'9

To complement the song, McLaren worked with Westwood on producing a companion garment: the 'Anarchy' shirt, made by accessorising dead stock McLaren had acquired for 430 King's Road during its retro-tailored period in 1973. 'We had boxes of about fifty cluttering the hallway in Clapham,' said McLaren. 'I got them from a warehouse in London, E1; they were manufactured in the sixties college-boy style by Wemblex Ltd. Most were pinstriped with rounded, pin-through collars with a tiny embroidered hole on each tip. I wanted to use them to make a visual statement the Sex Pistols could wear to express the mood they were celebrating.'

Westwood had begun the project by painting vertical stripes onto one of the shirts 'in deliberately dull and dirty colours; this had the appearance of a shirt worn by an inmate of Buchenwald or another concentration camp. It had impact but there wasn't enough energy,' said McLaren. 'There needed to be more of a collage to fit in with the mixture of messages in the song, so at the flat she and I started by turning the shirts inside out. We had done this with T-shirts – exposing the seams; interior detail gave garments more presence.

'Then we hand-painted them with dyes, and I chose a series of slogans from the Situationists and other anarchist movements which we stencilled using our son's John Bull printing set. I also wrote them on silk patches using a twig dipped in bleach, a technique I had learnt at art school. On each we placed a silk patch portrait of Karl Marx; I bought these at a Maoist bookshop in Chinatown. We chose Marx because we admired him; also he had lived in London and we liked his beard. In a final flourish we replaced the original generic shirt buttons with specific pearl stud buttons of the period.

'By this time the shirts had taken on a disorderly and uncared-for look, but deliberately and carefully constructed to appear this way. Each shirt took four to five days to complete and caused great excitement.'

The most impactful of their new designs was a strap-laden trousers-and-jacket combination called the 'Bondage' suit. The first production run used black sateen cotton; McLaren had noticed that this was the backing of waistcoats worn by British Rail guards and tracked down the fabric supplier, Cottrells, to its factory in Manchester.

The trousers derived from a pair of US military baker pants McLaren had brought back from the stay in the southern states with the New York Dolls the previous year.

'At that time, we needed to make a symbolic gesture in clothes that suggested bondage,' McLaren said in 2008. 'I decided to make a pair of trousers in order to dress an army of disenfranchised youth and the answer was to put a strap between the legs. I set about working with Vivienne using the marine trousers as a base and put zips in the back of the trouser leg on the thigh and at the bottom, so one could pull the trouser leg tighter together.

'The zipper went under the crotch and wound its way up the arse. When you undid them, your goolies fell out. They were about the explosion of the body, a declaration of war against repression, a Luddite uniform battling high-street consumer fashions. Then I added something that made the trouser feel primitive: an infant, Tarzan-like nappy at the back, dyed grey or black.'

The matching top was modelled on an oiled canvas jacket produced by the traditional British outerwear brand Barbour, but the collar integrated by McLaren and Westwood was removable, with a strap so that it could be tightened around the neck. With more straps across the chest and arms, the garment resembled a high fashion straitjacket. And for complementary footwear, the design duo created Bondage boots in canvas and soft leather, based on a military snowshoe and made by their Greek shoemaker in Camden.

The photogenic John Lydon proved a worthy mannequin by wearing the first of the Bondage suits with McLaren's Basque beret on the Paris trip, while McLaren designed a striking poster, based on the Smoking Boy artwork in pink and green. This attracted the leading members of Parisian demi-monde since the Chalet du Lac performances were organised by photographer Pierre Bénain with help from interior designer and writer François Baudot.

'The Sex Pistols seemed an excellent choice to reopen the club,' said Bénain, who had been put in contact with McLaren by Michel Esteban, a prime mover on the new punk scene as operator of the Paris mail-order music shop Harry Cover and the magazine *Rock News*.[10] Esteban had met the Pistols' manager in New York and London with his partner Lizzy Mercier Descloux and started handling the career of the Stinky Toys at McLaren's suggestion.

Bénain acceded to McLaren's demand for a performance fee of £1000 for two concerts; one on the opening night, a Friday, and another two days later. The Chalet's capacity was 800; on the Friday night more than 2000 invited guests attempted to enter the venue, while around 200 showed up for the 4 p.m. gig on the Sunday afternoon.

With Lydon in the centre in Bondage suit, creepers and Peter Pan-collared Peeping Tom shirt flanked by Jones and Matlock in Anarchy shirts, the group performed on Starck's dramatically underlit stage in front of the Parisian demi-monde, including Bénain, Esteban and Descloux as well as the record shop owner and band manager Marc Zermati and such fashionistas as Jean-Paul Gaultier, Yves Saint Laurent, Karl Lagerfeld, then designing for the upmarket labels Chloé and Fendi, and Kenzo Takada.

The latter was one of a number of Japanese designers who had by this time latched onto McLaren and Westwood's work; Yohji Yamamoto was another while Rei Kawakubo, who opened the first Comme des Garçons store in Tokyo around the time the Pistols played the Chalet, was particularly keen, buying entire new ranges of clothing as soon as they were stocked in the store.

'I had connections through all those clients and met Rei Kawakubo that way and Yohji Yamamoto and Lagerfeld,' McLaren said in 2005. 'They all drifted through the shop. I had no fucking idea who they were but after a while I got to know them. The whole bondage suit was unveiled at the Chalet du Lac, which was some crazy little folly in the Bois de Vincennes. And cross-legged on the floor in the front row were Kenzo, Karl, Yves . . .'[11]

Also present, of course, was Jean-Charles de Castelbajac. 'Malcolm called, told me they were coming and asked me to take care of the Bromley Contingent,' says de Castelbajac. 'He was always trying to fix me up with someone; I remember during that call he told me he thought me and Jordan would be perfect together! The whole thing was much more frenetic than when he came with the Dolls. There was a friction already developing between Malcolm and Johnny. I became close to Paul, Glen and Steve, but Johnny saw my friendship with Malcolm as a problem and so was more difficult.'

Back in London, with queues around the block, McLaren's 100 Club Punk Festival proved the point where punk broke through into public consciousness, amplified by the behaviour of the Pistols' self-appointed audience provocateur Sid Vicious.

He took part as a performer, drumming in the first line-up of Siouxsie & the Banshees, but it was Vicious's offstage antics that encouraged the media view that punk was in essence a violent movement: in separate incidents he was disarmed by the 100 Club's Ron Watts after threatening Elli Medeiros with a knife, attacked Nick Kent with a bicycle chain and was arrested and put on remand for blinding a concertgoer after throwing a beer glass at The Damned which shattered against one of the venue's pillars.

McLaren professed a blasé attitude to such mindless actions. This was heartless, and served to fuel the perception of him as the key advocate of a careering youth cult. 'The violence was magnificent; it was something that gave all those kids a terrific identity, made them proud of their future,' said McLaren much later. 'So someone got blinded? Well there are far worse things that happen for far worse causes. One person blinded, a couple of people badly hurt – the achievement outweighed it completely.'[12]

The effect of such events and the similarities between the groups that played the festival were to codify punk in the public imagination as articulated through youthful, belligerent mistrust of the status quo.

Despite considerable reservations, this provided purchase for Britain's out-of-touch music industry executives, upon whom it was finally dawning that the combination of bizarre fashion and abrasive music could prove commercially viable when packaged for mass consumption.

They were also aware that international coverage was beginning to gather pace; around this time the Pistols dominated an issue of the big-selling German teen title *Bravo*, with five pages of photographs of the group by Abba's favourite photographer Wolfgang 'Bubi' Heilemann headlined 'Wild Backstreet Boys . . . Trash Fashion'.[13]

McLaren himself cut a striking figure on the streets of London, as recalled by James Truman, then in his late teens but later to become a close friend when he was a prominent magazine publisher within the Condé Nast group.

'I first became aware of Malcolm by seeing him one Saturday afternoon on Charing Cross Road,' says Truman. 'London at that time was grey, depressed and broken, which seemed to be reflected in the drab wardrobe that almost everyone wore, of head-to-toe denim. Malcolm was dressed in a brilliant bright red suit with some kind of thick-soled brothel-creeper shoes and this wild mane of red hair, stopping the traffic.

'He looked like he'd come out of a vaudeville show, or maybe a Victorian madhouse, and bystanders just stopped in their tracks in front of him and stared, incredulous. I did the same. Malcolm was doing what he did best, talking loudly and without pause to his friend, who was dressed in a style that was already becoming familiar as punk, with the ripped T-shirt and so on. It may even have been one of the Sex Pistols. I don't remember because I couldn't take my eyes off Malcolm. I don't even remember if I knew who he was at that time. But I never forgot that first impression.'[14]

On the day of the Pistols' appearance at the 100 Club, McLaren signed the group to a three-year management contract with Glitterbest, an off-the-shelf company he acquired for £100. Under the terms of the deal, the group members assigned all aspects of their professional lives to Glitterbest, which took 25 per cent of earnings (5 per cent above the industry standard) while they shared 50 per cent of merchandise profits with the management. A clause in the contract set out that the name 'Sex Pistols' was created by McLaren and belonged to him.

At twenty-three, road manager Nils Stevenson was more worldly than the group's members and advised them against signing the Glitterbest agreement. 'I could see how heavily in favour of Malcolm it was,' he said. 'I'd always been led to believe that I'd get some percentage of the management, that I'd get some points out of it. I looked for my name and it wasn't there. Rotten was saying, "It's alright, if you don't want a part of it, I'm leaving", which was all nonsense.'[15]

This agreement formalised the relationship that had begun on McLaren's return from New York seventeen months previously; his co-director in the company was the lawyer Steven Fisher. Meanwhile Jamie Reid's partner and fellow radical from the Suburban Press Sophie Richmond became McLaren's secretary, while the QT Rooms rehearsal space bought by McLaren a year earlier was now among the new company's assets.

Cannily, McLaren secured the group a deal for their original song compositions (the members shared equal rights in these) with EMI Music Publishing's Terry Slater. In what he considered a 'cheap deal' Slater advanced £500 in cash to each of them in return for a three-year contract with an option of renewal.

Slater's prescience encouraged his counterparts at EMI Records, so McLaren – who had by now left Bell Street and moved back in with Westwood, Ben and Joe at Thurleigh Court – set about sealing negotiations for the Sex Pistols to sign to the country's biggest record label, previously home to the Beatles with a current roster that included such mainstream big-hitters as Pink Floyd, Queen and Cliff Richard.

McLaren was dead-set against signing with the new independent labels such as Stiff and Chiswick, which had sprung up in the build-up to punk; he knew that their distributive power was not as strong as the majors. The idea was to infiltrate the mainstream and place his chaotic charges as free radicals infecting the pop process.

While music business professionals were too blinded by the group's appearance and rough-hewn sound to recognise the Sex Pistols' importance, McLaren was aware that they tore a gaping hole in rock's continuum.

'The idea was to demystify the pop music establishment: Mick Jagger, Pete Townshend, Rod Stewart, David Bowie and Bryan Ferry,' McLaren said in the 1980s. 'There was no point in the Sex Pistols copying the rock 'n' roll movements like the Rolling Stones and the Beatles had produced because, more often than not, they had purely imitated music from America, be it in the south like the Rolling Stones with their more African and raucous rhythm and blues or the north with its sweet harmony groups that the Beatles were so good at imitating. With a third generation, you couldn't see yourself doing a weaker version of that to make a real contribution to rock 'n' roll. They did what the English do, which is to broaden things out, make them literary and more political, more international. That attitude was really what the Sex Pistols were about.'[16]

Meantime, armed with Fisher, the neophyte manager proved himself a dab hand at manipulating music business interest in the group. He romanced among others the major label Polydor Records, whose A&R executive Chris Parry was so convinced he had ensnared the Pistols that he booked studio time for them and, it is said, burst into tears when he found out that EMI had won the race with an advance of £40,000 against royalties for worldwide rights and delivery of two albums over two years. That these could have been double or even triple LPs, and the fact that the contract allowed for a maximum of eight singles a year ('all to be commercially suitable'), showed this to be a typical deal of the period with the onus heavily weighted on the artist.

The royalty rate of 10 per cent and the advance, which was due 50/50 on signature and delivery of the first album, were handsome enough for a group with no sales record. Crucially, monies, principally the advance, royalties and 'reasonable' recording costs, were paid by EMI to the group via Glitterbest, which shared approval of record packaging and choice of producer with the musicians.

They were put on a weekly wage of £25 – less than half the country's average at the time – and their rents were covered by Glitterbest from the advance (though Cook, Matlock and Lydon were all putatively still living at home). Some of the band members were bought new instruments; Glen Matlock chose a bass priced at £400. The cost of this, like that of the clothes they wore from 430 King's Road, was deducted from the advance monies.

With an eye ever on posterity, McLaren organised the acquisition with Glitterbest funds for a then-rare and expensive VHS video recorder for Julien Temple, who had left the National Film and Television School and been appointed in ad-hoc style the person in control of moving images of the group. This was forward-looking for the music business three years before the onset of video promos and was also to prove invaluable in documenting interviews and performances, which were often wiped by broadcasters.

'I was very excited by Malcolm's concept that the band had broken all the rules to achieve pop success,' says Temple. 'He had interesting ideas about how they could be projected in film. You had a sense that this was really important, that certainty that this would make a dent in what was going on.'

Temple's appointment complemented McLaren's earlier recruitment of Nils Stevenson's rock photographer brother Ray, who was granted access to achieve exclusive shots of the group. This enabled McLaren to maintain a grasp on the public image of the Sex Pistols at a time when most managers were happy for their group's likenesses to be featured across the media, whatever the quality of the image.

According to EMI press officer Brian Southall, McLaren netted the EMI deal by upping the tempo of negotiations with the record company's boss Nick Mobbs at the last minute. 'Once he decided on EMI, he wanted everything to be settled in double quick time,' says Southall.

This was the biggest challenge facing Mobbs. While the deal was relatively simple, McLaren's indecent haste to get it signed was anathema to a large corporation used to taking its own sweet time to work out the finer points of the contract. McLaren didn't want to hear about the technicalities. He got his way with the deal completed after less than twenty-four hours of intense negotiations.

This was definitely a record for EMI, which normally drew up drafts that were rewritten and then rewritten and drafted again. As the details of the deal began to trickle out of the A&R and legal departments it became apparent there had been some game-playing, suggesting McLaren had managed to up the advance by keeping Polydor waiting in the wings.[17]

McLaren and Fisher, however, committed egregious errors in failing to advise the young members of the group – at twenty-one, Steve Jones was older than the others by four months – to seek independent legal advice on either the Glitterbest or EMI contracts they signed.

'We were told, "If you don't do it tonight, there'll be no deal,"' said Lydon. 'At that age, you're naive, you don't think of these things. You just see: contract, the big time. You think of the hundred pounds you're going to get out of it, not how it'll be an albatross for the rest of your life.'[18]

This wasn't necessarily true; less than eighteen months later Lydon would lead a legal campaign to freeze the onerous contract and within a decade secured victory in the group's favour (during which time he and the other members had enjoyed the fruits of several more high-paying record contracts). But the principle stood; McLaren sought to burden the youngsters unfairly. The manner in which he achieved the Glitterbest and EMI contracts once again betrayed the mercenary aspects of his nature.

McLaren's justification was that he had already devoted considerable energies and finances to the group over the fourteen months since Lydon had joined, not least the purchase of the lease on the QT Rooms as well as his invaluable advice on presentation, live promotion and musical direction.

During contract negotiations on the group's behalf, McLaren was bolstered by a factor apparently unavailable to the upper echelons of Britain's entertainment complex of the period: an appreciation of British youth desires. 'I didn't know much about the record industry and didn't give tuppence for it,' McLaren said in the 1990s.

In those days there was a kind of snobbism. I would always get remarks like 'You don't know anything about music or making records or managing because you're a trouser-seller'. They took that for me to think that it was derogatory but I was very proud to be a trouser-seller. I was making more money than that guy sitting in Polydor Records. Someone who had the ability to make lots of trousers and sell them on the King's Road was someone who knew to some extent where it was at with young people.[19]

Chapter 22

Malcolm McLaren's counter-intuitive strategy in obtaining a recording contract for the Sex Pistols revolved around the notion that this was a group where spontaneity was of greater value than musical proficiency.

Just as the clothing business at 430 King's Road was positioned as 'anti-fashion', McLaren felt that the integrity of this musical project lay in the refusal of the professionalism then suffocating the record industry via such ponderous stadium acts as Genesis, Pink Floyd and Yes and the worthy, beery groups playing Britain's pub circuit. Both valued 'musicianship', but the celebrations of the amateur to which McLaren had been exposed during his art school years were now coming into play.

'I constantly paraded the idea that, like the New York Dolls, they couldn't play very well,' said McLaren of the Sex Pistols. 'I didn't see any problem with that.'[1]

This wounded members of the group, particularly Steve Jones, who challenged McLaren in an LA radio station encounter three decades after the group's demise. 'I always thought you could play,' McLaren reassured Jones. 'It just didn't seem a good way of selling the idea. I never thought the industry should be sold a group that could play because that would make you fit in too well. The point always was to not fit in with anyone. That, initially and ultimately, was its greatest success.

'Because you didn't fit in you related to a legion of disaffected youth who equally felt they didn't fit in and suddenly you became their rallying call, their flag. That's what made you notorious, celebrated and famous.'[2]

In 1976, once McLaren had pitched record labels against each other to achieve an impressive deal for 'the group that couldn't play', the building blocks of his reputation as pop's arch manipulator were laid. In fact, he was treading a path blazed by wily 1960s forebears such as the Rolling

Stones' charismatic manager Andrew Loog Oldham and the flamboyant stable-runner Larry Parnes. They, like Led Zeppelin's Peter Grant on an international scale, exploited the fact that the industry was almost entirely bereft of business convention and did not operate along necessarily financially prudent lines.[3]

The EMI advance monies enabled McLaren to install Glitterbest – essentially himself, PA Sophie Richmond and Jamie Reid – in a building in the heart of the West End. 27 Dryden Chambers was on Soho's northern edge, in a teetering warren of offices accessed by a winding staircase in a passage leading off McLaren's beloved Oxford Street. McLaren dedicated his time at Dryden Chambers to mapping out a strategy for the Pistols, and occasionally used the premises to work on designs for 430 King's Road.

In another mould-breaking move, McLaren appointed Reid the Pistols' art director. This was virtually unheard of in the ramshackle world of pop; heretofore, only a few groups had maintained single graphic artists and designers to handle their visual output, among them Hawkwind (who worked with the brilliant Barney Bubbles) and Roxy Music (fashion designer Antony Price oversaw stagewear, album-sleeve photography and design). But these collaborations had not achieved the integrated approach masterminded by McLaren, where Reid's advertising, record packaging, posters, handbills and other promotional materials were all of a piece with the clothing created with Westwood and the music and lyrics espoused by the group.

In this way, McLaren first realised his lifelong ambition to express 'the look of music and the sound of fashion'.

Among Reid's first tasks from McLaren was the coordination of a tabloid newspaper format Pistols fanzine named after the group's first single. 'Jamie had the Suburban Press experience and knew how to produce an effective publication for the fans,' said McLaren. 'Vivienne wanted to be involved and so they worked with Sophie on pulling it all together.'

Anarchy in the UK No. 1 used exclusive images taken by Ray Stevenson of the Pistols as well as The Clash and Suburban Sect in performance at the 100 Club. Most striking was a sequence shot of revels at the St James's apartment of Sex customer and dominatrix Linda Ashby featuring members of the Bromley Contingent. These resulted in the front-cover portrait of the young Pistols superfan Susan Lucas, known as Soo Catwoman for her feline haircut.

Reid leavened the offer with artwork he had previously run in issues of *Suburban Press*, including, on the back page, renditions of the US transit buses that had been détourned by the San Francisco Situationist group Point-Blank! as agitprop material in the early 1970s so that their destinations read: 'NOWHERE'.

Simultaneous with the Sex Pistols signing to EMI, punk started to break across the UK as major media outlets communicated the style and music to mass audiences. Having gingerly dedicated a split front cover to the Sex Pistols and Dr Feelgood in September 1976 – clumsily headlined in mockney 'Oo you screwing John?' and focused on the wave of aggressive attitudinising among the new groups – the *New Musical Express* now picked up on the spadework of journalists such as Caroline Coon at *Melody Maker* and Jonh Ingham at *Sounds*, appointing the young Julie Burchill and Tony Parsons to report exclusively on the new youth movement.

Punk features appeared in the national dailies and TV commissioners responded by producing news stories on the phenomenon, but it was cultural critic Peter York who most successfully placed McLaren and the Sex Pistols project in the context of the British avant-garde of the period.

Among York's waspish social commentaries for the glossy monthly *Harpers & Queen* was an extended and heavily illustrated feature entitled 'Them', about 'a happy breed of aesthetes who live by style. They wear clothes to knock your eye out. They are born of Art School by Rock Generation'.

'A group who take a dim view of much Themness are the people who run the Sex clothing store at the World's End,' wrote York. 'They represent the extreme ideological wing of the Peculiars. The Sex shop people, untypically, have political views, of a kind which they describe as anarchic. Their associated group the Sex Pistols are alleged to cause trouble wherever they go. The Sex people *hate* Retro, and seem perfectly sincere about it, yet they are working in a 1958 Council Flat Greaseball vein.'[4]

Among Them groups identified by York was the Bryan Ferry-approved Japanese quartet Sadistic Mika Band, whose producer Chris Thomas McLaren had approached in the summer of 1975 to work with what then remained of the New York Dolls.

Now McLaren was keen for Thomas to oversee the recording of 'Anarchy in the UK' as the first single for EMI, having struck out with his first choice, Roger 'Syd' Barrett. The founding member of Pink Floyd was by the mid-1970s a lost soul whose LSD excesses had combined with incipient schizophrenia to plunge him into a state of near-catatonia.

McLaren admitted later that this was among his 'craziest' ideas for the Sex Pistols, having been turned on to Barrett's wayward genius by Nick Kent's series of articles in *NME* a couple of years previously. Still, he arranged a meeting at a central London residential hotel through Barrett's music publisher Bryan Morrison.

'I thought, this guy is the perfect guy, I loved those early songs: "Arnold Layne" and "See Emily Play",' said McLaren in the 2000s. 'I thought he was culturally subversive and poetic. He showed up wearing a navy blue blazer and reading a newspaper about the Angolan crisis. I tried to talk to him [but] he couldn't speak, and the following day he left the hotel and I couldn't find him. It was an idea that just disappeared into thin air.'[5]

Then McLaren turned to Chris Thomas. 'This was another result of the shop being a forum and open house,' said McLaren. 'He was the only producer I knew and had brought clothing from me in the past. I may have met him via Bryan Ferry and arranged to visit him at his house in Ealing, where coincidentally a lot of Sex customers came from.'

McLaren played Thomas demos of tracks that had been made over recent months with Dave Goodman, who had handled the Pistols live sound and was angling to become their producer. This wasn't going to happen on McLaren's watch: Goodman's recordings were proficient but lacked impact and chart appeal.

Thomas was sufficiently impressed to want to meet the group. McLaren, ever nervous of Lydon's ability to estrange potential working partners, sent Cook, Jones and Matlock and consequently a deal with Thomas was struck to produce 'Anarchy in the UK' for late October release.

The backing track was cut without Lydon present; once again his feelings of being excluded were justified. 'John was being kept in the dark by Malcolm the whole time,' confirmed Thomas.[6]

Satisfied with the commercial potential of the outcome, McLaren won the first in a series of battles with EMI by insisting the packaging of the single was housed in a plain black paper sleeve. Picture sleeves for 45s were recently coming back into vogue, having been pioneered for the first time since the 1960s by such indie labels as Stiff, but McLaren announced that the sleeve would not bear any exterior information.

The record company wasn't to know that the use of black was consistent with McLaren's deeply cross-hatched portraits of the 1960s, nor his reliance on the colour for designs produced with Westwood at Sex. And McLaren's rationale that the sleeve quoted the infamous 'black page' in Laurence Sterne's eighteenth-century meta-masterpiece *The Life and Opinions of Tristram Shandy, Gentleman*[7] was pitched way above executives' heads.

But McLaren and the group had the contractual right of approval of packaging, so won the day.

Preparations for the single's release coincided with a visit to London by Bob Gruen; McLaren had by now patched up his differences with the New York photographer over what he saw as Gruen's intervention into the affairs of the New York Dolls.

Gruen broke the return to the US from a visit to continental Europe with a stay in the British capital. Eager that his American friend should document the burgeoning social scene around the Pistols, McLaren found Gruen a place in a rooming house in west London and took him directly to Club Louise, the Soho lesbian bar which had been adopted by the group and their followers – including Jordan, Siouxsie, Soo Catwoman, Marco Pirroni and Philip Sallon – as a late-night haunt. McLaren recalled the distinctive titular owner from his forays in Soho clubland as a teenager in the early 1960s.

'Malcolm introduced me to the Sex Pistols and encouraged me to take pictures of them and their crowd,' says Gruen. 'Even though I was intimidated because of their attitude, I got some great material; everybody in that room went on to do something special. I was used to people being a little different, but there was something about their hostility. In New York, things sucked, but we thought: "So what?" In England they were angry, and expressing that anger.'

Gruen found McLaren little changed. 'In a sense he was being the same kind of manager as when he was with the Dolls, particularly in the way he found me a place to stay and took care of me,' he says. 'I see now that Malcolm had more respect for me than I did for myself. I didn't understand my importance. These kids saw me as a media outlet, a route to publicity and coverage in American magazines like *Creem* and *Rock Scene*. To me they were little rock 'n' roll fanzines, but Malcolm had told everyone I was a bigshot. And I guess to them I was.'

At McLaren's behest, Gruen visited Sex, where he took photographs of the exterior and interiors as well as the likes of Westwood and Sid Vicious, at the time employed at the shop as a spectacularly poor sales assistant. Gruen's images, which soon appeared in US publications, became important in communicating the visual richness surrounding the Sex Pistols to the world's biggest music market. They also logged Sex in its final phase; McLaren had already decided that punk's breakthrough demanded an overhaul of 430 King's Road.

'Since we were now cultural terrorists, the store had to be the ultimate punk enclave,' said McLaren in the 2000s. 'I wanted the shop to appear inside like a ruin, albeit a perfectly designed ruin, with a discreet facade so that it felt secretive.'

McLaren was also aware that he and the Pistols weren't alone in using music and visual culture to provoke and disrupt; in October 1976, the ICA's Ted Polhemus invited COUM Transmissions, the art collective whose members included Peter Christopherson's allies Genesis P. Orridge and Cosey Fanni Tutti, to stage an exhibition with performances.

They chose the umbrella title *Prostitution*; exhibits included framed examples of Tutti's porn magazine interventions, a Perspex box of tampons with buzzing flies which had previously been shown at the Paris Biennale, and photographs and documentation of COUM actions dating back to the late 1960s. Several members of the Sex crowd were in attendance and an early version of Generation X supported a set of 'Death Music' from the recently formed Throbbing Gristle.

Outraged Tory MP Nicholas Fairbairn was also there, and made the headlines when he declared: 'These people are the wreckers of civilisation.' London newspaper the *Evening Standard* illustrated his remarks with a photograph of the Bromley Contingent's exotic-looking Siouxsie Sue, Steve Severin and Debbie Juvenile, all of whom were wearing Sex apparel.

Events such as *Prostitution* propelled McLaren in realising the new manifestation of the clothing business at 430 King's Road. He turned to customer Ben Kelly, who had just produced a stunning High-Tech/industrial facade and interior for designer Paul Howie's new boutique in Covent Garden's Long Acre (the store opening was attended by McLaren and Westwood).

British academic Catherine McDermott has described the Howie shop as 'one of [Britain's] most important retail interiors. Using Dexion frames, rubber flooring, metal mesh doors and casual understated display stands, it showed Kelly's acute understanding of materials and details.'[8]

In this way Howie proved to be a springboard for Kelly's designs for 430 King's Road in its new incarnation as Seditionaries, a name conjured by McLaren. 'I chose it because we had entered a political era,' said McLaren. 'Punk had made it so. We were at the forefront of a cultural change.'

This was communicated to Kelly. 'Malcolm called and asked me if I would work on his new concept for the shop, so we met in a caff in Covent Garden,' says Kelly. 'Malcolm was the art director; he knew what he wanted and needed someone to realise his ideas. For the technical drawings of the interior I approached David Connor, who had been at the Royal College with me, and he provided a kind of collage on Malcolm's theme for the shop as a bombed-out Dresden.

'Then David and I translated Malcolm's plan for the front of the shop. I did a drawing of the white painted frames, the door in the middle with the diagonal blue fluorescent tube overhead and the exposed air vents on either side. Vivienne contributed the idea of the milky white glass for the window, which I found for them. It's White Flashed Opal, used for lamp shades and absolutely beautiful.'

On reopening at the beginning of December 1976, the exterior of 430 gave the impression of anonymity and exclusivity. The glass rendered the interior impenetrable from view from the street and a small plaque was attached to the frontage, etched 'Malcolm McLaren Vivienne Westwood Seditionaries'.

'The place was so unusual,' says Kelly. 'It didn't look like a clothes shop, maybe a launderette or a betting shop, but when the brass plaque was added you wondered, was it a solicitor's office? I loved the ambiguity.'

The brutalism of the overall design activated a conversation with the built environment in the immediate vicinity: Eric Lyons's hulking red-brick World's End Estate, which loomed over the neighbour-hood, was finally completed within a couple of months of Seditionaries' opening.

Inside, all was stark, functional and post-apocalyptic: on the floor, a grey office carpet and brightly coloured, nylon-covered Adeptus seating, while monochrome photographic murals adorned the walls, one display-ing scenes of devastation in the aftermath of the Dresden bombings.

'The blow-up I loved the most was the old-fashioned photo of Piccadilly Circus printed upside down across the fitted cupboard doors at the back of the store,' said McLaren.

TV sets were positioned above the clothing racks, and overhead harsh film lighting beamed through jagged holes McLaren had punched into the false ceiling.

Kelly had contracted the rebuild to his sculptor friend Ted Walters, husband of one of the founders of Camden boutique Swanky Modes and also a shopfitter. 'Ted told me that he and his team were concerned about breaking up the existing ceiling since it evidently contained asbestos,' says Kelly. 'Malcolm would have none of it, so while they waited at a safe distance outside on the pavement he climbed up a ladder and smashed his way through. When he came out he was absolutely covered in the stuff.'

The cultural critic Jane Withers understands McLaren's design for Seditionaries as 'a stage for punk's anarchic celebration of chaos and destruction as creative principles. Articulating the inchoate nihilism of the punk revolt, it presented a vision of an apocalyptic utopia that sought to locate punk on the precipice of cultural collapse.'[9]

This was expressed in McLaren's instruction to the builders that they position a cage under the new sales counter. Containing a live rat, it was the final flourish in the transformation when the shop reopened at the beginning of December.

McLaren and Westwood's new clothing designs built on the transition into a tougher, militaristic aesthetic afforded by the introduction of the Bondage suit and Anarchy shirt earlier that autumn. The latter were accessorised by armbands with swastikas or encircled anarchy capital As, and clothing labels were silk bands printed black on black with 'Malcolm McLaren Vivienne Westwood Seditionaries Personal Collection' or white tags also bearing the anarchist A accompanied by the statement 'For soldiers, prostitutes, dykes and punks'.

Well cut with fine detailing, the new range represented the culmination of the design direction essayed in the shop's previous manifestations. Heavy mohair jumpers in geometric patterns were matched by jodhpur boots McLaren had selected from a George Cox catalogue and commissioned to be produced in suede with contrasting patent leather straps.

A new cardigan-like jacket with buttoned front pockets was inspired by a surprising source. 'I was always fascinated by the formal uniforms worn by British Rail guards,' said McLaren. 'We took one of the waistcoats they wore and Vivienne added the arms and made the pockets pouch-like. In a soft fabric they became something else.'

In sum, the reopening of their shop had marked a shift in the clothing designs produced by McLaren and Westwood; as her technical skills reached new heights and his conceptualising sharpened, they were now entering the realm of couture.

Just as 430 King's Road was undergoing the transition into Seditionaries, the *NME* finally granted substantial coverage to the Sex Pistols but once again McLaren, not the band members, was the interviewee. The erstwhile Nick Kent's double-page spread on the growing phenomenon featured a Pennie Smith portrait of McLaren in an Anarchy shirt sipping a cup of tea at Dryden Chambers underneath the headline: 'Meet the Colonel Tom Parker of the Blank Generation'.

Kent set the scene with a recollection of the Pistols' performance at Andrew Logan's warehouse loft the previous spring and ran through McLaren's CV to date, including the history of 430 King's Road and his work with the New York Dolls. Pausing bitchily to spill the beans on McLaren's voice lessons with Tona de Brett in 1974, Kent allowed McLaren to set out his stall:

From the start I realized the Pistols were not relevant strictly for the music. That was in fact all very secondary to the image they were projecting, which was something all these kids could instantly relate to. I mean, when we played the 100 Club, half the audience we were attracting were kids who normally would have been across the road in Crackers disco. These were young kids – mostly in the 16-17-18 bracket – who'd been into Bowie and Roxy Music but been left behind . . . who'd left *them* behind because those acts had just got too big, too distant.

Having been a victim of the 100 Club attack by Sid Vicious, Kent challenged McLaren on the violence pervading the punk scene. 'Well it's bound to happen, innit?' responded McLaren. 'I mean, rock 'n' roll is a violent music. It's about pent-up frustrations and pressures.'

As the first substantial profile of McLaren in a prominent national newspaper – read by journalists working in mainstream media as well as the target audience of fifteen- to twenty-five-year-olds, the *NME*'s circulation was then around 100,000 copies a week with a pass-on rate of three to one, so was seen by close to a million young people a month – the tone of Kent's article was telling in that it betrayed a distaste for McLaren, who was described as 'totally unimposing . . . awkward . . . effeminate . . . a fanatic'. This view of McLaren was to permeate media coverage and inform the views of music fans for the rest of his life, and may in part be attributed to his singular personality; as an interviewee McLaren could be abrasive, arrogant, combative, posturing and verbose, in fact, the embodiment of his late grandmother in her prime. Journalists, particularly males, don't like to be outwitted conversationally, and often ploughed their dislike into the copy they filed.

After this, rare was the affectionate McLaren profile, not that it seemed to bother him. But then, at that stage in his life in particular, McLaren didn't engender affection.

Kent's pay-off was a case in point. He ended on a quote from the charm-free ex-Doll Johnny Thunders on McLaren: 'He's the greatest con-man that I've ever met.'[10]

This was rich, considering not only that McLaren had invested considerable resources into propping up Thunders's career as a member of the Dolls but also because Kent's interview coincided with McLaren organising for Thunders and his fellow members in the Heartbreakers – Richard Hell had long since flown the coop, so the original three-piece had been reconstituted into a quartet based around Thunders and Jerry Nolan – to travel to the UK and join the Pistols and other support acts The Clash and The Damned on the forthcoming countrywide Anarchy tour.

But gratitude is a rare commodity among junkies. Thunders and Nolan were broke, unsigned and effectively kicking their heels in New York, and jumped at the chance when McLaren made the offer, the lure of acclaim from a new generation of fans and the availability of Britain's welfare heroin substitute methadone enabling them to overcome any qualms they felt about working with McLaren again.

Just ahead of the Heartbreakers' arrival on a flight funded by the tour support McLaren had wangled out of EMI, the Pistols were subjected to a slew of television coverage, including an appearance on the BBC's national teatime show *Nationwide*. Once again, McLaren assumed the role of spokesperson in a dual interview with Lydon.

When asked whether – as Steve Jones had informed Neil Spencer that spring – the group was more interested in creating chaos than music, McLaren, whey-faced in rocker leathers set off by a Ton-up boy's white scarf, stared fixedly at the floor as if determined not to meet his interlocutor's eye and adopted the Situationist viewpoint. 'That's an accusation from people who don't understand what kids want,' he said, his voice tremulous. 'Kids want excitement, things which are going to transform what is basically a very boring life for them right now. And young rock music is the only thing they have that they control.'

The programme-makers attempted to set up an oppositional element to the conversation by booking music journalist Giovanni Dadomo, who told McLaren: 'Destruction for its own sake is dull.'

McLaren's sharp riposte was to quote the view espoused by artists from Pablo Picasso to Gustav Metzger: 'You have to destroy in order to create that, you know that.'[11]

While this was potent material for early evening Britain (at a time when viewing figures for such programming on the nation's three channels was in the high millions) the exchanges were no match for those in the broadcast a few days later which became the single most important event in the short existence of the Sex Pistols: their appearance on the London regional teatime show *Today*.

The interview with the sozzled presenter Bill Grundy has attained folkloric proportions in the wider popular culture. The impact of Jones closing the encounter by calling Grundy 'a fucking rotter' – in the process uttering the expletive for only the third time in four decades of British television broadcasting – was to make the Sex Pistols both media demons and free speech causes célèbres.[12]

By all accounts McLaren's immediate reaction was to panic when all hell broke loose as the *Today* credits rolled. Jones records that after the interview the manager was 'white as a sheet . . . fair enough, on this occasion he thought we'd ruined all his plans and the EMI driver who came to whisk us home seemed to take it pretty seriously as well'.[13]

By the next morning the group were household names as a result of the hysterical media reaction. McLaren convened a press conference at EMI's Manchester Square HQ, and Glen Matlock found him much changed.

> He saw how he might turn it all to our – and his – advantage. His greatest strength was never that he was a great manipulator. He wasn't some Svengali with a giant master plan. He was an opportunist – something he might have learned from his years attached to the Situationists.
>
> The group took it quite lightly, but Malcolm saw it differently. He knew how he could exploit it to his best advantage. All that he had to do was rise to the occasion. And he certainly did that.[14]

Chapter 23

In what may be understood today as a Trumpian media blitz, Malcolm McLaren audaciously seized the moment over the winter of 1976–77 and networked furiously among British press and broadcast figures, feeding stories to them on a daily basis as the Sex Pistols indulged their natural inclinations for behaviour deemed offensive by polite society.

McLaren fed off the ensuing chaos as he went all out to maintain the group's dominance over news cycles, sidestepping the flow of scandals by changing the subject so that the press and even those closest to him were constantly playing catch-up.

'A lot of the ideas he never told us, just used to shove us out there and we'd do our thing,' said Steve Jones in the 1980s. 'He never told us half the things he was scamming. He's a complete con-man really. He used us in the same way Brian Epstein used the Beatles. He didn't look after the financial idea, it was just, "Another scam, another scam, what can we do to keep the ball rolling?" It made us more popular, which was great. I still think he's a great manager.'[1]

In a similar manner to Trump (and more to the point Edna Welthorpe, the letter-writing pest and alter-ego of one of McLaren's heroes, Joe Orton), McLaren adopted alternate personae to stir the pot and concocted with Sophie Richmond a stream of prank communications criticising the group to the music press. Unlike Trump, however, he satirised himself in the process. One such appeared as the lead missive in an issue of *Sounds* published in the aftermath of the *Today* appearance. Purporting to be from 'Roxy Music Follower, Leeds', this read in part:

> I'm a 16-year-old female, but if they think I'm going to be taken in by a bunch of bloody loonies, whose manager is just as bad, running

a sex shop, they can flaming well piss off and think again. Punk is supposed to be 'in' is it? Well, if punk is tatty clothes pinned together with last week's porridge, music that makes Doctor Magnus Pyke [an eccentric scientist often featured on television in the period] sound an interesting bloke and interviews on television that consist of four letter words fouling up meaningless sentences, then you can flaming well count me OUT.[2]

The national newspaper headlines generated by the Grundy incident – among them 'The Filth and the Fury', 'Must We Fling This Filth at Our Pop Kids?' and the *Daily Express*'s deathless Shakespeare quote 'Punk? Call It Filthy Lucre' – set in train the series of events that have become familiar in the retelling of the Pistols story down the decades: several local councils around the country reacted by banning dates on the Anarchy tour, religious groups held protests outside the few venues where the Pistols and their support acts were allowed to play, EMI factory workers refused to handle manufacture of the 'Anarchy' single (which had sold an impressive 50,000 copies up to that point) and, ultimately, the board of the parent company Thorn-EMI decided that the reputational risk of being associated with the group was too great and, by the dawn of 1977, cancelled the contract.

This was a genuine media furore, one which McLaren later credited to the group:

People thought I was the architect. I wasn't, but what I did do was feel that what they were doing was commendable. As a manager, that was my job, to make sure that whatever they did was correct. This was a young supposedly rock 'n' roll group with a sense of style and angst, and they were expressing themselves in no short terms. They had an avalanche of fans that exhibited very clearly their approval and my feelings to the record companies were: 'Well, so what? You know: Boys will be boys.'[3]

Unlike the musicians, who became bored and groused about the pointlessness of taking to the road to venues they weren't allowed to play, McLaren traced his delight in the restrictions to his dysfunctional upbringing.

'This was about destruction of anything ordered – something I had learned as a child,' he reflected. 'The Anarchy tour was a huge success for me because even though the group had been banned from most of the venues, I still got everyone on board the coach, travelled to the towns in question, checked into the hotels, gave everyone a meal and the next day we would drive off to the next town and the next town and the next.

'EMI were constantly on the phone saying, "We know they're banned, just come back to London," but I would reply, "It doesn't matter, we're finishing the tour." The idea that we were on tour but not playing was so attractive to me. It was a futile exercise and that was what I loved. We were on a tour literally going nowhere.'

Meanwhile he maintained his role as spokesman, notably for an interview with national news network ITN at a Leeds hotel. McLaren was presented front and centre in an Anarchy shirt with a mohair jumper wrapped around his shoulders Italian-style, while the Pistols snickered in the background.

Throughout the encounter McLaren maintained a focus on the importance of teenagers being granted agency, echoing the Situationists' cry of 'Totality for Kids', and also plugging into Guy Debord's theories, in particular that 'rebellious tendencies among the young generate a protest that is still tentative and amorphous, yet already clearly embodies a rejection of the specialised sphere of the old politics, as well as of art and everyday life'.[4]

Asked whether he had stopped the group members from talking to the press, McLaren responded, 'Not at all. They're disgusted at having to answer so many questions about something so simple. At least they're standing up and not tolerating any form of censorship in their act. In that sense, it's exhilarating a lot of kids around the country and giving them confidence to say what they want.'

When he was challenged about the group's reputation as 'the most revolting in the country', McLaren cut to the chase: 'Look, our group is creating a generation gap for the first time in five years, and a lot of people are feeling threatened by it. If the kids want to buy the record it's called "Anarchy in the UK", it's in the shops and they can make their own decisions. If their mothers care anything about their kids they should be up in arms about the fact that councillors, who they're paying taxes to, are not allowing their kids to go into the concerts and make their own choices.'

McLaren later qualified his role: 'I suppose I put forward certain feelings and attitudes in my comments to the press [and] created – not to be arrogant – an articulate response which lent phrases and slogans they could ultimately use.'5

Paramount among these was McLaren's reaction during the ITN interview to the unwarranted charge that group members vomited on stage during performances. Rather than point out that the claim was without basis, McLaren sucked the air out of the room by pronouncing: 'People are sick everywhere. People are sick and fed up of this country telling them what to do.'

After the Anarchy tour ended, McLaren also used the press to spread negative rumours about EMI, claiming that the group had been lumbered with £10,000-worth of debts because of the cancelled dates. Record company staffer Brian Southall recalled, 'An EMI spokesman set the record straight: "We are in regular meetings with Malcolm and the Sex Pistols and if they need money then I am sure the question has been raised and discussed. We have certainly fulfilled our obligations." That the corporation did not reply with a "no comment" or a throwaway line was an indication that McLaren was pushing things too far and that people at the top had had enough of his insolence.'6

But McLaren didn't let up, surprising the record company by announcing to the *NME*: 'They [EMI] cannot hold us to our contract and we shall break it. I can assure you that other record labels have expressed interest in signing us.'7

Push came to shove when McLaren was encouraged by the music entrepreneur Miles Copeland (who occupied offices in the same building as
Glitterbest and was soon to become manager of The Police) to add live
dates in Holland to a promotional TV appearance in Amsterdam organised
by EMI at the beginning of 1977. At Heathrow Airport members of the
Pistols acted up in the departure lounge, having been bated by the press.
This provoked overreaction, not least from London daily the *Evening
News*, which claimed the musicians 'shocked and revolted passengers and
airline staff as they vomited and spat their way to an Amsterdam flight'.[8]

There were shades here of Johnny Thunders's attack of biliousness
witnessed by McLaren in front of the ranks of the French media when
the New York Dolls had arrived at Orly four years before, but in this
case there was no substance.

'The situation at the airport was fabricated up to a point,' McLaren
told the *NME*. 'Yeah, the band might have looked a little bit extraordinary, they may have spat at each other. Big deal. And someone may have
appeared a little drunk. But they weren't flying the plane, they don't
need to be sober.'

No matter, this was enough for the EMI board to rescind the contract.
An exit was hashed out while the group was still in Amsterdam:
Glitterbest was paid the £20,000 balance of the advance as well as £10,000
from the music publishing deal.

According to EMI's point person Graham Fletcher, McLaren and the
group took the dismissal in their stride. 'It just seemed to be another
milestone ticked off along the way,' Fletcher told Brain Southall.[9]

The EMI rejection made waves in the music industry, McLaren having
publicly pointed to the Masonic connections among many of the top-
ranking execs in Britain. And, even though he had previously been jilted,
Chris Parry was still keen to do the deal for the group at Polydor, but the
powers-that-be at its telecommunications parent Philips quashed the
prospect.

While McLaren pondered his next move, even undertaking a trip to
the business's annual jamboree Midem in Cannes with Stewart Joseph,

manager of Generation X, he was simultaneously forced to deal with incoming on the domestic front. His son Joe was now nine, and Vivienne Westwood began to balk at the lack of attention his father was paying to him.

Glen Matlock tells a story of how she refused to let McLaren into their apartment after returning from an all-night party. 'She was hiding inside pretending she weren't there, so he climbed up a drainpipe and started shouting "Vivienne, Vivienne, let me in, it's Malcolm!"' said Matlock in the 1980s.

In the wake of the EMI pay-off, the first substantial cracks appeared in the group's facade as its young members bowed under the strain of living in the media spotlight. Within a few weeks of their return from Holland, Matlock announced his departure on the grounds that Lydon – whose confidence had been boosted immeasurably by the attention – had become insufferable, while Paul Cook and Steve Jones were too pliant to McLaren's will.

Unbeknown to Matlock, a replacement was already being put through his paces, but rehearsals with Lydon's friend Sid Vicious revealed him to be an utterly inept musician, so McLaren called Matlock in a last-ditch attempt to keep the original line-up together.

'We met in a Soho pub and Malcolm said: "Glen, I want you to be strong. I want you to go back there and kick the door down and prove the job is yours and . . ."'

'I said: Malcolm, I'm just not interested any more.'[10]

McLaren agreed that they should part on good terms, but 'then he went and did the dirty on me', said Matlock. Within a few days of their final meeting, the *NME* ran a telegram sent to the news editor Derek Johnson:

Yes Derek Glen Matlock was thrown out of the Sex Pistols because he went on too long about Paul McCartney STOP EMI was enough STOP The Beatles was too much STOP Sid Vicious their best friend and always a member of the group but unheard as yet was enlisted STOP His best credential was he gave Nick Kent what he deserved many months ago at the Hundred Club Love and peace Malcolm McLaren.

'I'd had enough of the band, so why couldn't Malcolm just say that?' asked Matlock years later. 'The reason was simple: if he'd told the truth it would have looked like he wasn't in control.'

Just as he had flipped on a dime over the Grundy controversy, the agile McLaren soon turned the recruitment of Vicious to the group's advantage, presenting the troubled nineteen-year-old as the living embodiment of punk attitude, the superfan as superstar. Handily and ironically given the new bass player's sponsor, this also provided a bulwark against the increasingly egotistical Lydon.

Born John Simon Ritchie and, like McLaren, abandoned by his father at a young age, Vicious was rangy, handsome and extremely troubled, having experienced a peripatetic childhood and adolescent exposure to his mother's heroin addiction. Predictably, Vicious fell victim at an early age; drug abuse and violent behaviour served to mask reserves of intelligence, sensitivity and wit behind a numbskull veneer.

The addition of Vicious piled on the Pistols' newsworthiness as McLaren worked on netting the group a new recording deal, checking in with his friend Rory Johnston, who was now living in Los Angeles, trying to catch a break in the entertainment business.

'I'd called Malcolm from a payphone on Sunset when the news about the Pistols filtered through to the West Coast,' says Johnston. 'I told him, "If you need any help, I'm here." He knew I'd be able to push things forward but keep it pure since I'd been around the band since the earliest days.'

In February 1977, McLaren's PA Sophie Richmond recorded in her diary: 'Malcolm is in a bit of weird mood. Thinking too much about record companies. It seems between A&M and CBS . . . Malcolm tells me about the different companies . . . CBS, very kosher firm & big. A&M a tight family concern based in LA. West Coast smoothies v New York Jews. A weird choice.'[11]

The power plays involved in courting entertainment companies inspired McLaren to channel his frustrations into a new disruptive design for sale in Seditionaries. 'While working in the office with Sophie Richmond one evening, toiling away on various recording contracts, I decided I wanted to make an ultimate, bigger statement, one that would wreck all established principles to do with order, power, right and wrong,' said McLaren in the 2000s. This artwork became known as 'Destroy', after the shattered lettering emblazoned across the top of a nihilist collage, echoing McLaren's pronouncement on national TV a couple of months previously ('You have to destroy in order to create'). However oblique, Destroy was evidence of McLaren's preoccupation at the time with taking on the music industry and bringing down the major conglomerates that controlled it.

Apart from the most simple and powerful, a circle, McLaren détourned each of the symbols overlaying it. The most prominent was a swastika, placed as the embodiment of evil as well as for its properties as a symbol of provocation three decades after the end of the Second World War ('I knew it always got people up in arms'). He determined this would be printed in unexpected colours such as industrial grey (with the circle in blood-red), lime green and acid yellow (both against navy blue).

Adjoining this, McLaren juxtaposed a Jamie Reid drawing of a British postage stamp bearing the decapitated head of the Queen; this represented not only the overturning of order but also McLaren's wish to embody a treasonous act in the design.

As the representation of good, McLaren depicted Christ on the cross (taken from one of his favourite artworks, Matthias Grünewald's sixteenth-century *Isenheim Altarpiece*), though this was heretically inverted.

At bottom right, McLaren hand-lettered the lyrics from the first verse of 'Anarchy in the UK'. At this time, Alex McDowell – the Central School of Art student who had laughed loudly throughout the Sex Pistols' first performance – was overseeing the screen-printing and production of Seditionaries T-shirt designs and, on viewing the artwork, suggested that it needed a title. McLaren proposed the word 'destroy', sketching the lettering which was incorporated by McDowell.

The Destroy shirt appealed to one of Seditionaries' more high-profile customers: Anita Pallenberg, true ultra-stylish Italian former model and actress who was Rolling Stone Keith Richards' partner. 'When punk came along and Malcolm and Vivienne made those wonderful rubber clothes, I felt in tune with them,' said Pallenberg in 2007.

'I bought a Destroy shirt for Keith but he didn't like it. Eventually Mick wore it onstage at an American show.'

In this period Westwood had worked up the design for a highly unusual long-sleeved top made from layers of muslin with the seams on display and extra-long sleeves, which were pulled back from the cuffs with dog-clip attachments. With Destroy as its artwork, this new top, which became known simply as a 'muslin', epitomised the creative exchange conducted between McLaren and Westwood: her technical daring combined with his graphic understanding and political discourse to produce the most surprising outcomes existing way beyond the purview of fashion.

The EMI advance monies were used in a variety of ways, principally to fund a fresh set of recordings by the group, which resulted in a clear choice for their next single once a suitable deal could be struck. Initially known as 'No Future', this bombastic track was soon titled after the first words of Lydon's opening line 'God save the Queen'.

The EMI cash also funded the compilation by Julien Temple of footage of the group in interview and performance into a short titled *Sex Pistols Number 1*. The intention was to distribute this to independent cinemas so that fans could witness the group in the absence of live bookings.

McLaren took a tape with him on a trip to LA to meet the A&M label's owners, middle-of-the-road recording star Herb Alpert and his business partner Jerry Moss, whose British MD Derek Green had been leading the charge to sign the group.

During the visit – McLaren's first to the city which was to loom large over the rest of his life and provide a home base over several years in the 1980s – he reconnected with Rory Johnston, who collected him at the airport. He spirited the eccentric figure, wearing Bondage pants and leather in Hollywood's early spring heat, to the A&M offices on the lot on La Brea which had been opened by Charlie Chaplin in the 1920s.

'I was always insistent in dealing with the people at the very top of the companies I did business with,' said McLaren in the 2000s. 'Derek Green seemed a nice enough man, and A&M were certainly the most excited about the group financially, but I had to see Herb Alpert and Jerry Moss for myself.'

Alpert, Moss and their fellow American executives weren't as taken by the group as Green, but nevertheless the bosses gave their assent, and McLaren returned to London, where he and Green set about finalising the deal. 'The Sex Pistols becoming available presented us with a unique business opportunity,' Green told the music press. 'The notoriety which they have already received was not a dissuading factor and would not be to anyone who has been around during the last 15 years of rock music and its fashions.'[12]

Not only was Green bowled over by the music recently recorded by the Pistols, he was charmed by their manager, describing McLaren as 'very funny, terribly amusing, so outrageous in his styled choice of language'.[13]

The two-year A&M recording contract was a testament to McLaren's powers of persuasion and his lawyer Steven Fisher's astuteness. Financially, it all but quadrupled the value of the EMI contract with annual advances of £75,000 against record sales. In return the group was required to deliver a total of eighteen individual tracks rather than committing to the industry standard of two albums (the half-dozen tracks which the group had already recorded were included in that total).

Again the money was to be paid to the group members via Glitterbest; McLaren took receipt of a cheque for £50,000 as the first advance payment on the day the group signed the contract.

Among the mistakes made by Green in his enthusiasm was a decision against meeting the members of the group; in fact, it was only on the day that they arrived to sign that Green learned Glen Matlock – arguably the Pistol with the greatest melodic sensibilities – had been replaced by Sid Vicious.

The Pistols' drunken and boisterous behaviour that day set the tone for the company's brief relationship with these new additions to their A&R roster. 'When we walked in, Sid collapsed in the marketing director's chair. He was completely gone having drunk two bottles of vodka between 10 a.m. and 3 p.m. when we arrived,' said Malcolm a few years later. 'Johnny Rotten was going around spraying swastikas on the photos of the record company's various artists, Steve Jones had gone in to the ladies toilets to try and thieve all the secretaries' handbags and Paul Cook was pissed off because his eye was all banged up.

'I'll never forget Rotten took a vase from a secretary's table and threw the daffodils at Sid, and they landed in his lap. It was marvellous. This wasn't a group which had entered the building. What had entered was a fabulous disaster.'

Such scenes of chaos were grist to McLaren's mill: 'The greatest technique in managing the Sex Pistols was always to create the right explosion and, knowing that it was going to happen, run into the toilet and then come out afterwards and say, "Really? What's happened?" '[14]

Green took the Pistols' first visit to his offices in his stride and succumbed to McLaren's proposal to stage a mock contract signing early the following morning. This was timed to catch the first editions of the two London evening newspapers then setting the agenda for the rest of the nation's media. A table was set up outside Buckingham Palace – an appropriate venue since 'God Save the Queen' was now scheduled for a May release – and journalists and camera crews assembled in wait for the group's arrival. 'I thought it was a very shrewd piece of media-playing,' said Green a couple of years later. 'That's what I like about [McLaren]. He knew how to manipulate the press.'[15]

The Pistols emerged from the A&M limo worse for wear, high and drunk from the night before and having indulged in a fistfight en route. Throwing peace signs and leering for the photographers, they 'signed' the contract and were then swept to a press conference at the Regent Palace Hotel off Piccadilly where they swigged from bottles of vodka and abused the assembled journalists during a press conference at which McLaren sat and observed, stage right, occasionally whispering advice in the clearly uncomfortable Lydon's ear.

Green was asked a single question, on the record company's contractual obligations over the group's behaviour. 'At the very moment I was about to answer there was none whatsoever, Sid Vicious farted,' he said in the 1980s.[16]

Green's good humour soon dissolved. A few days later Vicious was involved in an assault on the BBC television broadcaster Bob Harris (who had sneeringly dismissed the New York Dolls three years previously). Exactly a week after the Pistols had signed to A&M, Green called McLaren to a meeting and announced that the company was – like EMI before it – rescinding the agreement. McLaren left clutching a termination cheque for £25,000, representing the remainder of the first year's advance.

At a hastily organised press conference at the Glitterbest offices, McLaren announced: 'From my point of view I feel like we're some kind of contagious disease. When you walk in to a company and the guy says, "Just take this money and don't come back" what are you supposed to think about that?'

While the rest of the group members remained mute, Lydon – with crow-black dyed hair and taking a much more authoritative stance than he had at the Leeds encounter with ITN three months previously – interrupted McLaren to accuse A&M of hypocrisy and 'classic stupidity'. The tension between the Pistols' singer and their manager was shifting in full public view.

Meanwhile in LA, Rory Johnston found himself in an embarrassing situation. He had been set up in an office at A&M to coordinate marketing and promotion with the record company's UK wing, and was not informed that the group had been dropped. 'So I sat and waited for a few days and then one day called Malcolm in London and got him out of bed,' says Johnston. 'He said: "Oh, Rory, didn't you know? We got kicked off the label again!"'

According to McLaren, Steven Fisher was thrilled at the turn of events: 'My lawyer was amazed that we were doing so well, having not sold any records but taking all this money.'[17]

Fisher's observation was apposite: in five months McLaren had grossed £125,000 in non-returnable record company monies on the group's behalf. His and Fisher's financial manoeuvres were to win for the Pistols the accolade 'Young Businessmen of the Year' in *Investors Review*.[18] However ironic the tribute, Fred Vermorel – who had by that time started work with his wife Judy on a biography of the group – interpreted the magazine's cover story as a tribute to his art-school friend's audacity.

'It was McLaren who got that award,' said Vermorel in the 2000s. 'You have to make a distinction, I think, between the band and McLaren. Other people disagree with me, but I don't think they would have made it without him steering them through the precipitous route that they took. Plus, between Glitterbest and the band [there] was a big gulf of generation and outlook, education and aspiration. I would also add, talent, but that's more contentious.'[19]

Under the terms of the management contract, after Glitterbest's share, each group member was now due £25,000 – twice the average annual wage and a considerable amount for youngsters who had only just reached their majority.

Aside from their stipend, which had risen to £30 a week, and coverage of living costs, the musicians did not receive 'penny one', in Lydon's memorable phrase. A proportion of the cash was spent conventionally: on recording (producer Chris Thomas had negotiated a sizeable fee and royalty rate) and day-to-day expenses, including equipment hire and new rentals. Apartments were found for Lydon and Vicious first in a house in north-east London's Edmonton which, so they claimed, was haunted, and for Cook and Jones in Marylebone's Bell Street, close to Helen Wellington Lloyd's home.

Meanwhile Seditionaries provided McLaren with a separate cash stream. The fashion business was going well as a result of the publicity surrounding the band and punk breaking overground. McLaren and Westwood's new designs such as the muslins and 'Thalidomide' jumpers (with tiny arms which restricted movement in the upper body, named after victims of the early 1960s pharmaceutical scandal) were featured on television and in the mainstream press, and imitators led by the King's Road business Boy, which was launched out of the rival boutique Acme Attractions, sprang up around the country.

But rather than pay the musicians their due, McLaren devoted himself to a new side project which would eventually envelop him, directing funds from the smash-and-grab committed against EMI and A&M into a factional film based on the group and their exploits. Inspired by his trip to Hollywood and still frustrated by the failure of *The Story of Oxford Street* six years previously, McLaren became fixated on realising his cinematic ambitions. He courted potential screenwriters, including the comic actor and writer Peter Cook, whom McLaren and Lydon visited at his home in Hampstead, north London, and Johnny Speight, the ribald East Ender whose 1960s sitcom *Till Death Us Do Part* had translated into the US TV smash *All in the Family*.

Problematically, public prominence and an influx of cash had gone straight to Vicious's head. Within six weeks of joining the group, the doomed youth contracted hepatitis from his prodigious heroin usage. After a spell in hospital, McLaren gave the youngster a dressing down and placed him in the care of his King's Road friends Gerry and Pat Goldstein, both of whom were experienced with handling the dangers of hard drugs.

But hope of recovery was short-lived when Vicious hooked up with the hedonistic American groupie Nancy Spungen. She had followed the Heartbreakers to London from New York; Johnny Thunders and his pals had remained in town after the Anarchy tour and parlayed their reputation into a record deal with Track Records, a rickety label run by The Who's management team.

If a single element united the rest of the Pistols and McLaren, it was a shared hatred of the needy, wheedling Spungen. In her bad influence over the suggestible Vicious lay the seeds of not only the couple's destruction but also the group's dissolution.

Another flashpoint was the lack of live promotion, in part caused by the hit their reputation had taken among promoters, but exacerbated by McLaren's adoption of a policy of maintaining the group's unavailability as a way of adding to their mystique. Jeff Dexter, the veteran DJ then running a management company with the entrepreneur Tony Secunda, recalls a meeting with McLaren around this time about a performance by the Pistols at the large central London venue, the Lyceum.

'Malcolm asked that we keep their identity under wraps so I went ahead and got the gig only to receive a call from the bookers cancelling it a couple of days later,' says Dexter. 'They had found out that it was the Pistols. And when I asked around I discovered Malcolm had told them!'[20]

McLaren began to adopt a visual identity at odds with his position as the ringmaster of the situation: that of the innocent schoolboy. 'I can never forget wearing a schoolboy's suit with long trousers from John Lewis when I managed the Sex Pistols,' wrote McLaren in his notes on this period. In fact, he soon abandoned the grey serge trousers but kept the matching blazer, which didn't feature a badge on the breast pocket but still gave a jarring appearance when paired with his leather jeans, Bondage boots and black shirts. 'People thought it very odd but I felt very good in those clothes. It made me feel somewhat younger than I was and somehow enabled me to make the kind of mistakes that, ordinarily, you would fear making. By virtue of being seen in something young you could be young and immature. You could afford to be fearless and naive. I enjoyed that; and those clothes put me into that frame of mind.'

This outlook was seriously to disadvantage McLaren in business terms, for now the thrusting Virgin Records entrepreneur Richard

Branson had entered the scene. Four years younger than McLaren, 'Mr Pickle', as the Pistols' manager derisively nicknamed him in the mistaken belief that he was related to the family which produced the Branston brand of condiments, disguised his sharply honed commercial nous behind a permanent wolfish grin and tousle-haired, bearded facade. Branson was just as willing a risk taker as McLaren, but by far the smarter businessman and had been touting his freewheeling independent label as a sympathetic home to the group since the EMI debacle, and saw his chance in the wake of the A&M collapse.

Like McLaren, Branson was aware of the publicity opportunities the forthcoming Silver Jubilee would afford the Pistols' holdover single from A&M, 'God Save the Queen'. Causing a stir at the epicentre of punk action would help reinvent his company, which had become associated with stodgy progressive rock.

'Malcolm and Richard were so similar,' said one of Branson's aides-de-camp, Al Clark, in the 1980s. 'In Richard, Malcolm had met his match. He didn't like that.'[21]

Journalist Peter York put it more succinctly: 'Clever young Richard Branson, who was a merry prankster, thought, "I don't know what this punk thing is about, but there's some money in it." '[22]

Chapter 24

At twenty-six, Richard Branson was a successful entrepreneur with an established track record in Britain's business circles for exploiting the consumer aspects of the youth market.

Like McLaren, Branson was a suburban Londoner who had left school at sixteen, but there their similarities ended. Unlike the totally wired Sex Pistols manager, Branson was absent any sense of visual style or political sensibility, presenting a quiet-spoken bland persona underpinned by the self-assurance of a privileged WASP background. The grandson of a notable High Court judge and the son of a barrister and ballet dancer, he was also the product of Britain's upper-middle-class educational system (in Branson's case the Buckinghamshire boarding school Stowe).

From a young age, Branson had cultivated a knack of appropriating aspects of youth culture to his commercial gain. See, for example, the magazine *Student*, which he launched in his late teens at the tail end of the 1960s to appeal to those in further education by courting the likes of Mick Jagger and R. D. Laing and adopting the approaches of the underground press. Unlike his competitors, Branson had no qualms about accepting advertising from such unhip targets as the Playboy Club, the *Daily Express* and Lloyds Bank, and so his publication became a financial success.

This formula of applying an alternative veneer to sound propositions explained his subsequent prospering from *Student*'s mail-order record venture, which undercut the High Street retail chains, though Branson's willingness to cut corners led him into difficulties with HMRC over unpaid VAT payments and resulted in an eye-watering £70,000 fine; Branson was rescued by his parents, who remortgaged their house.

As early as 1970, when McLaren was lingering at art school, the British establishment had already recognised the enthusiastic youngster – then just twenty – as one of their own. That year Branson was paid a healthy £1500 as a youth consultant to the publishing conglomerate IPC (though he was accused of boasting it was twice that amount).[1]

Branson soon established the hippy-friendly Virgin Records retail outlets and then the companion music label whose first release, Mike Oldfield's instrumental *Tubular Bells*, became a million seller. But four years hence, punk's arrival threatened Virgin's sound footing, so netting the Pistols became a priority.

'I never trusted hippies, and he was one of these dreadful public school ones,' McLaren said of Branson in the 2000s. 'I couldn't really quite come to terms with the fact that he was always trying to pull one over on you. I never really liked anything about him or those that worked with him.'

McLaren, however, was coming under increasing pressure from the Pistols whose aims were not as radical as their manager's. Despite their rebel attitudes, apart from Sid Vicious each appeared set on establishing lifelong careers in the music business for themselves (as of course they did). 'Their ideas of being brilliant amateurs were fading,' noted McLaren. 'They were getting into this notion that they might be considered professional, that they could gain the obvious commercial success, and they wanted records out. So I behaved myself.

'Otherwise I was prepared to somehow figure how to mismanage this [and] really pull the carpet from under Branson's feet. Branson knew that all the time and was very, very cautious while working with me. He knew that I was far better than him with the media, he knew I could speak to them, he knew he couldn't. So he knew that I was a very useful tool in the mechanics of Virgin . . . he needed me.'[2]

Yet Branson was to prove frustratingly unrufflable, restricting his public comments about McLaren to a diplomatic description of the Sex Pistols manager as 'larger-than-life'.[3]

With the pair eyeing each other uneasily, a deal was agreed for Virgin to sign the Pistols for an advance of £45,000 against delivery of three LPs over a two-year period. Branson also advanced a further £50,000 for

European rights excluding France and Francophone territories, where McLaren had an agreement with Barclay Records' swashbuckling John Fernandez, which netted Glitterbest another £26,000.

In the unusual position – for a largely untested group – of being cash rich after just one single that had done middling business, McLaren agreed that the first £15,000 of the Virgin advance be paid in twelve monthly increments.

Rory Johnston viewed the Virgin deal as 'a radical move. I thought there must be an ulterior motive. Branson was a hippie, but he was no fool. Virgin would do for England I guess. Time was running out. They needed to get the single out before the Queen's Silver Jubilee.'[4]

Soon after signing with Virgin, McLaren took the group members back to Paris where the short compilation of footage of interviews and live performance edited by Julien Temple was given a promotional screening for Barclay. While in town, McLaren socialised with his friend Jean-Charles de Castelbajac, still living close to the Folies Bergère, and even made an approach to the *fin de siècle* cabaret music hall for a booking for the Pistols that summer. This didn't materialise, but the inquiry once again demonstrated that McLaren's ambitions for the group lay beyond the increasingly parochial purview of UK punk rock.

In America, negotiations continued with the music division of Warner Brothers, much to Branson's chagrin; he had wanted US rights but McLaren was determined to prevent the British entrepreneur from controlling the group's destiny in the biggest music market in the world.

Rory Johnston had been handling the negotiations in Los Angeles after striking lucky and being connected to the label's venerated boss Mo Ostin on his first speculative call to Warner's. Unbeknown to Johnston and McLaren, Ostin and another Warner's high-up had attempted to establish contact by visiting Seditionaries when they had been in London with their wives earlier in the year during the A&M fallout, but the message left for McLaren by the middle-aged and doubtless conservatively clad American tourists was not passed on.

'I called a bunch of labels from the phone booth on Sunset, which was by now my office,' recalls Johnston, who targeted Warner's head of A&R Ted Templeman, the exec who had scored big with such acts as the Doobie Brothers, Little Feat and Carly Simon.

'When I got through to his office his assistant asked me to hold and then Mo Ostin came on the line. He explained they'd been trying to reach Malcolm and said he was sending a car to bring me in to the offices.'

Back in the UK, McLaren set about promoting 'God Save the Queen' as both a rallying cry to disgruntled youth and an all-out assault on British traditional values. This, he felt, required an outrageous stunt to extract media coverage far in excess of the A&M Buckingham Palace signing and so secure the single's place in the chart during Jubilee week.

Branson drew on his considerable reserves of charm to talk down not only representatives of workers at the record pressing plant who downed tools in protest at the lyrics' reference to the Queen as 'a moron', but also plate makers at a record-sleeve printer who objected to Jamie Reid's design which détourned a Cecil Beaton portrait of HRH by positioning a safety pin as though it closed her lips.

Once again commissioned by McLaren, this drew on his and Reid's shared knowledge of potent revolutionary imagery and channelled the infamous May 1968 poster *Une Jeunesse Que L'Avenir Inquiète Trop Souvent* (A Youth Disturbed Too Often by the Future), where an anonymous designer depicted a staring face bound by bandages secured by a safety pin at the mouth.

Having learned that part of the official ceremony was to include a flotilla down the Thames, McLaren's first act after closing the record deal was to secure £750 funding from Virgin's marketing budget – which Glitterbest matched – to cover the hire of a pleasure boat called the *Queen Elizabeth*.

'Since the Sex Pistols couldn't play anywhere on land I decided they would come out of the closet on the river,' he said in the 2000s. 'That way we would beat the bans and play our music for the people on the bridges and the embankment.'

The boat sailed in the early evening, packed to the gills with international and domestic media, Virgin staff and hangers on. Accompanying McLaren were Vivienne Westwood, Jamie Reid, Sophie Richmond, Julien Temple and his crew, and fellow travellers such as designer Ben Kelly and Michael Collins from Seditionaries.

Positioned on the main deck, the Sex Pistols launched into a set that included a rendition of the new single as the boat dipped under Westminster Bridge alongside the Houses of Parliament.

Some of those present recognised that this was a situation engineered to cause maximum provocation. 'Malcolm saw the whole thing as performance art, an event,' says audience member Tony Parsons, then one of *NME*'s resident punk writers. 'It was about baiting the establishment until it howled. There were a lot of hippies on the boat, all these sweet people from Virgin. There wasn't actually a huge divide between hippies and punks back then that we made out there was. Both groups were determined that they were going to change the way society was ordered, but both wanted to do it while getting absolutely shitfaced.'[5]

When a fight broke out in the audience, the nervous boat owner – already rattled by the presence of the notorious Pistols – pulled the plug on the group and alerted the river police. Very quickly, the *Queen Elizabeth* was escorted to a nearby quay and officers heavy-handedly brought proceedings to a close.

Partygoers initially resisted police coercion, and, in the ensuing melee, several arrests were made on the grounds of obstruction, threatening behaviour and, quaintly, 'using insulting words'. Those transported from the scene in paddy wagons included Ben Kelly, Jamie Reid, Westwood and McLaren.

Branson's description that McLaren 'had some cheeky words' for the officers made light of his raised fist declaration at the end of the gangplank that the assembled constabulary were 'fucking fascist pigs'.

The response to McLaren's protest arrived, in the words of Tony Parsons, in the form of 'the worst beating I've ever seen. OK he was asking for it but what they did to him was shocking. There were 10 coppers kicking the shit out of him.'[6]

Kelly was arrested for obstruction, after witnessing such scenes as one officer restraining the prone teenage Sex Pistols follower Debbie Wilson by placing his heavy boot over her throat. 'Then I heard one say, "There's McLaren" and they went for him, carrying him to an arch under Charing Cross bridge to give him a proper hiding,' says Kelly. 'When I tried to stop them I was flung in the back of the Black Maria. And my girlfriend put her head in to ask for the keys to our flat and she was also arrested!'

Peter Culshaw, the world-music journalist and musician, believes that the roots of McLaren's goading of the police on the night of the Jubilee boat trip lay in his dysfunctional upbringing.

'With no restraining influence and no male figure in the house, you can see McLaren's own narrative arc as a quest to provoke the patriarchal authorities,' wrote Culshaw in the mid-2000s, by which time he had known McLaren for a decade. 'My thought on watching a video of Malcolm being arrested on the Jubilee boat trip, manhandled by police and shouting "you fucking fascist bastards", is that there was an element of masochistic thrill-seeking about it. Finally he's been spanked and told to behave by a father figure.'[7]

McLaren emerged after a night in the cells at Bow Street magistrates court and was released on £100 bail – put up by Branson – for insulting behaviour. 'I felt at the time that these sweet kids were wildly exaggerating punk's importance and the idea of repression and police brutality,' said Peter York, who was also present on the river trip. 'I'm fascinated by Malcolm, but what would be the point of being a Situationist if you couldn't get yourself arrested?'[8]

The assault of McLaren by the police was but the first of a series of unprovoked attacks on the Sex Pistols and their associates that summer: Lydon was the victim of two, one a stabbing, and Paul Cook and Jamie Reid were both hospitalised as the so-called 'Summer of Hate' ground out with regular pitched battles between Teddy boys – some furious that their former stamping ground Let It Rock had become the epicentre of the new youth movement – and punks in the King's Road.

For Branson, the reinvention of Virgin was complete as the furore fuelled bans on radio plays of the single and in turn sparked a huge demand; 150,000 copies were sold in five days alone. This would have placed 'God Save the Queen' atop the singles chart had the British Phonographic Industry not decided to remove it from listings.

McLaren was delighted. 'Here we were, the most successful band that no one could hear or see and had a number one record that they wouldn't even dare to print the name of,' he wrote in the 1990s. 'It was an extraordinary feat which I absolutely adored because it meant failure in the most brilliant manner.'

Some record chains replaced listings of 'God Save the Queen' in the pole position with a blank space, prompting McLaren to encourage his ten-year-old son Joe to visit the outlet in Clapham that reported sales for compilation into the chart. 'I sent Joe to the retailer WHSmith to ask for the record. "We don't sell anything like that here," he was told by the shop assistant.

'I told him to protest: "But it's number one!"

'The assistant said: "We're not allowed to mention that." The Sex Pistols were expressing everything I was trying to do with my own shop. They were anti-music and anti-business.'

However much fuss the release caused, there is no truth in John Lydon's subsequent claims that the release of the single prompted parliamentary calls for the group, and their lead singer in particular, to be tried for treason.[9]

Nevertheless, it made for a good story for Branson. 'Years later when I was knighted I did wonder whether the royal sword would be used to chop my head off rather than tap me on the shoulder,' Branson joked in 2016. 'Thankfully the Queen has been good enough to have forgiven me. Now "God Save the Queen" is so woven into the fabric of British society that it was even used in the Olympic Opening Ceremony to soundtrack the journey down the Thames to the stadium. All from a little boat party that cost us £750.'[10]

McLaren later claimed that the international notoriety generated by the release of 'God Save the Queen' resulted in congratulations from the Situationist International's Guy Debord. 'He was one of my mentors,' recalled McLaren in 2000. 'A total recluse, he avoided any form of media involvement but he called me and said: "Thank you very much for getting my record to number one." As far as he was concerned he owned that record and that idea. I thought that was brilliantly audacious and truly wonderful. I agreed with him; it was his idea.'[11]

Fred Vermorel doubts the veracity of this tale, or another version related by McLaren where emissaries of the author of *The Society of the Spectacle* set up a meeting with McLaren, though Debord failed to materialise.

'I don't buy it. There was no way he would want to meet the manager of a rock band who owned a fashion boutique,' scoffed Vermorel in 2015.

Debord loathed and despised popular culture and mass media. Fashion and popular music were anathema, examples of what his former mentor Henri Lefebvre decried as 'cretinisation'.

McLaren also misjudged the celebrity script. Debord detested celebrity, even, or especially, his own. He had no time or inclination for celeb encounters or accolades or top people confabulating. So the emperor of punk and the pope of Situationism never did get together. But in another way of course they did.[12]

'God Save the Queen' retained a special place for McLaren. 'I'm very, very proud to have been associated with it,' he said in 1983. 'It probably gave me the best moments of my life to date. The Sex Pistols were something I hold very close to my heart and the reverberations they made around the world – even to the front pages of *Pravda* – was a tremendous effort in showing very clearly that England did have something to offer. The Sex Pistols were probably the greatest contribution to English rock 'n' roll and "God Save the Queen" was their best song because it was the most pagan, the most anti-Christian.'[13]

'God Save the Queen' contained the keynote of provocation. 'The only rule I had was that if it didn't annoy anyone and create problems, it wasn't worth doing,' McLaren said in the 1980s. 'If it didn't have any politics, it was suspect. Then it had to have a lot of style and be sexy to sell.'[14]

Virgin's call sheet for the Jubilee boat trip recorded that McLaren planned for the actor Warren Mitchell – who had made his name as the racist good-for-nothing Alf Garnett in Johnny Speight's sitcom *Till Death Us Do Part* – to act as DJ, playing a selection of the type of bawdy music-hall songs so beloved by his grandmother Rose.

This unusual booking was triggered by McLaren's affection for Mitchell, who was twenty years older but shared the same anarchic sensibilities and Jewish Stoke Newington background. It also underscored McLaren's unwillingness for the Pistols to adhere to the growing codification of punk, where dub reggae was the acceptable alternative to the largely derivative three-chord ramalama then dominating live events.

In addition, the connection to Speight highlighted McLaren's growing preoccupation with the Pistols biopic, the script of which had already gone through several rewrites as resources were channelled into Matrixbest, the newly launched film production arm of his and Fisher's management company. After all, the deal with Virgin ensured that the music side was now taking care of itself. By the summer of 1977, sufficient tracks had been recorded for the Pistols debut album to start to take shape with a third single, 'Pretty Vacant', scheduled for early July.

Meanwhile McLaren's surreptitious manoeuvring against the group making live appearances was feeding public interest. In all, the Pistols performed just seventeen concerts before live audiences in Britain in 1977, fifty less than they played the previous year (and that total doesn't take into account the dozen or so cancelled Anarchy tour dates).

To the musicians' and Virgin's frustration, McLaren did his level best to close down media access, refusing to allow the group to join the promotional treadmill unless for cover stories and once again emphasising his view that the Pistols' music was but one element in the mix. 'We hate giving interviews for the purpose of giving interviews, there isn't any point,' he told fanzine writer Tony Drayton and *Sounds* freelancer Sandy Robertson when they visited him at Dryden Chambers. 'If we talk about ourselves then it's only a star-conscious interview, it's not about something. They have the album coming out, the thing is, that's just an album, records. You don't wanna talk about your records, you wanna talk about something else.'[15]

The group's inaccessibility infuriated early champions such as Tony Wilson, the Manchester broadcaster who had provided important exposure a year earlier on *So It Goes*, the regional music TV programme he presented.

As a student, Wilson had immersed himself in Situationist theory, and was a great admirer of McLaren, but became disillusioned when the manager declined an offer for the Pistols to take over an entire episode of the programme – with Julien Temple as director and Sid Vicious as presenter – on the basis that it represented a compromise.

'I totally sympathise with your fears of being swallowed up by the six billion dollar industry, of becoming the kind of commodity music you set yourselves up to destroy,' Wilson wrote to McLaren in a three-page tirade. 'More important than you, safety pins or Steve's rapidly improving guitar playing are the kids, all those youngsters with new reasons, new thoughts and new excitements. You were the first band to show them the potential in stepping outside the dried skin of the music world. Your greatest contribution has been almost as missionaries; but don't tell me the fucking mission is over.'[16]

What was McLaren up to? According to Fred Vermorel, there was no plan, just 'a gut feeling, to keep everybody on the edge, so nobody knew what would happen next. That was his modus operandi [to make] everybody wonder: "What the hell's going on? Is there any ground underneath us?"'[17]

In music business circles McLaren's restriction on the group's availability was viewed in terms of, say, Colonel Tom Parker's exertion of control over Elvis Presley's career in order to increase his mystique. But there was more to McLaren than industry gamesmanship. In truth, he had wearied of the group's constant demands, of having to deal with record company executives, tour promoters and studio personnel. After a lifetime stimulated by contact with figures on the fringes of the art, design and fashion communities, these were boring creatures whose ambitions were limited to technical knowhow and rivalry with other labels over chart positions.

As a way of satisfying the Pistols' appeals for live bookings, removing them from the dangers of everyday life in London and cutting off Vicious from sources of heroin supply, McLaren agreed a three-week Scandinavian tour. His decision not to accompany the group but leave the members in the care of Virgin executives and the group's road crew exacerbated already strained relations, particularly when Branson pulled a fast one and placed the 'Pretty Vacant' promo video on the much-despised weekly TV show *Top of the Pops* against the group's and McLaren's express instructions.

Now, McLaren focused all his attention on the film project. With a Johnny Speight script entitled 'Anarchy in the UK', McLaren had brought producer Sandy Lieberson on board; he was introduced to the American expat by Gerry Goldstein, who had known Lieberson since his production role in Donald Cammell and Nic Roeg's *Performance* in the late 1960s.

As head of European production for a major Hollywood studio – Twentieth Century Fox – Lieberson was something of a known quantity and sympathetic ear, having co-produced the rock 'n 'roll hit movie *That'll Be the Day* (which featured Let It Rock clothes) and with fashion connections through his marriage to *Vogue* journalist and costume designer Marit Allen.

On the basis of the script, Lieberson persuaded Fox to consider a development deal while McLaren weighed up potential directors, including the then largely unproven Stephen Frears, the veteran Richard Lester and *vérité* filmmaker Ken Loach. McLaren had heard that Nicolas Roeg had expressed an interest in working with the Sex Pistols, but John Lydon nixed the choice on the basis of his dislike of Roeg's David Bowie film *The Man Who Fell to Earth*.

Then McLaren conjured an audacious choice: American exploitation king Russ Meyer, whose taste-free, knockabout soft-porn movies such as *Supervixens* and *Beyond the Valley of the Dolls* had gained kitsch currency at London arthouse venues.

'The other directors seemed dull compared with Russ and his fully cantilevered ladies,' McLaren said later. 'He knew nothing about the Sex Pistols so would have a completely different viewpoint.'[18]

And the choice of Meyer gained a thumbs-up from the Pistols after McLaren escorted them to a screening at Notting Hill's Electric Cinema of *Beyond the Valley of the Dolls*, which had been produced by Fox. This aided communications with the LA-dwelling Meyer and, while the Pistols reacquainted themselves with live audiences on their tour of Denmark, Norway and Sweden, McLaren joined Rory Johnston in LA to cement Meyer's involvement.

Johnston had already visited Meyer in the Hollywood Hills, where he was introduced to the young Dutch screenwriter/director Rene Daalder, who was to focus on the early scenes to the story, tracking the birth pangs of the Pistols against the backdrop of class-ridden Britain's economic collapse.

'Rene was extremely excited to be on board and kind of became the lead on the project for a while, representing Russ because he was always uncomfortable with Malcolm,' says Johnston.

By the time of McLaren's arrival, Meyer had also recruited his script-writing partner, the film critic Roger Ebert, who first met McLaren at the Sunset Marquis hotel in West Hollywood. 'He was a ginger-haired, wiry man in his 30s, who wore a "Destroy" T-shirt and leather pants equipped with buckles and straps,' recalled Ebert the day after McLaren's death in 2010. 'These were, I learned, the infamous Bondage Pants he introduced at Sex, the celebrated King's Road store. On his feet he wore what Russ approvingly noted were brothel creepers.'[19]

After viewing *Sex Pistols Number One* and hearing tracks for the album at Rory Johnston's home, Ebert and Meyer rejected the Speight script and set to tackling the job of creating a new screenplay, using Ebert's room at the Sunset Marquis as an office because, as Ebert remembered, 'McLaren and Meyer could not be left alone in the same room for long without fierce arguments. McLaren thought of Meyer as a fascist. Meyer thought of McLaren as a source for money to make an RM film.'[20]

'McLaren was sincere,' Daalder told Meyer's biographer Jimmy McDonough. 'He really was a zealot, with fire in his eyes [but] I don't know if either of them understood how far apart they were.'[21]

The team emerged from a weekend at the Sunset Marquis with a new script, which revolved around the slaughter of a young deer by a cynical rock star dubbed 'MJ' and the discovery of the Pistols by the McLaren-esque entrepreneur, P. T. Boggs, 'a man in his mid-30s who fancies himself as the nation's leading and most uncanny TrendSpotter. His motto: "They said it was impossible until somebody did it!" He's well-preserved and filled with limitless energy and often inane enthusiasm. He comes on to people like a youthful Zero Mostel character in *The Producers*.'[22]

At McLaren's urging, the screenplay included fictionalised scenes of incidents from real life. These ranged from the innocuous, such as when the proudly sceptical John Lydon had betrayed an innocent side to his nature by succumbing to a personality test at London's Scientology Centre in the first year of the group's existence, to the damning: Sid Vicious's eyewitness accounts of his mother's heroin abuse, which were reconstructed into an episode that culminated in them both enjoying the drug and indulging in incestuous sex.

While in LA, McLaren and Johnston also set about finalising negotiations for the US contract for the Pistols with Warner's. They were joined by Steven Fisher, whose formal appearance provided a striking contrast not just with casual LA but also McLaren's all-black attire. 'Record company staff wore Hawaiian shirts, jeans and sandals,' says Johnston. 'Steven was almost in a wing collar, certainly a waistcoat and grey striped trousers. It was extraordinary. And there was me. I was in the mix because Malcolm knew I'd done a pretty good job in maintaining the integrity of the project and communicating the message of British punk.'

Johnston was paid for his efforts in T-shirts, muslin tops and other clothing shipped from Seditionaries and struck a deal with the local branch of Granny Takes a Trip to carry the latest designs, which were the subject of a fashion spread in the city's recently launched fanzine *Slash*, and so was responsible for introducing original punk clothing to the West Coast.

After a couple of weeks McLaren returned to London with Ebert and Meyer in tow; the director had managed to wangle not only a posh apartment in Cheyne Walk, the riverside avenue in Chelsea where neighbours included Mick Jagger and Keith Richards, but also a financial package that stipulated payment of £100,000 at a rate of £5000 a week for the duration of the production.

With Fox yet to approve the full budget, the acceptance of such terms was extremely reckless, but McLaren ploughed on regardless. 'Malcolm was quite desperate to have Russ involved,' says Johnston. 'His vision for the movie was essentially a Russ Meyer production.'

The singer Marianne Faithfull was signed to play Sid Vicious's mother and the veteran Texan rocker P. J. Proby agreed to take the role of MJ (whose moniker was changed to PJ to avoid legal heat from Mick Jagger). At McLaren's urging, Ebert and Meyer instituted a subplot into the script concerning a serial attacker called the Battersea Rapist.

The pair also spent time with the Pistols, whose Scandinavian dates had resulted in almost blanket positive front-page coverage, which had been engineered by Virgin's press office, in the music weeklies. McLaren was not only losing his hold over the group, but also appalled at their growing co-option by the media. 'Because the music press are basically Sixties culture freaks they imply we're not original, they try to maintain this facade of knowing every song, every riff, every lyric, as if they invented it,' he said. 'One recent headline had us as "John, Paul, Steve and Sid," like we were the Beatles! That's fucking disgusting! They were

trying to make us fun. It shows the vampire nature of the Sixties generation, the most narcissistic generation that has ever been!'[23]

The return of the group to the UK also necessitated new living arrangements for Lydon and Vicious, indicating a widening gap between the two
former college pals.

They had been sharing the top floor of a large house in Sutherland
Avenue in west London's boho Maida Vale, but Nancy Spungen's troublesome presence had made tenancy unsustainable, and, in the summer
of 1977, Glitterbest organised for separate accommodation.

This was also precipitated by pressure from the group members led by
Lydon, always the sharpest of the gang. He had become perturbed by the
chaotic accounting and non-payment of royalties, and forced McLaren
to release moneys for permanent residences.

Lydon acquired a duplex in Gunter Grove at the far end of the King's
Road on the Chelsea/Fulham borders for £12,000 and Paul Cook an
apartment in Marble Arch, not far from Helen Wellington Lloyd. Jones
stayed there until he spent £12,000 himself on a flat in Canfield Gardens
in north London's West Hampstead. Sophie Richmond's diary entry for
24 August 1977 records the fact that Glitterbest bought a mews apartment for Vicious, again in Maida Vale, with a lease of just seven years
(ending in 1984): 'When I phoned Malcolm to OK it he said, that's fine,
he'll be dead by then. True enough . . .'[24]

The issues over money increasingly put McLaren in Lydon's cross-
hairs; he later complained the Gunter Grove acquisition represented the
sole financial gain from his time in the group.[25] The average annual UK
wage was £3600 and house prices averaged £16,000, so the springing of a
proportion – maybe a fifth – of what the group members were owed
undercut to a certain extent the subsequent claims that the group
members did not benefit in any way during his stewardship. Their resentment was nevertheless justified in light of McLaren's channelling of the
majority of their money into what was palpably his film.

For the time being, however, the Pistols were happy enough for the
project to progress, having also been mollified by a short tour of the UK

– known as SPOTS (Sex Pistols On Tour Secretly) – where venues were played using pseudonyms.

Over this period Vicious gained a growing public profile and, less than five months after he had joined the group, was challenging Lydon's authority.

This served McLaren's divide-and-rule agenda and reinforced his position that the root of the Pistols' appeal lay in their ineptitude and the grotesque nature of their public image. And Vicious best exemplified those traits, though, to a rational music manager, these would have appeared as terminal shortcomings. This is instructive in viewing McLaren's understanding of the relationship between creative expression and morality, and accords with Walter Benjamin's formulation that 'at the base of every major work of art lies a pile of barbarism'.[26]

For example, one rumour, which gained currency in the latter half of 1977, was that McLaren had welcomed the nihilistic Vicious as a replacement for Glen Matlock because the bass player's realisation of his death wish – as demonstrated by suicide attempts, involvement in violent incidents and prodigious drug intake – would enhance the group's image. Even the addicted writer Nick Kent was surprised by Vicious's response to the gossip.

'Yeah, maybe that's true,' said Vicious. 'Maybe that's why Malcolm has me in his band. I mean, I could easily end up dead quite soon. But then again, that's just my tough shit, isn't it?'[27]

Roger Ebert and Russ Meyer were as taken aback as Kent when they showed Sid Vicious the scene in the screenplay in which he and his mother have sex after she has jacked up in front of him. 'Sid studied it,' recalled Ebert. 'Russ, Malcolm and I studied him. He read carefully, smoking. Finally he closed the screenplay. "I don't think me Mum will like the part about the heroin." '[28]

Robin Scott visited Thurleigh Court when McLaren was working on this particular scene. 'I gave my critique of it, saying "This doesn't ring true, because I can't believe this. It doesn't make any sense that someone living in the top floor of a council flat is a heroin addict, and is feeding her son heroin." Malcolm laughed at me and said, "That's what's going on. That's his life. It's true." '[29]

The film script described the McLaren character P. T. Boggs as an amoral 'destroyer, a consumer of youth, taking their genuine street culture with one hand and selling it back to them with the other. Although he's totally positive in a socko manner, none of his clients is indispensable. They're here today and gone tomorrow, and there are a hundred more to take their places. Being the ultimate opportunist, he is in fact as anarchistic as the Pistols themselves.'

Meanwhile Lydon's alter-ego Johnny Rotten was depicted as a sarcastic, narcissistic boozehound who mistrusts Boggs but is nevertheless ordered around by him (one scene reprised the incident at the 100 Club the previous spring when McLaren commanded Lydon to return to the stage after he had walked away during a performance).

The script closed with the assassination of the rock star and the following scene:

JOHNNY ROTTEN
(down at the body)
'Will success spoil Johnny?'
(pause)
(freaking out and kicking the lifeless body of BJ all over the stage
 as he continues)
'No. He will waste, spoil, smash, blow up and destroy success!'
Another pause. The room is hushed. JOHNNY ROTTEN looks up
 slowly, chest heaving from the exertion, and directly into the camera.
JOHNNY ROTTEN
(Quiet again)
'Did yer ever have the feeling yer being watched?'[30]

The character's final comment derived from footage from the Jubilee boat event captured by Julien Temple. Then, the wary Lydon remarked bitterly: 'Ever get the feeling you've been trapped?' And, of course, it would be paraphrased by Lydon himself at the final performance by the Sex Pistols with Vicious in the line-up, when he ended the concert with the words (as much to himself as the audience): 'Ever get the feeling you've been cheated?'

That this lay just a few months in the future was plausible given the maelstrom of events and the rolling media frenzy that surrounded the group's existence. Even the artwork for the fourth single, 'Holidays in the Sun', became the subject of an intense legal battle when the Belgian Travel Service sued Glitterbest and Jamie Reid over his *détournement* of cartoon panels from one of its brochures for the sleeve.

'They were the golden boys of Fleet Street and gave everybody what they were looking for,' said McLaren of the Pistols a few years later. 'The greatest storytellers of all time, the Charles Dickens of rock 'n' roll. I was a total catalyst, and one who saw the advantage and became ruthless in manoeuvring [situations] to their greatest heights. I was undoubtedly Fleet Street's most marvellous asset. After "God Save the Queen" came out one editor phoned me up and said, "We sold more papers than they did on Armistice Day." '[31]

On Rory Johnston's advice, McLaren accepted a request from *Rolling Stone* staffer Charles M. Young to visit London to interview him and the Pistols and also write generally about the punk phenomenon sweeping Britain. The fortnightly agreed to McLaren's condition that the feature appear as a cover story; tacit approval from the world's most influential rock read would help up the ante with Warner Brothers in terms of advance monies for American rights.

Through sheer persistence, Young eventually gained access granted to few other journalists at this stage in the group's trajectory. After two days of being ignored by McLaren, Young tracked him down to the West End punk club the Vortex where he found the manager and Meyer witnessing a performance by the young all-female punk band The Slits. Subsequently Young hung out with all four group members and also wangled an invitation to the apartment in Thurleigh Court McLaren shared with Westwood, Ben and Joe.

While he waited for two hours for McLaren to arrive, Young had time to take in the décor, later describing the flat as 'modestly furnished in black and white . . . the only color in the room is a poster of the equally depressing Red Ballet. The bookshelf includes Orwell, Dickens, de Sade and Wilhelm Reich's *The Mass Psychology of Fascism*. First in a pile of albums on the dresser is *The World of Billy Fury*.'

When he arrived at midnight, McLaren talked Young through his experience of working with the New York Dolls and how it informed his management style. 'I was trying to make them more extreme, less accessible,' he told Young. 'Most bands won't do that sort of thing, but they must find a means to provoke. I love to go the hardest route. It keeps you up. It keeps the truth happening. Too many of the new groups are getting sucked up by the record companies too early. The movement will get diluted.'

For a group still without a US deal, McLaren used the encounter with Young not to romance the American music business but rather to denigrate the members of its upper echelon. 'These record company presidents, they're all whores,' he informed Young.

Two months ago, their doormen would have thrown us out. We sell a few records and they phone and want their pictures taken with us. Mo Ostin (of Warner Bros) is flying in with his lawyer tomorrow, and I couldn't get past his secretary before. I've been in and out of CBS many times. Walter Yetnikoff (president of CBS Records Group) sang me 'Anarchy in the UK' at breakfast at the Beverly Wilshire to prove he knew the group. He said he wasn't offended by Johnny Rotten saying he was the anti-Christ. 'I'm Jewish,' he said.

McLaren reserved substantial vitriol for Young and *Rolling Stone*. 'This band hates you. It hates your culture. Why can't you lethargic, complacent hippies understand that? You need to be smashed,' he exclaimed. 'This is a very horrible country, England. We invented the

Mackintosh, you know. We invented the flasher, the voyeur. That's what the press is about.'

The encounter was interrupted by a phone call informing McLaren that Elvis Presley had died. 'Makes you feel sad, doesn't it?' Young recorded McLaren as telling his informant. 'Like your grandfather died. Yeah, it's just too bad it couldn't have been Mick Jagger.'

Young also witnessed a performance by the Pistols on the SPOTS tour. Despite the abuse heaped upon him, the *Rolling Stone* journalist recognised that McLaren and the group's impact extended beyond rock music across post-War culture in the west.

'I can't dislike Malcolm McLaren for figuring out that reporters are vampires, lurking in the night, ready to suck out every last corpuscle of titillation, leaving the victim to spend eternity as a Media Zombie,' wrote Young.

If he were merely a manipulator, he wouldn't have chosen such genuine fuck-ups for the band. If he were merely a greed-head, he could have found an easier way to run the Sex Pistols for number one group in the world. As it is, he chose not the politics of boredom, but the politics of division, Richard Nixon's way: amputate the wanking Sixties liberals from their working-class support. Kids destroyed schools to the tune of $600 million in the US last year. That's a lot of anger that the Southern-California-Cocaine-And-Unrequited-Love Axis isn't capable of tapping.[32]

By the time of the publication of Young's piece in October and despite his condemnation of Arista bigwig Clive Davies, McLaren had closed the deal with the label's Billy Meshel to represent the Sex Pistols' music publishing for £58,000.

In addition, he persuaded Warner Brothers to take US recording rights of the Pistols, for an advance of £50,000 against delivery of the group's debut album. Warner's also committed a further £200,000 to the film, which had a new title courtesy of Roger Ebert: 'Who Killed Bambi?'

With a further £50,000 each from Virgin and the British film and theatrical producer Michael White, the stakes had been upped sufficiently for Sandy Lieberson to add the young British producer Jeremy Thomas to the team.

'Russ Meyer was champing at the bit by this stage,' says Thomas. 'And working with Malcolm was an unusual experience. He was very charming but it was quite a theatrical process. He was an anarchist, in that he was very intent on being destructive even during the process of creating something.'[33]

During his time in London, Meyer confided in Ebert that he believed McLaren to be 'full of shit'. Gradually, as the weeks passed and the budget ballooned after Meyer insisted on the construction of expensive sets at Bray Studios to the west of London, the relationship between the film's progenitor and the director all but collapsed.

Amid this infighting, after three days of filming during which a fawn was shot in the Forest of Dean, Fox withdrew its £125,000 commitment to the project. Princess Grace of Monaco, a board member of the studio, was not only unimpressed by the combination of the Pistols and the Z-Movie King but also disgusted by such scenes as Vicious's incestuous encounter with his mother, and sealed its fate by announcing: 'We don't want to make another Meyer X film.'[34]

McLaren announced the news to Meyer, who had received £30,000 in cash. The director immediately announced that he would sue for the remaining £70,000 due to him.

In later life, when he was asked about 'Who Killed Bambi?', Meyer, who realised only two more movies – both poorly received – in the remaining twenty-six years of his life, was disinclined to acknowledge the central facts that a) it was Fox that pulled the rug and b) he received considerable compensation for his involvement. Instead he blamed McLaren. 'We had a chance to make a pretty good film but Malcolm muffed it,' Meyer told British TV host Jonathan Ross.[35]

With Meyer and Ebert back in the US, McLaren, Sandy Lieberson and Jeremy Thomas cast around for new backers to help keep the project afloat. Given that Meyer and Ebert had dibs on the existing script, the dazed team briefly reverted to the Johnny Speight version before bringing other scriptwriters on board, including the young US team of Jonathan Taplin and Danny Otashyu. 'They were brought over from America, installed in a flat in Baker Street and met all the Pistols but their script didn't quite make it,' says Thomas.

McLaren commissioned British scriptwriter Michael Armstrong, whose credits include *The Image*, a 1960s short featuring David Bowie, to concoct a new screenplay with the title 'A Star Is Dead'; according to the journalist Frances Lynn, 'Malcolm loved it but the film wasn't made. The script is outrageous and hilarious.'[36]

But then McLaren struck upon the idea of filling Meyer's shoes with the veteran British horror and sexploitation director Peter Walker. 'Malcolm's idea was that we would run counter to everything that was acceptable in the business by appointing him,' adds Thomas. 'It would be raucous and music hall, like the Pistols.'

But Walker also fell by the wayside, and, with Julien Temple on board as film archivist and assistant director, McLaren made contact with Ian Stuttard, a director who had filmed news items at 430 King's Road when it was Too Fast to Live Too Young to Die for the *Today* programme, the magazine show on which the Pistols had appeared with Bill Grundy.

'He called me out of the blue at Thames TV and told me "Who Killed Bambi?" had run into trouble and asked whether I would be interested in picking up the film where Russ Meyer had left off,' says Stuttard, who agreed to start work, though was kept largely in the dark as to the overall concept of the film.

'He was an incredibly tricky character, slippery as a bag of eels,' says Stuttard, who spent time with McLaren and Temple at the Glitterbest offices and over drinks at their local, the Cambridge Arms. 'The film didn't have a new name but soon the swindle was emerging in his mind,' says Stuttard. 'Then McLaren talked to me about it all being based on a con, that he was swindling as much money as possible out of record companies on the back of the group.'[37]

Meanwhile McLaren leaked to the press that the movie was heading into production once more, with Marianne Faithfull named as leading lady.[38]

The to-ing and fro-ing over the film played out against the release of the LP *Never Mind the Bollocks, Here's the Sex Pistols* by Virgin in late October 1977. Against a fluorescent sleeve the title appeared in the ransom-note font and was chosen by McLaren after a phrase repeatedly uttered by Steve Jones.

'We had been drinking vodka with journalists from *Pravda* who were possibly KGB officers, and Jones said "Never mind the bollocks" about something,' recalled McLaren. 'I thought, "That's good. We'll make this a commodity so it looks nothing like an album, unapologetically rude, crude, ugly and wonderful." We didn't want a smiling bunch of people on the cover, just the statement in hard black and white.

'Jamie suggested it be fluorescent so it would stand out in the dark. I thought, "Yeah, you're right." We understood not to use graphic letters that looked pure and designed, but instead use the lettering that would never look like a commodity, never look like you were behaving responsibly.'[39]

With advance orders for 125,000 copies, *Never Mind the Bollocks* was granted immediate gold disc status. The Pistols were a bona-fide commercial success.

But the LP title landed the group in hot water, resulting in prosecutions for record-shop displays on the grounds that the prominence of the word 'Bollocks' contravened the 1899 Indecent Advertising Act. Richard Branson was quick off the mark in exploiting the story, hiring the eminent barristers John Mortimer (the creator of *Rumpole of the Bailey*) and human rights lawyer Geoffrey Robertson to successfully defend the manager of Virgin's Nottingham outlet before the city's magistrates, thus pushing demand for the new release through the roof.

'The album sold truck loads, I mean literally truck loads,' acknowledged McLaren in the 2000s. 'Not to the extent that it was the best-selling album of all time, but still enough to keep the wolf from the door at

Virgin. The one thing that grated [was] it inadvertently made Virgin look vaguely hip. That was the thing that I absolutely just felt dreadful about.'[40]

As part of the promotional round for the album, Lydon and Vicious participated in a good-natured interview with BBC Radio 1 presenter John Tobler where they derided 'that oaf' McLaren but nonetheless accentuated his importance to the group.

'He was a miserable little artist from the East End with pretensions of being middle class,' Vicious guffawed. 'In his closet in Clapham he's got this ridiculous picture of an awful load of scribble which is meant to be a chair. He was going [adopts posh, quasi-academic accent]: "Well, you see, it's meant to signify the flow of air around the chair." He was trying to be all artistic and impress us but we were laughing our heads off. What an idiot! And there's that poxy Vivienne squawking away in the corner sewing things up, babbling away to herself, the old bag. I hate her as well.'

When Tobler asked Vicious why, in that case, the group put up with McLaren and Westwood, Vicious pivoted for comic effect: 'Because we like them. They're our friends . . . Where would we be without Malcy-Walcy?'

A discussion about the album track-listing – there had been disagreement about including the singles – was revealing about the band members' view of McLaren's role. Tobler asked Lydon whether McLaren had input on the subject. 'He had something to say about it and I hope he would,' retorted Lydon. 'If he doesn't he's a pretty bad manager. We expect him to have an opinion. In fact, we demand it.'

The casual listener may have observed beyond the grandstanding not only Lydon and Vicious's grudging respect for McLaren, but also the depth of their own friendship, though Vicious struck an ominous note in the final seconds of the recording after the interview had ended. Offered a cup of tea, he muttered: 'No, I don't want one. I want to go and take some drugs.'[41]

Meanwhile, Lydon's suspicions that he was being replaced in McLaren's considerations by Vicious were confirmed during a taxi ride to his Chelsea home shared with the manager and Julien Temple. 'Malcolm argued that he wasn't neglecting John, claiming he had visited Gunter Grove several times, banging on the door and getting no response,' recalls Temple. 'John challenged Malcolm to come up with the address or even directions, which he clearly didn't know, and, after some more goading, Malcolm waited until the cab stopped at a traffic light and jumped out!'

Working with booking agency Cowbell, McLaren devised a plan for what he called 'The Sex Pistols' Tour of the World', starting in the UK in December and taking in continental Europe, the US and South America over the following two months. With Lydon's approval, McLaren proposed that the group take an unorthodox approach and avoid the main entertainment centres such as London and New York. In America, he decreed, they would play the southern states, using his model of removing the drug-addicted New York Dolls Jerry Nolan and Johnny Thunders to the healthier climes of Florida three years previously.

During downtime before dates commenced, Spungen and Vicious kicked their heels in central London's Ambassador Hotel. Their stay ended in eviction when, in a drunken rage after his fellow Pistols failed to turn up at rehearsals, Vicious beat Spungen and made a dramatic suicide attempt. The police were called and the pair were arrested on drugs charges in a hail of front-page headlines.[42]

The other group members were now thoroughly tired of Vicious, and during a sit-down at Glitterbest with the errant bassist and their manager, elected to sack him. Only McLaren's intervention stopped the musicians from approaching Paul Simonon of The Clash for the forthcoming live appearances, as Vicious informed the *NME*'s Nick Kent: 'Malcolm came to my defence all of a sudden. He just realised that my side of things had a point. That what I was doing was just living out the original idea of the band as four complete nutters going out and doing anything and every-thing. Just having fun, which I always reckoned was the whole thing about the Pistols from the very beginning. It just got so fuckin' wet, so serious. That was what he said anyway.'[43]

McLaren was also cracking foxy. While the five talked about Vicious cleaning up his act and abiding by a condition not to see Spungen, his American girlfriend was in fact, at McLaren's instruction, being whisked in a car by Sophie Richmond and the Pistols roadies John Tiberi and Steve Connolly (known as 'Roadent') to Heathrow Airport, where a ticket on the next flight to New York awaited her. But the kidnapping failed; Spungen escaped and soon the doomed lovers were back in each other's needle-pocked arms.

After a few more dates around Britain and on the continent, McLaren made arrangements for the group to travel to the US (though even this process was marred by problems when US immigration balked at the band members' substantial arrest records). On Christmas Day 1977 the Sex Pistols played their final British shows, a response of McLaren's to a request for a benefit for the children of firemen and laid-off workers at an engineering plant in Huddersfield, Yorkshire.

With a financial contribution from Virgin, McLaren organised buses to transport the children and their parents to a nightclub for an afternoon Christmas party. And, as if to undercut the cheery family atmosphere, he designed an extraordinary flyer to be distributed at the event. This acted less as a promotion for the Pistols than a commentary on both his Jewishness and his strange relationship with the group.

The artwork reproduced an illustration from the original edition of *Oliver Twist* by the nineteenth-century satirist George Cruikshank. The choice from the Dickens book that had so delighted Rose Corré in McLaren's childhood was on the nose. Entitled 'Oliver introduced to the Respectable Old Gentleman', this depicted the central character's first encounter with Fagin, the miser who refused to distribute his accumulated wealth among the children to whom he provided shelter in exchange for their criminal acts.

This was supported by a statement about the Pistols scrawled by McLaren in spattered lettering:

They are Dickensian-like urchins who with ragged clothes and pockmarked faces roam the streets of foggy gas-lit London. Pillaging. Setting fire to buildings. Beating up old people with gold chains. Fucking the rich up the arse.

Causing havoc wherever they go. Some of these ragamuffin gangs jump on tables amidst the charred debris and with burning torches play rock 'n' roll to the screaming delight of the frenzied, pissing, pogoing mob. Shouting and spitting 'anarchy' one of these gangs call themselves the Sex Pistols. This true and dirty tale has been continuing throughout 200 years of teenage anarchy and so in 1978 there still remains the Sex Pistols. Their active extremism is all they care about because that's what counts to jump right out of the 20th Century as fast as you possibly can in order to create an environment that you can truly run wild in.

McLaren signed the artwork – which was also printed as a banner and later onto muslin tops sold in Seditionaries – 'Oliver Twist'.

'I used a wooden stick dipped in ink to write that,' said McLaren many years later. 'It was deliberately made for the last British performance by the Sex Pistols, because I didn't think there would be any coming back from where we were going.'

Chapter 25

'The management is bored with managing a successful rock and roll band. The group is bored with being a successful rock and roll band. Burning venues and destroying record companies is more creative than making it.'[1]

With this statement issued two days before his thirty-second birthday, Malcolm McLaren confirmed the Sex Pistols break-up to the world's media, less than three weeks after the group arrived in the US for the concert tour that comprised the final chapter of their story.

McLaren had been outgunned, not by the warring Pistols but, in fact, Warner Brothers. The American conglomerate was keen to protect its hefty investment in the Pistols and in the light of McLaren's insistence against the group playing major cities, Warner's sent a crew of tough security guards, some Vietnam vets, to oversee the musicians and keep them – especially Vicious – on the straight and narrow as they travelled across the flyover southern states by tour bus.

This heavy-handed approach intensified relations between the group members and their manager; one result was that, on the road, Lydon responded positively to the attentions of Warner's executives such as A&R head Bob Regehr. His sympathy for the isolated young man compared favourably against McLaren's borderline neglect.

'My relationship with John Lydon and the rest of the group was very poor,' McLaren conceded in the 2000s. 'My only concern was to make sure Sid didn't OD. Rotten was being poached by Warner Brothers, who said: "The manager's crazy, he's a communist." '[2]

Caroline Coon had at that time left *Melody Maker* and was set to replace McLaren's former partner-in-crime Bernard Rhodes as manager of The Clash after they nearly split over problems with the US major

CBS Records. She detected a failure of nerve on the part of McLaren and Rhodes when confronted with the might of the American entertainment complex.

'When bands get to a certain level you start talking hundreds of thousands of dollars to record companies, and if you're a male manager you have to deal in quite a confident way with men who have more authority than you,' she said in the early 2000s.

'Neither Bernie Rhodes nor Malcolm McLaren feel very comfortable with men who they perceive to have more authority. Rather than nurture them to the next level, they broke their bands up. It's very easy to do; you just have to set the band members against each other.'[3]

Coon's intervention helped pull The Clash back from the brink, but when it came to the Sex Pistols, McLaren was distracted, simultaneously channelling his energies into the film production and distancing himself from the car-crash spectacle the group had become.

'I was more interested in the ideas than the people, which was obviously my failing because as a manager I obviously didn't handle my nursemaid role well enough,' McLaren told the writer Johnny Black in 1982. 'That was the major flaw which led to the break up of the group, because I wasn't prepared to be their father. And from my own experience I realised that all singers need fathers. They need tremendous security, need to know they're right, need to know they're more important than anybody else in the group, they're the most scared, the biggest actors, the most dishonest, but onstage they're the greatest performers.'[4]

The tour had been booked from LA by Rory Johnston, who met the Pistols before their first date in Atlanta, Georgia. This was a much-changed group from the youngsters he had hung out with at the Portobello Hotel two years earlier. 'For a start Malcolm wasn't there; he arrived a day later,' says Johnston. 'The changeover from Glen to Sid was just one of the things that altered the dynamic. There was so much going on it was like experiencing a tornado. It was hard for them and in fact the rest of us to stay focused on any one thing. And when he arrived, there was definitely more anxiety with Malcolm, particularly negativity from Rotten, but then he was always like that.'

McLaren didn't travel on the bus with the group, opting to fly between gigs to observe the live appearances, many of which were beset by near riots and violent confrontations with audience members and angry locals.

McLaren later admitted his sloppiness, particularly in the mishandling of passport and visa applications, which resulted in the group missing a slot on *Saturday Night Live*. In those pre-MTV days, this would have beamed the Pistols, *Ed Sullivan*-style, direct into the homes of millions of Americans. Instead last-minute substitutes Elvis Costello & the Attractions reaped the benefits and soon became favourites among US new-wave fans.

Counter to claims that McLaren didn't have a plan, Fred Vermorel says McLaren set out in the US to unleash maximum chaos. 'He sat down and worked out how to deliberately fuck it up,' says Vermorel.

One way was to send them to the far south, where there were cowboys with guns. Maybe one of them would get shot, which would be great for promotion! He also deliberately booked them into places that were too small, where there would be panic and fights.

The whole thing worked like a charm, and apparently the FBI was following them and asking what was going on, because of the drugs as much as anything else. They were wondering: 'Were these people crazed with drugs? Who was the manager? Was he in control? Was he mad?'

No one was in control and deliberately so. That way, Malcolm held all the strings. At the end of the day he could emerge triumphant, and talk about 'cash from chaos', and other glib things like that.[5]

Glib or not, McLaren remained fixated on the visual aspects of the group until the end. For the American dates, he and Westwood worked up a selection of ingenious and eye-popping designs. One was for a new suit for John Lydon to wear on stage: this consisted of Bondage trousers and a bum-freezer jacket in vivid tartan, though Lydon eschewed the matching kilt-like lengths of fabric designed to be attached back and front. 'We wanted the Bondage suit to become more warrior-like,' said McLaren. 'Using my Scottish background, we selected five tartans in the best wool from the cloth merchants Hunt & Winterbotham in Golden Square, central London.'

McLaren commissioned the suits to be made by Mintos, the leather-maker in north London's Caledonian Road. 'We knew he had the skills of working with very good materials and was like a tailor in leather, cutting from the skin. He got the tartan to match with the pockets and other details exactly.'

Lydon also wore a pink cotton 'muslin' top featuring a new détourned graphic of McLaren's: an illustration of an ejaculating man being fist-fucked, framed by the slogan 'Fuck Yr mother . . . and run away Punk!' in lettering that mimicked the phallic font used by Russ Meyer for his film *Up!*

A T-shirt printed with the sex scene was among the haul McLaren acquired at the Pleasure Chest on Santa Monica in West Hollywood during one of his trips to Los Angeles the previous year. 'I never liked mothers per se, and this seemed the right message to convey to young punks across America,' said McLaren in the 2000s.

Lydon also baited the Stetson-hatted audiences by flaunting the Cowboys T-shirt that had caused such outrage on the streets of London when it was first stocked by Sex a matter of weeks before he joined the group. Now, thirty months later, it was all over. The final straw for Lydon came with McLaren's last-minute decision for the Pistols to be filmed performing with the fugitive British criminal Ronnie Biggs – notorious for his part in the 1960s heist the Great Train Robbery – in Rio de Janeiro.

The combination of the UK's most wanted felon cavorting with the world's most hated group amid the favelas during Carnival was too good an opportunity to let pass, McLaren believed. But Lydon was among those who pointed not only to the crass nature of the union but also the unsustainability of the scheduling; five days after the end of the US tour the Pistols were booked to play Stockholm, on the other side of the world and a couple of time zones away. To subject the already exhausted group to this punishing timetable was tantamount to driving them into the ground.

Bob Regehr advised McLaren against the Rio visit on the grounds that 'Latin American governments do not like rock 'n' roll and being predominantly Catholic would abhor the Sex Pistols lyrics. [McLaren] dismissed my warnings. I told him it was dangerous for the members of the group to go, meaning they might have difficulty getting out of South America and Latin American countries tended to be "trigger happy".'

When McLaren asked Regehr to arrange for Warner's to fund the exercise, he was reminded that the record company did not represent the group in Brazil. 'McLaren retorted he would ask Virgin Records to pay for it if I would assist him with the travel arrangements,' said Regehr. 'I told him I would offer the services of Warner's travel agency, but that we would take no part, financial or otherwise, in a venture I regarded as foolhardy.'[6]

McLaren's insistence looked increasingly like sabotage, and suspicions that he was pulling out all the stops to demolish the group were confirmed by his attempts to bait the venerated San Francisco promoter Bill Graham. He then instructed the rock critic Richard Meltzer to rile up the audience by abusing them roundly when introducing the Pistols at the last date on the tour at the city's Winterland Ballroom. According to Meltzer, McLaren's view was that 'it all seemed too placid, too pat – like a Grateful Dead show'.[7]

It was there, as the Sex Pistols played the last chords of their final show together in front of a baying mob of six thousand assorted freaks, that Lydon announced his dissatisfaction: 'Ah-ha-hah! Ever get the feeling you've been cheated?!'

In the wings, sipping from bottles of Heineken in the company of his friend, the New York photographer Joe Stevens, McLaren breathed a sigh of relief.

Warner's interventions had brought home to him the reality that the global music industry was now geared to assimilate punk. The parochial British music business had been relatively easy to cajole and manipulate. The news from slick, fast-talking Warner's was that McLaren would be expected to toe the line.

Accounts of the immediate aftermath of the Winterland show, first backstage and then over the next twenty-four hours at San Francisco's Hotel Miyako, vary wildly. Both Vicious and Jones subsequently claimed that they announced they were leaving the group, but it was Lydon's unwillingness to comply with McLaren's plan to hook up with Biggs that broke the band. With justification, Lydon viewed Biggs as a charmless nerk rather than an anti-hero deserving of glorification, not least since the train driver in Biggs's gang crime had suffered severe brain damage from injuries inflicted upon him during the raid.

'The fact that Rotten didn't want to cooperate was icing on the cake,' says Joe Stevens. 'Malcolm was really pissed off and didn't want to be manager any more. I think he could have rescued the situation but chose not to.'

Over the next few hours, while Rotten alternately sulked and raged and drummer Paul Cook and guitarist Steve Jones stewed, Sid Vicious absconded to a Haight-Ashbury shooting gallery where he promptly OD-ed, though he was brought back from the brink of death by a local homeopathic doctor hired by McLaren.

During a final confrontation with Lydon in McLaren's hotel room, the manager told the singer: 'You're turning into Rod Stewart. We don't need you. You're replaceable. Go downstairs and find some cocaine to take.'[8]

With that, the various factions went their separate ways. Vicious was accompanied by the roadie John 'Boogie' Tiberi on a tortuous journey by air back to London via Los Angeles and New York; on the snow-bound bi-coastal leg he slipped into another drug-induced coma and was rushed into Jamaica Hospital in Queens.

Cruelly stranded by McLaren without money, Rotten also returned to London via a stopover with Joe Stevens in New York, where he was feted by the city's punk elite and revealed the band's bust-up.

Meanwhile McLaren took Cook and Jones with him to Los Angeles and packed them onto a flight to Rio so that they could enjoy a bout of R&R and prepare for filming with Biggs.

With a series of meetings with record company executives, movie studio producers and financiers lined up in LA, McLaren stayed at the infamous Tropicana Motel on Santa Monica Boulevard, close by the Pleasure Chest and home to the likes of Tom Waits and visiting musicians from Bob Marley & the Wailers to the Ramones.

'We were pretty shell-shocked,' says Johnston. 'It had been mind-boggling; the whole thing had been on the precipice for so long before toppling over. To a certain extent that's what Malcolm wanted, but it wasn't the way I had envisaged things going. I was more aligned with Steve, Paul and Rotten. I wanted to continue, to keep building, not blow everything up. From a musical point of view we could have gone on to bigger and better things, maybe not with Sid, but Malcolm was undergoing tremendous anguish and aggravation. If he'd not decided on Brazil and instead separated from the band, gone back to London and done his own thing, they could have gone on to new adventures.'

During his stay in LA, McLaren hung out with Johnston and Fayette Hauser, a founding member of the San Franciscan troupe the Cockettes. Their gender-fluid performances as 'hippy acid freak drag queens' had matched the Sex Pistols for public outrage. Hauser had also visited London in the spring of 1977, where she had been exposed to punk rock and visited Seditionaries.

Hauser recognised McLaren across the bar of the Rainbow, the late-night rock haunt on Sunset Strip, the day he arrived in town from San Francisco. 'I pounced on him, simple as that,' says Hauser. 'He took me back to the Tropicana and we had wild sex that night and every night. We had a great time, with him telling stories and me listening, absolutely captivated.'[9]

According to Hauser, McLaren let his guard drop during the stay. When he and Hauser weren't out on the town, McLaren talked long into the night, often frankly about his life before the Sex Pistols, particularly his upbringing and adventures during his teens and twenties within the London art school system.

Attired in leather jeans and sneakers, McLaren took to selecting a handmade Sex Pistols T-shirt from a pile delivered to his room by a fan. 'Every day he would pluck one, wear it, and then throw it away,' says Hauser.

Often McLaren tinkered with a film script for the British all-girl punk group the Slits, whom he was considering managing, and took meetings with Johnston, who was coordinating with Julien Temple in London in corralling a film crew for Brazil.

By now there were considerable forces marshalling their resources against McLaren: in London, Richard Branson had picked up the option to sign Lydon to an eight-album solo deal with Virgin and provided backing for the singer to prepare litigation against his former manager.

Some in the media who had observed Lydon and McLaren's relationship at close quarters pondered the Sex Pistols frontman's vitriol. 'Malcolm McLaren is so much like an older version of his former ward John Rotten that a short time with him makes it apparent to how large an extent this sophisticated Chelsea shopkeeper must have become a crucial role model for the only just post-adolescent Lydon,' wrote journalist Chris Salewicz a few years later. 'One feels that in Rotten's ostensible loathing for the man who carried out the often sexually ambivalent task of manager towards him, there may well lurk the hurt of confused love.'[10]

Such emotions could not be attributed to Russ Meyer. During the Pistols break-up he had also initiated proceedings for the unpaid £70,000, while photographer Ray Stevenson was making legal his fight against McLaren's attempts to block publication of a Sex Pistols photobook. And now Warner's was breathing down his neck over the band's collapse.

According to Hauser, in this period McLaren maintained a buoyancy, which she captured in upbeat photographs taken on a weekend trip to

Las Vegas with Johnston. 'We didn't even get a hotel room,' says Hauser. 'There was just the hire car, a wad of cash and not a care in the world. We had a lot of chemical assistance – a bag of powder – and visited every casino, playing and watching the all-night lounge acts.'

Witnessing performances by 1950s doo-wop stars Little Anthony & the Imperials and 1960s soul survivors Smokey Robinson & the Miracles, McLaren insisted the trio haunt the funky, neon-lit downtown area of Vegas, where card games were dominated by authentic Western-dressed cowboys who didn't give a second glance to the trio.

Back in Los Angeles, McLaren avoided the newly established network of punk clubs in favour of the music business hive the Whiskey and also the Pleasure Chest, where he stocked up on more explicit T-shirts.

One day in the lobby of the Hyatt House hotel, Hauser and McLaren were approached by Linda Stein, co-manager of the Ramones and wife of the boss of Sire Records. Incongruously this matronly figure, who had not hitherto revealed a sartorial bent, was dressed head-to-toe in the most expensive Seditionaries designs: a multi-strapped black sateen parachute shirt and matching Bondage trousers.

'Malcolm absolutely flipped out, went completely berserk,' says Hauser. 'We had to leave the hotel because he was so furious with Westwood for having sold her those clothes: "How dare she do that? They're not meant for people like her!"'

'For blocks he ranted and raved and, when we got back to the Tropicana, he rang London and shouted at Vivienne that they shouldn't have even let Linda Stein in to the shop, much less buy anything. I thought it was fabulous that he could be so exclusive.'

When he flew back to London, McLaren began to pour all his energies into the Pistols biopic. At least he now had an ending. 'The group's success wasn't the doing of the music business,' wrote McLaren in the 1990s. 'It arose out of a concentrated effort to fail, at least by any of the conventional standards of the time. I was determined not to let any of the corporate record businesses appropriate the band and make it their own. Instead I was trying to use their money to fund a film that told an entirely different story, one that would undermine much of what the representatives of this corporate culture claimed to believe in.'

At the Glitterbest offices, McLaren was confronted by visiting Warner's executives over the £200,000 the company had invested in the film about a group that was no more. It is at this point that McLaren's nerves began to fray.

A factor may have been Fred Vermorel's publication with his wife Judy of the book *The Sex Pistols*. Coming as it did within days of the group's break-up, this was about as removed from a pop-band biography as one could imagine and served to immediately crystallise the myth of the Pistols and focus on McLaren's role, not always in beneficial terms.

McLaren had helped the Vermorels with introductions but declined to participate. With exceptional access, they included transcripts of interviews with the band members, their parents and associates, as well as extracts from Sophie Richmond's diary and, most significantly, a savage psychological portrait of McLaren.

'Malcolm's fascination with "evil" can be opportunistic and anti-human,' wrote Fred Vermorel.

> For example: his aesthetic use of the Cambridge Rapist motif in t-shirts etc seems insensitive to the feelings of rape victims.
>
> It should be said that Malcolm has a puritanical disdain for the sexual deviations – narcissism, exhibitionism and fetishism – he exploits through his work.
>
> It is interesting that Malcolm's style of flaunting and carping, fierce flash and studied resentment – arising from his chosen reaction to social marginality (Jewishness) and psychological rejection (by his family) – has now been taken up as a ready-made social attitude by so many people.
>
> Malcolm has the vision of an artist, the heart of an anarchist and the imagination of a spiv. There are signs that entrepreneurial success may flush out his receptiveness and creativity. I hope not.[11]

McLaren did not respond to Vermorel's public dissection of his personality – the book sold well on the back of the group's notoriety – but began to make choices that quickly rebounded upon him.

On hearing that John Lydon was holidaying in Jamaica on Richard Branson's coin – the reggae aficionado acting as an ad hoc A&R executive recommending acts to sign to Virgin sub-label Front Line – McLaren nuttily dispatched road manager John Tiberi to the Caribbean island with a series of signed declarations imploring Lydon to return to the group.

McLaren suspected Branson of trying to coerce Lydon into either uniting with the new wave group Devo or reforming the Sex Pistols without him at the helm, so also instructed Tiberi to capture images of Lydon relaxing by his hotel pool for possible inclusion in the film. After being ignominiously dunked, Tiberi returned disconsolately to London with a single, blurred frame.

McLaren and his faction had become the gang that couldn't shoot straight. 'The group didn't have to be over,' said McLaren in the early 1990s about this period. 'But it could never develop easily because there wasn't a common bond between the characters other than we all hated each other, and you can only hate each other for so long before you want to love somebody else. So it was a time in which the idea had come to fruition.'[12]

The events of the early spring of 1978 brought this home to McLaren. In the second week of February he joined Cook and Jones in Brazil, where several scenes were filmed with Biggs, including a performance on a riverboat of a new song 'No One Is Innocent', which had been given the alternate title 'A Punk Prayer' as a libertarian plea that tolerance should be extended to such figureheads of evil as Myra Hindley and Martin Bormann; McLaren hired the actor Henry Rowland – who had appeared in Russ Meyer movies in the role – to appear as the latter in full Nazi uniform as Sid Vicious's replacement.

The Brazil shoot was directed by Julien Temple and cost £20,000, funded by reserves of record company cash in Glitterbest's coffers. A fair chunk of this budget was swallowed up by damage to musical equipment when McLaren – mindful of the Situationist instruction 'Musicians – smash your instruments' – ordered the participants on the boat to attack the hired drumkit, amps and guitars and throw them in the river.

McLaren returned to London via Los Angeles, where Warner's had arranged a meeting to attempt rapprochement over the film with Lydon, who was himself en route to Toronto to visit relatives with his mother. The encounter ended badly. 'I said I would only appear if I could choose my own material, but he was unwilling to agree to that,' wrote Lydon in the affidavit he filed as part of the legal proceedings he instituted.[13] These also sought to restrict McLaren and the company's usage of the properties 'Johnny Rotten' and 'Sex Pistols', thus pulling the rug from under any attempts to make a documentary about the group.

In turn, McLaren and his co-director Steven Fisher countersued on the basis that the singer was in breach of contracts by failing to honour his agreement to participate in the movie.

Meantime, McLaren had come up with a new concept to link the material being assembled by Temple. 'By then I thought I needed to bring together all the pieces that we'd done, all the news footage, and create a movie that would exhibit the attitude of the group,' he said later.[14]

The title was now *The Great Rock 'n' Roll Swindle* and the footage divided into a series of portmanteaux linked by lessons mock-portentously delivered by McLaren on the subject of tricking the entertainment business by manufacturing a provocative rock group.

'I thought: "I'll be the blaggard, I'll be the Svengali" and dictate the ten commandments of how you swindle your way to the top,' said McLaren in the 2000s. 'It was a way of making an enigmatic final gesture in this story.'[15]

But the Pistols movie was just one project McLaren was juggling; on his return from LA he began to work himself into a frenzy, even planning an immediate return to management by proposing the Slits as the female Sex Pistols. Meetings were held with Island Records boss Chris Blackwell during which McLaren demanded a £100,000 advance. Part of the pitch was based around the film outline Fayette Hauser had observed him working on in LA: the sub-Meyer storyline, such as it was, consisted of them being lured into becoming a disco act indulging in promiscuous sex across Mexico.

McLaren also made contact with the German disco label Hansa as a possible home for the group, and wooed the quartet by sending Temple to film them in Paris, nominating his former Croydon Art College pal Robin Scott as their producer.

'I found it interesting that they were in a business that was predominantly chauvinist, i.e.: rock 'n' roll, and anything that was anti-rock 'n' roll at that time intrigued me,' said Scott the following year.[16]

But the Slits shrewdly rejected both McLaren and the tawdry film idea and were signed by Island for far less than he had demanded.

With Temple beavering away on compiling footage, Jeremy Thomas struck a deal for Ian Stuttard to become pick-up director of *The Great Rock 'n' Roll Swindle*. 'An amount was agreed in principle, but nothing was signed,' says Stuttard, who doesn't specify the fee beyond saying it was 'ample'. Stuttard gathered together a five-person crew including the award-winning cinematographer Nick Knowland and filmed intensively in London and Paris over three weeks. 'The Meyer script was out the window and we couldn't use the sets he had built, so Malcolm was improvising madly,' says Stuttard. 'Meanwhile I was hassling Jeremy Thomas not only for my money but also to ensure that the crew was paid.'

Stuttard is responsible for such scenes as an interview with a dazed and battered-looking Sid Vicious sitting in a Hyde Park deckchair. 'Nancy Spungen was also there constantly trying to interfere, but McLaren wasn't around,' says Stuttard. 'Sid was absolutely off his face. I could cope with it but McLaren seemed to find the whole subject of drugs completely distasteful. I was very struck by his rectitude in that regard, whereas he was completely amoral about everything else.'

Stuttard also filmed a sequence that didn't make the final cut: the funeral of the gamin Bromley Contingent member and Seditionaries sales assistant Tracie O'Keefe, who had died suddenly at the age of eighteen in the spring of 1978 after a diagnosis of bone-marrow cancer.

Proposing O'Keefe's death as the passing of the Pistols' greatest fan, McLaren's opportunistic nature and lack of compassion were on full display when he attempted to incorporate the ceremony into the film's narrative, arranging for a large floral tribute proclaiming 'Never Mind the Bollocks Tracie' to be displayed in the cemetery where her burial took place.

The event didn't make the cut and even Vicious took offence, attempting to physically attack Stuttard. 'Sid was upset because he thought our filming there was in bad taste, and he had a point,' says Stuttard, who nevertheless was soon shooting Vicious in Paris, wandering the streets affronting passers-by in a swastika T-shirt while buskers performed a French-language 'Anarchy in the UK'.

Stuttard returned to London to take over the edit and Julien Temple took the helm for the next leg of the Paris shoot. With Lydon definitely out of the picture, McLaren had persuaded Barclay Records' John Fernandez to put in £10,000 to fund the Paris scenes, another of which posited Vicious as the group's new frontman.

Having been frustrated in his attempt to present the Pistols at the Folies Bergère the previous year, McLaren was keen for Vicious to perform at the equally opulent *fin de siècle* theatre L'Olympia, where the New York Dolls had played five years previously.

Posters proclaiming the performance were produced for the film shoot, but the venue was unavailable, so Eddie Barclay swung it for the crew to film at the Théâtre de l'Empire close to the Champs-Élysées, using the stage set of an impressive staircase, backlit with strip lighting, which had been built for a Serge Gainsbourg residency.

McLaren readily agreed to Fernandez's condition that he should choose a song for Vicious from the Barclay catalogue. When the punk rocker refused Édith Piaf's 'Non, Je Ne Regrette Rien', Fernandez suggested 'Comme d'Habitude' by Claude François and Jacques Revaux, better known by the Anglophone version, 'My Way'.

McLaren determined that Vicious's performance should climax with the singer drawing a gun from his white tuxedo and shooting an actress playing his mother. This not only extended the Oedipal theme proposed by the 'Who Killed Bambi?' script and writ large across the front of the 'Fuck Yr Mother' T-shirt, but spoke to the complicated emotions surrounding McLaren's relationship with Emily Edwards.

This may in fact have been triggered by a brief encounter with his mother on the London Underground, the first time that they had been in proximity to each other for more than a decade.

'I was sitting in a tube carriage when I saw reflected in the window opposite that my mother was sitting just a few seats down from me,' wrote McLaren in the 1990s. 'I knew that she had seen me but we didn't exchange a word. After a few stops we both got off the train at Aldgate East and went our separate ways.'

In a version of the story related to LA punk magazine *Slash* in the aftermath of Lydon's departure from the group, McLaren claimed the near-encounter with Emily Edwards had occurred several years earlier. 'I thought, fuck, that's my mother sitting next to me. I was at art school at the time, going to some poxy art gallery, my mother was going to the factory.'

Curiously, McLaren also described how attractive his mother had been, and mentioned her affair with the magnate Sir Charles Clore. 'I was just intrigued, as a young kid, you know, completely obsessed with who was the next man in her life. Eventually I left home because I realised that I didn't fuck my mother and obviously had to interest other parties,' said McLaren, before making a declaration that countered Fayette Hauser's account of their time together in this period: 'I must've had about eight fucks in my whole life.'[17]

McLaren's weird filial perspective was expressed in his instructions to Temple for the end of the 'My Way' sequence. 'The crazy idea I came up with goes back to the old ideas of mothers, I suppose,' he said in the 2000s. 'You're going to shoot your mother, this is what you must do at the end. She's going to be in the audience, she's going to be happy and thrilled for you, and by the end of the song you're going to have to shoot her.'[18]

Ahead of filming, studio time was booked to record the track. But Vicious and Spungen's gargantuan appetite for opiates rendered them insensible in their hotel room and he repeatedly failed to attend a recording studio to tape his vocal.

'One morning I got back to the hotel after another night failing to get Sid to do it, and told Malcolm,' said Temple a few years later. 'Malcolm was in bed and got very annoyed and rang Sid's room and started telling him that he was completely finished and just a fucked-up junkie. While he was talking Sid gave the phone to Nancy and suddenly the door was kicked open and Sid appeared in his motorbike boots and swastika underpants and jumped on Malcolm and started kicking him.'[19]

Vicious also demanded McLaren sign a letter releasing him from his management. The bruised McLaren left Temple to complete filming the 'My Way' scene and slunk back to London, where another confrontation awaited him. Claiming the film funding had been exhausted, he informed Ian Stuttard that his services were no longer required.

'Malcolm was firing me,' says Stuttard. 'He said: "You've done a lot of work on this; I'll make sure you get paid." I thought: "You're fucking right you will."'

And Stuttard had an ace in the hole: having started the process of assembling the film with his editor while the rest were in Paris, Stuttard was in possession of virtually all the rushes, not just the scenes he had shot.

Before McLaren could act, Stuttard sequestered the footage from the cutting room and had a friend stow it at a secret location. 'It didn't take long for the phone to ring,' says Stuttard. 'McLaren was friendly to start with but then increasingly agitated. I told him that I would release it once the contract was honoured. I was hardcore about it. He was trying to con me like he'd conned the band. I told him: "You ain't gonna fuck me, pal."'

After a few days McLaren relented and sent Sophie Richmond with a carrier bag stuffed with pound notes to Thames TV's studios, scene of the Bill Grundy debacle, where Stuttard was working. 'I had my money, McLaren had his footage, and Temple was left to pick up the pieces,' says Stuttard.

With one fight over, McLaren picked another, injuncting the release of new film *The Punk Rock Movie*, directed by Don Letts. This was a prong of his legal defence against Lydon's lawsuit, based on Glitterbest's ownership of the Sex Pistols; Letts, who had become close to Lydon and holidayed with him on the Virgin-sponsored Jamaica trip, had, on the singer's say-so, included live footage of the group in his feature.

The loyal Westwood closed ranks with McLaren and decorated the often-shuttered facade of Seditionaries with offensive graffiti about both Lydon and Letts. She followed this with a regrettable review of Derek Jarman's punk movie *Jubilee*, which referred to Letts in racist terms. Her abuse-laden rant (in which McLaren was not involved) also included homophobic references and was published in the form of an open letter on the front and back of T-shirts sold at 430 King's Road. While Letts was maligned as an 'Uncle Tom', Jarman, according to Westwood, was a 'gay boy' condemned for displaying a homosexual's 'love of dressing up and playing charades' when he was not 'jerking off through the titillation of his masochistic tremblings'.[20]

The embattled atmosphere pervading 430 King's Road – where some staff had been fired for siding with Lydon while others were openly engaging in stock theft to feed their heroin habits – reflected a wider malaise. Now the Sex Pistols existed notionally, whatever McLaren's anti-Lydon claims that no one person represented the true spirit of the group. Still, the band's name appeared on the rush-release of a double A-side single pairing Vicious's rendition of 'My Way' and Biggs on lead vocals on 'A Punk Prayer'.

Vicious nonetheless confirmed that the Sex Pistols were finished and that he had formally separated from McLaren. 'As a clause [*sic*] of doing the film I said that I had the choice as to whether he manages me or not,' Vicious told broadcaster John Tobler. 'It was up to me. If I don't want him to manage me then he doesn't manage me.'[21]

Vicious also assured Tobler he was no longer a junkie, but this wasn't true. Over the summer Vicious returned to his bad habits with Spungen. Soon one of their drug buddies, nineteen-year-old John Shipcott, died from a heroin overdose at the flat the bassist shared with Spungen. Now the pair were entering their mutual endgame.

As Cook and Jones – who was developing his own heroin addiction – worked with McLaren and Temple on the task of completing the film soundtrack, Lydon's Virgin-signed new group Public Image Ltd (PiL) was proving an instant hit with critics and fans, establishing itself at the forefront of the new post-punk musical movement. Richard Branson's support had also secured Lydon's financial future, with a £75,000 advance to the singer paid just a few months after he had left the Pistols. According to Virgin's Rudi van Egmond, the record company also paid for 'the living expenses of John's colleagues in the group, expensive rehearsal facilities and studios which were being used 24 hours a day'.[22]

Meanwhile media and public sympathies aligned against McLaren. 'The pro-Rotten lobby of the music press derided the Diaghilev of punk as a desperate man,' wrote Johnny Rogan five years later. '[McLaren's] tactics were deemed self-aggrandizing, whimsical or irrelevant, rather like a Screaming Lord Sutch political campaign. Many of their objections were well-founded but they failed to appreciate McLaren's love of irony, his economic and artistic dilemma and, most crucially, his message that the Pistols were not a precious pop group but a mouthpiece for an absurdist rationale.'[23]

Under pressure, McLaren increasingly channelled the worst aspects of his grandmother's imperiousness; his behaviour on the film sets and in the edit suites was often ugly.

'It was a very, very unpleasant experience because Malcolm and Vivienne were really against me making it,' said Temple of the circum-stances surrounding the completion of *The Great Rock 'n' Roll Swindle*.

I think Malcolm probably distrusted me. I was nowhere near as prestigious a person as Russ Meyer and I was inexperienced. In front of everybody he'd say he was sacking me. He'd change things we'd agreed and was just very, very negative.

Once he fired me on the phone using the most extraordinary invective I've ever heard. He was calling me a middle-class arsehole and telling me he'd raised me – which is a contradiction in terms – from the gutter and had checked with the film school and they said I was completely talentless.[24]

At the distance of four decades, with a successful career as a film-maker under his belt, Temple is now sanguine. 'For a while we were very close,' he says. 'He genuinely liked working with younger people, but there was always an underlying sense of "When do I get rid of this guy?" He could be very brutal in that way.'

According to Temple, relations were made more fraught by McLaren's inability to deliver dialogue in front of the camera. 'We'd have to put up postcards all around the set with his lines on, even for a couple of sentences,' says Temple. 'He would panic and forget them, and when I made him do another take he would become frustrated. That became the source of friction between us.'

For a Hammer Horror-style comedic scene McLaren persuaded the keepers of the gothic cemetery in north London's Highgate to open an area that had long been closed to the public. Among the cata-combs, McLaren performed the 1950s song 'You Need Hands', writ-ten and made popular by the British light entertainer Max Bygraves. Crooning the schmaltzy lyrics, McLaren frolicked with Helen Wellington Lloyd, the duo alternately dancing a strange pas-de-deux and pasting Reid-designed 'Wanted'-style fluorescent posters onto the walls of a crypt.

In ransom-note lettering, these begged forgiveness – 'God Save' – for such criminals as Myra Hindley, the prostitute-killer Jack the Ripper, the highwayman Dick Turpin and, of course, Ronnie Biggs. Reid later described the artworks as 'hugely humanitarian'[25] in that they champi-oned redemption for every person, whatever their crimes.

As Rogan detected, McLaren's decision to take a vocal turn was part of the overall plan to destabilise expectations of what constituted a successful musical group. 'One of the things we were aware of was the need never to remain still, never to become stagnant,' said Reid in the 1980s. 'After three or four records have come out there begins to be a typical punk fan, who identifies with the band the way fans always do. When Rotten left and we put in Ronnie Biggs, they couldn't understand. It seemed a good idea to us.'[26]

During the film's production phase, McLaren was courted to become an A&R executive at RCA Records, home to David Bowie, Dolly Parton and the Elvis Presley catalogue. Flown to the company's New York headquarters for an interview for the job, McLaren worked up the concept of a cartoon pop character called Jimmy the Hoover; years ahead of the likes of Gorillaz, McLaren suggested animated performers as a far more preferable signing than living, breathing and demanding pop stars.

He didn't get the gig.

The suspicion with which the music business establishment treated McLaren, the Pistols and punk in general was brought home at the recording of the 'You Need Hands' vocal track at the north London studio owned by pop impresario Mickie Most.

'When I turned up he couldn't understand what was going on: "What are managers doing singing songs?"' said McLaren in the 2000s. 'He thought it was a ploy, that I had the Sex Pistols with me and that the studio was going to be robbed. All the doors were locked and when I finished, I couldn't get out. I could see him pretending to sweep up and clean out ashtrays, looking at me with a beady eye: "He's not really recording, it's a pretext." Eventually he opened the door and I scampered off, but this was [representative of] so much of the paranoia that existed throughout the life and times of the Sex Pistols.'[27]

The uneven financing didn't help the film. 'Some weeks there'd be none, and we'd be waiting around for Malcolm so we could film the next sequence,' says Temple. 'The whole thing cost £350,000, which was quite a lot of money for the time but still not enough for what we set out to achieve.'

McLaren and Westwood had once more become close – she was involved in the film, even contributing lyrics to a featured song named after the Meyer project, 'Who Killed Bambi?' – but his concentration on the *Swindle* had acted as a distraction from their fashion design relationship.

The eighteen months since the refurbishment of 430 King's Road as Seditionaries in December 1976 had been the first fallow design period since the pair started collaborating in the spring of 1972; those few new garments to appear on the shop racks represented tweaks on already established styles, such as the application of the range of tartans to the Bondage trousers.

This paralysis was broken by McLaren's introduction of a collection of new T-shirt artworks in the autumn of 1978. But their general tone was of peevishness rather than triumphant disruption.

The first, and most successful, returned McLaren to the practice of détourning his own creations, in this case combining two early designs made for the London Rock 'n' Roll Festival of 1972 onto the front and back of a shirt: Vive le Rock!, featuring the image of Little Richard, and The "Killer" Rocks On!, originally dedicated to Jerry Lee Lewis.

The former had been worn by Sid Vicious in the summer of 1977. 'There were some T-shirts left over from Wembley in our cupboards in Clapham; we had to do something with them,' said McLaren in the 2000s. 'Sid liked them just the way they were but I needed to throw some messages across them and reinvent them. So, I married the slogans and images of Little Richard and Jerry Lee Lewis with words and drawings from various texts such as "We are not in the least afraid of the ruins", the famous phrase of the Spanish anarchist Buenaventura Durruti.'

The new artwork marked his abiding fascination for the writings and theories of the Situationist International. Durruti, the militant who fought General Franco in the Spanish Civil War, was a Situationist hero, and the SI was paraphrased in a slogan on the front of the shirt: 'Ours is the best effort so far to leave the 20th century in order to join the punk rock disco'.[28]

Vive le Rock/Punk Rock Disco, as it became known, also contained renderings of recipes for making Molotov cocktails and other explosive devices from Yippie leader Abbie Hoffman's publication *Steal This Book* and William Powell's *The Anarchist Cookbook* as well as US Army field-training manuals.[29]

More successful than Westwood's disagreeable condemnation of Derek Jarman, Vive le Rock/Punk Rock Disco expressed the turbulent nature not only of the times but also of McLaren's mindset.

Meantime, his rise to public prominence provoked charges of 'recuperation' – the dilution of radical politics by incorporation into the mainstream – in a diatribe published by Dave and Stuart Wise, the King Mob founders with whom McLaren had associated a decade previously.

'Malcolm McLaren had been friendly with individuals versed in the Situationist critique in England, and had picked some of the slogans and attitudes of that milieu,' they wrote in 1978. 'Punk is the admission that music has got nothing left to say but money can be made out of total artistic bankruptcy with all its surrogate substitute for creative expression in our daily lives. Punk music, like all art, is the denial of the revolutionary becoming of the proletariat.'[30]

Two illustrated T-shirt designs, which accompanied McLaren's issue of Vive le Rock/Punk Rock Disco, were more straightforward, even childish, in their intent to shock, one depicting King Kong masturbating over Fay Wray and bannered 'Exposé' and 'Punk Rock Sex' in Meyer film-title lettering, the other showing Mickey and Minnie Mouse enjoying sexual congress, with one of Mickey's ears stamped with the encircled anarchist 'A'.

Similarly, a shirt displaying an image of Snow White surprised by the lascivious attentions of the aroused seven dwarves – retitled by McLaren 'Snow White & the Sir Punks' – enacted a commentary on the Disneyfication of Western culture.[31]

Satisfyingly, Seditionaries was subjected to a police raid on the basis of complaints from local residents (or pretend complaints by the shop's affiliates) about the design, and the stock of Snow White tops was impounded.

Westwood called on lawyer Nick Pedgrift, who worked with Glitterbest's Steven Fisher. 'I sweet-talked the desk sergeant into dropping the charges and handing back the shirts,' says Pedgrift. 'When Vivienne arrived she was furious and complained that I had spoiled her chances of appearing on the *Six O'Clock News*.'[32]

Like McLaren Westwood was, for the time being, hell bent on provoking the authorities. 'We were writing on the walls of the Establishment, and if there is one thing that frightens the Establishment, it's sex,' she announced. 'Religion you can knock, but sex gives them the horrors.'[33]

As provocations, these new designs worked well enough, but in the absence of a coherent clothing collection providing a framework, they lacked panache and indicated that the McLaren/Westwood design relationship was marking time.

The 'King Kong' T-shirt appealed to Sid Vicious, who wore it out and about in New York, where he moved with Nancy Spungen in the autumn of 1978. With publishing cash from the 'My Way' single, the duo's drug-fuelled mayhem amid Manhattan's downtown scene drew the inevitable ever closer.

Just eight weeks after they arrived in town, McLaren received a call from Leslie Hinton, the New York stringer for Rupert Murdoch's muck-raking British tabloid the *Sun*, informing him that Vicious had been charged with Spungen's murder, his inamorata having died from stab wounds in the room they shared in the seedy Chelsea Hotel.

The tragedy came as no surprise to anyone in the Pistols' circle, but there is no truth in John Lydon's claims in the years since McLaren's death that the Pistols' ex-manager responded by abnegating his responsibilities – 'Malcolm was just panic-panic-panic . . . I don't think he lifted a finger. He just didn't know what to do' – nor that Mick Jagger funded Vicious's defence.[34]

On hearing the news of Spungen's demise and Vicious's arrest, Jagger had made an overture to McLaren on behalf of the Rolling Stones to provide financial and legal aid.

'Jagger, dare I say not somebody who was a friend at that time, called me up and said, "I know how you must feel, I know how Sid must feel, we understand what these record companies do, we know what it's about, we feel really bad, is there anything we can do?"' recalled McLaren in 2004. 'I said, "Yeah, we need money." I never heard from him again! Perhaps I should have said, "Do a benefit concert and we'll take the money later." I'm afraid I wasn't thinking on my feet.'[35]

According to the music journalist Charles Shaar Murray, Jagger's offer was in fact withdrawn the following day.[36] By that time, McLaren had scrambled, hiring New York lawyer Michael Berger, who had handled the Sex Pistols' visa applications at the beginning of the year, to represent Vicious at the arraignment. He also deputed his New York friend Joe Stevens to scope out the situation at the Chelsea.

'Even though I was technically no longer managing Sid, I wanted to help,' wrote McLaren in the 1990s. 'I'm still not entirely sure why. Maybe because I felt there was no one more fun than Sid. He was chaos incarnate and made my blood flow. And I suspected if I didn't help him no one else would.'

Within a couple of hours of hearing the news, McLaren was on a flight to New York. If his assistance to Vicious is acknowledged, it is often interpreted as being not only exploitative (though he was not involved in Westwood's immediate production of a T-shirt showing the couple with the phrase 'She's Dead. I'm Alive. I'm Yours') but opportunistic, in that keeping Vicious alive and out of jail would maintain what remained of the Sex Pistols' viability. In this way, the argument goes, McLaren would have kept Branson and Lydon at bay.

Yet the strenuousness with which McLaren attempted to establish Vicious's innocence and survival belies a humane resolve, one that had been manifested previously in his 1974 testimonial that staved off a likely life-altering prison sentence for Steve Jones and also in his organisation and bankrolling of rehab for New York Dolls bassist Arthur Kane the following year.

In regard to Vicious, McLaren moved so quickly that he was in New York the morning after the arrest, arriving at the imposing New York

Criminal Court in Lower Manhattan in time for the arraignment. Jostling his way through the courthouse mob scene, McLaren was on hand to witness the charging of Vicious with second-degree murder under his birth name John Simon Ritchie. Bail was set at $50,000 and Vicious was ordered to the hospital wing of Rikers Island prison to undergo detox.

'Sid was frightened; he looked pale and fragile in the dock,' said McLaren. 'I needed to do something and raised my hold-all in the air as if it were loaded with money. I wanted the lawyers to know I could guarantee bail. But there was no money in the hold-all and I couldn't. Sid, vulnerable, dejected and confused, was escorted out.'

Having spent all available cash on the film, McLaren's only asset was the soundtrack he was compiling with Jones and Jamie Reid from past recordings, demos and new songs. McLaren approached Mo Ostin, the chief of the Pistols' American label Warner's, to front the bail monies against delivery of this and an album of cover versions he proposed Vicious could record once at liberty.

Having conferred with his A&R chief Bob Regehr, Ostin not only demurred but – as McLaren later claimed – Warner's used the murder case to terminate the recording contract with Vicious, Jones and Cook, keeping the relationship with Lydon and thus writing off the £250,000 the entertainment major had invested in the Pistols to date.

McLaren then solicited Arista's Billy Meshel, the group's US music publisher, who also declined. With Jagger in absentia and left with no other choice, through gritted teeth McLaren put in a call to Richard Branson. The Virgin boss readily agreed to the terms and arranged for the $50,000 to be transferred to Virgin's Greenwich Village office.

With the court's approval, a member of Vicious's legal team visited the room at the Chelsea – now a crime scene – where Spungen died. 'His photographs showed that the window catch was broken and the door lock was flimsy,' said McLaren, who also visited the hotel with Joe Stevens and interviewed staff and residents. 'Anyone could have broken in there.'

It is a fact that a knife found in the room and thought by the police to be the murder weapon was clean, bearing no fingerprints or blood. In the early 1990s McLaren made the unsubstantiated claim that he bribed an unnamed individual to tamper with the evidence. 'I was fairly confident there were enough clues around the Chelsea Hotel to suggest Sid hadn't killed his girlfriend,' McLaren announced at British music business conference 'In the City'. 'The knife was washed clean, which I paid a lot of money for ... but you know, fair's fair.' This appears to have been grandstanding; in the fifteen years since Spungen's death, McLaren had not mentioned this act, and backtracked in later life.[37]

The circus-like atmosphere surrounding the murder was escalated by the arrival in New York of Vicious's mother Anne Beverley, funded by £10,000 paid for her story by the *New York Post*. Rupert Murdoch's media empire was now driving the news cycle on both sides of the Atlantic, with McLaren feeding the fire, championing the apparently criminal Vicious just as King Mob and the Situationist International had trumpeted murderers and felons in the 1960s.

While he was banging the drum in the media, McLaren, who was by now joined by Steven Fisher from London, set about replacing Berger, who he described as 'clearly the wrong choice. He treated Sid like he was a kid.'[38]

Among the candidates approached in the search for legal representation with sufficient heft was the New York super-lawyer Gerald Lefcourt, whom McLaren decided against because 'he didn't seem terribly interested in Sid's case'.

'I wanted to employ the most conniving, toughest lawyer I could find,' said McLaren, who was very easy to spot among the city's detectives and reporters in their kipper ties and crumpled suits. He alternated his dress between black leather jeans with a T-shirt proclaiming 'Cash from Chaos' (designed for a sequence in *The Great Rock 'n' Roll Swindle*) and red tartan Bondage trousers, matching jacket and a T-shirt produced by Jamie Reid to promote the Ronnie Biggs single, which incorporated a photograph of the lunging Great Train Robber with the slogan 'Cosh the Driver'.

McLaren and Fisher had made their first stop the city's most infamous legal figure, the unsavoury Roy Cohn, Senator Joe McCarthy's right-hand man during the communist witch trials of the early 1950s, consigliere to the likes of Richard Nixon and Rupert Murdoch, bagman for Mafia boss John Gotti, and best known as the mentor of such disreputable figures as the convicted political 'ratfucker' Roger Stone and, of course, Donald Trump.

In later life, McLaren recalled Cohn's high-handed bearing. 'He greeted us brusquely: "I don't wanna know whether he did it or not. What I wanna know is whether Sid wants to live."' McLaren had barely finished glossing Vicious's suicidal tendencies before Cohn launched into a diatribe, telling McLaren: 'He's got to know what it's like in a United States prison. Rikers Island is for beginners ... We've got to make him understand that the last thing he wants is to be locked up in one of those hellholes.'

Cohn announced that his defence would be that Vicious was a victim of circumstance, someone who had fallen in with the lowlifes who populated the Chelsea Hotel, any one of whom could have committed the murder. Cohn also indicated that jury-fixing would be among his services.

'Cohn, I could see, was a hood lawyer, and there was no way he was going to sympathise with Sid's angst,' wrote McLaren in the 1990s. 'For $250,000 he virtually guaranteed victory. I looked at Steven; he blanched at the price and the impossible confidence from this booming, impatient man. We knew to move on.'

On the first evening of his trip to New York, McLaren accompanied Joe Stevens to a party at new-wave nightclub Hurrah. Here he was introduced to Allen Ginsberg. The beat poet had been following the case and made an introduction to a lawyer at the opposite end of the social and political scale to Cohn: the civil rights activist William 'Wild Bill' Kunstler, who had represented such radical organisations as the Black Panthers and the Weather Underground.

'We met Kunstler at his home in Greenwich Village, wearing jeans and an open-necked shirt, his hair dusted with cigarette ash,' recalled

McLaren. 'He led us to a study carpeted in kilims where he made points about the politics of the culture and rolled a joint. Steven Fisher's eyes widened.' McLaren, who admired Kunstler, realised he would not be a good fit. 'His music was, I suspected Bob Dylan or Joan Baez, possibly even Joni Mitchell. This was a concern. How would he ever understand the Sex Pistols?'

Eventually, McLaren and Fisher settled on F. Lee Bailey, famed for his defence of such accused as the US Army captain charged with responsibility for the Vietnam war My Lai massacre and the kidnapped newspaper heiress-turned-terrorist Patty Hearst.

The odd couple from London – manic McLaren in his punk finery and the owlish, besuited Fisher – met Bailey in a grand booth in a bar-restaurant just after a book signing for his novel *Secrets*. This may have explained his unusual appearance.

'As Steven briefly summarised our case, F. Lee leaned into the pool of light above the table and my first impression was of utter astonishment: he was wearing make-up!' exclaimed McLaren. 'I was transfixed by this extraordinary man, whose rugged features were glazed in Orange Max Factor pan stick. He wasn't effeminate but simply, from what I could deduce, someone who was always on stage. He wore a navy blue pinstripe Savile Row suit with a fresh gardenia in his lapel and immediately fell into a reverie about the British legal system.'

Like Cohn, Bailey's concern was Vicious's capacity for proclaiming his innocence, but believed there would be strength in casting the youth as 'an innocent rock 'n' roller' adrift in 'lonely, dark, miserable' New York.

The august lawyer pointed out that his team would choose a sympathetic jury made up of 'toilet cleaners and road sweepers' and suggested McLaren work on Vicious's image. 'You're good at publicity,' he told McLaren. 'Get him jogging in Central Park and dating librarians.'

Bailey also suggested that once he was bailed, Vicious should spend time with him at his estate outside Boston. 'I flinched at the thought of reinventing Sid as a friendly jock,' said McLaren. 'And a librarian to take the place of Nancy . . .?'

McLaren and Fisher agreed the super-lawyer's terms of $50,000 upfront and control of resulting book and film rights, and Bailey's associate, a distinguished counsel named James Merberg, was assigned to the case.

Soon, Richard Branson made good on his promise; within a few days the bail money arrived from Virgin and McLaren and Stevens were outside Rikers to greet Vicious and reunite him with his mother at a Madison Avenue hotel. McLaren immediately arranged for an assessment of Vicious's mental condition by forensic psychiatrist Stephen S. Teich, who recommended constant surveillance. Beverley scored her son heroin, however, and within a couple of days McLaren was forced to accept the twenty-one-year-old's committal to Bellevue psychiatric hospital for his own safety after he slashed his wrists.

'Sid had taken a light bulb from the toilet and gashed his arms,' said McLaren. 'His hands were dripping with blood as we came through the door. His mother was bruised, they'd obviously been in a fight together. She couldn't look after him but maybe nobody could.'[39]

Vicious begged McLaren to score him some more drugs. 'Sid screamed, "Just get me something – anything, anything! Get me some pills! Please Malcolm!"'

'I told him I'd get him some Quaaludes. He was very frightened and his mother was in bad shape. Steven and I left the room and went down to the lobby and sat trying to figure out what to do. I felt terrible. I had no intention, of course, of getting Quaaludes.'

McLaren contacted Teich. 'They had got his arms compressed so the bleeding was contained, and we decided to put him in the hospital and called emergency medical services to come over,' said Teich in 2007.[40]

'In New York if you call an ambulance they call the police and, with Sid being such a high-profile character, it was going to be a rough ride,' said McLaren.[41] When the police arrived, Vicious had to be restrained by McLaren and Teich from throwing himself from the open ninth-floor hotel-room window and was transported to Bellevue in a straitjacket on a stretcher.

McLaren, meanwhile, maintained a brave face for the press. 'Sid is all right now they patched up his arms. He was anxious to get himself clear of drugs, and was trying to come off it too quickly,' McLaren dissembled to British music weekly *Melody Maker*.

Speculating that the murder trial would be held in six months, McLaren explained that his client was best served by focusing on a covers-album project: 'I want him fit mentally and physically for the ordeal, and felt he would need an objective to steer himself away from all the problems that will constantly nag at him until the trial is over. That's why I suggested some recording to him. Also, the enormous cost of getting the strongest defence lawyer I can find will provide us with considerable financial problems, which a record will help solve.'[42]

In his heart, McLaren knew Vicious's life expectancy, let alone the likelihood of recording, remained under threat while his primary carer was his similarly addicted mother.

'The important thing for the lawyers was that Sid was cooperative, that would be a beginning,' said McLaren. 'We tried and tried and tried to get Sid to do that but it was impossible. His relationship with his mother was something we didn't have a great understanding of.'[43]

On arrival back in the UK, McLaren fulfilled an unusual booking: a debate with theatrical songwriter Tim Rice on the subject 'Is pop music popular?' at the Cambridge University students' union. 'When I got there I realised everyone was out to get me,' he recalled much later. '"What about Sid?" they kept asking. I had become the symbol of anti-pop. I was anti-music. In my mind was a picture of Sid in the straitjacket. I could think of little else except the two looming court cases: Sid's on one side of the Atlantic and mine on this one. I was, I felt, on trial. It filled me with rage.'

McLaren responded by denouncing 'the fraudulence of the music industry. "What's so important about the music?" I shouted. "Nothing. Unless it creates chaos. A deadly, sexy chaos." The chairman of the student union called for order. Tim Rice looked at me with alarm. People were everywhere, screaming at me, shouting me down. And yet, unsurprisingly, we won the motion.'

After Vicious was released from Bellevue, James Merberg entered a plea of not guilty to the murder charge at a court hearing in late November 1978. 'Our defence cannot be disclosed but I can say that it points away from Mr Ritchie,' Merberg told the court, while the press revealed that Bailey's team had hired the private investigator who had cracked the Boston Strangler case in the 1960s.[45]

But the distraction of Vicious's travails had rendered the undisciplined McLaren and the beleaguered Fisher incapable of mounting a sound defence in Britain against John Lydon's High Court proceedings to dissolve the partnership as set out in the onerous 1976 management agreement. And now Lydon was using press interviews and even the debut Public Image LP to denigrate McLaren. On the group's first single Lydon declared 'I will not be treated as property' and the album track 'Low Life' was clearly aimed at the former manager, describing him variously as an 'egomaniac traitor' and a 'bourgeois anarchist'.

The disenchantment felt by such key figures as Paul Cook, Steve Jones and Julien Temple posed additional problems. 'The rest of the members of the band – who I needed to have on my side – were becoming isolated from me,' confirmed McLaren. 'They didn't understand why I was spending all this time with Sid, this was not the objective as far as they were concerned. And to some extent they were correct but what else would one do? You have to show compassion.'[45]

Chapter 26

Over the winter of 1978, as Malcolm McLaren and his lawyer Steven Fisher struggled with preparations for the court battle with John Lydon in London and maintained contact with F. Lee Bailey's counsel James Merberg over the defence being mounted for Sid Vicious in New York, the tussle to complete *The Great Rock 'n' Roll Swindle* was underway.

Not just principal actor, scriptwriter and conceptualist, McLaren was the project's auteur demanding oversight of every aspect, pushing Julien Temple hard during the editing process, having worked with Jamie Reid, Sophie Richmond and Vivienne Westwood on realising the look of the feature, including the costumes, sets and graphics. Most frames in the resultant movie feature McLaren or his voice; he was the viewer's guide and de facto star, eagerly cultivating the role of the self-mocking 'Embezzler'.

This was to saddle McLaren with a reputation as a Fagin-like creature who swindled entertainment companies by using and then discarding the talents of young creatives.

'By the end of the Pistols, he had fallen foul of punk's ideologues, who disapproved of his opportunism and flamboyant barnstorming,' wrote Michael Watts. 'Considered once to have been a visionary, he was now held to be just another crooked self-promoter.'[1]

In later life, McLaren realised he was to blame. 'I thought everyone would realise it was a joke!' he exclaimed in 2008. 'I was sending myself up. No true swindler would declare himself as such. But people took it at face value and I suppose I've had to live with it.'

Temple had his hands full meeting McLaren's demands. 'It all came to a head when we were in this tatty cutting room owned by a "launderette king" above one of his laundrettes in Berwick Street,' recalls Temple. 'It was fucking freezing; there was a hole in the roof and the snow came through covering the edit machine. Things were fraught enough and then Malcolm told me that he wanted me to be his "slave" and that I was only to speak when spoken to.

'I think this partly came from my sympathy for the group's position – they moaned about their money being wasted on "the fucking film" – and partly because, as director, I'd had to tell him what to do, and he didn't like that. I felt that I should fight. If I let him fire me, it wouldn't bode well for the rest of my life, so I had to stand up to him. But he fired me anyway, so, for a very brief spell, I wasn't working on the film.'

Jeremy Thomas came to Temple's aid. 'Malcolm could never see that Julien was exactly the right person for the job,' he says. 'Julien was very smart and knew the subject, but Malcolm would constantly undermine him by trying to change the nature of the film we had all agreed. That meant that Malcolm and I fell out to certain extent.'

With Temple reinstalled and Branson gaining the upper hand by supplying a further £150,000 for the film's completion, McLaren's position was made even more unstable by the concise and detailed lawsuit filed as *Lydon v. Glitterbest and others*. This included affidavits from Joe Stevens and Bob Regehr of Warner's.

In New York, Vicious's descent spiralled; soon he was sent back to Rikers Island after an arrest for glassing Patti Smith's brother in Hurrah, the nightclub where McLaren had connected with Allen Ginsberg just a few weeks previously.

'So he was back inside and we were in London thinking, "Shall we get him out again on another bail?" and meanwhile the wolves were at the door,' said McLaren in the 1990s.

Via the legal team, McLaren sent Vicious a list of suggested songs to contemplate for the forthcoming covers LP. While some spoke to his circumstances, among them Elvis Presley's 'Suspicious Minds', Brecht/Weil's 'Mack the Knife' and the Bobby Fuller Four's 1960s garage-rock classic 'I Fought the Law', McLaren also proposed the chanson 'La Vie en Rose' and the Village People's recent disco smash 'YMCA'.

McLaren was also sending money to Vicious's mother Anne Beverley via Frankie Pisaro, who ran Ian's, the Greenwich Village clothing outlet that stocked McLaren/Westwood designs. Pisaro informed him that Beverley was revelling in her role as the mother of the infamous Sid Vicious, punkily dyeing her hair and providing interviews to the New York tabloids in return for drug money. 'Everything I hated about mothers came to the surface,' wrote McLaren in notes he made two decades later. 'I was so angry. But I couldn't leave London. I still had my film to finish, my court case to face and money to raise. Vivienne was haranguing me. Things were closing in on us in the most menacing way. Couldn't I just quit?'

'During the time Sid was being tried or in jail, Malcolm had a permanent red "M" on his forehead,' Temple observed to Pistols chronicler Jon Savage several years later. 'He was very wired, deranged. I think the whole Sid thing was far more complicated in his head than he let on. He did feel responsible in some ways. I don't think he did anything wrong, but he did feel very humanely about it.'[2]

Asked about the red mark on his forehead, McLaren said that it was a physical defect which appeared, as Temple correctly surmised, at times of stress. 'People used to think "He's got the mark of the devil,"' said McLaren, who was convinced that some observers connected it to a ring he wore in this period. The centrepiece of this was the seven-pointed Star of Babalon symbol representing the British early twentieth-century white magician Aleister Crowley's order AA. This was inscribed on the inside: 'There is no law beyond do what thou wilt.'

'People thought, "Oh, it's that ring . . . look at the forehead." I think it added to the myth,' said McLaren. 'It was illustrative of what you were being accused of, so naturally it sounded like a good story.'[3]

After eight weeks of forced detox, which lowered his tolerance for hard drugs, Vicious was released from Rikers Island upon an application by the persuasive Merberg. This put a fatal kink in McLaren's plan to meet Vicious and whisk him to a Florida studio where he would record the much-touted covers album with Paul Cook and Steve Jones.

Within twenty-four hours of gaining his freedom, Vicious was dead of an overdose after a celebratory gathering at his new girlfriend's Greenwich Village apartment, his mother having not only paid for the fatal doses but, according to some, administered one of them.

'We got a message from someone who was at the party,' said McLaren in the 2000s. 'We thought, "It all smells so terrible." The mother said she was feeling much better [because] "Sid passed away with a smile on his face".'[4]

Describing Vicious as 'an incredible romantic' to the US national press, McLaren's reputation for insensitivity was bolstered by his reaction to Vicious's death.[5] 'There was no frame, there were no goalposts, he never saw a red light, he only saw green,' said McLaren in 2007. 'Danger wasn't something he'd ever consider. He never thought that his life was important.'[6]

Few acknowledged McLaren's attempts to ensure the doomed youth's survival. Among them was the psychiatrist McLaren hired in the wake of Spungen's death and Vicious's subsequent suicide attempt. 'It's hard to find words to express what I feel,' Steven S. Teich wrote to McLaren. 'I have just learned about Sid, and I'm searching my mind to find what else I could have done. I, for one, feel you did as much as possible to help him in the way you knew. You acted beyond the formal role in your relationship. Clearly he was someone you cared for.'

But this provided small solace as McLaren finally faced Lydon's serious charges of financial and personal mismanagement at the High Court. McLaren later claimed that Virgin had obtained Anne Beverley's support for Lydon's case by paying her bail when she was arrested for cannabis possession on her return from New York. 'This led to her subsequent betrayal at the trial,' wrote McLaren. 'She switched camp.'

McLaren had already received intimations from Steven Fisher that victory was unlikely. The Glitterbest case relied on affidavits from the likes of Eddie Barclay and two Virgin employees, John Varnom and Rudy van Egmond. The latter had accompanied Lydon on the Jamaican trip and claimed in his testimony that the singer in fact harboured deep admiration of McLaren, but this was far from enough to shore up the defence.

'My trial. It doesn't look good does it?' McLaren asked Fisher before the hearing commenced. 'Steven – portly, bespectacled, round-faced – stared at me with an expression of remarkable blankness and said nothing. It was an ominous silence. Rotten's case was that the Sex Pistols was a partnership and since he was no longer a member it shouldn't continue. But he also argued that the assets should no longer be controlled by the management, that the management had misused the funds. I had to admit, some people might think he had a point.'

After a disastrous pre-trial meeting to discuss a last-ditch attempt to settle with Richard Branson on the Virgin boss's houseboat in London's Little Venice (at which, according to his later accounts, McLaren contemplated or actually carried out urinating against the entrance to the vessel to express his dissatisfaction), McLaren dedicated the evening before the commencement of the case to the *Swindle* film. In a film-editing suite, McLaren and Temple assembled the sequence that followed the announcement of the film's final 'lesson', 'Who Killed Bambi?'

'I spent hours trying to figure out how to bring the long, winding dialogue to a close,' said McLaren. 'I finally wrote Lesson 10, which ended with the following exchange:

' "So what are you going to do with all the money?"

' "That's the most ridiculous question I've ever heard." '

On the commencement of the hearing, Lydon's QC John Wilmers went in hard at McLaren, describing him as a Svengali whose dubious character was made evident in the film script's pleas for clemency for such evildoers as Jack the Ripper, Myra Hindley and the Cambridge Rapist.

And what there was of Glitterbest's case collapsed when Paul Cook and Steve Jones agreed to an offer by Branson for a record deal for their new group. Enlightened by the proceedings to the fact that £90,000 of their money had been plunged into the film, the pair promptly followed Anne Beverley in joining Lydon's side.

After a few days Mr Justice Brown-Wilkinson recorded that the Sex Pistols partnership was over when Lydon exited the group in January 1978, but left the key issues of the validity of the management agreement and ownership of the name 'Sex Pistols' to be resolved. In regard to Lydon's bid to render void the five-year Glitterbest contract, Brown-Wilkinson suggested that the parties find common ground after appointing Russell Gerald Hawkes of receivers Spicer & Pegler to safeguard and oversee the exploitation of the group's principal assets: *The Great Rock 'n' Roll Swindle* and its soundtrack.

And the broad financial detail revealed the extent of McLaren's profligacy: of the £880,000 earned by the Sex Pistols in advances, royalties, performance fees and other income in the previous three years, Glitterbest retained just £30,000, having spent £343,000 on the film. Where had the rest gone? Certainly not to McLaren; he had never claimed the 25 per cent share due to him under the terms of the contract but ploughed that, along with the band members' monies, into his various schemes.

Given Lydon's stance, there was no chance of a rapprochement in regard to the judge's guidance; in fact, settlement of the dispute over the management company and ownership of the Sex Pistols properties was to take another seven years of legal wrangling.

Brown-Wilkinson appointed McLaren 'sub-manager' of the film, to work under Hawkes as – notionally, if not temperamentally – the person best placed to oversee completion. But the day before the judge handed down his ruling, McLaren had bolted to his safe space, Paris. Fearing fraud charges and having fallen out with Steven Fisher, whose professional standing was besmirched by having been involved in a project that so boldly declared itself a swindle, the French capital offered a new beginning. Eddie Barclay was dangling a contract for McLaren's own version of Vicious's covers album, including a track that the recently deceased bassist had rejected, 'Non, Je Ne Regrette Rien'.

McLaren later claimed he made a pitstop before leaving town: the bank that held the Glitterbest account. Here, he said, he withdrew the remaining £30,000 in cash and secreted it about his person before hailing a taxi and heading to Heathrow Airport.

In McLaren's retelling in the late 1990s, the experience was nerve-wracking. 'During the drive I took the money out of the bag the teller had given me and started putting it in my socks, my knickers, inside my shirt, my jacket, my trousers. And then I noticed that the driver was looking at me in the rear-view mirror. "Aren't you . . ." he said.

'I cut him off. "No, that's my brother."

'The taxi driver said: "He's in a lot of trouble at the moment, but good luck to him."

'At Heathrow, I looked for the first flight to Paris. I bought a ticket and then realised in a panic that I was going to have to go through a metal detector. British notes have a silver metallic strip in them, and with so many on me I was certain to set off the detector like an alarm bell.

'And then an improbable stroke of luck: a security guard spotted me. "Oh," he said. "It's Malcolm McLaren!"

'I told him I was late for my flight and he said, "Oh, come on then," and I jumped the queue and avoided the machine, as I had no bags.'

In this version of the story, McLaren had £40,000 on him. 'I got on the plane to Paris. "A fascist regime," I sang to myself. "God save the Queen . . ."'

Staying first with Robin Scott, who was working for Barclay Records, and then Jean-Charles de Castelbajac, McLaren initially fumed over the turn of events. 'I bear enormous anger when I think of Rotten and Branson,' he told the British music press.

> I think Branson has been enormously clever. I know now that it was a hoax on Branson's part to say that we could all go to Miami and record because he knew the trial was coming up. And I just wasn't prepared for that trial. I was thrown by Sid's death.
>
> You see, the next case may not come up for three months, and they're all of the opinion that 'If McLaren doesn't have the money by then, then there'll be no trial' and all my assets will be wound

up. First they take away every means of you making a living and then they send you into the bankruptcy court. I just think my number has come up on this case. It was writ there after the second day. I knew then I'd lost.[7]

Within a week of the hearing, Virgin rushed out *The Great Rock 'n' Roll Swindle* soundtrack as a double album. Since the film wasn't released for another year, this provided a taste of the satiric tone and surprising juxtapositions proposed by McLaren: straight-faced symphonic and disco versions of Sex Pistols classics were presented alongside alternate takes and live performances of the singles and rare tracks.

Then the British producer/director Don Boyd kicked in £50,000; McLaren had considered Boyd for the director's role the previous year at the suggestion of their mutual friend Gerry Goldstein. Now Boyd's input proved crucial. 'This gave us enough to set about finishing the film,' says Jeremy Thomas.

Soon McLaren returned to London to fulfil his sub-managerial duties, but all hopes of his cooperation with the fifty-seven-year-old accountant Russell Gerald Hawkes were nixed by an edit carried out by Temple at the receiver's behest. Among the excised scenes was an animated retelling of the 'Who Killed Bambi?' sequence featuring Vicious and his mother.

After just one day, McLaren terminated his involvement. In a five-page diatribe to the producers, McLaren wrote from Paris:

I believe that the film is in no better shape than a completely misdirected rough cut which makes no sense at all. [It] does not work for a number of reasons, but the major and extremely serious one is the film's total disregard in providing the one possible anchor for the audience: that is, two people telling the same story from two points of view. These two people are Steve Jones, a lone, typical cliché crook, and McLaren, an underground fetish Lucifer, both part of the Sex Pistols . . . I wish my name to be struck off this film's credits entirely and myself taken out immediately of all scenes . . .[8]

McLaren understood that undertaking the sub-manager role would signal capitulation to the court, the still-formulating Sex Pistols partnership and Virgin Records. 'I don't mind being sold down the river, but I'm not gonna drown in it too. It's like wiping your face in your own shit,' he told *Melody Maker*. 'The facts are that without me that group wouldn't have existed, and I feel that if I couldn't spend that money on the projects that I thought were right, then they should have thrown me out years ago.'[9]

The former 'slave' Julien Temple now took the reins, a move which earned him McLaren's undying mistrust.[10] In the 1980s, Temple claimed he relied on the class distinction between himself and Hawkes – both with solidly patrician English family backgrounds – and the Portuguese/Scottish Jew McLaren to wrest the movie from his former boss.

'I used the receiver to get control,' admitted Temple in 1989.

I played my card, which is being a privileged upper-class Englishman. We have codes of behaviour that Malcolm wouldn't understand. It takes 500 years to learn the secrets. So I let off a pyrotechnical display of my knowledge in front of the receiver and anyone else who was financially interested in finishing the film. And then I plucked a few chords that I knew would hit home, just doing it with the movement of an eyebrow. And they know what the code is, they know who's from where.[11]

In 2018, Temple was more measured about his approach. 'I don't actually recall saying that, and I'd be surprised if raising an eyebrow made any difference, but I probably gave the receiver a sense that I was capable of delivering,' he says. 'Given the fact that I'd been on a precarious ride I wanted to reassure everyone. Film finances are all based on trust; a big part of my strategy was to convince the receiver that I could finish it. You have to remember that young directors were a rarity in those days.'

Meanwhile Hawkes, who died in 2018, told McLaren's 1980s biographer Craig Bromberg that he was taken aback by McLaren's demeanour.

'I had anticipated, because I heard about the amount of money that was involved, that I would meet somebody with all the trappings of wealth, having misapplied so much money to his personal benefit,' said Hawkes. 'I was quite surprised to find a chap who didn't spend any money on himself, who didn't drive a motorcar, and who showed no outward sign of having got any money.'[12]

In fact, so McLaren claimed to journalist Michael Watts in a wide-ranging profile for *Melody Maker*, he was £60,000 in the hole as a result of losing the court case. Of course, this did not take into account the £30,000 he may or may not have appropriated from the remaining Glitterbest funds.

Watts noted McLaren's cheerfulness in the face of the loss, as the man who had cut his teeth in central London as a teenager led a tour of Soho and the surrounds with Westwood and photographer Barry Plummer.

'Malcolm had a few set ideas about where he wanted to be photo-graphed,' says Plummer.[13] These included the entrance doorway to his offices in Shaftesbury Avenue, next to billboards for music gigs outside the adjacent ticket agency, in front of the property developer Harry Hyams's brutalist Centre Point office tower, over tea in the Regent Palace Hotel and against the Tin Pan Alley Club sign in Denmark Street.

Just down the road from this afternoon drinking establishment, McLaren attempted to gain entry to the QT Rooms, the live-in rehearsal space he purchased for the Pistols in the autumn of 1975, but heavy padlocks barred entry and, in any case, McLaren had been forced to give up the keys to the premises by court order. Through a window, McLaren pointed to scattered lettering piled in the courtyard; these were the cut-outs which formed the opening credits for *The Great Rock 'n' Roll Swindle*.

'If I had expected McLaren to be visibly depressed by events, I was wrong,' wrote Watts.

His nature is too buoyant; he's a cork that always bobs to the surface, propelled by the chemistry of excitement. He is very good at hiding his depressions.

He has personally been driven by the constant need to escape from the boredom of his circumstances; he wanted to find an audience to whom he could show off his skills as a theatrical ringmaster, and he took an undisguised pleasure in the commotion he created with the Pistols, the thrill of living dangerously. 'I was always one for being as childish as possible,' he said.

McLaren evidently felt liberated, and readily talked about his family and art school years, relaying the story of the tube encounter with his mother once again. Watts subsequently contacted Emily Edwards with an interview request; she declined on the basis of the Sex Pistols' notoriety.

McLaren claimed to Watts that the Barclays LP was to contain music-hall covers, including the Marie Lloyd song 'A Costermonger in Paris', yet he had clearly kept an eye on post-punk musical developments: synth-pop was by now on the march as cheap new electronic technology had arrived, prompting the ascendance of such acts as Gary Numan and the Human League. 'The age of the guitar is over, don't you think?' he asked Watts. 'I blinkin' well do.'

Meanwhile, McLaren entertained a wild variety of schemes, from the preposterous – joining the Stock Exchange ('but I am a little old') – to the forward-thinking: hosting a TV chat show for regional broadcaster Granada, staging an exhibition of Pistols artwork in Paris, obtaining the British rights to the *National Enquirer* (this a decade ahead of the rise of sensationalist supermarket tabloids in the UK) and establishing a members' club for teens in the premises of an established site such as the Garrick.

As they drifted into the venerable Soho pub the French ('where failed painters and clapped-out anarchists regularly gather', according to Watts), McLaren said that he remained guided by the randomness of the *dérive*. 'I'm a great believer in digesting things and walking round, and suddenly somebody grabs you off the street and you walk into a situation, God knows what it's going to be,' he told Watts.

McLaren had still not lost his interest in returning to the unfinished student film *The Story of Oxford Street*, and in fact used some of the material for the opening Gordon Riots section of *The Great Rock 'n' Roll Swindle*.

Now, he told Watts, there were plans to realise a full-blown update of the Oxford Street movie for Dutch TV, having been introduced to executives in Holland by 'Who Killed Bambi?' scriptwriter Rene Daalder.

McLaren's appearance had evolved since the break-up of the Pistols. His tartan Bondage trousers and kilt attachments contrasted jarringly with a sober V-neck sweater, business shirt, Paisley patterned tie and a smart Burberry Raglan raincoat. McLaren also wore a pair of military-style leather boots he had recently designed with Westwood for sale at Seditionaries. These were thick-soled in vivid red, with the tongue elaborately displayed on the outside and adorned with silver studs and metal appliqués.

Westwood told Watts these were part of a new collection, which she described as 'an extension of punk'.

'McLaren alerted [Westwood] to her own potential,' wrote Watts. 'Despite certain domestic disruptions and abnormalities (such as the fact that McLaren now works from Paris), the partnership has been fruitful: he, fizzing with ideas, subtle and exploitative; she, protective, a sounding-board, bullishly single-minded.'

'We're just sort of rebels, really,' said Westwood, who described her son Ben, then fifteen, as 'a sweet boy' and their son Joe, eleven, as having 'a very good mind; he's very much like Malcolm'.

According to Westwood, 'to be creative is like food and drink to Malcolm. He's more clever; he uses people. My reasons are more simple. I'm just a freedom fighter.'[14]

McLaren and Westwood's next fashion collection would take another year to realise, but in the meantime there was a trickle of new designs, which extended the violent and sexually challenging nature of McLaren's artworks since the collapse of the Sex Pistols.

One in particular stands out: a T-shirt graphic comprising McLaren's response to two recent and contrasting cultural events, the October 1978 publication of *Prick Up Your Ears*, theatre critic John Lahr's biography of the controversial 1960s British playwright Joe Orton, and the February 1979 release of Walter Hill's low-budget dystopian gang epic *The Warriors*.

Prick Up Your Ears, which became the title of the new design, had struck a chord with McLaren in its identification of Orton as a remorseless cultural provocateur; in defining Orton, Lahr quoted the Hungarian scholar Karl Kerényi's view of a societal role McLaren believed himself to fulfil: 'The trickster's function is to add disorder to order, and so make a whole; within the fixed bounds of what's permitted, an experience of what is not permitted.'[15]

Meanwhile McLaren was impressed at *The Warriors*' impact on mass culture (prints were withdrawn from distribution in some regions after copycat crimes among America's gang population).

McLaren hijacked yet another Pleasure Chest T-shirt as his basis for the design. This depicted an illustration of a gay orgy involving at least a dozen figures which he détourned by adding tattoos (among them 'Joe Orton', 'The Warriors', 'Destroy' and 'Chaos') to the writhing bodies, with anarchy armbands, spiky haircuts and punk paraphernalia.

And so, having noted the orgiastic scenes detailed in Lahr's extracts from Orton's diaries, McLaren used the illustration to celebrate the impish 1960s dramatist as a punk-rock kindred spirit, and tied the abandon with which Orton lived his life into the brutalism expressed by Hill's film. Across the top the slogan 'Prick Up Your Ears' (the title of an unproduced screenplay Orton produced for the Beatles) appeared in *The Warriors*' distinctive spray-can lettering.

The artwork was overlaid with a two-colour screen of a photo close-up of a sexual encounter, and at the lower edge appeared a paragraph from a 1967 entry in Orton's diary, which referred to an aphoristic exchange between the dramatist and the showbiz lawyer Oscar Beuselinck and theatrical producer Michael White:

' "You look very pretty in that fur coat you're wearing," Oscar said, as we stood on the corner before going our separate ways. I said, "Peggy bought it me. It was thirteen pounds nineteen." "Very cheap," Michael White said. "Yes, I've discovered that I look better in cheap clothes." "I wonder what the significance of that is," Oscar said. "I'm from the gutter," I said. "And don't you ever forget it because I won't." '[16]

Orton's response to White, thought McLaren, expressed punk attitude to a T. 'You must never forget that you have to draw inspiration from the gutter, the most basic material,' said McLaren a few years later. 'I'm a Joe Orton fan for life, and I'm concerned with never losing sight of the idiot and the most vulgar of society's dispossessed. 'Cause if you lose sight of that, you lose sight of any answers to anything. And if you want to solve things, inspire things and make question marks, then how the hell do you do it unless you work with the dispossessed?'[17]

Another new artwork featured a monochrome 1952 photographic portrait of a smiling Marilyn Monroe, with streams of urine spurting from red phalluses on the sleeves and pooling to form the words 'Piss Marilyn' across her face.

'I purposely printed the Marilyn image in a faded light grey,' said McLaren in the 2000s. 'Marilyn Monroe was a symbol of America and as punks we needed to piss on all that.'

That this was a dual tribute to McLaren's artistic role model Andy Warhol – representing both his silkscreens of the Hollywood star and the 1978 'oxidation' artworks produced by urination on copper plates – was made all the more satisfying when the great American pop artist purchased a Piss Marilyn T-shirt on a visit to Seditionaries.[18]

'Warhol also asked if we would make him a T-shirt featuring just the names "Johnny Rotten" and "Sid Vicious", nothing else,' said McLaren. 'We told him we didn't make T-shirts to order and there was just what we had in the shop.'

Though McLaren was regularly checking in with Westwood, Paris was his base pro tem. Not only had his relationship with the former Sex Pistols disintegrated, but Steven Fisher was also out of the picture now that Glitterbest was in administration. Meanwhile Sophie Richmond and Jamie Reid had withdrawn, the latter beaten down by the demands of meeting Virgin's design needs for the stream of singles spinning from *The Great Rock 'n' Roll Swindle* soundtrack.

The final Sex Pistols packaging to be designed by Reid – the sleeve for the 45 of Sid Vicious's cover of the Eddie Cochran classic 'C'mon Everybody' – included text by McLaren and Reid barred by Warner Music from appearing in a Pistols songbook. This communicated – in the style of King Mob graffiti – the despair the pair felt at punk having been swallowed by the entertainment business:

> The Sex Pistols are an undoubted success based on an idea called punk rock, which sets out to trail blaze a path of anarchy and ruin within a culture that chooses to destroy us by making our decisions for us.
>
> Punk rock's cause is to create as much fuss, havoc, excitement as possible. Crime pays us. Punks slogans are – Cash From Chaos – Believe In The Ruins – Never Trust A Hippie – Anarchy Is The Key, Do It Yourself Is The Melody – in other words, Rot 'N' Roll.
>
> The media was our helper and lover and that in effect was the Sex Pistols' success as today to control the media is to have the power of government, God, or both.
>
> It is all that matters to explain our Great Rock 'N' Roll Swindle. A true swindle of ideas that gives you back the right to decide for yourselves.

Such bitterness reflected a response in many quarters to the recent general election installation of Margaret Thatcher as British prime minister. This was already instituting a harsh new era of materialism in the wake of the collapse of the ineffectual James Callaghan's Labour government after the strike-hit so-called 'winter of discontent'. Thatcherite hardline capitalism would, McLaren figured, favour the bottom-line-obsessed music industry by now benefiting from the punk-powered revival of its fortunes. 'The industry is happy that the culture is on the move again, and they'll do better under Mrs Thatcher than Jim Callaghan,' he predicted to Michael Watts.

McLaren was nevertheless proud of his and the Sex Pistols' cultural contribution and remained so for the rest of his life. 'I put anarchy back into rock and made it, for that moment, a tremendously subversive, stylish and above all sexy platform that had never before been seen in England,' he said in the 1980s. 'I never considered the Beatles subversive or sexy or stylish. I think the Pistols were more provocative and created a generation of thinkers, whereas the Beatles created a generation of sheep. That was my contribution, to be involved in creating a generation of thinkers, and they have personified changes in culture you have today.'[19]

PART V

World's End

Chapter 27

'I was somewhat lost but I knew one thing: Paris loves anyone the English hate,' said Malcolm McLaren of his sojourn in the French capital at the end of the 1970s. 'I was welcomed, almost, with a red carpet, and wined and dined. It was a sexy time for me. I didn't know what to say to Vivienne because I had left all that back home. In Paris, I wandered the streets and worked in various capacities.'[1]

In 2004, McLaren was asked by the curator and writer Louise Neri whether this flight had been in conscious emulation of artistic figure-heads, such as Oscar Wilde and Alexander Trocchi, who had previously exiled themselves in Paris.

'They were inspirations of sorts,' confirmed McLaren. 'But it was interesting to think about it from the other perspective: that the French Revolution was clearly influenced by London's Gordon Riots; Guy Debord's concept of *dérive* was directly inspired by the writings of Thomas De Quincey, and so on.'[2]

In this period McLaren revisited southern Europe and stayed in Madrid, but life on the continent wasn't as leisurely as he made it out to be a quarter of a century later. The single version of 'You Need Hands' was a hit in France, prompting TV appearances and a degree of local celebrity, but plans to record an album of covers for Barclay Records drifted. At one stage, there were talks with a British promoter to coincide the LP release with a series of dates back across the English Channel at such light entertainment venues as the London Palladium, but these foundered and the recording sessions did not materialise.

Meanwhile, as the mysterious 'M', McLaren's Paris-dwelling friend Robin Scott, scored a surprise worldwide hit with the electro-pop anthem 'Pop Muzik'. Combined with the imminent release of *The*

Great Rock 'n' Roll Swindle, this seemed to send McLaren into a paroxysm of activity.

With one breath he was contemplating working with visiting American contemporary dance theatre troupe Calck Hook and then, with another, Serge Gainsbourg on a follow-up to the Frenchman's recently released reggae record 'Aux Armes Et Cætera' (which contained a dubwise version of 'La Marseillaise').

McLaren met Gainsbourg in a bar on the Champs-Élysées not long after the death of Sid Vicious to discuss the project. 'He drank twenty-six Bloody Marys to my five over a couple of hours,' recalled McLaren. 'As he was dragged out to his car by his chauffeur I wished him goodbye. All he said was, "J'adore Sid Vicious." I learnt later that he kept a framed photograph of Sid on stage singing "My Way". This stood on top of his grand piano.'

An overture from Chrysalis Records to reconnect with Debbie Harry and manage Blondie didn't work out and, for a month or so, McLaren made ends meet by advising a young Iranian heiress interested in breaking into the music industry. He claimed at the time to be paid 1000 francs (approximately £120 at 1979 rates and £650 today) a lesson to teach the twenty-two-year-old, who was apparently related to the recently toppled Shah, such wistful music hall songs as 'Only a Bird in a Gilded Cage'.

For most of the period, McLaren resided at Jean-Charles de Castelbajac's apartment in rue de Trévise. 'He was staying on my couch and enjoying the freedom away from the Pistols,' says de Castelbajac, who led the Englishman to one of Paris's great attractions, Père Lachaise cemetery. 'Malcolm had never been, so I insisted we make a day of it wandering the graves of Jim Morrison and Oscar Wilde. He was entranced by what he found there, the legions of cats and the fact that it is built along the lines of a city. I always loved Père Lachaise and was so pleased that my dear friend was just as spellbound.'

De Castelbajac also introduced his friend to the Hungarian punk rocker Péter Hegedüs, also known as Peter Ogi, who later recorded a raucous electro-pop song with lyrics by McLaren entitled 'She Wolf, Woof!'

Aside from such distractions, a meeting organised by Barclay's John Fernandez with executives from a Marseillaise adult-film distributor resulted in a gig producing background music for sex scenes using out-of-copyright and library tracks.

'They thought I was of interest musically,' said McLaren. 'I could give them a bit of class, a bit of rock 'n' roll. I lent humour to them. You don't necessarily learn about making films, what you learn is how to get the job done fast under amazing conditions. I thought it was a great way to get an idea across. You'd have to be bloody sharp and on the ball, without feeling precious and being aware that your film will look bad.'[3]

Among the features that included McLaren's contributions was the grubby flick *Trois Filles dans le Vent* (Three Girls in a Boat), still available to view online today and scored with a patchy soundtrack.

It was during research for one of these productions that McLaren made a discovery that set him on a new musical and visual path, ulti-mately leading to complete creative reinvention.

'In those days you used classical music for sex pictures, preferably recorded by East European countries or members of the Communist Bloc because you didn't have to pay copyright,' said McLaren. 'I listened to a lot of African rhythms and realised they were special. Nicely primi-tive and quite different from the old 4/4 banging away on the cymbal and hi-hat. Very tribal.'[4]

With African music undergoing one of its periodic revivals among the Parisian nightlife set, McLaren embarked on a research phase by haunt-ing the section containing ethnic records at the vast public library at the Centre Pompidou in Beaubourg.

This contained racks of the recordings produced by the Folkways label, founded in New York in the late 1940s as an educational documen-tation of the entire world of sound, from contemporary electronic music to traditional and spoken word. Quality control was high: Folkways releases were packaged in handsome card sleeves with exemplary graphic design and photography completed by illustrated explanatory inserts. For such a visual creature as McLaren, they proved irresistible.

Another reason for the frequency of McLaren's attendances was the attractiveness of one of the librarians. One day he came across the LP *Burundi: Musiques Traditionelles*, released in 1967 by Radio France's ethnographic label Ocora. McLaren's eye was drawn to the last track on side two: 'Tambours Ingoma', a field recording by the drummers of the Bukirasazi region of central Burundi. Unknown to McLaren, 'Tambours Ingoma' had featured on the French novelty hit 'Burundi Black', released in 1971 with overdubbed rock instruments by the producer Michael Bernholc using the pseudonym Mike Steïphenson. This became a 12-inch French club release in 1978.

McLaren asked the librarian to play the track as a pretext to striking up a conversation and asking her for a date. But all romantic thoughts disappeared when he heard the thunderous drumming and raucous call-and-response chants of the Burundi. 'By accident, instead of 33rpm she played it at 45,' said McLaren. 'It sounded so powerful, so out there, and I thought '[whistle] That's a beat . . . my God, that's incredible!'[5]

For McLaren, the Burundi beat connected him to the primal rock 'n' roll of such Let It Rock heroes as Bo Diddley. Much as McLaren's musical understanding has been retrospectively maligned by rock writers and the performers and producers with whom he worked, it was he – antennae atwitch – who was the first to recognise that, when subjected to the intervention of tempo increase, this could form the basis of a new direction in pop. So he took the Ocora LP back to de Castelbajac's and recorded 'Tambours Ingoma' at 45rpm on cassette for future reference.

By this time McLaren was investigating funding for a new film company, Tour d'Eiffel Productions, to focus specifically on porn projects. As part of the pitch to investors he provided a couple of speculative film scripts: 'The Mile High Club' was another Meyeresque conceit revolving around an orgy on an inflight plane, which included such characters as Lieutenant Lush and Jimmy the Hoover, no longer a kids' cartoon figure but an oral sex expert. The other, 'The Adventures of Melody, Lyric & Tune', was a musical about the three titular fifteen-year-old girls featuring songs written by McLaren with rock critics Pierre Grillet and Stephane Pietri as well as pianist Eric Watson, partner of a member of the Calck Hook troupe. These included 'Sexy Eiffel Towers' and, in a nod to his grandmother's recurrent description of his own mother, 'Man-Mad'.

This project in particular represented the development of the most tiresome, not to say misguided and divisive, aspect of McLaren's creative outpourings, one which was predicated on the countercultural conceit that teenagers should be allowed the agency to enjoy and participate in sexual activity.

Unlike David Bowie, Johnny Thunders and other rock stars whose sexual exploits with such young groupies as Lori Maddox and Sable Starr are well documented, McLaren derived no sexual pleasure from, and was not interested in engaging in, sexual acts with underage teens. By nature he was more of a romantic than a libertine, though it is true that he had cultivated a prurient view of sexual matters, largely as a result of his strange upbringing. His promotion of liberating young desires sprang from radical political grounding; not only had the Situationists propagated the idea of 'totality for kids' but the European and American underground press of the late 1960s and early 1970s, which informed his worldview, had brimmed with such views – take for example the furore surrounding the obscenity trial of the 1970 'School Kids' issue of *Oz* magazine.

McLaren's point was that true power in popular, and in particular music, culture resided with the youth, not preening performers in their twenties or self-indulgent, middle-aged music-biz hacks, and that the sexual and social potential of young people outstripped that of any of the rock stars of the era, be they Mick Jagger or Johnny Rotten. McLaren constantly referred to record company executives as 'child molesters' in that they corrupted and stifled fans' desires with a forced diet of corporate gloop.

Overriding such concerns was the simple fact that McLaren not only enjoyed but was addicted to upsetting social mores. In the style of his outrageous grandmother, the espousal of these views in the baldest and most sexually charged terms amounted to sheer troublemaking. As in his invoking of the swastika at a time when the Second World War was present in the popular memory, McLaren knew that banging on about teenage sex was an effective means of causing a stir. This is why he blithely described his Paris film projects to the music press as 'child pornography for kids'.[6]

McLaren's stays in Paris in 1979 were never extended. When in town he hopped between de Castelbajac's residence and the apartment of the British fashion designer Jane 'Spider' Fawke, who assisted de Castelbajac and had previously worked with the inventor of prêt-à-porter Daniel Hechter, but every few weeks or so he visited Westwood in London.

The fallout from working with the Sex Pistols had left them in a daze but, rather than discussing their personal future, the couple deflected, and poured their energies into making a decision about the one thing aside from their son Joe they truly shared: the design practice at 430 King's Road. Here, McLaren and Westwood's customer base was no longer drawn from the cutting edge of the capital's cognoscenti. Now, visitors comprised curious provincials, cookie-cutter second-wave punks, Johnny-come-latelies and Sid fans.

That Seditionaries had lost its place at the forefront of street fashion was made clear by the raft of exciting new retail outlets springing up across the capital, including the retro Johnson's The Modern Outfitter, which was powering the visual sensibilities of the burgeoning multicultural mod-based two-tone movement, and Antony Price's Plaza, where military stylings – silk sashes, shirts with epaulettes, pilotkas – foreshadowed the coming of New Romantic. Both of these were in close proximity to Seditionaries in the King's Road, while Kensington Market housed the new rockabilly look of such shops as Rock-A-Cha, run by Pistols follower Jay Strongman. In central London, Covent Garden was home not only to Paul Smith's tailored menswear-with-a-twist, but also PX, run by Helen Robinson, her partner and Acme Attractions founder Steph Raynor, and a group of friends pioneering industrial chic.

PX sales assistants Julia Fodor – known as 'Princess Julia' – and another former Pistols acolyte Stephen Harrington, who styled himself 'Steve Strange', were at the forefront of a generation of art students, fashion designers and scenesters including George O'Dowd and Robert Elms who were creating their own youth movement around such Soho clubs as Billy's. With the ascendance of new electronic music by the likes of the Human League, these boutiques, individuals and musicians had taken their cue from McLaren and Westwood but were collectively challenging the couple's hegemony.

'They climbed on the shoulders of punk, but had a far greater sense of confidence and were determined to use the 80s, to use their teenage lives, their own time, in a way that previous generations had been too repressed to,' McLaren said in the 2000s. 'The new generation was totally, unquestionably, more open and optimistic. The whole scene had changed. Club life had never existed like this before: more kinds of drugs were consumed in London than ever before; more people gathered on a Saturday night outside mainstream pop culture than ever before.'[7]

The deaths of Sid Vicious and Tracie O'Keefe and the disintegration and legal squabbling of the Pistols had rendered the Seditionaries crowd numb. Michael Collins and Jordan had succumbed to heroin addiction themselves and were stealing stock and selling clothing to support their habits undetected, since the finances were so ramshackle: taxes were unpaid and there wasn't even a business bank account. Instead the company was run from Westwood's personal account at the local branch of NatWest.

'There were sycophants – many of them gay – and fag hags hanging around Vivienne,' was McLaren's take in the 2000s. 'She was protective towards them as long as they continued to flatter her, but all of them had their own agenda. A couple were clearly junkies and always looking to get their next fix. Furthermore, they had the shop to themselves. Vivienne and I rarely entered the store during that time. I could never understand why they were seemingly living it large, until I realised it was at our expense. I was told clothes were literally being stolen from the store with both of those assistants' eyes open in clear view. The tills were often robbed of cash by Michael Collins.'

Jordan meanwhile channelled her celebrity into managing Adam & the Ants, the group led by the former Bazooka Joe bassist Stuart Goddard, which peddled punky songs with a sub-Allen Jones line in S&M imagery.

This was not for McLaren and Westwood. 'We weren't interested in sticking to the forms we had come up with for punk or embellishing garments,' said McLaren. 'No, no. It was over. The shop wasn't crowded or particularly well stocked. We'd get the odd tourist in. Punks on the streets were lost. There was maybe a slight depression. The shop wasn't going broke – of course not – but it eked out a living. It wasn't as strong or anywhere near as fruitful as the periods before.'

During one of his London stopovers, McLaren was asked by the disillusioned Westwood whether they should close Seditionaries so that she could study for a degree. This would free him up to focus on film and music. The response from the self-proclaimed fashion victim, grandson of a tailor and son of womenswear manufacturers, was pointed. 'Fashion every time,' he told Westwood.

Searching for fresh inspiration, Westwood turned to researching the construction of garments from the age of Romanticism, principally via the British historian Norah Waugh's 1964 pattern book *The Cut of Men's Clothes: 1600–1900*.

And so Westwood began the flight from chaotic postmodern assemblage into the historicism that became the hallmark of her design approach. McLaren returned to the UK from Paris to work with her on the new direction, picking up reference texts of his own at the venerable Charing Cross Road bookseller Foyles, later claiming he stole the following from the outlet: a new edition of *My Life*, the 1906 autobiography of the native American chieftain Geronimo, and two Time-Life publications: Benjamin Capps's *The Great Chiefs*, which was packed with tales of the leaders of various tribes, and Douglas Botting's *The Pirates*, which provided an illustrated and comprehensive overview of the dastardly deeds of the buccaneers of the high seas. McLaren also acquired from Foyles *Indian Rawhide*, a compendium of the folk art produced by American tribespeoples and reproduced in detailed coloured drawings by the author, Mable Morrow.

'With memories of reading as a kid about Blackbeard and Geronimo, the last great Apache outlaw, they suddenly leapt to life in my imagination as being very colourful people in terms of their look,' said McLaren in the 2000s.[8]

As he absorbed this exciting material, McLaren was contending with the impending release of *The Great Rock 'n' Roll Swindle*. Virgin began to gear up for this in the autumn of 1979 with a set of promotional interviews by Julien Temple. During one, Temple suggested McLaren's 'greatest achievement' was his talent for media manipulation.

'I don't think he manipulated the Sex Pistols at all, those guys are just themselves,' Temple told the *NME*'s John May. 'What he did do was manipulate their image and manipulated the way the press received their image. He understood how gullible the press can be and how you can play the press off against each other in a fantastic way. I think that's a very interesting thing he's opened up. It was shock tactics. It was trying to get as much mileage out of shocking people into thinking about certain things; not actually saying what they should think but making them think.'[9]

In fact, the film was several months away from its spring 1980 release, but the prospect propelled McLaren forward. He persuaded Charles Levinson, MD of the UK branch of major record company Arista who had recently signed the Godfather of Punk Iggy Pop, to invest £10,000 in the development of the 'Melody, Lyric & Tune' script rather than a new pop act.

'I had the idea of Apaches, tribes, kids being modern-day pirates,' said McLaren a couple of years later. 'I was going to put it all into a film plus

soundtrack album plus videocassette, which I knew was the modern way
ahead. It would only have cost £50,000 and Arista was going to do it, a
kid's rock porno film, and on video there was no censorship.'[10]

With contributions from Westwood, the script was merged with that
of 'The Mile High Club' and took place on a plane circling Paris that had
been hijacked by a gang of homosexual Apaches – apparently based on
the scenario he imagined for his 'Prick Up Your Ears' T-shirt – who
condemned 'heterosexual filth in libraries throughout the world'. The
lyrics to their theme song ran:

> Give us your vote straight away
> To restore our tribal way
> Ridding us of their company
> Heterosexuality
> Uomo Uomo, Uomo Sex Al Apache
> Bow-wow-wow-wow-wow-wow

Levinson and other Arista executives were unimpressed and pulled
further funding.

Convinced that the Arista proposal contained sufficiently powerful
material for a new musical project to match the design vision being
nurtured with Westwood, serendipity intervened as McLaren became
embroiled in another former Pistols fan's endeavours.

With Westwood, McLaren attended a wedding where the other guests
included Adam Ant, who had split up his art-punk group the Ants after
a couple of years slogging around Britain's toilet circuit and the recent
release of a debut album, which was already proving to be a critical and
commercial damp squib.

'Malcolm knew about the split and seemed genuinely interested in
what I was going to do next,' Ant wrote in the 2000s. 'For almost three
hours he lectured me on the music business in the way that no one else
had (or could). Among the various bits of rubbish he offered as advice, he
did hit upon something. We decided between us that the live show was a

thing of the past and the future belonged to the artist who could make the best videos.'[11]

By December 1979 an agreement had been hammered out: after a month of instruction by McLaren – for which he received £1000 – the reconstituted Adam & the Ants would be launched in the New Year with a new image and set of songs. 'I got involved with him on a mercenary basis, that I would be paid a certain sum for a certain period,' McLaren said a couple of years later. 'I wasn't interested in working with another band, I was quite happy to go back to my tacky Parisian friends and make porno movies. So I said to Adam, I'll give you a new image if you listen to everything I say and do, exactly what I say, nine to five, for four weeks. After which: you do as you like.'[12]

To provide inspiration and help hone songwriting skills, McLaren furnished Ant with an extremely eclectic mixtape. 'Burundi Black' was among the seventeen songs, as was 'Belly Dance Nights' by Farid El-Atrache, another ethnic track McLaren had discovered in the Beaubourg library.

The Village People's 'YMCA' survived from the previous year's suggestions to Sid Vicious and the others ranged from the surprising – Toots & the Maytals' raucous ska anthem 'Broadway Jungle' (recorded as the Flames) and the blue-eyed Brit-soul of 'I'm Not Tired' by Cliff Bennett & the Rebel Rousers – to the self-referential ('Got to Pick a Pocket or Two' sung by Ron Moody as Fagin on the soundtrack to Lionel Bart's *Oliver!*). There were some novelty tunes (among them Buck Clayton's early 1950s swing song 'Hot Dog'), a couple of Elvis Presley tracks and wild rock 'n' roll favourites of McLaren's since the days of Let It Rock: 'Cast Iron Arm' by Peanuts Wilson, the Johnny Burnette Trio's 'Tear It Up', Lloyd Price's 'Where Were You On Our Wedding Day?' and Buddy Holly's 'Rave On'.

On receiving the management fee, McLaren told Ant to absorb the Botting book on pirates as well as the tome about Geronimo 'because they would be his images, and they would be what he should write about'.

While Ant worked up a new set of song lyrics – including the future hit 'Kings of the Wild Frontier' – and undertook a solo promotional interview tour of the UK for the recently released LP, McLaren oversaw practice sessions with the musicians his charge had assembled: guitarist Matthew Ashman and drummer David Barbe, both leftover Ants, and new bassist Leigh Gorman.

McLaren drafted in a team of professionals to help out, including the late British orchestrator Simon Jeffes – who had produced the string arrangements for songs on *The Great Rock 'n' Roll Swindle* soundtrack – to instruct the band members and the record scout David Fishel to advise on the project's commercial prospects.

Barbe, a dextrous player whose Mauritian extraction appealed to McLaren's multicultural sensibilities, was ordered by the new manager to strip his kit to the basics, losing the hi-hat cymbals and snare drum so that the floor tom dominated. This enabled Barbe to swiftly master a streetwise version of the Burundi beat, and earned him a new surname, which McLaren had located in *The Pirates*, that of the sixteenth-century seagoing Turk Hayreddin Barbarossa, who was nicknamed 'Redbeard'.

Meanwhile Ashman developed a sound based in equal parts on the circular rhythms of African high life, early 1960s surf guitar (the Surfaris' classic 'Wipe Out' was on the mixtape) and the snaking lead lines from Ennio Morricone's spaghetti western soundtracks.

'I played them Aboriginal music, Latin American stuff, but mostly ethnic primitive sounds, very simple,' McLaren said in 1982. 'I was extremely interested in the chant aspect, all the noises created by pygmies and aboriginals and African tribes. I wanted to weld that into his images of pirates and Red Indians, with the Burundi drums and some slogans. It was a cartoon. That was as far as I could take it, to deliver to [Ant] what he needed – a pop package.'[13]

Among this was advice on a new look, which shook off punk leather-wear in favour of the twin references of piracy and Native Americans, who painted broad stripes across their faces to terrify their foes.

'The white line of the face paint that I gave to Adam is what the Apaches put on when they went to war, as well as pirates braiding gold in their hair. I had this wonderful picture of Bluebeard [Blackbeard] the pirate boarding the boats of the British or Portuguese navy with his hair alight so that he looked like the devil,' said McLaren. 'I wanted Adam to do the same on *Top of the Pops*.'[14]

During the time he was working with Ant and his colleagues, McLaren was drawn into a new television project being hot-housed at Granada TV, the UK's influential regional northern broadcaster. It was there that the presenter Tony Wilson had not only given early exposure to the Sex Pistols but used his position as a pop authority to launch Factory Records, now making its mark with post-punk's most powerful act, Joy Division.

Granada's London production heads John Slater and Gus Macdonald (now the Labour peer Baron Macdonald of Tradeston) had initiated a documentary series of *Insider's Guides*, and tasked Wilson's young researcher Andy Harries with the job of finding a host for a programme on the music business. Having considered such hit-makers as the subsequently disgraced Jonathan King, Mickie Most – the label and studio owner who had been suspicious of McLaren's intentions when he recorded the vocal track for 'You Need Hands' – Ed Bicknell, the talkative manager of bland up-and-coming million-sellers Dire Straits, and radio DJ Paul Gambaccini, Harries lit upon McLaren as the best candidate.

'Tony talked about Malcolm all the time,' says Harries. 'Because he was obsessed with him, so was I. They were very similar, particularly in the way they wanted to use the mainstream to effect radical change, so I contacted Malcolm while he was in Paris and when he came back to London to work with the Ants we spent a lot of time talking it through. Malcolm came up with some brilliant ideas and was always charming and funny, though one got the impression he was still slightly on the run.'[15]

McLaren rejected Granada's proposition of walking the viewer through the process of creating a successful record, from songwriting to recording, manufacture, sales, marketing, promotion and retail, and suggested a typically perverse route that undercut the music industry's raison d'être: its commercial basis.

As ever looking to the current event and entranced by technological developments, in France and on his travels around southern Europe McLaren had been turning over the rising popularity of music cassettes and the recent introduction of affordable boomboxes and Sony's portable player the Walkman.

Understanding that pop consumption was on the verge of dramatic change since the new devices enabled mobility and choice on behalf of the consumer, he also recognised that blank tapes were effectively handing the power over music recording to the fans now actively reproducing and distributing music for free. Since the record-business terminology for such activity was 'piracy', a conceptual light-bulb exploded over McLaren's head after an encounter in one of the American-style fast-food chain restaurants now spreading around London.

'I was eating at McDonald's in Wood Green having just been to see Barbarossa when this elegant black guy strolled in with a massive ghetto-blaster playing. When the staff complained, he simply picked it up and sauntered out with it on his shoulder. He looked heroic,' said McLaren.

Two decades before file-sharing became commonplace and drove a stake through the heart of the post-war global music business, McLaren was not only celebrating a younger generation of music consumers rampaging and pillaging the music world at will, he was also drawing parallels between them and the buccaneers of the high seas.

He later said he identified with pirates because he thought of himself as one. 'It was again a kind of bricolage,' McLaren said in the 2000s. 'Pirates stole all kinds of things and mixed them all together and so did I.'

To Granada, McLaren proposed the slogan 'Music for Life for Free' as the programme's theme, even writing a song celebrating home-taping to the rhythm track of the sped-up Burundi beat.

The title took its name from cassette durations – 'C30, C60, C90 Go!' – and actively encouraged consumers to take up the principal message of punk and do it themselves:

C30 C60 C90 Go
Off the radio, I get a constant flow
Hit it, pause it, record it and play
Turn it, rewind and rub it away

It used to break my heart when I went in your shop
And you said my records were out of stock
So I don't buy records in your shop
Now I tape them all 'cause I'm Top of the Pops

'He brought a beatbox in and played the demo he'd done with the rest of the Ants,' says Andy Harries. 'It was fantastic. Malcolm wasn't particularly interested in interviewing other people for the show, probably because he was far more interesting than them in the first place.'

Harries recommended that, instead, Granada make a documentary about McLaren but Macdonald and Slater balked and pulled the project from production, ending the series. This did not stop Harries harbouring an ambition to realise a film about McLaren and his life over the coming years.

McLaren meanwhile was contending with the fact that the four-week management period with Adam Ant had come to an end. The twenty-five-year-old had a clutch of new compositions and a new sound he dubbed 'Antmusic'. But McLaren had bonded with the young musicians – Barbe was the oldest at twenty-two – during the intense rehearsals, and, to Ant's irritation, began to act in an unsavoury manner.

'Malcolm was a bit weird because of his constant 1950s-style London spiv act, always trying to get the band off with "tarts", as he called them,' wrote Ant in 2006. 'It was as if he had studied Laurence Harvey in *Expresso Bongo* and believed that was how managers had to behave. He'd always be talking out of the side of his mouth with a mockney accent, giving it "Cor boys, what about 'er?" and almost physically nudging Matthew or Dave as a woman walked past us.'[16]

Was this, as Ant suspected, McLaren's heavy-handed attempt at recreating the camaraderie he had experienced with such laddish figures as Paul Cook and Steve Jones in the early, pre-fame days of the Sex Pistols? Or a response to his self-described 'sexy' times in Paris?

While McLaren had long held oddly immature views on sex, such behaviour marked a regression for this erudite man and likely belied all manner of insecurities, from the grinding legal fallout over the Sex Pistols' collapse to his relationship with Westwood, which was on the brink even as their design partnership had been sparked anew.

And McLaren's later claim that he longed to return to Paris was false. In fact, the realisation hit that he had struck upon a number of exciting new musical ideas to complement his and Westwood's fresh fashion design direction.

'I didn't want to conceptualise, like a Damien Hirst with his dead shark,' McLaren told his friend Peter Culshaw in the 2000s.

> I wanted to work with real, living people. The problem with that is that people don't like being used. I take that into consideration, but many bands have been created by people other than the bands themselves. If it's done with excitement and provocation, it has a value. But it's really very simple. You're on the shelf. Do you want to come off the shelf and come on an adventure trail. Or stay on the shelf? And when I do a piece of work I can never be sure if it will last five minutes or five years.[17]

In Adam Ant's case, the duration was exactly the twenty-eight days of the agreement. At the end of this period, McLaren decided that the three musicians should provide the backdrop for a younger and more easily manipulated performer, so engineered for them to announce to Ant that they no longer wanted to work with him.

Out of the picture, Ant soon began an extremely fruitful collaboration with guitarist and former Sex customer Marco Pirroni, first in the highly successful Adam & the Ants Mk II and then as a world-beating solo artist. Ant has long credited McLaren with catalysing his career. 'He was the only person that sat down with me, talked to me about the construction of songs,' said Ant in 2013. 'He said: "Do you want to continue making this kind of independent record or make a pop single?" No one had ever attempted to give me any kind of education before, but he did.'[18]

As McLaren cast around for a suitable replacement, his concept for a new, Romantic youth movement crystallised. Westwood had by now thoroughly absorbed Norah Waugh's book, in particular the sections that mentioned the clothing worn by the post-French Revolutionary dandies Les Incroyables and their female counterparts Les Merveilleuses.

However, her new samples were faithful but uninspired. 'Vivienne dutifully copied from the pattern book, but a lot we couldn't use because they were respectful of the past,' said McLaren in the 2000s. 'I was, in a way, an absolute fascist dictator and Vivienne was diligent and compliant. Whenever I saw something Vivienne created and didn't like, I simply threw it in the trash. She knew better than to allow anything to enter that store that I hadn't approved because my temper was horrendous. I would go stark raving mad if something was in that store that I didn't like. Vivienne was terrified of my wrath in that regard.'

In this case, McLaren recognised that Westwood's Waugh-based explorations didn't contain youth cultural references. 'Vivienne was diving into 18th-century fashion with these cheesy ball gowns,' he told *Vice* in the 2000s. 'I said, "If you're going to do that, Vivienne, you're going to have to give it a label that kids will understand." Vivienne was like, "Fuck the kids! I want to sell to elegant women." But we didn't have a shop like that. We had to stay in the pop culture.'[19]

Infused with the visual and informational overload provided by his own research, McLaren determined that there was one item Westwood had taken from Norah Waugh's book which would form the basis of a new range: a billowing man's shirt dated 1700–1810 with which he and Westwood experimented in a variety of prints to be worn by both men and women.

'It looked like the shirt a slave girl would wear from her master's bedroom on a galleon,' he said, and together they agreed designs for complementary breeches, sashes, tiny bodice-style patterned waistcoats, tricorn hats and slouchy buckled boots in suede and leather.

A recurring motif was the usage of a continuous, looping print which became known as 'the squiggle'. McLaren had been introduced to this serpentine design by Jean-Charles de Castelbajac during his recent stay in Paris. 'I was fascinated by heraldry, and this snake figure occurs across heraldic artefacts,' says de Castelbajac. 'I showed it to Malcolm because we shared ideas. He immediately understood how it could fit into his new vision.'

Once again, the McLaren/Westwood partnership was firing into the future. 'I added the vision of pirates to give it all a certain look and style and pop panache,' said McLaren.

Meanwhile, with himself as lyricist, McLaren started the search for Ant's replacement and encouraged the musicians to write a number of backing tracks based around the music he had played them; one such outcome was the track 'Jungle Boy', which used another Pompidou library find, 'Umculo Kawupheli' by South Africa's Mahotella Queens.

Determined to hire a female frontperson, McLaren organised auditions over the first months of 1980; among those who attended were the late Kirsty McColl, daughter of the folksinger Ewan McColl, who had already launched her solo career via a single on Stiff Records, and models and club faces Kate Garner (soon to become a member of pop act Haysi Fantayzee and these days a respected fashion photographer) and Lizzie Tear (who worked at 430 King's Road and had a solo musical career later in the decade).

None made the grade for McLaren, who was meanwhile indulging his unpleasant bid to make the musicians more sexually active, cajoling them into attending the new gay superclub Heaven and paying for them to have sex with Soho prostitutes. Years later both Barbe and Gorman complained that this was likely designed by McLaren 'to make us more subservient and pliable' (in the latter's words). Gorman has related that McLaren set up Robert Fraser to introduce the bassist to a famous rock star's ex-wife, and then successfully urged Gorman into sleeping with her.

In the early spring of 1980 – by which time he was working out of an office in the heart of Soho at 25 Denmark Street, trading as Moulin Rouge Ltd – McLaren was alerted by David Fishel to the vocal talents of Annabella Lwin, a fourteen-year-old Anglo-Burmese girl he had heard singing along to the radio while going about her duties in a West Hampstead laundry. Totally untutored, Lwin was largely unaware of pop music beyond a liking for Stevie Wonder.

McLaren's rationale was that, since the Second World War, young teens had been at the forefront of changing social attitudes. 'They were at that level of teenage-hood where they were virgins and still experimenting with their sexuality,' said McLaren. 'I thought Annabella was perfect.'[20]

Soon Lwin became an Eliza Doolittle figure for McLaren to mould into a frontwoman.

' "C30 C60 C90 Go!" was an idea for which I needed a group, and when I found this young Burmese girl in a launderette, I knew that was it,' said McLaren, who recorded the newly formed quartet at Morgan Studios with the assistance of engineer Martin Levan. 'I produced it and paid for it myself, the best way I could, but I didn't have much expertise.'

From the outset, the positioning of a fourteen-year-old girl at the front of a McLaren-steered musical project was fraught. Though Western showbiz had long hot-housed pre-teen and pubescent talents – from Shirley Temple to the likes of Lena Zavaroni and Bonnie Langford, both British light entertainment stars by the age of ten, and Brooke Shields and Mariel Hemingway, who made breakout appearances in mainstream American movies at the ages of thirteen and fourteen respectively – McLaren's presence invited suspicion as to his intentions.

'McLaren's use of 14-year-old Annabella Lwin was wildly over-determined, like the ad campaign for a new product,' wrote the US artist and curator Dan Graham.

Child nymphets like Brooke Shields were used to open up a new market of both child consumers and adults imitating or observing kids. Aimed ostensibly at newly 'liberated' women and girls, the actual effect was one of retrenchment and reversal of the values of the early 70s Women's Movement. McLaren's use of Annabella was a counter-spectacle in calculated symmetry to the appearance of Brooke Shields. Both young women were used to exploit the new buying power of the 13- to 17-year-old consumer.[21]

McLaren ensured that the media was aware that educational and other regulatory bodies were informed of Lwin's participation in this latest musical venture, telling the music press that he was dealing with 'courts and orders. You can't believe it. Police. Scotland Yard. Criminal records. Are you chaperoning her? Tutors on tour. Maaaan. In front of magistrates Monday morning to take from here to there and back. School authorities. The ILEA [Inner London Education Authority]. Can we have weekly reports? Boy . . . man that's heavy.'[22]

For the time being Lwin's mother was, in McLaren's words, 'gung-ho' about her daughter's role in the group now named by the ex-Pistols manager Bow Wow Wow (from the chorus to the Apaches' theme in 'The Mile High Club' script).[23]

And so McLaren began a round of record companies, just as he had done three-and-a-half years previously, but the climate had changed and, with one surprising exception, all were naturally wary of McLaren's reputation.

The odd one out was EMI, whose new head of A&R Terry Slater – the man responsible for signing a publishing deal with the Sex Pistols four years earlier – rocked the UK music business by signing Bow Wow Wow in the spring of 1980 for a one-year deal offering an advance of £50,000 against delivery of the single, with an option of £20,000 for further tracks.

'They didn't know what the record's about but they liked the drumbeat and the feel; I think you can say the ground floor love it and the top floor are shaking by the knees,' said McLaren of EMI, which he claimed was 'the only record company in Britain' since they had on their roster stalwarts such as Cliff Richard and new stars including Kate Bush and that spring's number-one act Dexys Midnight Runners.

In case EMI needed reminding, McLaren's waywardness and unreliability were foregrounded around this time by the release – finally – of *The Great Rock 'n' Roll Swindle*. Julien Temple's edit excised all but a couple of appearances by John Lydon at the singer's insistence, while McLaren was depicted in full bloom as 'The Embezzler'. Enough remained of McLaren and Jamie Reid's version to convey bitter humour and brilliant flourishes, particularly in the opening sequence, which recreated the Gordon Riots with the Sex Pistols and McLaren hanged by the mob at Tyburn, as well as the 'auditions' for a new frontman ('Anyone can be a Sex Pistol') intercut with an aerial view of Helen Wellington Lloyd's assemblage of the giant lettering, which made up the opening credits.

In an introductory monologue to camera, for which he adopted a breathy, comedic, Fagin-like accent akin to an exaggeration of his grandmother Rose's timbre, McLaren – in a rubber inflatable mask and catsuit outside Seditionaries – presented his extraordinary CV and claimed ownership over the youth movement he had nurtured:

'My name is Malcolm McLaren.

'In my time I have brought you many things. Teddy Boy revivalism, Zoot suits, Sex clothes, bondage, whips, chains, the whole bloody lot . . .

'But the most successful of all was an invention of mine they called . . . the Punk Rock.'

When asked for his views on the film, McLaren was breezy in his dismissal, conveying none of the sense of betrayal he had harboured a year earlier. 'Could have been a good film . . . bad director . . . had a lot of hassles mind you,' he said. 'But ultimately, badly edited and a lot of film was cut, unnecessarily in my view. And the story went out the window. I don't think I acted well in all the scenes. Overall, disappointing to me.'

Similarly, McLaren expressed no anger over the *Lydon v. Glitterbest* court case which had derailed his plans for the film. 'Me, I'm never disillusioned,' he said. 'You get upset, right, when you have a court case and get blown out of a movie that cost you five hundred grand. But you just have to fuck off for a bit.'

Doubtless the former Sex Pistols noted McLaren's use of the possessive in regard to the film funding, 75 per cent of which, of course, stemmed from them.

Gone, also, was all semblance of exasperation with Lydon, who had recently produced the avant-garde and critically acclaimed *Metal Box* LP with his group PiL:

All that stuff with John Rotten is water under the bridge to me, mate. I think he was a very good singer, wasted on (Virgin). He is good as a performer and – I don't say his new lyrics – but he was a fine lyricist. But without the blood and guts of a team, a management team, a sense of music, which he doesn't have in my opinion . . . I don't find his thing musical. And, if they're not musical, I don't care how experimental they are, at the end of the day it's only a bloody Mickey Mouse medium anyway.[24]

For Bow Wow Wow's graphic identity and the campaign around the release of 'C30 C60 C90 Go!' McLaren turned again to Jamie Reid, who worked on concepts, logos and packaging and summarised McLaren's new approach as being concerned with 'the freedoms conferred by pleasure technology, the possibilities that blank cassettes and the ability to copy give you, and the ability to look rich even though you were poor'.[25]

Reid produced a simple design for the single's release as a C10 cassette, providing a black sleeve with the title on the front and the credits on the back in yellow. For the 7 inch, the packaging was again black with the song lyrics emblazoned across the front. These were references to the debut single by McLaren's previous signings to the record label, when 'Anarchy in the UK' first appeared in an all-black cover.

'The idea was to reiterate the EMI/Sex Pistols connection,' said Reid, who also proposed a poster for the single based on a 1974 collage of Eugène Delacroix's painting *Liberty Leading the People* with Croydon skyscrapers, as featured in his underground paper *Suburban Press*. The artwork declared 'Out of the Dross and into the Age of Piracy'.

This was rejected, but Reid received the thumbs-up for packaging commissioned by McLaren for a promotional canister designed to appear as a tin of dog food as a commentary on the processed nature of pop, containing a press release, a photo of Lwin and the cassette. This was toned down by EMI when execs ordered the removal of the 'Music for Life for Free' slogan McLaren intended to carry over from the Granada documentary.

Almost as soon as the single was released, they realised their mistake in having allowed McLaren back into the henhouse; using EMI's platform, he was after all proposing that young music fans stop buying records entirely and step up their home-taping activities.

Rival record companies and the music industry trade body were up in arms, and the hysteria led eventually to the launch of an industry-funded campaign based on a logo of a cassette bearing the skull-and-crossbones on record inner sleeves with the slogan: 'Home Taping Is Killing Music'.

McLaren was again in the thick of controversy; it's notable that – as when the Sex Pistols began – he was the focus of news stories and interviews, not the members of Bow Wow Wow, who were nevertheless featured in photographs dressed head to toe in the latest designs cooked up with Westwood to form a new collection, which he christened 'Pirate'. The group also appeared in Pirate gear in a Jean-Luc Godard-style promo video for 'C30', which was shot at EMI's pressing plant outside London in Hayes, Middlesex. Lwin and the musicians, who brandished boom-boxes, progressed in primitively choreographed dance steps among the office workers and through the factory floor as boisterous representatives of the new leisure era.

Meanwhile, McLaren was using press encounters to test out his theories, this time about the conformity of life in Britain now that Margaret Thatcher's hardline Conservative government was entering its second year. He also projected an international outlook at odds with post-punk's introversion. 'I can't see Labour getting in again,' he told Neil Spencer, the first journalist to write about the Pistols four years previously.

Thatcher's sold off so much they wouldn't be able to do anything anyway. It's divide and rule: kids in the army looking after kids who are unemployed. There's a greyness in the culture that's beating everyone down to a pulp. There's too much poverty around the music. You can't sell poverty to anyone in Europe, the only band that happened there was Madness. The reason? It didn't look too poverty-stricken, didn't look too English. They're fashion conscious over there and there was a fashion feel to it. I hated 2-Tone; all that black and white. Why not blue, green, yellow, gold?

The latter colour (and material) became a keynote of press interviews, as McLaren preposterously proposed that the unemployed be paid in gold dust and recalled the Croydon student who had demanded the art college's authorities make gold available for sculpture during the sit-in he, Reid and Robin Scott organised in 1968. McLaren also summarised the brief he had given Westwood in developing the new clothing range in three words: 'Sun, Gold & Piracy'.

'The outrage of such a suggestion in our context just thrilled me,' said McLaren in the 2000s. 'So suddenly I thought, why don't we make everything in gold, pirates and so on? I'll dismantle the shop and turn it into a galleon, setting sail for the high seas!'[26]

Chapter 28

For the fifth and final iteration of the retail business Malcolm McLaren operated at 430 King's Road with Vivienne Westwood, he chose the name Worlds End (absent the apostrophe) from the area occupied by the premises, which was also the destination of the local buses.

'The thought of the world ending, the apocalyptic, suggested to me the potential for cultural change,' said McLaren, who produced interior and exterior design ideas for the outlet, which crossed piratical references – in particular the prows of ships and facades of eighteenth-century houses on Bristol dockside from an illustration in Douglas Botting's book – with the Old Curiosity Shop in London's Holborn, a sixteenth-century structure built from disused boat timber, which became the basis for the Dickens 1841 novel and exists to this day.

The twisted fairy-tale elements of McLaren's concepts were manifested in a drawing of the facade by David Connor, the interiors architect who had been brought on board by Ben Kelly during the Seditionaries refit four years previously. McLaren desired a wilder and weirder proposition than Connor's rendition. Funded by £2500 from his share of the Bow Wow Wow advance and other sources, McLaren oversaw the overhaul, which was carried out by Roger Burton, a former clothes dealer and partner in the boutique PX, and the electrician Andy Newman, a fellow Clapham-dweller and one-time member of 'Something in the Air'-hitmakers Thunderclap Newman.

'The shop was to represent a kind of pirate galleon setting sail outside of this muddy hole called England, a place I had learned to loathe due to the conditions I had to meet because of the English courts and the music industry generally,' said McLaren in the 2000s. 'This store became a way for us to sail away from the King's Road.'

Inside, McLaren created an environment as unsettling to visitors as Let It Rock's 1950s sitting room, Sex's pervy gymnasium and Seditionaries' brutalist clinic of horrors. He decided the new wooden flooring was to be tilted at an angle so that visitors felt as though they were on board a listing ship. 'I wanted the store to "float" as on waves,' he said later. 'You sort of keeled over when you went in. The uneasiness and difficulty in getting around made everything more interesting.

'I made the interior turquoise blue with brass-shellacked naked bulbs shooting out from copper tubes, as fitted by Thunderclap Newman. These gave the place an air of romance. The old-timey little windows at the front were to create that part of the galleon where the captain would often have his chambers. All that was left was to hoist the Jolly Roger, but we couldn't do that because it was too much of a cliché.'

For McLaren, pirates were 'the ultimate bricoleurs, raping and pillaging, stealing from all cultures and mixing everything up; they represent a stand against authority'.

And so he located a suitably defiant logo in Botting's book: in a spread entitled 'Emblems to strike terror upon the high seas' the only one not containing a skull-and-crossbones or a skeleton was the seventeenth-century privateer-turned-pirate Thomas Tew's white-on-black flag of an arm brandishing a scimitar. 'This expressed the direction I wanted to go in perfectly,' wrote McLaren many years later.

Jamie Reid contributed preliminary designs of the logo housed in a roundel, but McLaren felt these weren't imposing enough for the facade. Soon he came up with an ingenious *Alice's Adventures in Wonderland* device: a giant clock placed above the front window's sloping slate shingle and perpetually spinning backwards through thirteen hours, not twelve. It was, he later declared, 'something impossible to conceive. Something unreal. Something magical. That clock was one of my greatest ideas.'

On the timepiece's face McLaren reproduced Tew's marque with the shop's name in curlicue-laden lettering, derived from *The Pirates'* map titles. These were repeated on a smaller backward-spinning clock hung on the central pillar inside, as well as across the woven labels for the new clothing ranges (which included the tagline 'Born in England').

David Connor and Roger Burton's subsequent claims to certain design aspects of Worlds End were hotly disputed by McLaren. 'Sadly [Connor] continues to pretend that he designed the store,' said McLaren in the late 2000s. 'He NEVER designed anything. And Roger Burton simply carried out some structural drawings that enabled him and the builders to realise the concept I created.'

Another driver behind the new direction was the desire to sever all connections to the now-degenerating movement they had created. 'Vivienne in particular wanted to destroy and not have anything further to do with punk,' said McLaren. 'She hated it.'

This gave impetus to a money-raising venture of Westwood's to which McLaren was not party but nevertheless haunted the pair for decades. Keen to rid the shop of any trace of the recent past, Westwood struck a deal with Steph Raynor and John Krivine, whose King's Road outlet Boy had rested its reputation thus far on imitations of Seditionaries-wear: heavily-zippered trousers, combat-style tartan jackets, poorly designed 'provocative' T-shirts.

For just £200, Westwood – never a capable business head – provided the pair with what little remained of the stock and an apparently limitless licence to reproduce virtually all of the designs she and McLaren had created over the preceding six years: around thirty T-shirt artworks, including such big sellers as You're Gonna Wake Up, Cowboys and Destroy, as well as Bondage trousers and jackets, Seditionaries boots, muslins and parachute and Anarchy shirts.

If there was a duration to the agreement, it wasn't respected. Using original Sex and Seditionaries screens and taking patterns from existing garments, Boy was quickly launched anew, predicated on a range of fifty or so McLaren/Westwood reproductions, which were bowdlerised in terms of quality and cut over the next decade. On the back of this business, Boy's takings went gangbusters as many thousands of garments were sold and outlets were opened as far afield as Los Angeles and Hong Kong.

Worse still, the intellectual property rights weren't protected or policed. Soon, reproduction bondage gear and copies of the most popular T-shirts were available around the world, from new-wave boutiques and market stalls to regional outlets with no association to Boy, let alone McLaren and Westwood. Yet they took their cue from the Situationists' disavowal of original creation and, for the time being at least, ignored the aggressive exploitation of their work.

For a brief while, McLaren considered raising money for Worlds End by publishing his memoirs. These were dictated over a few vodka-fuelled nights to journalist Barry Cain, who had run expansive pieces on McLaren the previous summer in the fourth-rung music weekly *Record Mirror*, and comprised salacious, hammed-up anecdotes. The tenor of the project was best summed up by the working title: 'The Great Jewish Bastard'. His friend Fred Vermorel later described the Cain manuscript as McLaren's 'most boorish stroke yet'.[1]

McLaren wisely abandoned the Cain collaboration and poured his energies not only into the refurbishment of 430, which took four months in the winter of 1980–81, but also Bow Wow Wow and their debut album, which was released on cassette in a style aimed at its target audience of teen consumers: a 'flip-top' container akin to cigarette and confectionery packaging.

With vinyl sales crashing as a result of the uptake of the new format, McLaren drew parallels between the major music labels and the Hollywood studios that had been ruined by the advent of television in the 1950s. He suggested the music industry would be better off taking on board the home-tapers and 'sell their music to more people for less money. The situation we're in is that record shops are becoming like antique shops. The cassette should be half the price of the album and be available at your local Mobil gas station. If the record industry does that and accepts less profit and the artist accepts a lower royalty you'll have a more buoyant industry with more music. Like any popular culture, rock 'n' roll in particular needs the ability to carry information fast.'[2]

For *Your Cassette Pet*, Reid came up with inventive logotypes of contrasting cassette 'happy' and 'sad' faces. Already deflated by the gruelling experiences of his punk years, Reid had been losing faith in the months since the release of 'C30 C60 C90 Go!', during which time he embarked on an investigation into the corrupt world of chart returns (where bribery often generated the reporting of individual record sales for the top forty). 'I'm convinced that EMI had second thoughts and didn't want ["C30 C60 C90 Go!"] to be a hit; it's quite possible that they actually prevented the record becoming bigger than it did,' said Reid. 'All this left me feeling frustrated with working within the format of pop music. I needed to move on.'[3]

A collection of rambunctious rock topped off with Lwin's impassioned performances, *Your Cassette Pet* contained eight tracks, all – apart from a cover of the Johnny Mercer classic 'Fools Rush In' – with lyrics by McLaren, who was also the arranger and producer. The majority were survivors from 'The Mile High Club', including the title track, 'Uomo Sex Al Apache', 'Giant Sized Baby Thing' and 'Louis Quatorze'.

The inclusion of the latter on *Your Cassette Pet* prompted the Parisian musicians Pierre Grillet and Stephane Pietri, who had worked on the 'Mile High' musical proposal, to pursue a claim through the French publishing rights body Sacem. They kicked up a fuss over copyright infringement on the basis that 'Louis Quatorze' and an as-yet-unreleased track called 'Cowboy' contained contributions for which they deserved credit, though their claim was on shaky ground from the start since both songs had been subject to substantial changes and, as the *NME* noted, the pair had already been compensated.

'Pietri and Grillet did get paid for the two script treatments for the musical they worked on with McLaren, who later did a third treatment with an English writer and a fourth and final treatment on his own,' reported Paul Rambali, who quoted Grillet: 'Malcolm wrote a final script himself when he got back to London. He kept the basic characters but changed the plot. "Louis Quatorze" was in it, for instance. But probably he thought he wouldn't be able to make the film so he used the song and the idea for Bow Wow Wow. I don't mind that he should get credit for it. But I want the money!'[4]

In the event this wasn't forthcoming. The duo backed off from bringing a suit and instead settled for a credit on 'Cowboy', which wasn't released for another year.

Meanwhile another 'Mile High' track, 'Sexy Eiffel Towers', attracted attention for Lwin's simulation of the sounds of orgasm (an echo of the Serge Gainsbourg hit favoured by McLaren, 'Je T'Aime ... Moi Non Plus'). Lwin naively defended her performance in the recently launched British lifestyle publication *The Face* – 'I know everyone thinks it was Malcolm's idea to get a sexual kind of turn-on but the actual thing is I was supposed to be falling off the Eiffel Tower. It's meant to be fun'[5] – but the American journalist Mary Harron, who had observed McLaren on both sides of the Atlantic since the mid-1970s as a founding writer for New York's *Punk* magazine, sagely observed in the *Guardian*: 'Just because it's Situationism doesn't make it right. This is the usual McLaren paradox because everything else – the music, the spirit – is very healthy. The same was true of punk rock, where eventually the kids took what they needed from McLaren's fantasies and used them for their own ends.'[6]

McLaren's involvement with the group ensured attention from mainstream media; the BBC detailed a crew under producer Alan Yentob and music journalist Robin Denselow to trail Bow Wow Wow and their high-profile manager for a documentary to be shown as part of the prestigious *Arena* strand.

And, to promote *Your Cassette Pet*'s release to the widest possible audience, McLaren obtained EMI backing for the production of a dedicated magazine featuring the lyrics to the album tracks with band photographs. Akin to the songbooks produced for performers of the period, some of which had been designed by prominent artists and designers such as the painter Derek Boshier's publication for The Clash and Barney Bubbles's titles for John Cooper Clarke and Ian Dury, McLaren conceived 'Playkids' as a stapled forty-eight pager in the style of the popular fortnightly *Smash Hits*. The latter had been launched just two years previously and was selling hundreds of thousands of copies a month to teenage fans of the zingy 'new pop' then elbowing aside dour post-punk in the charts.

McLaren's concept also contained an ingenious element, at least in music business terms. He envisaged 'Playkids' increasing *Your Cassette Pet*'s in-store visibility by featuring the release on the cover; for just £1.99 the pop fan obtained a new album and magazine at the same time. In this way, Bow Wow Wow would circumvent the traditional distribution of music via specialist record shops and instead be racked on the shelves of the tens of thousands of independent and high-street newsagents around the country.

'The non-visual aspect of cassettes is a bit of a problem,' McLaren pointed out a few months later. '[This way] you could introduce Bow Wow Wow to a much larger audience, rather than putting it in a little corner of a record shop and have it disappear because it's too small.'[7]

This smart solution to the knotty problem of promoting audio cassettes later became standard industry practice; within a year a cassette-only monthly music magazine *SFX* was launched, and though this was short-lived, by the end of the decade the covers of music mags regularly featured the add-on.

Yet McLaren's provocative nature didn't allow him to stop there, and his decision on the content of 'Playkids' – billed as 'pleasure technology for the primitive boy and girl' – was to lead him into questionable territory. Just as *The Story of Oxford Street* film project haunted McLaren for years after his failure to deliver it, so, in the early 1980s, he seemed unable to shake the near-obsession with teenage sexuality that had informed the discarded 'The Mile High Club'.

The coarsening of McLaren's worldview had taken hold; from cajoling the male members of Bow Wow Wow to frequent prostitutes (and even proposing – unsuccessfully as it mercifully turned out – that one of them deflower Lwin) he now appeared to be regressing to realising his dangerous 'pornography for kids' idea.

'I thought all the songs were very sexy, because they'd come out of the idea of a sex picture I'd been writing in Paris,' he explained later to journalist Chris Salewicz. 'I felt they should be put in the context of a cheesecake *Playboy*-type magazine.'[8]

EMI released funds and McLaren set about gathering an editorial team including Fred Vermorel and commercials photographer Jay Myrdal. In Jamie Reid's absence, the British artist Brian Clarke, by now close to McLaren, was on board to help realise the look of the magazine, and Vivienne Westwood contributed styling suggestions.

The overarching 'School Kids' *Oz* theme was that young people would be responsible for the copy; through EMI, McLaren contacted a fifteen-year-old who had been named Young Scientist of the Year in a national competition, and commissioned him to review new entertainment technology, including the latest hi-fi systems and the Walkman. The cassette-player's manufacturer Sony agreed to take out advertising, unaware that there was a seamy side to the project.

For example, Leigh Gorman was persuaded into filing a report on visiting Soho prostitutes, and, after a few weeks McLaren announced that the title was to change from the relatively innocent to the suggestive: 'Chicken', a term used in American paedophile circles for their prey. This exposed the lack of musical knowledge among EMI execs and it is surprising that nobody in wider music business circles didn't pick up on the reference, which appeared in such blues songs as 'Back Door Man', as popularised in the 1960s by the Doors and written by one of McLaren's favourite artists, Howlin' Wolf.

McLaren organised for a promotional leaflet using the Bow Wow Wow cassette logos to be issued to potential advertisers:

Scheduled for release in mid-November, Chicken is to be published by EMI and Buccaneer Books.

Chicken's readership is boys and girls from 11 to 18 (roughly the same audience as Smash Hits).

Chicken will be about pop and fashion, focusing around pleasure tech: roller-skating, cassette-swinging microchip kids, and on the swashbuckling and romantic 'new look' which is just coming in.

McLaren subsequently pointed out there was to be no nudity – 'How would we get something like that in the shops?' – but Fred Vermorel claims that things came to a head during a photoshoot at a modernist house in Hampstead which, it should be noted, he didn't attend.

'I wasn't there but was told Malcolm shouted at a young girl who was being photographed and she burst into tears,' says Vermorel. 'Apparently she was clothed but upset and her mother intervened and took away any photos that had been taken of her daughter.'

Scheduled for release in mid November **Chicken** is to be published by EMI and Buccaneer Books.

Chicken's readership is boys and girls from 11 to 18 (roughly the same audience as **Smash Hits**).

Chicken will be about pop and fashion, focusing around pleasure tech: roller-skating, cassette-swinging microchip kids, and on the swashbuckling and romantic 'new look' which is just coming in.

Flyer for cancelled 'Chicken' magazine project, 1980.

At the Hampstead session, an Indian boy of around twelve agreed to pose for a photo-story illustrated by the lyrics to the song 'Jungle Boy', starting off in school uniform before stripping to a loincloth and climbing trees. In one shot he sat jubilantly on Leigh Gorman's shoulders; the Bow Wow Wow bassist wore a transistor radio suspended from chains to cover his genitals (the lyric to the song ran: 'Radio G string say something to me').

Vermorel says he was unsettled by this information when he undertook direction of a photoshoot with Annabella Lwin and other group members a few days later at Robert Fraser's apartment in Piccadilly. With the statue of Eros visible through the open window and Lwin posing for photographs on Fraser's bed, Westwood made an appearance.

'She begins to work her way around the room, muttering to people conspiratorially. I wonder what she's saying,' Vermorel wrote in 1996. 'When she gets to me she says, almost conspiratorially: "Malcolm thinks Annabella should be in the nude for this session." This is the first I've heard of it. I ask Annabella if she wants to strip off. She declines and I don't press the point. I continue directing the shoot. All the while Vivienne continues to whisper to onlookers, as if trying to get their support for the idea."⁹

Then McLaren arrived at Fraser's flat with a stills camera and began photographing the entire scene. 'He was taking pictures of all of us, including me and the photographer, whose name I can't remember. It wasn't Jay,' says Vermorel. 'I asked him what he was doing. I'd never seen Malcolm with a camera before. He kind of smirked. I believe he intended to use the images he was taking to implicate all of us in some sort of scandal. That was enough for me. I called a halt and walked out.'

That night Vermorel confronted McLaren and Westwood at Thurleigh Court. When McLaren again refused to be drawn on why he had taken the photographs of the session at Fraser's flat, Vermorel flipped. After seventeen years, the friendship formed in the Harrow Art School canteen was at an end.

The following day McLaren, Westwood and members of Bow Wow Wow visited Vermorel at his home to wrestle him back onto the project. 'I shout "I'm finished with it Malcolm! You're just a cunt! A dirty old man!"' recorded Vermorel. 'Then I slam the door.'[10]

Vermorel made the incident public by contacting the music papers, which reported that EMI's response was to put 'Chicken' on hold indefinitely. Meanwhile the BBC abandoned the documentary; no footage has emerged.

'The initial idea behind "Chicken" was that it should promote McLaren's beliefs in leisure and not work as a way of life for unemployed teenagers,' reported *Smash Hits*. 'Because the preparation of the mag was being followed by a film crew from BBC TV's *Arena*, it has been suggested that McLaren simply couldn't resist the temptation of grabbing some inexpensive publicity.'[11]

Such reports as well as the unverified ones that there was a police investigation stemmed from the incandescent Vermorel, who launched a passionate personal attack on McLaren six months later in the music weekly *Sounds* 'for trying to implicate us in a child porn rap as publicity for himself'.

Vermorel wrote:

For the first time I saw a new Malcolm McLaren. Someone who seemed concerned to hurt people and was quite unconcerned with their feelings and integrity. Who was a greedy person: greedy for power, acclaim and success. Who was casual about people getting injured or even dying.

The student who had been arrested for burning the American flag because, so I thought at the time, of people getting hurt and dying in Vietnam, was now the man who exploited and even gloated over the tearful confusion of an outraged little girl. For years Malcolm was my most generous and stimulating friend, and I owe him many perceptions and ideas. But what he is about now is dubious and possibly evil.[12]

Though he never met her or her mother, Vermorel also made the unprovable allegation that the girl who had been at the Hampstead photoshoot had been identified and was being subjected to schoolyard taunts at school as well as obscene phone calls. The three-page article was in essence an attempt at all-out character assassination, depicting McLaren as 'a frequently dithering individual' whose incompetence ran from failing to use colour samples to obtain the correct tone of red for the *Your Cassette Pet* packaging through poor acting ability in *The Great Rock 'n' Roll Swindle* to being 'a lousy businessman whose boutique mentality renders him incapable of large-scale organisation and planning'.

More pointed was Vermorel's charge that McLaren treated Lwin – and by implication other musicians – 'as an object'. Meanwhile, in *The Face*, Chris Salewicz's view was that 'Chicken' and McLaren's manipulations of Bow Wow Wow were evidence that he had 'become hampered by his own previous iconoclasm . . . the trouble with Malcolm McLaren is that no matter how many excellent scams he's come up with, there is the over-riding sense that, basically, he's a pretty dodgy individual'.[13]

McLaren presented an airy front just a few weeks after the publication of Vermorel's diatribe. 'It got blown up out of all proportion, and EMI got worried, and *voilà*: they stopped everything,' he told Salewicz. 'A very stupid move, because had we brought out the magazine that cassette would have been a very, very big hit.'[14]

And a couple of years later McLaren maintained his unrepentant stance, employing the second person singular and the third person plural as he often did when appearing to defend the indefensible. 'Let me tell you, great art, or any real idea, has never worried about running a few people over,' McLaren announced. 'You never worry about it, because the idea is more important. If we had an idea and we believed in it, then, by hook or by crook it was the idea that got through.

'That's why we've been accused of being evil, or Svengalis, manipulating, conniving. All absolutely true. I wouldn't deny for one minute. There are great elements of truth in it all. Yes, we did do some very dastardly acts, but don't regret it for one minute, otherwise it would have been a hell of a boring job.'[15]

There are signs however that McLaren recognised 'Chicken' as, at the very least, a foolish venture. He never featured the escapade among the scandal-ridden anecdotes of his life that he loved to turn over for public consumption in his later years.

It's arguable that McLaren was privately chastened by the 'Chicken' episode and the loss of his friendship with Vermorel. Inescapable was the fact that McLaren's interest in Bow Wow Wow was now wavering. In the wake of the genuine international media furore surrounding the Pistols, controversies relating to his new charges appeared seedy and second-rate. They also soon dissipated. Vermorel recounts how McLaren had complained to him that the Bow Wow Wow musicians were needy. 'It wasn't like the Pistols, who would just go out and create havoc,' says Vermorel. 'The Bow Wow Wow guys were onto Malcolm all the time: "What should we do now?" He hated it.'

And EMI executives began expressing their unease, not least at McLaren's insistence that *Your Cassette Pet* must not appear on vinyl. This rendered the release ineligible for the British album chart, and so it stalled at a paltry fifty-eight in the singles listings.

On the bright side, the bout of promotion and extensive coverage of the band had enabled the public unveiling of the Pirate collection now stocked in Worlds End and proving popular with a fresh raft of shoppers drawn from London's Blitz club and art school crowds.

At the time, McLaren described Worlds End as 'probably the most successful' of the retail manifestations at 430 King's Road on his watch. 'It's taken on very, very quickly,' he declared.

> That's because the clothes have been understood by more people right across the age groups. There's not really a generation gap in those clothes.
>
> You should be able to get *anybody* wearing Pirate clothes, if you can get across those clothes' politics. That's often very difficult just

on a visual level, so you have to blurb it and blag it. That's why it's very nice having songs. You can get those songs to exploit the ideas and tie them in with the visual, so you can get an identification going and makes the clothes have a certain purpose.[16]

On opening, the shop's new manifestation was greeted as representative of a fresh fashion aesthetic. Notably, Vivienne Westwood was now available for interviews, during which she claimed sole authorship. 'I took things like Apache Indians who were just great, those people after the French Revolution who were called the Incroyables and pirates,' she asserted. 'Those three things are basically what this whole collection's been based around.'[17]

This repudiation of McLaren's conception and contribution was done with his blessing; he remained an equal in the design partnership, as reflected in the labels carrying both their surnames, yet was content that his partner step into the spotlight and accept the recognition. 'Vivienne was determined to become a mainstream fashion designer and I was absolutely supportive,' said McLaren in the 2000s. 'I believed 100 per cent that it was possible to make an impact in the mainstream high-fashion arena even though it ran against what I believed in at the time.'

Elsewhere, McLaren paid tribute to Westwood's undeniable talents. 'Vivienne was so sweet and dedicated and clever,' he wrote in the 1990s. "Although I'd come from that world and my grandfather was a tailor and my stepfather was a dress maker, it was what I knew and what I hated, so it was difficult for me to go along with anything other than the kind of philosophy I had been working on for the past ten years. I really felt that Vivienne needed to be pushed to the fore and announced as a designer.'

The full force of Pirate was exhibited at an 'unleashing' of Bow Wow Wow McLaren cooked up for north London's Rainbow, a former dancehall within walking distance of the first home his parents had occupied in Islington after their marriage.

For the show, McLaren ordered the removal of the ground-floor seating and installation of fairground rides and attractions such as coconut shies. In tribute to the venue's past, he booked a forty-piece swing orchestra, which played Glenn Miller classics. Bow Wow Wow's set, meanwhile, was augmented with an encore rendition of 'Cast Iron Arm' – the rockabilly song from back in the days of Let It Rock which McLaren had previously tried to persuade Sid Vicious and Adam Ant to perform – by an apparition billed as 'Lieutenant Lush' from 'The Mile High Club' script.

This was eighteen-year-old Londoner George O'Dowd, a gender-defying club kid noted for his soulful singing voice, sassy demeanour and outrageous appearance. O'Dowd had heard rumblings of dissatisfaction about Annabella Lwin's abilities from Bow Wow Wow guitarist Matthew Ashman, and so offered himself as a replacement.

With an eye once again to building a talent roster, McLaren opted to grant O'Dowd this opportunity as a test. 'I went mental, dancing around all over the stage,' says O'Dowd. 'Matthew was grinning away but the drummer and the bass player were looking at me obviously thinking "What's Malcolm doing making us play with this poof? It's bad enough playing with a teenage girl." And I got a very confused reaction from the audience; they didn't know what to make of me. I don't know what Annabella felt but Malcolm's mate Dave Fishel wasn't at all impressed.'

McLaren was encouraged enough to book O'Dowd for cameos on the opening dates on the group's forthcoming British tour, but was soon redirecting his energies into fashion after an offer came from veteran British entrepreneur Jeff Banks for Pirate to be shown on a catwalk at the London Designer Collection (the forerunner of London Fashion Week) at exhibition centre Olympia in the west of the capital.

Banks – who had been married to singer Sandie Shaw and began his career with the south London boutique Snob in south London in the mid-1960s – was among the most forward-looking of UK fashion industry executives and keen to shake up the country's staid business as a means of challenging Paris's domination.

This was important at a time of national economic decline. One of the unintended consequences of McLaren and Westwood's redefinition of

British style as the preserve of the young, the eccentric and the extrovert is that punk and post-punk had enlivened the domestic rag trade, and while sales in music and other popular culture sectors were plateauing, growth was being generated by independent boutiques who had taken their cue from the pair while the high-street chains continued to copy their silhouettes.

Meanwhile there was also a boom in what was then known as 'designer fashion', since the national clothing manufacturing industry was in steep decline, and so the value of the UK fashion exports exploded by 500 per cent in the five years to the start of the 1980s.[18]

Of course, McLaren and Westwood weren't solely responsible, but Banks knew their participation would provide crucial credibility and encourage other, younger homegrown talents to follow suit. He introduced them to the young fashion publicist Marysia Woroniecka, while pattern maker Mark Tarbard had been a visitor to 430 King's Road since the mid-1970s. They became part of a makeshift team, which included shop manager Michael Collins, former Bromley Contingent member Simon Barker and Yvonne Gold, who had helped out on the Let It Rock stall at the London Rock 'n' Roll Show at Wembley nearly a decade previously and was now an innovative and in-demand make-up artist.

Gold worked on the successive catwalk shows McLaren and Westwood staged together over the next couple of years, and testifies to McLaren's involvement against the received opinion that from hereon in his interest lay purely in music while Westwood concentrated on the clothing. 'Before each one, Malcolm used to gather all of us models and backstage staff together and give us a rousing team talk, going through the ideas behind the clothes and getting us all steamed up,' said Gold in 2013.

Many of the Pirate models were not professionals, but drawn from the multicultural generation now gravitating to Worlds End. Wearing clothes they selected themselves from a pile dumped backstage by Westwood, these dreadlocked and gold-painted youths cavorted jubilantly on the catwalk, sporting Walkmans to McLaren's soundtrack of the latest Bow

Wow Wow tracks in pirate shirts, squiggle-print tops and layered outfits emulating the images of such nineteenth-century braves as Cochise in Benjamin Capps's *The Great Chiefs*.

This book was also the source of one of the most enduring designs of the partnership – the suede Pirate boots which could be adjusted at knee or ankle height. These were based on an 1886 photograph of Geronimo and other warriors wearing Apache boots, also made of suede and worn at mid-calf but adjustable to be pulled over the knee as protection against cactus. The addition of several leather straps with buckles represented the couple's effortless abilities as collagists, since they referred not only to the bondage clothing introduced five years earlier, but also to the enclosures that featured on the footwear worn by brigands centuries before.

McLaren's more outré contributions included Wehrmacht-style helmets, as worn by the actress Antonia Ellis with the Too Fast to Live outfit in Ken Russell's *Mahler*, painted with designs he had found in Mable Morrow's *Native Rawhide*. McLaren also added to the assault on the senses by cladding the hall pillars in paper printed with the new Worlds End scimitar logo.

Contemporary fashion commentators such as Britain's Tamsin Blanchard have credited Pirate and the couple's other catwalk shows of the period as achieving Banks's aim of making London the style capital of the world for the first time since the Swinging Sixties, with 'a mix of historically researched clothing, sex and anarchy and a band of followers who were as fanatical about music as fashion. Westwood's shows were irreverent, and raised a one-fingered salute to the grand traditions of fashion.'[19]

No less a publication than *Women's Wear Daily* described Westwood as 'the hottest designer of the new look', and buyers from American department stores formed a queue for orders at the couple's new workshop in Kingly Court (again, resonant of McLaren's past, since it was a few feet from the site of Keith and Heather Albarn's gallery where he had staged his labyrinth exhibition in 1967).

McLaren was genuinely pleased with the acclaim heaped upon

Westwood. 'I tried very much to make Vivienne into a fully fledged designer because that is what she had wanted, and put a lot of money into doing that, creating shows and co-designing with her on various collections,' he said in the 1990s.[20]

While it is true McLaren resisted the fashion world respectability that Westwood craved, his motive for prodding her forward wasn't entirely altruistic. For a while he had been conducting a love affair with twenty-year-old African American/German fashion student Andrea Linz, who was studying at Saint Martin's, the college where he began his journey into creative expression nearly two decades before.

Of all the flings and relationships over the years, it was this that prompted McLaren to finally end his relationship with Westwood and move out of Thurleigh Court. First, he opted for a flat in Whitechapel close to his family's East End stamping ground, though he spent a lot of his time at Linz's apartment above an Italian restaurant in Queensway, the transient central London neighbourhood near Hyde Park.

Unsurprisingly, the split hit the devoted Westwood hard. 'I felt so emotionally distraught I went through a sort of door, as if I died,' she told her biographer Jane Mulvagh. 'I hadn't realized before I was capable of such passion. I think I cared so much because I had put so much into the relationship.'[21]

Her sons Ben Westwood and Joe Corré have said that the emotion they felt above all others at the final disintegration of the relationship was relief, having witnessed at first hand the constant arguments and the wear-and-tear on their mother of McLaren's inconstancy, belittling remarks and stinging rebukes. Seventeen-year-old Ben was relatively phlegmatic, but McLaren's desertion naturally caused severe damage to his relationship with Joe, then thirteen.

There were, of course, to be repercussions. McLaren may never have been a traditional father but this exit had all the impact of betrayal.

It is interesting to note that Jane Mulvagh, whose book about Westwood was not well-inclined to McLaren, believes he was 'gasping for liberation from a sequence of domineering females. He had been ignored by his hedonist mother, smothered by the overpowering grand-mother and overwhelmed by Vivienne's bossiness and ardent demands'.[22]

Those who sided with Westwood after the separation dismissed Linz in casually racist and misogynistic terms as a groupie. The fact is that, though she was thirteen years younger than McLaren, Linz was more than a match for her new partner; as a teenager she had gained an under-standing of the pop process as a member of Germany's successful disco covers act Chilly, and funded her course work in London herself from the proceeds of having performed their hits on the continental live circuit for a couple of years.

In fact, Linz's instinctive take on fashion and ready wit impressed McLaren as much as her beauty when they met after Linz accompanied a friend to an audition for dancers for Bow Wow Wow.

After a first date – McLaren the oenophile and lover of Parisian haute cuisine took Linz to a Kentucky Fried Chicken outlet where they talked for hours – Linz became something of a muse, her trim physique lending itself to his plans that she become the Worlds End fit model.

Over the next three years Linz observed at close quarters the design relationship between McLaren and Westwood, even at this emotionally charged stage of their collaboration. 'It was always Malcolm, not just his ideas and concepts but also his designs,' says Linz. 'Vivienne always listened to him because he was such a great critic with a fantastic eye for detail.'[23]

As well as nursing huge resentment over McLaren's departure, Westwood was now thoroughly disenchanted with Bow Wow Wow; she couldn't connect to Annabella and the group members, whose laddish behaviour held none of the danger or subversive charm she had detected in the Sex Pistols.

One day she appeared at Linz's first-floor apartment to remonstrate with McLaren, ostensibly over funding for Worlds End, but the argu-ment soon became physical and McLaren was forced to bundle her out. Later, while Linz was on her own, a brick smashed one of the windows. As related by Mulvagh, Westwood had previously threatened over the phone to leave the business unless McLaren made more cash available for expensive fabrics: 'She slammed the phone down, returned to her sewing machine and, head down and shaking with fury, started to sew maniacally. A few minutes later she stood up, screamed, and marched out of the door. After an hour she returned with a huge smile across her face.'[24]

McLaren revelled in the drama, claiming that he had been at the apartment with Linz when the incident happened. The smashed window was unrepaired when George O'Dowd paid a visit to talk through Lieutenant Lush's participation in the Bow Wow Wow tour. 'When I arrived a waiter downstairs was pointing up at it and saying "Crazy lady, crazy lady",' says O'Dowd. 'Malcolm was a bit upset about his new girlfriend but seemed to take it all in his stride. He offered me a retainer and said I could sing "The Mile High Club" with the band, which I did at the first date in Manchester. It didn't go down well and the *NME* ran a story afterwards saying I was no longer performing with them, so that was that.'

Within a matter of weeks O'Dowd was rehearsing with the musicians who would form Culture Club as he became their frontman Boy George; initially the group's name was Sex Gang Children, from the lyrics for 'The Mile High Club', and their early songs mimicked Bow Wow Wow's appropriation of ethnic rhythms.

Soon, however, the group transcended their influences and O'Dowd's charisma, soulful voice and songwriting skills propelled Culture Club to global fame and considerable fortune. Unlike other younger musicians and performers with whom McLaren worked, O'Dowd's strength of character guaranteed that he could not be manipulated. McLaren later countered by claiming there was little countercultural about Boy George. 'Having been a fashion designer and before that a painter and after that a rock and roll manager the three things only work together if you're interested in doing something subversive, and that wasn't something George was going to achieve,' McLaren said at the height of Culture Club's fame. 'He was strictly a commercial enterprise.'[25]

Among the songs O'Dowd had rehearsed with Bow Wow Wow was a McLaren composition constructed as an introduction for teenagers to the new uses of leisure afforded by technology. Entitled 'W.O.R.K. (N.O. Nah, No No My Daddy Don't)', this, believed Dan Graham, amounted to McLaren's 'analysis of leaders of a new society based on mass unemployment and total leisure . . . the end of patriarchal subordination to "your parents . . . to your teacher . . . to your boss". McLaren used late 1960s Yippie ideas and applied them to the current situation in Britain.'[26]

These were to be driven home by a promo video McLaren hoped to shoot in the British Leyland car factory producing the recently launched family car the Mini Metro, again in the style of Jean-Luc Godard's 1966 critique *Made in USA* as a conceptual follow-up to the 'C30' clip shot at the EMI plant at Hayes.

'I wanted it very Mao-istic, with all the robotic plants to be going round in the background of Annabella,' said McLaren. 'I wanted to get it on *Top of the Pops* with very big slogans like Godard used: "DEMOLITION OF THE WORK ETHIC!" Do it as a very hardcore, brutal slogan, and make it a big *up*. Make it as choreographed a dance routine as possible: Busby Berkeley at British Leyland.'[27]

The frantic, yelped rap of 'W.O.R.K.' was housed in Jamie Reid's final collaboration with McLaren, a vividly coloured sleeve presenting on the front a graphic exercise, which used the lettering of band's name and the first word of the song's title to form a swastika (a recurring leitmotif of Reid's to critique the output of major record companies).

On the back was a statement of McLaren's: 'Demolition of the work ethic takes us to the age of the primitive'. This was surrounded by photographs of Lwin lying on a recording studio desk draped in a tartan blanket.

'I wanted to create an image of how she would record and wanted her to look ecstatic,' said McLaren many years later. 'This idea went against all the bureaucratic record companies' opinions of how you had to record rock 'n' roll. Pretending they were serious, like Brian Eno.'

The single failed to dent the top fifty and soon EMI announced it wasn't renewing the group's contract; over a year the label had spent at least £100,000 on a project for virtually no return. But McLaren wasn't fazed. Ultimately, EMI had proved disappointing in its unresponsiveness to his demands. The company was also, McLaren felt, too focused on Britain, so he worked with Rory Johnston in the US on securing a new deal.

'On a visit to London we went for a meal at a Jewish deli in Wigmore Street,' recalls Johnston, who'd witnessed Bow Wow Wow in performance at the Rainbow gig with Boy George. 'I said I was in, but with the stipulation that this time I needed to be paid. Of course he was fine about it. Then we started talking to RCA.'

The New York-based label, which had tried to lure McLaren to an executive position two years previously, was then looking to revitalise its offer, since its catalogue had been overly reliant on the likes of Elvis Presley and Dolly Parton, while David Bowie was about to jump ship.

Swayed by the impressive publicity surrounding Bow Wow Wow, British A&R head Bill Kimber and his US counterpart Nancy Jeffries signed a two-year deal, with delivery of three albums starting in the summer of 1981, for a package worth a whopping $750,000.

'It was a very good deal but in music business terms Malcolm had already had an incredible level of success,' says Johnston. 'He may not have made much money but he'd created worldwide attention for the Pistols and the feeling was that he would do this again.'

By this time, McLaren had a new operational base: a wood-panelled apartment in a mansion block in Grenville Mansions, Hunter Street, not far from Russell Square in historic Bloomsbury.

From here he worked on a new set of songs with the musicians and cast around for a replacement art director to step into Jamie Reid's sizeable shoes. During a visit to EMI a few months previously McLaren had noted the work of Nick Egan, a twenty-three-year-old art school graduate who had designed for The Clash in partnership with another young designer, Peter Barrett, with whom he also realised inventive packaging and promotional material for the hit act Dexys Midnight Runners.

'We went for sushi in Leicester Square and got on immediately, talking for hours,' says Egan. 'The great thing about Malcolm was that he didn't bother asking whether I'd been to art school or been trained in any way. If the vibe was right, it was on.'[28]

Soon Egan became McLaren's right-hand person and emissary in the worlds of music and fashion. 'Malcolm was always invited everywhere but was rarely interested, so I would go to all the parties and openings,' says Egan, who took a desk at the Moulin Rouge office. 'He encouraged me. I was happy to up my social standing by riding on his coattails but I could also see how vulnerable he was. Often in meetings I would inter-ject on his behalf, lead the way, so that he could then close the conversa-tion in the way he wanted to.'

McLaren's generosity extended to providing Egan and his girlfriend Anne Witchard with the funds for a deposit on a flat in central London's Marylebone. 'It was great that Malcolm gave us the money but it came with a price,' recalls Egan. 'I was constantly on call. I'd get back from a night out and he'd be sitting on the doorstep waiting for me at one o'clock in the morning, and then we'd talk through whatever was on his mind. He was a lonely man, in that he had very few friends he could relate to, and he drove them crazy because he could also be shy and uncomfortable around people he didn't know.'

At their first encounter, McLaren informed Egan 'the album cover was virtually dead as a form because of the rise of cassette-taping and videos. But in the same breath he said he needed a sleeve for the next Bow Wow Wow record.'

McLaren's concept was that the image should use a photograph of the band members to reconfigure references to the past, consistent with the new clothing designs being hatched with Westwood and the recasting of 430 King's Road.

Egan was then led on a bout of intensive research, spending hours looking through Impressionist and Romantic era art at the library of London's

National Gallery. The pair gave serious consideration to three: *The Bolt* by Jean-Honoré Fragonard, in which a young man holds his lover and reaches for a lock to detain her in a bedroom, Eugène Delacroix's French Revolutionary depiction *Liberty Leading the People*, which Reid had used to great effect in *Suburban Press* and then in the rejected poster for Bow Wow Wow, and Édouard Manet's *Luncheon in the Grass* (*Le Déjeuner sur l'Herbe*).

After a few try-outs, the last won the day. McLaren was enchanted not just by the societal tremors the painting had caused in the 1860s by depicting a female nude with two clothed males but also Manet's life, his deep associations with Paris and friendships with the likes of the Romantic and Symbolist poets Charles Baudelaire (creator of the flâneur) and Stéphane Mallarmé.

A couple of years before his death, McLaren recalled having visited the 1983 National Gallery exhibition *Manet at Work* with the British artist Francis Bacon, to whom he had been introduced by Robert Fraser.

'Francis asked: "What do you think?"' related McLaren in the 2000s. 'And I said "Well, he is a great painter." Francis said: "No, no, he's not a great painter, he's more than that! What you have to understand is that Édouard Manet is a magician! He is an alchemist! He takes ordinary things and he puts them together and shows you something different. He is a sorcerer! Remember that!"

'Sometimes you take from someone something that helps you under-stand what you do. [Bacon] made me understand why I do what I do, understand that idea of sorcery.'[29]

This revelation lay in the future when McLaren and Egan settled on *Le Déjeuner sur l'Herbe*. For McLaren, the image conveyed the senti-ment of a favoured dictum: 'I knew that if we set it up properly, it would show that the band would all be clothed but Annabella would represent the truth, which loves to go naked,' he said in the 2000s.

The portrait was also intended to reflect the theme of one of the new songs for which McLaren had provided lyrics: 'Go Wild in the Country'. This drew on his experience as a teenage runaway, when he took to the road with the tramp Charlie, and the chorus referred to the night they slept in a wood outside Eastbourne and McLaren feared attack by snakes: 'Wild, go wild, go wild in the country, Where snakes in the grass are absolutely free.'

To realise the portrait, Egan recommended young British photographer Andy Earl, who found a suitable location on the lakeside in Priory Park, near Reigate to the south of London.

'I was still at college when Malcolm saw my work and liked its painterly quality,' says Earl. 'He came up with the idea of copying *Déjeuner* on Saturday and we shot it on Monday. Annabella didn't know about it until she turned up and Malcolm showed her the painting. She said: "What, I've got to take my clothes off ?" Malcolm said: "Well, you're not going to let the band down, are you?" I had no idea she was only 14.'[30]

In Manet's painting, the nude is a pale Caucasian; equal to McLaren's interest in presenting Lwin's body as a way of upsetting polite society was the fact that she was of Burmese origin. This linked the image to another of Manet's works, *Olympia*, in which a girlish prostitute is attended by a black serving maid.

'In a Britain fearful of the loss of Britishness through interracial coupling, Annabella is unnervingly ambiguous,' wrote Dan Graham.[31] But such academic considerations went out the window when Amy Dunn-Lwin learned of the venture, and called all holy hell upon McLaren, attacking him in the national media and demanding a Scotland Yard investigation.

Dunn-Lwin's claims – that her daughter had been pressed into disrobing over a five-hour lunch before the shoot, where she had been plied with vodka – were dismissed.

Nick Egan, who assisted McLaren on the shoot, also refutes the charge of coercion. 'I saw first hand he was far more interested in attention to detail,' he says. 'He was a perfectionist, and that comes through in the final image. You look at it today and it's amazing what he pulled off there.'

McLaren was exonerated from the charge of exploiting a minor for immoral purposes since this was clearly an art-directed project and not titillating; Lwin posed so that her private parts were covered. But

McLaren's reputation as a wicked manipulator of the young gathered momentum and the relationship with Dunn-Lwin deteriorated.

Rory Johnston recalls a visit by Lwin's mother to the Moulin Rouge offices around this time. 'I was on a call to New York when she furiously stormed in. I'm trying to conduct a calm business conversation and they're at each other.'

Soon the singer was spirited away, according to McLaren, who claimed Lwin and her mother stayed for a period in a remote part of Cornwall. 'I was given forty-eight hours to find her by the record company otherwise I'd be sued for not fulfilling the contract, blah, blah, blah.

'It was ridiculous. I became a detective who had to find this girl on the moors, with her mother who thought I was a disgrace and was trying to make her daughter commit some cardinal sin. But deep down I adored the photograph.'

RCA execs were horrified they had become mired so quickly in a McLaren mess, and confirmed to Amy Dunn-Lwin that the photograph would not be appearing on the cover of the forthcoming LP, to be titled *See Jungle! See Jungle! Go Join Your Gang Yeah, City All Over! Go Ape Crazy!*

While Dunn-Lwin railed against McLaren to the media and to RCA executives, he held his position and leaked the photograph to the *Los Angeles Times*, New York's *Soho News* and *The Face*, which reported 'McLaren continues to tread a thin line between "fun" and exploitation'.[32] The *Sun* newspaper also printed part of the image. This had the trickledown effect of diluting Dunn-Lwin's protests. 'Others, particularly musicians, used to get upset when Malcolm said: "I use people like others use paint,"' says Egan. 'I never thought there was anything wrong with that. In fact, I thought it was part of his genius.'

Meanwhile, McLaren set about promoting the album, which was scheduled for November release. The first single for RCA, entitled 'Prince of Darkness', was based around a duet between Annabella and a manipulative, devil-like figure: post-*Swindle* McLaren was bent on processing his public image – and in this case his disputes with Dunn-Lwin – in real time.

This release was housed in an Egan sleeve and fold-out poster of a draped Lwin and the band members from the *Déjeuner* shoot, but once again failed to chart. Eighteen months in, Bow Wow Wow still hadn't broken through while their former collaborator Adam Ant was receiving commercial and critical plaudits.

'Malcolm would have liked me to move back to London and work with the band while he kept the management but went off and did other stuff,' says Johnston. 'It was in his nature. He didn't like standing still and, compared with the daily, sometimes hourly fire-fighting around the Pistols, this was routine stuff.'

And so McLaren turned once again to New York for inspiration. A series of US dates had been booked for Bow Wow Wow in the summer of 1981 as a precursor to a British tour to accompany *See Jungle!*'s release. McLaren took the opportunity to return to Manhattan and kibitz with Johnston and RCA execs as well as participate in the industry gabfest, the New Music Seminar.

Also in town was McLaren's sparring partner Bernard Rhodes, who had returned to managing The Clash and was overseeing a seventeen-night residency at Bond's International Casino near Times Square. The British punk rockers were taking the city by storm, receiving blanket media coverage, which helped establish their name nationally. McLaren and Johnston took in some of the performances, where The Clash used their pull to showcase the rising stars of the emerging rap scene, notably Grandmaster Flash & the Furious Five. The group's leader had been name-checked, and their musical style co-opted, by Blondie's international hit 'Rapture' a few months previously, but nevertheless Flash and his crew went down badly with The Clash's white rock audience.

This registered with McLaren. During his stay an invitation arrived from an expat friend, the artist Stan Peskett, to one of the art happenings he held under the banner 'Canal Dreams' at his vast warehouse space downtown at 533 Canal Street. These gatherings showcased artworks and installations by new artists; Peskett's fellow organiser was Michael Holman, a twenty-four-year-old San Franciscan who had recently been exploring the city's emerging hip-hop scene with his video and stills cameras.

A couple of years previously Holman had located the pioneering graffiti artist Fred Braithwaite, otherwise Fab Five Freddy, through a *Village Voice* ad and engineered for him to decorate the interior of Peskett's loft for the first 'Canal Dreams'.

This was an important occasion: not only was it the first time graffiti was brought in off the streets but it was also where Holman met the struggling young artist Jean-Michel Basquiat, with whom he formed the experimental jazz/rap/noise outfit Gray.

It was at the tenth 'Canal Dreams' that Holman was introduced to McLaren. 'Stan and Malcolm had known each other for years; weren't they at the Royal College together?' asks Holman. 'I seem to recall they studied together somewhere in London. I immediately went in to a pitch, telling Malcolm to check out this scene which wasn't even called hip-hop yet, where the kids were going crazy to music based on mixing and cutting existing beats and melodies from records, where graffiti and street style merged with breakdancing.

'Malcolm listened politely and, I guess, was struck by my passion and said he was interested, so I offered to take him along to an event so he could see for himself.'[33]

Holman seized the moment and used Peskett's phone to contact Lance Taylor, the DJ who organised weekend block parties in the South Bronx as Afrika Bambaataa. These were intended as a means of uniting the various neighbourhood gangs under the umbrella 'Zulu Nation'.

'Bam said he had a Zulu Nation party coming up at the Bronx River Projects on Friday night. When Malcolm said he would like to come I told Bam to pull out all the stops because the guy behind punk rock was going to be with me.'

On the Friday evening Holman met McLaren and Rory Johnston in the foyer of Le Parker Meridien, the midtown hotel where they were staying; both were dressed to the nines in Pirate clothes. 'I was wearing low-rise Keds, jeans, nylon shirt, nylon jacket and chain,' says Holman.

'We were going to the Bronx. I knew we had better fit in but was too embarrassed to ask them to change. I thought they might be scared off. Anyway, I figured they were intrepid London types who had seen it all, so would be OK.

'The penny didn't even drop with them when cab after cab refused to take us. We didn't get lucky until the seventh, a gypsy cab driven by a Puerto Rican woman who said, "That's good for me, I live a few blocks from there so can knock off for the day."'

The taxi driver was nevertheless cautious. 'She said, "Here's what'll happen,"' recalls Johnston. '"You pay me up front, I'll pull up, you jump out and then you're on your own, I'm out of there." And that's exactly what happened.'

The Bronx River House Projects at East 174th Street consists of nine 100-storey low-income social housing buildings; at the time the neighbourhood was still devastated by the economic blight which hit New York in the late 1970s.

'We arrived at these burn-out projects, broken windows, garbage on the streets,' says Holman. 'We got out of the cab and started wending our way to a huge community centre surrounded by tenement buildings like a circle of wagons, and could hear a beat, like something out of Africa, so heavy and sweltering, vibrating through the area.

'By this time Malcolm and Rory were looking apprehensive and I was wondering whether this was such a good idea. Then we got inside the community centre and it was like Moses parting the waves. There must have been 1000 high school kids in there, shouting, dancing, fighting, throwing bottles. Seventy per cent black, 20 per cent Latino and about 10 per cent white.'

Johnston remembers a serious altercation after an audience member flashed a knife. 'It kicked off and Bambaataa's guys came and formed a wall around us,' he says.

At one stage Holman recognised that Bambaataa was playing the break from 'Mary Mary' by the Monkees, soon to become a hip-hop staple, and mixing it with the Jimmy Castor Bunch's early 1970s funk classic 'It's Just Begun'. 'I saw some kids were actually pogoing!' exclaims Holman. 'They must have seen white kids do it to punk on TV. But Malcolm and Rory hadn't noticed. They were concentrating on getting out alive. Malcolm said: "Michael, I think we'd better go," but I told him it was too late, that now we were safer inside than out on the street. That didn't make him or Rory feel any better but I steered them through and we got behind the rope with Bam, Jazzy Jay, Ikey C and some others.'

Soon Jazzy Jay – later to be a founder of Def Jam Recordings – took over the decks and started scratching. 'The kids went wild and in that flash of an instant, I saw Malcolm got it,' says Holman. 'His eyes widened and he understood and started raving about it. We stayed for a while but then he didn't need to see any more. He already had a plan. Three of the biggest Zulu Nation guards walked us back to our cab and he was off, talking about what he wanted to do.'

During the ride back to Manhattan, McLaren asked Holman to create a package of DJs, rappers, dancers and graffiti artists to act as a support for Bow Wow Wow's US debut at The Ritz in September.

'Malcolm told me he would get me $3000 to put together a revue – he didn't use that word but that's what he meant,' says Holman. 'This was more than I could have hoped for. Here was the guy who had done so much already recognising the worth of this scene which didn't even have a name.'

Although The Clash and Blondie had been first to make the links between rock and the new genre, McLaren's role in popularising hip-hop in America and around the rest of the Western world should not be underestimated, even if he was prone to exaggerate some of the aspects of this first encounter, later claiming, for example, that it was he who had struck up conversation with Bambaataa after he noticed the DJ was wearing a Sex Pistols T-shirt on a street in Harlem.

Importantly, McLaren related the new urban genre to punk. 'I've always been a punk rocker,' he explained a couple of years later. 'The Sex Pistols had a lot to do with the street and what was going on. It had a lot of politics and social awareness. Rap music seemed to be the natural black American true music of what was going on, on the streets of most cities, particularly New York.'[34]

For the former art student, the major attraction was that hip-hop's exploitation and manipulation of 'found' material slotted with his artistic practice.

'It was extraordinary,' McLaren told a group of hip-hop fans in the mid-1980s. 'As far as I could see the sound coming out was totally inarticulate, a load of rough noises that sounded a little like a guitar but sort of like a concrete chisel, right? And I realised the sound came from the way they were messing around with their hands on the decks, moving records backwards and forwards, moving back and forth between the two. In fact, it was making music out of other people's music.'[35]

The day after the visit to the South Bronx, McLaren was on fire with enthusiasm, and, during a meeting at RCA to discuss Bow Wow Wow providing music for a TV advert for Japanese make-up brand Shiseido, could barely contain his excitement about the revolutionary new approach to music that encompassed street art and style. Fellow Brit Steve Weltman, then an international executive at the company, suggested that McLaren make a record with the Zulu Nation. From this seed, an entirely new musical direction would blossom.

Chapter 29

Malcolm McLaren kept Steve Weltman's suggestion in mind when he returned to London in the summer of 1981 to prepare Bow Wow Wow for their US debut and work with Vivienne Westwood on a second catwalk collection.

His personal interactions with his former partner remained fraught and often centred on what he saw as her deliberate profligacy with the funds he was providing, such as insisting on using reams of expensive fabrics during sampling. These arguments were interspersed with brief sexual encounters, as McLaren later confirmed and as recorded by pattern cutter Lorraine Piggott's observation: 'If she got too difficult, he would fuck her and then he'd get what he wanted.'[1] Still and all, their fashion collaboration was by now fully reinvigorated. Having achieved their first substantial coverage in international media, Worlds End's rise to prominence coincided with the media-generated attempt to lift the downturn-hit country's mood by trumpeting the marriage of the fogeyish Prince Charles to the pert young aristocrat Lady Diana Spencer.

High fashion magazine editors pounced on the collection's sensual fabrics and voluminous cuts. 'Romance in recession?' asked British *Vogue*. 'Sounds like a non-starter (the Royal solution apart!). It's been in the air for months . . . swashbuckling out of Vivienne Westwood's Worlds End shop and blossoming into the fashion world.'[2]

Pirate garments were also featured across several pages in the same issue with a shoot in the Caribbean. Westwood's ambition of bringing the design business at 430 King's Road into the mainstream was being realised, and the heading 'The New Romantics decked in castaway cottons, pirate smocks, pantaloons' confirmed Worlds End's place at the forefront of the burgeoning new youth movement.

McLaren wasn't the only one who was struck by the coincidence that this edition of *Vogue* ran a Tony Snowdon portrait of Spencer in a ruffled collar shirt along with a giddy profile ('her fashion sense is far removed from the Royal tradition' gushed staff writer Antonia Williams).

'*Vogue* magazine start raiding the shop,' McLaren wrote in present-tense notes in 1997. 'We don't want their attention but we get dragged into the fashion press becoming their darlings. By creating a pantomimic display of piracy the shop attracts a much wider audience, including Diana Spencer and her fashion followers. We are the victims of an overnight success. Vivienne wants to become a "real" designer. I am trying to stay underground.'

One way of achieving this was to maintain engagement with cutting-edge music. Having brought in more cash for Bow Wow Wow by instructing bassist and de facto musical leader Leigh Gorman to organise a session for the lucrative Shiseido advertisement, McLaren returned to New York with the musicians at the beginning of the first British youth-quake in America since the 1960s.

The recent domination of East Coast media by The Clash was preceded by notable performances by Public Image (fronted by McLaren's former charge John Lydon) and followed by the arrival not only of Adam Ant with his McLaren-inspired mix of tribal beats and rapped lyrics but also a bunch of flamboyant young Londoners who were in town to showcase new British fashion and music heavily influenced by McLaren and Westwood. The hardcore of the New Romantic scene, this group included members of Spandau Ballet and Sade Adu, both of whom were set to become US million-sellers along with other Worlds End clientele such as Culture Club and Duran Duran.

Bow Wow Wow made a strong impression at The Ritz. 'Annabella skips un-self-consciously across the stage and sings engagingly, if somewhat tunelessly, while the group's guitarist, bassist and drummer pump out a brisk, precisely modulated rhythmic barrage,' wrote the *New York Times*'s influential critic Robert Palmer. 'The group's rhythms are still influenced by the Burundian recording, but they are varied and flexible rather than slavishly imitative. They seem able to synthesize their influences into appealing trash-pop as easily as they subvert Malcolm McLaren's image manipulation.'³

Palmer's latter suggestion was mistaken; for the time being Bow Wow Wow remained cast as their creator wished. Meanwhile, the Michael Holman-organised Zulu Nation collective of scratchers, rappers, DJs and dancers represented, for McLaren at least, the future.

'The audience was a bridge-and-tunnel new-wave crowd and here were breakdancers from the Bronx spinning on their heads while one guy on stage kept the beat with a basic rhythm machine from an organ,' says Leigh Gorman. 'At the same time there was a hierarchy of fifteen MCs who came on and rapped. We were standing by the stage with our mouths agape. When they finished we looked out at the audience and they were just as stunned.'⁴

With Rory Johnston now handling the day-to-day management, Bow Wow Wow embarked on the first of a series of intensive tours across America. 'We steadily built an upward trajectory,' says Johnston. 'The live reputation grew and everything came together.'

The touring gave McLaren the space to dedicate more time to his mushrooming plans for a solo musical career, as well as the design relationship with Westwood. Their next showcase at the autumn London Designer Collection was billed as 'Spring/Summer 1982', confirming the partnership was now in lockstep with the fashion business's seasonal schedule.

'Savage' – as the pair titled the new range (the title was soon corrupted to 'Savages') – demonstrated the pace at which they were turning over exciting new concepts and represented a shift towards the primitive and pagan cultures that had preoccupied them since McLaren's revelation in the Centre Pompidou library two years earlier.

McLaren wrote the text for the Savage showcard, which described the couple's intent to show 'clothes that are a mixture of old and new, put together to arouse those instinctive creation rites and work out the taboos that befell us'.⁵

Based around a number of prints of the tribal patterns in his copy of *Native Rawhide*, Savage scored the designers yet another positive reception from the fashion industry and the style media. For the collection, McLaren commandeered ideas from popular culture, even designing a heavy brimless hat with a veil that exposed only the eyes in tribute to the mask worn by the actor John Hurt in that year's arthouse hit, David Lynch's *The Elephant Man*, as well as Aertex vests with a dangling 'trunk' that connected the wearer's breasts.

Westwood continued to be foregrounded, but McLaren's contribution was recognised by those working behind the scenes. 'Malcolm was so busy and all over the place but it was strange: he was also always so on it, making sure that everything from the fit to the look to the silhouette fitted in with their latest collections,' says Carolle Payne, McLaren's assistant tasked with juggling his frenetic diary at Moulin Rouge.[6]

The Savage invitation also featured the *Déjeuner* image, sealing the synergy between Bow Wow Wow and the clothes, to Westwood's further discomfort. McLaren's publication of Andy Earl's photograph – he was paid £2000 for the picture – marked a downturn in the hostilities with Amy Dunn-Lwin, at least in the media. The sealing of the RCA deal, Johnston's even-handed involvement and her daughter's imprecations caused Dunn-Lwin to begin backing off from openly condemning McLaren. And, though the initial release of the *See Jungle!* LP featured a photograph of a clothed Lwin on the front, this was later replaced, with Dunn-Lwin's blessing, by the *Déjeuner* shot.

When the album stalled outside the top thirty in the British charts and at an unpromising 192 in the Billboard 200, the coincident success of Adam Ant – whose *Prince Charming* LP went to number one in the UK and spawned such worldwide hits as 'Stand & Deliver' – grated on the trio of musicians who had thrown their lot in with McLaren.

'Adam's success hurt them a great deal,' he admitted a couple of months after *See Jungle!*'s release, by which time a routine dispute became indicative of the widening gap between the group and their manager.[7]

During one of McLaren's increasingly frequent absences Leigh Gorman scheduled a meeting with RCA's Bill Kimber to discuss the single release of 'Go Wild in the Country'. 'Bill asked if he could cut the chorus in earlier to make it more radio-friendly,' says Gorman. 'I was impressed with his edit and told Malcolm it gave the song a more powerful structure.'

McLaren protested and urged Gorman to tell Kimber to revert to the original. 'I said: "I'm sorry Malc, I can't do it. I think he's right." And that act of defiance was really the beginning of the end.'

Gorman's instinct proved on the money. 'Go Wild' reached the top ten in Britain, providing Bow Wow Wow with the first of a run of hits. 'Malcolm admitted to me he had been wrong,' says Gorman. 'I could tell he was thinking, "I'm gonna do something else now."'

McLaren sprinkled oblique hints to the new musical project germinating in his mind during an encounter with journalist Johnny Black while 'Go Wild' was riding high in the charts. 'I don't think this is good time to put a rock band together,' he declared. 'If I was to do it again I would create a band that would be very instructional, not a social service, you can't have that arrogance now. What I mean is to invite people to become more intimate with each other, maybe in the form of dance.'[8]

This talk was inspired by exposure to another collection of ethnological field recordings he had encountered in the Centre Pompidou library. Released by Folkways Records in four volumes in the late 1950s and recorded across different continents, *Dances of the World's Peoples* compiled every style from Scottish waltzes to Italian tarantellas and Irish fairy reels. By the record company's own description, these were 'scholastic releases of interest', encased in sleeves with woodblock illustrations of such folkloric figures as medicine men and zombies. And the packaging contained the record label's illustrated inserts detailing dance instructions with potted histories as to how the steps had been developed and their social purpose. These were a gift to the research-minded McLaren.

Homing in on volume three's musical renditions from the Caribbean and South America, given the regions' slave-trade connections to Africa,

McLaren conceived a contemporary update, a musical travelogue with the working title 'Folk Dances of the World'. This, McLaren felt, would communicate his notion that the authenticity he identified from 1950s rock to hip-hop also existed in pre- and non-Christian and pre-industrial societies.

'Rock 'n' roll is jungle, it is ethnic, it's ultimately going to send you into a trance because it's magical and comes from Africa where it existed long before Jesus Christ was born,' McLaren told American broadcaster Peter Gordon. 'It's nothing new, but all about the pagan ideals that are ultimately very anti-Christian and have nothing to do with stepping in line and very little to do with the church-going minorities. With respect to the white man, the only thing I found that retained those wonderful pagan ideals was the square dance in the hills of the Appalachian mountains where they still don't realise this country's called the United States of America.'[9]

McLaren had been led to this conclusion by yet another Folkways release, a compilation called *All About Square Dances*. This featured a character named Piute Pete, actually Morris Kaufman, a Jewish clerk from the Lower East Side who had made his name in the 1940s on CBS radio shows calling the changes on such traditional songs as 'Buffalo Gals' and the rambunctious 'Duck for the Oyster', both of which featured on the *Square Dances* release.

McLaren said that the roots of the square dance lay in the primal urges that drove rock 'n' roll, reducing life to 'the real game of pursuit and capture or pursuit and rejection, not wholly unlike Rubens's famous painting *The Rape of the Sabine Women*, where marriage wasn't yet introduced into society but you had to find your mate: "Go round the outside, go round the outside, do-si-do your partner". This dance still exists and is often thought of as silly. People teach it at high schools but they don't know it meant something that was far closer to what we're talking about when we mention rock 'n' roll. A hundred years ago the church banned it and called the fiddle the instrument of the devil. "Duck for the oyster" means find that sweet part of that female body opposite you, "dig for the clam" is going a little further sexually and when you say "knock a hole in the old tin can" then you've laid the egg.

'I honestly believe that those guys in the Appalachian mountains calling out "Buffalo gals go round the outside" have something in common with the rapper who lives in the South Bronx in New York City. There's not much difference to that guy, in his magic man manner, scratching Ricky Nelson with James Brown, shoving in a sprinkling of Gary Numan and hollering over the top whatever social comment he may have.'

Years ahead of widespread appropriation of found sound in the form of sampling, the international explosion in club and dance culture, the coincident re-evaluation of folk, roots and Americana and the acceptance of world music in the West, it was McLaren who understood that these were the areas where popular music's destiny lay.

'I believe people will be more interested in dancing, getting involved in communication,' he told New York art periodical ZG. 'I'm going back to the roots and finding that people will gain inspiration from it. Putting something back in, rather than constantly taking out. I want to make the audience the stars. I want to do a record that can really inject a lot of ideas in people's cultures and the way to do that is to get them to dance. I think it's going to be very big.'[10]

Personally, McLaren related the expedition he was about to undertake to his involvement in punk. 'Having been responsible for an earlier DIY culture, I couldn't help feeling that I would be unquestionably a fraud if I didn't attempt to do it myself,' McLaren later wrote. 'So I stepped out from behind the curtain.'

Steve Weltman had by now left RCA for Charisma Records, the British prog rock-associated label run by the ebullient music entrepreneur Tony Stratton-Smith, whose boozy, gambling public persona was equated with the overblown music he released, and so utterly out of step with the austere early 1980s.

Undeterred by McLaren's troublemaking reputation, Weltman was a fellow London Jew who became enchanted by his spiel about fusing contemporary urban black sounds with world music, and signed McLaren to deliver the travelogue project as his debut LP for an advance of £45,000. McLaren announced that he would assume the role of the 'caller' – the person who bellowed instructions to square dancers – on the record and was given relatively free rein as to what music would appear. Wisely, Weltman instituted a security measure by assigning as producer Trevor Horn, who had made his name working with such glossy hit artists as ABC, Dollar and Spandau Ballet. Back-up was provided by Gary Langan, described by McLaren as the 'Rolls-Royce of recording engineers'.

Among those who had also been considered to produce were Robin Scott – still riding high from the success of 'Pop Muzik' – and, bizarrely, the British performer Jona Lewie, who scored major hits with unusual songs such as 'Stop the Cavalry' and 'You'll Always Find Me in the Kitchen at Parties'. These featured a conversational vocal style which, it was felt, might have favoured McLaren.

In the event the choice of Horn and Langan proved savvy, though McLaren had a job on his hands persuading Horn's late wife Jill Sinclair – who was also the producer's hard-bargaining business manager – as to his good intentions. Forthright by nature, the sceptical Sinclair hailed from a similar London Jewish background and marked McLaren down as a shyster.

'Jill constantly threatened me by phone: "What have you done to my Trevor? You'll never get me to pay to see *The Great Rock 'n' Roll Swindle*!"' said McLaren. 'I retorted, "I used to go out with girls like you when I was thirteen but I don't any more!"'

Horn countered McLaren's claim in 2019, pointing out that his wife recognised that the collaboration might bring benefits. 'She said, "Malcolm's risky but you might learn something,"' says Horn. 'And boy, did I learn something. I just loved Malcolm, he was so much fun to work with. So eccentric but essentially a very kind and considerate person, not like people think.'[11]

Just as Horn and Langan brought professionalism to the project, McLaren noted that his addition to Charisma's roster enhanced the label's credibility, in the same way as his delivery of the Sex Pistols to Virgin had transformed Richard Branson's company.

'There was naturally an excitement at Charisma to break the mould and do something different,' explained McLaren a couple of years before his death. 'Here I was, they thought, a manager-turned-artist. No one bothered to think that I had always been an artist from day one. Not a musician, but an artist.

'I decided to organise a tour of the places and origins of those exotic and magical sounds I had heard in the Beaubourg library. I wanted to record in places that would excite me, seduce me, and take me as far away from this Anglo-Saxon culture that I felt truly oppressed by. I wanted to escape from this muddy hole and find something cool elsewhere.'

Before recording began in earnest, McLaren was engaged in a frenzy of activity, which resulted in one of the high marks of his clothing collaborations with Westwood.

'Maybe fashion is the last enclave, maybe at the moment it is the most credible aspect for people in terms of media creativity,' said McLaren at the time. '[Fashion] is relevant now. Music and film mags and TV gossip is surrounded by an avalanche of fashion. Ten years ago you left art school and became a musician. Now you leave to become a fashion designer.'[12]

Just as McLaren's near-maniacal obsession with the look of music and the sound of fashion was reaching one of its customary peaks, so his enthusiasm for the latest refurbishment of the Chelsea premises as Worlds End diminished. 'Very bored with this Worlds End thing,' as he recalled two decades later, McLaren began a campaign to dismantle the interiors and facade – backwards-spinning clocks and all – in favour of a new manifestation he wanted to call Nostalgia of Mud, a phrase denoting the romanticising of primitive souls encountered in the writings of American social commentator Tom Wolfe.[13]

Sanely, Westwood would have none of it. She had poured her life into supporting McLaren and his ventures over the previous

decade-and-a-half and since they were no longer in a personal relationship, stoutly refused to countenance the move, which threatened to
undermine her fast-growing recognition.

Drawing on his Charisma advance, as well as funds from a £60,000
publishing deal with CBS and a US recording contract with Chris
Blackwell's Island Records, McLaren took a two-year lease on another
shop, 5 St Christopher's Place, in a narrow back alley leading off the
thoroughfare that had preoccupied him for so long: Oxford Street.

'It was filled with ridiculous boutiques,' McLaren wrote of St
Christopher's Place. 'I wanted to do everything I had done before, but
more extremely. I wanted the shop to look permanently closed down,
making it appear as if we were digging up the place to find the London
that lay under the pavements and eventually I found that all that lay
under there was mud.'

McLaren instructed Roger Burton, who had carried out the work on
Worlds End, to whitewash the windows and drape lengths of tarpaulin
from scaffolding across the double frontage 'to make it appear like an
archaeological dig under permanent excavation'. In front of the tarpaulin
were placed large clay renditions of the continents of the world, with
Africa in the centre and the shop name daubed on it by Nick Egan.

Inside, the ground floor was designed to resemble a ruined Regency
drawing room, with a gaping hole in the floor where rope-tethered steps
led to a basement in the centre of which was a cauldron of bubbling mud.
'I want a shop where the mere act of entering will cause physical harm,'
wrote McLaren in the 1990s. 'On opening the door visitors either have to
jump into a trough of mud or climb down the scaffolding.'

In one respect, Nostalgia of Mud, which opened in March 1982, can
be seen as an outcome of the investigations into the history of Oxford
Street McLaren began in 1969; he noted that St Christopher's Place is
parallel with the cul-de-sac Stratton Place, the location of Thomas De
Quincey's acquisition of his first bottle of laudanum. 'Under the paving
stones, the beach . . . The real London lies under the pavement,' wrote
McLaren. 'This is what Nostalgia of Mud means to me.'

In another light, the shop was a prime example of McLaren's singular practice, 'the idea of moving backwards through history and across cultural boundaries', remarked interiors expert Jane Withers. She described the edifice on completion as 'a crumbling world layered to reveal its own past, stretching from pseudo-classical grandeur to primitive origins'.[14]

And, as the 'ultimate in anti-fashion and anti-design', Nostalgia of Mud was also the culmination of McLaren's interest in creating disorienting environments masquerading as retail spaces. For more than a decade, from In the Back of Paradise Garage onwards, he had provoked expectations with the series of increasingly confrontational installations, and in his wake had inspired waves of challenging boutiques; contemporaneous with Nostalgia of Mud were such early 1980s outlets as Demob, run by a collective of former fashion students out of a barely refurbished fishmonger's in Soho, and Scott Crolla's ornately decorated Dover Street outlet.

'Living Yesterday Tomorrow . . . only interested in ruins,' wrote McLaren in notes about the outlet in the 1990s. 'Search for the authentic . . . same search for the original in music.'

Later, McLaren proudly recalled visitors' confusion on entering 5 Christopher Street, recounting how the film star Jack Nicholson delighted in skidding in the mud swashing around the basement floor. But for McLaren, Nostalgia of Mud represented a full stop. Now he was done with shopkeeping, 'anti-fashion' or otherwise.

For the fashion collection timed to coincide with the shop opening, he and Westwood advanced the Savage theme, abandoning the colourful prints on cotton and jersey in favour of such basic materials as roughly cut sheepskin and coarse sackcloth. As was usual, Westwood's initial samples, which included reproductions of eighteenth-century ballgowns from Nora Waugh's pattern book in delicate black cotton, were subjected to McLaren's fierce critique, not least because they lacked a unifying concept, and he memorably demanded that she 'listen to the caller and stop all this water-treading and voyeurism'.

Deeply affected by the tonal subtlety of Giorgio Morandi after a visit to the travelling retrospective of the Italian painter's work at New York's

Guggenheim Museum, McLaren declared the palette of the collection be restricted to earthy hues, and the high plains look gave rise to the name by which the clothing range also became known, 'Buffalo'.

And he provided Westwood with a copy of *Dances of the World's Peoples*, urging her to think about designing for 'a disco on Hadrian's Wall where all the kids would be folk dancing'.[15]

The hats, full skirts and toga dresses illustrated by William Johnson on the front of the LPs were given life by Nostalgia of Mud, and the connection was reinforced by repeat-printing the woodcuts onto a number of garments in various fabrics.

McLaren also inserted art references such as Matisse cut-outs on the trains of the toga dresses and included hoodies – at the time the preserve of sportspeople and b-boys – into the look. These were also printed with the *Dances of the World's Peoples* characters, as were stockings to be worn in the dishevelled style of the bag ladies then populating Manhattan's streets, as well as suede shoes that emulated the plastic bags these vagrants often wore on their feet. 'Hobos and tramps represent a different kind of adventurer and wanderer,' wrote McLaren in the 1990s. 'Buffalo Gals are my interpretation of romantic hobos swaggering through London.'

Other important stylistic additions from McLaren's researches included the tall, dented 'Appalachian Mountain Hat' (this was popularised in the twenty-first century as the 'Buffalo Hat' by Pharrell Williams), as well as the addition of a line of luxurious brassieres as outerwear.

McLaren had noted photographs of native tribeswomen adopting this approach, and led his girlfriend Andrea Linz to HRH The Queen's lingerie supplier Rigby & Peller in South Molton Street to be fitted for a cerise silk bra with satin insets. This became the sample for a Worlds End range to be worn over the hoodies and dresses, in keeping with his concept 'that, in the post-industrial age, the roots of our culture lie in primitive societies'.

And McLaren's sense of the absurd was present in the range of suits with baggy, hiked-up trousers and high-cut, double-breasted jackets based on that worn by Chico Marx, recalling his enjoyment of Marx

Brothers films at Euston's fleapit Tolmer Cinema in his student days. The 'Chico' jacket was produced in a range of materials, most successfully in sheepskin when sported with a Mountain hat.

Since Nostalgia of Mud marked a major leap forward in the fashion design partnership, McLaren engineered for the collection to be shown not just in London but also during Paris Fashion Week. Westwood's application to participate in the official prêt-à-porter schedule was declined, but McLaren's friend Pierre Bénain, who had organised the Sex Pistols' appearances at the Chalet du Lac, made the right connections; the resultant show at the Belle Époque tea salon Angelina's in the rue de Rivoli caused a stir, rendering the city's haute-couture shows out-of-touch in a single stroke. McLaren proclaimed to anyone who would listen that Westwood was the first British fashion designer to take to the Paris catwalks since Mary Quant in the Swinging Sixties.

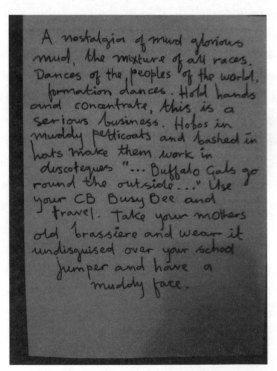

Notes for Nostalgia of Mud London catwalk show,
1982. Malcolm McLaren Estate.

The new designs very nearly didn't make it to Paris after it was decided that the entire collection should be driven from London by Nick Egan in the company of Gene Krell and the young Irish jeweller Tom Binns, who assisted Westwood in the Kingly Street studio and had fallen in with McLaren. 'We got held up at customs for six hours at Dover and nearly missed the show,' says Egan. 'We later found out that another designer had alerted them to us bringing the clothes over that way without the right carnets, but it all got sorted in the end. But it was still chaotic and very last minute, which is what I loved about working with Malcolm.'

In fact, McLaren's contemporaneous notes underscore his commitment to detail, complete with instructions to himself for such tasks as organising lighting and a sound mixer, the price of cladding for spray-can graffiti, organising photography for London's *Evening Standard* and booking video-mastering equipment so that Egan could transfer footage from U-Matics to domestic playable cassettes.[16]

The Angelina's show took place five days after another riotous appearance at Olympia's Pillar Hall. 'Paris had never seen or heard anything like it,' said make-up artist Yvonne Gold. 'Backstage, a mix of family and friends did everything: Vivienne's sons Ben and Joe, Gene, Tom . . .

'Nick Egan modelled, towering over heartthrob Nick Kamen who opened the show, heading up the convoy of models, Buffalo girls and friends. The concept or term "street casting" didn't exist back then, and those on the front row weren't celebrities but press and confused buyers from Bloomingdale's.

'I spent most of the show backstage, because it was just me and one assistant, with only seven minutes per face. The look was a two-toned rose and peach freshly fucked flush blush with mascara-less (unheard of) moody, hollowed eyes. Natural hair mingled with classical Greek headbands, braids and the occasional blonde, mud-caked dreadlock.'

For McLaren, the embrace of seasonal showcases of new collections made him increasingly uncomfortable, in that they eroded the sturdy independence that had been maintained at 430 King's Road. 'Catwalk shows changed the notion of the store completely,' he noted in the 1990s.

'Suddenly you were selling clothes and you intended to compete in the mainstream. You had become part of the fashion business.'

A key element of the Paris and London shows was McLaren's eclectic and ambitious ten-minute soundtrack. This was at a time when haute couture was presented silently or to the accompaniment of bland classical music. The Nostalgia of Mud extravaganzas opened with a sweep of the theme to William Wyler's 1958 cowboy epic *The Big Country* and segued into C. W. McCall's 1975 novelty country hit 'Convoy' as teams of Mountain-hatted girls and boys (in velvet suits with lapels beaded with shells at McLaren's instruction) strode the stage before breaking out into a square dance to Piute Pete's rendition of 'Buffalo Gals'. Tracks from *Dances of the World's Peoples* – a mazurka from Martinique, a song of the Peruvian Collaguas, a Haitian merengue – were interlinked by bursts of CB radio announcements with a recording of the bells of Notre Dame Cathedral (as a tip of the hat to the location) and the British comic singers Flanders & Swann's rendition of 'The Hippopotamus Song' (otherwise known as 'Mud, Glorious Mud') and, of course, Muddy Waters's 'I'm a Man'.

The soundtrack was created with Nick Egan – who also designed the catwalk invitations by reproducing the Nostalgia of Mud logo over a *Dances of the World's Peoples* insert – at the Camden Town recording studios run by Bernard Rhodes. 'Malcolm was formulating his ideas for what would become *Duck Rock*,' says Egan. 'By mixing up all those musical genres he basically made the demo for his album.'

One of the fallouts from the Nostalgia of Mud shows was that Westwood finally gave in to pressure from McLaren and others and sacked Michael Collins, who had worked at 430 King's Road since the mid-1970s. In the showcard he was credited with co-producing the Paris and London showcases with Mark Tarbard, and also for contributing ideas to the soundtrack. But the accusations surrounding Collins's drug abuse and pilfering came to a head. Westwood's biographer Jane Mulvagh confirmed that the designer for too long 'seemed oblivious to the fact that Collins was controlled by his addiction to heroin and funded his habit by selling large amounts of stock for cash at retail prices, register them as wholesale deals and pocket the difference'.[17]

This had become a source of fury for McLaren, since the money he was pouring into the Worlds End business was either being frittered away by Westwood or drained by dubious characters.

The Nostalgia of Mud shows closed to the aural backdrop of a trio of Bow Wow Wow songs, including their new single, a version of the 1960s garage-rock classic 'I Want Candy'.

'RCA could see it was going to be a hit and decided to shoot the video in LA,' says Egan. 'Malcolm sent me in his place to keep an eye on things. His only instruction was that I should make sure there were no candy canes in it. But me, I was having a great time and the video ended up being really corny with, of course, candy canes in shot.'

But the weight RCA put behind 'I Want Candy' added to McLaren's disillusionment. 'I was ashamed of it,' he announced the following year. 'It wasn't anything to do with what I originally intended that group to be. I suddenly saw my position as useless. I'd rather be working selling books in Foyles than have to sit in an RCA marketing meeting discussing how we'd flog "I Want Candy".'[18]

With MTV taking off, the clip increased Bow Wow Wow's profile across the Atlantic, and the newfound interest in the group threw McLaren's absences further into relief.

One distraction was yet another attempt to create an artists' stable by signing the singer Pip Gillard to Charisma Records in a country-lite guise McLaren named She Sherriff. His plan was to recast the big-selling but middle-aged country-and-western genre for a young audience; he told industry execs he was aiming for a 'sound which is ambient, truthful and untreated, not bastardised in studios'.[19]

With a great deal of media interest, promo photos by *The Face* photographer Janette Beckman and a Charisma-funded video, She Sherriff failed to deliver on the promise. Her only release was a perfunctory single version of the obscure Skeeter Davies track 'I Forgot More Than You'll

Never Know About Him', backed by a limp McLaren-penned slow blues pastiche, 'This House Is for Let'.

This failed to chart and Gillard was soon dropped by Charisma, but McLaren was moving too fast for this blip to become a setback. 'It's difficult to put Malcolm into perspective these days,' says Nick Egan, who designed the She Sherriff single sleeve. 'His influence was so huge that if he had an idea he wouldn't even have to demo it to a record company. He'd tell them, "I'm gonna make a single" and a company like Charisma would go, "Great! Go and do it." There was trust in him to deliver a record that people would be reading about, wearing the clothes on the sleeve and dancing to. This was good news for Malcolm, because he was easily bored. If it didn't work, it would all be done and dusted within three months and he'd move on.'

That this restlessness was undoing his relationship with Bow Wow Wow was not of great concern. After two-and-a-half years, the length of the existence of the Sex Pistols, working with the musicians had become a pedestrian experience. 'Pop culture is no longer subversive, it's all-round family entertainment,' McLaren announced. 'I think clothing is more subversive now; I know that because my clothes are selling across the board from kids off the street to extremely wealthy people worldwide. The concept of things is becoming more important than the product. Bow Wow Wow are talked about more as a concept than as an act. The people in it are irrelevant, buying the record is irrelevant, but it is important that their sleeve looked like the *Déjeuner sur L'Herbe*, or the cassette packaging, or Annabella's hairstyle, or the concept of the sound: now most of these are my ideas so maybe it's my fault that they haven't succeeded.'[20]

Such was McLaren's disinterest that Leigh Gorman took matters into his own hands, tracking him to a New York hotel room and reversed the charges on a call from a phone-box at Liverpool Street railway station.

'By this time he was never around, either when we were on the road or back at home,' says Gorman. 'On that call I confronted him and asked, "What the fuck's going on?" He started talking about recording his own album, things got heated and I told him to eff off. We didn't speak again for a decade.'

It fell to the diplomatic Rory Johnston to negotiate a path between the disgruntled group members and McLaren when he next visited the UK. 'In a traditional curry house in Regent Street Malcolm asked me whether I would be willing to move to London and manage the group in partnership with him. He even said I could take his apartment in Bloomsbury, because he was going to be travelling the world. That wouldn't have worked, with Malcolm off the scene but still pulling the strings.'

After some discussion, McLaren agreed to relinquish his role, and an industry-standard settlement was reached in which he received his commission for the duration of his agreement with Bow Wow Wow.

During this trip Johnston gained further insight into the increasingly curious relationship between the separated McLaren and Westwood and their son, ferrying the pair by car to a posh boarding school in the countryside attended by Joe Corré, then fourteen. 'It was strange to see them in that context, and also for Joe to be there in the first place,' says Johnston. 'I really felt for him. It was weird.'

The boy wasn't to see much of his father over the coming months as McLaren went in search of the field recordings that would comprise his debut LP.

Since the Sex Pistols collapse and his Paris sojourn of 1979, England had lost its allure for McLaren. 'We're all very sophisticated in this country, more than any other country in the world, so we tend to overexaggerate what people really care about and need,' he explained to Johnny Black. 'It's because we're an island and we're protected; since the seventeenth century we've been the heart of the world, the industrial revolution, the first civil war, the inventors, and we've never been invaded, very secure, cocooned, extremely eccentric, great purveyors of taste, tremendous colonisers, terrible snobs, eclectic and the most un-European, most worldly, most original and without a doubt the most creative, not necessarily in the visual arts or writing, but more in the terms of understanding how to put things together.

'Mind you, in the last couple of years, London has lost its edge, maybe due to an age of conservatism. It used to be a radical hotbed, more conniving, more sly. It no longer has an underground, and that was an important thing. It had it in the fifties, the sixties and the seventies, when it was punk, a vulgar, media-oriented form. It produced the word anarchy, and gave every child a critique, whether he painted it on his back or spouted it in class.'

Now, as well as planning the recording of his forthcoming debut LP, McLaren talked excitedly about an invitation he had received from the culture department of the West German government to mount an exhibition in Berlin. This would, McLaren said, convey his renewed interest in the visual arts and in particular painting, the form he had forsworn back in 1969.

McLaren described the show – which did not materialise – as 'an exhibition of pictures and music which tries to bring painting to the modern world and make it as modern as the world it exists in. Revitalise the idea of painting as a fast, expressive, simple way of putting across ideas. The pencil is a far quicker and better means of expression than video.'[21]

McLaren's response to the apathy he identified was to become even more actively engaged in the project still known as 'Folk Dances of the World'. He eschewed the option of using the new and expensive technology to build tracks from samples such as the Fairlight system – which his friend Robin Scott had shown him – in favour of recording indigenous music makers in situ and then using the musical results as the basis for a volume of contemporary aural collages.

In this way, McLaren intended the LP as a postmodern pastiche, reinventing the Folkways scholastic exercises just as he had presented Let It Rock as a 1950s sitting room in early 1970s Chelsea, Nostalgia of Mud as an archaeological dig in the centre of London's shopping district or Le Déjeuner sur l'Herbe as a portrait of an untameable rock group. But this time McLaren would be the central figure, the caller and musical overseer.

With Steve Weltman's backing and funding for a series of promo films made by pick-up teams in various locations so that a long-form video would coincide with the eventual album release, McLaren gathered up Trevor Horn, Gary Langan and Nick Egan and left for the melting pot of

New York, where the kaleidoscopic flavours and mix of nationalities would bring the world of ethnic music to them.

With a budget that eventually ballooned to £100,000 (five times the average cost of most LPs in this period), time slots were booked at the state-of-the-art Power Station studios in Hell's Kitchen but, initially at least, McLaren gave no indication as to exactly what he intended to record.

Horn and Langan became swiftly acquainted with their client's unusual methods when he went missing for their first week, checking out various musical avenues with Egan and a friend, the fashion agent Terry Doktor, who represented his and Westwood's designs on the East Coast.

'It was alarming at first because there was nothing to rest back on,' said Horn. 'Even though the idea of working with Malcolm and not having any particular rules appealed to me, of course it's like wanting to go swimming and you know it's cold but when you jump in you're a bit freaked by how cold it really is.'[22]

McLaren eased Horn and Langan into the tempo of the project by taking them to Negril, the club at 12th and 2nd Avenues in the East Village where Michael Holman had opened the world's first hip-hop night. 'It was one of the most enlightening things I'd ever seen,' says Langan. 'It had a whole culture of entertainment there with all these different people reacting to the music. It was a pivotal moment in my life – these kids showed me that we really could do anything we wanted.'[23]

McLaren also made a beeline for Folkways's offices in midtown's West 46th Street, and struck up an acquaintance with an Afro-Cuban employee known as Kuango, who set up a session which proved uninspired, though one of the musicians turned them on to a group of seven drummers who were also Santería priests devoted to the Lucumí cult.

When brought to the Power Station, the priests drank and stripped to their waists before playing a single track 'calling down their ancient deities' on their batá drums over several hours. This mesmerised McLaren but bemused his production team. 'The rhythms they played go way back to the days before they were slaves, back to their original homelands in West Africa,' said McLaren. 'They made me appreciate the magic in music. I literally went into a trance in the studio when they were playing their drums. So did Trevor Horn. Neither of us could understand the music the following day, except that I just believed the understanding of it wasn't important as long as you could feel its power.'[24]

According to McLaren, Horn announced he was quitting over the prospect of condensing the beats into tracks that would appeal to Western ears. 'He complained he couldn't "find the one" in this long, meandering groove,' said McLaren in 2008. 'It wasn't commercial. He felt he was wasting his time. But I found a musical anthropologist who explained to Trevor that the "one" was in the spaces, so no one could steal the music. He convinced Trevor to continue.'

Soon other musicians were summoned by McLaren to the studio to record more backing tracks, including a collective of Peruvian pipe players, a Dominican group called Lewis Khalif and his Happy Dominicans, most of them bakers and car mechanics by trade who played semi-professionally at weddings and parties and provided a furious merengue, and a Colombian marching band.

Through Holman, McLaren had also been turned on to the wild rap radio show hosted by a crew known as the World's Famous Supreme Team on New Jersey FM station WHBI 105.9. He decided to bring on board their most prominent members, Larry Price and Ron Larkins Jr, known respectively as See Divine the Mastermind and Just Allah the Superstar.

By day Price and Larkins were 'Three-card Monte' hustlers on 42nd Street who used the takings from gullible tourists to fund their hilarious programme, which featured phone-ins, MC skits and raps over scratched records. Recordings of these, McLaren determined, should be intercut with the album tracks and provide links for the LP.

'Hip-hop is simply black punk rock and they were my ideal Afro-American punks,' McLaren said of the World's Famous Supreme Team in the 2000s. 'Their music was ecological, recycled. Their ideas were genius! The radio shows had to be the way to re-introduce, re-invent, re-locate pop music to its authentic roots across the globe, by simply cutting up and rearranging those tracks I'd spent time collecting at the Beaubourg library. I now had a firm grip on the concept.'

Dedicated to incorporating the square dance at the heart of the project, before he left for New York McLaren had picked music historian and publisher Tony Russell's brains. 'I went to his offices in Denmark Street and played him a bunch of albums of old-time music,' says Russell.[25]

According to Russell, McLaren had already done a deal of research and hoped to record a Virginian outfit called Whit Sizemore and the Shady Mountain Ramblers. 'Unimpressed when he heard them on record, McLaren cast about for something closer to his ideal of archaic purity,' wrote Russell a couple of years later.

A few weeks before he encountered McLaren, Russell had been reconnoitring for a Channel 4 documentary on Appalachian music in East Tennessee and, in the remote Roan Mountain community, encountered the Hilltoppers, a family group led by Joe Birchfield – a blind seventy-five-year-old fiddler – and his banjo-playing brother Creed, seventy-seven.

Russell played McLaren some of their songs. The Hilltoppers' 'musical and visual impact' made a good impression. 'I gave him directions for finding them, a considerable operation in itself,' wrote Russell. 'None of the band members is on the phone and the only way to arrange anything with them is to call up a relative in the nearby town of Hampton who can pass messages to them.'[26]

McLaren visited the Birchfields and set up a recording session at Tri State Recording Co studios in Kingsport in June 1982. The Hilltoppers arrived with several children in a purple VW traveller van complete with purple carpeting. Some family members were under-nourished in appearance and afflicted by strabismuses. 'McLaren had met them before, of course, so he knew what to expect,' said Langan. 'But Trevor and I just looked at each other and our jaws dropped.'

The culture clash between the British production team and the Birchfields was magnified when McLaren attempted to pay the musicians for the day's recording session with a $100 bill. They hadn't previously encountered such high amounts in single denominations and, believing the note not to be legal tender, insisted it be broken down into $5 bills.

According to Horn, the Hilltoppers' music did not match their authentic look, and after they were sent packing the Tri State proprietor provided utility pickers to lay down the basics of two songs, 'Buffalo Gals' and 'Duck for the Oyster'.

'A bunch of guys showed up,' recalled Horn in 2013. 'They all had that slightly tough, hard-bitten American look until they smiled. They set up and they could obviously play really well. They were crazy guys. I remember going to the toilet and there were five of them doing great big lines of blow off the sink.'[27]

Enthused by the Tennessee trip, in particular the sessioneers' tumultuous version of 'Duck for the Oyster', McLaren struck on a new name for the LP during a conversation back in New York with Nick Egan and Terry Doktor.

'We were sitting in Times Square shooting ideas about what it could be called and someone, I can't remember who, suggested *Duck Rock*,' recalls Egan. 'First off we all went "No . . ." and then suddenly all three of us said, "Yes". It was too funny and weird to pass up.'

With his confrères, McLaren was absorbing new cultural experiences like a sponge, becoming fascinated by the fad among teams of black teenage girls for jump rope competitions on the sidewalks and in hoop courts.

The sport – known as Double Dutch – had been devised by New York police as a means of diverting black youth from crime, and became part of the hip-hop world when McLaren's British acquaintance, the influential night-time entrepreneur Ruza 'Kool Lady' Blue, staged Double Dutch competitions at her Chelsea nightclub The Roxy.[28] 'The hip-hop scene was so male-dominated I wanted to infuse some female energy,' says Blue, who had seen the skipping performed on a McDonald's TV advert and invited McLaren along to witness the athletic enthusiasm of the participants.[29]

'Back in the day when New York was called New Amsterdam, rope-skipping was one of the Dutch colonial games played along the water-front,' McLaren later observed. 'The NYPD had reintroduced Double Dutch to teenagers and their teams had various names: Five Town Diamond Skippers, the Ebonettes, Ford Green Angels, the Golden Angels . . .'

So popular was the activity that it had already inspired local hits such as the previous year's 'Double Dutch Bus' by funkster Frankie Smith, but McLaren believed that it could have international appeal way beyond the five boroughs.

He also learned that Afrika Bambaataa took his surname from Bambatha kaMacinza, the early twentieth-century African warrior who led a victorious revolt against British rule in the South African district of KwaZulu-Natal. This information provided the spark for a shift of base from New York to South Africa for the next burst of recording, where McLaren set about working with local black musicians, then a rarity in the apartheid era.

'The Zulus fought against the Redcoats with wooden clubs and a Zulu dance that magically gave the brave warriors nine lives,' said McLaren in 2008. 'They decimated the English army, sending a message around the world of England's shameful motives. So inspired to film and record that dance performed by Zulus, I found myself following the name Bambaataa all the way to Kwazululand.'

There, with help from A&R staff at Charisma's local record distribu-tor, he enlisted musicians to record more tracks for *Duck Rock*, with night-time sessions overseen by Horn and Langan at RPM studio in Johannesburg. The city's curfew sometimes necessitated the musicians sharing the visitors' rooms at the posh Carlton Hotel in the city centre when they weren't working nights in the studio.

'No one black was allowed to be seen on the streets after 7 p.m.,' explained McLaren. 'On certain nights, Trevor, Gary and I had to share with seventeen Zulus dotted around our beds as curfew became a problem. I would open my hotel door in the morning to several surprised waiters with trolleys crammed full to feed all these Zulus huddled on my floor.'

During downtime, the musicians told McLaren tales of the dance, which granted warriors nine lives during the Zulu wars that led to the Bambatha Rebellion.

'A hundred years ago, faced with the onslaught of an English army with muskets and Gatling guns trying to trample over his turf, King Chaka took out a simple drum and beat it and made sure his warriors did this dance by stamping in time with their bare feet on the ground until the earth beneath them cracked,' said McLaren the following year. 'Thereafter they would swing up one foot so that it hit them in the face as a demonstration of their prowess and they finished by falling on their arses so hard they ultimately pissed blood. Having finished the dance they realised they didn't have to fear anybody. They confronted the English army with nothing more than a few sticks and a dance which they did in unison. The English were so frightened they were massacred. That's why the Zulus are noted for being powerful warriors. They are not much bigger than you or me. But they had a wonderful dance.'[30]

McLaren was compelled to make a record 'to put history right', and concocted lyrics for himself to chant for the song 'Zulus on a Time Bomb'. This became one of the first recording sessions where McLaren made a vocal contribution to the project, though Trevor Horn later appeared set on diminishing his efforts.

'One particular day I said to Malcolm: "OK it's time to do the vocals," ' related Horn a couple of years after the South African recording sessions. 'He went into the studio and put his headphones on and it began to dawn on me and Gary that Malcolm had never done this before. He was making the strangest noises, [sound] like nothing I'd ever heard before was coming out of him. My engineer was on a percentage of my income – that was the way I was paying him – and I said to him: "There goes your bonus for the year." '

McLaren recalled the occasion differently: 'We were working nights and most of the Zulus were kipping on the floor of the studio and everyone was smoking various herbal tobaccos so I decided to sing, and woke everybody up!'[31]

However the session began, it is a fact that McLaren had recorded in a studio previously, not just the voiceover sections for *The Great Rock 'n' Roll Swindle* but also the perfectly serviceable vocal for 'You Need Hands' at Mickie Most's RAK. It is not as though the milieu from which McLaren emerged – which included the likes of Richard Hell, Johnny Rotten and Joe Strummer – produced traditionally proficient singers. But it seems likely that the seasoned technician Horn remained uncomfortable that McLaren's willingly amateurish spontaneity couldn't be tamed by any amount of knowhow and was thus effectively beyond his control.

'I think my voice is quite hooky,' said McLaren during that period. 'The difference between working with me and most other artists for Trevor is that I don't give a damn. I'm not really very precious. I go for spontaneity because I get bored in these studios. I'm a one-take kind of guy. Also, in terms of the interpretation of the song, I don't really hold anybody to anything too rigid. If it seems to be working then I go with that and fit my idea around it. I don't hang people up. Get on with the job. Get the money.'[32]

The latter remark did McLaren no favours in the 'straight' music business circles such as those occupied by Horn. Once again insecurity was leading McLaren to play up to the 'Swindler' role even though his untrained vocal technique provided one of the most beguiling elements of *Duck Rock*'s success. Nick Egan, however, confirms Horn's view.

'Malcolm could be terrible in the studio,' says Egan. 'He was often very nervous and needed to drink a lot to get in the zone. Trevor did a great job in patching together the best bits from vocal takes, though on songs like "Duck for the Oyster" that is undeniably Malcolm: impish and there to cause trouble.'

Less attractive was McLaren and Horn's repurposing of existing songs without credit to the originators. In mitigation, Horn later claimed that the various groups who provided musical accompaniment were paid £1000 each for two weeks' work in the studio, 'many times the going rate in South Africa,'[33] and, according to McLaren, 'when one of the musicians got married during the session, Trevor and I gave him a wedding reception and a night of his own in a Carlton Hotel suite'.

McLaren was so delighted at the musicians' response to his tales of the Sex Pistols that he wrote autobiographical lyrics for a song entitled 'Punk It Up':

A Sex Pistol, a Sex Pistol
That's what I am
Irresponsible I say
Mummy yeah!
I know you think I'm horrible
Believe me babe
Never did like school
No! Never! Yeah!

McLaren also raised the discomfort levels for Horn and Langan by insisting that the recording sessions move to Soweto, the poverty-stricken all-black township bordering Johannesburg's mining belt. Here he wrote the lyrics for a song named after the locale, about the inhabitants' hard lives, recording with local superstars the Mahotella Queens.

'It was a very frightening experience,' said Horn. 'That song is about the road to Soweto. Those people were like the song, chirpy and optimistic despite the horrible circumstances.'[34]

When taping edged towards dusk, Horn and Langan high-tailed it back to the Carlton Hotel, but McLaren was happy to hang with the locals after dark.

'Sometimes I found myself sleeping in a garage in Soweto so I could rehearse the following day,' he said. 'There was no electricity. We used car batteries to power the electric guitars.'

Once recording had ended, Horn and Langan returned to London, but McLaren stayed to organise the filming of three video clips for potential singles recorded there.

Directed by Ian Gabriel, the joyous promo for 'Zulus on a Time Bomb' was made outside the all-male Zulu Mine Hostel in Johannesburg's

Jeppestown and featured a re-enactment of the slaughter of British troops during the Bambatha Rebellion. These were intercut with scenes of general mayhem, including dancers who had appeared in the West End hit *Ipi Tombi*, and the sacrificial slaughter of a bull before a feast.

With the film crew, McLaren returned to Soweto for the clip for the song he had named after the township. Tanned, and in a grubby white Chico suit from the Nostalgia of Mud collection with matching white bucket hat, McLaren appeared wild-eyed and evidently having the time of his life, rolling in the clay earth and declaiming through a bullhorn.

According to Trevor Horn, this film, and another for 'Punk It Up', were made on the hoof. 'He couldn't get a permit so, with two armed bodyguards and a suitcase full of money he and the film crew got the train to Soweto,' says Horn. 'He bribed the train driver and the station master with cash so that they would take the train back and film it coming into the station, and walked around spotting people: "Here, you, the guy with the donkey, here's $200, wanna be in my film?" '

Back in London, Horn and Langan had begun assembling the basic tracks recorded in New York, Tennessee and South Africa, working with session musicians and arrangers Anne Dudley, J. J. Jeczalik and Thomas Dolby on overdubbing a range of instrumentation including synthesisers as well as samples and an orchestral string section, while McLaren finalised his lyrics and recorded his vocals.

McLaren was by now particularly close to Nick Egan and jeweller Tom Binns. 'Tom and I became Malcolm's foot soldiers,' says Egan. 'If he and I were dissatisfied about some aspect of *Duck Rock* while it was being made, Malcolm would push us forward, telling me: "You go in and tell Trevor Horn that he can't get away with that. You fucking tell him." So I would be upfront, telling Trevor "Malcolm thinks this or that", and Malcolm would wait and then step in.'

With passion from everyone involved in the project, the musicians' empathic contributions, and Horn and Langan's technical knowhow and skill, McLaren began to make sense of the tapes that had been amassed:

for example, from the recording with the Lucumí cultists came three tracks named after Afro-Cuban deities: album opener 'Obatala' (the god of iron and war), 'Song for Chango' (storm and lightning) and 'Legba' (fertility). Here were McLaren's ambitions for contemporary takes on Folkways-style field recordings made manifest.

Initially attempts at laying down a straightforward version of 'Buffalo Gals' came to naught, and one night, over dinner, McLaren revealed to Horn he had written a new rap entitled 'ET Come Home'. He announced that he wanted to record this to scratching and MCing by the World's Famous Supreme Team in tribute to the Spielberg movie, which had taken the Western world by storm.

'I said: "Why don't we do a rapping, scratching version of "Buffalo Gals"?' and he said: "Yeah!"' says Horn.[35] McLaren arranged for See Divine and Just Allah to be flown to London from New York. While they were happy to contribute, they refused to sing the 'Buffalo Gals' lyrics – 'Nah, we can't do that – that's Ku Klux Klan shit. That's what the KKK dance to' – so McLaren took up the task, with Horn beating time on his chest so that he maintained the rhythm.

According to Horn, the track took two weeks to complete. The result was stunning, from the opening war whoop and samples from a Kool & the Gang live track, through the Tri-State sessioneers' rootsiness and the various verbal interjections – 'All that scratching is make me itch', 'You know it', 'Promenade!', 'Too much of that snow white' – to the World's Famous Supreme Team's epic rap, McLaren's clipped instructions and the Zulu choir providing the refrain: 'She's looking like a hobo.'

That this was a stylistic aural collage to rival McLaren's work in fashion, interiors and design was entirely lost on the record company. Not only were the bills arriving from his overseas adventures, but Charisma was deeply in debt as a result of the owner Tony Stratton-Smith's profligacy, so tensions were running high when McLaren cued up 'Buffalo Gals' for executives.

'It was greeted poorly by almost all at the record company,' recalled McLaren. 'The radio plugger Phil Hardy was so outraged he refused to take it to radio and declared it was "not music", claiming it was McLaren's *Great Rock 'n' Roll Swindle Part 2*. Tony Stratton-Smith didn't believe me when I said people danced on their heads to this beat in the middle of the streets of New York. He only wondered if I was going to dance on my head too. He suggested I think about how I was going to repay the company for what this project had cost them so far. It all suddenly looked bad. The only person who stood up for me was the press lady: a young American, new in her job.'

Charisma execs announced that they were preparing legal proceedings, on twin bases: that McLaren had grossly overspent (Nick Egan's hotel costs in New York came to $20,000 alone) and that he was in breach of the contractual obligation to deliver music of acceptable commercial value. McLaren responded by plotting with Nils Stevenson, who had moved on from his days as Sex Pistols roadie to work in the music business managing Siouxsie & the Banshees, to leak the track.

Over a weekend, Stevenson passed a tape to David 'Kid' Jensen, a prominent DJ at London's influential Capital Radio on condition that it be played that day.

'Nils explained it was exclusive to them,' said McLaren. 'His parting shot was, "It looks as if McLaren may have another court case on his hands. Check it out!" That clinched it and within the hour all of London heard "Buffalo Gals" for the first time. By Monday morning Charisma was fielding calls from radio stations all over the country demanding why they hadn't been serviced with the track. Charisma couldn't help but bite the bullet and release the record. The rest is history.'

Often there was justification in accusations of hyperbole in regard to McLaren, but his claim holds that the release of 'Buffalo Gals' caused a sea-change of significance in popular music terms to rival the advent of punk. It remains a hip-hop touchstone and one of pop's most sampled songs. The success may also be attributed to the promo video, which was overseen by McLaren and shot guerrilla-style by the cinematographer Ron Fortunato on the sidewalks and amid the skyscrapers of New York.

With models square-dancing in Times Square in full Nostalgia of Mud regalia and striking eye make-up McLaren had taken from Darryl Hannah's replicant character in Ridley Scott's *Blade Runner,* the clip shone a light on the vibrant street culture that had exploded out of the South Bronx since his visit to the Zulu Nation with Michael Holman and Rory Johnston the year before.

Graffiti kingpin Donald 'Dondi' White was filmed creating a giant spray-can backdrop while breakdancing members of the Rock Steady Crew did their thing and McLaren, in an ensemble which included a sheepskin Chico jacket and Mountain hat, revelled in taking on the persona of the demented caller.

'With the evolutionary process of capitalist society, where we suddenly realize there's going to be less rather than more for everyone, it's making people decide what's important in their lives,' he told *Sounds*. 'People aren't so concerned with product, they're getting more concerned with content. Suddenly quality's come back in a very major way. People are looking to see what's in the magic boxes they buy. And if they buy too many boxes that turn out to be empty, then they stop buying. That's the record industry now, they're crying wolf because they've sold too much rubbish for too long.'[36]

On release 'Buffalo Gals' went top ten in Britain and other countries around the world, but US resistance emanated from the country's conservative, white rock-oriented music business and its relatively new vehicle, MTV.

With the backing of his US label Island, McLaren lobbied the channel's top brass, but to no avail. 'They objected that the people in my video were the sort who would terrorise, rape and steal from his suburban, white viewers,' claimed McLaren. 'I protested: "I invented the Sex Pistols, discovered Billy Idol, gave Chrissie Hynde her first shot, delivered Adam Ant a new look, created Bow Wow Wow, and, with them, put Boy George on the map. You owe me!" It fell on deaf ears.'

On Island's advice, McLaren travelled to Birmingham, Alabama, where the song had proved a breakout at an urban music radio station. 'I was greeted by a large African-American DJ who bawled, "Malcolm *McLaine*, you can't be Malcolm *McLaine* ... Malcolm *McLaine* is black!"' recalled McLaren.

'I explained, "I am Malcolm McLaren and I am from London, England." The DJ took a moment, spun around as if to face his audience and declared "Malcolm McLaren, he ain't black, he's white! But he's all right! He's from London, England ..."'

Without MTV's support, however, the single failed to break into the Hot 100 and peaked at number thirty-three in the US dance club chart. Nevertheless, the popularity of the song in the UK proved sufficient for Charisma to back off from its legal posturing and pave the way for the release of more singles, though the company's financial difficulties continued to delay the *Duck Rock* LP.

At Charisma's Christmas party that year, McLaren was confronted by singer and label-mate Peter Gabriel, who scolded him for exploiting the work of others. 'He accused me of treating musicians like cattle. I was reminded vaguely of Alfred Hitchcock when he was asked to comment on actors,' said McLaren who noted that, not long afterwards, Gabriel founded the world music festival WOMAD.

Nick Egan witnessed the attack. 'Malcolm gave as good as he got,' says Egan. 'Gabriel had no idea what he was talking about. His accusations of cultural appropriation weren't valid. What Malcolm was doing was taking a mix of elements, blending them with loads of others and in the process coming up with his own interpretation. Apart from anything else, the *Duck Rock* musicians were paid and treated really well.'

Trevor Horn was also adamant that contributors had been accommodated. 'The Africans got married on what we paid them,' he pointed out to journalist Paul Rambali. 'The Cubans charged us a lot of money, they really had their heads screwed on. The Dominicans charged us a fortune. *They* screwed *us*!'[37]

The majority of the *Duck Rock* tracks had been completed at Horn's studio a couple of months earlier, as confirmed by the inclusion of several in the soundtrack for McLaren and Westwood's fourth catwalk collection 'Punkature', which was again shown in Paris – this time as part of the official programme at the Chambre Syndicale in the Louvre Palace – and at London's Olympia.

As well as songs by Afrika Bambaataa, Leadbelly and Sam Cooke, the sequence concocted by McLaren with Nick Egan and Gene Krell included 'Buffalo Gals', 'Soweto' and 'Legba' and ended with the frenetic 'Merengue'.

Also known as 'Hobo-Punkature', the new clothing range demonstrated that, in spite of his prolonged absences and growing detachment from Westwood, the design relationship remained intact, at least for the time being, and was replete with his concepts and cross-cultural flourishes, from the overprinting on full skirts of stills from *Blade Runner* to the graffiti-style decoration of pillars with such slogans as 'She's looking like a hobo'.

Among the designs were items made from domestic materials: clingy tops in stitched and dyed dishcloth patches, a cardigan with giant buttons fashioned by Tom Binns from the lids of Vim scouring-powder containers.

For the showcard, McLaren wrote a largely unpunctuated sing-song statement, which quoted the Supreme Team's 'Buffalo Gals' rap: 'Grand grand grand p p punkature – punk punk punkature looking looking looking like a hobo medi-evil yeah my medi evil hobo girl! check it out! check it out! yeah inside out! back to front! wet like velvet dry like rust – it's a pity she's so dirty she's only dancing to be friendly – so silly she makes me blush so so pretty she drives me loco! Vivienne Westwood – pregnancy in its infancy made to look pretty old and crazy – anarchy in a black country!'[38]

After the Paris show, several players in the Italian fashion industry began to flock around McLaren and in particular Westwood. *Vogue Italia*'s influential Lucia Raffaelli introduced them to her husband Alberto, who, after a special showcase, reached agreement to manufacture Worlds End lines through his Italian company GLR. The negotiations with Raffaelli had been smoothed by Carlo D'Amario and Giannino Malossi, two publicists for the larger-than-life industry character Elio Fiorucci.

Little did McLaren and Westwood know it, but these discussions were to sow the seeds for their partnership's destruction within a year.

For the time being, however, business appeared to be as usual. In an interview after the London show for Japanese television, McLaren was voluble, explaining that Punkature set out to accentuate authenticity and integrity, through 'the discovery of people's roots, because most clothes look so packaged. The idea is to make the clothes look as unpackaged as possible, with real values.'

The exchanges with the TV crew provided insights into the complicated tensions existing between the pair, drained but elated in the afterglow of the standing ovation that had just been granted them.

Backstage among groups of well-wishers, Westwood was animated and sociable but in the full glare of the camera next to McLaren, though they were clearly comfortable in each other's company and shared glances and smiles, she was shy to the point of inarticulacy.

When asked why he thought punk was still a phenomenon six years after its emergence, McLaren said that he was 'the main person who set the sparks alight and gave the opportunity for a lot of those kids to do their own thing'. He also explained that the essence of punk lay in its anti-hierarchical, DIY nature.

'Punk rock had a success because it enabled people to do things which before they thought was impossible,' he said. 'Prior to that, being in a group and expressing yourself in that way seemed very difficult and quite mysterious, not within your grasp. With punk rock you could learn three chords, get up on stage and do your thing. That has progressed so that a lot of the attitudes that were prevalent in 1977 have given people confidence. It will always come back in new forms because the attitude is so very, very good, to do with people doing things for themselves and controlling their own methods and their own culture. Punk rock's greatest asset was that it questioned everything. That's why it stayed alive. It was a critique and an attitude which developed into a lifestyle.'

Asked the same question, Westwood muttered that she didn't know the answer and looked to McLaren for support, apologising: 'I'm sorry I'm so quiet today, I don't know why that is.'

After her repeated stonewalling, McLaren urged his former partner to elucidate on the ideas behind Punkature. 'Explain about the hobo and why you made the clothes look old, as if they're dug up out of the earth. What's the spirit behind that?'

Smiling, Westwood again faltered – 'I can't tell you, I can't. I'm sorry you have to make excuses for me' – so McLaren defended her to the crew. 'She's very tired. It's post-show blues. You caught her at a bad time,' he said, before they descended into giggles. 'Usually she'll yap on for ages.'

McLaren refused to denigrate those youngsters around the world who continued to wear punk clothing. 'It means that style was very, very good, wasn't it?' he asked. 'That they can still do it five years later, you can't say that for many designers today, Thierry Mugler, Saint Laurent, Claude Montana, Ralph Lauren, but you can say that about punk rock. People are still wearing that. It will become like Chanel, but have a hell of a lot more content.'

When asked where he would be a decade hence, McLaren said: 'I've always considered myself an artist, but I've never been in the position to make that announcement because I've always had to hide behind other things or have people do the things I couldn't do myself, whether it be a group I managed or designing clothes and somebody else wearing them. Now I'm in it more myself. I'm doing my own project and making my own record and ultimately my own show. That's me coming out of the cupboard, within the next six months.'

Having – conceptually at least – escaped the muddy hole called England, McLaren was preparing to step out and slip the bonds of personal relationships into self-imposed exile.

Chapter 30

By the turn of 1983, Malcolm McLaren had become Britain's unlikeliest musical phenomenon, 'one of the more mischievous sights on *Top of the Pops* . . . a pale, puckish figure with a Groucho Marx walk and a megaphone, instructing athletic New York guttersnipes in the art of square dancing [to] a culture clash of disco and hillbilly music that has made him, at 36, a pop star at his first attempt'.[1]

Though 'Soweto', the follow-up single to 'Buffalo Gals', failed to repeat its predecessor's success by stalling at number thirty-two in the charts, the song's emotional charge and the by turns poignant and exuberant promo clip persuaded even the most disinclined towards McLaren that he was onto something.

'McLaren has been much more than an audacious publicist: he can claim artistic responsibility for performers he has launched,' wrote Michael Watts. 'Now he has tested the hypothesis on himself, compelling the press and record industry, which has often thought him a distasteful maverick, to reconsider.'[2]

And McLaren was using the interview format to predict the changes coming down the pike for the music industry, where traditional gig-going was set to be challenged by the rise of DJ, club and dance culture as primary youth activities.

He told *Smash Hits* journalist and soon-to-be Pet Shop Boys frontman Neil Tennant that a positive response to 'Buffalo Gals' from street kids in south London offered signposts to the future. 'These are the people I can very easily see getting hold of their brother's or mother's record players and fitting them up and piling up a load of old records and figuring out what's a good groove and a good beat,' said McLaren. 'Suddenly a whole different attitude will take place. Live discotheques where deejays will be grooving along to their favourite records with their friends coming in to give them a hand, scratching one record into another.

'Discotheques will be more vigorous and exciting than any concert on the stage of the Hammersmith Odeon. Live discotheques. I really think that'll happen.'[3]

Subsequently, McLaren invited Tennant to a square-dancing night at the Mud Club, run by Philip Sallon and decorated with graffiti by Nick Egan. On Tony Russell's recommendation, a seasoned caller from the English Folk Dance & Song Society was on hand 'to lead London's *nouveaux hobos* in Virginia reels'.[4]

McLaren also participated at an event in front of hundreds of screaming teens at London's Lyceum Ballroom on a bill with PAs by such heart-throbs of the day as Nick Heyward and Bananarama. The event was hosted by DJ Gary Crowley and was an offshoot of his pop-oriented *Tuesday Club* show on the city's Capital Radio.

Crowley had been introduced to McLaren a couple of years earlier by Nick Egan and socialised with him and such mutual friends as Egan's girlfriend Anne Witchard, who worked in Nostalgia of Mud, his design partner Peter Barrett and Bananarama's Siobhan Fahey.

'I was in awe of Malcolm at first; it was very exciting to meet him,' says Crowley. 'He was incredibly entertaining. He called me "Boy", like he did a lot of people, which I loved. We would go to dinner at Kettner's, with him regaling us with tales of Russ Meyer. Sometimes we'd also be at his apartment in Bloomsbury, and Nick and Anne's place in Weymouth Street was also a bit of a hub.

'You could see why Malcolm had the reputation for being a Pied Piper. You enjoyed being around him. Always had that twinkle in his eye. Very, very bright. You put fun and gossipy in there and why wouldn't you want to hang out with this guy?'

Via his connections, Crowley had been an early champion of 'Buffalo Gals' and featured McLaren in promotional jingles. When the Lyceum party was announced to mark Crowley switching from the *Tuesday Club* to a Saturday slot on Capital, McLaren agreed to take part. 'It bordered on the surreal,' says Crowley, who, like McLaren, wore a Mountain hat and Nostalgia of Mud gear for the occasion. 'Instead of miming to a track, the idea was that I should attempt to interview Malcolm. We played the record and he tried to teach me how to do-si-do. The audience was primarily teenage girls and pretty soon they started yelling for Nick Heyward. Malcolm was oblivious, and carried on talking about the adventures they'd had recording the album as the cries for Nick mounted. Eventually my producer told me to cut it short and, though we didn't need a hook to drag him offstage, it had to be swiftly curtailed before the crowd turned.'

McLaren was taken by Crowley's upbeat charm, and announced in a music press interview that he planned to take the young Londoner to New York and introduce him to the World's Famous Supreme Team and the world of scratching. Crowley feels that McLaren's belief in him stemmed from the fact that they shared an enthusiasm for pop culture and its by-products.

'Malcolm was a fan of young energy and mismanaging it to see what would happen,' says Crowley, who remains a popular British broadcaster. 'I think he identified me as an eternal fan, as he was. I was really pleased that Malcolm had mentioned the idea of going to New York in print but sadly for me it never happened. Who knows? I could be a superstar DJ now with residencies in Ibiza and a private jet . . .'[5]

In a surprise move, McLaren gave a revealing interview to the veteran British broadcaster Charlie Gillett, whose book *The Sound of the City* was an authoritative rock music text. A former music journalist, Gillett had been presenting roots music shows on London radio stations since the early 1970s and also managed Ian Dury's group Kilburn & the High Roads before their career was taken over by McLaren's friend Tommy Roberts.

Importantly, Gillett was a pioneer of the various international genres soon to be lumped under the banner of 'world music' and, impressed by the depth of research for *Duck Rock*, invited McLaren onto his Capital

Radio show to select and talk about ten of his favourite recordings. These provided Gillett's guest with the opportunity to map out a biographical narrative, from 'Take This Hammer' by Leadbelly, the song that had appeared in the Punkature soundtrack which he had known from his art student days, to 'The Coster Girl in Paris' by Marie Lloyd, the early twentieth-century music hall artiste favoured by McLaren's grandmother Rose.

'Marie Lloyd didn't give a damn for anybody and was probably as rock 'n' roll as you could be in those days in England,' he told Gillett. 'And Paris was the place I imposed myself in exile while the record industry was paranoid after having gone through the years of the Sex Pistols.'[6]

The Pistols' 'God Save the Queen' appeared in the selection along with Pink Floyd's 'See Emily Play', written by Syd Barrett. This enabled Gillett's guest to relate his approach to Barrett to produce *Never Mind the Bollocks*. McLaren also chose 'Buffalo Gals' and other *Duck Rock* tracks and at one stage – trailed by Gillett as 'a British radio first' – made the calls live on air to a recording of the square dance 'Alabama Gal' by an authentic group, Kyle Creed, Bobby Patterson & the Camp Creek Boys.

'It has a marvellous fiddle technique,' McLaren told Gillett before exhorting his listeners: 'If you're in your bedrooms or discotheques or wherever you are, get out of your car and dance the do-si-do away!'

Claiming that square dancing was becoming popular with young pop and rock fans across America, McLaren related how he had been the caller at an event at the recently opened Buffalo Ballroom on the site of the 1920s Hollywood Athletic Club in LA. So taken was Gillett with McLaren that his guest stayed beyond the allotted time so that they could listen to an eleventh track, the 1928 recording of 'Hallelujah I'm a Bum' by the itinerant American Communist Party member Harry 'Haywire Mac' McClintock.

'Haywire Mac was the main man of American music, singing his songs on the street corner long before vinyl,' declared McLaren.

While McLaren was vigorously promoting his singles in an effort to persuade Charisma to release *Duck Rock*, Nick Egan had spent weeks in New York working on the album sleeve, which McLaren determined should include contributions from the super-talented Dondi White as well as the brightest star of New York's incandescent early 1980s art scene, the graphic artist Keith Haring.

Importantly, Terry Doktor and Michael Holman were providing conduits to these and other such figures as the gallerist Tony Shafrazi, an early champion of Haring's work, and Jean-Michel Basquiat. 'Michael told me that Keith was working on the door at the Mudd Club,' says Nick Egan. 'I'd said to Malcolm I wanted to immerse myself in this culture rather than just being a recipient of ideas, so met Dondi and went down one night to watch him working with his crew on trains on the subway, which was pretty scary. Then Malcolm and I met up with Keith at The Roxy, where Malcolm commissioned him to produce the album artwork for £1000.'

With audacious colour usage accentuating orange, powdery pink, mint green and baby blue, Egan's kinetic *Duck Rock* sleeve presented a collage as vibrant as the music it contained; the backdrops on the front and back comprised Haring's rendition of interlocked snake-headed men framing a pair doing the Latin-American club dance known as the Huevo (or Webo).

On the front, Haring also provided the block lettering for the all-caps credit 'MALCOLM McLAREN!'; this overlaid the multiple aerials in a photograph of a customised boombox known as the 'Duck Rocker'.

Adorned with – what else? – buffalo horns as well as tribal furs, feathers, badges and multicoloured dials, the Duck Rocker announced the album title in Dondi White's graffiti lettering on its speakers along with a nod to the World's Famous Supreme Team with their radio station frequency 105.9FM.

A half-dozen Duck Rockers were customised to McLaren and Egan's designs by Ron West, a college friend of the latter, and McLaren had taken one to South Africa, where he was filmed carrying it in the promos for 'Soweto' and other tracks.[7]

'Malcolm told me that the Duck Rocker was treated like a deity there,' says Egan. 'The Zulus were amazed at how it looked and the fact that it conveyed music.'

The Duck Rocker was made the star of the album design, appearing three times on the back: surrounded by tribespeople, carried on the head of a Zulu woman and with a behatted McLaren twiddling its dials and slyly looking to camera. There were also images of a tracksuited New York breakdancer spinning on his head and Double Dutch girls twirling ropes and skipping, while graphic effects abounded amid bold announcements: 'DOUBLE DUTCH', 'Z-ZULU', 'BREAK' and 'ELECTRIC BOOGALOO'.

These last declamations – both dance instructions – are cleverly wrapped around the sleeve so that the person holding the LP cover feels impelled to turn it around for the full effect.

During the design process, Egan admits to having felt overwhelmed. 'There was so much information coming in,' he says. 'Keith, Dondi, the Duck Rocker, the Zulus, the breakers . . . Also I had started to question why I was doing what I was doing. One day I complained to Malcolm that it was just a square, that it felt restrictive. And he came back with a brilliant response. "Forget the square. That's just a part of the big picture. Imagine there's a giant wall packed with visuals and you've just taken a square out of it. If some of the words aren't in full it won't matter; in fact it will make you wonder what the rest of it is like." I thought that was genius.'

At McLaren's insistence, *Duck Rock* contained a six-page tri-fold information sheet with lyrics, credits and information about each track, an updated version of the inserts produced for Folkways releases in the 1950s and 1960s. To cement the connection, one photograph from the Piute Pete square dances collection appeared in the *Duck Rock* sheet along with more Haring illustrations of dog-headed men, UFOs and a full-bleed photograph of McLaren outside Nostalgia of Mud with two models in Punkature clothes.

Back in London, Charisma was by now in considerable financial disarray and continuing to fob off McLaren with delayed release dates for the LP. He maintained pressure on the label and also dedicated energies to his role as chief conceptualist and art director in the fashion design relationship with Vivienne Westwood.

The pair were now focused on a new collection he titled 'Witches', continuing the pre-Christian themes of his most recent work and having been inspired by a new set of research.

Among the reading materials McLaren had assembled during the recording of *Duck Rock* was *Voodoo and Magic Practices*, an English translation of a book by Jean Kerboull, a French missionary priest in Haiti in the 1960s and 1970s. Billed as 'an incomparable voyage into the world of magic and sorcery', Kerboull's examination of pagan rituals dovetailed with McLaren's deliberations.

Kerboull's book is filled with references to those who practise witchcraft, as well as to zombies, medicine men and the devil. Some had been featured in William Johnson's illustrations of capering figures on the covers of the *Dances of the World's Peoples* series. And there is a section in *Voodoo and Magic Practices* on Legba and Obatala, the Lucumí cult's deities after which McLaren named instrumental tracks on *Duck Rock*.

'Our latest clothes not only needed graphics and representation but also a big idea,' McLaren said towards the end of his life. 'That's where the voodoo book came in.'

Keith Haring's work for the *Duck Rock* LP made him the ideal candidate for the graphics for Witches, and, as well as using the dozen or so artworks he had already produced, McLaren commissioned Haring to come up with updated representations of Johnson's *Dances of the World's Peoples* characters.

Simultaneous to his cultivation of Haring, McLaren had made a connection with the enigmatic New York street artist Richard Hambleton, whose eerie, brush-painted 'Shadowmen' had sprouted on walls downtown over the previous couple of years. On attending an exhibition of the elusive Hambleton's work at the Alexander Milliken gallery on Prince Street, McLaren arranged via Terry Doktor to license one of these figures for inclusion on a jersey skirt in the forthcoming collection, which was peppered with pointed hat references in the exaggerated shoulder and elbow shapes on trench coats, jackets, jersey tops and cardigans.

Simon Withers, a graduate of a fashion course at Saint Martin's who had been a customer at 430 King's Road as far back as the beginnings of Seditionaries, was recruited as studio assistant and pattern cutter at Kingly Court as Witches was being pulled together, and describes the clothes as 'articulated, with points and shoulder and elbow hinges, as though made for a marionette when you moved in them. It was quite comical and very much based on the defined silhouette. There was a shift of scale, so jackets and coats would be overlarge. That was all Malcolm, because Vivienne, if left to her own devices, tended towards softer, unstructured design, quite hippy.'[8]

Withers was a designer in his own right, having supplied clothes to the likes of Spandau Ballet and been a member of the New Romantic inner circle for years, and knew McLaren, having attended a memorable dinner at the Hunter Street flat with Nick Egan and Anne Witchard the previous year. 'Very exotically Malcolm had been to the deli counter at Safeways and served quails' eggs and various exotica,' says Withers. 'He'd just got back from a trip to Japan and proudly showed us a lavish Japanese book about Brigitte Bardot.'

Subsequently, Withers was invited to Bloomsbury for early morning meetings. McLaren, as was his wont, lay in the bath (as he had done in scenes with Helen Wellington Lloyd in *The Great Rock 'n' Roll Swindle*) while discussing whatever was on his mind with Withers and Andrea Linz sitting on the edge. 'Hunter Street felt proper, grown-up, on the louche side,' says Withers. 'It was a compact mansion flat, very nicely appointed, with a service shaft. I remember once we walked from there to his solicitor's Christmas drinks in Kingsway, so not far, and Malcolm told me very proudly he was worth a quarter of a million pounds. How much of that was available and liquid or even existed I don't know, but it really meant a lot to him.'

Nick Egan emphasises that McLaren's input into the design partnership with Westwood remained crucial. 'He would arrive at Kingly Court, look at what Vivienne had been up to and make a series of edits and suggestions: "Cut that, re-arrange that, put this here,"' recalls Egan. 'This transformed the designs from being pretty great to extraordinary. Hence the puff screen-prints and the three-tongued sneakers in Witches.'

One day, during the run-up to the public unveiling of the new collection, Westwood arrived unannounced in New York. 'I got a call at the Mayflower Hotel from immigration at JFK,' says Egan. 'They said, "There's a woman here with no luggage, just some garbage bags full of clothes, who says she knows you. Can you vouch for her?" It was Vivienne.'

Westwood stayed for a few days, during which time she insisted on being introduced to Haring; no longer was she prepared to be the mere recipient of McLaren's ideas, but wished to be involved at ground zero. 'Keith was always suspicious of Malcolm, because of his reputation,' says Egan. 'These were early days for Keith; he was pretty paranoid about being ripped off. So he gravitated more towards Vivienne, who jumped on the bandwagon and went crazy with his stuff.'

'Vivienne found me and asked if I would do some drawings for her that she could use in clothes, so I made two black and white drawings that she took away,' said Haring a couple of years later.[9]

To these illustrations were added the artworks Haring supplied for *Duck Rock*, and so his pop-art glyphs were printed in heavy fluorescent colours on a range of garments, including college scarves, apron dresses, knitwear two-pieces, handkerchiefs and jersey tracksuit pants and tops, while one of his barking dogs decorated the front of the showcard for the Witches catwalk presentations in London and Paris (where the collection was shown again at the Louvre Palace). In addition, Haring's version of the *Dances of the World's Peoples* shaman was on the invite.

Egan and others believe that Westwood's appearance in New York and enthusiasm for Haring indicated her wish to make things whole with McLaren. 'He was definitely the love of her life and to a certain extent she was his,' says Egan. 'They were like Jagger and Richards or Lennon and McCartney. There was something about the tensions between them which made their work brilliant.'

Back in London, Simon Withers was called in to Kingly Court three days before the Paris show. 'Malcolm phoned and said Vivienne would like to give me a trial,' he recalls. 'I went in early in the afternoon and we worked through the next two nights. I left at one o'clock on the third day. They were loading the vans; Tom Binns had arrived with the jewellery. I was so tired. I was living at my mum's at that point and knew if I went there they would find me so I dropped by Anne and Nick's in Weymouth Street to get some rest. Within half an hour a bike turned up with the message: "Get your passport, you're coming to Paris."'

The soundtrack McLaren concocted for Witches contained choices that acted as a signpost to the next avenue of McLaren's musical explorations: excerpts from Giacomo Puccini's opera *Madam Butterfly* which were mixed with hip-hop tracks by Egan.

'I was bored with playing pop music at fashion shows and was looking for something more grand, more dramatic,' said McLaren in the 2000s. 'I discovered the world of opera, the diva, the heart of the prima donna. Their voices appealed to me; they sounded larger than life. They had real drama, even though I understood nothing of what was being sung. I became spellbound by the world of Puccini and thought if only I could graft this sound onto a simple hip hop beat then my models could walk to it.'

A few events had pricked McLaren's interest in the musical form. While he had been in Alabama on *Duck Rock* promotional duties, McLaren judged a local television talent contest and awarded first prize – an audition for a recording contract with Charisma – to a Birmingham secondary schoolteacher, a Mrs Froggett, who was, in McLaren's words, 'a very eloquent opera singer'.

McLaren claimed that he would be the producer of her first single, an aria from *Madama Butterfly*, but while this project didn't materialise, the blue touch paper had been lit.

During interviews for *Duck Rock*, the subject of opera popped up with increasingly regularity. 'I've just discovered it,' he told London's *Time Out*. 'I'm working with something with Puccini. I'd like to use that and put it in the context of the street and maybe even introduce it to the South Bronx.'[10]

After the Paris Witches show McLaren was congratulated on his musical choice by a *Vogue Italia* editor who was nonetheless shocked by the hip-hop and folkloric references in the collection. 'She came rushing back stage: "Malcolm, the music is bellissimo! Simply bellissimo! But the clothes! Why do you have to make the people look poor?"' said McLaren. 'I had to think very seriously before replying – as I had no real answer – "Robin Hood, that's why, Maria. I am designing clothes to make the rich look poorer so the poor can look rich."

'This was something Paris could in no way understand. I was completely outside that frame of reference. People just thought I was totally nuts anyway. She looked at me and said: "Malcolm, it's not going to happen in Italian *Vogue*." Of course I realised I was on a very dodgy wicket. I had to rethink my whole career, whatever that meant.'

The journalist was out of step with the general view of Witches, which marked the point where international recognition for Worlds End clothes crossed into the mainstream; US *Vogue* promptly commissioned a portrait of McLaren and Westwood in clothing from the new collection from the top-flight fashion photographer Steven Meisel. He captured them throwing poses with model Talisa Soto spinning off the ground in Haring-decorated knickers and top.

Madonna, whose career was taking off, had been introduced to Witches by her close friend Haring and wore a skirt from the collection in the promo for her third single 'Borderline', enthusing to a New York interviewer: 'Worlds End is a great clothing shop. Whenever I go to England that's where I buy my clothes.'[11]

Behind the scenes in Paris there was much excited activity. On the first night after the show the McLaren/Westwood gang was treated to dinner by Italian manufacturer Alberto Raffaelli. 'Keith Haring was there; it was an amazing evening,' says Simon Withers, who was envious the following morning when he missed out on a breakfast with Karl Lagerfeld attended by McLaren, Egan and Gene Krell. 'There was a really good atmosphere, very dynamic. It was a phenomenal achievement to be the first British people since Mary Quant to be in the tents, and on the streets it was very exciting to be in a Witches raincoat and have people stopping you and asking where it had come from. From this tiny operation in London you were walking on top of the world. We were told it had cost £20,000 – a lot of cash for such a small business.'

Keith Haring was delighted to be involved until he was informed a few days later that his payment would be in the form of clothing. 'I had to make the call and tell him we would be paying him in women's jumpers,' says Withers. 'He was not thrilled.'

'Malcolm steps on a lot of people's feet to do what he does and he uses and takes advantage of a lot of people,' said Haring the following year. 'But at the same time he gets things done. I guess he made a breakthrough in some ways for some people, but he takes advantage and walks away and I don't think that's right.'[12]

Among those in Paris was the Italian publicist and fashion biz fixer Carlo D'Amario, with whom Westwood had become quite taken, his glass eye enhancing his raffish charm. Soon they began a physical relationship, which developed as he proffered advice. D'Amario's not unreasonable view was that McLaren's avowedly anti-establishment position was restricting Westwood from gaining the industry credibility she not only craved but deserved.

This was confirmed by Westwood's assistant Lorraine Piggott, who told Jane Mulvagh: '[D'Amario] certainly saw her business potential first. She was very, very flattered by this man who was coming onto her sexually, but also fed her this yarn. Most people thought he was a bit of joke, but Malcolm recognised that he could be dangerous.'

And McLaren confessed to Mulvagh: 'I just didn't like this man. I felt let down by Vivienne's choice. I just could not deal with him. Vivienne clung to him, and she was trying to get at me when she thought she'd lost me.'[13]

Whether the latter is true or not, Westwood was soon taking D'Amario's advice over McLaren's, particularly in regard to garment manufacture in the more professional setting of his home country. In possession of a newly independent spirit, due in part to the flattery of a recently acquired self-styled 'guru' named Gary Ness,[14] Westwood had given up on projects that they had worked on, such as the Nostalgia of Mud shop, which was permanently on the verge of closure due to mismanagement, pilfering by staff and customers and complaints from local retailers and the council.

D'Amario brought with him the promise of an end to Westwood's dependence on McLaren and his record company funds. Now talk began of substantial investment in the Worlds End label from Elio Fiorucci, who had a reputation as a pirate among British fashion retailers but was well-funded and ambitious. Recently Fiorucci had set up a glitzy new King's Road boutique and was intent on becoming a force in Britain's now-vibrant fashion scene, understanding that control of exploitation rights over the McLaren/Westwood designs going back to Let It Rock would include the commercially precious punk and New Romantic ranges.

After Witches, Simon Withers was required to establish his credentials to become part of the team. 'I had to do two tests for Vivienne, both essays, one on the movement of Christianity from the Tigris and Euphrates basins to the cities, and the other on alchemy,' says Withers. 'I loved researching and writing them both. It was refreshing that, while the rest of fashion relied on post-war pop culture, they were interested in the whole of history and by using it they were immediately better than anyone else. I remember walking with Vivienne from the studio to an obscure bookshop in Museum Street, talking all the way. Shortly afterwards they employed me at £60 a week. It was low, but having been running an eponymous label and pattern-cutting for absolutely nothing it made life much easier.'

Withers's job was to reorganise the patterns cut by Mark Tarbard for the shows for commercial production and also assist, along with Lorraine Piggott and others, on beginning the next collection. One evening during this period Westwood asked Withers to stay behind after the rest of the staff had left for the day. Actress Julie Christie arrived for final fittings of garments that had been made exclusively for her.

By now a couple of assistants had introduced heroin to the workshop, says Withers. One was a dealer while his partner was an addict who, on one memorable occasion, accidently set fire to himself in the studio's tiny lavatory after nodding out over a lit cigarette. 'Smack was one of the things which was destroying the atmosphere at Kingly Court just as it was at Nostalgia of Mud,' says Withers. 'I walked in there one day and three members of staff were nodding out. This was serious.'

To add to the mounting chaos, personal interactions between McLaren and Westwood were by no means on an even keel; one argument over the follow-up to Witches escalated despite the fact that Nick Egan and Simon Withers were present. 'I remember her annoying him so much by being air-headed – he used to refer to her as "Snake Pass" because of her country roots – that soon they were struggling together on the floor with their hands round each other's throats and she was screaming: "You're going to have to kill me Malcolm! You're going to have to kill me!"' says Egan.

Withers recalls that this took place after they had thrown bowls of Chinese takeaway soup over each other. 'Every time Malcolm was away, the clothes became loose, soft, without shadow,' says Withers. 'Vivienne had been talking to Gary Ness a lot about esoterica and it played out in an odd way. When Malcolm was there, there would be a manic focus on the silhouette and the meaning, the story. We didn't start the design process properly until that fight. We had a big board where the "manifesto", if you like, of the collection was pinned – visual references, sketches, fabrics – and that was completely reordered that day with Malcolm as editor.'

The decision was to continue investigations into pre-Christian cultures by dedicating the new range to the legend of the Greek god of sleep Hypnos.

With McLaren, Withers had visited the British Museum to study the bronze head from a statue of Hypnos, which has wings sprouting from his temples. One time they were accompanied by Withers's friend, the photographer Neil Matthews.

'The drive to use the god of sleep was from Malcolm; he was fascinated by the winged head,' says Withers. 'When we went with Neil we had a camera and tripod and stole a few moments to document it. Meanwhile I was visiting the Wallace Collection with Vivienne to study armour. The idea was to make a connection to classical Greece but step outside the orthodox set of references.'

In the early summer of 1983 Westwood vacated Thurleigh Court in Clapham and moved to Italy. Her son Ben, now twenty, remained in London while Joe, fifteen, travelled with her and stayed with D'Amario's mother. This shift of base represented at least a temporary turn in Westwood's fortunes; she was later paid handsomely to produce a one-off jeans collection for Fiorucci called 'World School'.

That this traded on the Worlds End name and was in breach of the 1973 partnership agreement with McLaren didn't bother Westwood, who compared this business decision to McLaren's abandonment of her for Linz two years previously.

Westwood soon made clear her disillusionment with England and, by extension, McLaren. 'The reception I get in Japan, in Italy and in France is so much better, and not just financially,' Westwood told fashion journalist Helen Roberts. 'London's just a waste of time for me.'[15]

The spell had been broken. After sixteen years, Westwood was envisaging a creative and personal life beyond McLaren. Withers was summoned to Italy to work with Westwood on patterns for the next collection. She had been installed by D'Amario in a house in a village in the foothills of mountains south of Brescia, equidistant from Milan and Verona. By Withers's account the conditions were rough-and-ready; there was no money and no arrangements for food. He organised a couple staying nearby to cook for them and at one point locals invaded and ransacked the rooms.

Meanwhile McLaren was being pulled back towards his music career. Charisma relented and scheduled the release of *Duck Rock* in the early summer of 1983. This, and the issue of the LP's third single, 'Double Dutch', which gave him a number three hit in the UK, served to remove McLaren from Westwood's orbit as he hit the international promotional trail.

On occasion he was accompanied by Andrea Linz; Bob Gruen took photographs of them in Witches finery in New York, him leaping and her doing handstands by a Richard Hambleton Shadowman painted on a wall of the Westbeth Artists Community, the West Village studio complex that housed Gruen's living/work space.

But mostly he travelled on his own in the company of local record-company reps. In media interviews, McLaren recounted the increasingly familiar tales of the album's genesis and realisation but took time to muse about Westwood. 'What I probably do for Vivienne is bring her the outside world,' he told Paul Rambali for a cover story for *The Face*. 'I see what she's got, and I push it in a direction. I'm the concept man, but she's the tailor. She's a wonderful person, a brilliant craftsman. London people aren't craftsmen; they're very lazy about that. She comes from the Pennines, and she is one of those English hard rock people. She's got the ability to be able to live and survive in the woods.'

He also confirmed that his partner was now slipping out of his ken. 'She's working in uncharted territory,' he said. 'She'll either sink or swim; she's involved in very big money, and she's competing with the world, who are much better at production than we are. They look upon you as curios. Sure, you're influential, but you're not considered a competitor.'[16]

Rambali's report incorporated significant quotes from Trevor Horn, who revealed that, contra to McLaren's claims, recordings had not been made outside of New York and South Africa in such locations as the Dominican Republic and Peru. 'Malcolm will probably tell you it was recorded all over the world, so if he does, write that instead,' said Horn. The journalist also noted that the advance copies of the LP credited the tracks to McLaren/Horn. 'That'll have to be changed. It should be "Trad. arranged by",' said Horn.

This didn't occur and, in any case, would not have been appropriate, since some of the songs were clearly compositions owned by others. That this was standard practice at the time – for example the Specials' 1979 UK hit single 'Gangsters' used the melody and rhythm of ska star Prince Buster's 1960s song 'Al Capone' without credit – does not excuse McLaren and Horn's approach. A case in point became 'Double Dutch', which was based on a Zulu *mbaqanga* hit, 'Puleng' by the Boyoyo Boys. The group's Petrus Maneli and publisher Gallo Music subsequently took legal action, which resulted in a hefty payment without addition to the song credits.

South African record plugger Phil Hollis worked with Gallo on instituting more legal proceedings against McLaren, Horn and their music publishing companies on behalf of several other musicians whose work had been registered with the local performing rights agency but had not been credited on the LP. 'To use them you would have to do a split, usually at least 50/50,' said Hollis in the 1980s. 'Malcolm said he'd give me a small percentage and I objected. I said, "You're treating me like a monkey and I'm not a monkey." '[17] Although Hollis won the judgment, the case was settled out of court for legal fees. The credits remain McLaren/Horn to this day.

The issue of *The Face* containing the McLaren cover story also carried Bob Gruen photographs from a wild video shoot for the single 'Duck for the Oyster'. McLaren had returned with Gruen, Egan and director Ron Fortunato to film himself with the Hilltoppers at their ramshackle rural retreat in East Tennessee.

As the day wore on, the extended Birchfield family became increasingly disgruntled at the interlopers' presence, possibly since they gathered that their contribution to the LP had been replaced by the session musicians' version.

'Bob and I met Malcolm in this place they had built themselves in the middle of nowhere, straight out of the nineteenth century, no plumbing or anything like that,' says Egan. 'We paid them with a pig, no word of a lie. They seemed happy enough with that but couldn't get their heads around the fact that we wanted them to mime to a song which they hadn't played on. Then the moonshine was being passed around and it started to get dark.'

During the shoot, McLaren – dressed in a huge 'Buffalo' sheepskin coat and no less than three Mountain hats, one on top of the other – asked the fiddle-player Joe Birchfield to announce to camera some of the lines from the song. McLaren's coaxing of the seventy-five-year-old was reminiscent of his cueing of his grandmother for *The Story of Oxford Street* voiceover a decade-plus before. 'No, no, no,' he chided the elderly man before slowly enunciating the lines for him to repeat. At the end of the process, Birchfield paused, before asking with a baleful tone: 'What's your meaning of that?'

The exchange was to provide the opening scene for the clip on the *Duck Rock* long-form video, but that day Joe Birchfield's wariness was a portent of the change in mood among the locals after McLaren suggested in blunt terms that more photogenic females be fetched from a nearby town to join the dancing.

'Malcolm could be oblivious to danger even when his mouthing off had started it,' says Egan. 'Trucks started showing up and there was this general feeling that we'd insulted their women. This guy came over and said, "You'd better leave."'

Gruen was oblivious and having a whale of a time. 'I was negotiating to buy a jug of moonshine when Malcolm rushed over and told me to get in the car,' he says. 'We were out of there.'

In New York it became clear that the Appalachian footage wasn't sufficient so McLaren organised for Egan to shoot sequences of strangely garbed male and female black and white models – leering in false noses and sportswear – performing the Lindy Hop, since the dance could be traced back to Harlem in the early twentieth century. This was then intercut with the Birchfields scenes to produce a promo of considerable comic force.

McLaren's notes for the New York 'Duck for the Oyster' shoot provide a flavour of what he was seeking to achieve: 'A group of Duck Rockers! Peruvian Indians in coloured sweaters! Baseball shirts over ragged old jumpers . . . Venezuelans! Bowler hats, football sox, fluorescent kneecaps with knitted stockings striped from London . . . Badges . . . Ponchos . . .'[18]

In between this and participating in the filming of skippers at a Harlem gym for the 'Double Dutch' promo, McLaren toured the world in support of *Duck Rock*.

In New Zealand it was a hit, but Phonogram, the local record company, didn't have a clue as to which consumer group was driving sales. 'We found the answer at a local TV station,' said McLaren in 2008. 'Outside, in the car park, a group of Maoris arrived and rolled out corrugated cardboard to demonstrate that they could breakdance.'

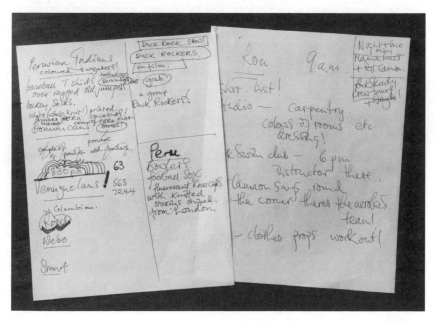

Notes for 'Duck for the Oyster' promo video shoot, 1983. Malcolm McLaren Estate.

In America, McLaren was embraced by the black musical community. Jazz pianist Herbie Hancock was inspired by 'Buffalo Gals' to record his international number one 'Rockit' (which featured the turntablist Grandmaster DST) and dedicated his 1984 Grammy for best R&B instrumental to McLaren.

'I like his taste,' explained Hancock to the *NME*. 'The thing that really caught my ear was "Buffalo Gals". I said, *"What is that???* I want to do something like *that*!" '[19]

And McLaren later proudly proclaimed that veteran producer/ arranger Quincy Jones 'who I treat as a friend, told me I was the only white man who he felt was a competitor'.

Later, McLaren wrote, 'Russell Simmons, founder and president of Def Jam, thought of me as a hero. Elvis Costello, who I casually met in a bar, simply told me how he loved the song "Jive My Baby". Much later, Paul Simon asked me somewhat cagily at a party, what was I plotting next? He had recently been successful with his album *Graceland*. *Duck Rock* had played a part in that too.'

It was always McLaren's intention to shake up the international music industry, which he saw as having grown once more complacent in the years since punk. 'With this journey I wanted to demonstrate that the field holler, the square-dance caller, the rapper in the South Bronx or the Peruvian baker in the wilds of New York City has got more to offer than Blancmange, Diana Ross, Darryl Hall, Lionel Richie or any other aristocratic hit-maker,' he said.

'Here you have a group of dances, all the lyrics are purely instructional, you have a music that is born out of non-professional people with all the colour and resources of tradition gone by and all the soul and magic that goes with it, into a package illustrated with a simple booklet that gives you the origins of those dances.

'[The plan] was to compare the Zulus with Inca rituals, or the paganism of the square dance or the rappers who break and electric boogaloo or skip to the Double Dutch. All together to demonstrate there is more culture and excitement on those streets and in those traditions than anything the industry has concocted over the past ten years.'[20]

McLaren's dedication to his burgeoning music career and the widening wedge after D'Amario's arrival on the scene precipitated the collapse of his working relationship with Westwood. There was one last shot when they were reunited to work on 'Hypnos', which became their final catwalk collection together. Contributors again included Tom Binns, who produced inventive rubber jewellery to be worn as bracelets, necklaces and anklets, as well as Roman phalluses as fasteners. The new designs accentuated activity and acted as a counterpoint to the overarching concept by emulating modern sportswear with such garments as bodysuits and cycling tops.

But the jig was up with Westwood. *The Face* noticed that her disaffection started with the relationship with D'Amario: 'Last spring colleagues noted Vivienne stopped saying "Malcolm says . . . Malcolm thinks". Her love affair with Italy had begun.'[21]

Dangerously, Westwood's claims to D'Amario of Worlds End's shaky financial structure provided Fiorucci with an opening to initiate a take-over plan. Instantly, McLaren set about asserting his rights, changing the name of the new collection to 'Worlds End 1984' as a tribute to the shop and label they still owned together.

The invitations for the shows in the British and French capitals carried distorted images of one of Binns's phalluses with the Latin phrase *'Hic habitat felicitat'* (Here happiness dwells) but the irony hung heavy in the air backstage where the team had split into two rival factions. In a defiant jab at McLaren, Westwood and her camp removed the Worlds End labelling from the clothing just before the show started. The wrong-footed McLaren discovered that, instead, the garments bore 'Made in Italy' tags.

'On each chair they had placed an A4 information sheet in Italian,' says Simon Withers. 'Malcolm and I ran around and finally found someone who could translate. They told us it was an announcement that Fiorucci was taking over Worlds End. It was horrible. Meanwhile we didn't have our London models, so the show didn't have the swagger of Witches.'

There was, however, an injection of energy from the participation of two seventeen-year-old New Yorkers who had contacted McLaren and asked to appear on the runway since they were such fans of the clothes. One was Andre Walker, soon to make his name as one of the most brilliant designers who rose to prominence in the 1980s.

'Andre and his friend, a Latino, were an incredible pair,' says Withers. 'That was the first time I'd seen anyone wearing Birkenstocks. You couldn't get your head around it, the German hippie thing and kids from Brooklyn wearing it. They had also been sending tapes of new music to London, stuff that had only just come out, and Malcolm had chosen one of the songs for the soundtrack for them, but when they heard that, they refused to go on because it was three weeks old, so the music was reordered.'

The reception to Worlds End 1984 was far cooler than to any of the preceding five collections. 'Die-hard Brits remained tight-lipped,' reported *The Face*. ' "Too safe," said one. "The only balls that show had were on the invitation." The reason of course was Vivienne's new Italian connection. They'd not only tamed the sex to make it palatable, they'd also castrated the hardcore. It turned out later that much of the collection did not make the catwalk.'[22]

Withers confirms McLaren's claim that he was outnumbered in Paris by a large Italian contingent led by Fiorucci, who was either unaware of the existence of the partnership agreement or hadn't been informed by Westwood about it. It is also likely that Fiorucci proceeded on the basis that McLaren would not fight him. This was to severely underestimate McLaren's pride in his achievements with Westwood.

Both McLaren and Westwood took to the stage after the Worlds End 1984 show to accept applause, but at a Paris after party a furious confrontation broke out between McLaren and Fiorucci, with Westwood pitching in on the side of the Italians. 'I can't tolerate this man,' she said of her former partner a few weeks later. 'His behaviour has been inexcusable, conjuring up what seems to be a soap opera. Malcolm has one more chance to be good. And if he can't, I will have to carry on on my own.'[23]

Westwood's schoolmarmish statement didn't tell the full story. And McLaren knew that he had right on his side. Any attempts by Fiorucci to exploit the couple's intellectual properties would fail since McLaren had a 50 per cent share backed up by the decade-old legal deed.

'I wasn't about to let her give what we'd done together away, to Fiorucci of all people,' said McLaren in the 2000s. 'For once I had the law on my side.'

Meanwhile Westwood appeared oblivious to the fact that the Italians were intent on gaining possession of the archive of the patterns and clothing created with McLaren dating back to the early 1970s. Much of this was stored in the attic of Kingly Court. 'Vivienne was always spectacularly uninterested in the archive,' says Withers. 'She didn't seem to understand that it was really precious.'

Back in London, tensions frayed publicly at the Kingly Court studio. Withers hadn't been paid for a long time, nor had he been reimbursed for sizeable accommodation and other expenses in Paris. With reporters from *Women's Wear Daily* waiting to interview Westwood, Withers asked her for the money. 'She became really angry, screaming at me and then slapped me round the face,' says Withers. 'Regrettably I punched her, and she went flying. The *Women's Wear Daily* people saw the whole thing from the next room through the glass door panels. The next issue had a page-one headline "Assistant swats Westwood". It was an appalling ending. I left. There was no going back after that.'

At the time McLaren told David Johnson, the London-based journalist who chronicled the collapse of the partnership:

I will fight tooth and nail. Worlds End may continue with or without Vivienne Westwood. There is no financial trouble. But we are having grave discussions about where Worlds End collections are to be produced. The Worlds End marque is more significant than the likes of Fiorucci.

For the past four years I have personally financed and developed our concepts. I haven't struggled for 10 years to see them go off to Italy. What we create on the streets out of the dustbins of England is an extremely exportable commodity. Worlds End was born of

something subversive. If Vivienne wants to go down a more bourgeois road, fair enough, but she owes some consideration to the
partnership here.

McLaren also pushed the possibility that Westwood would make an
agreement with D'Amario and Fiorucci that would effectively hand
them the rights. 'She does tend to get embroiled in spaghetti dinners
and fall for Italian charm,' he told Johnson, making an oblique reference to a countryman of D'Amario's who had wooed Westwood way
back in the 1960s. 'I am concerned that the Worlds End marque remains
English. I'm not going to throw it away easily. I hope Vivienne continues with Worlds End but I'm not incapable of designing the next collection myself.'[24]

Westwood's refusal to back down forced McLaren's hand as he was
apprised of the licensing agreement Westwood had negotiated with Boy
a few years earlier without his knowledge. 'We went through the papers
and came across the deal letter; it was terrible,' says Simon Withers. 'It
promised a penny a garment which, of course, she never saw. The whole
thing was beyond bonkers. Malcolm would never have been party to
something so monumentally stupid. Things like that were coming to
light.'

McLaren instructed GLR to cease manufacturing, setting in train a
typically internecine Italian dispute in which GLR's Raffaelli claimed not
only that he was the primary creditor of the collapsing Worlds End but
also threatened to sue Fiorucci rather than Westwood or McLaren.

McLaren had new locks placed on the Kingly Court studios – which,
in any case, were abandoned after he retrieved patterns and samples –
changed the bank account and pondered his future. Within a matter of
weeks, his lawyers produced a document dissolving the partnership,
which he presented to Westwood and D'Amario in Rome in the early
spring of 1984, by which time Nostalgia of Mud was permanently closed
and Worlds End darkened by disconnection of the water and power
supplies.

Recognising the partners' shared ownership in the designs they had produced to date, the dissolution handed existing goodwill and the future business to Westwood, with a clause providing that she should be entitled 'to continue to trade as Worlds End' on the basis that she 'represent herself as carrying on the business formerly carried on by the Partnership as a sole proprietor'.

Westwood's agreement meant that not only did she gain full control of the business, but she accepted liability for the debts. The second clause of the agreement read: 'You [Westwood] will use your best endeavours to procure that all debts incurred by the Partnership are repaid.' Despite this, Westwood was to claim that McLaren lumbered her with the debts, omitting to mention that as part of the agreement she had taken them on.

The contract nominated an accountant – a Mr Jones of Pavie and Associates – to monitor the progress of payment of the debts and allowed Westwood to appoint a replacement if she so chose with McLaren's agreement.

The agreement did not, as Westwood would otherwise interpret for decades to come, mark McLaren's relinquishment of authorship of the designs they created together, particularly those in the life of the document after October 1973.

The purpose was to allow Westwood to use the Worlds End name for her own designs created after the date of the deed, which was signed by both parties on 11 May 1984. In the 1990s McLaren told Jane Mulvagh: 'It was only a partnership, not a limited company, so – as we didn't know what these Italian guys were like – if we started to manufacture and nothing sold I'd be liable.' He was also convinced that Westwood was motivated by his multiple betrayals. 'She broke it over my head. She knew she couldn't have me and she couldn't be in business with me so she smashed the business to smash me.' Mulvagh cast this interpretation as 'self-serving'.[25]

Acceptance of the dissolution enabled Westwood to show her first solo collection in Paris. Entitled 'Clint Eastwood', this contained such McLaren elements as designs for shoes that were tweaked by Westwood's footwear designer Patrick Cox, but sales were poor since there were no retail outlets and, by all accounts, the organisation of the catwalk show-case was shambolic.

D'Amario stuck by Westwood and organised a bank loan to fund the revivified Worlds End label in Italy, all the while negotiating a mighty seven-year investment by Giorgio Armani's partner Sergio Galeotti. This was to including a $3-million fee for Westwood, and was to set the stage for her emergence as a major player in mainstream international fashion, but was poleaxed the following year by Galeotti's death from complica-tions arising from Aids. Westwood remained in limbo and didn't return to London for another two years.

Meanwhile, McLaren poured his energies and finances into a collec-tion of his own. With the working title 'FAN MM', a range of extraordi-nary and transgressive designs were realised to sampling stage with Simon Withers and Andrea Linz, whom he installed in a design studio in the King's Cross area of north London.

'Malcolm's concept centred on a beautiful army captain's wife attend-ing a ball in clothes which had been "militarised" with camouflage and other elements,' explains Withers. 'We researched camouflage books from the Second World War. It was really hard work and bleak some-times in the workshop but we produced some fantastic things.'

The collection included handcrafted lace-up boots in calf with exposed stainless-steel toecaps and armature-structured bodiced leather jackets bearing imprints of small metal objects such as keys burnt into their surfaces as if by branding.

There were also gowns in pinstripe material threaded with tiny gold chain to provide a chainmail effect. 'We used everything from hessian as interlining to Bedford cord,' says Withers, who recalls obtaining the steel toecaps from specialist Dinkie Heel and located a loom operator on a Scottish isle who was prepared to risk their equipment by feeding dispa-rate material through it. 'That's where we made the stunning gold-chain pinstripe,' says Withers. 'It was breathtaking. We even got them to weave a crude, porcupine-like corduroy out of rubber.'

Trevor Myles, who had figured large in McLaren's life as the proprietor of Paradise Garage in the early 1970s, was asked to provide an industry insider's view. 'Those guys were coming up with mind-blowing stuff,' says Myles, who accompanied McLaren and his lawyer on a trip to Rome to check out a potential investor. 'We stayed overnight, sharing a room,' says Myles. 'Then, first thing in the morning, as the meeting got underway, Malcolm pointed to his solicitor and said: "He knows what I want. Talk to him because me and Trevor are going for breakfast." Then we walked out.

'I think Malcolm was demanding £100,000 upfront. He never got it, but it was worth the trip just for that moment.'

McLaren also developed on the theme of underwear as outerwear from Nostalgia of Mud by sampling a design for a conical brassiere in looped rolls of gold metal. Having poured his own money into the project and still without adequate outside investment he made a return to Paris, where he encountered the young designer Jean-Paul Gaultier, who was mining a similar vein. During their conversations, McLaren showed Gaultier some of the FAN MM prototypes, including the conical bra. Of course, a Gaultier variant achieved notoriety when worn by Madonna and her dancers several years later on the 1990 Blonde Ambition tour.

There are various versions of how this transaction proceeded. McLaren himself said that he gave the design to Gaultier in the spirit of comity. Others believe he sold it to the French designer. Withers, whose first-hand testimony is difficult to deny, says: 'I think Malcolm got over-enthusiastic and gave his visiting card away, as it were.'

The gesture was an indication of McLaren's waning interest. He visited the King's Cross studio less often and became increasingly diverted by the commitment to Charisma to record a follow-up to the half-million-seller *Duck Rock*.

Simon Withers recalls the end of FAN MM to the day. 'On 22 June 1984 Andrea and I visited the Denmark Street office and Malcolm told us it was over, that there was no more money and no sign of an investor,' says Withers. 'He'd put quite a bit in himself. It was no big deal. We'd done our best and produced some great work, I thought.'

Among the collection's accessories had been a range that conveyed McLaren's new musical direction: belts with large metal buckles proclaiming names taken from the world of opera, including pairs to be worn together such as 'Giacomo' and 'Puccini' and 'Cho Cho' and 'San'.

The origins in the new project, which he entitled *Fans*, lay not only in the inclusion of the Puccini arias in the Witches soundtrack the year before but also the aborted plan to produce a record by the Alabaman schoolteacher Mrs Froggett. McLaren later related that Trevor Horn had asked him what he wanted to do next musically, and, half-jokingly, he mentioned opera.

But there was no desire from either McLaren or Horn to continue the working relationship established by *Duck Rock*; McLaren was later to make derogatory references to 'these producers, they're big pot-belly farts who sit in their studios and blind you with science' (a dig at Horn's *Duck Rock* colleague Thomas Dolby, who had scored a British hit with a song entitled 'She Blinded Me with Science').[26]

With a limited budget and ensconced in Greene Street Studio in New York's Soho, McLaren reworked outtakes from *Duck Rock* with production duties handled by the hot New York club DJ Johnny Dynell, a former art student who had been a key player in New York nightlife since the late 1970s at such nightspots as Danceteria, the Mudd Club and Club 57. Together they added raps and vocals from R&B singer Angie Stone – at that stage known as Angie B – and pioneering female MC Sharon Green, who went by 'Sha Rock'.

Then, at the suggestion of Charisma's Steve Weltman, McLaren transferred to Synchro Sound, a Boston studio run by producer Stephen Hague and engineer Walter Turbitt, who had recently scored a hit with the World's Famous Supreme Team's McLaren-approved 'Hey DJ!' featuring samples from 'Buffalo Gals'.

As well as 'Duck Rock 2', McLaren struck a deal to deliver a third LP to Charisma. There had been talk of reviving the plan of recording an album of interpretations of standards which he had contemplated in Paris in the wake of the Pistols break-up. 'The record company had put Stephen Hague in charge of me supposedly singing songs like "A Foggy Day in London Town",' McLaren related in the 1990s. 'Well if you think I was gonna do that, you're much mistaken. I told the guy, "No, it's all changed." He had all the music sheets up, he'd prepared dodgy synth-pad stuff and it was all seemingly rather dreary and far too kosher. I thought I would do something a bit more drastic.'[27]

McLaren later claimed that while tinkering at Synchro Sound studios he received a call from Nick Egan in London informing him that Horn was planning to record a pop-opera record of his own. This was enough for McLaren to abandon the remaining *Duck Rock* tracks and direct his energies into the musical form that he had been talking up but about which he knew little. In a record shop in Cambridge, Massachusetts, McLaren purchased a compilation of Puccini's most popular tracks. 'I thought I'd better start simple,' he said. 'I don't want to sit here listening to three hours of opera. I'll never know whether I'm coming or going.'[28]

With Hague's help, McLaren established contact with the New England Conservatory of Music and recorded a choir of singers, with solos from soprano Betty Ann White and mezzosoprano Valerie Walters, performing Puccini compositions at Synchro Sound and in a church in neighbouring Belmont.

These performances then provided the beds for McLaren's by-now trademark audio collages, with beats, rhythms and vocals overlaid back in New York at Unique Recordings, a studio where one-off dance music tracks were the day-to-day constituency. As replacement for Hague, McLaren's right-hand man was the American musician, composer and arranger Robbie Kilgore, whose rap track record extended to acts such as Jazzy Jay (of the Zulu Nation), the Treacherous Three and Man Parrish, while he had also been responsible for such club hits as Shannon's 'Let the Music Play'. Unique and Kilgore provided, according to the *Boston Globe*'s Jim Sullivan, 'a sleazy, funky feeling where [McLaren] concocted a wild sort of, as he puts it, "porridge".'[29]

Entire opera storylines were condensed and given the Burroughsian cut-up treatment. 'I had never been to an opera and never listened to one from start to finish,' said McLaren. 'I began by recording a track with the task of reducing the story of *Madam Butterfly* to one song. I took "Un Bel dì Vedremo", the most famous aria from this opera, and began to arrange a beat and an R&B vocal interpretation with my pop producers. It wasn't easy but I managed to combine both an opera student's voice and an R&B session vocalist to tell the story, casting myself as the character Pinkerton. The song ended up being six-and-a-half-minutes long, and I had still not completed the whole story. I left the death of Cho Cho San to the end.'[30]

Released in the summer of 1984, 'Madam Butterfly' contrasted Betty Ann White's swooping soprano with the gritty vocal of soul singer Debbie Cole, leavened by McLaren's 'Yankee'-mimicking Pinkerton voiceovers. It was a seductive hit, reaching number thirteen in the British charts and confirming McLaren's position as a musical shape-shifter capable of not only championing vital new music genres but also of creating them from surprising juxtapositions.

'Opera is about the most irrational art form ever in the sense that it gets to your emotions better than anything else,' McLaren told Charisma press officer Stephen Alexander. 'What is great about opera and the story of Butterfly in particular is that it's so poignant; it's the absolute opposite to anything that's bland. The video for *Madam Butterfly* is actually gonna be very cinematic and has no mimed playback whatsoever. I want to create a moment and an expression that would enhance the record and allow you to listen, rather than be bamboozled by a variety of images. I think the content is in the record and in the vocals mainly. The vocals are what you want to listen to and you don't want to be completely disillusioned by seeing my face on screen and burst out laughing, so I've just opened it up to a lot of girls sitting about in a Turkish bath, waiting and crying their eyes out.'[31]

McLaren's abilities in harnessing astounding visuals to music were foregrounded in the promo, which was directed by the fashion and commercials photographer Terence Donovan.

As suggested to Alexander, McLaren conceived a scenario intended as the antithesis of the hyperactive videos dominating pop in the period. To the pulsating opening of the song, several beautiful young women in bathing suits emerged from the steam of a Turkish bath to self-consciously pose, stroll and drape themselves.

The television executive Andy Harries had by this time left broadcaster Granada and become a freelance director and producer. He had maintained contact with McLaren, and at one point the pair proposed a one-hour documentary about McLaren's engagement with Africa to Charisma's Tony Stratton-Smith, who failed to bite.

Now McLaren drew upon Harries's experience to pull the 'Madam Butterfly' video shoot together; Harries came up with the late Victorian Turkish baths in Harrogate, Yorkshire, as the location. 'I offered to direct it but Malcolm turned me down, saying he wanted "my mate Terence" and I could produce,' recalls Harries. 'I said, "He doesn't do videos does he?" and Malcolm said, "Doesn't matter, let's go and see him."

'So we walked through Mayfair and turn up at his plush office near Park Lane and, you couldn't make it up, but there was Terence sitting with Terence Stamp. But of course. Malcolm told him what he wanted and Terence Donovan said, "All right Malcolm, you want a few birds, some naked, some semi-naked and a couple with the gear on, that right?"'

Harries called the Virgin Records' video commissioner Tessa Watts – the late wife of Michael Watts, who had written perceptive profiles of McLaren earlier in the decade – and Donovan promptly ferried the pair in his 1960s open-top Bentley to the record company's offices in Ladbroke Grove, west London.

'Terence swept into Virgin with us trailing behind him and of course Tessa was completely bowled over and wrote him a cheque, which he put into his production company,' says Harries. 'Come the day of the shoot he came over and said, "Now Andy, as producer you can take cash", and pushed a couple of hundred quid into my top pocket with a wink.'

Harries says that McLaren acted as art director during the making of the promo, discussing angles, lighting and other elements with Donovan. Once again and unbeknown to the average pop fan, McLaren was engaging in an act of appropriation. The film emulated the approach of the American fashion photographer Deborah Turbeville and in particular her 1975 American *Vogue* shoot 'The Bath House'. But by activating Turbeville's mysterious *mise en scènes* and combining them with his strange new sound in the context of the MTV generation, McLaren presented, in his own words, an anti-pop moving portrait of 'the English feeling death-like . . . dull, bored and senseless'.

In the by-now cliché-ridden world of the promo, McLaren's film was hailed as radical. 'The most common critical complaint about rock videos is that the images they present detract from the images that a listener conjures up when listening to music,' wrote New York arts journalist Glenn O'Brien.

After seeing a video often, those predetermined images supplant the imagined images of the listener. McLaren has conquered that problem here. He has made a transparent video. Although the images are as strong and sexy as any others in rock video, they are ephemeral. The song and its literal images are present only in the minds of the women we see. Although the visible images are strong, they are static and defer to the invisible images. The women are dreamers and we seek their dream. Our own reverie is accelerated. The images are almost like a hypnotic drug.[32]

The mood was also evoked in the series of record sleeves accompanying *Fans* and its single releases. These were designed by Nick Egan and featured not McLaren but fashion-style portraits of such fresh new models as Susie Bick, as well as copious and instructive notes on the operas that had been co-opted.

The 'Madam Butterfly' promo format proved popular; Donovan himself repeated the foregrounding of groups of bored-looking attractive models in a series of popular clips for the British R&B/soul singer Robert Palmer.

'Malcolm was really pissed off about that,' says Andy Harries. 'Malcolm felt Terence had ripped him off. Much later he asked to show one of the Palmer videos as part of a presentation showing his influence and Terence wouldn't give him permission. They fell out quite heavily.'

In one respect, 'Madam Butterfly' was a musical realisation of McLaren's plans for the stillborn FAN MM collection. 'I was putting the diva into the modern context of a discotheque,' he said decades later. 'Unfolding that in front of people's eyes as a Cupid who doesn't have a bow. It was an attempt to change lives. When the track was first played in a New York nightclub, people were convinced that the operatic voices they heard in the dance groove were coming through the walls from the theatre next door. It was a collision of worlds. This genuine experience of breaking through the boundaries of your "lifestyle" into something bigger.'

The process of the recording of the tracks for *Fans* was captured in the hour-long film about McLaren's life and work broadcast when the LP was released in the winter of 1984 as part of the Sunday-night British television arts strand *The South Bank Show*. This episode was the brain-child of director Andy Harries, who had been nurturing the project since the collapse of the *Insider's Guide* film for Granada.

Harries initially pitched it to the BBC TV arts strand *Arena*, whose head of programming Alan Yentob had been hankering to realise a McLaren documentary since his own failure to realise such a project due to the 'Chicken' furore. But the BBC passed and *The South Bank Show's* main man Melvyn (now Lord) Bragg gave it the green light.

'I can't remember Melvyn's exact words, but the gist was, "I don't know anything about the Sex Pistols and I've never heard of Malcolm McLaren, but I'm told by everyone here that we should be doing this film and you seem a bright young chap and the person to do it," ' says Harries.

'In those days it was difficult to take a crew to New York but Melvyn told me not to worry. They set up an NY bank account, the programme's production accountant transferred £20k and I had the budget to hire crews and equipment there. That meant I could produce it under my own steam and at the end of the day they would buy it.'

Inclusion in *The South Bank Show*'s rollcall – previous subjects had ranged from Paul McCartney to Laurence Olivier via Satyajit Ray and Francis Ford Coppola – conferred importance to McLaren's position in British cultural life. 'Over the past ten years, McLaren's name has been synonymous with the development of British youth culture, fashion and pop music, and he's sought, and found, controversy and commercial success for his many and varied projects,' said Bragg during his opening remarks as he introduced Harries's mission to discover 'what motivates the man who had been described as the Diaghilev of punk'.[33]

With McLaren's participation in sequences filmed at the Moulin Rouge offices and various locations in Boston and New York, the inventive film contained contributions from Trevor Horn and such major stars of the day as Boy George and Adam Ant, as well as rap diversions from the World's Famous Supreme Team and interviews with Steve Jones, representing the Sex Pistols, and Annabella Lwin of Bow Wow Wow. Although his time at 430 King's Road was covered, Westwood declined involvement.

McLaren's life was traced back to Stoke Newington (the houses where he grew up in Carysfort Road were included in footage) and the idiosyncratic relationship with Rose Corré was explored. Since *Fans* track 'The Boy's Chorus' paraphrased his grandmother's refrain with the chant 'All work, no joy, makes Mac a dull boy', McLaren's time at Clissold Park's Avigdor school was recreated with a segment miming to the song in front of a classroom of eight-year-olds at the Simon Marks Jewish Primary School (also in Stoke Newington).

Cannily, Harries filmed McLaren in sites where he would open up. A visit to the Guggenheim prompted McLaren to talk about his relationship to the visual arts and his art school years, and a set-up paid tribute to McLaren's considerable abilities as a raconteur, positioning him at the head of a long table in conversation with Nick Egan and Rory Johnston as they shared food and wine. This was filmed in the Upper West Side home of the up-and-coming twenty-one-year-old club kid and fashion designer Marc Jacobs, who was fascinated by McLaren and had just left Parsons School of Design on West 11th Street with the coveted Golden Thimble award as young fashion designer of the year.

They shared similar backgrounds; a fellow Jew, Jacobs's father died when he was seven and he was very close to his grandmother Helen (it was, in fact, her apartment in the art deco Majestic Apartments at Central Park West where the 'dinner party' sequence was shot).

'Marc was a kid, a pop-culture junkie whose fix was music, style, gossip and art,' said Egan, who, along with his girlfriend, *Details* fashion editor Ellen Kinnally, was soon sharing an apartment with Jacobs and his boyfriend, the nightclub impresario Robert Boykin, owner of Hurrah. 'Marc's eyes were wide open and enthusiastic like any fan. I saw both a young kid who wanted to have fun, but I also saw a dedication and a maturity that most don't have at that age. He was never driven by fame or money. For Malcolm and I to walk into his life at that time must have been a huge inspiration to him – not in his designs, because Marc always had his own style – but more in his attitude. It made him more street-savvy.'[34]

'I didn't know anything about Marc; you had to be deeply involved in the fashion business to have even heard of him at that stage,' says Johnston. 'I remember Malcolm telling me, "This is a really, really important guy. He's going to be huge."'

During the filming of the New York sequences, McLaren stayed at the Hotel Mayflower on the Upper West Side. 'One of our biggest problems was that Malcolm would never get up before twelve noon,' recalls Harries. 'I'd often be sitting at the end of his fucking bed, begging him, "Malcolm, will you please get up?" He'd be going, "No man, I just have to make a few more phone calls," totally oblivious to the fact that the crew had been waiting for hours.'

But the subject's lack of punctuality was a minor consideration. The completed programme was impressive in its scope and narrative thrust and benefited both McLaren and Harries. 'It really helped put me on the map,' says Harries. 'I remember Melvyn told me that Paul McCartney loved it.'

The South Bank Show was also well received critically, though *Fans* on the other hand served to confuse reviewers and music consumers, not least because it contained only six tracks, the majority of funds having been ploughed into 'Madam Butterfly'; McLaren was now paying for the recording of *Duck Rock* going way over budget. Within a few months, he was describing *Fans* as 'really a demo' and claiming that, once again, he was facing legal action from his record label because he had not delivered the goods.

'They feel I've cheated, I've ripped them off, because the album's a little too short,' he said. 'I say never mind the quantity, it's quality that counts. There's a court case about it right now. It's a lovely little album, very pretty. It's a marriage of the uptown, white, moneyed opera students I found in Boston, and the hip-hop, downtown, braggart-kid who's desperate to get a few bucks. Having manifested the Sex Pistols I've taken advantage and continued the saga. This is the closest thing to "Anarchy in the UK" I can muster in 1985.'[35]

McLaren drew upon the brightest new talents of British fashion for the *Fans* sleeve, with contributions from John Galliano and stylists Paul Frecker and Amanda Grieve (now Harlech). 'What we did was a very cheap album, which is why I dressed it up in the very classy sleeve with the fans and girls and all,' he said the next year. 'It made the album glamorous. I could imagine people going to discos with fans, because it does get rather hot in there.'

To promote the release in New York, McLaren organised an 'opera night' with DJs Kurtis Blow and the World's Famous Supreme Team scratching classical tracks at a New York venue. 'We sent out fans as invitations; you had to bring them along to get in, and then to the ugly people in The Who Final Tour satin jackets we'd give masks to cover them up,' claimed McLaren. 'People danced to opera. It changed the whole ambience. Then suddenly they put on Shannon or Michael Jackson and they sound terrible, packaged, less emotional, duller. The records made the bloody place look cheap, while the opera made it romantic and glamorous. Wouldn't it be nice to make that transformation all the time? Well, wouldn't it?'[36]

McLaren was convinced that *Fans* was surfing the zeitgeist, citing the recent release of Francesco Rosi's film *Bizet's Carmen* and claiming a rise of interest in the musical form in European capitals. 'Jean-Paul Gaultier, the French designer, is quite operatic, although it may be unconsciously,' McLaren told Glenn O'Brien. 'But the whole flamboyant atmosphere – Paris, Germany, Europe loves that; it's fulfilling their 19th-century ideals. It's the *Empire Strikes Back* mentality.'[37]

It is a fact that, from the mid-1980s on, opera began its journey to mass appeal as it was incorporated initially in arthouse and then mainstream film soundtracks and soon in TV advertising. This blossomed to such an extent that, by the end of the decade, mass recognition had been achieved by such figures as Luciano Pavarotti, who, McLaren claimed in 1985, was 'more over the top than these rock & roll singers. Yeah, it's true man, your Keith Richards ain't got nothing on these geezers. Pavarotti really is a fucking god-man.'[38]

McLaren adopted the role of Don Juan for one of the album's standouts, 'Carmen', which contrasted Angie B's street edge with Valerie Walters's lines from Bizet, but in total *Fans* was too one-note – and insubstantial at thirty minutes playing time – to become the standard-bearer of McLaren's dreams. Aside from the genuinely heartfelt nature of 'Madam Butterfly' (which, with 'Carmen', had benefited from Hague's musical adroitness), the record lacked *Duck Rock*'s variety and warmth so failed to find an audience, stalling just inside the top fifty in Britain and making virtually no mark in the US.

McLaren's lack of application during the recording process was a factor, though he could be excused for his flagging energy. Coming off the decade-long explosion of activity since upping sticks for America to work with the New York Dolls in late 1974, McLaren was handling the emotional and financial fallout over the rancorous final split with Westwood, the failure to establish a name for himself in fashion and alienation from Charisma and the record business at large.

These all took their toll on the thirty-eight-year-old who was quick to confess that Robbie Kilgore had carried the weight of the production. 'Every day I'd play Robbie opera records and tell him the stories, to let him know what he was doing, what feel I was looking for,' he recalled within six months of the album's release. 'I'd tell him not to give me heavy hammer-to-the-head beats. I'd have to do that, because you know musicians are very coarse. They did a jolly good job at keeping with the sentiment of the material [but] I couldn't stay around with them banging in my ear all day. I'd go to the galleries and everything. And I'd read the biography of Puccini. And then I waited for Angie B to show up and that was my next bit. I have better things to do than hang around a studio.

'The thing I really hate is the way record company people want you to be as simple as they are. They want you to go buying antiques with them on Saturdays. They don't like you going off having mad ideas. Contracts being contracts, they want to know exactly where you are every day. They've always got some nonsense, like doing a 12-inch remix or something, and they won't leave you alone.'

Fans contained sufficient theatrical elements for McLaren to consider a new direction, onto Broadway, or off-Broadway at least. The impetus lay in the title track, which blended the 'Nessun Dorma' aria from Puccini's *Turandot* with an R&B instrumental. For this he had encouraged Angie Stone to compose a fan letter, which she read against the solo from the tenor Michael Austin while in the background McLaren barked curtain calls in the manner of an insolent stage hand.

'I threw in the "Fans" track at the last minute because I was running out of money and I only had five songs done, and trying to do *Tosca* was giving me trouble,' admitted McLaren. 'So I sketched out the song, wanting some emotional, sentimental thing. I thought it should be a love letter rather than a song. I forced Angie B to write it herself. Then we chucked in the chorus bit and the end. The track is like you're tuned just between two radio stations, and you're picking up opera and R&B at the same time by accident. You can't focus on what you're supposed to be listening to, a fabulous dynamic.'

The tensions between the fan and the superstar, between high culture as represented by opera ('uptown') and the street culture of black urban life ('downtown'), provided the impetus for McLaren's pitch for a full-blown stage version of *Fans*, and his reputation was sufficient to open the doors for meetings with such New York theatreland bigwigs as impresario Joseph Papp.

He later claimed to Boston journalist Jim Sullivan that they had welcomed him with open arms: ' "We've been waiting for guys like you, Malcolm! You're the guy with his finger on the pulse. You're the guy who showed us Boy George. You're the guy who showed us the Sex Pistols . . . You're the sort of guy who ought to be on Broadway!"

' "If you say so," McLaren responds to that spiel. "Where do I begin?" '[39]

PART VI

Wilde West

Chapter 31

Though Malcolm McLaren's plans for 'Fans: The Musical' eventually faltered, the initial development phase provided a bridge from the record industry treadmill to another area of focus, cinema.

His proposal for the theatrical production of 'Fans' was that the action should take place on a split-level stage set, to reflect the project's uptown/ downtown tensions. Three singers were to represent the characters Carmen, Cho Cho San from *Madam Butterfly* and Tosca on the upper deck, and the lower would present three urban girls, a Puerto Rican, a Japanese and an Italian, whose passions and love lives were manipulated by those above them.

'It's perfect!' exclaimed McLaren. 'Just cut the fucking stage in half horizontally – heaven and earth – slipping from opera to R&B with relative ease and without being too self-conscious about it.'[1]

Never one to give up on a concept, this was the latest – though toned-down – manifestation of 'The Adventures of Melody, Lyric & Tune' film idea from Paris in 1979 blended with another, more recent, proposal to stage a musical in London's West End presenting the African dancers and music from *Duck Rock*. This, he felt, would have been a way of entering another medium and simultaneously disrupting the smug Shaftesbury Avenue set by exposing central London to the tribal heartland. In several aspects it was a precursor to the contemporary phenomenon of refreshing collections of pop songs by particular artists for the stage (the most successful of which is, of course, the Abba-based *Mamma Mia!*). It also awoke in him the theatrical ambitions harboured by his long-dead grandmother.

McLaren had discussed this plan in 1982 with the Chelsea playwright Jonathan Gems, the former lover of Vivienne Westwood who he had tracked down to Sloane Square's Royal Court Theatre. Now Gems was drafted in to create the book for 'Fans'; in fact he had already utilised the two-tier staging for his 1984 Royal Court play *Doom Doom Doom Doom*.

McLaren meantime had retained his friendship and working relationship with Rory Johnston, who had advised on promotional aspects of both *Duck Rock* and *Fans* and was now free of his managerial input into Bow Wow Wow. The group McLaren had formed amid the embers of punk had disintegrated the previous year when the three male musicians unceremoniously dumped Annabella Lwin following the poor reception of their third LP.

Now Johnston became McLaren's de facto business manager, helping him pitch at Joseph Papp and executives from his Public Theater on Lafayette Street, New York. 'We got a really good response from Papp and his people,' says Johnston. 'They liked Malcolm and his ideas.' However, these discussions were to drag on for years, during which time McLaren developed a near-obsessive ambition to realise another theatrical production which, while also never realised, never left him. To the end of his life, a plate McLaren kept spinning was the concept marrying the tale of 'Beauty and the Beast' with the life of a leading fashion designer. For the time being it was to be a fantasy but he was eventually to settle on the life of Christian Dior, whose brilliant career was cut short by death under mysterious circumstances in the Italian town of Montecatini in the mid-1950s. Subsequently his place at the pinnacle of Paris couture was taken by his twenty-one-year-old artistic director Yves Saint Laurent; there has long been conjecture that they were conducting an affair. At different times the project was entitled 'Fashion Beast' and 'Diorama'.

McLaren described it as 'a life of Dior', though the story's flight of the central character from his mother chimes with McLaren's personal history. 'Dior has a spell cast on him by his mother who's completely gorgeous, or thinks she is, and would never wear anything other than La Belle Epoque,' said McLaren. 'In order to remove the spell he has to fall in love. So this fashion beast surrounds himself with beauty. No one's ever made a fashion movie from a gothic point of view. It's Dior's world bastardised and transposed in a future imperfect. I love his story, especially at the end where Yves St Laurent becomes his lover . . . or at least thinks he does. St Laurent, who, if you wish, could be a girl, is the love interest from another world, coming to break his spell.'[2]

Simultaneously this also became a companion film proposal, which had been prompted by Jonathan Gems, who told McLaren's 1980s biographer Craig Bromberg that while he was wrestling with the 'Fans' outline he had suggested a cinematic collaboration based around the 'Beauty and the Beast' myth. It was McLaren, according to Gems, who added the Dior element. As Bromberg tells it, club DJ and producer Johnny Dynell then connected McLaren to a screenwriter, Kit Carson. Excited by the proposal, Carson in turn introduced McLaren to a William Morris agent named Erica Spellman.

Finally, McLaren was closing in on realising the plan to become a fully fledged auteur which had been sparked in the late 1960s by his student project *The Story of Oxford Street* and thwarted by the failure of 'Who Killed Bambi?' and the subsequent loss of control over *The Great Rock 'n' Roll Swindle*.

Johnston and Carson accompanied McLaren on a trip to the West Coast in the autumn of 1984 to pitch 'Fashion Beast' in a series of meetings arranged by Erica Spellman with top brass at such majors as Twentieth Century Fox, Columbia and Warner Bros as well as a number of prominent independents. 'They all opened their doors for Malcolm,' says Johnston. 'He was such an exciting prospect for them because *Duck Rock* and "Madam Butterfly" had caused a stir and he brought a rock 'n' roll edge with him.'

Craig Bromberg's book essays the reaction among Californian film executives to the Londoner's punk attitude and frenetic behaviour. Among McLaren's worst characteristics, even for that stab-you-in-the-back town, was his constant shifting of loyalties. He started with abandonment of Carson and Spellman.

'Before they left for LA we agreed if there was a deal to be made with anybody I had sent them to, I would make the deal,' Spellman told Bromberg. 'The next thing I knew, it was as though I had not done anything and was not to be involved. Malcolm had decided to do everything on his own. It was the single most distasteful thing that happened to me as an agent.'[3]

Soon Carson was off the team when Lynda Obst, a senior at David Geffen's film production house, expressed interest in 'Fashion Beast'. Carson was to successfully sue McLaren for $35,000 on the basis that it was his treatment that had enabled McLaren to close in on a deal.

But the project wasn't to travel past discussion stage. Eager to annex original thinking amid the dross that passed for discourse in Hollywood in the 1980s, Obst was initially enchanted by the unlikely looking McLaren, who had allowed his hair to grow into the long ringlets of his spoiled childhood. Never a conventional fashion figure, McLaren matched this Sideshow Bob cut with long, widened culottes, tight pink polo necks, long socks and slim loafers or Converse boots. This oddly comical silhouette empowered him to embark on wild flights of fancy during Hollywood conflabs, just as his leather and bondage gear had made the difference in the entertainment epicentre when he was proclaiming on behalf of the Sex Pistols in 1977.

Obst later described her first encounter with McLaren as 'the most memorable pitch of my career . . . a performance of stellar quality which I have since discovered was entirely rehearsed, because later on he did the same pitch for David Geffen word for word, beat for beat'.[4]

For McLaren, the performance was everything. He later told his friend Peter Culshaw about the meet with David Geffen: 'For two hours, his room was my stage. It felt like a movie even though there was no story and no characters, or only the most mythic characters.'[5]

One has to ask: what did Obst expect? The fact that McLaren made the presentation appear extemporaneous was surely to his credit. But nevertheless, the suspicion in the wider film community lingered. Bromberg, whose book manifestly sympathises with his compatriots in

Recreation of Manet's *Le Déjeuner sur l'herbe* with Bow Wow Wow art-directed by McLaren, Priory Park, Reigate, Surrey, summer 1981. *(© Andy Earl)*

With Vivienne Westwood and models (including centre, standing, Nick Kamen) in Worlds End, October 1981. *(© David Montgomery/Getty Images)*

Nostalgia of Mud team outside 5 Christopher's Place, central London, including (top) Vivienne Westwood, (second right standing) Yvonne Gold, (second right crouching in Mountain hat) Gene Krell and (second left crouching) Herbie Mensah. *(© Robyn Beeche)*

With Andrea Linz and a Richard Hambleton Shadowman, Bethune Street, West Village, New York, spring 1983. *(© Bob Gruen)*

Wearing three Mountain hats with Duck Rocker and the Hilltoppers at their homestead, Roan Mountain, Carter County, East Tennessee, spring 1983. *(© Bob Gruen)*

Portrait of the artist as a production executive at CBS Theatrical Films, Los Angeles, 1985. *(© Deborah Feingold/Getty Images)*

With World's Famous Supreme Team members Larry Price (aka See Divine the Mastermind) and Ron Larkins Jr (Just Allah the Superstar), London, February 1983. *(Iconic Images © Gered Mankowitz)*

Downtown Tower Records window display to coincide with the exhibition *Impresario: Malcolm McLaren & the British New Wave*, autumn 1988.
(New Museum of Contemporary Art)

With Lauren Hutton, Madison Square Garden, New York, 20 February 1989.
(© Ron Gallela/Getty Images)

Promoting *Waltz Darling* with dancers including Willi Ninja (centre beneath McLaren), 1989.
(© Bob Gruen)

On the set of *The Ghosts of Oxford Street*, London, autumn 1991.
(Middlemarch Films for Channel 4 © Rebecca Frayn)

The cover of *Paris*, 1994.
(© Jean Baptiste-Mondino)

Thumbprint label for the 'Malcolm McLaren' tailored menswear collection, 1994.
(© Malcolm McLaren Estate)

With Françoise Hardy at the New York launch of *Paris*, 1994. *(© Bob Gruen)*

With Jungk at their New York unveiling at the Convent of the Sacred Heart, Upper East Side, New York, 1998. *(© Henri Struck)*

With Young Kim in Beijing, September 2003. *(© Shutterstock)*

Vinyl featuring the infant McLaren on its label for the 'Fashion Beast' party at Pitti Immagine, Florence, spring 2004.

Promotional shot for *I'm A Celebrity… Get Me Out of Here!*, 2007. *(© ITV/Shutterstock)*

Still, *Shallow 1–21*, 2008. *(© Malcolm McLaren Estate)*

Being manhandled
by harbour master
Michael Watt after
informing the
residents of the
Scottish village of
Gardenstown that
'Jesus is a sausage',
2008.
(© ITV/Shutterstock)

(above) History Is For Pissing On,
Edinburgh Festival, August 2009.
(© Geraint Lewis/Shutterstock)

(left) Still, *Paris, Capital of the XXIst
Century*, 2010. *(© Malcolm McLaren Estate)*

LA, describes McLaren in this period as 'a con man', a view that was held by many.

For the time being, Obst was interested enough to recommend a screenwriter to replace Kit Carson. Dutchman Menno Meyjes was hot-to-trot, having just completed the script for Steven Spielberg's in-production big-screen version of Alice Walker's novel *The Color Purple*, and worked with McLaren on polishing the treatment not only for 'Fashion Beast' but also that for 'Fans: The Musical'.

'We'd just got back from filming *The Color Purple* in Carolina,' says Meyjes. 'We met at a restaurant and it was sort of social. Lynda said that Malcolm had some interesting projects that I might like. I'd obviously known about him for years; when I was a student in San Francisco I was going to go to the last Sex Pistols gig but got waylaid. I liked him and we started spending time together.'

Meyjes counters the impression given by Bromberg's book that there was widespread dislike and mistrust of McLaren in LA. 'It's important to point out that people really liked Malcolm there,' he says. 'LA is always looking for something new. It's not a particularly conservative place so people wanted to meet him and hear his ideas. The way he looked and expressed himself meant there was a certain amount of fascination. They may not have known what he was on about sometimes but were very happy to help steer the energy he exuded in a direction. He was an exciting guy.'[6]

Backed by his powerful lawyer Peter Dekom – who had also been recommended by Obst – McLaren then demanded a two-project deal. Concerned that what had begun as a relatively straightforward contract for a mid-level budget movie was spiralling out of her control, Obst was also alarmed by McLaren's pestering of David Geffen, since this shattered the protocols of the industry caste system. Her alarm was compounded by a confrontation with Erica Spellman, who pointed out to Obst that she was due commission on any agreements, and since McLaren wouldn't play ball, Geffen would have to pay up.

This was but one of a number of bars to the Geffen deal going through. Freaked at the story McLaren was putting around town that the company was going to pay him $1 million, when in fact their offer would have been in the $50,000 range, Geffen pulled the rug. Once again, the constant spinning, which had worked so well in the relatively parochial milieu of the British music, fashion and media industries, came up against the obdurate, risk-averse American entertainment complex.

'He [was] one of those people who's perfect for his time, because he's like cocaine and that's when everyone was into it,' said Spellman in the 1980s. 'You get very euphoric when Malcolm comes bouncing into your life. There he is – attractive, charming, all the rest – and then before you know it you're down on your knees with your eyes all bloodshot.'[7]

In an act of generosity following the failure of the Geffen deal, Lynda Obst introduced McLaren to the super-producer Ileen Maisel at CBS Films, where she suspected there might be a fit as a production executive at the TV and stage arm, CBS Theatrical Films.

With negotiations over terms underway with CBS, McLaren returned to London to settle his affairs and prepare the shift of base to LA. His relationship with Andrea Linz had foundered as a result of his absences, and she declined a last-minute offer to join him in the US where, he said, they could become engaged. This repeated the pattern of the failure with Vivienne Westwood; having neglected his partner for too long, McLaren overcompensated in dramatic fashion just at the point when she slipped away.

The Moulin Rouge offices vacated, the FAN MM project dead and the Hunter Street flat shuttered, McLaren had no emotional ties to Britain, having been detached from his immediate family for decades and harbouring few, if any, paternal feelings towards his son Joe, now seventeen and living in London. Again, a circle remained unbroken, that of parental abandonment.

The return to the US slotted with his final promotional duties for the flagging *Fans* LP. Music, and the music business, no longer held his interest and he had not only tired of the pop routine but was once again plagued by litigation. Unique Recordings, where taping the tracks for

'Duck Rock 2' continued with Robbie Kilgore in desultory fashion, was claiming $100,000 in unpaid studio-hire bills.

Meanwhile, in the fickle world of the charts, the Duck Rocking court jester had been supplanted by the likes of Frankie Goes to Hollywood, the Liverpudlian quintet to whom his former collaborator Trevor Horn successfully applied McLaren-like marketing shock tactics.

Now McLaren was entering a peripatetic phase that would make his recent existence appear that of a homebody. From here on, McLaren's restlessness and feelings of grievance against his home country spelled an end to long-term residence there. He was to return to live in London, but often used it as a base for travels around the world in the ensuing years.

A factor was the legal dispute over his management of the Sex Pistols, which rumbled through the British courts in *Jarndyce and Jarndyce* fashion. In 1984 John Lydon sought to break the deadlock by initiating an action to exclude McLaren and divide the existing and future Sex Pistols royalties income and ownership of the name between the three ex-members and the estate of Sid Vicious (represented by his mother). McLaren responded with a counterclaim, on the basis that this was unreasonable. Continuing legal argy-bargy meant that, five years in, a court date had still not been set for resolution.

In the final media encounters for *Fans*, McLaren did not disguise his disenchantment with the music business. 'I'm doing this promotion for the record company right now, but I don't have much interest in it,' he told LA music journalist Mark Leviton. 'It's nice they've paid for my flight and hotel and all, but I really can't wait to get in a cab and go over to Paramount and try to sell them an idea.'[8]

In later life McLaren related that the promotional trip had culminated with two weeks on US record company Island's coin at LA's Sunset Strip hotel, the Mondrian. Finished with *Fans* and the negotiations with CBS continuing, McLaren stayed on. 'Nobody presented me with a bill, so I lived there for six more weeks, avoiding any messages reception left for me and nipping out of side doors to have meetings and go to dinner,' he said in the late 2000s. 'I didn't know what to do. The CBS deal wasn't done and I couldn't return home. I prayed the hotel staff had forgotten I was staying there. Then, one day when I was hiding in my room, a loud voice came over the Tannoy: "Paging Malcolm McLaren! Paging Malcolm McLaren! Would Mr McLaren please come to the front desk?!" I wondered whether I should just pack my bags and slip away, but kept on hearing this voice and approached the lobby with some trepidation.'

But there was no staff confrontation awaiting him. They had been receiving calls for McLaren for several weeks from the team at Steven Spielberg's Amblin Entertainment and resorted to the Tannoy after becoming frustrated in their efforts to track him down.

Menno Meyjes had mentioned that he was working with McLaren over lunch with the director. 'Steven didn't really know who he was and had no idea about the Sex Pistols, that is just not in his wheelhouse, as they say over there,' says Meyjes. 'But I played *Fans* to him and he loved it. Then I got a call from [Spielberg's production partner] Kathleen Kennedy, who said Steven had been playing *Fans* to Harrison Ford, who also loved it. So Steven then became involved.'

Soon a car arrived and McLaren – who was yet to learn to drive – was whisked across to the Amblin production suite on the Universal lot. There he was met by Spielberg, sat at a long table and flanked by a retinue of expectant executives.

This encounter ended in a desultory fashion, with Spielberg asking McLaren whether he was contemplating recording another album in the style of *Fans*. McLaren later told his partner Young Kim that he asked the director why he would do such a thing. 'So I can watch you,' Spielberg remarked, according to McLaren, who said that the director described McLaren as 'like a film director without a camera'.

At a follow-up meeting Kathleen Kennedy asked McLaren whether he could come up with a talk for a high-profile Aids benefit dinner hosted in Los Angeles by Armani and attended by Spielberg, Martin Scorsese and Bob Dylan among others.

'Thinking on my feet, I started telling them all the story of how Oscar Wilde discovered rock 'n' roll in America,' said McLaren in the 2000s.

McLaren had recently absorbed *Impressions of America*, the Irish playwright's account of the marathon lecture tour of the US he undertook in 1882. The identification with Wilde ran deep; the acerbic dandy's visit was set up by the theatrical impresario Richard D'Oyly Carte after Wilde was satirised in the Gilbert & Sullivan production *Patience; or Bunthorne's Bride* (1881), and so it was felt that American audiences would be more inclined to the production by encountering the original model on the tour, which was granted the theme 'On Beauty'. But Wilde used the exercise to extend his own celebrity in the place he is credited as having described as 'the only country that went from barbarism to decadence without civilization in between'.

Given his experiences with the New York Dolls in Manhattan and Florida, those with the Sex Pistols in California and the Deep South, and his *Duck Rock* adventures from the South Bronx to the Appalachians, McLaren was in agreement.

'Wilde was brought in to define his notion of beauty during a time when America was changing,' said McLaren, who related the episode where the playwright was invited to visit a newly built opera house in the rowdy mining boomtown of Leadville in Colorado and addressed an audience that the night before had attended the public lynching of a pair of criminals (the bodies still hung over the streets).

Wilde then visited roughhouse bars populated by rambunctious brass bands and, according to contemporary accounts, 'wildness and wickedness to satisfy the most insatiate seeker of excitement . . . female bathers, daring tumblers and other dramatic attractions . . . the final show, at one o'clock in the morning beggars description for all that is vile. Even the bedizened girls in the boxes turn their back for shame. Yet the drunken crowd hoots with glee, mainly, I believe, at the effrontery of the show.'[9]

In McLaren's interpretation of the evening, Wilde was 'stopped in his tracks by a cacophonous sound. Venturing through the smoke he found this polyethnic creature chanting and wailing. The guys were throwing coins and dollar bills and a man was banging a tin plate in time with her music. Oscar felt that he'd discovered beauty and that he had to take her back with him to England, but the girl escaped and it took another fifty or sixty years before such a thing elevated itself to the status that would bring about a change in America's popular culture. That thing was called rock 'n' roll.'

According to McLaren, Spielberg was intrigued and told him to work on the idea and return in a year, while he continued to hover around formal involvement in 'Fans: The Musical'. 'Steven thought Malcolm was a curious, interesting guy,' says Menno Meyjes. 'He was in his butterfly-collector mode and thought, "Oh, I like this man." '

In the meantime, 'Wilde West', as the pitch was now titled, was added to 'Fashion Beast' and 'Fans' as one of the properties tied into McLaren's two-year contract as an in-house producer with CBS Theatrical Films, which commenced in May 1985 with an annual six-figure salary, an office on the lot and a rented house at 1580½ Glencoe Way, a winding cul-de-sac in the heights above the Hollywood Bowl.

On signing the deal McLaren requested the entire interior of his office be painted black, like the hallway in Clapham he had decorated after leaving Goldsmiths and the Paradise Garage interior, which had so impressed him in the early 1970s.

McLaren was assigned a secretary and employed a young development assistant, Paige Simpson. 'An agent at ICM I knew called me and told me about this British producer who had a deal with CBS Theatrical,' says Simpson. 'I was a pretty naive Midwestern girl and didn't know who I was meeting and embarrassingly had never heard of the Sex Pistols or Malcolm. So I arrived at his office on the lot in my cheap three-piece suit with heels and was shocked to meet this guy wearing a pink cashmere sweater backwards over a long-sleeved, elegant white tuxedo shirt with culottes and Vans.

'He had such a thick accent I could barely understand what he was talking about. He showed me the video he made for "Madam Butterfly", which I thought was the most beautiful thing I'd ever seen, and then he talked about Sid Vicious and his past. He really tried to educate me about his life and when I left I thought there was no way I was going to get the job because I wasn't hip enough.'[10]

But Simpson received the call the next day and was to work with McLaren for the next couple of years, allocating writers for scripts and helping develop the properties generally. 'The productions he had in mind were considered quite eccentric but I thought they were wonderful,' says Simpson, who recounts a familiar issue in regard to McLaren's consistency.

'Malcolm would arrive in the morning with a brilliant idea, we'd talk it through, and I'd prepare an outline, but the next day he would want to drastically change it or be off in another direction, so it sometimes became difficult to pin him down. It was challenging but always very rewarding working with Malcolm.'

It's impressive that, exactly a year after the formal dissolution of his partnership with Vivienne Westwood, McLaren had achieved a reinvention far ahead of any of his peers in the British music and fashion businesses. He had a prominent position in the film industry, a good salary, a very comfortable home in the Hollywood Hills and a regular day job, the first in his adult life. As if that wasn't an unexpected turn of events, more surprising was the fact that he had a new partner, one whom he would soon proclaim as another first: the love of his life. This was the renowned beauty and model-turned-actress Lauren Hutton, famous for having graced the cover of US *Vogue* fourteen times and appearing in the box-office hit *American Gigolo*.

Hutton approached McLaren with her friends the actors Beverly D'Angelo and John Cusack as he was on his way to dinner one night with Rory Johnston and the photographer Michael Halsband at the Beverly Hills steakhouse and celebrity haunt Morton's.

'I had just read an interview with this guy who said all this stuff that Hollywood people would never say in a newspaper, the kind of stuff that gets you sued upside down and backwards,' she recalled not long after McLaren's death in 2010. 'I remember thinking "Boy I've got to meet this guy" . . . When I asked him if he was Malcolm McLaren, he jumped up in the air, spun around, landed and said, "Yes!" His hair went out like a giant red puffball, like an exploded bunch of red dandelions all over his head. That's how it started.'[11]

'To be honest I'd never heard of her,' said McLaren a couple of years later. 'She said, "Which one's Malcolm McLaren?" I spun round and went as bright as a beetroot. I was extremely embarrassed but said, "Actually it's me."'

According to McLaren, D'Angelo and Hutton joined the Brits and Halsband for dinner after ordering the then-teenage Cusack home. 'About halfway through the meal, Beverly D'Angelo got up and started singing "I Can't Fuck Without Falling in Love". It left the entire restaurant speechless and me thinking this was the nightly routine, with me as the schmuck.'

After the meal the actors took McLaren, Halsband and Johnston to Peanuts, an old-school West Hollywood lesbian and transvestite bar. 'I danced all night with Beverly but kept looking out of the corner of my eye at Lauren Hutton, dancing atrociously I'll have you know,' said McLaren. 'I couldn't look at her properly. I was too shy. I didn't know too much about her but I liked her a lot. After they left I said to my friends, "I'm gonna get that girl." I spent the next two days working up the courage to call her and she called me! She had obviously spent a few days in Tower Records finding out about me because she started singing "Madam Butterfly" down the phone.'[12]

The pair became a notable couple about town; the beautiful actress who was three years older than her avant-garde British beau. 'I got to know him inside and out,' Hutton said. 'He was extraordinarily intelligent, but, boy, was he complicated.'

McLaren's friends recall how smitten he became with Hutton. Andy Harries stayed with McLaren while working on a Barbra Streisand documentary in LA for six weeks around this time. 'One night he woke me up at 2.30 a.m. to have an urgent talk about how confused he felt about Lauren,' says Harries. 'It had hit him that he had fallen in love, so he was flooded with emotions he'd never previously had to deal with. It was genuinely daunting for Malcolm, so I sat up with him and tried my best to talk him through it.'

One night during Harries's stay it was decided that Hutton would be moving back into the house on Glencoe Way after a period apart, and as a result Harries would take her hotel room at the Chateau Marmont. McLaren had recently passed his driving test and insisted on driving Harries down the winding roads of the Hollywood Hills to Sunset Strip.

'How he passed that test I'll never know,' says Harries. 'He was a nightmare behind the wheel of a car. So we set off with me fairly terrified and, as we entered the car park, instead of braking he hit the accelerator and drove straight into the front of the Chateau. He dented the car, it wasn't a big smash, but it was hilarious. He kind of shrugged it off.'

In private McLaren told Hutton about his upbringing, magnifying elements by claiming his grandmother had not only told him his mother was his sister, but also dressed him as a girl and barred him from attending school until he was ten. 'Every night he had to sit in the corner of a sitting room on a chamber pot while her sisters read to him from the novels of the Brontës and Dickens,' Hutton said. 'That's where he got his love for Fagin and the Artful Dodger. Those were his really formative influences.'

McLaren also drew Hutton into his art-infused world, insisting she accompany him to exhibitions. 'To go to a museum with Malcolm was an education in itself,' said Hutton. 'We'd be looking at a Goya or a Raphael and he'd be telling me the whole history of what was going on in Europe when the painting was being made.'

Hutton recalled that McLaren was not daunted by the provenance of the Glencoe Way house, which had been built at the behest of the movie director Cecil B. DeMille. 'Right away, Malcolm wanted to tear the walls out. That was him, always wanting to tear down the walls.'[13]

'Fans: The Musical' rumbled on. In September 1985 McLaren was back in New York with Menno Meyjes for a meeting with Joseph Papp at the Public Theater. 'Joe was very keen,' says Meyjes. 'It began to look like a real prospect. I thought of all of Malcolm's projects in that period, this was strongest, not least because the music was already in place. We were always trying to figure out how to keep Steven [Spielberg] involved. That's like using an atomic bomb to conquer Luxembourg. But if Steven was fully on board then he would want everything, including control over the musical and that made Joe Papp naturally cautious.'

Paige Simpson believes the musical to have been the most powerful project she worked on with McLaren: 'The trifecta of Malcolm, Spielberg and Joe Papp was so exciting. Had it all come together I think that would have been sensational, and showed Malcolm to be on a par with those people to the general public. Malcolm's idea was that it would play twice a day, so the money would go further. He also wanted to get younger people to appreciate opera, which was really smart.'

But it wasn't to be, and soon the theatrical producer and choreographer Tommy Tune emerged 'out of the mist', to use Menno Meyjes's phrase. 'Tommy was really up for it, and that became slightly problematic because people in theatre are so straight. We had a meeting where Malcolm and Tommy visited me in San Francisco, and apparently the noise of the engines of the plane they were on really freaked Tommy out. Every time he left the room, Malcolm would look at me and imitate the terrified Tommy. It was mean but very funny.'

Tune's interest carried weight. He persuaded the arts faculty at the University of Texas in Austin to workshop the musical and worked hard with Meyjes on the scene-by-scene structure. 'That made Malcolm uncomfortable,' says Meyjes. 'I think he thought it was getting too straight. Then I got a call from Tommy telling me that Malcolm didn't want me to work on it any more. I wasn't that bothered. I knew that that was coming and we remained mates.'

Not long afterwards, Meyjes received another call from Tune. 'It all blew up between them,' says Meyjes. 'Tommy was saying, "I can't cope, I've got all this shit from Malcolm, he keeps changing everything, I can't make head or tails of it . . ." By that time I had figured out that there was going to be a huge rights issue over the music from the Puccini estate or whoever so that it was likely never going to happen. Malcolm was never a great one for due diligence.'

Another film proposal arose out of McLaren's interest in the West Coast surf scene, which he recognised as California's only contemporary youth cult to rival the many that had been incubated in Britain in the post-war years. He met surfers and researched the fashions, the music and even the types of boards they rated.

'I came up with the idea of these gangs made up of second-generation American Vietnamese, Haitians, Puerto Ricans, Mexicans and Pakistanis encroaching on the privatised beaches searching for money, water and food,' said McLaren.

This is LA in the future where there is no water, where the sun never shines, where the skies are always grey, where the American dream, the land of milk and honey has turned into a nightmare where the darkside of society ride surfboards at night.

This is a California that had nothing to do with the Beach Boys. And on top of this you throw in a girl who can magically call up a wave – a girl who doesn't have to wait for waves like surfers do. And in calling up a wave she can cause havoc by flooding the towns and cities. This, and the thought of surfing by night, seeing the ocean come to life after dark like a stage really fascinated me.[14]

While developing the film project, McLaren made an approach to West Coast funk/rock act the Red Hot Chili Peppers and offered himself as producer of their second album *Freaky Styley*, proposing they abandon their multi-layered sound in favour of three-chord 1950s rock 'n' roll with the focus on singer Anthony Kiedis.

'He started throwing out words like "cacophony" and "epiphany", and we were going "What does he mean by a cacophony of sounds?" At last he got to the point,' wrote Kiedis in 2004. 'By way of demonstration he took out some pictures of surfers who were wearing hot pink punk rock colours.'[15]

Kiedis and co. weren't interested in working with McLaren, who had by now conjured an in-your-face title for his film: 'Heavy Metal Surfing

Nazis'. Using the term for particularly competitive and territorial surfers, this soon became 'Heavy Metal Surf Nazis' and has no relationship to the film 'Surf Nazis Must Die' produced by the B-movie production house Troma later in the 1980s. 'I thought this suited Hollywood to a tee; I also thought it was profound,' said McLaren of his project many years later. 'How can you co-opt the Beach Boys, co-opt Nazi movies and co-opt rock 'n' roll all in one go?'

Paige Simpson confirms that there was no lack of interest from the Hollywood scriptwriting community. 'As we tried to figure "Surf Nazis" out, we talked to lots of people, who all jumped at the chance to have a meeting with Malcolm,' says Simpson. 'It was never a problem but their interest got to the point that they would offer to write for free just to be part of it. Then I'd get an angry call from their agents, yelling that there was no way their writers weren't getting paid. So I had to explain to Malcolm about the screenwriters' guild and the unions and he'd be like, "What union?" He was a rule-breaker.'

Tales of McLaren's activities filtered through to Tina Brown, the English editor who had transformed the fortunes of the revived *Vanity Fair* for Condé Nast over the previous three years. She commissioned star photographer Annie Leibovitz to capture the transplanted Englishman in situ for the front-of-the-book 'Fanfair' section. Leibovitz set up a portrait of McLaren in Converse, baggy shorts, long socks and a lifeguard top crouching next to the renegade Californian surfer Christian Fletcher at the Point Dume promontory in Malibu. The snarling Fletcher appeared in the shoot as the main 'Surf Nazis' character, his hair dyed red, his body blue, in a loincloth and seaweed necklace clutching a board made by the premier Australian outfit Rip Curl.

This is where Craig Bromberg entered McLaren's life for the first time. *Vanity Fair* features editor Sharon DeLano commissioned a caption for the Leibovitz portrait from the twenty-six-year-old New York freelancer who also contributed to such magazines as the *East Village Eye* and the Australian art journal *Art & Text*, run by Bromberg's friend, the Manhattan-based Aussie critic and curator Paul Taylor. The well-connected pair were bewitched by McLaren and his CV. 'He embodied the contradictions of Postmodernism,' says Bromberg. 'I was extremely intrigued. And I was a fan. As a Jew, the Jewish thing was fascinating to me.'[16]

In fact, the *Vanity Fair* caption arose because Bromberg had made it known in media circles he had recently signed a deal with the British publisher Music Sales to produce a biography of McLaren. Through *Vanity Fair*, Bromberg obtained McLaren's phone number and after the publication of the Point Dume photo in the April 1985 issue was invited to meet him during a stay at New York's Morgans Hotel.

'He kept me waiting for about an hour, and then, when we met, was warm and effusive, giving me four hours a day over the next four days to talk about his life,' says Bromberg. 'I was completely under his spell. He was funny and charming, talking intensively about his family, the Pistols, Lauren Hutton, you name it. He was a dream. Nothing was off limits. I was coming at it from the perspective of a fan and was 100 per cent up for telling his side of the story.'

As open as McLaren was, he remained wary, 'His attitude was, "I don't really know about this. My story is my story. I'll talk with you, and let's see what happens,"' says Bromberg. 'He wasn't a dick about it.'

Soon thereafter Bromberg left for London to research and interview figures in his subject's life. Like any good reporter, he thumbed through phone books, scanned birth and death certificates and wore out shoe leather tracking down friends, family members and individuals who might throw new light on McLaren.

Around this time, Bromberg's pal Paul Taylor approached the directors of New York's New Museum of Contemporary Art with a proposal for a retrospective of the work of the ex-Sex Pistols manager. 'My ideas for the exhibition are quite unconventional, as is McLaren's art,' wrote Taylor in his pitch. The New Museum's director Marcia Tucker and senior curator William Olander were persuaded. 'Had Paul Taylor suggested an exhibition of, say, rock musician David Byrne or performance artist Laurie Anderson, both celebrated figures of the "downtown scene", we could have reached a decision rather quickly,' wrote Tucker and Olander later. 'Yet after talking with our colleagues, a decision was reached after little discussion – we wanted to do this exhibition.'[17]

The show was to take three years to realise, but the increase it brought to McLaren's cultural equity among Bromberg and Taylor's East Coast set was of no value at his workplace on the other side of the country. As could be expected, the 'Surf Nazis' title alone proved too much for LA's disproportionately Jewish film community. Now the proposal entered the inevitable watering-down process and the name changed many times – at one stage it was 'All She Wants to Do Is Surf with Nazis', based around an update of the 1950s rocksploitation flick *The Girl Can't Help It* – to eventually settle on 'Wave Warriors'. During one phase, McLaren addressed rewrites with Gabrielle Kelly, a consultant to Marvel Comics, who had been drafted in to help steer him through development. The comic book connection proved useful.

On a trip to New York, where he and Hutton sometimes stayed at her loft apartment in the rapidly gentrifying NoHo district, McLaren paid a visit to St Mark's Comics in the East Village in search of inspiration. Here he was introduced to the work of British writer Alan Moore, who had revolutionised the field as a contributor to such magazines as *2000 AD* and *Warrior* and as creator of the strip 'V for Vendetta'. More recently Moore had reinvented the DC Comics characters Marvelman and Swamp Thing to great acclaim.

'Me and Lauren got talking to all these kids there,' said McLaren. 'I asked one kid who he thought was the best comic book writer and he said Alan Moore. Lauren asked the kid why, and he said: "Are you kidding? He sits by the left hand of God!" I thought, if a black 13-year-old from New York thinks Alan Moore is the best, then he's got to be good.'[18]

McLaren sought out the reclusive Moore in his Midlands hometown of Northampton. Moore was – and remains – chary of the movie business, which was to bowdlerise his work (in the process earning his undying enmity) with big screen translations of *V for Vendetta, From Hell* and *The Watchmen*. But he was intrigued by McLaren. As early as 1978, Moore had introduced McLaren into his work, in an illustration for the *NME* of his version of Aubrey Beardsley's 1893 drawing *The Climax*, so he agreed to meet and talk about delivering his first film script. 'I liked the upfront way McLaren had treated the music industry, and also his self-promotion as a rock 'n' roll Fagin figure, some of which was probably self-projection and the rest hype,' says Moore. 'In the hyper-world even minor celebrities have to live it to a certain degree, and McLaren seemed to create a persona that could handle that process.'[19]

The pair spent a pleasant afternoon. 'Malcolm understood ahead of a lot of people that comic writers produce for a visual medium, so could be great for film,' says Moore. 'This was before I'd written *The Watchmen*, so I wasn't that well known. Malcolm told me about the conversation with the kid in the comic book shop in St Mark's Place. I thought the left hand of God comment was wonderful. If I ever write an autobiography, that will definitely be the title. That or *My Struggle*.'

McLaren talked through three of the film properties he was developing for CBS: 'Surf Nazis', Oscar 'Wilde West' and 'Fashion Beast'. 'Surf Nazis didn't appeal and Malcolm's explanation of the Oscar Wilde movie was that it was going to be Madonna touring nineteenth-century America. While I'm big on Oscar Wilde I'm not so big on Madonna,' says Moore. 'I thought "Fashion Beast" as he explained it was really good. Looking back, I think that was the one he wanted me to work on all along.'

They shook on a deal for Moore to receive £10,000 to start on the script, the same amount halfway through the draft and the same again on delivery. 'That was the going rate for a first-time screenwriter back then,' says Moore, who seized the opportunity to deliver one of McLaren's *Great Rock 'n' Roll Swindle* epithets to its creator. 'He gave me a deadline to which I agreed and chortled when I told him: "You realise you're going to have to trust a hippie, don't you Malcolm?"'

Moore absorbed the research materials McLaren provided, including two biographies of Dior, as well as Jean Cocteau and René Clément's haunting 1946 film *La Belle et la Bête*, and duly delivered a sparkling script, for which he received the full £30,000.

'Malcolm thought it was good,' recalls Moore. 'His main advice was that I ought to leave more for the director to do. Being a control freak comic writer my scripts have got everything in them, including the camera angles, the lighting, the expressions on the character's faces. Of course I'd left nothing for the actors or the director to contribute.'

The final version – in which the story is credited to both of them – is set in Paris against the backdrop of a military threat triggering an environmental crisis. Themes of androgyny and thwarted sexual desire play out as the central character, the grotesquely deformed designer Jean Claude Celestine, pursues his muse Doll Seguin. The screenplay contains biographical touches, such as an exchange between two characters that points up the tyranny of the fashion industry's seasonal schedule, which became a major source of frustration during McLaren's work with Westwood on their catwalk collections:

Doll: So what are you doing holding a Spring collection when it
    looks like we're on the brink of a nuclear god-damned winter?
Jonni: Don't be stupid. We don't have nuclear winters in the Salon.
    Here there's just Spring and Autumn.

'I had an extremely interesting and educational experience working with Malcolm,' says Moore. 'It occurred to me he was playing at being a film producer. When I say play, I mean that he had a serious approach but at its core was childish delight.'

Moore pinpoints an aspect of McLaren's experimental approach that can be found across the creative spectrum. As the American author Gore Vidal said of the British writer Anthony Burgess: 'He was encyclopaedic and very daring. As things struck him, he did them, like a child. "Ah that's a pretty thing, oh, that's a good thing, oh, let me play with this." '[20]

'Malcolm had a mercurial mind,' agrees Alan Moore. 'If he saw something that interested him – whether fashion, pop music or movies – he would play with it, mess it about, improve it or simply have fun with it. Maybe that was never going to happen with Hollywood, which is a place I've avoided. I encountered him at the start of his film career and disillusion hadn't set in, but understood even then it was always going to be a tricky fit.'

Among other proposals McLaren was hot-housing at CBS was a film based on *Hammer of the Gods*, the recently published unauthorised biography of Led Zeppelin in which their heavyweight manager Peter Grant looms large. As a student of post-war popular culture, McLaren understood that Grant – who began his career working as a bouncer at the legendary Soho skiffle club the 2i's – embodied the criminal roots of the business.

McLaren was also taken with a screenplay entitled 'Art Boy', pitched by the writer Megan Daniels, about the nomadic life of the precocious American artist James Mathers, and organised funding for Daniels to travel to New York to research the city's art scene. (A couple of years before, Andy Warhol had organised an exhibition in Manhattan for Mathers when he was just nineteen years old.)

Despite the diversity of his activities, McLaren was soon acquainted with the trickiness of the fit with Hollywood identified by Alan Moore. After just six months his job was pulled from under him when CBS Theatrical Films – which had been haemorrhaging money long before his appearance, while its parent was under threat of takeover by the media mogul Ted Turner – closed in November 1985. McLaren was paid in full on the remainder of his contract, providing him with a financial safety net. Meanwhile the properties he had been developing were put into turn-around, film parlance for when a studio writes off projects as tax losses. This allowed McLaren to pursue them with other backers; for a while he retained the CBS office as a base, with Megan Daniels provided with a desk. According to Craig Bromberg, when they upped sticks, he and Daniels scrawled 'FUCK YOU' in large letters on the walls of his office.

In one sense McLaren was free and clear, an independent once more, no longer questioned on his whereabouts or intentions. He was also in possession of several projects at various stages of development and retained Paige Simpson as his development executive, working out of the Glencoe Way house. McLaren's reputation as a bad boy was cemented by a drunken incident at the upper-echelon hangout the Ivy. Showing off in front of such young stars as Darryl Hannah and John Cusack, McLaren pulled a chair from underneath CBS's Ileen Maisel just as she was about to take her seat at a table, causing the executive to lose her poise and collapse to the floor. In such a small town, ill-mannered behaviour is tolerated only when you're delivering the goods, though Menno Meyjes says that McLaren was mortified and repentant. 'He called me the next day and told me what he'd done,' says Meyjes.

McLaren had hot-housed more than half-a-dozen pitches into development in the six months he was at CBS, and was impatient to make things happen. This breaks another golden Hollywood rule: unless you have the juice, the wheels of the American film industry do not spin fast. And McLaren didn't have the juice.

'Getting something done in LA is almost an abstract notion,' says Rory Johnston. 'It's the place where people think they're going to realise a creative vision and get sucked into the scene and end up doing nothing, just biding their time. That wasn't Malcolm's way, so he was bound to come up against it sooner or later. I always hoped that his skills would enable him to overcome those barriers but he got pigeon-holed as the guy with lots of exciting ideas nobody actually wanted to do.'

Meanwhile, McLaren heard Craig Bromberg had attempted to make contact with his mother and stepfather in London during the course of a three-week stay where he interviewed around thirty people from McLaren's past.

Bromberg adopted brazen tactics and doorstepped Emily and Martin Edwards at the house where McLaren had lived in the late 1950s and early 1960s. He arrived in Cheyne Walk, Hendon, on a Sunday morning tricked out in a suit and clutching a bouquet of flowers to ingratiate himself, but was met with the belligerent suspicion Londoners reserve for those they regard as slick interlopers.

McLaren's mother – 'Dyed ginger hair. Lots of make-up. Tiny 50s-style specs. Big breasts and bushy eyebrows. Little legs,' according to Bromberg – slammed the front door on the New Yorker after giving him the bum's rush: 'You want to talk about my son Malcolm? Go away, just go away. I have nothing to say about him.'

Bromberg resorted to pleading with Emily Edwards through the letterbox, believing mistakenly that a claim that the flowers were a gift from McLaren's 'wife' Vivienne Westwood might change her mind. Eventually Martin Edwards informed Bromberg from an open window that he would punch him on the nose if he didn't leave. And he culminated his tirade with a caustic north London payoff: 'As for those flowers: let me tell you, you can stuff 'em!'[21]

From here on, relations between McLaren and his biographer became chilly. 'The psychological warfare between Malcolm and I began when he realised I was going to home in on his family, his relationship to Vivienne and to the children Ben and Joe,' says Bromberg. 'As that came into focus, so my awareness of his infidelity to the people around him sharpened. I vaguely remember getting through to Malcolm and asking him about the family and he said "I don't want to talk about them. I haven't seen them in years." He was definitive that he didn't know his family and they were dead to him. After that his response to my calls was "Leave me alone."'

This reluctance spurred on Bromberg, even though his UK publisher Music Sales had gone to the wall. 'I was particularly convinced there was a book there because of Malcolm's unwillingness to talk about his family; this was the most interesting shit in his life,' says Bromberg, who struck a new deal with New York-based Harper & Row.

Bromberg's persistence over the next couple of years was to provide a low-level but constant irritation for McLaren as the writer tracked the highs and lows of his life. Bromberg returned to London and frequented Thurleigh Court, where he got on with Vivienne Westwood, who was by now back from Italy after the collapse of the Armani deal and preparing to reopen Worlds End. Her wounds over her relationship with McLaren were far from healed. 'We got along very well and I saw a lot of her,' says

Bromberg. 'I found her maddening and crazy. I thought she was nuts. She was also extremely emotional; angry one moment and then chatty and carefree the next.'

Meanwhile, McLaren's departure from CBS had coincided with the release of the third and final album on his contract with Charisma, which had been subsumed into Virgin Records. What had started out as 'Duck Rock 2' was now entitled *Swamp Thing*, part in tribute to Moore, the 'Fashion Beast' scriptwriter, and also an affectionate nod to Lauren Hutton (the title was McLaren's nickname for her).

The LP is rightly forgotten. It is a hotchpotch of half-baked ideas and outtakes that weren't included in the original *Duck Rock* release with good reason; the title track is a lame retread of the Troggs' 1960s song 'Wild Thing', while the bottom of the barrel is scraped with a reworking of the 'Mile High Club'/Bow Wow Wow song 'Sexy Eiffel Tower'.

McLaren didn't stir himself to promote the release, and not just because there was no contractual obligation. The end of 1985 brought pressing news: early in the New Year the High Courts of Justice in London were to cast judgment on the long-standing issues surrounding rights to the Sex Pistols and their catalogue.

After holidaying with Hutton at Jean-Charles de Castelbajac's chateau in the French countryside, McLaren arrived in London in the second week of January 1986 to contest John Lydon's case that he should be excluded from the division of the £880,00 accrued in Sex Pistols royalties since the appointment of the receiver to Glitterbest seven years earlier. This not only meant that the monies would be paid to Lydon, Paul Cook, Steve Jones and the estate of Sid Vicious, but they would also obtain rights to the name Sex Pistols and all associated works, including the music, *The Great Rock 'n' Roll Swindle* and the artworks he had commissioned from Jamie Reid.

The first day in court was dedicated to the issues surrounding the Pistols' bitter demise in the late 1970s, which were revisited with a lengthy submission from Lydon, by now a Los Angeles resident and represented by Mr John McDonnell QC, as well as presentations on behalf of Jones, Cook and McLaren, whose claim included the assertion that he had 'put together the violent and aggressive Punk style; it was his original literary work'.

The charismatic Lydon was an ebullient presence in and outside the courtroom. Also in attendance were the more retiring Cook and Vicious's mother Anne Beverley. Jones was by now another expat LA resident, and unable to make the trip as he struggled with drug and visa problems. No one was in any doubt that the complicated case boiled down to McLaren having earned Lydon's hatred. 'There he is, looking like a pervert and all,' Lydon was overhead to comment on the velvet-suited McLaren by the journalist Jon Savage, who doggedly covered the legal wrangle and noted the tactic of Lydon's QC of dragging out proceedings on the first day. This resulted in news reports that the case was likely to last two months at a cost of hundreds of thousands of pounds and had the desired effect on the agitated McLaren.

By the third day a settlement was reached; McLaren gave up his counterclaim on the basis that the former members of the Pistols pay all costs. These ate into the amount of money in the pot, but nevertheless the media rounded up the figure and proclaimed that the band members had emerged victorious with a £1 million payout. 'It's all mine!' cried Lydon gleefully, ignoring the fact that a quarter was his due.

As well as the considerable legal fees that had mounted up over the years – the three days in court alone cost £30,000 – the band members' income was also reduced by a number of claims from creditors such as Chris Thomas, producer of *Never Mind the Bollocks*, who had been pursuing his share of the LP's royalties ever since Glitterbest went into receivership.[22]

In the manner of Vivienne Westwood and her dismissal of McLaren's role in her fashion career, Lydon refused to accept McLaren had made a quantifiable contribution to the Pistols. 'I wrote the songs, I gave it all the direction, I was the brains, not him,' crowed Lydon. 'In hindsight, he claims it was all him, but then he conceded so badly in court that he obviously knows that he is wrong. Malcolm wouldn't know one end of a console from another. To him it's a big lump of metal with flashing lights. And he's got a cheek putting his name to all those records that were made by Trevor Horn and all the rest.'[23]

Steve Jones is marginally more sympathetic to McLaren. 'It was a shame for Malcolm that it ended the way it did and he came away from the Sex Pistols with no financial reward,' Jones said in his 2016 memoir *Lonely Boy*. 'But he had no one to blame but himself. If he'd just taken credit for the things he did do instead of spending all our money on making a film which made us out to be a bunch of muppets who couldn't play our instruments, it would've been fine.'[24]

The day after the court ruling, Jon Savage tracked McLaren by phone to London's Brown's Hotel. 'The whole thing was like two old men arguing over tomes. It was the end of an era,' sighed McLaren, who cited an observation of Paul Cook's. 'He said something very shrewd: "Whatever we try, Rotten will take you. You see Rotten loved you. You didn't pay enough attention to him." And it's true, I was more involved with Sid. I was always thinking about event after event and not in terms of personal relationships.'[25]

That day, McLaren had scheduled a meeting about the 'Fashion Beast' script with Alan Moore, who arrived at Brown's to find him in a buoyant mood. 'I was a few minutes early and Malcolm was finishing up with a photographer from the *Sun*,' says Moore. 'He asked Malcolm to look glum and pose with his pockets turned out. Malcolm agreed; he was into the pantomime aspect of it as much as anybody. Once he'd gone I mentioned that it had been a bit of a bad result for him. He responded, "Do I look like someone who's just lost £1 million?" and burst into peals of laughter. I guess he was covered. It was all good publicity.'

This sanguinity accorded with his parting remark to Jon Savage: 'It's constantly nagged at me for eight years,' McLaren had said of the Pistols' break-up. 'Now I'm shot of it.'[26]

The sense of relief expressed in that brief sentence informed McLaren's attitude to the Pistols and punk. Although he would have liked to have emerged from the legal dispute with at least the rights to *The Great Rock 'n' Roll Swindle* (the music and the money weren't priorities), McLaren didn't harbour bitterness at the outcome.

Instead, just a few days after his fortieth birthday, McLaren was mourning the death of the art dealer Robert Fraser, who had succumbed to complications resulting from Aids. 'I certainly loved him for his romantic air, and in many respects found him to be a great friend always,' he told Fraser's biographer Harriet Vyner several years later. 'It all seemed much more romantic with him than without him. It made you feel like you had potential, made you feel like you could do something. He was that kind of guy, he gave you that kind of sense. It's a wonderful and rare talent. He was a wonderful man.'[27]

Returning to LA to continue developing his portfolio of film ideas, McLaren was invited as the star guest to the Sydney arts biennale. His New York champion, the curator and critic Paul Taylor, had recommended to Biennale director Nick Waterlow that he include McLaren's interpretation of Manet's *Déjeuner sur l'Herbe* in the festival, which was entitled 'Origins, Originality + Beyond' and investigated themes of quotation and appropriation in artistic practice. Waterlow may as well have named McLaren when he discussed in the Biennale notes 'the artist as transgressor, the artist as code cracker'.

Pleased to be included in a diverse line-up of internationally renowned fine artists such as the Swiss painter Miriam Cahn, the American Eric Fischl, the Czech-German installation artist Magdalena Jetelová and the British absurdist Glen Baxter, McLaren took Nick Egan on the trip to Sydney.

By this time Egan had also joined the British expat community in Los Angeles and was continuing to design record sleeves and direct music promos. 'This is what he was like: Malcolm traded the business-class ticket they had given him for two economy ones,' says Egan. 'We flew via Tahiti and shared a room. We had a great laugh. He was a bit like Charlie Chaplin, a comical character. We went swimming and there was naked little Malcolm walking around our room reminding me of Vivienne's quote about Malcolm's proud member standing up when they camped in the south of France. I've seen that.'

Upon arrival in Sydney the pair realised the seriousness of the endeavour Waterlow had put together across several venues centring on the prestigious Art Gallery of New South Wales. The absence of *Déjeuner* photographer Andy Earl made Egan and McLaren feel like imposters. 'We had to come up with something that didn't make us fraudulent,' says Egan. 'Malcolm suggested we turn our appearance there into an over-the-top merchandising opportunity, "We're Only in it for the Manet". We printed T-shirts and a few other things with that as the slogan, and set up a stand near the blow-up of the photo.'

Egan used a spray-can to draw a baroque-style frame around the photograph in fluorescent pink. 'That put our stamp on it,' says Egan. 'Then Malcolm gave a talk where he said artists were the rock stars of the day, people like Basquiat doing cocaine in the backs of limousines. This shocked a few people. Malcolm was also heckled by feminists over Annabella's nudity, so caused quite a stir.'

Less perturbed was Australia's very own rock-star painter, Brett Whiteley, who had known acquaintances of McLaren's such as Robert Fraser and David Litvinoff and befriended the Brits, introducing them to people in his circle including the street photographer Jonny Lewis. 'We had a great time,' says Egan. 'Malcolm was riling people up and the *Déjeuner* photo had new life breathed into it by being recognised as a fine art piece.'

In the US, McLaren reconnected with Spielberg. Having developed 'Wilde West' for Amblin, he garnered sufficient interest – so McLaren later claimed to his friend Peter Culshaw – that Spielberg provided $50,000 in seed money and flew the British dramatist Tom Stoppard over to consider writing the script.

McLaren also claimed that Martin Scorsese expressed an interest in directing. Then he was told to hit the bricks. 'One day they said that it wasn't such a good idea any more because they were concerned that it might not be liked by the American public; the thought of an Irish homosexual discovering rock 'n' roll was something they wouldn't buy,' said McLaren in the 2000s.

' "Could I change his name to Billy Wilde?" they asked. It was very difficult for me to understand that because I didn't know who the fuck Billy Wilde was.' Here lay McLaren's issue with the film business: however extraordinary the facts of a particular story, there was a compunction to gloss over the authentic. 'Let's only sell fake life, fake desires, fake dreams,' he railed. 'At that point I realised that my lot was hopeless. You always have to choose your way, a commitment to a point of view, otherwise you end up making things [that are] incredibly grey, uninteresting and devoid of emotion.'

Another pitch for Spielberg returned him to a person with whom he had wished to engage in a variety of musical schemes in the mid-1970s: Chrissie Hynde. As another 'Beauty and the Beast' riff, McLaren proposed a film pairing Hynde with Stephen Hawking. In this scenario McLaren planned to transform the paraplegic theoretical physicist into 'the most brilliant pop star, and have him make love to Chrissie Hynde . . . I tried hard to sell that as a bridging between art and science.'[28]

Again, the director and his production house Amblin passed, but 'Fans' was optioned and McLaren provided with a screenwriter to produce a film-worthy script.

The exit from CBS Theatrical had by now impelled McLaren to work up another property; he persuaded Peter Grant to give the thumbs-up for a film about his life, with British film sales company Glinwood Films, *Chariots of Fire* director Hugh Hudson and the British scriptwriter Barrie Keeffe on board.

A screening of *The Great Rock 'n' Roll Swindle* impressed the Led Zeppelin manager; the sections in the film that showed how McLaren played record companies against each other chimed with his experiences. 'Peter said he'd got it exactly right,' Keeffe told Grant's biographer Mark Blake.[29]

In the summer of 1986, media coverage of the tenth anniversary of punk breaking through in Britain and Vivienne Westwood's reopening of Worlds End brought forth many reminders of McLaren's former life. The story goes that the locks at 430 King's Road hadn't been changed; the premises had remained undisturbed in the intervening two-and-a-half years. Westwood – contending with the business's sizeable debt, which she hadn't addressed during the prolonged absence in Italy – was able to set up shop again, assisted by her sons and mother, and at first using candles to light the place until enough money could be found to reconnect the electricity supply. McLaren was blamed for her financial dilemma, rather than the failure of the potentially lucrative Armani deal.

The same month as 430 King's Road opened its doors again, *Sid and Nancy*, director Alex Cox's film about the doomed Sex Pistol and his lover, was released into cinemas. Despite a spirited portrayal by Gary Oldman, the cartoon-like acting and dialogue as well as clunking anachronisms sparked critical dismissal, particularly from those who were depicted such as John Lydon.

Alan Moore recalls encountering McLaren the day after he had seen *Sid and Nancy*. McLaren was played by the British actor David Hayman as a fey figure with a penchant for wearing matching pink shirts and ties. 'The film suggested, in its overblown portrait of Malcolm, that he had more or less encouraged and profited from the demise of Sid Vicious,' says Moore. 'I asked him what he thought of the portrayal. He said: "Well, I would NEVER, EVER wear clothes like that!" I thought: "Fair enough."'

According to McLaren the film failed to grasp the dynamic between Lydon, Vicious and Spungen – 'Sid and Johnny were lovers in the sense that they were virgins, buddies, and Nancy forced a wedge' – as well as the bass player's true nature. 'Sid was a lot more horrible than he appeared in the film, harder, much more the bully,' said McLaren.[30] He chose to appraise his association with the Pistols with a three-day workshop at – where else? – an art school, the Art Center College of Design in Pasadena, the verdant city to the west of Los Angeles in the San Gabriel Valley. McLaren gave the event a series of titles – 'Punk Is Not a Fashion Statement' aka 'Punk Was Not a Fashion Statement' aka 'Punk Might Be a Fashion Statement' aka 'Punk Lives, It's Just Gone Somewhere Else' – and staged activities including a screening of *The Great Rock 'n' Roll Swindle* with a Q&A and a catwalk show where models 'posed in a scene from a punk-style "Madam Butterfly" to a song by a short-lived band called the Sex Pistols screaming forth from the PA', according to local reporter Larry Wilson.[31]

Over the long weekend, McLaren strolled the campus and dined in the refectory and college boardroom with Lauren Hutton, making himself available for conversations with curious students. 'Unlike so many in the hipper-than-thou entertainment industry, McLaren never tired of answering questions, never mumbled, never refused to go over anecdotes he must have related endlessly over the years,' wrote Wilson.

The surf scene continued to fascinate. Now McLaren talked about taking his VW Rabbit convertible on a cross-country drive visiting man-made inland surfing spots which had been made possible by wave machines.

'When I think of rock 'n' roll I think of action and stepping out, that's what it is,' he told the audience at one talk in Pasadena. 'And when people in California step out, they step into water. They go surfing. It's the only sport that's inspired a rock 'n' roll sound. I really wanted to leave you with the thought that you're in the right place at the right time. With surfing, people can express themselves on a one-to-one basis. I want to rewrite Johann Strauss to a salsa beat for a new surf sound. It's the same kind of challenge as when I founded the Sex Pistols.'

The reference to Strauss is instructive; three years ahead of McLaren's return to record releases with the album *Waltz Darling* he was already turning over in his mind the inclusion of the form in a new musical melange, having signed a contract with CBS Records London's head A&R honcho, Muff Winwood.

As this idea was germinating, New York DJ and producer Johnny Dynell made contact. He was keen for McLaren to view a showreel for a film about the city's drag ball scene being made by the artist, photographer and film studies student Jennie Livingston.

The extraordinary footage of flamboyant black and Latino gay men competing at underground venues by striking dramatic poses and indulging in hyper-athletic dance steps stemmed from the 'Paris Is Burning' ball held by one of the scene's founders, Paris Dupree, that summer. Livingston was using the showreel to raise money to complete the film, and Dynell, himself a member of the ballroom troupe the House of Extravaganza (later Xtravaganza), hoped McLaren would have a route to funds. 'I told Malcolm about the ballroom scene because I thought it would be perfect for him,' Dynell told dance-music chronicler Tim Lawrence, though he would later come to regret having passed on the information.[32]

But the West Coast was too square; there was no sympathy in the Hollywood film community for these minorities who were living on the margins of Reagan's America, facing poverty, harassment, drug addiction and Aids.

McLaren recognised that the scene that was coalescing around one particular dance style, Voguing, represented the true dispossessed of the age, rising above their unfortunate circumstances to create beauty and drama. He was also spellbound by every element of the ballroom hierarchies: the heroic pseudonyms – Willi Ninja, Venus Extravaganza, Pepper LaBeija, Octavia St Laurent – the fact that there were 'houses', each with a 'mother' and a 'father' who looked after 'children' (mainly runaways), and the competition categories, which were given bold titles: Executive Realness, European Runway, Town & Country . . .

The music was overwrought and often magnificent. Ball favourites included such disco classics as MFSB's 'Love Is the Message', Cheryl Lynn's 'Got to Be Real' and Loose Joints' 'Is It All Over My Face?' 'These are more than just bitchy songs; they form a soundtrack of power, control, manipulation, escape and fantasy,' commented online Voguing source the House of Diabolique in 2018. 'They glorify gayness and femininity.'[33]

The appropriation of white high fashion by street kids of colour naturally held great appeal for McLaren. 'By taking the name from a magazine that suggests for the rich to look rich, to buy rich, suddenly it's the domain of the street,' he said a couple of years later. 'The black gay community has given kids with holes in their trousers the opportunity to look as glamorous as mannequins on a Paris runway.'[34]

These days ballroom is a recognised subculture, its jargon having entered the mainstream: contestants 'threw shade' at each other, for example, while the Netflix series *The Pose* manicures the lifestyle and the grittiness of the life and Livingston's film. But at the time, McLaren was unable to stimulate sufficient interest in the film and Livingston eventually secured funding, but all from non-Hollywood sources, to make *Paris Is Burning*. Nevertheless, McLaren began to turn over Voguing as an element of the look and sound of the music he was developing for CBS Records.

Meanwhile a new version of 'Surf Nazis' by the screenwriter Lewis Colick, which included at McLaren's insistence the surf pools he had visited in the Midwest, was turned down by indie producer Ed Pressman. Ultimately, Hollywood was proving an orthodoxy against which McLaren was struggling.

'At first it seemed a place to reinvent yourself,' McLaren said of the film business. 'Finally, I have to admit, its malevolence creeps in through the walls at night and slowly depressed the hell out of me.'[35]

Chapter 32

Two years into his career as a movie and theatrical producer, Malcolm McLaren was chafing at the slow pace in realising his visions for Hollywood and on Broadway, and so – as he attempted to propel various projects through the circles of development hell – he used the freshly inked CBS Records deal to return to music-making as a means of self-expression.

The commercial landscape had changed enormously since McLaren was signed to Chrysalis Records in the early 1980s. The advent of the CD and the rise of the post-Live Aid global figures such as Madonna and U2 had altered the dynamics of the increasingly corporate industry which had once reeled in fright at the antics of the Sex Pistols and their ilk. Rebellion had been co-opted and such behaviour was now lauded for its marketability. In the words of journalist Dave Rimmer, the music world felt 'like punk never happened', but McLaren retained an edge not only through his grasp of grassroots movements such as the ballroom scene but also his willingness to break the rules.

The recording of what was to become *Waltz Darling*, which took place over two years and swallowed up a huge cast of contributors, was inspired in part by a conversation with Steven Spielberg. During one of their meetings, the superstar director expressed a desire to record an album, and asked McLaren's advice. 'I had to explain to him that I didn't know how to make a record, I don't play and I don't sing,' said McLaren in the 2000s. 'The man turned round to me and said. "I know. That's why I want to go into the studio to see how you do it." I thought, "He's really smart."'

Spielberg's desire to adopt McLaren's wilful amateurishness acted as a trigger to attempt to solve the knotty issue of marrying the three-four time of the waltz to dance music's four-on-the-floor rhythms. 'Spielberg made me try to make in the studio something that Oscar Wilde might have heard in the 1880s,' said McLaren. 'I thought that the waltz must have been the thing of his day but I wanted to mess about and put some rock 'n' roll with it.'

On a visit to London, McLaren explained how his new music would merge his interest in surfing with the German musical form. 'I was driving down Santa Monica Boulevard, thinking of my surfing soundtracks and seeing all those grey skies and mile upon mile of beaches, and I was pumping Strauss on the cassette deck,' he told *i-D*'s Dylan Jones. 'I found it a great contrast to the modern world of machines, power stations, Caterpillar pool rigs, fluorescent boards stuck on the beach, and the enthusiastic surfers running around being modern. And Strauss seemed to add romance to the whole set up. I thought it was so big, so epic and so gallant that it had to work.'[1]

The meeting with Jones took place in the Hiroko sushi bar situated near the sizeable lobby of London's Kensington Hilton. As Jones later discovered during transcription, when he interrupted the interview for a ten-minute search for a hotel lavatory, McLaren continued to talk into the cassette recorder as if Jones were still there and, in fact, when he returned to the table at the Hiroko, continued as if Jones hadn't absented himself.

Much of McLaren's loquacity was concerned with Hutton, and how their relationship instilled in him a newfound tenderness. 'It's only since going to Hollywood and meeting Lauren that I've understood being in love means a certain amount of understanding, listening to their needs and desires and generally being aware of [partners]. It's the first time in my life that I've worked hard at developing a relationship. That's not to say it will ultimately succeed . . . I don't know. I'm not selfish any more. I care about caring for somebody.'

He also revealed that he did not deal emotionally with the death of his grandmother until the end of his relationship with Vivienne Westwood more than a decade later. 'I suddenly looked back and wondered what the hell I was all about,' said McLaren.

Vivienne must have thought, 'What a strange fucking person!' At the time I had no sense of what it was like to be engaged physically with a woman. I had no sense of romanticism. Vivienne must have been madly in love with me, but I never ever contemplated the thought of being in love with anyone really. Looking back on it I think I probably was in love with her, but I don't think I did it justice. I don't think I was ready for it, I don't think I ever really understood the idea of sacrifice in any shape or form.[2]

A sign of this thaw lay in a resumption of contact with Westwood; he also made sure to see his son Joe when he was in town. Westwood's biographer Jane Mulvagh recounts how the designer had made the first move when McLaren first started living with Hutton. 'She periodically telephoned him in the middle of the night seeking advice and comfort: "I'm over 40! I've got to prove a point and become a great fashion designer," she told him,' writes Mulvagh. 'They discussed the best plan and decided that couture, not street fashion, was the route to the prestige she craved. Their interpretation of "couture" was not strictly accurate; they did not mean handmade clothes crafted on the body for individual customers, but rather a refined version of ready-to-wear.'[3]

McLaren was in the audience for the London catwalk show for Westwood's collection 'Harris Tweed', which confirmed her return to the cutting edge of fashion after the Italian sojourn. With Joe's aptitude and Carlo D'Amario's support, Worlds End was now on the up and up. A new studio was established in Camden Town and D'Amario – with whom Westwood had temporarily resumed her affair – had instituted legal proceedings over the failed Armani deal, suing the Italian fashion giant for loss of earnings to the tune of $3 million. This was to rumble on for years, and in the meantime money was still extremely tight, but for Westwood credibility was restored by a hefty cover story in *The Face*. The style bible's imprimatur placed Westwood as the figurehead of contemporary clothing design, and the text provided by Kathryn Flett foregrounded Westwood almost entirely at McLaren's expense.⁴

The relative cordiality of their relations ran counter to those with his oldest friend, Fred Vermorel. He and McLaren never spoke again after their argument over the 'Chicken' photography session in 1980, and the 1987 publication of a revised and updated edition of Vermorel's biography of the Sex Pistols with his wife Judy served to drive the wedge wider.

It is here that Vermorel diagnosed McLaren as a sufferer from Tourette's syndrome and also identified him as an appropriator of Situationist tactics. 'Malcolm has never been a thinker, but he is easily carried along by the force and inner logic of an idea,' wrote Vermorel. 'And Situationism was one of the best ideas this century.'⁵

McLaren didn't comment publicly about Vermorel's observations. At this stage he was far more interested in talking up his new musical ambitions and film properties. A script for the *Hammer of the Gods*-inspired proposal, now entitled 'The Rock 'n' Roll Godfather', had been delivered by Barrie Keeffe, and the late Bob Hoskins, star of the Keeffe-written 1980 hard-nut drama *The Long Good Friday*, was touted to take the lead role.

Elsewhere, Alan Moore's screenplay for 'Fashion Beast' had enabled McLaren to attract the attention of Marc Jacobs's partner, the entrepreneur Robert Boykin, who agreed to provide development money. The project was subsequently optioned by the newly founded LA indie Avenue Pictures, which was hot on the back of its owner Cary Brokaw's executive producer credits on such art-house hits as Jim Jarmusch's *Down by Law*.

But once again, McLaren failed to gain traction as the script became bogged down in rewrites. Eventually all impetus was lost when Boykin's health suffered; he died of complications arising from Aids in 1988.

Against these travails, life was comfortable in LA. The Glencoe Way house had undergone an interior redesign courtesy of the expat Englishman Paul Fortune, as recalled by another Brit living in the US, James Truman, who had recently completed a spell editing music magazine *Spin* and was living in the city with record producer Roger Trilling.

'One afternoon we drove up to the Hollywood Hills to pay a visit to Malcolm,' says Truman. 'He had gone LA and done so with good taste, though not punk taste. He was holding court, and I remember a good-looking, charismatic guy with impressive hair was paying rapt attention. I didn't realise until he'd gone that it was Michael Hutchence of INXS, which was just becoming a big band in the US. Again, I didn't really put this together till later, but Malcolm had arrived in LA as the oracle of youth culture. Everyone wanted to meet him, and he was happy to meet everyone.'

Among those who sought out McLaren in this period was David Bowie; they had last encountered each other when the rock star visited Too Fast to Live Too Young to Die in 1974. 'We met one afternoon in the Formosa Café, which was totally empty apart from us,' recalled McLaren later. 'Bowie told me that when he came into the shop his life was in turmoil. He was splitting up with Angie and having an affair with his son's nanny. Everything had got very complicated and he felt he had to leave England.'

That day in the 1980s McLaren discovered the greatest regret of Bowie's life: that he had not attended an art school. 'Bowie asked about my times there and talked about how he had always wanted to train as a painter, which of course he became anyway.'

James Truman identifies the attraction McLaren held for the city's residents and visitors: 'To LA, he was the star who'd revolutionised music, fashion and culture in general; in Hollywood this was seen for the majestic, mythical achievement that it was, though it was also my impression that most people didn't have the first clue about what the detail of that achievement was. For Malcolm, it was an amusement, a cabaret, and he also had no problem being feted, so he rolled along with it, and, I would say, enjoyed it.'

Soon the recording of *Waltz Darling* was underway. An important person in McLaren's life was Paige Simpson's replacement, his right-hand person Carol Ann Blinken. She was a movie executive in her own right and Hollywood royalty since her grandfather Howard W. Koch was a major producer, so she helped McLaren negotiate some of Tinseltown's trickier waters. Working from the Glencoe Way home office she, like Simpson before her, became part of McLaren's professional and personal life. Close to Lauren Hutton, Blinken represented McLaren through the life of the *Waltz Darling* album from its inception to its release.

Overseen by producers Robbie Kilgore (from the *Fans* and *Swamp Thing* sessions) and his partner Mary Kessler, the majority of the *Waltz Darling* recording took place at Abbey Road studios in London, a suitable location for large orchestras and also handy for CBS to keep an eye on the budget.

Being back in his hometown enabled McLaren to reconnect with Nils Stevenson, the King's Road scenester and forward adopter of punk who had tour-managed the Sex Pistols in their early days. Stevenson had fallen foul of hard drugs after a stint managing Siouxsie & the Banshees but was now in recovery and became an important sideman for McLaren.

The romantic aspects of the LP were inspired by McLaren's affair with Hutton. The intention, he said, was to 'make a very romantic record about courtship, partners, foreplay, being swept off your feet, with pre-pubescent lyrics. It's the romantic period that everyone seems to have forgotten but wants to get back to. I've decided to write from that point of view – get my head into being a nine-year-old – and try to think myself back there.'[6]

Waltz Darling demonstrated McLaren's developing role as a musical director. While he wrote or co-wrote every track and made vocal contributions to many, he also harnessed several surprise contributions, not least from rock god Jeff Beck, who had first made his name in the 1960s as a member of the hard-driving British R&B group the Yardbirds.

Beck had been bowled over by McLaren's first single: 'When I first heard "Buffalo Gals" I got the same charge as when I heard Elvis Presley's "Hound Dog". It really got me going. I loved the way he manipulates people and wanted to see what he'd do with me.'

Incongruously, at a party at London nightclub the Hippodrome to celebrate the final performance by pop duo Wham!, Beck had approached McLaren and asked him whether he would like to collaborate on a project. 'To my amazement he said "Yeah, I'd love to," because I thought my style would have been a bit out for him, not useable enough, that kind of deal,' said Beck.

McLaren adopted his usual approach of providing potential collaborators with packages of existing material that outlined the areas he wished to investigate. 'It was strange because he sent me cassettes of wonderful 1890s music hall music, surf music and classics,' recalled Beck. 'And he said, "What do you make of that?" One thing led to another.'[7]

Beck contributed to a number of tracks, including 'Call a Wave', a musical outcome from the shelved 'Surf Nazis', as well as 'House of the Blue Danube', an instrumental funk/house/waltz collision enlivened by the appearance on bass of Bootsy Collins, veteran of James Brown's backing group the JBs, a P-Funk collective member of Funkadelic and Parliament and frontman of his own Bootsy's Rubber Band.

McLaren later confessed that the making of *Waltz Darling* was 'horrendous, because I chose the most ridiculous idea. It was like having two people who could never marry each other – Strauss and James Brown – and doing my utmost to persuade them to marry. I didn't know what the hell I was doing because I'm musically incompetent.'

According to McLaren, things reached a head at Abbey Road when one recording engineer, overwhelmed by his client's demands and having to record waltz after waltz performed by the sixty-piece orchestra, suffered a debilitating attack of eczema. 'Beck and I found him on the floor one day covered in powder and bandages because he was so nervous he couldn't do what I was asking him,' said McLaren. 'He said, "It cannot be done. It's impossible, man." I said, "Right, then, OK, you're fired." But when we would endeavour to find somebody else, they were just as bad. I mean, everything ended up sounding like "Frankie Goes to Hollywood Hooked On Classics". I couldn't live with that. I'd kill myself. We needed a witch doctor.'

This was where Collins entered the scene. McLaren, who hadn't previously heard of the bass player and his achievements, tracked Collins down to his residence in Cincinnati, Ohio, and later claimed the splendour of Collins's sleeping quarters convinced him. 'I realised he was the man for the job, because his bedroom was quite extraordinary, man,' gushed McLaren.

It had this extraordinary red velvet giant double-sized queen bed. He pressed a button and the bed started to rise up and the bed posts were like traffic lights and they whizzed around through 360 degrees and as it rose half way up the room, it started to rock, man. It was the most brilliant thing I'd ever seen. It looked like a witch doctor's dream and I thought, 'Well, any guy who can conceive of a bed like that has to be definitely *not* "Frankie Goes To Hollywood Hooked On Classics". He's coming from another planet, man. And then he turned around to me and said that at 13, whilst in high school, he was playing bass with James Brown on "Sex Machine". Man! No more to be said. That's checkmate! And Bootsy Collins, man, he was my orchestra, he was my band, and I didn't know what the hell I was doing but he made it all make sense to me.[8]

Recording took place in Detroit with Collins's own session players (dubbed for the venture the Bootzilla Orchestra) and a rap duo he worked with who performed under the soubriquet Pretty Fatt. Collins subsequently credited the *Waltz Darling* sessions with rekindling the enthusiasm for music-making that paved the way for his successful collaboration with dance trio Deee-Lite a couple of years later.[9]

Others McLaren brought into the fold included the model Lisa Marie Smith, who had been photographed by Robert Mapplethorpe and made her name appearing in Bruce Weber's campaign for Calvin Klein perfume Obsession as well as *Let's Get Lost*, Weber's biopic of the tragic jazz trumpeter Chet Baker.

Lisa Marie, as she was known professionally, took the lead vocal on the jaunty track 'Something's Jumpin' in Your Shirt', which accorded with McLaren's ambitions for the overall theme of adolescent awakening.

One of the music hall songs McLaren was circulating to participants was 'Algernon's Simply Awfully Good at Algebra', written by Paul Rubens, whose work was performed by such big stars of the late Victorian and Edwardian eras as Vesta Tilley.

McLaren had been introduced to the novelty ditty as a child by his grandmother and her sisters and claimed this was the first track to be recorded for playing on a phonograph. McLaren used Rubens's lyrics – which were long out of copyright – without credit as the basis for a new composition, and, for the recording session, united the talents of Beck, Collins and British musician Dave Stewart, who had by now branched into a successful production career after being a member of Eurythmics with Annie Lennox.

'That was a *mad* session,' recalled Stewart, whose introduction of McLaren to the American soul singer N'Dea Davenport led to her taking the lead vocal. 'It was rude in a way, but that was covered up in the lyrics,' said Stewart. 'It was a crazy session, because "Algernon" isn't in any sort of groovy time at all, and Malcolm wanted it to be a dance track.'[10]

'Waltz Darling' led to an approach from British film director Steve Barron for McLaren to create a soundtrack for his film 'Teenage Mutant Ninja Turtles'. Barron wanted to emulate Stanley Kubrick's 'A Clockwork Orange' and juxtapose the film's fight scenes with orchestral compositions scored by McLaren and his team. In the event, 'The House of Blue Danube' was featured in the hit movie's trailer.

While he continued to encounter roadblocks to achieving his film ambitions in Los Angeles, McLaren was made an accredited member of the English expat contingent, named 'The Britpack' by *Spy* magazine. Described as 'a media manipulator', McLaren was caricatured alongside his former collaborator Julien Temple, who had also gravitated to Hollywood, and classified by writer Richard Stengel as a member of the generation that 'grew up in post-war England, where ambition was not, for the first time, a sin. They were youngsters in a hurry, eager young men and women attracted to the aggressive style and quick rewards of American-style business.'[11]

And in New York, two projects appeared to be heading towards realisation. One, the Broadway production of 'Fans' was to fall at the last post, even though theatre publication *Playbill* announced that Tommy Tune was slated to direct and choreograph as late as June 1988.[12]

The other, curator Paul Taylor's McLaren retrospective at the New Museum, opened a few months later.

Impresario: Malcolm McLaren & the British New Wave posited its subject as a post-Warholian visual artist working at the crosshatches of commerce, as well as 'a "bad guy" of popular culture' with 'a reputation that, in these times, makes him all the more appealing'.

And Taylor provided a ringing endorsement of McLaren and his activities since he had left Goldsmiths close to two decades previously. 'To many in the worlds of art and social criticism, McLaren is like a new type of artist,' wrote Taylor in the *Impresario* catalogue.

A 'producer' in more than one sense of the word, he has literally orchestrated new musical events and created provocative 'cultural texts' within the mass media. He has also shown that art in the post-avant-garde era is a matter of synthesis, of combining elements from radically different sources . . . McLaren has applied the artistic methods and ideologies of the Cubists, Futurists, Dadaists and Constructivists to everyday life and spectacular popular culture alike. McLaren is a popularizer, which is to say he is a pioneer.[13]

Funded in part by American advertising mogul Jay Chiat and designed by artists Judith Barry and Ken Saylor, the exhibition at the New Museum's premises on the Bowery was accessible and thorough, with Jamie Reid artworks and the likes of the Bow Wow Wow *Déjeuner sur l'Herbe* portrait contrasted with mannequins in clothing designed with

Westwood from Let It Rock to Nostalgia of Mud surrounding monitors blasting forth *Duck Rock* videos and Sex Pistols performances.

Other mannequins were flown from the ceiling over visitors' heads towards giant blow-ups of the various retail outlets at 430 King's Road and portraits of the Pistols. Banks of the provocative T-shirt designs were arranged against a wall, and throughout were peppered familiar McLaren-related phrases, including 'Craft Must Have Clothes But Truth Loves to Go Naked'. McLaren's more recent work was also covered, with images such as Annie Leibovitz's 'Surf Nazis' Point Dume photograph.

'By this stage Malcolm had become a glamorous international figure,' says Jane Withers, author of an *Impresario* catalogue essay, who had been introduced to the exhibition's subject by her brother Simon earlier in the decade. 'He moved in "society" and was now very much part of that world.'[14]

For the two-month run of the show, McLaren appeared inescapable in downtown Manhattan; even the local branch of Tower Records dedicated its window space to a giant cartoon cut-out of him in a T-shirt scrawled with 'Opportunist'.

Dismissed by critic Peter Schjeldahl as 'a deliberately tacky phantasmagoria attuned to the attention span of a hummingbird on amphetamine. It's all immediately engaging and instantly forgettable', the show in fact foreshadowed the presentation of pop culture through the prism of contemporary art. But Schjeldahl objected to the overall tone as manifested in the catalogue, which featured lengthy essays from Jon Savage and Dan Graham as well as Withers: 'Implicit is a sort of ethic for avant-garde capitalism; it's okay to cash in, as long as you do it as loathsomely as possible,' wrote Schjeldahl.[15]

In *New York* magazine, Michael Gross speculated that *Impresario* marked a transition from McLaren's 'career of prolonged problem adolescence' into maturity. 'Ironically, this portrait of the send-up artist as a young man coincides with McLaren's declaration that he's finally growing up,' wrote Gross, who quoted McLaren speaking in the second person about himself: ' "You were an instigator, never an architect. You did everything for effect. You have a duty to keep the fires burning, but these days nobody wants to light fires." Briefly a shadow dulls his twinkly blue eyes. "After a while it becomes a bit tiring." '16

McLaren declared himself happy with *Impresario* and had been at once a cooperative subject and enthusiastic contributor, corralling loans from his son Joe Corré, ex-partner Andrea Linz and Nick Egan. And he was sanguine about an American – rather than British – institution being the first to stage an exhibition with him as the subject. 'London and the English have always been concerned not to make anyone successful,' he told the French/English television magazine programme *Rapido*. 'In a way Americans are the exact opposite, and adore to make everyone successful even if you're just a tourist.'

McLaren described the show as a biography of both the 1970s and popular culture. 'They've used me to start to rewrite history and to propose that characters like myself can be construed as artists,' he said.'17

Lauren Hutton had been at McLaren's side at the glitzy opening of *Impresario*, but behind the scenes the relationship was coming undone. A factor was the frequency of their separate absences from the home on Glencoe Way, her travelling for movie roles and him keeping his projects in motion out of town.

'I idle life away in Hollywood watching the neighbours come and go and watching Lauren come and go,' McLaren told the British journalist Tom Hibbert. 'Lauren's like that. She's a triple Scorpio, man.'18

When Hutton wasn't there, McLaren felt isolated far from the centres of his world: New York, Paris and London. 'It's very easy to get lonely in Hollywood; it had a strange effect on me,' said McLaren. 'I was sitting in this massive house courtesy of CBS all on my own, waiting for the phone to ring from some film company, with Lauren away on some gig or other, and I'm thinking to myself, "What the fuck am I supposed to do next?" '

But if they were together on Glencoe Way, he was bored by the lack of cultural stimulation, while her love of the outdoors held little interest.

'There's only about five decent restaurants and the place shuts at 11.30 because everyone's got to get up and make movies,' McLaren complained. 'Hollywood is OK if you're working but it's not the best place in the world to come up with ideas; in the end you become like a camel that's run out of water and you have to go somewhere for a drink. I used to go to New York at the weekends just to get a sense of the world.'[19]

The situation was further complicated by Hutton's tangled relations with her manager and sometime lover Bob Williamson, who she had known since she was twenty-one and described as her protector, calling him 'Bob God'. Although Hutton's trust in Williamson was misplaced – by the time of his death a few years later Williamson had appropriated millions of dollars of Hutton's earnings and left what remained to a woman he married ten days before his death – such instability was exacerbated by the now emotionally exposed McLaren's decision to return to Britain at the end of the year and confront his mother over the whereabouts of his father.

By this time, McLaren had achieved celebrity status in his home country, and visits routinely included appearances on TV shows, his manic laughter and meandering answers about the strangeness of life in LA puzzling audiences but nevertheless attracting repeat requests from bookers.

His guest spot on Jonathan Ross's late-night David Letterman-style programme *The Last Resort* a week before Christmas 1988 arose out of an encounter with the talk-show host and Ross's director and McLaren's friend Andy Harries.

They had been in LA filming Russ Meyer for Ross's Z-movie series *The Incredibly Strange Film Show*, and featured McLaren among their interviewees. In contrast to his appearance in that programme, which was replete with jocular references to Meyer's 'fully cantilevered' female stars, McLaren's turn on *The Last Resort* made for uncomfortable viewing. McLaren appeared at the least distracted, and, at first, would not answer the question as to why he was in London. When Ross requested an update on McLaren's film activities, McLaren described his former

employer CBS Films as 'a Zionist organisation', and said about the failure of 'Heavy Metal Surf Nazis': 'You have to be very careful when you
use words like "Nazis" ... humour's slow coming down the path for
things like that.'

And to Ross's inquiry as to whether he was disillusioned at the fact
that none of his projects had made it into production – 'At least we got
to see and hear the Sex Pistols but with your movies all we know are the
titles' – McLaren paused for a long time, crossed his arms and muttered:
'Maybe.'

Pressed on his view of Hollywood after three-and-a-half years,
McLaren said that he felt as close to realising an unnamed film project as
he had during his time there, and also outlined CBS Records' response to
the tracks he had recorded for *Waltz Darling*. 'Record companies being
what they are, a bit paranoid, they think I've ripped them off again,' he
said. 'I guess it'll be out and about New Year's Eve.' Ross corrected him;
the message from the label was that it would be released in March 1989.
'That's what they think,' drawled McLaren.

Noting McLaren's befuddlement, some viewers believed he was
drunk, stoned or both. McLaren appeared to confirm these suspicions
when he blamed Ross's team on air for having been too generous in their
servings of pre-broadcast wine in the green room. But, at the halfway
point in the ten-minute encounter, the reason for his distraction became
clear.

Appearing to go on a tangent, McLaren told Ross with a serious
expression on his face: 'I've really got to make a lot of trouble, seriously,
and I'm gearing myself up for that . . . I'm going to see my mother, and I
haven't spoken to her in twenty-two years so I suppose it's time to make
amends. That's the real reason I'm here.'

The sincerity expressed in this statement was at odds with the knockabout exchanges of just a minute before. Ross, a consummate professional,
was palpably confused, and the audience responded with a smattering of
sniggers. As Ross struggled to frame another question, McLaren recovered,
sat back in his chair, put a foot on the desk and changed the subject: 'Well

you know I made this record, man . . .' and the host and audience relaxed as he headed into more familiar chat-show badinage, discussing Jeff Beck, Bootsy Collins, the female singers' contributions to *Waltz Darling* and the possibility of repeating *Impresario* at London's Royal Academy.[20]

This drew a veil over McLaren's determination to confront his mother, as he told the journalist Ginny Dougary in the 2000s: 'I said to my brother, "Look, if we can find our father, if he is still alive, maybe we'll have the last piece of the jigsaw and it will help us to understand everything. I think I should know what it is that our mother had a major problem with and then we can understand how we came to be who we were . . . these kids who were not wanted and brought up in the most dysfunctional way." '[21]

Stuart Edwards arranged the meeting with Emily Edwards over Christmas dinner at his home an hour north of central London in St Albans, Hertfordshire. The gathering was an unmitigated disaster. McLaren arrived before his mother and was so tense that, in a blue funk, when she appeared, he fled to hide in an upstairs bathroom, locking the door behind him.

'I was so fucked up; in a real state,' wrote McLaren in the 2000s. 'Stuart had to come up and say, "It's OK, just let me in." I told Stuart I wasn't coming out until I had got the answers and he said he would protect me. Stuart came in and locked the door. It was like a madhouse when I think about it.'

McLaren confessed to having been taken aback at the appearance of the woman he hadn't seen for a quarter of a century. 'I was so shocked at what she looked like,' he wrote. 'When I last saw her she was tall and had olive skin and was very dominant looking, but now she was all shrivelled.'

Once he was coaxed to the dining table, the exchanges were desultory, with Emily studiously ignoring her wayward son. Then he and Stuart asked her to clarify the circumstances of Peter McLaren's disappearance and Emily berated McLaren not only for his lifestyle and celebrity but also his resemblance to her own mother.

'She said I looked the spitting image of my grandmother, who was the most hideous woman who ever lived on the planet, and as it was getting a bit over the edge, I decided to leave,' McLaren said.[22]

A few days later, the brothers made another attempt to discover the truth from Emily by visiting her in Brighton. 'She told us that the last time she had seen him was at Charing Cross station,' said McLaren. 'He was going to Australia and that she'd never seen or heard from him since. She said he was a cheap criminal and a thief and was no good.'

Then the trail went cold: a few weeks after the Brighton visit, Emily Edwards died of a heart attack at the age of sixty-six. While McLaren did not grieve publicly, the unresolved schism between mother and son took its toll and was expressed in extreme and unusual behaviour.

This was noted by a friend, the fashion journalist Natasha Fraser, daughter to novelist Antonia Fraser and stepdaughter to Harold Pinter. She was then a twenty-four-year-old expat living in New York where she had been employed at the recently deceased Andy Warhol's Factory. She had also been among the members of McLaren's circle who encouraged him to see his mother, and a few months earlier received McLaren's support when Factory gatekeeper Brigid Berlin attacked her 'Anglofile' column in *Interview* magazine.

'Malcolm could be a mensch,' Natasha Fraser-Cavassoni – as she is now – wrote in a 2017 memoir. 'I called Malcolm and within half an hour he was at the diner opposite my office,' she says. ' "Why did [Berlin] do that?" I kept asking. "Because she's a nutter, a fruitcake," Malcolm replied, and then explained Brigid was one of "those old birds" who was "a casualty of the 60s. She's probably forgotten what she said." '

This consoled Fraser-Cavassoni, who believed McLaren's immersion in the New York art scene was providing him with a bulwark against the multiple disappointments he was suffering in Los Angeles. In the New Year she attended the presidential inauguration of George H. W. Bush dressed to the nines. 'A few admiring glances came in my direction,' wrote Fraser-Cavassoni. 'But I could only think of Malcolm.'

According to Fraser-Cavassoni, these feelings were reciprocated in spades. She has written that when she saw McLaren after his return from London, he declared his undying love. 'I adore you, I adore you,' Fraser-Cavassoni says he told her, pausing to relate how this espousal had been at the suggestion of *Fans* scriptwriter Menno Meyjes 'that he should just be honest and voice his passion'. She says McLaren asked her to move into an apartment he was renting in New York. 'I was convinced that his chronic commitment problems stemmed from his lack of relationship with his mother,' wrote Fraser-Cavassoni, who surmised that the encounter with Emily Edwards 'didn't make an iota of difference. In fact, he then disappeared for 12 days without a trace! I gave up on him there and then.'[23]

During McLaren's processing of his mother's death, Craig Bromberg published his biography. Entitled *The Wicked Ways of Malcolm McLaren*, journalist Michael Gross had given a foretaste in his *New York* piece on *Impresario*: 'Biographer Bromberg paints [McLaren] as a lying, amoral exploiter,' reported Gross on eyeballing the manuscript.[24]

Bromberg was no longer 'the 100 per cent fan' of 1985, but a full-throated critic and apparently wronged Boswell figure. The book represented a solid work of reportage but the overwrought tone upset the balance; by aligning himself with those he felt McLaren had abused, Bromberg too appeared to have an axe to grind, though from where this stemmed remains difficult to divine. After all, McLaren had granted Bromberg unlimited access over the range of topics during sixteen hours in New York, and had made no move to block others from speaking to him nor halt publication.

Wicked Ways also suffered from unfortunate timing. Apart from a short coda, it had been delivered in 1987 and thus did not capture the series of personal turning points triggered by such events as the staging of *Impresario*, his meetings with his mother and the aftermath of her death.

Bromberg remains unrepentantly anti-McLaren thirty-odd years later, declaring the subject of his book as variously 'an asshole', 'emotionally incompetent as a person' and 'a clinical narcissist'.

'That narcissism lit sparks which sometimes benefited people but more often they got burned,' says Bromberg. 'He wasted a lot of money and opportunities and was careless with his relationships. He insulted a lot of people who would have been important to him. That incompetence in his affairs was a reality that everyone who knew him was on guard against. I am sure there are people who are still angry at Malcolm.'

It appears that Bromberg is among them (though, once again, the source of his ire remains elusive). Bromberg also claims he didn't update the biography 'because it was tedious. I mean, how many more chapters about Malcolm's narcissism are there to write?'

Given his dislike for his subject, it is ironic that Bromberg believes his book assisted McLaren. 'It helped establish him and got his story out,' says Bromberg. 'In a therapeutic way it got him to a place where, for better or for worse, he could reconnect with his family again.'

Bromberg didn't hear from McLaren after publication. They met again once more in the early 2000s when he encountered McLaren on the street in New York:

'I said, "Malcolm?" and he looked at me and said, "Bromberg?"

'I said: "Why haven't we talked?" and he said, "I don't want to talk to you."

' "Why not? I did a good job, I wrote you a nice story, man! Get over it. C'mon, man, let's shake," and I put out my hand.

' "I'm not shaking hands with you." '

Bromberg persisted and says that McLaren relented and gave him 'a very feeble English handshake. That was it. Then I walked away.'

On publication, the book failed to make much of an impact in the US, though it drew interest in New York; Johnny Dynell, the nightclub host and sometime confrère of McLaren's, DJ'd at the launch party. According to Bromberg, Harper & Row was nervous of the potential for libel action, and subjected the manuscript to intense legal scrutiny before reducing the print run to 3000 copies. Bromberg says that Richard Branson's publishing wing Virgin Books also backed off; *Wicked Ways* eventually emerged in the UK via the music publisher Omnibus two years later, in 1991.

Back in the spring of 1989, McLaren was preparing for *Waltz Darling*'s release. The title song was the first single to trail the album, and the B-side contained the track that would ignite international interest in the ballroom scene.

McLaren's spoken word intro to 'Deep in Vogue' opens listeners to a world of transgression and exoticism:

> This has got to be a special tribute to the houses of New York,
> LaBeija, Extravaganza, Magnifique, St Laurent, Omni, Ebony,
>   Dupree

The song featured raps from two of ballroom's biggest stars, Willi Ninja and David Extravaganza and, since this was the era of the dominance of the club remix, McLaren commissioned one from the young British DJ/producer Mark Moore. He had recently scored a UK crossover hit with the song 'Theme from S-Express' and was delighted at the invitation, having been a teenage customer of Seditionaries.

In turn Moore brought on board another young remixer, William Orbit, who would go on to make his name with Madonna and Björk, and together they created a nine-minute epic, which included sampled dialogue from a rough cut of *Paris Is Burning*.

Moore and Orbit's interpretation lit up the US club scene and went to number one on the US Billboard dance chart in July 1989, but a familiar complaint hounded McLaren, who once again had played fast and loose with the intellectual property of others.

The last verse of 'Deep in Vogue' is a word-for-word lift of the final paragraph of an article about the ballroom scene which appeared in New York's *Details* magazine the previous year[25] and was written by Johnny Dynell's partner Chi Chi Valenti. She successfully sued McLaren and his publisher for infringement.

Yet this disagreement cannot subtract from McLaren's achievement in recording 'Deep in Vogue' and presenting Ninja, Extravaganza and the ballroom houses to the wider public, particularly in the extended promo video, which featured these dancers and dramatic *Paris Is Burning*-style title inserts such as 'McLAREN'.

The visual and aural stylistic flourishes found in 'Deep in Vogue' were, of course, to be refined by Madonna, who not only scored a worldwide hit a year later with her song 'Vogue' but also added major ballroom figures to the dance troupe featured on her tours and in the smash-hit movie *In Bed with Madonna*. In the same way that 'Anarchy in the UK' and 'Buffalo Gals' are touchstones for punk and hip-hop, so 'Deep in Vogue' is a major reference point for popular music's celebration of sexual fluidity.

'McLaren's track – and its iconic video showcasing the talents of Willi Ninja – was key to Voguing's infiltration of mainstream culture,' wrote British music writer Mark Lindores in 2018. 'The fashion scene which had inspired the dance was first to adopt it, designers such as Thierry Mugler and Jean Paul Gaultier featuring voguers in their catwalk shows. But ball culture's true coming out moment arrived on May 10, 1989 with The Love Ball, a glitterati-filled fundraising event which exposed ball culture to New York's elite and powerful, including Madonna.'[26]

The Love Ball was held within weeks of the release of *Waltz Darling*. But the fact that it was McLaren's strongest and most coherent musical statement since *Duck Rock* did not allay media suspicion.

'Malcolm McLaren is the musical equivalent of Andy Warhol,' declared *People*.

> He's a marketing genius and schemer who uncovers material the avant-garde will disdain and the average person will dislike – but it's material that will also capture a moment and earn him a bundle. He's in the novelty business.

Now McLaren is back to prove you don't have to actually play on an album to put your name on it. In fact, it's unclear precisely what McLaren does musically on *Waltz Darling*, though he did, of course, conceive it (ah, art). McLaren does talk on some of the songs. The impresario also had a hand in writing all the tracks and coordinated the performing talent ... this is mostly music that appeals to the chronically hip and sneers at them (this is, after all, a masochistic age we live in). The songs on *Waltz Darling* are best heard at dance venues, not around the house. This is not an album anyone will bond with. It may serve primarily, in fact, to illustrate how McLaren has declined. The Sex Pistols made you feel – you loved them or hated them – but *Waltz Darling* just kind of makes you wonder.[27]

PART VII

'That's My Dad'

Chapter 33

Before *Waltz Darling*'s release, Malcolm McLaren's relationship with Lauren Hutton disintegrated when she left him for good for her manager Bob Williamson.

This resulted from Hutton's consultations with a female Freudian psychotherapist herself about the complex relationship with Williamson, who she identified as her 'Daddy replacement'. Hutton in turn recommended that McLaren start sessions with the same therapist; this was to cause problems down the road.

McLaren was deeply perplexed at this turn of events: the person who had been urging him into therapy over his damaged childhood was now seeking similar relief, all the while seeing another man. 'It was a terrible thing to do,' admitted Hutton the day after McLaren's death. 'I went to a shrink for the first time and figured out how to stand on my own two feet.'[1]

The unravelling of McLaren's relationship with Hutton was soon followed by the commencement of that with photographers' agent Eugenia Melián.

During press interviews McLaren talked about Hutton as though they were still together, but in fact he was already forming a strong bond with Melián, who came from a cosmopolitan background. Born in the Philippines of a Spanish father and an American mother, raised in Andalusia among her parents' milieu – which included Maria Callas and Jackie Onassis as well as landscape gardener Russell Page, photographer Slim Aarons, interior decorator Jaime Parladé and abstract expressionist Fernando Zóbel – Melián had been educated at a British boarding school before attending the American University in Paris.

Melián also had deep roots in the fashion world, having modelled and interned at Yves Saint Laurent in the early 1980s before setting up as representative of the American illustrator and photographer Tony Viramontes from offices in Milan. By the time Melián met McLaren, Viramontes had died from Aids.

Melián was hired by CBS Italy to organise the international launch party in Milan for *Waltz Darling* as McLaren undertook a European promotional tour. Melián arranged for a lavish event featuring kilims, thousands of red roses and wine from Tuscany. This was backed by the fashion house Romeo Gigli and held during Milan Men's Fashion Week at what would become the renowned fashion store Corso Como 10, attracting crowds in their thousands and impressing McLaren.

'Malcolm called me from London three days later to thank me, saying that no one had ever given him a party like that,' says Melián. 'That was we first time we "met", and this by phone and fax, even though we posed together for a photograph at the party. After dozens of calls and faxes, a month later he came to visit me in Andalusia.'[2]

That trip to Spain occurred after a life-changing encounter. By some coincidence, Chrissy Iley, the British journalist who recorded Lauren Hutton's remarks in 2010, played a pivotal role in McLaren's existence at the height of the summer of 1989. During an interview for the *Sunday Express* about his new LP, McLaren told Iley of Hutton's belief that his psychological make-up was comparable to both the rock guitarist Eric Clapton and the American mass murderer Ted Bundy on the basis that he had told her he grew up under the misapprehension that his mother was his sister and his grandmother his mother.

'One of the questions was, "What is your real wish?" and I said, "Well, I really want to find my father," ' McLaren wrote in the 2000s. 'They said that they would try and find him on the condition they get the scoop. Then these calls came to the paper. There were six people who said they were my father and we vetted them and got one person.'

McLaren's appeal had resonated in an untamed corner of Britain's Kentish shoreline. In the flat above the Oasis Café on the edge of Romney Marsh, co-owner Barbara Nicola showed the interview to the man who had been her partner for the past sixteen years:

Peter James Philip McLaren.

Just a couple of weeks shy of his seventieth birthday, Peter McLaren had been following the exploits of the son he hadn't seen for forty-two years in the media for decades, but abstained from making contact because of the contract he reached with his first wife and her family in the late 1940s: that he would keep away from Stuart and Malcolm until Emily's death. 'He abided because he was an honourable man,' says Nicola. 'He'd given his word and his word was sacrosanct. That overrode any paternal urges.'

But now, as Malcolm McLaren had informed Iley, Emily was dead.

Not a lot is known about Peter McLaren's life in the years immediately after he left Carysfort Road in 1947. 'I think Peter stayed in London after the divorce for a while living at his mother's and became something of a "wheeler-dealer", mostly to do with second-hand cars and possibly other vehicles,' says Nicola. He did not emigrate to Australia as Emily had claimed. In fact, he didn't ever possess a passport and didn't leave England until he was seventy (and only then for a visit to Scotland).

Peter McLaren married a second time in the mid-1950s and fathered two more children, Ian and Christine. He and his wife ran a café in Swindon before another move to Kent where his wife was stricken with cancer while still in her thirties, and died within ten days of the diagnosis in the mid-1960s.

'He'd had a very poor existence bringing up the two children against all odds,' says Nicola, who met Peter McLaren in 1974 when he was running a café on a caravan site on Winchelsea Beach on the Sussex coast; she ran a market gardening concession there. 'There had been all sorts of jobs, anything to make ends meet. He told me that at one stage social services threatened to put the children into care because there were no provisions for single men with kids in those days.'

At the time he met Nicola, Peter McLaren was in a relationship with a partner named Gloria Donovan, by whom he had another son, Simon, who was to die in a motorbike accident on his sixteenth birthday. When

McLaren and Donovan split up, he, Ian and Christine moved into a cottage owned by Nicola and her husband.

But Nicola's marriage also didn't last. 'One night, after I had separated from my first husband, Peter said typically bluntly: "You look terrible. Do you want to go out for a drink?"' recalls Nicola.

And so their relationship began. 'Life had made him a bit of a lone wolf,' says Nicola. 'It took me a very long time to get to know Peter properly. He wasn't secretive but would never allow his emotions to come to the fore. But he didn't have a bad temper, and never swore.'

In 1976 the couple took over the Oasis, by which time Peter had told Nicola about his failed wartime marriage. As punk was breaking big, he produced a photograph clipped from the *Daily Mirror*. 'Peter said: "This is my son, have you heard of him?"' says Nicola. 'Well, I had, because my own son was an absolute Sex Pistols fanatic and drove me nuts with their music. So I said: "Oh please, it's not him is it?"'

Nicola describes Peter McLaren as 'lean, not terribly tall, about five-nine, five-ten, with a London accent, not particularly cockney; he was quite proud of the fact that he had Scottish blood'.

Peter was also dapper, sharing his most famous son's appetite for good clothes. 'Peter loved dressing well,' says Nicola. 'Given the money, which he didn't have at that time, he was a very snappy dresser. He liked hand-made shirts and trousers from a company that made them by royal appointment and always said he had a champagne lifestyle on a brown ale income. And he was very sociable and charismatic. I had to sweep women off him all the time. He liked women and much preferred their company.'

There was also an interest in visual artistic expression – 'He painted nude portraits,' says Nicola. 'I had to sit for him because we couldn't afford a sitter' – and a literary bent: 'He'd had a very poor education but read every word Shakespeare and Dickens wrote. He knew that education was essential to get ahead, which is why he was determined that his son Ian would go to Oxbridge.'

In the event, Ian McLaren became a professor of cognitive psychology after studying theoretical physics at King's College, Cambridge, and by the time Nicola and Peter were running the Oasis in Old Romney in the 1980s, their situation had improved. 'When we got going in the café he started to enjoy a better life,' says Nicola. 'We had a really nice time together.'

As Malcolm McLaren's fame grew, so the couple pondered making an approach. Notes that Peter McLaren dictated towards the end of his life are illuminating, and not just because he adopted his son's penchant for the third person singular: 'His father had followed his career for years, keeping newspaper cuttings in his worn wallet. Then increasingly articles began to appear that M wanted to find his Father. P and B talked a lot about the possibility of making contact, and what might be the ensuing results. Might M hit his father in the mouth for apparently deserting him? Would he be angry? Sad? Glad? Pleased? Snobbish? Helpful?'

On reading Iley's interview Peter and Nicola felt they had no option but to make contact. 'It was a risk we had to take,' says Nicola. And there were deciding factors beyond the demise of Emily Edwards; while Peter understood Malcolm was thriving and making his mark on the world, he knew nothing of his eldest son Stuart. It was time his adult children were united.

'Peter felt he should at least put them all in touch with each other before he died,' says Nicola. 'At seventy, it was time to look at his life and sort out those things that had been left undone.'

And so Nicola responded to the *Sunday Express* appeal. Iley rang the Oasis on the morning of 5 August 1989, a Saturday, and spoke to Peter McLaren, confirming that his youngest son by Emily was still in the country, staying at the Mayfair hotel the Westbury. Malcolm McLaren was passed the number of the flat above the café, and within a few minutes he was engaged in conversation with his long-lost father.

'Malcolm called me from London that day,' says Eugenia Melián. 'He was in a terrible state. Anxious, nervous, babbling, incoherent ... a frightened mess.'

Two days later McLaren and his brother Stuart were delivered by car at the behest of CBS to the Oasis, subsequently described in McLarenese as 'a greasy-spoon shack, with an abandoned garage of old petrol pumps from the 1930s and clientele of Hells Angels'.

Arriving three hours later than the assigned time, the brothers remained suspicious and planned in advance the tack they were going to take, working out a series of questions at the Westbury.

'My brother said to me, "I'll do the talking, you keep quiet, I'll sort this guy out and see if he's for real," ' recalled McLaren a decade later. 'So we got out and went into the house – it was like the House that Jack Built, all crumbling down. My brother grilled him for an hour.'

McLaren's jitters were similar to those which assailed him during his penultimate meeting with his mother, and he used the second person singular when answering a question as to whether the encounter had been emotional.

'Of course, you would be, yes. You were curious. You were scared,' he said. 'There was this guy with a shotgun and an Alsatian, wearing a pair of white Levi jeans and an emerald green shirt, with very flaxen grey hair, small, with an incredibly lined face – a bit like W. H. Auden, and I thought, this is a well-travelled man with a really weather-beaten sailor's face.'[3]

Stuart asked questions as to their father's whereabouts after the war as they were shown photographs, including the wedding portrait. For the most part, McLaren abided by his agreement to remain quiet. 'He was drinking whisky, very arrogant,' said McLaren in 2004. 'He looked a lot like my brother but certainly didn't look anything like me. I saw in him there was a connection . . . I just thought, "This is the guy." '[4]

The following is an extract from the notes Peter McLaren dictated to his third wife a few months before he died in 1999. These have never before been published.

The stilted sentences, formal usages, references to himself in the third person and occasional quaint terminology and phrases reinforce the clarity of Peter McLaren's memories, as well as the barely suppressed emotion with which this enigmatic man recalled the events of early August 1989:

The two men spoke to each other for the first time in forty-two years.

The die was cast.

A meeting was arranged for the following day, Malcolm to drive down to his father's modest home in the middle of the windswept 'sixth' continent, the Romney Marsh.

But that meeting was cancelled and another one set up for Monday afternoon at 3 p.m. when Malcolm would appear with his elder brother, Stuart, a London cab driver.

It's difficult to say what the atmosphere was like in the older McLaren household. A normal day's trading had to be accomplished, even in what might turn out to be a family crisis, a living needs to be earned. But by three o'clock Peter's nerves were becoming a little frayed.

It was early August and very hot. The waiting seemed interminable. Four o'clock came and went and no sign.

B, instructed by P to watch out for a black cab, kept a watchful eye on the A259 trunk road that runs alongside the Café, but cars came and went and no cab. Perhaps they had chickened out and would not turn up. Maybe the anxiety and eternal discussions about should we, shouldn't we, had all been a waste of time.

But eventually with an unpunctuality which was to become accepted as the norm for Malcolm, a chauffeur-driven Daimler approached, flashing indicator a signal to leave the window vantage point and compose oneself for a meeting. P went down to meet the two brothers and bring them up to the small flat above the shop.

Stuart, correctly attired in slacks and shirt, settled down to a cup of tea and a series of searching and sometimes impertinent questions about P's past, recollections and the nineteen-year age difference between P and his partner.

Malcolm, dressed in check trousers cut off below the knee and a blue oversized cotton shirt, the cuffs hanging loose below the end of his arms, refused refreshments and sat quiet and almost motionless facing his father. He answered when questioned, but he appeared struck dumb, rigid with fear, until asked by S if he wanted to ask P any questions to establish his identity, he replied quite simply, 'No. I'm quite satisfied he is who he says he is.'

Over several hours Peter McLaren unravelled to his sons the story of his unhappy, brief marriage to their mother: how they had met in north London in the summer of 1941, her announcement that she was pregnant, the hastily arranged wedding at Liverpool Road Register Office, Stuart's birth in Crane Grove, the move to 47 Carysfort Road and his delivery of the newborn Malcolm.

He also told them about their mother's dalliances with the bookies at the dog track and the ne'er-do-wells of the Mozart dance hall, as well as the installation of the tarty young woman known as the Local Old Bag, the final separation and his acceptance of the proviso that, since her family paid for the divorce, he would not seek to contact the boys during Emily's lifetime.

'Malcolm was expected for dinner in Kensington with friends but simply ignored the time and his commitments,' says Barbara Nicola. 'After forty-two years he was face to face with the father he had never known. All he could ask was: "Why did you never get in touch?"'

This was a reasonable question.

A few evenings later the two brothers returned; their father booked a table at an off-the-beaten-track hotel:

It would be a quiet family dinner.

So much for romances.

They were of course late and arrived in a hire car driven by M, according to S, very badly.

The central table in the restaurant had been cleared for us, and far from not being recognised, the packed restaurant seemed to be fully aware of M's identity immediately he stepped out of his father's car. But apart from a photograph or two, no one bothered us.

A pleasant evening was spent. Back at the café M produced photographs on which he wrote a message and signed them for his father to exhibit them. Addresses and telephone numbers were exchanged with enthusiasm.

The relationship was on the threshold of success.

Peter's already planned seventieth birthday was discussed but, as it was only days away, M had previous commitments and S was on his way to a holiday in the States that very weekend so we would all get together later.

Within a week, the confusion stirred by these encounters was expressed in a heart-rending, Byron-quoting postcard McLaren sent from Spain, where he had joined Eugenia Melián's family to ask for her hand in marriage even though they hardly knew each other. 'My father had kicked Malcolm out of our home after the tabloids started calling, wanting to talk about Pete with Malcolm,' says Melián. 'That's the way my father found out about the Sex Pistols, punk rock, "God Save the Queen", his arrest, etc. Even though my father had "given me away" and accepted his marriage proposal, he hadn't known about Malcolm's past.'

On the card from Seville, McLaren wrote:

Dearest Peter

I don't know where to begin. I have never written a letter to you before. Perhaps I should just think of you strutting in a debonair fashion across the Romney Marsh and whisper 'That's my dad'.

This message of tears and joy, of trust and suspicion, this pagan love this son of yours sends is simply best wishes from the land of Andalucia . . . I wish you much happiness in the years to come and I hope I may have some of those days with you.

Your lost and foolish son, whose virtues might be written in water.

X X X X[5]

Settled with a steady job as a taxi driver, Stuart Edwards was content to have finally communicated directly with his father, and kept in contact, though was unimpressed by his thirst for whisky and bohemian lifestyle.

In contrast, Malcolm McLaren – though he found his father 'very, very aloof' – threw himself into the new relationship with a characteristic vigour. The brothers also made contact with their step-siblings, visiting Ian McLaren in Cambridge. 'He didn't look anything like me or Stuart,' said McLaren in 2004. 'Black hair, quite a short, stocky guy, very smart. He was a very nice guy.' Ian McLaren revealed that, as a student, he had attended McLaren's 1978 Cambridge University debate with Tim Rice which had ended in uproar.

'We became friends a little bit; I came back a few times to see him at Cambridge and kept in contact,' said McLaren. 'He came down to London and we would go out for dinner.'[6]

According to McLaren, his father's great hope was to visit the village of Balquhidder, the central Perthshire home of the McLaren clan. He did so in his seventieth year and, at one stage, McLaren talked about buying his father a cottage there.

Peter McLaren was undoubtedly a complex person. 'Peter was very, very proud of Malcolm,' says Nicola. 'But he didn't understand his fame for one minute. I guess he never got his head round the fact that Malcolm was famous. We used to walk on the Marsh with Malcolm and people would come up to us and start talking to him.'

Peter offered a detached assessment of his son in his notes: 'On the plus side, he is an attractive young man, with a babyish skin and pleasant though whiny voice. He speaks quietly with a touch always of anxiety. He thinks a lot, only formulating a question after much consideration. He becomes and remains in his father's presence just a son, no longer the International Celebrity noted for his arrogance, outspokenness, even bloodymindedness, he seems anxious to please when with his father.'

And when Peter offered his sister Ivy as a possible source of information in regard to his upbringing, McLaren wrote urgently from

LA, using the headed paper of his production company San Simeon Films:

> Ask her please to write or fax me. I would love to know anything, anything at all about Rose and my early childhood. I would be so grateful.
>
> Thanks again for all our talks. It helps me no end. I hope to meet Ian on my return.
>
> Regards and fondest wishes,
> Your son,
> Malcolm.[7]

Peter responded to his son's engagement to Eugenia Melián by proposing marriage to Barbara Nicola on the basis that, as father of the groom, it was time they were wed too. Their nuptials in the late spring of 1990 were planned as a quiet ceremony, but an intervention by McLaren proved an indicator as to the ways in which his overcompensation was tempered by the tendency to withdraw when situations became fraught or commitment was anticipated at a higher level than he was ultimately capable of contributing.

In the first instance he faxed a series of instructions for a lavish party to the closest 'quality' hotel, the Imperial in Hythe, including that the wedding rooms be decked as a Scottish glen, with wild flowers and heather. Bollinger was to be served with black and red caviar, devilled crab claws and prawn bouchées, to be followed by a roast beef traditional lunch for immediate family. McLaren also announced that he would pay.

Peter and Barbara acquiesced and met the hotel's banqueting manager and florist. 'Even the wedding cake was specified, no sugar, no icing and only fresh fruit as decoration,' recorded Peter. 'We were to have the Scottish flag flying, the red carpet, etc, etc. A bride's dream? A nightmare. After most of the friends and family had been informed, Malcolm withdrew completely and decided it would be better if he didn't pick up the bill after all.'

In the event the ceremony took place at a local venue of their choice, with fifty in attendance and a cake which, as Peter noted, was iced and sugared. McLaren wasn't in attendance.

Clearly struggling with his filial responsibilities, McLaren wrote a soft-pedalling note to his father:

Have a most wonderful wedding and an abundant holiday. Keep healthy and please accept my apologies for not attending. I have just a schedule that is ridiculous during that period in Los Angeles.

A sweet present is on its way although as yet I don't know *what* it is.[8]

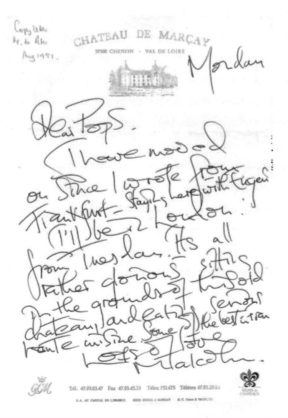

Letter to father, August 1991. Malcolm McLaren Estate.

This cut little slack with Peter: 'He did send a magnificent present: a complete set of bedding, including duvet, sheets, pillows, cases, etc. . . . This was very nice indeed but he had started a venture probably with the very best of good intentions and then run out of it, leaving someone else to pick up the pieces (he never even cancelled the hotel) and a very unwanted expensive bill with a total disregard for his father's feelings.'

McLaren's father was steely in assessing his son's personality traits: 'Malcolm displays an amazing amount of insecurity for someone who has built an empire out of an image. Very insecure in his relationships. Constantly at the psychiatrists to see how to map out his life, he says he is in search of a wife . . . He seems to be a catalyst sending sparks round within the family, and then having lit the blue touch paper he retires to the safety of the USA, returning months later as if nothing had happened.'

Over the following years, McLaren settled into a rhythm of contact with his father, addressing him by his first name or as 'dear Pops', introducing him to his own son Joe Corré – according to Nicola, Peter didn't approve of his grandson's use of bad language – and attempted to build relationships with his siblings.

Still, McLaren's father appears to have harboured a view of his most famous son which verged on dislike. Perhaps this stemmed from guilt surrounding his decades-long absence.

MALCOLM's public image is well known. But what about the private man? The man searching for his father? WHY?

Faced with a reunion with his father he hid behind his elder brother, then a girlfriend and then his own son Joe, P's grandson. He cannot face his father alone apparently. He makes promises he can't or won't keep.

Promising his father first tape cassettes, records, compact discs and a video recorder for his father's seventy-first birthday in 1990 which never materialised. He even said he would send a TV as well 'to be certain they were compatible' but nothing appeared at all.

He is easily influenced, especially by his older brother, and now by his newly found half-sister, checking with them each time he arrives in England before ringing or visiting his father. He stands in awe of his half-brother, a Cambridge Don.

This evaluation ill behoves Peter McLaren's position in his son's narrative; even the dispassionate observer can't help but agree that whatever the Isaacs' faults and eccentricities, they shouldered their responsibilities and provided a home, albeit tumultuous, for the child Malcolm McLaren. Meanwhile their manipulative, antagonistic, comic and fanciful outlook inadvertently set him on the path to committing the acts of subversion and radical expression that ran through the wider culture.

By the time of his father and stepmother's wedding Malcolm McLaren had been living with Eugenia Melián in Los Angeles for six months and drawn her into two hip-hop associated projects on which he was working.

One, *Round the Outside! Round the Outside!*, was a mini-album released by Virgin Records early in 1990 and arose from a *Duck Rock* album remix project which was stymied by Virgin's loss of the masters. *Round the Outside!* featured artwork by Shawn Stüssy, the legendary surf-wear designer who had proved an important conduit during the 'Surf Nazis' years, hotwiring McLaren to the SoCal scene. They had remained in touch and Stüssy's shop on La Brea in West Hollywood was by now an important youth nexus.

'Malcolm was very active in, and curious about, the LA hip-hop and rap scene,' says Melián. 'He found the music exciting, akin to street poetry. Some of the *Round the Outside!* kids – singers, artists, engineers or producers – belonged to gangs, either the Crips or Bloods, so no red or blue items of clothing were allowed in the studio. No blue baseball hats, no red bandanas, nothing that could spark a shootout in the parking lot where huge pimped-up cars of gang-member friends waited to pick them up, engines on, music blaring.

'I cooked lunch for them every day just to bring a "motherly" touch to the studio because they were so young. It was a great gig and we had a lot of fun. One song in particular was a defining moment that created unity in the studio: "II Be or Not II Be" rapped by MC Hamlet. In order to get the kids to understand the tone of what he wanted for the song, Malcolm played the 1948 black-and-white film with Laurence Olivier in the studio. The kids were roaring with laughter describing "dudes look like girls running around in pantyhose". Malcolm had to tell the kids that that was how men dressed then. When Olivier's soliloquy started, there was a huge silence in the studio and the kids were enthralled and respectful, and Malcolm told them to read Shakespeare if they wanted to sing. The kids said they wanted to meet Shakespeare, "being all English like you".'

Simultaneously McLaren was researching the city's urban music scene for a film idea called 'Night Brother' to be shot in downtown LA and Compton Beach. 'From the kids around Shawn's shop and from *Round the Outside!*, we got tips as to where artists were playing or DJ-ing and we would go to impromptu word-of-mouth live rap gigs that were held once a week but hardly ever in repeat venues because the police would close them down,' says Melián. 'Malcolm pitched "Night Brother" around Hollywood but the response was that rap and hip-hop was too niche. As usual Malcolm was way ahead of his time.'

During this period Madonna's co-option of the ballroom scene was making headlines as the superstar's single 'Vogue' became a hit and she assembled the dance troupe which included members who had been featured on *Waltz Darling*. 'Malcolm was very, very upset with Madonna for basing her "Vogue" video on his for "Deep in Vogue" and taking his dancers and going on to tour with them, thereafter claiming Voguing's mainstream success,' says Melián. 'I was at the Glencoe Way house at the time; it was a drama because Willi Ninja called Malcolm and told him about what was happening. Malcolm was deeply hurt.'

This fuss coincided with the disastrous effects of McLaren's commencement of the therapy sessions with the psychoanalyst who had been consulted by his ex, Lauren Hutton.

According to Melián, the counsellor's advice resulted in her being ejected from the Glencoe Way house. 'I was given twelve hours to pack up and leave, because, according to the shrink, "the women around Malcolm were too strong and he would never get strong and heal with us around".'

This referred not only to Melián – who left for Paris where she once again set up base and relaunched her agency – but also to McLaren's assistant Carol Ann Blinken, who was similarly dismissed, though rehired after a brief spell. It took a few months but, by the spring of 1991, McLaren had come to his senses. 'He travelled back to Europe to try to get me back,' says Melián.

The imbroglio served to underline the fact that McLaren's time on the West Coast was up. In a letter written from Glencoe Way to his father around this time, McLaren thanked Peter for birthday greetings and responded to enquiries after his wellbeing by writing: 'Things are going quite well. It's still hard work though.'

This was an understatement. After six years in Hollywood, and not for want of trying, McLaren had yet to haul a project into production. Recently he had turned his attentions to re-energising 'The Rock 'n' Roll Godfather' script when Walt Disney Co. relinquished its option. This, he decided, would be a straightforward biopic of manager Peter Grant.

'I thought, what a wonderful character to travel through what was an extraordinary world of thuggery, danger, rock 'n' roll gangsterism and all the things that made up a cowboy operation that suddenly turned into a megalopolis of accountants,' said McLaren. 'To parade that twenty years through the life and times of Peter, and dramatise the story of Led Zeppelin, we would have a great English rock 'n' roll movie, seriously hardcore, that the Americans couldn't necessarily do so well because they are more nostalgic about it, and not as exploitative or as flagrant.'[9]

The project reunited McLaren with super-producer Jeremy Thomas, who had seen *The Great Rock 'n' Roll Swindle* through its difficult realisation and subsequently risen to the top of the game with such Oscar winners as Bertolucci's *The Last Emperor*. By this time Hugh Hudson and Barrie Keeffe were no longer in the frame as director and writer; their places were assumed by the British filmmaker Mike Figgis and his screenwriting collaborator Mark Long, while McLaren hoped that Daniel Day-Lewis would fill the lead role, 'fattened up like Bobby De Niro in *Raging Bull*'.[10]

With Figgis and Long, McLaren spent hours interrogating Grant, who was forthright with his fellow former rock-band manager. 'I remember Peter Grant telling Malcolm, "If you make me look like a cunt, I will kill you." And he meant it,' says Eugenia Melián. But the project again foundered, this time over Figgis's distaste for the less savoury elements of Grant's past. Add to this difficulties in licensing Led Zeppelin's music and the fact that Grant's family were unhappy with the script (his biographer Mark Blake quotes Grant's daughter's summation: 'It was a bit sensationalist') and the film idea remained on the backburner.[11]

A similar proposal based around the last days of the tragic Beatles manager Brian Epstein crashed and burned as well. This would have returned McLaren to the territory he had covered in his Cambridge Rapist T-shirt design of the 1970s; the trail went back to the art dealer Robert Fraser's revelations about Epstein's penchant for S&M, and McLaren's film proposal replaced gangsterism with the darker sexual elements he believed to also underpin the music business.

During development, McLaren attached director Peter Medak, who had covered similar territory with *The Krays* (1990), to the film and discussed it with the British screenwriters Neal Purvis and Robert Wade, who have latterly made their name with an extraordinary run of credits for James Bond movies. At the time they were working up an idea based around the wrongful 1953 hanging of the epileptic teenager Derek Bentley for the murder of a policeman. Over a lunch, McLaren enthusiastically shared his interest in post-war adolescent culture and was taken enough by their script to pass it to Medak, who, in the event, directed Purvis and Wade's film – titled *Let Him Have It* after Bentley's words to his accomplice Christopher Craig – while the Epstein project foundered.

Such are the vagaries of the cinematic trade. 'Hollywood was, and still is, a business that trades on dreams,' said McLaren in 2005. 'They buy other people's dreams, whatever they might be: making a movie or being an actress. It's the only town that you can sell ideas. Name me any place on earth where you can sell ideas. It's very difficult to sell an idea. But Hollywood trades in them. It might be called the city of angels but it's really the city of crushed dreams.'[12]

Alone in LA, McLaren had come to realise after a great deal of effort that his life in the city was 'to a great extent, a waste of time. There were too many barriers, too many hurdles to jump, and inevitably, without the necessary experience, it was very difficult to climb over all of them. It's defeated better people than me.'[13]

Menno Meyjes suspects that McLaren wasn't ultimately interested in success on conventional terms. 'I would watch him blow things up in meetings,' says Meyjes. 'When he was in full will-o'-the-wisp mode, he'd come in full of ideas he got from some brainwave the night before and change everything. It was very difficult to keep a project on an even keel with him around.

'Also it was odd for Malcolm that they genuinely liked him in Hollywood. Within a few months of being there he had Spielberg really excited about his ideas. Some people spend their entire lives in LA and never get to that point. But I don't think Malcolm was eventually up for it, maybe because he thrived in a more adversarial environment.'

Towards the end of his West Coast sojourn, McLaren recounted advice he had received from Orson Welles. 'He said, "When I came to Hollywood I was 26. They gave me a beautiful chair. When I got up I was 66",' McLaren told British journalist Jim Shelley. 'He told me, "go home boy".'

It was time to return to Europe where he persuaded Eugenia Melián to resume their relationship. In London, McLaren rented an apartment in Oxford Gardens, Notting Hill, from the heiress Sabrina Guinness, whom he had met in Los Angeles as a fellow member of the *Spy*-nominated 'Britpack'.

McLaren regularly visited Melián in Paris, where he also caught up with Jean-Charles de Castelbajac and reconnected with Karl Lagerfeld, with whom he would regularly breakfast on 'rounds of bread and jam and four or five Cokes'.[14]

According to Melián, staff at Lagerfeld's atelier urged the designer into hosting McLaren because it would lend the man they called 'The Kaiser' credibility. 'I hated those breakfasts at Karl's,' she says. 'When Malcolm introduced me as Spanish, Karl said without missing a beat, "Oh I hate Spain, it smells of garlic and it's dirty." I thought to myself, "Well, I love you too, Karl." During the breakfasts Karl would say very personal and mean things about his clients and staff. I was shocked so only went to a couple.

'In January 1991, Karl talked to me backstage after his couture show. Gleefully he broke the news, in a fake-sad way, that Malcolm had spent Christmas with Natasha Fraser in Brittany while I was with my family. "Oh so sorry! Didn't you know?" Heartbroken, I tracked down Malcolm in LA. He swore over his father's head that he had never slept or had an affair with Fraser. I believed him. Malcolm was not a playboy and he took our engagement very seriously.'

Now Melián proved an inventive creative collaborator for McLaren. Through their time together she originated a flow of projects, some of which not only foregrounded his unique talents but also enabled a reversal out of the dead-end the film business had become. One in particular provided a cultural treasure trove to which McLaren would return until the end of his days.

In the early 1990s Melián set about developing an event for New York's Museum of Modern Art based around the rich advertising archive she had researched at France's CNAP (Centre National des Arts Plastiques). Founded by Anne Saint Dreux and her husband Bruno Zincone, the archive consisted of hundreds of commercials dating back to the beginnings of cinema, with many made by directors of note.

Melián's MoMA proposal was to stage an event called 'La Nuit de la Publicité', emulating the raucous *Rocky Horror Picture Show*-style participatory occasions held every year in Paris. The New York venture did not materialise, but McLaren saw potential for a television project, and he and Melián discussed a series based on the archive with BBC TV arts commissioner Alan Yentob. In the autumn of 1991 Melián signed a BBC contract for the project, entitled 'These Are the Breaks', to be presented and co-written by McLaren.

McLaren's west London base had brought him up to speed with old acquaintances such as Yentob and the design entrepreneur Tommy Roberts, by now dealing in collectable furniture in nearby Cambridge Gardens. Nights were spent socialising at the local brasserie 192 with Roberts and other friends including the design authority Jane Withers and her partner, the artworld mover-and-shaker Anthony Fawcett. 'I saw a lot of Malcolm around that time,' said Roberts in 2011. 'We became very close again. He was lost after LA and looking around for the next big adventure.'

This took the form of the television special *The Ghosts of Oxford Street* for Britain's alternative TV network Channel 4. Returning McLaren to his earliest foray into film – the unfinished psychogeographic degree project he had started twenty-two years earlier – *The Ghosts of Oxford Street* acted as something of a homecoming when it was broadcast on Christmas Day 1991.

The film stemmed from a meeting about a much smaller project between the critic Waldemar Januszczak, who was head of arts commissioning at Channel 4, producer Belinda Allen and her partner the filmmaker Rebecca Frayn, the girlfriend and soon to be wife of McLaren's friend Andy Harries. Allen and Frayn had recently launched an independent production company called Middlemarch, and first on the slate was 'The Great Picture Chase', a one-off documentary about the so-called 'war rugs' produced in the Middle East in the wake of the Soviet invasion of Afghanistan in the late 1970s featuring AK-47s and other weaponry in their designs. Like 'These Are the Breaks' at the BBC, this was to be presented by McLaren.

'It was a fairly straightforward proposition for a half-hour documentary with a budget of around £30,000,' says Frayn. 'Waldemar was keen to meet Malcolm so we brought him along to Channel 4. When Waldemar asked Malcolm, "So you're only in town for a few days?" Malcolm drawled, "Yeah man," talking out of the corner of his mouth like a pastiche gangster and waving a cigarette like a conductor's baton. "Then I gotta split. Places to go. Other fish to fry." '

Interrupting back-and-forth between the others about 'The Great Picture Chase', McLaren launched into a monologue about the Oxford Street film he had wanted to revisit since his student days. 'We were flummoxed and looking apologetically at Waldemar but, to our amazement, he leant forward, slapped the table and said "Great! I'll take it! I'm going to give you my entire budget for the year!" ' says Frayn. 'Looking back I realise Malcolm had read the room and knew that Waldemar would be up for working on a much bigger idea.'

The budget was £240,000, much less than the figures McLaren had juggled in LA but impressive in British broadcast terms. Januszczak insisted on Harries's involvement as executive producer as a guard against McLaren's potential for waywardness, while Allen oversaw production and Frayn worked on the script with McLaren. He assumed the position of director and also starred as the narrator, playing up his prankster character, flitting around the nocturnal West End in dark velvet suit, fedora and anti-pollution mask.

The experience of working with McLaren, bruised from Hollywood's rejection and still assimilating his father's presence in his life, was to scar Allen, Frayn and most of the other participants. 'From the outset Andy warned us we would be in for a rocky ride,' says Frayn, who later wrote a private memoir entitled 'The Horrors of Oxford Street' about the making of the programme. 'On more than one occasion, as things began to get more and more chaotic, Andy urged us to jump ship and abandon the whole thing. "This could ruin your careers before they've even begun," he would say.'

Frayn spent months hammering out a narrative at McLaren's Notting Hill flat. 'His ideas were often dazzling but hampered by the fact that they seldom made much, if any, logical sense,' says Frayn. 'Every time we made some sort of progress he would deliberately turn it on its head and, like a pack of cards, the whole thing would collapse. He described the process as "beating each other up" but it was really down to the fact that he was resistant to my attempts to impose a linear narrative. Chaos was his default position.'

The process was further undermined by the constant flow of phone calls on which McLaren thrived. 'It might be Harold Pinter wanting to know what Malcolm thought of his latest script, though Malcolm confessed to me in a state of some panic he had only read a few pages before inadvertently leaving it in a Notting Hill café,' says Frayn. 'Or it could be his father trying to persuade him to buy a decaying Scottish castle on a loch overlooking the McLaren ancestral graveyard. Or Eugenia insisting he name the day of their marriage so she could book Siena cathedral.'

Finally Januszczak was able sign off on the script, which presented McLaren as the viewer's guide into the past with a series of visits to various locations where performances were to be made by popular musicians of the day, including Sinéad O'Connor, Happy Mondays and the Pogues, all of whom had been corralled by McLaren's pointman Nils Stevenson. 'There was no problem attracting talent,' says Frayn. 'Everyone wanted to work with Malcolm.'

On the day before filming was to begin Frayn discovered that McLaren hadn't learned any of his lines. 'I went to Oxford Gardens to prep Malcolm but couldn't get him to focus because he was distracted by phone calls to the tailor who was making the velvet suit he wore in the film,' says Frayn. 'Then Belinda called to check if everything was OK and he launched into the most vile diatribe, not only about the shortcomings of the production but also her as a person, quickly reaching a pitch of vitriol I had never heard from him before.'

The shocked Frayn left McLaren's apartment to gather her thoughts and returned to ask him what he thought he was doing. ' "But sweetheart," he said to me, his voice treacly, "don't you think it upsets me too? I'm afraid that sometimes an artist just has to kick arse." '

The four-week shoot was fraught for the producers and the crew. The production manager, Joyce Hurley, had worked on *The Great Rock 'n' Roll Swindle*, so had McLaren's measure and attempted to lock down the script to halt his constant changes and introduction on a daily basis of new set-ups. According to Frayn, McLaren was incapable of delivering even a single sentence to camera satisfactorily, so she was forced to laboriously talk him through each line, resulting in many fluffed takes.

Meanwhile, the budget was blown as the staff at the Middlemarch offices grew from six to forty to cope with the production, which was also blighted by resistance from the owners of properties where filming was to take place. On the first day, Selfridges balked at the size of the crew, and the shop management's refusal to grant permission to shoot on the premises was only lifted when McLaren persuaded the singer Tom Jones to play the part of the department store's titular founder.

Frayn accepts that some of the difficulties may be attributed to her and Allen's inexperience, but says that McLaren's role as a director who couldn't direct was the root cause of the technical staff's problems.

'It wouldn't happen now but this was the era when the director, particularly if he was deemed to be a bit of a "bad boy", wasn't questioned,' says Frayn. 'We would arrive to find that Malcolm was arranging for ten set-ups when only four were marked out for that day, and people were flying around everywhere trying to cater to his wild plans.'

It is true that McLaren would suggest, off-the-bat, such late-stage ideas as Lauren Hutton and Angelica Huston playing Gordon Selfridge's companions/lovers the Dolly Sisters (this could have made for a brilliant flourish but the proviso that their London hotel bills were met by the already overspent budget meant this was a non-runner), but there were other issues beyond his control.

Plagued by bad weather and crowds of late-night West End revellers who made nightly attempts to invade the set, the alcohol and drug problems suffered by Shaun Ryder and Shane MacGowan, the respective leaders of Happy Mondays and the Pogues, hampered their participation. Eventually a stand-in was found for some of Ryder's dance sequences and he stumbled through their cover of the Bee Gees' hit 'Stayin' Alive'. McLaren's suggestion that the crew film Shane MacGowan in the hospital bed where he was drying out was not taken up when the lead Pogue arrived in shaky condition and announced that he could not remember any of his lines from the group's biggest hit, 'Fairytale of New York'.

At the end of the first week of the Selfridges shoot, McLaren became manic, firing off a series of wild and conflicting demands that left the crew confused as to what they were supposed to be shooting. 'The whole thing descended into chaos and disaster,' says Frayn. 'Not only did Malcolm not know any of his lines but he didn't know how to direct a sequence. He was like a child suffering from ADHD, wandering around the set shouting commands while I followed him around trying to calm everybody.

'The second AD had confided in Belinda that the crew were all hoping to get fired so that they wouldn't have to work with Malcolm any more, and then the editor, Martin Walsh – these days a very successful feature film editor in LA – walked off the project, declaring the film uncuttable.'

The next morning Frayn received a call from McLaren. 'He sounded like a frightened child,' she recalls. 'He asked me to help him and confessed, "I lost control last night." Martin's decision had completely terrified and humiliated him.'

Thereafter Frayn took over direction (she was listed as McLaren's co-director in the credits) and filming limped on, though McLaren continued to cause mayhem, not only complaining about Belinda Allen behind her back to Andy Harries, which prompted her also to exit the production for a while, but also admitting to having promised the production to an irate Alan Yentob at the BBC.

Eventually, Allen and Frayn brought the film home, Harries having also left the production in order to preserve his friendship with McLaren. 'It was a huge relief all round when we were done,' says Frayn, who nevertheless remained on good terms with McLaren, even renting him her Notting Hill apartment when he left the Oxford Gardens flat.

The Ghosts of Oxford Street bears all the marks of a difficult production, but there are several bright points, including the biographical elements such as the conflation of McLaren's childhood visits to Selfridges with the King Mob Christmas invasion of 1968. He also claimed that a McLaren was among the hundreds hanged at Tyburn for his part in the Battle of Culloden, and one scene recreated the art school tale of him wrapping bricks with ribbons and flinging them through church windows to reveal the message 'Magic's Back'. Bit parts were granted to Tommy Roberts, playing a street hawker, and Anne Lambton, who had appeared on the 'wrong' side of the 'You're Gonna Wake Up' T-shirt in 1974, was the gambling Georgian aristocrat Lady Sarah Archer. Even the Australian performance artist and nightlife legend Leigh Bowery appeared as mad King George III.

The script – the opening line of which quoted a sentence from King Mob's 1968 leaflet ('Christmas was meant to be great but it's horrible') – drew heavily on McLaren's student texts and communicated his adherence to the Situationist theories about the stultifying effects of consumerism: 'Oxford Street. How many times have I walked this street only to discover misery, boredom and loneliness?' asked McLaren over the house track he wrote as the programme's theme, sung by Brit soul artist Alison Limerick.

There were sequences that worked well, such as the child McLaren intoning Fagin's song 'You've Got to Pick a Pocket or Two' from Lionel Bart's musical *Oliver!* and Rebel MC's performance at Marble Arch. The section concerning Gordon Selfridge's retail achievements and tragic decline had McLaren clambering over the ornate facade of the department store, while some of the footage is of historical value: Sinead O'Connor's performance of 'Silent Night' as Thomas De Quincey's muse was located in the subterranean Victorian cobbled shopping parade located underneath Oxford Street, which was referenced in the original Goldsmiths project and has long since been inaccessible.

But the narrative arc was fragmented and McLaren proved too cloying a presence when stretched over sixty minutes. The finale, a masquerade inside Marks & Spencer on the site of the Pantheon, was a damp squib. 'The film was one of the more lively Christmas offerings as long as you could stomach McLaren's camp chic,' opined the *Guardian*, while McLaren himself later dismissed the venture as 'some pathetic Christmas musical to pay the rent'.

By the time *The Ghosts of Oxford Street* was broadcast, McLaren had found another means of realising that objective in the lucrative role of freelance music consultant for international advertising agencies.

This career shift had started when Anthony Fawcett engineered for McLaren to hook up with Saatchi & Saatchi, the advertising giant run by the former Let It Rock customer Charles Saatchi with his brother Maurice. Fawcett, who had been arts correspondent in partnership with Jane Withers at *The Face* and associated with the likes of Yoko Ono since the 1960s, was a pioneer of enticing brands into contemporary arts sponsorship, having succeeded in attracting bottled beer Becks to support the British duo Gilbert & George.

McLaren took the opportunity to apply his talents at fusing contemporary pop with classical music to a commercial for British Airways by working with the Greek composer Yanni (Yianni Chryssomallis). Their arrangement for a British Airways advertisement melded a wordless version of the lilting 'Flower Duet' from Léo Delibes's 1880s opera *Lakmé* with contemporary beats to produce the enduring 'Aria on Air'. This mined the seam McLaren had worked on *Waltz Darling* and provided the aural backdrop to the sixty-second clip directed by Hugh Hudson and known in industry circles as 'Face' (aerial views showed crowds of people in coloured clothing coalescing to form a visage).

'Aria on Air' became one of the most recognisable adverts of all time and the airline's signature tune, winning a coveted Gold Lion at the ad industry's annual bean feast in Cannes. This prompted McLaren to release a spin-off single featuring the Los Angeles gospel-trained singer Monalisa Young; the sleeve used a still from the advert decorated with lettering by Shawn Stüssy.

While the track – issued by Virgin Records – failed to make the charts, 'Aria on Air' established McLaren's name in the advertising community and he soon found himself in demand and matching a furious pace of commissions from Fawcett, including a Nike advert shot in New York to an opera/hip-hop hybrid created by McLaren.

Although Nils Stevenson was acting as McLaren's co-producer, the pair required technical and musical skills beyond their means. One day in Westside recording studios in west London, while working on a Coca-Cola campaign with the tagline 'Get Together with the Real Thing', Stevenson mentioned that he had heard the former Bow Wow Wow bassist Leigh Gorman was now operating as a dance music producer and arranger, having scored a degree of success working with the post-acid house duo Soho.

Gorman's last contact with McLaren had been to instruct him to 'eff off' a decade previously, so he was surprised to hear from his former manager.

'I'd produced a bunch of songs with Adam Ant and Marco Pirroni, who had passed my number on to Nils,' says Gorman. 'The first thing Malcolm said was, "Hi Leigh, I hear you're a producer now. Would you like to work on a Coca-Cola commercial?" That evening he faxed me the company's briefs: "PM Dawn/Spandau Ballet meets Public Enemy" and "Aretha Franklin's 'Respect' done by Queen Latifah". The next morning I turned up at Westside studios with a programmer and guitarist Boz Boorer and we started putting together some maquettes. Nils was great at finding people, so he got a rapper and a fantastic soul singer, and they both nailed it.

'I took my time putting the tracks together and Malcolm would disappear and then check in, sometimes being doubtful, so I'd have to reassure him I was still working with roughs. Then they came together. The clients loved them; the Coke people were jumping up and down. Malcolm was the hero and he paid me very handsomely.'

This set the working pattern for McLaren and Gorman for the next eighteen months; in all they produced tracks for thirty-plus commercials, many for blue-chip brands such as Levi's and Pepsi. They also created the musical bed for the Christmas remake of 'Aria on Air', and the ads were often directed by top-flight filmmakers, including Steve Barron and Tony Kaye.

In time, with Gorman's assistance, McLaren's reputation in the advertising world as a premier source of music reached a par with those of the British composer and arranger Brian Eno and Japan's Ryuichi Sakamoto.

'We had a good working relationship and really clicked creatively,' says Gorman. 'Now we were peers rather than me being just a bloke in a band. We also laughed a lot; our ideas were always kind of silly but then we'd make them work. I'd really got to grips with using electronics to make interesting sounds – basically EDM as you'd call it now – and Malcolm would be amazed: "How did you do that?!" He saw a new side of me that hadn't existed during Bow Wow Wow.'

Working with lavish budgets meant that the pair collaborated with top-quality recording engineers and session musicians, and recorded in the best studio facilities. Soon Gorman assumed the organisational aspects of the partnership from Nils Stevenson while McLaren maintained his position as conceptualist and creative director. 'We were usually working on very tight deadlines,' stresses Gorman. 'This wasn't like recording an album where the delivery is months away. We might have to turn it around in a day or two and if you didn't hit the deadline of 9 a.m. on Tuesday then they would find someone else.'

McLaren could still be mercurial. 'One commercial was for Citroën, directed by Ridley Scott,' says Gorman. 'I suggested we have a trumpeter do a jazz-but-fucked-up version of the theme to *2001*. Malcolm came in to hear the finished track and slammed me. "This is terrible, Gorman! You've fucked it up and lost me £50,000!"

'But I persuaded him that it would be fine, and, on hearing it, the clients said, "Ohmigod Malcolm, you're a genius!" Me and the engineers who had heard him say it was bollocks smiled at each other. After they left I asked, "How much are you getting for this Malc?" He denied it was fifty grand. "Just a couple of bob," he said.'

Gorman's musical relationship with McLaren extended to an odd contribution to the soundtrack of flop British film *Carry On Columbus*. This was an attempt to resurrect the bawdy *Carry On* franchise from the 1960s with a cast culled from those who had risen to popularity from the alternative comedy circuit appearing with the now elderly survivors of the original films.

McLaren had been introduced to the film's producer John Goldstone by a mutual acquaintance, the BBC arts correspondent Alan Yentob. 'I thought it was a huge hoot,' says Gorman, who recalls the memorable words of the series producer Peter Rogers: '*Carry On* is all about brown ale and farts.'

Gorman decided to go in the opposite direction and suggested to McLaren they put together a rave track. Entitled 'Fantastic Planet' with music by Gorman and lyrics by he and McLaren, the happy hardcore song incorporated an opera singer performing a classical theme by Spanish composer Isaac Albéniz as well as vocals comprising a yelped Annabella Lwin-style refrain by dance performer Jayne Collins.

The film sank without a trace and with it 'Fantastic Planet', which was played over the credits which mercifully closed the farrago. Nevertheless the track proved another example of McLaren's versatility and openness. 'Malcolm was supportive,' says Gorman. 'He'd encourage me to come up with ideas and most of the time was very positive. If he liked an idea you'd say to yourself, "Wow. Malcolm McLaren just said that was great," and you'd make sure that it was brought to fruition so that it lived up to his expectations.'

Gorman found McLaren much changed from the Bow Wow Wow era. 'We'd hang out and go for meals,' he says. 'There was money around. We weren't desperate, as we had been back in the day. Malcolm seemed more settled, happier.'

Soon McLaren abandoned his occupancy of Rebecca Frayn's flat for a home in the heart of the central London bohemian neighbourhood, Fitzrovia. Scala Street is in a quiet terrace of three-storey late eighteenth-century houses within walking distance of Soho and the West End, and number 16 was to provide him with a London sanctuary for several years.

Meanwhile, the excitement of producing music for adverts was palling. 'Though the money was great, it was a grind,' acknowledges Leigh Gorman. 'The deadlines were tough. We'd often work through the night in the studio to meet them. Malcolm had enormous energy and I'd try and keep up with him but it was physically demanding on both of us.'

The bigger the commercial, the greater the pressure. Gorman recalls a pitch for an ad for the chocolate bar Bounty. 'It had a huge budget, but that meant we had to produce several mixes,' he says. 'At five o'clock in the morning after four days of no sleep Malcolm asked me, "Why do we do this?" My only response was, "Because we want to get paid."'

For McLaren this was not enough. Beneath his jocular veneer, dissatisfaction was brewing. 'The commercials really drove me mad,' he confessed in the late 1990s. 'I hated meeting all those advertising people. We did all these demos and then they would be rejected or one might not be rejected and it just went on and on and on. It was the most boring fucking life. I made more money than I ever have for less work in some regards, but it was pointless.

'I was working for Golden Shred marmalade, Prudential insurance . . . it was fine if you didn't want to have to think about anything. And I didn't want to think about anything because I was just fed up, fed up with having been in LA working on all those movies that never happened. Oh God, they were also very terrible times.'

Chapter 34

Malcolm McLaren's presence in London in the early 1990s facilitated more regular contact with his son Joe Corré, who was by now in his mid-twenties and working hard behind the scenes to ensure the viability of his mother's company.

Westwood was on the rise. Anointed as 'the designer's designer' by the influential *Women's Wear Daily* publisher John Fairchild,[1] she won the British Designer of the Year Award in two successive years and also attained academic acceptance as fashion professor at Vienna's Academy of Applied Arts. Media attention came in the form of a *South Bank Show* TV documentary celebrating her life and work, and in June 1992 Westwood's prominence was boosted in the form of an OBE for her services to the fashion industry in the Queen's Birthday Honours List.

Importantly, Westwood had finally shaken McLaren from her life by falling in love with the twenty-five-year-old Austrian fashion student Andreas Kronthaler, who moved in with her at the Thurleigh Court flat found by Rose Corré way back in 1970.

McLaren took to sending his former partner adulatory notes after each of her collections were publicly unveiled. These were viewed with suspicion by Westwood and her circle. 'Vivienne was irritated by the way that, as she saw it, he was sucking up to her after she had found success, sending her congratulatory letters saying "I'm proud of you",' wrote Westwood's biographer Jane Mulvagh. '"I don't need him to be proud of me," she said. "He's a bit egotistical in that way, he doesn't like anything that he thinks belongs to him to sort of slip away."'[2]

Eugenia Melián counters this by explaining that McLaren's intentions were honourable. 'Malcolm was set on having a peaceful relationship with Westwood as part of the plan of becoming a more "normal" family after reuniting with his father and brothers,' she says. 'Same with Joe. He just wanted to be nice. It was not premeditated. Malcolm called Joe every day and spent hours chatting with him and brainstorming about his lingerie project [which became the successful Agent Provocateur]. Also, Malcolm never sucked up to anyone, it was not the way he was made. The concept of being nice to someone for a purpose was alien to him.'

Midway through 1992, Melián's BBC 2 TV series 'These Are the Breaks' had gone into production with a two-day shoot in Paris with McLaren as co-writer and presenter. But budget cuts had enforced the replacement of chosen director Jeff Stark and the finished result did not pass muster with Melián and McLaren, who persuaded the BBC's Alan Yentob to cancel the project.

Yet the lure of the subject matter proved irresistible and Melián set about helping McLaren to develop a new musical project. This would be his fulsome paean to Paris, the city he had adored since his teenage years in Soho, and started as an African/French patois demo called 'Paris Blacks' featuring the model Dominique Figaro, who is from the Antilles, and her west African friend Maggie Bond.

'Malcolm was inspired by the powerful diversity and ethnicity of the "beautiful black girls of Paris",' says Melián, who reports that the project was abandoned when it became clear that the duo's vocal limitations would not carry an entire album.

The sessions did, however, provide a musical direction for McLaren. To demonstrate how he wanted the vocals to sound, he entered the recording booth and proceeded to 'mouth a load of words, a stream of consciousness and then I started reading a letter from my girlfriend which I happened to have in my pocket. When I'd finished, everyone was quiet, and then they all clapped.'[3]

McLaren had alighted upon a style that suited him: ardour-filled, sexually charged spoken-word sections segued with sung romantic lyrics.

Years later, McLaren gave full credit to Melián for having not only set him on the path but also collaborated all the way to *Paris*, as his next album was inevitably entitled. 'Quite frankly, it wasn't my idea at all, it was Eugenia who suggested it,' said McLaren. 'I was reluctant to make a record again. It felt like going backwards. But after a few weeks I decided she was probably right.[4]

Melián's concept was for 'a soundscape album which could be an incredibly new idea because Paris was like the Tower of Babel with so many dialects, quarters, ethnicities, colours, feelings, odours. By then I had taken him on all my walks of the city: Clichy, Pigalle, Belleville, Saint Denis, Canal Saint-Martin, Montmartre, Buttes Chaumont park, Saint Germain where I had lived since 1979, the "guingettes" or dance halls on the Seine outside Paris . . .'

And she describes *Paris* as 'a love letter to the city that we roamed. I have many of Malcolm's love letters of those years, funny or poetic, romantic or naughty. I would never pretend that any was used on *Paris*, but Malcolm was feverish with the ideas and inspiration that came from those walks.'

For a brief while, before they settled on the final title, the project was called 'Ballades d'Amour'. 'Musically it is very much a pop record loosely inspired by Erik Satie and Saint Saens,' wrote McLaren to his Paris lawyers in October 1992 using that title. 'Each track will have a specific story involving particular references to Paris. My ambition is to perform this album live. It will be the first time I have ever done this.'[5]

Again at Melián's suggestion, McLaren set out to blend the expression of his adoration for the French capital with a showcase for the grand dames of French film and music. Having lived in the city in the late 1970s and early 1980s, she had connections to many of these. 'I knew Catherine Deneuve lived on Place Saint-Sulpice because I had lived there for two years,' says Melián, who was also friendly with the socialite and former call girl Susi Wyss, who received a credit on *Paris* and was well acquainted with Françoise Hardy and her husband Jacques Dutronc.

Actress Jeanne Moreau and singer Juliette Gréco were added to the list, as was Vanessa Paradis, and Serge Gainsbourg's daughter Charlotte, for whom McLaren wrote a song entitled 'Fathers', but she rejected it and did not appear on the record.

Meanwhile, the music he proposed was to be a light touch melange of African rhythms, jazz and the piano compositions of the early twentieth century. In one respect it became an easy-listening album, just as the revival of interest in this previously denigrated MoR form was occurring across the Western world.

A two-album deal was netted by McLaren with the venerable Disques Vogue, which had started as a jazz label in the 1940s. According to McLaren the label chief Fabrice Nataf stipulated a proviso. 'The company was dying on its feet, it had kind of ceased to exist since the 1960s and this was the 1990s,' said McLaren. 'They agreed to do the album, but on one condition: that I had to guarantee to use three of their five major French chanteuses: Catherine Deneuve, Françoise Hardy, Jeanne Moreau, Juliette Gréco and Vanessa Paradis.'[6]

Eugenia Melián located a recording studio in the basement of the Montmorency-Fosseux, an eighteenth-century *hôtel particulier* over-looking Saint-Sulpice church in the sixth arrondissement, south of the Seine. The facility was run by an acquaintance, the musician and producer Frédéric Bouveron, who became the engineer on the sessions.

Melián's connection was that she had been in a relationship with Bouveron's late brother. 'Eugenia, regardless of the situation, decided to revisit this place,' said McLaren. 'Of course the people there were delighted to have this famous guy from England come work in this some-what amateur studio. One thing we knew was that Eugenia's deceased boyfriend had always held *Waltz Darling* up to his brother and said: "We have to make a record like this!"'[7]

The ghosts of the Left Bank and the present occupants of the locale acted as inspiration; Au Nom de la Rose, the flower shop in the hotel's courtyard, triggered the writing of the song 'Revenge of the Flowers', which was based on Émile Zola's novel *The Sinful*

Priest in which an innocent girl creates a deathbed out of petals, thorns and leaves.

Zola's book was one of many from Melián's research for 'La Nuit de la Publicité' and 'These Are the Breaks' that influenced tracks on *Paris*. The companion track to 'Revenge of the Flowers', titled 'Driving into Delirium', was prompted by a reading of Bram Dijkstra's 1986 feminist study *Idols of Perversity*, described by the *Observer* as 'an astonishing . . . encyclopaedia of misogyny, proving once more that men always love the thing they kill'. Subtitled *Fantasies of Feminine Evil in Fin-de-Siècle Culture*, the book's chapter 'Dead Ladies and the Fetish of Sleep' provided particular food for thought, according to McLaren.

Boris Vian's *Manual of Saint-Germain-des-Prés* became 'a guide and inspiration', wrote McLaren in a diary about the experience, while the song 'Anthem' drew on Francis Carco's 1914 novel *Jésus-la-Caille*, whose characters include a Montmartre prostitute who returns from 'exile' in Belleville.

McLaren delighted in citing the singer and actress Léonie Marie Julie Bathiat, known professionally as Arletty and found guilty of treason after the Second World War. 'She said, when accused of sleeping with Nazis during the occupation, "I give my heart to Paris but my arse belongs to the world." This in one sentence sums up the lexicon of Parisian morality.'

In keeping with McLaren's previous musical efforts, a diverse group of musicians were assembled, including the funk keyboard player Didier Makaga, superstar percussionist Luís Jardim and guitarists Jean-Marc Benaïs and Babik Reinhardt (son of the jazz pioneer Django). Meanwhile, Melián recruited the French-Tunisian singer Amina Annabi, who was a star of North African pop and had crossed over when she was placed second in the Eurovision Song Contest earlier in the 1990s. 'Amina was huge in Paris at the time,' says Melián. 'I loved her voice and wanted *Paris* to show diversity and incorporate the multiculturalism of the city.'

Given the intensity of their recent bout of music-making for commercials, McLaren made the eminently sensible choice of bringing on board the multi-talented Leigh Gorman as musical director.

'Malcolm once said to me, "When you're making music for commercials, you're actually not producing anything,"' recalls Gorman. 'The chance to work together on an album showed we were intent on creating something of substance.'

The team worked on the record for a year from the early spring of 1993. In Paris McLaren and Gorman wrote material in an attic writing room at the *hôtel particulier* and recorded backing tracks with Bouveron and the musicians in the basement. 'In contrast with the writing room, that was rough,' recalls Gorman. 'There was no AC and the pee from Parisians using the street outside would come down the tiles.'

As the tracks took shape, McLaren was introduced by Disques Vogue executives to the British record producer Robin Millar, whose credits included million-selling LPs by artists such as Sade. Importantly, Millar had recently produced an album by the singer Patricia Kaas, which had sold well in Francophone territories. On his website years later Millar wrote:

I wanted to know why he had chosen me for one of his brave, cutting edge works. It was going to be an art work, with no singles coming from it and not even translated into English. Was it my jazz sense, perhaps, that had brought him to my door? My broader perspective on the music and cultural scenes? My reputation for making voices sound wonderful?

'Why me?' I asked.

'Well,' he wheeled round on me. 'You speak French, don't you?'

'Yes.'

'I just need a producer who can speak French.'

'Isn't there anything else?'

'How difficult can producing be? I need someone to translate. How much money do you want?'

'Less than usual,' I said, since everything he said was endearing him to me.

'That's good.'

'Thirty thousand.'

'You'll probably only get half of it.'

'Why?' I wondered.

'Because that's the way with my projects. They always run out of money.'

How could I resist such a lack of bullshit?[8]

Millar, who is blind, says that he felt secure in McLaren's company. 'We were going to be in Paris for five or six months, with Malcolm as my guide and my eyes,' says Millar. 'I have never felt as safe in my life, because he just goes wherever he wants to go. He doesn't stop for anyone or anything, confident that the traffic will stop for him if he steps in front of it. I simply had to hang on to him and he never walked me into anything.'

According to Millar, McLaren's enthusiasm for the project 'and his imagination seemed boundless'. For example, Millar was asked to record the bells of Saint-Sulpice through the open windows of a room in an apartment where McLaren believed Miles Davis and Juliette Gréco had first made love.

McLaren also took Millar on a nocturnal visit to Jim Morrison's grave in Père Lachaise to consult with the dead rock star about a track he had written for *Paris*.

'Malcolm persevered, leading me deeper with a torch,' says Millar.

I wasn't bothered. I'm pretty good in the dark. When he found the large, graffiti-covered mausoleum, Malcolm climbed on top and called out to the spirit world.

'Jim? It's Malcolm here, Malcolm McLaren. I'm doing this song, and I want to do it in your style, about Père Lachaise and the cats pissing on your sepulchre. I wondered if you minded.'

He turned back to me. 'I'm fucking petrified!'

'Sing the song to him,' I said.

'Okay.' So he started, his eerie quiet faint voice ringing through the silence of the graveyard. That's commitment.

The producer was interested in McLaren's insistence that *Paris* be an art piece: 'The effect he wanted to achieve was like hip-hop, made up of bits of other records stitched together into a rhythm tapestry, with rapping over the top. Since there were a variety of reasons why all the music he wanted to use couldn't be used, my job was to recreate it, musically and sonically, mimicking the sounds of Fifties jazz and Sixties pop and sewing them together with sounds from old movies and monologues written and read by Malcolm.'

But Millar is a traditional producer, and was unacquainted with the montage methodology that had been developed by Gorman and McLaren, so his comments downplay Gorman's contribution; it was due to his intensive labours before, during and after Millar's involvement that the sonic aspects of the tracks on Paris were laid. 'Robin was very kind to me and we worked well together but he didn't quite fit,' says Gorman, who points out that Millar's presence provided a bonus in terms of an increased budget. 'But he got through what we had already done very quickly so it was kind of zero sum. The extra budget went very quickly.'

Vocal sessions took place in one of the city's grander studios once McLaren had made approaches to the women whose lives he wished to celebrate. The song 'Jazz Is Paris' was about the jazz trumpeter Miles Davis's affair with the young Juliette Gréco, who was identified by McLaren as 'one of the first teenage rebels in Europe. They left home in the suburbs and lived in the small hotels of Saint-Germain-des-Prés. Gréco wore the cast-offs of Left Bank poets and philosophers such as Jacques Prévert and Jean-Paul Sartre and became their muse, always wearing black. One day she saw the silhouette of someone playing trumpet in a club close by. Running back to the Café Flore she exclaimed to Sartre that she had seen an Egyptian god. He laughed and told her it was Miles Davis. She immediately fell in love with him.'

But Gréco rejected McLaren's request to participate after he sent her a demo tape (part of the chorus ran, 'I wore black, you were black').

'Her agent called me and screaming down the phone said that I had first been insulting to suggest that the queen of the French chanson should sing anything in English, but furthermore, that she should sing about an old love affair that ended badly,' recalled McLaren. 'I learnt later that she had committed to plastic surgery in the US and was disliked thereafter by Miles Davis and returned to Paris alone.'

And so McLaren's lead vocal remained on the track supported by backing vocals not only by the British singer Tracy Ackerman but also Yves Saint Laurent's muse Loulou de la Falaise, a friend of Melián's, who also asked her to contribute translated lyrics. 'She was delighted,' observed journalist Eve MacSweeney of de la Falaise. '"Jazz" and "Paris" being, coincidentally, the names of YSL perfumes.'⁹

Events conspired for McLaren to also strike out the possibility of working with Jeanne Moreau, star of such *nouvelle vague* masterpieces as Truffaut's *Jules et Jim* and part of Jean Cocteau and Jean Genet's circles.

With Gorman and Makaga, McLaren wrote a song called 'Paris Lutece Paname' for Moreau and visited her to play the demo. 'She was dressed very sexily in a see-through leopard-print chiffon top and holding the longest cigarette holder I had ever seen,' said McLaren. 'As I explained the concept of the album she got excited and loved the idea of working with Amina. She was not too struck by Juliette Gréco, considered Françoise Hardy rather ordinary and had little to say about Catherine Deneuve. She was seductive to say the least, and when I asked her what key she sang in in order to prepare her track properly, she replied, "Key! Quoi key?!"

'I said, "How do you sing?" and she said, "In the morning I sing like this" – and she let out a groaning, smoke-ridden sound – "and in the afternoon I sing like this", and let out a rather high-pitched, fragile, canary sound. Finally she told me she would agree to contribute to the project but on the condition that her performance be the last on the record. On asking why, she said, "Because I am the best."'

McLaren agreed and prepared the recording session for a few days later, but news came through that Moreau couldn't attend. Depending on which version of McLaren's tale you believe, she either took umbrage at his insistence that she bring along a love letter to read out or she was incapacitated by a stay in hospital recovering from alcohol poisoning. There is the third story McLaren told Robin Millar: that Moreau had thrown him out of her apartment when they first met because she objected to singing the line: "I like to make love before I put in my curlers."

Late in the recording schedule, Eugenia Melián made another approach to Moreau with a proposal: she would interview the actress in French so that samples of the conversation could be used against a backing track. But by the time Moreau's agent responded positively, it was too late for her inclusion.

Melián also established contact with Catherine Deneuve through her powerful agent Bertrand de Labbey, who did not speak English. 'So I ended up having to deal directly with Bertrand for the lyrics, proposal and legal deal,' says Melián. 'It slowed down the process a lot having to translate everything between Malcolm, Disques Vogue and Bertrand.'

McLaren had decided that Deneuve should sing 'Paris Paris', a celebration of the city's 'dark side, the Arab quarter and prostitutes', according to Gorman, but the actress rejected the lyrics and recommended a rewrite by the singer and composer David McNeil, the illegitimate son of the painter Marc Chagall and his former housekeeper Virginia Haggard. McNeil's new version referenced Jacques Prévert, Josephine Baker and Simone de Beauvoir among others. A duet between McLaren and Deneuve, on the recording McLaren referred to himself in the song as 'a lonely fan' begging to be held by her.

According to Leigh Gorman, it took six months from McLaren's first approach to Deneuve to the recording of 'Paris Paris'. Gorman and McLaren booked Plus France, the most prestigious studio in the city at the time. 'Malcolm and I had plotted out the music on a napkin at the Flore,' says Gorman. 'The Latin American/hip-hop loop came from the Bounty commercial we had worked on in London the year before. But when it came time to play the backing track it wouldn't work, was all snarled up. There was a phalanx of people waiting on me: M. Deneuve, her hairdresser, the head of Disques Vogue, all the studio assistants.

'Malcolm came over and whispered in my ear, "Get this thing going Gorman or you're fucked!" I literally reprogrammed it on the spot from memory while she sat there looking at her watch. Once I was done and it was time for her vocal she started to get nervous, so we gave her a brandy.'

Deneuve was positioned in the vocal booth and asked for the lights to be turned low as she recorded her main part, a spoken-word section, but began to falter when it came to the singsong rap. 'I could hear her chair shaking and told Malcolm to get in there and offer some support,' says Gorman. 'He was very encouraging and asked her to stand up. We got through a huge chunk but there was still the middle section where she was supposed to sing.'

Robin Millar recalls the spontaneous exchange that made it to the finished version.

We did another take and then Malcolm's distinctive north-London voice chipped in. 'Sing away Catherine, sing away.'

'My God, no, I can't!' she protested.

'Come on,' he chirped, 'sing away.' And started to croon himself: 'Paris, Paris, Paris . . .'

She hesitantly started to join in with him and then gave up again. 'No, I can't sing . . .'

When he came to mix the track, Gorman proposed leaving this out, but McLaren insisted it remain because it showed Deneuve's vulnerability. As Miller says, the dialogue between the two 'gave their voices a coquettish, teasing sound, like two lovers in a movie'. On hearing the final version, Deneuve's manager announced that his client would never allow its release, but McLaren and Millar visited the film star at her home and played it to her.

'We held our breaths as she listened to the track in silence. We reached the end,' says Millar. '"It's great," she said. "I love it. Now go away."'[10]

Françoise Hardy was another less-than-willing participant when she was invited to provide the vocal for 'Revenge of the Flowers'. 'She had become a recluse, living in a house in Montparnasse whose interior was painted black, the shutters permanently drawn,' said McLaren. 'Her linen was black, even her toilet bowl was black. To find her hi-fi I needed a match. But she was sympathetic to the lyrics; I thought she was well-suited to this song and its poetic, downbeat nature.'

Robin Millar accompanied McLaren on the visit to Hardy's house, and the singer insisted on discussing the song only with the producer after McLaren insulted her husband, the venerable French singer-song-writer Jacques Dutronc, as 'a posy git'.

Once they were alone, Hardy told Millar that McLaren terrified her, and that she wanted to record without him present, so Millar organised for Hardy to arrive at the studio two hours before McLaren, and managed to coax two strong takes out of her before McLaren burst in with five alternative versions of the song with new lyrics. 'Poor Françoise was cowering in the corner, assuring us that she couldn't sing any of these versions,' says Millar.

'You've gotta have a go, Françoise,' Malcolm kept assuring her.

Eventually I persuaded him to give her a break and let her go downstairs. Once she was out of the room I played the tapes to him, telling him that she had changed her schedule at the last minute and turned up early.

He cocked his head to one side as he listened. 'Well that's marvellous then, isn't it?' he said when I'd finished. 'Job done.'

'Yup,' I agreed.

'So what are we hanging around here for, then? Let's go.'[11]

For the track Hardy sang on the album, she changed the key to suit her register. 'The song's tone changed a little,' said McLaren, who thought after the album's release that Hardy's version 'wasn't as good as the original demo'.

Some of the songs on *Paris* contained samples and extracts culled from the CNAP advertising archive Eugenia Melián had researched for their earlier projects. 'In the Absence of the Parisienne', which recounted

McLaren's teenage visits to beatnik Soho coffee bars such as Le Macabre and La Bastille, starts with a voiceover of Serge Gainsbourg from a 1970s commercial for the magazine *Sortir*, and 'Walking with Satie' contains dialogue from a 1971 advert directed by Jean Luc Godard for the aftershave Schick in which a young couple argue about a report about the situation in Palestine. 'She is trying to make coffee, he is trying to shave,' said McLaren. 'They both keep changing the radio stations, he wants to listen to the news, she wants to listen to music. Finally they stop arguing when she smells his scent and says, "Mmmm . . . bon! C'est froid!"'

The album sleeve came about via an introduction by Lauren Hutton to Joan Juliet Buck, the editor in chief of Paris *Vogue*. After receiving a demo of *Paris* Buck set up a portrait shoot of McLaren with Helmut Newton at Père Lachaise. 'Newton shot it fast because we had no permit and just a pocket flashlight for lighting,' says Melián. 'The portrait was wonderful and we decided to use it as the cover. We asked Newton, I sent him the album and he approved because he loved the record. I also had a bunch of artwork proposals made by an art director friend of mine, Edgar Becourt, but Disques Vogue binned them and we went on to produce it with Jean-Baptiste Mondino in a shoot featuring Malcolm with Amina, Deneuve and Hardy.'

Despite all her efforts, Melián received a credit for just one song on *Paris*: as production manager for a late addition to the American issue of the album released via the Island Records distributed imprint Gee Street. This had arisen from a demand from one of France's greatest designers, Sonia Rykiel. 'She rang me up very angry because I'd never asked her to be on the record,' McLaren told *Vogue*. 'How come I'd missed out on her, she wanted to know? "After all," she said, "I am the queen of the Left Bank. I always make clothes in black. You talk about black on black and Juliette Gréco – I was there Malcolm!"'[12]

McLaren arranged for Rykiel at join him in a studio to ad-lib to a backing track. 'The funniest lyric is Sonia saying "I would love to be a dress,"' said McLaren, who provided the cheeky refrain that gave the song its title: 'Who the Hell Is Sonia Rykiel?'

That sole credit to Melián for the Rykiel track on the record sleeve does her a disservice, given her significant role in the conception and realisation of the whole of *Paris*. Melián says she was told that McLaren's contract only allowed for two producer credits, for himself and Robin Millar, so that there was no obligation to name her as executive producer nor her assistant Rita Dagher as production manager, even though these were the responsibilities they fulfilled. 'I was pretty mad at Disques Vogue about this since I only got a "very special thanks to . . .",' says Melián.

Meanwhile, with Leigh Gorman's assistance, McLaren also delivered an album of instrumental Paris mixes, entitled *The Largest Movie House in Paris*. This fulfilled his commitment to the record company, while several *Paris* songs featured in a film about the fashion world for which McLaren provided the original score, again at Melián's recommendation.

Catwalk was a backstage documentary directed by Robert Leacock and starred many of the major international names of the period, including designers John Galliano, Jean-Paul Gaultier, Karl Lagerfeld and Isaac Mizrahi and models Naomi Campbell, Kate Moss and Christy Turlington. With Gorman, McLaren wrote the latter her own theme, since the extended opening sequence is dedicated to her. Also on the *Catwalk* soundtrack were 'Deep in Vogue' and 'I Like You in Velvet' from *Waltz Darling* and other tracks that reflected McLaren's abiding interest in classical music, such as a Chopin waltz and the Puccini song 'Chi il bel sogno di Doretta'.

While McLaren was creating the most mature work of his career – *Paris* presents bewitching melodies, rhythms and lyrics with warmth, reflection and humour – he later recalled the experience with bitterness.

'It was so horrible making that record,' wrote McLaren in the late 1990s. 'I was stuck with those French guys. They were so difficult and it went on and on and on.'

During the recording, Eugenia Melián had initiated a television project for McLaren to complement the album's release and act as a follow-up to the Channel 4 Oxford Street film.

Entitled 'The Ghosts of Père Lachaise', this was to pay tribute to the 'permanent Parisians' who populated the necropolis McLaren first visited with Jean-Charles de Castelbajac at the tail end of the 1970s. The fascination for the vast cemetery founded in Napoleonic times lay in the romantic and profane nature of its occupants, from the legendary lovers Héloïse and Abelard and novelist Honoré de Balzac to composer Frédéric Chopin, dramatist Molière, rock star Jim Morrison, singer Édith Piaf and Oscar Wilde.

' "The Ghosts of Père Lachaise" came from the research I did for "These Are the Breaks" and *Paris*,' says Melián, who – like her partner a decade previously – haunted the public library at the Centre Pompidou. 'I spent every day for months there and photocopied whole books on the subject. I also researched necrophilia happening in the cemetery and took Malcolm to a full-moon party they held once a month late at night on the tombs. You just needed to know where you could jump over the wall. We also went to the catacombs of Paris for research purposes; there were weekly parties there as well if you knew how to get to them, but I got scared and left Malcolm there alone, watching the crazies partying with loud music and drinking among the tombs.'

First, Melián pitched the film idea to British TV production house Initial as being centred on five segments directed by Jean-Baptiste Mondino and using the *Paris* tracks 'Mon Dié Séigné' and 'Père Lachaise' as well as those featuring Amina, Deneuve and Hardy. The plan was that funding would come from Disques Vogue, which would be able to use the segments to promote the album's release.

Melián worked with French production company Le Sabre to handle French rights, and a new treatment was produced by McLaren with British filmmaker Mary Soan and, in London, Jane Withers, who was then completing her postgraduate studies in design at the Royal College of Art, was recruited to write a treatment.

'I did a lot of research into the characters at the cemetery, the obvious and the not-so-obvious, and wrote up their stories,' says Withers. 'Malcolm was particularly interested in life after dark and the territorial cats that lived there, the hidden life of the place.'

Withers visited the cemetery with the brothers Jez and John-Henry Butterworth, the script doctors brought on board by McLaren to produce a treatment for the film. The association proved particularly fruitful for Jez Butterworth. Conversations with McLaren about Peter Grant's London rock 'n' roll scene of the late 1950s led to a breakthrough for the young dramatist, who was inspired to write *Mojo*, about gangsters kidnapping a bright young singer, which became one of the most acclaimed British plays of the 1990s.

'[McLaren] was talking about Soho and the wonderful collision between early rock and roll and gangland violence,' said Butterworth in 2013. 'It wasn't something I knew anything about, but the collision between these two things that sparked something. Who knows where plays come from, but in this case it came from Malcolm.'[13]

Soon Melián and McLaren came up with a more ambitious plan to develop the project into a six-part series financed and produced by Channel 4 in the UK, Le Sabre and Arté in Paris and Premier in Germany, and McLaren produced outlines for more episodes to be filmed at prominent European cemeteries.

But 'The Ghosts of Père Lachaise' hit an insurmountable problem when permission to film within the grounds of the cemetery itself was refused. According to Melián the head of the Cimitières de Paris was disturbed when he was shown the Oxford Street film, which he described as 'profane'.

Increasingly disillusioned with Disques Vogue, for a brief period McLaren pinned his hopes for *Paris* on a management deal with John Reid, one of the most powerful rock managers in the world, having steered the careers of such artists as Elton John and Queen.

McLaren approached Reid, who visited him at Melián's Paris home. 'His chauffeur parked the Rolls-Royce in front of the soldiers guarding my offices because they were right next to the prime minister's residence and his offices at the Hôtel Matignon, 59 rue de Varenne, two doors down,' says Melián. 'The guards went berserk and shouted at the chauffeur, machine guns in hand. I opened my window and begged the guards not to menace or shoot anyone because "l'Anglais" was my guest and a few minutes later in floated John Reid, loving the drama.

'Malcolm launched into a monologue on his many projects, and particularly the worldwide launch of *Paris* continent by continent. My only contact with John thereafter was to fax him a detailed list of the ongoing projects but Malcolm started calling him daily to give him orders and ask him what he was planning to do with his career. Reid stopped taking Malcolm's calls after a while. I think he was overwhelmed and couldn't see where the money was but Malcolm was really hurt by Reid's silence and subsequent disappearing act.'

In fact, though they continued to work together, McLaren's personal relationship with Melián had ended on a sour note during the final bout of recording of *Paris*. While he was taping the vocal for the track 'Walking with Satie', McLaren uttered the line 'All I do is think about you, Charlotte.' This was a clear reference to a person Melián thought was on the periphery of their social circle, the London-based British architect Charlotte Skene Catling.

'It was a terrible betrayal for me,' says Melián. 'The love relationship was over and I broke off our engagement.'

McLaren first met Skene Catling at his west London haunt 192 when she was dining with her brother at an adjacent table to him and the musician/producer Martin Glover, aka Youth. 'They kind of gatecrashed our table; Youth was an old friend,' says Skene Catling. 'Malcolm got my phone number and called me. He was quite persistent but I was still in a relationship. Then I went to dinner at Jane Withers and Anthony Fawcett's and found him there. Not long after he came to my flat in Soho to take me out to dinner. He was so funny and magical.'[14]

When Skene Catling threw a house party McLaren arrived uninvited with art dealer Jay Jopling and the young artists Damien Hirst and Marc Quinn. 'They were all friends anyway, so it was "What are *you* doing here?" It was quite a party. At that point we started seeing each other.'

Soon after they met, McLaren invited Skene Catling on an unusual date. He asked her to accompany him to the funeral of his half-brother Colin Edwards, who had died at the age of forty.

'It was a very Jewish affair, with women sat on one side and men on the other, so we weren't even together,' says Skene Catling. 'So Malcolm.'

Skene Catling had already been introduced to Stuart Edwards under different circumstances. 'We came out of Le Caprice and got into a taxi and the driver started going, "Oh fuckin' hell, it's fuckin' Malcolm!" I thought he was a bit forward and then they started joshing each other and it became clear he was his brother. It was funny.'

Skene Catling also joined McLaren on a trip to Romney Marsh, she thought to visit Peter McLaren, though his son was evidently still struggling with the reality of having found him. 'Malcolm talked a lot about his father and the weirdness of Romney Marsh on the way down,' recalls Skene Catling. 'We came to a very pretty vicarage surrounded by hedges with roses in the garden. Malcolm told me his father lived there. I suggested we say hello but Malcolm said we shouldn't bother. So we sat outside in the car and then drove back to town, actually passing the biker café where he really lived. Malcolm even pointed it out. It was very strange.'

Another time Skene Catling met Peter in the flat above the Oasis. 'He was surrounded by all these paintings of titty women on velvet,' she remembers. 'His wife was very nice but I thought the father was a bit self-obsessed. Malcolm sorely wanted him to be a romantic figure, one of the wild McLarens rampaging around Hadrian's Wall.'

Not long after their relationship began, McLaren repeated the pattern of his life since parting with Westwood and asked for Skene Catling's hand in marriage. For the engagement he applied an unusual tactic in winning over his fiancée's mother. 'He wrote her an ardent letter, a declaration of his love for me,' says Skene Catling. 'She was slightly puzzled because he decorated it with drawings of cocks with wings flying around the borders of the page.'

In London, the new couple divided their time between McLaren's Fitzrovia house and Skene Catling's Soho apartment in Lexington Street above their favourite restaurant, Andrew Edmunds. Leigh Gorman was by now dedicated to working on an album with Spandau Ballet's Gary Kemp and, for a period, McLaren toyed with new music along with British producer Andy Whitmore, who had collaborated with him on a version of Gainsbourg's 'Je T'Aime . . . Moi Non Plus', which was added to the US release of *Paris*.

'Gee Street wanted extra tracks to make its album different from the French import,' said McLaren. 'I don't believe it is in any way comparable with the original.'

A drum and bass version of 'Je T'Aime' was in a selection of *Paris* tracks that appeared on the soundtrack to a showcase of a catwalk collection by Jean-Charles de Castelbajac, who had recently completed a spell as head designer at the venerated haute couture house Courrèges.

McLaren worked on the remixes for his old friend with de Castelbajac's musical director, the composer and arranger Henri 'Scars' Struck. 'He was cutting stuff together, overlaying a lot of percussion and inserting spoken-word pieces,' says Struck. 'At one stage you could hear Malcolm's voice say, "This is for you Jean-Charles." I know Jean-Charles was very touched at the care Malcolm took with the mix. The show was a great success. After that Malcolm and I became quite close. I was twenty-three years old and learnt a lot from him; he became a bit of a mentor. He even gave me some equipment to work on my demos, and when I visited London I stayed at Scala Street.'[15]

McLaren promoted *Paris* hard. The tony New York launch at the prestigious Augustus Van Horne Stuyvesant house on 5th Avenue and thereafter at the Ukrainian Institute on the Upper East Side was attended by Catherine Deneuve, Claudia Schiffer, Paris *Vogue*'s Joan Juliet Buck and McLaren's friend James Truman, who told *New York* magazine at the party: 'Malcolm is the best pitch artist in the world. Some say con artist. His main love is chaos. When you ask him his profession, he says criminal.'[16]

On Australian TV McLaren outlined the album's raison d'être. 'It was a way of acknowledging a debt that the English try hard not to make,' said McLaren. 'I don't honestly believe that any of the bands that made up the sixties British invasion of rock 'n' roll would ever have happened without that Parisian tinge, that extreme angst, that very dark, vengeful, bored attitude. I don't even believe that Bob Dylan and Jim Morrison would have existed without having some kinship spirit to what was one of the most influential, nihilistic and valid forms of rock 'n' roll philosophy which the French invented.'

McLaren, now approaching fifty, explained that Paris also resulted from a growing sense of maturity. 'I felt I was at an age capable of doing it,' he said. 'Believe it or not I never had the confidence to do it by placing myself in front of the microphone and not acting like some kind of Alfred Hitchcock figure that I'd done in the past.'

Unbidden and revealingly, McLaren added: 'Black has been a notorious colour in my life and something I've been totally obsessed with, its invisibility, darkness, attractiveness and sexuality. I would never have adopted the colour black for the Sex Pistols if I didn't think so lovingly of that whole schtick. But I decided to make a black-and-white album about Paris and put myself in the frame; that was something like an act of catharsis.'[17]

This serious reflection informed McLaren's deflated mood after the completion of *Paris* and the companion album of remixes. Once again, dissatisfaction was setting in. BMG, the international conglomerate that owned Disques Vogue, couldn't find a place for *Paris* on the release rosters of its UK imprint RCA, which was scoring big in the pop charts with such dance acts as M People. Boybands, Britpop and drum and bass were all in the ascendance; there was no room in his home country for McLaren's soft-focus romanticism nor recognition of the grand dames or the Left Bank heroes and heroines he idolised. He appeared a man out of time.

Support came from another friend of McLaren's, the film producer Hamish McAlpine. He loved *Paris* enough to launch the label No! Records as an outcrop of his sales and distribution company Metro Tartan to ensure the British release, but to little avail. 'Hamish tried to get it on the radio and employed pluggers but the DJs said, "Who's Catherine Deneuve anyway?" I don't want to have to go through a fiasco like that ever again,' said McLaren in the late 1990s.

Funding was found for some fine promo videos. David Bailey's clip for the single 'Paris Paris' starred not only the cockney photographer's second wife Deneuve but also archive footage of their 1967 wedding, and Michel Gondry helmed the short for 'Le Main Parisienne' featuring Amina, but the clips failed to make their mark on MTV and *Paris* sank with little trace.

'I didn't really know what I was doing,' wrote McLaren about this period of his life. 'I came back to London because Charlotte was here and she didn't have anywhere to live. She'd given up her flat in Lexington Street but then she got the person out and she went back to live there. The record company didn't want anything to do with this thing I was working on with Andy Whitmore. I'd already put my own money into it, so I thought "Oh fuck it, I'll carry on." Then I realised I'd spent £50,000 on this rubbish. It was all so horrible and I thought, "I don't want any more of this."'

PART VIII

The Casino of Authenticity and Karaoke

Chapter 35

At his home in Scala Street, which also operated as a workspace with an office on the upper part of the split-level ground floor, Malcolm McLaren considered his options after the commercial failure of *Paris*.

With Nils Stevenson, he looked into reviving the prospects for the Peter Grant film. 'I sat down with Nils and tried to work out the script and get it going again,' he recalled later. 'We really did go a long way with that. It was looking in good shape; we were really very close.'

This was despite the resistance from Grant's family and the unavailability of Led Zeppelin's music, but when the manager suffered a fatal heart attack resulting from a combination of diabetes and the ravages of cocaine addiction at the age of just sixty, 'The Rock 'n' Roll Godfather' was permanently shelved.

'Then I tried to decide with Charlotte what we were going to do,' said McLaren. 'I thought maybe we could do food as fashion here in England – cafés that sold fashion too. I was just trying to sort out all this crap and decide where to go with everything.'

As McLaren pondered his future, he also dwelt on his son Joe's lack of higher education. On McLaren's behalf, Jean-Charles de Castelbajac organised a meeting with Vivienne Westwood in a Paris nightclub after she showed her career-high collection 'On Liberty' in the spring of 1994. According to Westwood biographer Jane Mulvagh, Carlo D'Amario and Westwood's partner Andreas Kronthaler, 'fearing that she might still love McLaren, felt threatened by the meeting and attempted to break up the conversation. But de Castelbajac held them at bay while Westwood and McLaren huddled in a corner and talked intimately for over an hour-and-a-half.'[1]

Among the points of discussion that night was McLaren's belief that Joe should attend university. Through a friend, U2 manager

Paul McGuinness, he had arranged an entry interview at Dublin's Trinity College, but the twenty-something, who had long since made his own way in the world without his father's help, understandably wasn't interested. 'I told him education was everything,' said McLaren. 'But he just wouldn't listen.'

Meanwhile, McLaren's long-severed connections to Westwood came back into play when two of her ex-employees made an approach proposing his re-entry to the world of fashion. Simon Barker and Derek Dunbar were among the first fans of the Sex Pistols in 1976, and both had worked for Westwood on production of her clothing designs since her return from Italy in the mid-1980s.

They had recently left her employ after falling out with Carlo D'Amario and had sourced funding for a fashion venture of their own. Barker and Dunbar's proposal was for a Japan-only range of updated versions of Sex, Seditionaries and Worlds End garments.

McLaren signed a contract agreeing to supply designs and concepts for two collections, for which he was to be paid a design fee of £10,000 each. The first, entitled 'ANCIEN Dead in England', replicated the originals, while 'Malcolm McLaren', the label of which featured his signature across a reproduction of one of his thumbprints, was to be reserved for a range of new, tailored separates.

The timing of the approach, and the territory of distribution, was significant. By this time Joe Corré had also left the Westwood company after feuding with D'Amario. His final act had been to force through a lucrative licensing deal for McLaren/Westwood designs with the Japanese retail giant Itochu. This would capitalise on the burgeoning interest in Japan for the couple's original collaborations and, as Corré later explained, simultaneously ensure his mother a flow of regular income should the fortunes of her company start to slide.

Essentially, Barker and Dunbar were setting McLaren in direct competition with his former partner, but he saw the new venture as a way of creating recognition for his 50 per cent input into the now much-sought-after punk and post-punk clothes. And the thumbprint label provided an opportunity to draw on his extensive knowledge of tailoring to head in a fresh direction.

Installing Charlotte Skene Catling as project manager, McLaren was initially enthusiastic, providing Barker and Dunbar with sketches, fabric books of tartans, tweeds, shirtings and suitings, original patterns, swatches and even wool samples from the days when mohair jumpers were knitted for Sex by Chelsea outworkers.

He graded and vetted tailors' paper patterns and edited down selections of seventy fabrics to six for shirts and eight for suits. Black jackets were named after the coffee bars of his youth, such as Le Macabre, and shorts versions of the Bondage trousers were produced in serge. McLaren's inventive flourishes included French-cuffed shirts with hidden messages stitched into the seam, including Thomas Fuller's phrase 'Craft must have clothes but TRUTH loves to go naked'. McLaren even commissioned black rubber mice to be made and secreted in the 'Dead in England' trouser pockets, but the relationship with Barker and Dunbar wasn't sustainable; he found them uninspired and only one collection made it to Japan. This featured such garments as Bondage trousers, moleskin Peter Pan-collared blousons and Cowboys T-shirts in pastel pink and baby blue. The young Leonardo DiCaprio modelled the clothing, including a mohair sweater, for a Japanese youth magazine.

With a second collection in development and a third at sampling stage, relations with Barker and Dunbar fractured. 'We didn't like working with them,' says Skene Catling. 'Malcolm regretted having done the deal; he knew it was a mistake.' Soon McLaren undertook the option in the contract to withdraw from the deal.

Displeased, Barker and Dunbar retaliated by retaining McLaren's archive of approximately 250 pieces, described by Dunbar as 'his life's work' in fashion.[2] McLaren would never be reunited with his possessions. The venture was not mentioned again.

For McLaren, the sour taste left by this brief association with his past was alleviated by requests for advice from Joe Corré and his wife Serena Rees about their upmarket lingerie brand Agent Provocateur. McLaren provided encouragement and contacts at French manufacturers but regardless of his input it was due to the young couple's combination of business nous and fashion flair that it became a retail success, transforming the international market for women's underwear in the process.

McLaren later reflected that his son had 'gleaned from my failures' and was dispassionate about what he perceived as Joe's need for security. 'He saw his mother being left with this shop as McLaren wandered off into the nether regions, the hinterlands and further adventures,' said McLaren in 2004. 'And he probably felt he needed a much more secure premise. He decided that early on. I think he was trying to figure out how and what I meant and what I was doing, but it was difficult for him because he was torn between the emotional relationship between his mother and me. His mother was by his side more than I was, unquestionably so. He's done very, very well.'[3]

While his son and Rees were laying the foundations for their multi-million pound business, McLaren was at a loose end. Skene Catling had moved to Germany to continue her architecture studies and, in between visits to her, McLaren kicked his heels in Paris for several weeks, rooming again at Fred Bouveron's *hôtel particulier*. 'There was nothing to stay [in London] for,' said McLaren later. 'I was just going round, visiting friends, helping Fred on a couple of projects. I had to change. I thought I'd better change. I had to do something.'

McLaren returned home and threw himself back into work, the breadth of which was grasped by a new friend, the musician and writer Peter Culshaw, who McLaren met at a London party given by U2 manager Paul McGuinness.

Culshaw was a London-based music journalist who had cut his teeth in the 1980s on such magazines as the activists' journal *Undercurrents* and the style bible *The Face*, and was by now establishing himself as an authority on worldwide ethnic music. Also a practising musician, Culshaw was a member of the collective the West India Company. 'I was wearing a purple silk jacket I'd had made in India while we were recording there,' says Culshaw. 'Malcolm spotted it and asked me where I got it. We fell into conversation. He was fascinated to hear all about Bollywood and told me he had an idea for an album with twelve tracks, each based on an astrological sign. He needed an Indian singer and asked me whether I could recommend someone.'[4]

Culshaw suggested McLaren work with a young Anglo-Indian performer and arranged for her to visit Scala Street for an audition. 'She was only twenty-one but quite sussed and told me that she was going to test Malcolm by pretending she'd never heard of him,' says Culshaw. 'I was really impressed with Malcolm's response. Rather than challenging her with "Don't you know who I am?" he took her at face value and went through his history, playing songs by the New York Dolls and the Sex Pistols and tracks from *Duck Rock* and *Fans* to show his background. In a way he auditioned for her. The project didn't happen but Malcolm and I became friendly. I'd drop round and see him for a cup of tea or we'd go out for meals.'

In this period Culshaw came to understand the sheer range of McLaren's activities; unbeknownst to many, McLaren was the music consultant for one of the bigger budget TV mini-series of the 1990s: Francis Ford Coppola's production of Homer's *The Odyssey*, directed by Andrei Konchalovsky and starring Greta Scacchi and Armand Assante.

McLaren had already brought *Paris* singer Amina Annabi on board as vocal coach and scored Culshaw a research gig. 'My job was to find out what the music would be like in 500 BC Athens so that they could create approximations,' says Culshaw. 'It was a fun gig, looking at how, say, African rhythms could have come to Athens from the outer edges of the Greek empire.'

McLaren rarely discussed the past with Culshaw. 'I remember he once mentioned his belief that Sid Vicious should have been the biggest international star to come out of punk and that he regretted that it didn't happen,' says Culshaw. 'Once I tried to draw him on his similarities to Johnny Rotten, and he accepted that they were both, in his words, "magnificent failures", but for the most part we concentrated on the here and now. He was very interested in politics, always reading the newspapers and discussing what Tony Blair was up to. His interest in Blair lay in the fact that he was like a failed rock star, having been in bands. I think that intrigued Malcolm, because, in a funny way, Blair had learnt from Malcolm: the whole spin doctor bit and how you manipulate the media.'

Through advertising connections in Poland – the only country where *Paris* achieved gold status with 50,000 sales, sparking usage of McLaren's version of 'Je T'Aime' in a TV commercial – he was invited to attend a festival entitled 'Art & Fashion' in Warsaw in late 1995. The other guests included the prominent Spanish designer Paco Rabanne, but McLaren grabbed the local headlines and charmed the city's luminaries with his insights and ready wit.

He was soon invited back as 'a kind of informal cultural attaché' by the office of the newly installed Polish President Aleksander Kwaśniewski, who had been Minister for Youth in a previous administration and defeated Lech Wałęsa in only the second post-war free elections as the country continued its march towards democracy. Taken on a tour of clothing manufacturers and universities with strong humanities curricula, McLaren was asked to deliver his thoughts on how Poland could rebrand itself by activating its creative communities.

'Poland stands on the edge of Europe and at the frontier of Asia and there's a sense there – due maybe to how people have lived through a whole Marxist revolution and a Stalinist purge and now they've broken free of all that and gone back to a socialist government – that they're on the verge of creating a point of view that hasn't been seen in Europe for a while,' he pronounced. 'Maybe that being on the edge of it all and looking in and wanting to join has made them more driven and ambitious.'

'I thought that was a really smart move by the Poles,' says Peter Culshaw. 'These days branding is *de rigueur* for cities and countries all over the world, but to do it then, and to choose Malcolm, was pretty forward thinking.'

An address to Polish fashion designers, during which McLaren told them to abandon clothing and become chefs, was not empty provocation; it signalled that he remained an inveterate zeitgeist surfer. Those culinary preoccupations foreshadowed the foodie explosion which occurred in Britain and across the affluent West in the second half of the 1990s.

'I thought [the Polish designers] needed food more than fashion,' said McLaren.

> Food is one of the last arenas now where people can have a point of view. People have discovered that what you eat is who you are, and it's a question of do you want to be a McDonald's hamburger, a saddle of lamb or an exotic risotto?
>
> You feel different after you eat an Indian meal from after you've eaten an Italian one. And I think we've got into that now: we never knew it before because we weren't allowed to know it. School dinners proved that 100 per cent because they made you not care about food.[5]

With funding from the Polish authorities, McLaren was assigned an apartment in Warsaw and a studio ninety minutes away in Łódź from which he intended to launch yet another fashion label. 'I was going to have a production company working with young Polish designers and maybe some English ones if I could,' he said. 'I really wanted to set something very serious up there.'

But his British advisers, including the music business accountant Ronnie Harris, counselled against doing business in the country which was only relatively recently liberated from the Eastern Bloc by the fall of the Soviet Union. 'They said, "They're all gangsters there." I became concerned that I wouldn't make any money and get in too deep. It is a very dodgy place, lawless in that regard. It looked too difficult, too tough. But it was exciting.'

McLaren's loss of bearings can also be identified in the variety of musical projects he was manically entertaining. One was drawn from his experiences in eastern Europe: a dance record using the *Waltz Darling* formula but replacing Strauss with the music of Polish composer Frédéric Chopin; another was the creation of a new group comprising black British drum-and-bass musicians from Tottenham in north London with two Belgian female singers 'who are equally disparate and desperate'.

Neither project was realised. 'I was thinking mad things then,' said McLaren later. 'I realised I was completely mad – sometimes I am mad.'

This private admission, made a few years later, was countered by the impression McLaren gave to the media at the time.

'McLaren is very happy to be back in London,' recorded the *Independent*, which detailed his excitement at the optimism then expressed by such mid-1990s phenomena as Britpop and Britart, many of whose movers-and-shakers hailed from the UK regions. McLaren wasn't alone in recognising that social changes were afoot; soon eighteen years of Conservative government were to end with the installation of Tony Blair's New Labour administration.

'What's happening at the moment is everything's bleeding into everything else,' McLaren announced.

> It's all becoming very egalitarian: the snobbism's going, the class structure that this country has always been weighed down with, even in pop music sometimes, seems to be suddenly blowing away.
>
> I think maybe it's due to all these salt-of-the-earth Northern creatures: Damien Hirst, from the North, Pulp is North, Oasis is North, Goldie is from the North [he is in fact from the Midlands], Björk is from the very, very North. They've all descended on London and cracked a few skulls and things are beginning to happen.

Although his former partner was famously born in northern England, McLaren didn't reserve the same praise for her. 'I think we're not looking to history in the same way we once did,' he said. 'People like Vivienne Westwood are always going on about returning to the 18th century. Although Vivienne was my girlfriend and I worked with her for years and years, I was never into that. The 18th century Vivienne looks at is the 18th century of about five people who never had to work. It's got nothing to do with us. Of course there was creative thinking going on then, but there's creative thinking going on now as well.'

Similarly, McLaren dismissed as backward-looking the recently announced tour by the original line-up of his former charges, the Sex Pistols. 'I wish I cared more,' he sighed. 'I try to but I can't. I suppose it's because it's antique, it's in a vacuum, it's in a frame – it's part of a compilation of oldies. If you think about it, is it really any different from a Gerry and the Pacemakers reunion?'[6]

McLaren took a more favourable view of a coincidental retrospective of his and Westwood's punk clothing designs held at the small gallery above the Eagle, one of London's first gastropubs, near King's Cross.

Entitled *I Groaned with Pain* after the first line of the 1974 Trocchi T-shirt sold in Sex, the modest but well-organised show, curated by art dealer Paul Stolper and academic Andrew Wilson, was the first comprehensive effort to view the clothing produced by the pair through the prism of McLaren's involvement in radical politics.

'Pop has always been linked with rebellion but in their earlier Vive Le Rock! shirt, McLaren and Westwood uncovered something more than just a disco-led youthquake,' wrote Wilson in the accompanying catalogue. 'They proposed a link between Little Richard and outright sedition, between pop and Molotov cocktails, and between revolution and its commodification – an image that, real or not, has never quite faded away.'[7]

During the show's run, McLaren agreed to be filmed by Stolper and Wilson. Set up in the centre of the gallery surrounded by framed Destroy muslins and Cowboys T-shirts, McLaren speculated that even punk's central participants did not comprehend the true nature of the movement. 'I don't think the Sex Pistols ever understood who the Sex Pistols really were,' said McLaren. 'I think their fans picked up on some of it and those at a distance were able to understand it even more because they could look at it as an extraordinary spectacle and explosion . . . It was never called punk or punk rock by me. It was always an art thing.'

And his view of the artistic merit of the Sex and Seditionaries collections was characteristic. 'I don't know whether it's art,' he said. 'It might be bigger than art. Art has been defined today as not much more than a commodity, and I don't think these things are. They remain, even now, set up in frames, as artefacts, enigmatic.'[8]

A contradiction aside – post-1976, McLaren often delighted in referring to himself as a punk-rocker – this was a view that was increasingly taking hold at bodies such as the Costume Institute of New York's Metropolitan Museum of Art, which began to collect original McLaren/ Westwood designs. Simultaneously, a high-ticket commercial trade gathered pace with the emerging market in collectible vintage wear.

But punk clothing wasn't at the forefront of McLaren's preoccupations as he moved through the 1990s, as evinced in another filmed interview, by the American-Israeli filmmaker Ariel Van Straten for a video-cassette issue of the magazine *Don't Tell It*.

Van Straten was gathering material for a short to raise awareness of the plight of British graffiti artist Simon Sunderland, who had recently been jailed for five years for committing criminal damage on the rail network in South Yorkshire using the tag 'Fista'.

He was hoping to draw McLaren on the background and artistic value of graffiti art, but the interviewee not only provided a thoroughgoing history of the development of rap, during which he recounted such anecdotes as his first meeting with the Zulu Nation in the South Bronx, but also took the opportunity to provide prescient commentary on the impact the digital era was going to have on the global entertainment industry.

Remarkably, a year before the introduction of the first commercial MP3 player and three years before the launch of the online service Napster, both of which rocked the music industry to its core, McLaren forecast the current era of social networks, free downloads and streaming services.

'Web TV, downloading music, graphics and so on is definitely the future, definitely where it is going to go,' McLaren told Van Straten. 'These guys [a reference to small dance music labels who were distributing their music on the internet] are on the verge of suggesting in the years to come you won't purchase your music from shops. Your cultural information is going to come through the net.

'Now it's about buying the technology so that you can broadcast from your goddamn bedroom across the planet. I think the reason why the industry is holding back is because they know that it is only a question of the technology being affordable and that's when it will happen.

'The establishment still aren't quite able to understand interactive; it's the street which understands it and is able to use it in a simplistic but very real way. They will be the people who break through; they will make it the most sexy. It won't be as cerebral as the likes of Peter Gabriel or Eno and that lot.'[9]

McLaren's views on technological developments were drawn from his friendship with the educational and entertainment software inventor and developer Graham Brown-Martin, founder of interactive record label EXP.

Brown-Martin was introduced to McLaren by EXP's A&R head Richard Norris, a DJ and producer who had scored dance hits as The Grid. 'I gave him my spiel about the music industry and how I was going to fuck it. He loved it and we clicked,' says Brown-Martin, who is on the spectrum and believes that McLaren was a high-functioning autistic. 'A lot of people I connect with are like that. I believe his form of that gift was the ability to forecast events and spot trends so he could join up the dots far quicker than anybody I'd come across. He was super-smart and ate up new ideas. Disorder is the wrong word but it definitely was an ASD [autism spectrum disorder] thing.

'After that we hung out or I visited him at Scala Street regularly. Sarah Bolton was looking after the office. She was really good for Malcolm, very friendly and straightforward and a bit of a gatekeeper, which is what he needed.'[10]

Brown-Martin often socialised with McLaren and Nils Stevenson at members' club Soho House (where McLaren successfully proposed Brown-Martin's membership to the owner Nick Jones). 'But it wasn't always so flashy,' says Brown-Martin, who left EXP and oversaw animation for the movie *Lost in Space* from a studio in South Bank Polytechnic in south London's inner-city neighbourhood Elephant & Castle. 'Malcolm would come down to see what I was up to there and we'd pile into Pizzeria Castello underneath the roundabout. One evening there'd be [gangster] Mad Frankie Fraser eating pizza opposite us there, another we'd be at St John and I'd be introduced by Malcolm to Brian Eno or Jay Jopling.'

Around this time, McLaren's literary agent Ed Victor proposed his client write a long-form memoir for the *New Yorker*; appearing in the prestigious magazine, said Victor, would net a US publishing deal for his autobiography.

With the *New Yorker*'s Bill Buford as editor, McLaren assembled an episodic feature which told the story of 'The Boy in the Blue Lamé Suit'. Published in September 1997 with a monochrome portrait of a diabolical-looking McLaren in black cape wielding a tall cane and a cigarette, 'Elements of Anti-Style' moved from the establishment of Let It Rock in 1971 to its reopening as Sex a few years later, the collapse of the Sex Pistols, the encounters with Roy Cohn, William Kunstler and F. Lee Bailey when he auditioned representatives to defend Sid Vicious and the fallout from John Lydon's legal actions against him.[11]

'It took a long time to get together, assembling and ordering Malcolm's memories, but we were pleased with the outcome,' says Skene Catling. 'It read really well and did the trick. Soon Ed was dealing with offers for Malcolm's book.'

The rights to the autobiography were snapped up by New York publishing house Alfred A. Knopf, which paid McLaren a six-figure advance. Now tasked with a deadline and the job of knuckling down to write the book, McLaren called upon his girlfriend to give him further support.

McLaren's assistant at Scala Street, Sarah Bolton, interviewed various people from his past and pulled together a great deal of source material, while Skene Catling worked on the nuts and bolts of turning this raw material into a narrative. The process was often frustrating;

just as in Rebecca Frayn's encounters over *The Ghosts of Oxford Street* script, McLaren seemed unable, or unwilling, to stick to a coherent storyline.

As well as assisting him through the process of assembling the materials for his life story, Skene Catling often found herself reminding her partner of his familial responsibilities, for example when McLaren's granddaughter Cora was born to Joe Corré and his wife Serena Rees.

'It's not as though he didn't have the tools to deal with a situation like that,' says Skene Catling. 'It was more that he needed prompting because it hadn't occurred to him. He hadn't been taught emotionally. I remember saying to him, "You know, we must do something to help them celebrate." He leapt up, "Of course!" and we rushed there with bottles of champagne. I took pictures of them all together, Malcolm and Joe smoking big cigars. There were tears and a lot of hugging.'

McLaren later recalled his granddaughter's birth equally fondly. 'It was kind of extraordinary – Joe coming out full of tears, holding this baby,' he said in 2006. 'He's such a different person and he just adores family. That's what he adores.'[12]

Meantime, McLaren welcomed distractions from the autobiography. One was a music project cooked up with French producer and arranger Henri Struck as a reassessment of the early 1980s hip-hop excursions that appeared on *Duck Rock*.

Dubbed *Buffalo Gals Back to Skool*, this was introduced and interlaced with spoken-word excerpts from McLaren's *Don't Tell It* interview and resulted from a two-album deal with Virgin Records (which no longer belonged to McLaren's 1970s nemesis Richard Branson but had long since been subsumed into the empire of EMI, the British major which signed and rejected the Sex Pistols and Bow Wow Wow).

One album for Virgin was to be a greatest hits compilation but, since rap and hip-hop formed popular music's dominant genre in the 1990s, McLaren proposed that the first release should be a contemporary take on the originals with contributions from big names such as De La Soul, KRS-One, Nas and Rakim.

'We wanted to include the original tracks with remixes by the people who represented where rap was at,' says Struck. 'The record was also an audio-text book of Malcolm's views of hip-hop culture, including break-dancing, graffiti and scratching.'[13]

It is here the recent Van Straten interview came into play. McLaren had been self-mythologising his role in popular culture arguably since before *The Great Rock 'n' Roll Swindle*, when he was the primary inter-viewee on behalf of the Sex Pistols, and *Buffalo Gals Back to Skool* made this explicit from the opening track 'It Was a New York Phenomenon', which features McLaren telling an anecdote about his first engagement with Afrika Bambaataa.

Though the story he related was the fictitious version in which the Zulu Nation leader was wearing a Sex Pistols T-shirt rather than the fact of Michael Holman's introduction, this and the other voiceovers made for beguiling contributions, with tales such as the World's Famous Supreme Team's 42nd Street hustles inserted at intervals throughout the record.

Working on the album over a period of a few months with Struck at his Hardboiled Studios in New York, McLaren adopted his usual role of musical director. 'A lot of people wanted to give shout-outs to Malcolm because he was the white guy who told record companies to sign them up,' says Struck. 'They gave him props, particularly since he had worked with the World's Famous Supreme Team.'

A measure of this respect came one night when Struck and McLaren were approached by A Tribe Called Quest's Q-Tip at New York hip-hop club Life. 'Q-Tip recognised Malcolm and came over and sang to him, "We on the world tour", from the Supreme Team's rap on Malcolm's World Famous "Hobo Scratch",' says Struck. 'That was a cool moment.' (The refrain was later sampled for A Tribe Called Quest's 1993 track 'Award Tour'.)

Buffalo Gals Back to Skool was released in the US by Priority Records, one of the leading hip-hop labels of the period, with a catalogue that included landmark releases by NWA, Dr Dre, Ice Cube and the Geto

Boys. 'In London, Virgin didn't know how to market a hip-hop album,' says Struck. 'There was a lot of fighting between us in New York and Virgin to get decent promotion, so Malcolm came up with a solution: a Buffalo Gals female breakdancing troupe.'

An urban take on the then-dominant Spice Girls, the five dancers, all late teens – some of whom had performed with the breakdancing pioneer Crazy Legs (Richard Colón, leader of the Rock Steady Crew, who appeared in the original 'Buffalo Gals' clip) – plus a nine-year-old Latina appeared in the video promo for the first single from the album, Rakim's 'Buffalo Gals (Back to Skool)'.

McLaren organised funding from Virgin for a digitally animated video to be produced by Graham Brown-Martin's new company Visual Arts. 'Malcolm showed me the Rakim video which was pretty good but a hip-hop clip . . . not splashy enough and without references to what he had done,' says Brown-Martin. 'Malcolm didn't even appear in it and thought that he should, not in a narcissistic way, but to tie the whole package together. After all it was his stuff and he shouldn't have been airbrushed out of it. So me and my creative director Mike Maxwell went to New York with Malcolm and made a new film with the Buffalo Gals. It was pretty much cut-and-paste, made on the fly, because we didn't have the budget for permits. We literally shut down a road near Times Square and shot Malcolm in a mad cowboy hat and the Gals walking down the middle of it. There was also some 3D animation in there; it was quite video-game-like, slightly Manga.'

The Buffalo Gals were also sent on a promotional tour to appear with McLaren as MC in European cities where the album was released; for example, in Paris, they performed at the venerable nightclub Les Bains-Douches.

But *Buffalo Gals Back to Skool* was too unwieldy a project to make a mark against the dominant rap leaders of the time such as Puff Daddy, and soon slipped from record retailers' shelves and the music business's radar. Meanwhile, the greatest hits compilation remained undelivered, but the formation of the Buffalo Gals troupe and a trip around south-east

Asian nightspots triggered a new project, which McLaren intended to use to investigate popular culture in the fast-emerging Asian consumer economies.

On the tour, McLaren was bewitched by the blending of Western pop with traditional Eastern music he heard during visits to the karaoke bars that were springing up across the region.

'I thought this is *Blade Runner* territory, this is totally new,' said McLaren. 'This is like an Asian invasion. Bells rang in my head.'[14]

Chapter 36

Malcolm McLaren's journey into karaoke culture began in November 1996 when he undertook a speaking tour of south-east Asia at the invitation of the regional network of record companies represented by BMG.

This, he determined, would be in the mode of Oscar Wilde's 1882 visit to America. McLaren's talk, entitled 'Living Yesterday Tomorrow', was patterned on his life story and filled with references to the figures that loomed large, from grandmother Rose to Sid Vicious.

The wellspring, as he later explained, came from the years he spent pitching film ideas in Los Angeles. 'Hollywood teaches you to tell stories as succinctly, quickly and efficiently as possible because out there they don't have a long attention span,' said McLaren in 2003, though his comments didn't account for his own notoriously long-winded approach to monologue.

> If the story lasts longer than five minutes, you're gone. Forget about it. They're taking another call. That's where I really learned. Also, this massive lecture tour was really freaky because I had to talk in front of two thousand people in huge spaces.
>
> Imagine a big fucking stage and you walk on and all that's there is a lonely little microphone. And you look into the audience and you see nothing because it's pitch black, you're looking into this giant black hole. You can hear all these shuffling feet and mumbles and grumbles but you can't see anyone. Everyone is looking at you. I had to speak for two-and-a-half hours. I mean, it was this whole show and people were paying forty dollars for it. I came back with a packet of money.[1]

During a stop-off in Singapore to speak at Zouk, one of the first super-clubs to open in the region, McLaren's eyes were opened to the fertile Asian youth culture then plugging into fast-paced technological change.

In a diary later published by a British magazine, McLaren wrote:

I meet a lot of hip, young Chinese entrepreneurs who take me on a tour of 'Post Karaoke' bars, a strange mix of singing, dancing, sensuality and kung fu. It seems foreign, curious, strange and dangerous. Back at the hotel 4 a.m. All I'm thinking about is a sexy ninja, cyber pop Mandarin THING! An Asian invasion could not be long coming in Europe. These people feel loud! Feel WILD! They are not Japanese, with those silent smiles you see in Tokyo. They seem so much fiercer here. Even though everything appears so organised and bland, it's volatile and young, very young under-neath. It is all beyond my references: unknown. Old and new at the same time. It's scary.

Visits to other destinations including Kuala Lumpur, Hong Kong and Jakarta accelerated McLaren's excitement at the digital uptake among young Asians. 'The Internet and the computer seem the centre of their homes – they're all so WIRED, this exciting computer generation,' he wrote.

One night I had a dream, more a nightmare, and woke up thinking: 'Why is there no Chinese pop cultural voice in the world?' Beijing and Washington, the two world powers. I know the sound of Washington but what is the sound of Beijing?? This is half the plan-et's population, with no pop voice. The new generation of Chinese will mark the way for change in the 21st century.

Memories of the Sex Pistols come hurtling back, but this is not the same. It's girls here who want to change things. It's tough for girls in China. The kids I met were a complete dichotomy – on one hand they were wired to the future and far beyond us in the West, on the other they lived by the most ancient code of honour.[2]

Back in London, McLaren entered his trademark phase of research, buying books on Taoism and Chinese calligraphy, iconography and art. For McLaren, the lure of karaoke as a cultural form lay in the purity of its expression of the meaninglessness of consumer society. Here was a vibrant, late 1990s update on the existentialism he had sought to investigate with the *Paris* album just a few years earlier.

'The Japanese word means "empty orchestra", a lifeless musical form unencumbered by creativity and free of responsibility,' McLaren wrote in the 2000s. 'Simple, clean fun for the Millennial nuclear family. You can't fail in a karaoke world. It's life by proxy, liberated by hindsight.'

By contrast, added McLaren, before incanting his lifelong axiom, 'authenticity believes in the messy process of creativity. It's unpopular and out of fashion. It worships failure, regarding it as a romantic and noble pursuit: better to be a flamboyant failure than any kind of benign success.'

McLaren felt, however, that the two need not be mutually exclusive. 'Karaoke and authenticity can sit well together, but it takes artistry to make that happen,' he said. 'When it does, the results can be explosive. Like when punk rock reclaimed rock and roll, blowing the doors off the recording industry in the process. Or when hip hop transformed turntables and records into the instruments of a revolution.'[3]

And so this interest in Asia and karaoke informed one of McLaren's most misunderstood excursions, his creation and management of Jungk, a girl band set up as an Asian response to the Spice Girls and the latest in his series of attempts to marry polar opposites to create radical new stepping-off points for youth culture.

That Jungk failed ignominiously and, in the eyes of some, represented a shift towards out-and-out cheesiness should not deflect from McLaren's continued attempts to shake things up even as he entered his early fifties.

With the assistance of Asian record executives, McLaren set about auditioning the line-up of Jungk, the name selected since it conjured both travel around the region and narcotic bliss, 'a boat navigating an opiated map of Oriental feelings stretching from Mongolia to Australia'.[4]

Five women were selected, aged between nineteen and twenty-three. Malaysian model Ling Tang, who was described in the British press as 'The Kate of Kuala Lumpur', became a member after an approach by McLaren in Paris. 'He gave me an audition,' said Ling. 'That's when he learned I only knew how to sing in Chinese. It was a funny audition, but he liked my voice and I loved his creative ideas and energy.'[5]

In the style of the Spice Girls, each was assigned particular personality characteristics by McLaren: Ling was 'the most glamorous and dangerous . . . looks like the daughter of Genghis Khan'; Singaporean Chinese model Celest Chong, 'the most spiritual, an operatic Chinese diva'; Teh Seow Ching 'a punk from Shanghai'; Tsang Hing Wan (who adopted the name Rosa), 'a wild dancer with a "Fuck You!" attitude from Hong Kong'; and Sammy Frith, 'a funky, slightly Aboriginal' Australasian from Perth.

'In the next millennium, music will be presented in so many new ways that will be predominantly visual rather than oral,' McLaren told the *Sunday Times*. 'Jungk's manga cartoon look and knockout Ninja style are perfect for interactive technology and the virtual world.'[6]

Using photographs of the girls and relying on his spiel, McLaren secured seed funding from a Swedish music executive without any music being recorded, and then assembled the Jungk members in a London recording studio with Henri Struck as co-producer and arranger. They taped electro cover versions with shrill vocals of such obvious choices as the Frank Loesser pop standard 'Slow Boat to China', Kraftwerk's 'The Model', David Bowie and Iggy Pop's 'China Girl' and Carl Douglas's 1970s novelty hit 'Kung Fu Fighting'. There was also a song that heavily sampled 'The Message' by Grandmaster Flash & the Furious Five, and Struck produced a cover of the Beatles song 'I Want You (She's So Heavy)'.

During the recording sessions the UK's handover of Hong Kong back to China took place. According to McLaren, the Jungk members watched the ceremony on the studio TV. 'They sing the Chinese national anthem and, watching them solemnly with their hands over their hearts, I realise these girls are serious,' McLaren wrote in his diary. 'The anthem inspires them to sing in Mandarin with English – they want people in the West to understand a few words of Chinese. They're on a MISSION!'[7]

McLaren immersed the Jungk girls in London's demi-monde; they were photographed by Rankin for *Dazed & Confused*, dined with the magazine's publisher Jefferson Hack at Soho House and paid visits to Goldie's Metalheadz jungle night at the Blue Note in Hoxton Square.

Despite creating a fair amount of media goodwill, McLaren's attempts to inject outrage into his tales of the girls' behaviour – mentioning that one of the band members wielded a banana at the Swedish music exec and shouted, 'Show me your arsehole and I'll give you my stick!', for example – did not take, paling in comparison not just with the media savviness of the Spice Girls but more particularly with the genuinely shocking antics of the Sex Pistols in their pomp.

After a year the project assumed an air of desperation with a record contract still not signed, however eloquent McLaren's pitch. 'While Western culture seems to be in an endless act of repetition, the East represents a new sensitivity and demeanour for the *fin de siècle*,' he told *Newsweek*. 'Anything Chinese is very happening.'[8]

The play-it-safe music industry, now utterly wary of this self-declared 'mismanager', wasn't convinced and in any case was content to rake in the cash from Oasis et al. as globalisation of the industry through such outlets as MTV created the final sales high before the onset of the digital era. At one stage, music publisher Warner Chappell expressed interest in rights to the songs and Island Records founder Chris Blackwell – who had recently launched the multimedia company Palm Pictures – contributed to the recording budget and was hovering, as was producer William Orbit, who had contributed to the remix of 'Deep in Vogue' back in the late 1980s and was now a big name after working with Madonna.

In a final push, McLaren saw an opportunity when Ling was appointed the face of Estée Lauder's cosmetics brand Prescriptives, and persuaded the beauty company to showcase Jungk at its New York launch at the Convent of the Sacred Heart girls' school on the Upper East Side. He invited the world's media and persuaded Willi Ninja to choreograph Jungk's performance and Michael Halsband to take their photographs.

'Half of the attendees were from fashion, and the other half hip-hop,' says Henri Struck. 'A lot of money had been spent and now we wanted to attract people to help us realise Jungk as a multimedia project, including a video game, a TV show and the record.'

At the party Jungk faithfully parroted the party line: 'We're actually forming a marriage between Western and Chinese music and it's something different,' said Celest Chong while Sammy Frith exclaimed, 'Asian Spice, hotter than Western Spice!'[9]

When one journalist raised the absence of a record deal for McLaren's so-called 'Rice Girls', he casually deflected. 'Not a problem,' said McLaren. 'They're closer in spirit to the likes of Lara Croft than the Spice Girls. Now girl power reigns and this is Asia's answer. The Spice Girls are like maybe their godmothers. This is the second wave.'[10]

The New York event generated a degree of interest. McLaren persuaded film director Abel Ferrara to shoot Jungk's performance and Fox News broadcast a segment featuring McLaren and group members. In turn, he used this to leverage more funding from Chris Blackwell and put together a seven-minute electronic press kit (EPK) for Jungk filmed on the Strait of Jahor between Malaysia and Singapore.

The intention was to use this to loop in a documentary about the group's formation and progress on an American television network – shades here of the Bow Wow Wow film McLaren proposed to UK broadcaster Granada TV in the early 1980s – but none took the bait.

'Malcolm told us, "OK guys, it's over," ' says Struck. 'We'd worked for a year-and-a-half for nothing, though it was a lot of fun. Malcolm was always excited about selling something that was crazy and new. That meant that people would need convincing, that's what he enjoyed. But he also always told me that when he became bored by a project he gave it up immediately. That's what happened to Jungk, though he was sincere about the rise of Asian culture. Just look at where we are today. Twenty years ago he was alone in music, fashion and art in recognising that China was going to become the next cultural explosion.'

Some of the group members returned to modelling and Celest Chong became an actress, while Struck says his partner at Hardboiled Studios, Chris Percival, had a major disagreement with McLaren over ownership of the music they had produced for the project.

According to his future partner Young Kim, the main issue was that McLaren was angered by Struck's handling of the *Buffalo Gals* remix album, since this had given Virgin Records an excuse not to proceed with the greatest hits package. 'It was sad, I never saw Malcolm again,' says Struck. 'I wrote him a long letter much later telling him how much I had appreciated working with him and thanking him for his help but I'm not sure it got through to him. I owe him a lot; Malcolm sent a letter on my behalf when I was applying to US immigration to work in New York.'

McLaren's preoccupation with the East was never to leave him and informed a burgeoning friendship in London in the late 1990s with the indie music mogul Alan McGee.

The pair had met when the British magazine *Punch* organised an encounter between the Sex Pistols manager and the man who saw himself as the inheritor of McLaren's manipulative skills as owner of the successful Creation Records, which released million-selling albums by such hedonistic groups as Oasis and Primal Scream.

McLaren liked McGee: he was clubbable, wealthy, Scottish and a fan. The music executive – who qualified his approval of any turn of events with the catch-all 'double punk-rock' – feted McLaren as 'a genius', having long since modelled his stewardship of young musicians on the tactics depicted in *The Great Rock 'n' Roll Swindle*. McGee owns to watching the film obsessively when he was determined to turn the noise-rock group Jesus and Mary Chain into 'the Sex Pistols of the 1980s', stoking the press with sensationalist stories so that their chaotic live appearances descended into punch-ups with audience members invading stages and destroying equipment.

McGee enjoyed indulging McLaren, treating him to lavish four-hour meals with expensive wines and allowing him to dominate the encounters with his incessant storytelling, apart from the fifteen-minute spells 'when he'd want a rest and eat his dinner, during which time I would be allowed to talk'.

The younger man also absorbed McLaren's insights into the future delivery of music: 'He was going on about China, how they were going to become the world's biggest economy, about the internet and MP3s and how that was going to transform the music industry. It's all come true,' McGee said in 2013.[11]

In this period, and much to Skene Catling's exasperation, McLaren continued to avoid focusing on the autobiography he had signed to deliver to Alfred A. Knopf. Instead, he returned to 'Diorama', the film musical formerly known as 'Fashion Beast' based on the life of Christian Dior. This was the subject of constant revision and rewriting, and McLaren remained confident that it would become a reality even unto his dying days.

All the while, McLaren continued to process the information to which he had been exposed during his trip around south-east Asia. These helped formulate his views on society at large when he was invited to speak at the London international marketing conference Promax in November 1998.

McLaren began with what was becoming a familiar refrain. 'Today our culture can be summed up by these two words: Authentic and Karaoke,' he declared. 'Today we live in a karaoke world. A world without any particular point of view, where high culture and low culture have had their edges blurred.' McLaren depicted Tony Blair, who had been in office for eighteen months, 'the first karaoke Prime Minister. Television has made his Cool Britannia a successful brand. However there is a counterpoint to all this product placement and branding: the undeniable thirst and search for the authentic.'

McLaren believed that multiculturalism offered a way forward. When he was asked to define Britishness by the *Guardian* in 1999, McLaren led with the inevitable karaoke-singing before heading into more diverse territory to explain that being British was also about 'eating Chinese noodles and Japanese sushi, drinking French wine, wearing Prada and Nike, dancing to Italian house music, listening to Cher, using an Apple Mac, holidaying in Florida and Ibiza and buying a house in Spain. Shepherd's pie and going on holiday to Hastings went out about 50 years ago and the only people you'll see wearing a Union Jack are French movie stars or Kate Moss.'[12]

The Promax talk triggered an invitation from Dutch curator Ton Quik to contribute to the group exhibition *On Taste* at the Bonnefantenmuseum in Maastricht. McLaren proposed a biographical installation. Described as a 'self-portrait', this was named after his current musings: *The Casino of Authenticity and Karaoke*.

McLaren's concept was for an interactive exhibit based around large-format video installations controlled by custom-built slot machines that allowed visitors to access four areas of his life at a pull on a lever: fashion, music, the Sex Pistols and his early years.

To realise this ingenious plan, McLaren enlisted the help of two British architects, Wyn Davies, who handled the content and interactive elements, and the Hamburg-based Stephen Williams, who produced the exhibition build in Maastricht and also at the ZKM gallery in Karlsruhe, Germany, which became home to the show after six months.

'We talked about being able to build an autobiographical casino, where visitors could "play his life, like a game of chance", developing the idea over a couple of evenings,' says Davies. 'The momentum developed from there as it rolled into a fully fledged project. What started out as an immersive virtual casino had to be pared back to something that we could exhibit within six months and a tight budget.'[13]

Williams recalls working on the project as 'really exciting. Malcolm would call from somewhere at two in the morning and say, "Stephen, listen, I have an idea . . ."' said Williams in 2007 before recalling McLaren's bursts of bad temper during the preparations for the show. 'Malcolm's not arrogant at all; he's a great team player. To some people he was really mean, but he was always nice to me.'[14]

A Dutch arcade company supplied the four one-arm bandits that were modified to activate the archive film, music, images and sounds from McLaren's life, while the installation structure created by Williams and his team realised a series of clever display devices: seven lighted and grave-like trenches set in the floor with corresponding vertical glass fins filled with ephemera and mementos from the Sex Pistols, Bow Wow Wow, 430 King's Road and Nostalgia of Mud between 1971 and 1984.

The visual identity of the show was realised by Mark Molloy of Why Not Associates, which had made its name working for clients from the Labour Party to the Royal Academy. Molloy produced graphics for the reels and rebranded the gels for the fruit machines while McLaren threw himself into the simultaneous role of curator and subject with gusto. À la Francis Bacon on the final day of the set-up, McLaren joined the installers in painting the exhibition walls black without changing out of his Savile Row suit.

With three hours to go, news service Reuters found him on his hands and knees, placing a Sid Vicious doll in one of the floor vitrines alongside Seditionaries T-shirts, boots and newspapers carrying front-page headlines of the Sex Pistols' demise.

During a tea break, McLaren said that the show was as much about the disappearance of the counterculture as it was about his past.

'Life has become karaoke,' he said. 'Anyone can be a star for fifteen minutes. You get up, you sing George Michael, you are George Michael. Everything is mainstream.'

According to McLaren, the end of the twentieth century had witnessed the passing of the desire of young people to dress outrageously. 'The new form of dressing, more often than not, is some kind of disguise to look like nothing,' said McLaren. 'You can walk through every country and not worry about passport control. We don't dress up like peacocks any more and get out on the street to confront everybody at the bus stop.'

This, he decided, was a reflection of karaoke's dominance as an egalitarian form: 'It's the way we've all decided culture should be,' he said. 'I've come to a point where I'm trying to understand how the whole culture works and how I can work in it. I'm still a student.' At the same time, he declared himself an artist, one who 'tries to find a position in the world. The life of an artist is whatever he paints or creates. You try to take the past and ram it right into the future. That's when you change the culture and move on.'[15]

To celebrate the show's opening, McLaren flew Charlotte Skene Catling, Peter Culshaw and a sizeable group of friends from London to participate in the vernissage. 'It was incredibly generous of him,' says Culshaw. 'I assumed it was the gallery's largesse.'

In spite of its technological whizz-bang, the content of the *Casino* exhibition communicated a more mature and layered reflection on McLaren's life than Paul Taylor's *Impresario* at New York's New Museum eleven years previously. This was due in part to McLaren coming to terms with the facts of his early life after the reunion with his father, who died of emphysema at the age of seventy-nine during the preparations for the Maastricht show.

There is no doubt that addressing his abandonment issues helped rebalance McLaren's psyche. In the decade left to him after his father's death, McLaren came to believe that neither Peter McLaren nor his absence were as important factors in his personal make-up as he had previously assumed. He was matter-of-fact about this in the 2000s. 'In the end, we found this guy who lived in a clapped-out building on the edge of Romney Marsh,' said McLaren. 'I went down there with immense trepidation. I'd never even seen a picture of him. He was a strange, weaselly creature who painted nudes on velvet and drank like a fish.

'Turns out I also had a step-brother who was a lecturer in parapsychology at Cambridge, who I got to meet. We also had a half-sister. My brother and I did follow the story, but in the end it wasn't very satisfying.'[16]

In reaching such conclusions, McLaren was asserting that he remained Rose Corré's grandson, unbiddable to the highest authority, the father figure.

*　　*　　*

While *The Casino of Authenticity and Karaoke* was still open to visitors, McLaren thrust himself to the forefront of the media glare for the first time in several years by announcing his candidacy for the newly created role of Mayor of London.

Since the 1980s dismantling of the Greater London Authority by Margaret Thatcher's government (in an attempt at defanging the city's left-leaning constituency), the British capital had been without a political voice. The New Labour win by Tony Blair in 1997 set the scene for redress with a referendum vote in favour of a new mayoral role. Answerable to the London Assembly made up of local government politicians, the office is a largely strategic position but, as the capital remains the generator of the country's economic and cultural wellbeing, it also wields substantial political heft not just nationally but also on the world stage.

The initial runners and riders in the first election set for May 2000 were an uninspired bunch, led by the stolid northern Labour MP Frank Dobson, whose place on the ticket was engineered to ward off the candidacy of the popular Ken Livingstone, leader of the Greater London Authority at the time of the Thatcherite crackdown, as well as disgraced novelist-cum-Tory Party chairman Lord Archer and the Liberal Democrat Susan Kramer.

A poll of readers of the British political weekly *New Statesman* as to their choice of Mayor made for interesting reading at 16 Scala Street. While Richard Branson scored highest, McLaren was in the top five. 'So Malcolm said, "Why not?"' recalls Culshaw, who promptly met McLaren and Skene Catling at their favourite Soho restaurant, Andrew Edmunds. 'Malcolm would have made a great figurehead for London as a successful artist and businessman. We jotted down a series of ideas, back of a fag packet stuff, and then he wrote an article for the *New Statesman* declaring his candidacy.'

Bugbears about a range of topics, from globalisation to the Blair government's obeisance to the US and concomitant lack of substance, were to the fore. 'I have never seen so many restaurants, coffee shops, so many places to go to buy things, yet London has never seemed so dull,' said McLaren in the magazine. 'The cappuccino bar culture that Tony Blair raves about looks set to dominate the whole of central London's lifestyle.'

In relation to his role in forming and steering the Sex Pistols, McLaren made a powerful point in support of his bid for Mayor. 'My effect on London was to create the best and most profound statement of useful protest since the end of the last war,' he wrote. 'I think it inspired a generation. I don't think today you would have as many artists living in London if it had not been for punk rock.'[17]

According to Alan McGee, McLaren asked him to sponsor the mayoral bid soon after the Andrew Edmunds lunch, but the Creation Records boss politely declined the request. A week later while on holiday, McGee learned not only that McLaren was in the running but that he had 'agreed' to fund the bid.

'I had absolutely no say in the matter,' said McGee. 'I was in the Caribbean when I heard I was putting him up. I hadn't agreed. I clearly remember *not* agreeing to put him up as Mayor of London. So he just announced it anyway!'

McGee was unfazed; in fact his mentor's mischievousness served to impress, and he persuaded Sony Music UK, which part-owned Creation, to part with £20,000 for what he described to them as 'an art project'.[18]

Wittingly or not, McLaren was pitching himself into the middle of a politically delicate situation. McGee had been a prominent Labour Party supporter and was one of the government's youth advisers, while Tony Blair and his team were extremely nervous that McLaren's candidacy would undercut Dobson and provide the room for Livingstone to announce his standing.

It is against this backdrop that McGee provided campaign headquarters in north London's Primrose Hill and a publicist, Andy Saunders, who had been head of press at Creation and was experienced in dealing with national media on the back of the frenzy around the Gallagher brothers from Oasis. Culshaw became campaign manager and a media blitz was launched to communicate a manifesto, which included legalising the brothels situated close to the House Of Parliament and allowing the sale of alcohol in public libraries ('why not drink a Guinness as you read Dickens?').

These both grabbed the headlines, but the sixteen-point manifesto's mix of anarchic thinking, utopianism and practicality identified substantial issues pertaining to urban existence, the decriminalisation of drugs, public housing, the survival of independent businesses, occupation of public spaces and sustainable living and transport.

McLaren proposed a list of policies, including replacing buses with electric tram networks and greater use of the Thames and other waterways; a housing lottery system to address homelessness; the provision of affordable adult education; free entry at galleries and museums funded by an entry tax on overseas visitors to the capital; and a 'multi-ethnic flag for the 21st century to reflect the true population of London'.

The reclamation of parks, squares, churches and the Thames was intended to open such spaces to access night and day, and an annual carnival taking over – where else? – Oxford Street would be accompanied by 'a Don't Buy Anything Day, and a No Car Day to allow kids to play in the streets'.

McLaren understood the pernicious aspects of the rise of the soon to be all-pervasive food and beverage multiples. 'Restructure rates in order to tax business according to scale,' he said. 'Chains such as Pret a Manger, for instance, now pay the same rates as a local florist. If we don't save small businesses, London will lose its soul and become like Singapore or Hong Kong – a shrine to capitalism.'

Nearly a decade ahead of the growth of artisan capitalism, which grew as an outcrop of the 2008 financial crisis among the hipster enclaves of the Western world before moving to mass acceptance, McLaren was focusing on the word as a means of resisting corporatism. One manifesto declaration was in favour of 'artisans in Oxford Street. With more e-commerce, old-fashioned department stores should be more diversified, welcoming artisans. Shoemakers could set up their workshops in

John Lewis, table-makers in Selfridges. Subsidise artisans and allow Londoners into the process of production.'

The legalisation of the Westminster brothels, wrote McLaren, would 'help get rid of sleaze scandals in the government and allow us to focus on the real bullshit that the elite produces', and the introduction of street-level digital information stations – featuring a hologram of the trusted 1960s TV neighbourhood policeman Dixon of Dock Green – would provide 'street directions, train and bus information and suchlike'.

A key plank was described by McLaren as 'responsive website democracy, with local voters using the web to voice their opinion on anything from whose statue should be put up or taken down to one-way streets'.

And, as suggested by the Oxford Street proposal, the Situationist McLaren was alive and kicking in the form of manifesto points that covered popular protest – 'London has a proud history of freedom of expression; anarchists, revolutionaries and dissidents have written their pamphlets here. Street protest is every Londoner's right and should never be stomped upon', and the idea derived from the *dérive* that no licensing restrictions be placed in certain twenty-four-hour zones of the capital 'so that we encourage chance encounters'.

McLaren's central point – and one which was to foreshadow developments around the world more than a decade later – was that the mayoral post was too important to be taken by a politician.

'The mayor of London must not be associated with any political party – he or she should be wholly independent,' wrote McLaren in his candidacy declaration in the *New Statesman*.

Surely, rather than represent any particular political group, the mayor should represent London – the general public at large. He or she should be free to lobby all parties and apply all the necessary pressures for and on behalf of the general good of those who live in London.

We are living in the spectacle of our city's commodification. Our freedom of choice has been removed. I have never seen so many

corporate franchises – and, as a result, London is destroying independent artisans. London's independence and its individuals
are being hounded out of existence.

McLaren accepted that he was not viewed as a heavyweight. 'I have
often been seen as a cartoon and sometimes enjoyed it (the perfumed
garden of fame – a primrose path to *Hello!* magazine),' he wrote in the
New Statesman.

But the demand for success and celebrity at all costs has made me
feel that I am living under the legacy of those we fought against
during the last war. For the Nazis invented the media and branded
a nation. They created logos, uniforms and a mission statement to
die for. Theirs was the first government-controlled corporate lifestyle. We have stepped into their mould: today, you no longer
watch the advertisement – you are part of it.

It is no coincidence that postwar America turned itself from a
manufacturing economy into an information society and sold its
culture and products across the world. Cool Britannia is its bastard
offspring. The mayor of London is an important role. Let's keep it
from the politicians.[19]

The impact of the candidacy announcement was immediate; McLaren
was in demand from media outlets across the world. 'It was an art piece
and simultaneously quite a serious proposition,' says Culshaw, who
approvingly recalls the late humourist Miles Kington describing
McLaren's candidacy as 'a serious joke' in the *Independent* newspaper.
'It was way ahead of its time.'

This is particularly true in the way McLaren capitalised on the increasing suspicion of mainstream politics among the populace and presaged
the exploitative tactics of contemporary populist figureheads from Beppe
Grillo to Donald Trump. 'We plugged into the feeling which viewed
politicians as corrupt,' says Culshaw. 'It was very Trumpian in that there

was a belief that anti-politicians could be successful in the political arena because they have a certain authenticity.'

McLaren was explicit in his stance as a non-politician. 'You are not a member of their club,' he told the BBC in second person singular mode. 'You are definitely not a politician and in essence you don't want to be treated like one, because basically your platform is that you don't like politicians.

'You often think, every day of the week, politicians fail you. What you really care about is London and that in essence makes you a very different kind of ego to those that are standing for and on behalf of their political parties.'[20]

And McLaren understood that his appeal relied in great part on punk's contribution to the cultural equity of the British capital. 'My effect on London was to create the best and most profound statement of useful protest that has existed since the end of the last war, something the media labelled punk rock,' he told *BBC News*. 'I think it inspired a generation. I don't think today you would have as many artists living in London if it had not been for punk rock.'[21]

McGee used his prominence to support McLaren, appearing with the candidate in news interviews and at an Oxford University debate.

A visit to the opening of an exhibition at London's ICA provided McLaren with collaborators on his campaign's visual identity. *Crash!* was the title of both the show and the savage art publication which was put together by the British graphic artist Scott King and the academic Matthew Worley.

A tabloid fold-out lampooning the posturings of New Labour, the YBAs and the bogus cultural nostalgia that infected Britpop, *Crash!* took aim at contemporary radical chic, whose exponents were described as 'fickle victims and perpetrators of the encroaching "lifestyle" culture. They remain proudly political and eternally grounded in the halcyon days of university bar banality.'

McLaren was impressed with both the exhibition, which included such contributions as UK artist Mark Leckey's film *Fiorucci Made Me*

Hardcore, and the magazine, which was King and Worley's end-of-the-century response to Wyndham Lewis's First World War publication *Blast*, the Vorticist statement of intent celebrating Modernism.

And he agreed wholeheartedly with their condemnations, particularly of the YBAs, whose work, in the words of the British curator Mark Beasley who also attended *Crash!*, 'he fathered from a distance but ultimately had little time for, describing them as "the worst aspects of the culture of desire" but that "their unbridled energy changed the British art world for the good"'.[22]

King's graphic vigour displayed many of the design flourishes of McLaren and Jamie Reid's broadsides from punk's heyday, including washes of fluorescent colour and bold Situationist-style sloganeering, and the first issue of *Crash!*, published in 1997, had quoted Sex Pistols lyrics and folded out into a giant poster of a soccer field which marked the positions of two teams, each opposed in terms of cultural worth in the style of the 'You're Gonna Wake Up' shirt sold in Sex in the 1970s.

One side was taken up by such mediagenic figures as the TV presenters Chris Evans and Chris Tarrant, the novelist Nick Hornby, the latterly disgraced musician Morrissey and the comedian David Baddiel. On the other were massed the likes of Shaun Ryder of the Happy Mondays, Johnny Rotten, Iggy Pop, Guy Debord and Belgian writer Raoul Vaneigem. Upfront, among the strikers' positions held by Oscar Wilde, Jean Genet and André Breton, was Malcolm McLaren.

'We met Malcolm at the launch and a few days later he asked us along to Scala Street to discuss how we could contribute to the campaign,' says Worley. 'We went for a meal at his local Italian restaurant and he talked throughout it, which was wonderful, and then at the end said, "Well, I guess we'd better have a proper meeting," so a week later we went to Alan McGee's offices in Primrose Hill.'

There they found McGee in agitated mood. 'Andy Saunders lay on a sofa in a baseball cap while McGee paced up and down, really wired,' says Worley. 'At one stage, while he and Malcolm were discussing how to get more funds, he shouted, "I know! I'll call Bono!" and proceeded to try and track him down in Dublin. I was wondering whether I really wanted to be involved in something Bono was backing, but it came to nothing so we started to talk sensibly to Malcolm about the kind of approach he wanted us to take.'[23]

McLaren was by this time receiving support from unexpected quarters. Auberon Waugh, satirist and son of the great British novelist Evelyn Waugh, praised the proposal for alcohol to be available in libraries. 'The British genius survives,' wrote Waugh in his column in the *Literary Review*. 'At last somebody has come up with a good political suggestion. McLaren must learn that politics is a tricky business, and there are endless armies of public employees and would-be bureaucrats waiting to jump on every bandwagon. McLaren must be bold and strong. He has the massive backing of *Literary Review*, and no candidate with this magazine behind him has yet failed to sweep to power.'[24]

Having announced his candidacy, McLaren took a break to spend Millennium Eve with Skene Catling and Peter Culshaw and his girlfriend at Jean-Charles de Castelbajac's chateau. 'We were looking to the future and meantime there was all that Y2K fear going around,' says Culshaw. 'At one point we went to a party at another chateau owned by one of the people who runs French fashion and drank the finest wines known to humanity. At the end of the stay Malcolm suggested we buy Jean-Charles a case of wine to thank him. There was a certain lack of empathy there. Malcolm didn't quite realise I was a struggling alternative musician-stroke-journalist who found it really difficult to find the £500 for my share.'

Chapter 37

Back in London in the new Millennium, Malcolm McLaren gingered up his mayoral candidacy by updating the media manipulation that had served him so well during the punk years.

These days, campaign manager and friend Peter Culshaw views the tack taken by McLaren through the prism of the daily shock-and-awe tactics that enabled Donald Trump to ride successive news cycles.

'One morning we'd put out a press release announcing that the brothels should be legalised opposite the Houses of Parliament,' says Culshaw. 'It didn't matter that it had already appeared in the manifesto. Most people don't have the attention span and didn't read the *New Statesman*. This would be taken up by the press and then discussed on the evening news programmes and chat shows.

'Then the next day, as those headlines appeared in the morning papers and before it had had a chance to subside, we'd send out a press announcement that drink should be served in libraries, and that would then be taken up, and so on. It was a great success and kept Malcolm in the news, though I have to say it was better when pundits commented and argued. Malcolm was never one for a snappy soundbite; he preferred the baroque story.

'Also he tended to use phrases that weren't voter-friendly. On the hustings he referred to the police as "the filth". I told him that there was no way we were going to get any votes unless he cut that out, but he wouldn't listen.'

A website, malcolm4mayor.com, was launched to underpin the dissemination of information, allowing McLaren to deliver insights into the ways digital would impact on politics.

In the style of the various 'czars' who became popular appointees in British politics a decade later, McLaren proposed a 'cabinet of ideas' made up of people with personal experiences of their subjects. John Bird, the editor of *The Big Issue*, the magazine which provides income for homeless people, was to be given oversight over policies in regard to housing those who lived on the streets of the capital. Doreen Lawrence, mother of the murdered black teenager Stephen Lawrence whose case had been grievously mishandled by investigating officers, was approached to assist in the rooting out of racism in the Metropolitan Police, and the world champion Formula One racing driver Damon Hill was asked to advise on traffic problems.

Dangerously, McLaren proposed a close working relationship with London's financiers.

'The City are a great bunch of freewheeling geezers out to basically earn lots of money for themselves,' he said. 'Basically they are people that are very intelligent and if they weren't making lots and lots of money in the City they probably could run this town a hell of a lot better than the government.'[1]

McLaren was on safer ground criticising the erection of the £789-million Millennium Dome (now the 02 Centre), which he was not alone in as viewing as one of the great Blairite follies. After he and Culshaw were refused entry when they attempted to visit the site, the campaign was rewarded with a front-page story on the nation's biggest-selling tabloid, Rupert Murdoch's the *Sun*. McLaren suggested the money would have been better spent on rail tickets for every eighteen to twenty-four-year-old to tour Europe.

And he told British chat show host Gloria Hunniford that he saw the mayoral role as 'protecting London and Londoners from government, not someone who sleeps with them. It would be a form of devolution where people can control their destinies.'

And McLaren proudly informed Hunniford, 'I'm someone who has done something for this town. I am a fourth-generation Londoner. In London we're able to culturally put things together to make up a unique flavour. We're known, and watched by the world, for our ideas which move the culture forward.'[2]

Since mass transit was one of the central concerns of the campaign, Culshaw located a professor of urban studies at Liverpool University and suggested they seek his advice. 'We went up to see him on the train,' recalls Culshaw. 'I shared not only a hotel room with Malcolm but the bed since we were on a tight budget. He kept me awake, snoring, by the way.'

The following day McLaren gave a talk at Paul McCartney's Liverpool Institute for Performing Arts and arrived elated for dinner with Culshaw and the Liverpool University professor. 'This was one of the world experts in regenerating cities and transport systems, what they'd tried in Jakarta and what did and didn't work in Amsterdam,' says Culshaw. 'As far as I was concerned, with this guy behind us, we would be unbeatable. But Malcolm was pretty high after his talk, where he'd obviously had a few drinks and flirted with some people. He was in that mood to talk where nobody else could get a word in edgeways. I'd gone to a lot of trouble to set this meeting up and Malcolm messed it up. That was the point where I wondered whether we were going to make it.'

Nevertheless, McLaren's campaign polled well. 'We climbed from 6 per cent to a high of 18 per cent of the vote at one stage,' says Culshaw. 'It's still interesting to me to ponder how serious Malcolm was. McGee used to say, "Of course you're not going to win," and Malcolm would become quite upset. "Maybe not," he'd say. "But you don't tell that to a boxer before he goes into the ring." We felt that McGee wasn't as dedicated, and nowhere near as radical, as Malcolm. On the other hand we were impressed that he and Saunders had turned Oasis, who were basically pub rock, into the biggest band in the world, so there was a certain amount of respect.'

With Oasis and Primal Scream lined up to perform concerts in support of the campaign, McGee came under direct pressure from Tony Blair's government.

Culshaw says he was shown a letter questioning McGee's loyalty from the prime minister's notoriously aggressive spin doctor Alastair

Campbell. 'I said, "This is gold dust. We have to release it. It shows we've got them on the run,"' says Culshaw. 'But McGee refused, so we fell out.'

It's worth pointing out that McGee says he was expelled from the Labour Party for supporting McLaren, but his withdrawal meant that McLaren was forced to switch his campaign HQ from the music executive's Primrose Hill offices to Scala Street.

By this time King and Worley had responded to the commission with a Warholian campaign logo of a dayglo pop-art bubble pierced by a safety pin. This appeared on a series of posters and sticker designs, which communicated the campaign website's URL with such statements as 'It's the biggest job in London – Don't give it to a politician' and 'Churches open 24 hours – Sanctuaries where you don't have to buy anything'.

MALCOLM McLAREN NEEDS YOUR HELP!

Malcolm McLaren, the man who created the **Sex Pistols**, is running as an independent candidate for London Mayor and he wants YOU to help him.

He is protesting against the great political swindle of the mainstream Parties who are plotting to make London expensive, oppressive and boring.

But in order to stand Malcolm needs at least TEN signatures from each of London's thirty-three boroughs.

If you are on the electoral register in London or have been resident in London since October 1999, YOU can nominate Malcolm McLaren.

That means your name will appear on Malcolm's nomination papers....

ANYONE CAN BE A SEX PISTOL

Malcolm McLaren

- **To nominate Malcolm, make a donation to the "Malcolm McLaren Fighting Fund" or to get involved:**
- **tel: 020 7586 3903,**
- **fax: 020 7586 6382**
- **e-mail:** info@malcolm4mayor.com.
- **Write to Malcolm:**
  "BCM Malcolm4Mayor", London, WC1N 3XX

Leaflet for Mayor of London campaign, 2000. Paul Gorman Archive.

But the stickers and posters didn't make it into full production. Around this time, an approach was received from representatives of Ken Livingstone, who had been observing the campaign's headline-grabbing from the sidelines. 'We'd always thought that if he entered the race – and this is long before the anti-Semitic business [charges of anti-Semitism, which he denies, have been levelled against Livingstone since 2004] – we would support him,' says Culshaw. 'Initially Ken's people told us that he wasn't interested in leaving Labour and they quite liked the idea of victory going to an independent candidate, not a party hack, but then Ken saw an opportunity. Malcolm's running on independence triggered Ken to announce he was joining the race after all. This meant it was over for us. It petered out.'

According to Culshaw, McGee and Saunders issued a press release announcing the termination of the campaign without deferring to McLaren. 'I think at the time Malcolm was disappointed we didn't see it through to a vote,' says Culshaw. 'Later on he thought of it as one of his projects which was strangled before it reached fruition. We wouldn't have won but it would have made things much more interesting.'

In the immediate aftermath of the election – which Livingstone won comfortably with 58 per cent of the vote – McLaren described his candidacy as 'a stand for the soul, for principle, for the artist' and condemned New Labour for its contrasting lack of principles. 'It's all bollocks,' he told *GQ*.[3]

Throughout their friendship when he was living in London, McLaren was wont to arrive at Peter Culshaw's apartment unannounced and sleep overnight on a sofa. But one weekend in 2000 he stayed for an entire weekend. 'He took me around his childhood haunts, showing me everything from where the Vogue cinema had been and the premises where his family bought eggs to the school he had lasted a day at,' says Culshaw.

The reason for the stay was that McLaren's relationship with Charlotte Skene Catling had finally disintegrated. A couple of years earlier, in

March 1998, he had started seeing Young Kim, a twenty-eight-year-old Korean-American who had approached him at the after party for a Vivienne Westwood show in Paris, where Kim was studying fashion at the private training institute Studio Berçot.

'Besides a few flirtations, I'd never had a relationship before,' said Kim in 2013. 'I had practically no experience. How did I look past the celebrity and see the real person? Why did I know Malcolm was right for me? And I for him? I just did. He wasn't so sure. It took a lot of convincing. Though he was attracted to me, he pushed me away constantly, listing all the differences and difficulties: age, background, experience and culture. But in the end I was proven right.'[4]

McLaren and Kim had visited each other in Paris and London and they had also holidayed together in Portugal and Sicily. Kim was also with him in the French countryside when he had resumed work on his autobiography. After she returned to New York he had met up with her when he was in town and she had started to contribute to his projects, sourcing clothes for Jungk and vintage T-shirts for merchandising for the *Casino of Authenticity and Karaoke* exhibition.

Eventually, her residence in New York offered an exit from London. For the remainder of his life, the couple divided their time – when not travelling the world – between Kim's Manhattan apartment and a series of rented flats in Paris, where the multilingual Kim felt equally at home.

As he had with previous partners – apart from the untameable Hutton – McLaren drew Kim to the centre of his life and work, which were pretty much indivisible. She soon became collaborator and sounding board, but also took on the duties of both assistant and manager which previous girlfriends had resisted.

Since his mid-forties, McLaren had settled on a smart, suited appearance which gave him, in the eyes of one journalist, the appearance of 'an insane academic'. Such judgements underestimated the care and attention that McLaren poured into his look at a time when most middle-aged men are happy with nondescript clothing.

Now he favoured clothes from Dries Van Noten, Maison Margiela, Prada and Jil Sander as well as made-to-measure suits that ran to €2000 from the Saint-Germain-des-Prés tailor Arnys, which opened in the 1930s and was popular during the pre- and post-war period with artists and intellectuals, numbering Le Corbusier, Jean Cocteau and Jean-Paul Sartre among its clientele.

'I kind of like the anonymity of a tailor's suit,' McLaren explained to *Fantastic Man* magazine during a discussion about menswear in which he communicated his deep understanding of the tailoring process.

> When you reach a certain age, as you get older, it's much better to look more anonymous. I don't know why. It feels more comfortable not to strut around like a peacock. Arnys is a bit French-dandyish. That's the part I don't like, that dandy look. Otherwise they are very nicely made and they used nice cloth. They are not brilliant cuts, so you have to compromise. The shoulder is the most important part of the suit. The better suits have the shoulder put in by hand. It's not so square. I like it sloped and rounded. Square is good on a young figure. But on an old figure, square doesn't work well. You need a suit that goes with the flow.[5]

McLaren also favoured the more avant-garde tailoring of the American Thom Browne, whose suits he also wore for the rest of his life.

In New York and Paris, McLaren continued to nurture 'Diorama'. One doleful track was the result of merging the melody from a work by the twentieth-century composer Francis Poulenc with samples from blues legend Bessie Smith's 1920s performance of 'St Louis Blues' and 'She's Not There', a song by the British 1960s group the Zombies. The demo was given the title 'Smith Ballad'. Another, titled 'The New Look' after Dior's revolutionary post-war collection, crazily mixed the wild outpourings of the 1950s beat performer Lord Buckley with a twenty-first-century Charleston rhythm.

'The music was made with the intention that I wanted to bury myself into the bowels of pop culture and grab-bag it, reinvent it, cut it up and destroy its product,' McLaren explained a couple of years later. 'You know how songs in the end become products and clichés, and the value is lost. The outlaw spirit is gone – all that you initially picked up on at the very beginning when you first heard those songs. I knew that if you could grab-bag a chorus here, a verse there, a little backing vocal from somewhere else, and just stick it on some generic groove, then you could make these things have a different kind of resonance.'[6]

There were other projects that came and went, including a treatment to stage the *Paris* album as a Broadway musical and a proposal for a TV series called 'The Magnificent Appelbaums'. This was to be 'a history of pop culture told through the life and times of a family growing up in the entertainment business from 1945 to the present day'.[7]

Neither of these was to be realised, but no matter; McLaren's creative processes were re-energised as he prepared to leave London. The now widespread reappraisal of the punk years by all manner of media, however, meant that McLaren was never to escape this two-and-a-half-year period deep in his past. And for the most part, he ensured that he made a contribution, even appearing in voiceover segments in a film produced by the remaining Sex Pistols as a riposte to *The Great Rock 'n' Roll Swindle*'s positioning of him as the movement's (and the band's) prime instigator.

The group and their management chose *Swindle* director Julien Temple to helm *The Filth and the Fury*, which roundly lambasted McLaren's legitimacy (though the greater proportion of the content derived from sequences he created for the 1980 original). 'Malcolm's had his opportunity and all he's done is sabotage, wreck, ruin and destroy, all according to his pontificating ego throughout the years,' said John Lydon in an EPK interview for the film. Steve Jones was more succinct. 'Everyone on the planet knows that Malcolm's full of shit,' declared the guitarist.

In the film, Lydon accused McLaren of complicity in supplying Sid Vicious with heroin on the US tour of 1978. 'That's sad,' said McLaren. 'How can anyone say that? God, if Sid could only hear those words. It's like blaming Warhol for Lou Reed's heroin addiction. What are we saying here? Oh, you're eighteen and you don't know whether you should do heroin or not? Oh, Malcolm was a big junkie and he knew every Chinese dominoes player on Gerrard Street? You ask anybody, Malcolm doesn't know a drug from a skunk, I mean from a cigarette.'

Expressing equanimity over the accusation that he played Fagin to the Sex Pistols' gang of young criminals ('In many respects I was'), McLaren now championed *The Great Rock 'n' Roll Swindle* in comparison to Temple's latest Pistols effort. 'That film caused punk to become an enigma, tried to prevent it becoming just another page in the rock 'n' roll almanac,' he said.[8]

McLaren also decried the cheerlessness of Temple's film, which stressed such elements as Britain's high unemployment and off-the-scale industrial action during the period, as well as the poor backgrounds of the group members and Vicious's decline. The decision to present the surviving Pistols in interview as outlandish blacked-out silhouettes – apparently to mask the effects of aging on their faces – added to the doc's gloominess.

'I don't remember punk rock being like that,' said McLaren. 'I always remember it as a ticket to the carnival for a better life. This movie made it feel very downbeat. I don't think that was the case. The manipulation that I was accused of – all of that is absolutely true. But ultimately, it was to express something that was going to be a vital ingredient in changing culture and life within the British Isles.'[9]

For McLaren, *The Filth and the Fury*'s revisionism qualified it as an exercise in bogus nostalgia. 'The question I find most interesting is how you reclaim history,' he wrote in notes in 2000. 'This is a very different thing from repackaging it. It's not about nostalgia, which is basically dead tissue. Living yesterday tomorrow should be about reclaiming history then reversing it into the future. If you can discover how to do that, you are probably doing everything an artist genuinely wishes to be involved in. One must aim to use certain disruptive practices to challenge the dominant cultural forms and relax the grip of authority.'

But the fashion world, like the music business, could not resist the desire to look back. Punk signifiers from studs and safety pins to torn T-shirts and spiky haircuts were now catwalk staples, while the demand for original examples of the clothing McLaren designed with Vivienne Westwood reached new heights with such events as an exhibition at New York's Visionaire Gallery.

The show – where Piss Marilyn T-shirts were displayed alongside Snow White & the Sir Punks tops – was curated by Katy Rodriguez, co-owner of Resurrection, a new and soon to be dominant type of fashion outlet, the upscale vintage clothing store. 'Not a lot of this stuff was made, and it really wasn't sold in the US, so it became a treasure hunt,' she said of her two-year search for authentic garments. The *Village Voice* reported that Rodriguez tracked down designs from members of 1970s punk groups, while many loans came from the collection of Massive Attack and Björk producer Nellee Hooper.

Rodriguez also identified the growing market for fakes and reproductions. 'The Japanese have been making forgeries since the '80s – they love Westwood,' she said. 'And there's a guy in Camden Market whose whole business is repros of this stuff. He's used it for couches, lawn chairs, even coffee mugs.'[10]

Little was McLaren to know, but questions over authenticity in regard to the designs he made with Westwood were to become an abiding preoccupation in the ensuing years.

Meanwhile, McLaren's presence in Paris provided an opportunity to work with the digital youth television channel Jimmy after an approach was made by his friend and a director of the company, Sylvie de La Rochefoucauld. He responded by scripting and presenting *Being Malcolm*, a series of shorts on a variety of cultural subjects.

The three-minute films used the latest digital technology to present McLaren in a variety of ways. One, 'The Private Case', about the huge cache of erotica dating from the seventeenth century that is secretly stored in the British Library, followed McLaren in grainy detective-style around Paris; another, 'Subversive Trousers', positioned him in a tailor's cutting room wielding shears discussing the creation of the Bondage trousers.

A two-parter on Sid Vicious's New York trial recounts the encounters with Roy Cohn and F. Lee Bailey in the aftermath of Nancy Spungen's death and posed McLaren in a sepia-toned police poster headed 'Wanted for Talent', and 'The Biology of Machines' rendered his face in code as he discussed the coming of AI as predicted by *Wired* editor Kevin Kelly's 1994 book *Out of Control*. Arguably the best of the series is 'Shoppertainment', which blue-screened McLaren against sweeping footage of shop facades and boutique interiors. This pondered the growth of consumerism as a lifestyle choice, taking as its cue from Walter Benjamin's descriptions of the flâneur of the Parisian arcades of the nineteenth century, and the ways in which, in the words of museum curators Christoph Grunenberg and Max Hollein, 'the browsing, selection, purchase and consumption of commodities has been recognised as a defining activity of modern urban life'.[11]

There's a line from 'Shoppertainment' to the student McLaren's Situationist-influenced thoughts in the 1960s on the ultimately unfulfilling nature of consumer society. 'The entertainment is not in the spending, it's in getting your purchase back home,' explained McLaren in the Canal Jimmy film. 'You're supposed to believe it's offered you some knowledge and some salvation, quenched your thirsts and desires, but more often than not, you're not certain it has, so you go back to the shop the next day to spend more.'

In quintessential McLaren style, he used *Being Malcolm* to further process his more recent ideas, such as the mayoral campaign's point about the havens provided by churches in the West from the nightmare of consumerism.

Asked during the 'Shoppertainment' episode to recommend a safe space, McLaren responded: 'I'd probably take you to a church where I can smoke a spliff. These are places which are almost permanently closed in this day and age [but are] sanctuaries where you don't have to buy anything, you just make love in the aisles.'

Being Malcolm used a format made for McLaren; fast-paced, eye-catching and edited with style, it curtailed his tendency to verbosity and produced pithy dialogue. Rightly, it was awarded French television's prestigious honour, the Prix Ithème, for best cultural TV programme of 2001.

Paris had long since suited McLaren, but as he settled into life with Young Kim, he felt particularly comfortable in the city. This may have been due to the fact that their stays were always open-ended – the couple tended to head for New York for the seasonal fashion and art shows in the autumn – but also the French recognition of his role as a creative figurehead made life easier than in London, where he was plagued by (and sometimes played up to) the media impression of a Machiavellian schemer.

Now there was domestic harmony in his life. 'Once we started living and working together, we were hardly ever apart,' said Kim in 2013. 'Over the course of a day, it would be unusual if we spent more than an hour beyond shouting distance. "We have to be together," he'd instruct me. "We're like Bill and Ben, the Flowerpot Men."'[12]

Over Christmas 2001 the couple were invited to holiday at a house rented by McLaren's ex Lauren Hutton on the French-speaking Caribbean island of Saint Barthélemy. The vacation magnet for monied celebrities, St Barth's was to become a regular destination for McLaren and Kim. On this first trip they were accompanied by a couple of friends, including Stephen Williams, the Hamburg-based Welsh architect who had designed the *Casino of Authenticity and Karaoke*, and the 2001 visit set a pattern with parties and barbecues populated by artists including Brice Marden and Francesco Clemente, gallerist Tony Shafrazi and actors such as Daniel Day-Lewis and Lisa Marie, who had sung 'Something's Jumping in Your Shirt' on *Waltz Darling*.

At mealtimes, McLaren chose the wine and arranged the food on the table as well as a soundtrack of romantic French and German songs sung by such stars of the 1930s as Marlene Dietrich and Zarah Leander.

These choices were informing the music McLaren was concocting for 'Diorama', based around a musical hybrid he christened 'bastard pop'; new songs featuring spoken-word extracts against backing tracks composed of samples. One, 'Mexico, Manhattan & Malibu', blended beat poet William Burroughs reading from his novel *The Naked Lunch* with 1950s pin-up film star Jayne Mansfield talking about fashion, all against a mambo beat with swooping strings.

Another, a version of the Jimi Hendrix Experience's 'Foxy Lady', incorporated samples of Mick Jagger speaking. 'I was feeling stifled by the tyranny of the new,' wrote McLaren later.

iPod this. PowerBook that. Listening to albums, like Madonna's latest, that were made using Pro Tools – software that reduces virtually every mix-down effect to a mouse click – left me with a depressing sense of sameness, like everything on TV.

I decided to make an album about the 'look' of music: the visual gestalt of youth culture. For me, music has always been a bridge between art and fashion, the two realms I care about most. Now it was lost in the hearts and minds of a karaoke world. I couldn't find my place in it.[13]

Tom Silverman of American hip-hop label Tommy Boy funded the sessions and expressed an interest in releasing the LP, which McLaren had predictably named 'Fashionbeast', but clearances proved expensive or unavailable. With representatives of the Rolling Stones unwilling to play ball, Silverman bailed.

But music wasn't McLaren's sole focus. In 2002 he announced the formation of a film company, Malcolm McLaren Productions (MMP), after being invited by the major studio Universal to advise on ways of reviving properties held in its vast back catalogue. Recognising the impact of the hit musical *Mamma Mia!*, McLaren opined: 'The cheapest way besides putting it out on DVD is to turn the film into a stage musical. If that works, turn it back into a musical on film.'

Having considered comedies made by Britain's Ealing Studios, including the classic *Kind Hearts and Coronets*, McLaren settled on an unlikely title as suitable for the musical treatment: Joseph Losey's 1963 adaptation of Robin Maugham's homoerotic novel *The Servant*, which was based on a darkly subtle script by Harold Pinter.

McLaren was persuaded by the fact that the film was released on the cusp of the rise of Swinging London, in the same year McLaren made his first steps towards becoming an art student. 'I love the idea of *The Servant* as a very intriguing, sombre, quintessential English pop musical with the world of the Kinks, the Herd, Anthony Newley, the Zombies and so on,' McLaren explained. ' "Waterloo Sunset", "A Well Respected Man", "Chalk & Cheese", you're never going to be able to write songs as good as that. They were written at a time when songwriting was so fresh and new.'

In interviews McLaren foresaw no problems from Pinter – 'I've known Harold for many, many years,' as he told one journalist – and believed that the film would follow the formula of Baz Luhrmann's recently released *Moulin Rouge*. 'I love the idea of using existing songs and weaving them in,' said McLaren. 'It's an old-fashioned post-modernist way.'

Also on MMP's slate were two book options: Rolling Stone reporter Eric Schlosser's best-selling exposé *Fast Food Nation: The Dark Side of the All-American Meal* and *Among the Thugs*, the *New Yorker* literary editor Bill Buford's chronicle of his travels with English football hooligans, which had been recommended by Young Kim.

Cleverly, McLaren hit upon the idea of adapting Schlosser's nonfiction work into a narrative feature, and soon persuaded Jeremy Thomas, the British producer of *The Great Rock 'n' Roll Swindle* a quarter of a century previously, on board. 'I had remained pally with Malcolm; our paths crossed in various places, when he was in LA and elsewhere,' says

Thomas. 'I was always genuinely happy to see Malcolm. He was portrayed as a malign person, but he wasn't that at all. He was a joker, he was a jester, a creative, talented person.'

McLaren's idea for *Fast Food Nation* was to 'make a drama about the young and the new generation who work within the fast-food industry at many different levels'. Among the directors he pitched was the Mexican Alfonso Cuarón, since he intended the movie to be largely Spanish-language (the workforces that endure the scandalous conditions in abattoirs and meat-packing plants are predominantly Latinx).

'This will be the first real Spanish-speaking American movie that combines both the lives of the new second generation of Mexicans with the Anglo-Saxons and the Caucasians that live in the United States,' said McLaren. 'That's where the new teen culture is.'

Thomas said he was familiar with the book – 'it was a huge hit at the time' – but didn't consider it since he didn't make documentaries. 'Malcolm bought me the book and said he had Ridley Scott interested at that stage, I think,' says Thomas. 'I hadn't thought of it as a feature because it wasn't my métier. But as I reflected on it I thought it could work with the right director.'

Meanwhile, *Among the Thugs* was proposed by McLaren as a combination of 'hooliganism and the rave culture that got bound up with it. It's from Ibiza to Millwall and back. It has the uncanny quality of the mob, the drug aspect, and then the aspect that these people who were sent down, as soon as they got out of jail, were the guys organising the raves in Ibiza.'[14]

While the Buford project was never realised, it showed that McLaren's antennae remained atwitch since it was just ahead of the curve of films such as *The Football Factory* and *The Business*, both directed in the mid-2000s by Nick Love, the British filmmaker who has also made the connection between soccer-loving hardmen and Spanish criminality.

Fast Food Nation remained a hot property with McLaren attached, and became his sole focus in the film world when *The Servant* also failed to make it out of development hell.

As McLaren continued to work on the film with Thomas and simultaneously considered what to do with the songs recorded as the basis for 'Diorama', celebrations of the Queen's Golden Jubilee in Britain brought reminders that it was now twenty-five years since 'God Save the Queen' was released. In the interim, Vivienne Westwood and John Lydon had both declared themselves supporters of Her Majesty, while the latter fronted a tour by the reunited Sex Pistols to cash in on the anniversary. Punk had become subsumed, with such symbols of 1977 as Jamie Reid's safety-pin portrait of Queen Elizabeth offering toothless protest.

'Vivienne these days is becoming a bit of an old bat,' sniped McLaren.

She's becoming terribly reactionary. She keeps telling us how the Queen is her favourite person, just because she has an OBE. It's so hypocritical.

The so-called golden jubilee will be nothing more than a beer commercial for fascism. Oxford Street will flaunt images created in the 70s with a safety pin through the Queen's nose, as well as very pretty pictures of the Queen with diamanté-studded slogans that say 'Isn't she brilliant! She's a one-off!' And most people will probably buy them both.[15]

PART IX

Wild Strawberries

Chapter 38

In the autumn of 2002, a chance encounter at a party in Zurich led Malcolm McLaren in a new and encouragingly contemporary musical direction.

'Some friends of mine had a vague relationship with a small-label dude who caught my attention rattling on about lo-fi,' said McLaren. 'He soon had me playing phone tag with a clique of "reversible engineers" working illegally in Stockholm. I didn't know what that meant, but I was eager to find out.'

McLaren had stumbled upon a network of tech-heads who had been creating 'chip music' by sampling the analogue sounds from out-of-date gaming consoles since the 1990s. McLaren learned that the exponents were connected worldwide by a network of websites and fora, and was introduced to French music producers Thierry Criscione and Jacques Fantino, who ran the label Relax Beat.

Criscione and Fantino invited McLaren to their studio in a former warehouse in the south-eastern Paris suburb of Ivry-sur-Seine, where they played him their current project, a concept album about Game Boy music called *Boy Playground*. His response was akin to the first time he heard the New York Dolls: 'It sounds ugly ... but this music is so beautiful!'[1]

'To my surprise, I found myself in an Ali Baba's cave of outdated studio equipment,' wrote McLaren in *Wired*.

The chamber was stuffed floor to ceiling with hardware from the dawn of the 1980s: dinosaurian Amigas and Ataris once prized for their sound chips and arcane applications, giant echo plates, and knob-studded analog synthesisers. In the centre was a pair of dusty turntables, one with a 45-rpm single on its platter. Thierry put the needle to the groove. I reeled as the record player emitted a din like screaming dog whistles. It sounded like a video arcade gone mad.

McLaren likened the experience to the revelation he experienced on attending the Zulu Nation party in the Bronx River House Projects two decades before. He also noted that one of his guides wore a T-shirt with the slogan 'FUCK PRO TOOLS'.

According to McLaren, the phrase 'described perfectly what I'd been feeling for months. Like any fashion victim who comes across a new and stylish idea, I was smitten. Fashion is most easily used as a disguise – it allows you to be something you're not. It's much more difficult to use it to express who you are. I understood immediately that this was no facile fashion statement.'

The chip musicians' interest in vinyl, as evinced by an EP he spotted at Relax Beat by a Stockholm artist called Role Model, fascinated McLaren. 'The last time I had come across this format was in the 1960s, when I bought my first Rolling Stones record,' said McLaren, who recognised that vinyl records offered an authenticity which would soon cross over into the mass market. 'In a world where information is free and experience is virtual, delicate vinyl discs, black and fetishistic, are precious. They're treasured, collectible, real. The fashion for record players is growing – just look at the display window of Colette on the rue Saint-Honoré, or in the pages of *Jalouse* and *Vogue*.'

For McLaren, this 'lost tribe' of musicians using old-fashioned 8-bit technology (Pro-Tools started at 24 bits) represented '*Le Resistance*. Chip musicians plunder corporate technology and find unlikely uses for it. They make old sounds new again – without frills, a recording studio, or a major record label. It would be facile to describe the result as amateurish; it's under-produced because it feels better that way. It's the Nintendo generation sampling its youth.'

Unlike hip-hop in 1981 or New York punk in 1975, chip music had been rumbling for years, generating commercial releases and live acts.

But this didn't diminish McLaren's enthusiasm. Over a few months, McLaren worked with Criscione and Fantino at the Ivry-sur-Seine studio; they produced a number of new tracks including 'Ride a Fashion Horse', which was based on a sample of bluesman Sonny Boy Williamson's 'Mighty Long Time'. This featured contributions from the classically trained Chicago chip musician Mark DeNardo, who had appeared on Criscione and Fantino's Game Boy project and was introduced to McLaren by them.

'We translated the modernist classical music of Francis Poulenc into Game Boy sequences and arpeggios,' wrote McLaren. 'Chip music is mutating into a growing taxonomy of styles – post-karaoke, rock-and-roll Game Boy, bastard blues – that represent the most anarchic display of the antihero in pop culture. The sound is raw, noisy, and at times poorly played and sung. Still, repurposing defunct devices to end-run a music industry in total decline constitutes a revolution. Chip music is the final repository of the marvellous, its makers the last possessors of the wand of Cinderella's fairy godmother.'[2]

This drew fire from the purists; once again McLaren was seen to be exploiting a fertile subculture for his personal gain. Gareth Morris, a 'chiptunes community leader' who recorded as gwEm, lambasted McLaren in an online address that questioned his motives and undercut his claims that the genre was a recent phenomenon.

'In *Wired* you make the statement "then I discovered chip music",' wrote Morris. 'Chip music existed since even before 1977 – the year attributed by many as being the birth of punk. Perhaps you can understand the outrage of many chip musicians that you make this statement – claiming that you personally discovered the music?'[3]

As noted by chiptunes historians Kevin Driscoll and Joshua Diaz, Morris's screed was hampered by minutiae that would have evaded all but the most hardcore aficionado: 'Unfortunately, despite his claims of an "already well developed" style with "25 years of chip music history", Morris's letter does little to clarify McLaren's image of a "video arcade gone mad".'[4]

McLaren was unbothered by such rants as Morris's, having by now embarked on another new venture that was informed by his experiences not only with chip music, but also his 'bastard pop' experimentations and the stillborn Jungk.

According to Peter Culshaw, McLaren recognised that the 8-bit world's 'overall vibe was a little nerdy but then, with the likes of Bill Gates, the nerds have taken over the world. And these were geeks with attitude. Nevertheless, for the scene to go global, clearly it would have to be sexed up a bit, and Malcolm was the man to do it.'[5]

McLaren saw his opening when he was invited by ad agency Ogilvy to visit its Beijing office and work with a female rock group called Wild Strawberries on music for a campaign for one of its clients. 'I had worked hard mashing things up, using those sounds for the purpose of making a record for myself,' said McLaren. 'But I realised it would be much more exciting to have some youthful creatures onstage who would actually take it further, so when I got invited to work with Wild Strawberries I thought, "Well, that's exciting, what can I bring to the table for them?"'[6]

By the early 2000s, the creation of musical acts as branding devices had become an advertising and marketing norm. More than three decades after Malcolm McLaren claimed he put together the Sex Pistols to sell Sex clothing, mavericks such as the Diesel entrepreneur and McLaren's friend Renzo Rosso were getting in on the act. In 2000 Rosso conceived the fictional pop star Joanna to promote his label's jeans, with a model posing as the rocker in performances and in a catalogue published in the form of a scandal sheet reporting her fall from grace after she was turned away from a nightclub for wearing dirty denim; Joanna's single, released by EMI Italy, was, naturally, entitled 'Dirty Country Girl'. The track became a minor hit in a couple of continental European countries, but Joanna soon faded from view, Rosso's construct too postmodern for the target teen audience.

A couple of years later in China, the four-piece thrash guitar band Wild Strawberries were selected as the perfect front for a series of Beijing fashion commercials. The Nirvana-worshipping guitarist Fu

Shuming, known as Ming Ming, had formed the group with bassist Zhang Na in 2000 and recruited the Mongolian drummer and drama-school student Huang Dongmei and keyboard player Chen Chen just a few months before McLaren's arrival in Beijing as their producer in September 2003.

McLaren was still high on the possibilities offered by chip music's collage processes and also had a readymade track in mind: Jungk's cover of 'Foxy Lady', which had been cleared by the Jimi Hendrix Estate.

'Looking back, I launched Jungk too early for a xenophobic music industry,' he told the local press. 'They couldn't understand why anyone would appreciate these strange Chinese voices. Wild Strawberries will shine a light on Beijing in a way people will not anticipate. People in the West won't expect this. Generally when they think of Chinese pop music they think of synthetic, over-produced Canto-pop, which has no integrity.'

The quartet of twenty-year-olds – whose name came from Ming Ming's adoration of Irish rock group the Cranberries – had performed a few times in small clubs in the city, but had never entered a studio before they were corralled by McLaren for a week of rehearsing and recording. A translator was on hand throughout, since the musicians, who had never heard of McLaren or the Sex Pistols, didn't speak English. 'We wondered what this old guy could teach us,' said Zhang. 'But his energy and creativity were amazing. He kept experimenting with different sounds and pushing us harder and harder.'

It's clear that McLaren was genuinely enthusiastic about the project, trotting out quotable lines about Wild Strawberries being part of 'the lo-fi, bastard blues, bastard rock, post-karaoke, rock 'n' roll, Game Boy generation' and comparing them to such back-to-basics acts as White Stripes and the Strokes.

And he was thrilled to be in Beijing. 'This place is a real Gotham City – piping, fuming, polluted skies – definitely a Batman city,' he announced. 'Beijing makes New York feel antiquated. Mark my words. The Eastern invasion is coming.'[7]

With tracks produced by superstar producer Stephen Hague, who had worked on *Fans* in the 1980s, Wild Strawberries were deemed ready for a Western showcase in the early spring of 2004, when McLaren repeated the formula he had applied to Jungk, by booking the Chinese group into a fashion event. This time Pitti Immagine, the seasonal trade fair held in Florence, was chosen. 'Malcolm McLaren's Fashionbeast Party' presented the Wild Strawberries in performance along with such chip musicians as Covox from Stockholm and Belgium's Lo-Bat.

The Beijing band's set duly included 'Foxy Lady' as well as a cover of Serge Gainsbourg's 'Harley-Davidson', as originally recorded by Brigitte Bardot. 'In the mix are bits of old video game bleeps, while the big screens surrounding the stage feature graphics from antiquated arcade games,' wrote Peter Culshaw. 'The whole event fizzes with a kind of glamour that would seem equally at home in Italian *Vogue* or *Wired*, and the audience, a weird mix of computer nerds, fashionistas and alternative Florentines, seems to love it. For once, the new new thing isn't coming from New York, Los Angeles, Paris or London, but Florence via Beijing. The vibe is anti-corporate, DIY and global with just a touch of high-end gloss – and very Malcolm.'[8]

The invite featured Space Invaders-style graphics and McLaren announced that Wild Strawberries releases would appear as 'black and fetishistic' vinyl 45s. The purpose of the appearance was to snare a record company deal; executives from Universal Music and the UK independent Mute Records were in attendance. In the event, none bit and Wild Strawberries returned to the East unsigned, like Jungk before them.

Not that McLaren seemed to care. 'When I do a piece of work I can never be sure if it will last five minutes or five years,' he told Culshaw, who used the Pitti party as the entry point for a wide-ranging twelve-page profile for the UK's *Observer Music Monthly*.

Culshaw described his friend as 'surprisingly uncynical, rather child-like in his enthusiasm for new ideas, constantly trying to explain a world in which he has always felt himself something of a misfit. He is brilliant, funny, usually charming and very good value. He is exasperating and totally chaotic too.'

Despite his international lifestyle and friends and acquaintants all over the world, Culshaw asked whether McLaren was in fact a loner. 'I've always been a misfit in a way,' accepted McLaren. 'Old friends tend to have families, so you don't tend to go on holidays with them, and they have their own lives.' To Culshaw's belief that he took pleasure in being acclaimed as a genius and 'sleeping with beautiful women' McLaren responded: 'But it's not enough. You have to keep working.'

Culshaw declared McLaren 'happier than he has been in years'. This was, he thought, attributable in part to Young Kim's presence. 'She is bright and organised and works with him on the eternal problem of turning a whirlwind of brilliant ideas into reality,' wrote Culshaw, who observed that often their realisation was hampered by the fact that 'McLaren's past never quite leaves him alone'.[9]

One such event turned out to be pleasurable. While visiting television executive Andy Harries in this period, McLaren was accosted by a young woman who jokingly referred to him as her 'father' in the reception of Harries's company. It turned out this was the actress Jodhi May, whose mother Jocelyn Hakim had married McLaren in 1972 so that she could obtain British citizenship. May was born in 1975, long after their separation though her birth surname was registered as Edwards, McLaren's legal name at the time of the union.

McLaren's friend, the educator Graham Brown-Martin, believed that Young Kim was now providing him with 'a rock-like presence. Malcolm wasn't easy by any stretch of the imagination and also needed someone who was dependable, and Young certainly was that.'

Yet, there is a sense that McLaren was never quite comfortable, nor firing on all cylinders, when life was without conflict. As Dorothy Parker wrote in her poem 'Fair Weather', 'They sicken of the calm, who knew the storm', and certainly McLaren continued to thrive on confrontation late into his life.[10] Here was the chaos in which he felt most secure, as was apparent in his quite reasonable decision to fight for credit in the Victoria and Albert

Museum's staging of a huge retrospective of Vivienne Westwood's fashion designs.

Westwood was cut from similar cloth. Contented marriage to Andreas Kronthaler, life no longer in the cramped rented accommodation at Thurleigh Court but a fine Georgian townhouse in Clapham's posh Old Town and international success for her company along with popular acclaim for her work in the twenty years since the split had not dimmed her determination to dimish McLaren's role in her creative life.

Working with V&A fashion curator Claire Wilcox, Westwood displayed this in her instructions against McLaren's name appearing in captions to the clothing they had designed together, as well as in the catalogue, the show guide and on the V&A website. In the book, Westwood mentioned McLaren's name once in her introduction, even though more than a third of the display items – some seventy-plus exhibits – were produced during their time together.

As an expert and historian, Wilcox was duty bound to abide by accuracy and her catalogue overview was more generous to McLaren, accepting he had 'galvanised' Westwood's career and detailing his role in the development of the various retail manifestations as well as the fusing of fashion and music via such ventures as the Sex Pistols and Seditionaries, and Bow Wow Wow and Worlds End.

Nevertheless the cumulative effect of the book, as well as the information and images splashed across the V&A site, was to portray Westwood as the sole creative force in regard to the clothing produced when she was with McLaren. The V&A compounded this by including in the catalogue a glossary of McLaren/Westwood garments held in the museum's collections.

Not one of the 130-plus clothes produced by the pair in the V&A archive – from Let It Rock peg pants, Sex T-shirts and Seditionaries Bondage trousers and muslins to Pirate boots, Savage dresses and Buffalo hats – featured a credit to McLaren.

Once he absorbed the catalogue's import, McLaren and his legal team fired off a volley of letters to the museum, informing, for example, the

V&A's head of publications Mary Butler he was 'shocked and appalled that you've already published this book without ever consulting me, much less gaining my approval. I was never shown text or a proof for my comments and approval [yet] you have used my quotes, my image and my designs.'[11]

The catalogue also blurred the lines around the McLaren years, claiming, for example, that Westwood opened Let It Rock with her former partner in September 1970, eighteen months before McLaren persuaded her to give up her teaching job to join him on the departure of Patrick Casey.

But such omissions amounted to minor quibbles when compared with the museum's failure to credit McLaren in the exhibition itself. This was exacerbated by Wilcox's failure to establish contact with McLaren until a month before the show opened, even though it had been planned for four years.[12]

Wilcox had sent two letters, in December 2003 and January 2004, to the long-vacated 16 Scala Street before striking lucky with talent agent Les Molloy, who McLaren described himself as 'being vaguely acquainted with. He does not represent me. I do not know why you have had difficulty in reaching me since nobody else has had any trouble in this regard. It has been public knowledge for the past two years that I no longer live in London. My email, which has never changed, is publicly listed on the internet.'

McLaren's response on returning from Beijing and viewing the catalogue was to instruct his lawyer Tim Osborne from London practice Wiggin Osborne Fullerlove to seek recourse on several grounds, including copyright infringement.

'It's like calling Dolce & Gabbana simply "Dolce", or Viktor & Rolf simply "Viktor",' railed McLaren. 'And how about calling the Victoria and Albert the "Victoria"? Through this exhibit, the V&A is effectively erasing my life and destroying my career and legacy. Vivienne Westwood became the fashion designer she is today because of what she learned from our partnership and my inspiration and guidance.'[13]

The V&A's legal department accepted that the book contained factual inaccuracies and committed to make corrections in future editions, while

Wilcox apologised not only for the false information that was repeated on the museum's website – which included a huge number of errors in terms of dating as well as at least one fake garment – and in the show guide, but also in quotes, attributed to her by the *Independent* newspaper, that omitted McLaren's involvement. Wilcox blamed the journalist for not including quotes by her which, she claimed, would have corrected the impression she gave.[14]

'Why on earth I was never consulted on my own work, I do not understand,' McLaren thundered to Wilcox.

I am not credited for the early catwalk shows though I was totally involved in all aspects. They were not solo shows by Vivienne as the V&A website suggests. Furthermore, all the shops I personally conceived, named, designed and created do not mention my name at all. For your information I was co-designer and co-owner of all designs during this partnership and obviously remain so. You have only to look at the labels between 1980–83 where it clearly states my name on the clothing itself to figure this out!

I shouldn't have to tell you this since you are the senior curator of modern fashion.[15]

By now extremely suspicious, McLaren requested copies of the labels that would accompany each exhibit, but Wilcox declined on the basis that 'it would not be appropriate'. Just over a week before the show opened, the museum agreed to insert 'By Malcolm McLaren and Vivienne Westwood' on all labels 'deemed relevant'.

To add insult to injury, the museum sent the invitation for McLaren to attend the private view to the wrong address, and so he insisted on travelling to London to view the show before the opening.

McLaren was furious, particularly at the hastily inserted attempts to fix the label credits; by some accounts Wilcox was reduced to tears, though the museum declined to change the text on the information panels since they were made of metal and formed 'an inherent part of the architecture'. These remained riddled with inaccuracies and more credit omissions throughout the three-month run, though a sentence was added: 'All outfits designed by Malcolm McLaren and Vivienne Westwood'.

Just before the show was opened to the public, McLaren warned the V&A director Mark Jones that his lawyers 'were champing at the bit to sue' and, on the day of the private view, he issued a press release via his website accusing the museum of complicity in deception and claiming the museum 'constantly stalled for time, doing just the minimum to placate me'.

McLaren didn't progress his legal threats. This would have been costly and, anyway, the show was up-and-running within days of the row developing. Instead he took to the media, describing the garments produced with Westwood as 'labours of love. We made everything ourselves; we customised the items in our bathroom and kitchen in Clapham. We tore pieces of material, but they were beautifully torn. Maybe Vivienne doesn't remember. Maybe they were too close to her relationship with me.'

He also derided Wilcox's efforts to make amends. 'All they did was take a few white cards, print my name on them and put them on the floor next to certain things,' claimed McLaren. 'They didn't agree to change the text in the catalogue or to amend their archive. I'm not going to have some curator write me out of history.'[16]

Given Westwood's 'national treasure' status, McLaren was shouting into the void. The exhibition received plaudits from fashion and general press, and became one of the best-attended events in the museum's history, travelling to several overseas venues in the ensuing years and setting the scene for the venue's highly commercial, though curatorially suspect, juggernaut pop-culture shows such as that dedicated to David Bowie in 2013.

And his attack on the show caused a further rift not only with Westwood, but also Joe Corré, who had sourced items for it and was defensive over McLaren's denigration.

McLaren was right to be concerned that the catalogue and show would have the lasting impact of downplaying his contribution. The V&A only fixed the attributions for the clothing in its collection in 2013, some three years after his death. Westwood did not formally acknowledge this until the following year, when her company staff, under pressure from the Malcolm McLaren Estate, amended the timeline of her fashion career on her official website to more accurately reflect the duration of their partnership.

Some might speculate that McLaren had invited this lack of respect for the part he played in Westwood's life and work, given his tendency to mock her and willingness to cast himself as a Svengali figure who leeched the talents of others. But the mid-2000s had witnessed a character change; as he approached sixty, McLaren's feelings of self-worth rose and he adopted a more mature attitude to his achievements. 'It's my legacy and now I've got to face it,' he said during this period.

Consolation over the lack of recognition in the Westwood exhibition arrived in the form of a McLaren song being featured prominently in Quentin Tarantino's hit film sequel *Kill Bill: Vol. 2*.

'About Her' was the slow-mo trip-hop composite of the Zombies and Bessie Smith McLaren had demo-ed for 'Diorama' a few years previously; produced by Stephen Hague it made for a majestic track in Tarantino's movie.

McLaren had met the puckish American director by chance when Tarantino was premiering *Kill Bill: Vol. 1* in Paris and a reluctant McLaren was persuaded by Young Kim to pass on a CD of his latest music to the film director. Inclusion on the big-selling soundtrack provided a much-needed fillip, and McLaren was in high spirits when encountered by video-game designer and film critic Theresa Duncan for a piece for *Artforum* around the time of the film's release.

Duncan found McLaren 'impeccably dressed, his youth magically preserved like the Countess Bathory's (does he, too, bathe in virgin's blood?)' as she interviewed him at the Café de Flore. There was, Duncan later wrote, a consistent line from his recent chip-music investigations to the musical montages of 1983's *Duck Rock* LP.

'The nomadic life of McLaren and the Game Boy musicians and the mercurial nature of their music and thus far primarily Web-based distribution techniques make for a nascent subcultural current that is (perhaps deliberately) difficult to pin down,' wrote Duncan. 'But the use of this inexpensive, discarded digital technology (the first Game Boy programmers found their secondhand machines in Paris's *puces*) is no doubt meant to challenge that primary symbol of baby-boomer rebellion – the guitar.'

Duncan drew a line from McLaren's place in 8-bit music to his punk pioneering of the 1970s. 'For decades the art world was unperturbed by all manner of scatology and profanity, but the appearance of digital art got middle-aged critics harrumphing,' said Duncan. 'And, if punk rock delivered the first blow to the record industry, it is software engineers in their 20s creating primitive digital production tools and file-sharing technology on their basement computers who are poised to deliver the coup de grace.'

McLaren told Duncan: 'Using whatever tools are available, running your electricity in from a pole out on the sidewalk. It's DIY. It's punk.'[17]

This enduring anarchic stance was not incompatible with McLaren's increased acceptance in hifalutin circles in New York and Paris. Consequently, he was among the attendees of the funeral of Susan Sontag, the so-called 'Dark Lady' of literary criticism who he had dined with on New Year's Day 2003 in Paris. Sontag was interred in Montparnasse Cemetery, a fact which impressed McLaren. 'To be buried in Montparnasse is not an easy job,' he said.

It's not a big cemetery. There's no space. They must have dug someone up who was less illustrious and sent him off to the suburbs. Maybe a lesser-known poet from the 19th century. She had this grave that was right bang in the middle, round the corner from her was Samuel Beckett. To the left was Serge Gainsbourg. And I thought, 'She's got the best seat in the house!'

It was quite extraordinary. But when you left this cemetery, you definitely preferred to be alive. It's like what Balzac said – he used to go for walks in cemeteries and it would cheer him up. He'd walk around Père Lachaise then go for a nice big lunch.[18]

It was McLaren's own pleasure in sensual experiences that prompted a return to St Barth's with Young Kim at the end of 2004; he admitted this was 'the most decadent thing . . . besotted by so many pretty things, I was immediately transported back to the Cote d'Azur in the sixties.'

Once again, he was part of a set which ran from producer and arranger Quincy Jones and Def Jam founder Russell Simmons to actors Robert Downey Jr and Uma Thurman, fashion designer Tom Ford, singer Bryan Ferry, film directors Quentin Tarantino, George Lucas and his former sponsor Steven Spielberg, and even the son of Libyan dictator Muammar Gaddafi. 'Night and day, everybody is doing everything to everyone everywhere,' McLaren wrote delightedly in a diary. 'I bumped into Nick Rhodes, a Duran Durannie, and he's still wearing all his pan stick and eyeliner. Quite a feat in the heat! I do love him, though. He darlings everybody, always with a silent teenage girl in tow.'

McLaren also noted the fashion stylist Isabella Blow 'queened out in her Joan Crawford gold lamé bathing suit and diamante studded stilettos', her husband Detmar Blow 'sat shrouded in a Philip Treacy sun hat. Detmar is hysterically critical, refuses to be clever, an absolute English invention, extraordinarily funny although he doesn't know it' and Giorgio Armani strolling on the beach 'in his ever-so-brief black bathing trunks, ultra-tanned chest and the toned body of a 30-year-old. Astonishing.'[19]

McLaren was still fizzing with excitement about the trip to St Barth's in the early spring of 2005 when he was visited in Paris by the Dutch journalists Jop van Bennekom and Gert Jonkers.

Their gay erotica photography magazine *Butt* had taken the print publishing world by storm, and Van Bennekom and Jonkers were dedicated to ensnaring McLaren for the first issue of their soon-to-be-launched menswear title *Fantastic Man*.

Noting that paparazzi were forbidden on the island, McLaren cast an anthropological eye over its visitors and the reasons why his stay was so pleasurable. Much of this, he believed, was because it had once been part of Guadeloupe, an overseas department of France.

'One good thing about the French is that they make everything French wherever they go and they do it much better than anyone else does,' said McLaren. 'You go to the equivalent English island and it's all kind of rough and the food is naff and the native islanders hate them. So you get a lot of angry islanders who were once African slaves and they haven't forgiven the English.

'But in St Barth's you have nothing but the French because it was a desert island and nothing could grow on it. The soil wasn't good. It doesn't have that bad vibe.'

Admitting that the cost of the holiday approached $5,000 a day ('Getting close. You can do it on a budget'), McLaren told van Bennekom and Jonkers that one night he and Kim joined a party on Paul Allen's notorious megayacht *Octopus*. During the evening the Microsoft founder entertained attendees with a set on guitar backed by session musicians flown in from Nashville.

'You were the most expensive rent-a-crowd ever,' said McLaren. 'It's like Paris meets Hollywood in the Caribbean with people flying down from the New York art set. And on the island there's this little shopping strip with all these Hermès, Louis Vuitton, Bulgari, Dior stores, all shack-like. It's not like Paris. They're selling the same stuff, but shopping grass hut-style! It's a tax-free island. You think it's gross but it's cool.'[20]

Chapter 39

When he was visited in Paris by *Fantastic Man*'s van Bennekom and Jonkers, Malcolm McLaren revealed that he was planning not only a return to the film business but also to live again in Los Angeles, this time with Young Kim.

'We have our eye on this condo in Venice, one street off the beach,' he told the Dutch pair.

It's the best air in town, down in Venice. The air's shit in LA and the light is harsh. It's almost like there is a hole in the sky. You are permanently wearing sunglasses. Down in Venice the light's a little softer. And there's a sea breeze blowing all the shit away, and you can walk. It's the only part of LA where you can walk. You don't have to drive to get a pint of milk.

Bit of a clamber up the motorway to Hollywood if you are doing business or to Bev Hills, but it's a nice area. Living in LA, people don't talk to you. People spend so much time in cars they don't know how to communicate. Venice is more of a community. People talk to you. It's a cooler place. You don't have the space there and you won't get very big apartments. I don't need a big space as long as I can get a decent studio.[1]

McLaren was contemplating this move because he was once more a Hollywood player now that *Fast Food Nation* was heading into production with *Slackers* and *School of Rock* director Richard Linklater on board, the Austin-based filmmaker having been suggested by McLaren. Both Linklater and the writer Eric Schlosser agreed with McLaren's concept of the film adopting a dramatic narrative in place of the book's reportage but, as it turned out, weren't happy to work with him on the day-to-day business of filmmaking, so the move to LA didn't transpire.

With Linklater and Schlosser's approval, producer Jeremy Thomas decreed that McLaren – who retained his own producer credit – should not be involved once the shoot was underway. Thomas's actions appear to have been informed by his experiences working with McLaren on *The Great Rock 'n' Roll Swindle* all those years before.

'There was some argy-bargy,' says Thomas. 'I knew how to work my world. I couldn't make the film with Malcolm there, with all his guessing and second-guessing and willingness to destroy what he had created. I didn't know whether that impulse was still within him, but I couldn't risk it.'

It seems unnecessarily harsh to have judged McLaren on the fraught circumstances of a quarter of a century back in time, where one of the principals refused to appear in the film and another was arrested for murder and subsequently died of an overdose during production.

But Thomas defends his decision. 'When you're making a movie there's an inside and outside the citadel,' he explains. 'When you're inside, you have to love it and protect it from those outside who are trying to get in and kill it.'

So did Thomas suspect that this was McLaren's aim? He won't say, but this was clearly his suspicion, though Thomas denies that he opted McLaren out of the film he had conceived. 'I opted Malcolm *in*,' claims Thomas. 'I just couldn't let him be involved in the process of shooting the movie. There was no place for him in script rewrites or the direction.'

McLaren was quite reasonably upset that the version of *Fast Food Nation* delivered by Linklater didn't accord with his vision, and the diplomatic Thomas allows for McLaren's disgruntlement. 'He was on the edge of being unhappy about it, because it wasn't what he had envisaged,' says Thomas. 'I don't know whether he ever came to the set. Maybe he was very busy on other projects during the making of the film.'

That's as maybe, but having been blocked from involvement in the production, it is hardly surprising that McLaren didn't visit. After all, this was the second occasion involving Thomas where he had been effectively removed from a film project he had originated, with a repeat of any acclaim going to others.

There were, as usual, a number of other activities on McLaren's plate, including a plan once more to address the writing of his autobiography. McLaren told *Fantastic Man*'s van Bennekom and Jonkers that he was intending to get together with a literary editor in Berlin in the summer of 2005, and that the resultant tome would be a tell-all, including such revelations as his claims of arson of the Goldsmiths library in the early 1970s.

Once again, the book didn't happen, though a long-form email dialogue with the Belgian fashion designer Martin Margiela – or in fact representatives of his 'house', Maison Margiela – provided autobiographical insights when published by the *New York Times T Magazine* in the spring of that year.

The self-confessed fashion victim had long been a Margiela fan. 'His trousers are very nicely cut; a very 19th century Incroyable mixed with a stovepipe. They are a marriage of the two,' said McLaren. 'They have no waistband. Even if you are a little plump, Margiela's trousers make you look quite elegant.'[2]

And the e-conversation with Maison Margiela included ruminations on events, both distant and recent, that McLaren was evidently turning over for his book: the 'benign failure' encounter with the arts teacher at Harrow, the King's Road promenade by 'The Boy in the Blue Lamé Suit', Marianne Faithfull playing Sid Vicious's mother in *The Great Rock 'n' Roll Swindle*, the theory of 'Shoppertainment', 'Diorama', his involvement in the chip-music scene, *Kill Bill 2*'s inclusion of 'About Her', all were thrown into the mix.

'Television has been eclipsing all cultural institutions and life itself for some time,' wrote McLaren to Margiela. 'But the digital generation has struck a blow to the heart of television, and there is no stopping, now that the Internet is free. No matter how much government and industry

try together to control the new media, the Internet's inherent lawlessness is its appeal, its sexiness. We are seizing the automated stuff of our world: I am excited.'[3]

During a visit to LA for meetings on *Fast Food Nation* and Wild Strawberries, McLaren accepted an invitation to appear on *Jonesy's Jukebox*, the local FM radio show fronted by Steve Jones. Over the previous couple of years the former Sex Pistol had gained a cult following for his humorous, freewheeling style and non-playlist format. His guests were usually culled from the city's rock fraternity, with a fair proportion in recovery from drugs and alcohol abuse like their host, so McLaren was something of an outlier.

His hour-long appearance made for entertaining listening; the pair hadn't seen each other for at least two decades and Jones was affectionate and extremely animated. And their barely suppressed peals of laughter lent the encounter an edge of hysteria.

McLaren was on good form, talking about his mayoral bid, chip music and the rhythmic qualities of Mongolian drummers, while Jones maintained a comical refrain of 'Where's the money Malcolm?!' to much guffawing.

Meantime, McLaren theatrically delivered stories about the meeting with Bradley Mendelson that led to his occupancy of 430 King's Road, the formation of the Pistols, the recruitment of John Lydon and the recording of the vocal for 'You Need Hands' with the suspicious Mickie Most.

At one stage, Jones asked McLaren whether he could recall being driven by the Sex Pistol to East End tailors to pick up suits for Let It Rock, as well as their visits to the Roebuck pub and the Speakeasy nightclub. 'They were the early days which shaped and formed you,' McLaren told Jones. 'They turned you in to a true rascal. Now you're Artful Dodger-ing it all around LA on this radio show.'[4]

Back in Paris McLaren returned to recording at Ivry-sur-Seine and socialised with friends such as the French-British artist Philippe Bradshaw, who had attended Goldsmiths at the same time as Damien

Hirst and arrived in Paris in the early 2000s after living a harum-scarum existence on the fringes of the YBA pack in London, creating art pieces from 'amateur porn, grotesque sex toys, throwaway debris, KY wrestling and techno music'.[5]

McLaren and Bradshaw enjoyed each other's company, frequenting such offbeat premises as Paris's only lesbian tapas bar. The older man spent time talking Bradshaw through his various personal dramas and was pleased when his career took a turn for the better with a collaboration with the choreographer Merce Cunningham, commissions from major collectors and exhibitions at key European galleries. As a result, McLaren was affected by Bradshaw's death at the age of thirty-nine in the late summer of 2005. The artist went missing from his apartment one Friday and his body was found in the Seine two days later, an apparent suicide.

A few months after Bradshaw's sad demise, McLaren was presented with a lawsuit from a French engineer named Benjamin Béduneau, who had assisted in the production of the first version of 'About Her' three years previously.

By claiming £70,000 in lost earnings on the basis that he had written the track, Béduneau was on very sticky ground. He admitted that McLaren had paid him to render on a synthesiser the melody from Francis Poulenc's composition 'Improvisation no. 13 in A Minor' and incorporate it with the Bessie Smith and Zombies samples selected by McLaren. That he registered the work in his own name with the French recording rights society Sacem did not give him authorship over the demo, then known as 'Smith Ballad'.

This had been intended for McLaren's 'Diorama' musical, but formed the basis for 'About Her' when McLaren collaborated with producer Stephen Hague.

McLaren's lawyer Bruno Ryterband told a court in Angers, western France, that his client was the true author of the song, since Béduneau had carried out McLaren's instructions. 'In the same way that Picasso, when he made collages, was considered to be a painter, Malcolm McLaren is a producer who uses musical collages,' said Ryterband, who persuaded the court to dismiss Béduneau's claim on the basis that he did not 'compose the melodic line of the piece, which is inspired by a work of Francis Poulenc'.[6]

The Béduneau case proved a distraction from an unexpected venture into upmarket children's clothing with the Fashionbeast label McLaren had developed with Young Kim to market '8-bit fashion'. Manufactured and sold by Italian online retailer Yoox, the collection of knits was aimed at four- to twelve-year-olds and featured graphics of Space Invader-style creatures and retailed at $275 for a sweater and $130 for a ski hat.

'Before passing judgment on Mr McLaren's suitability as a fashion role model for children, one should consider this: If children are taking their cues from Britney Spears and Jessica Simpson, how bad can he be?' asked the *New York Times* fashion reporter Eric Wilson.

McLaren explained to Wilson that he had been inspired by chip music.

'I'm so bored and uninterested in the real world, one that is looking less attractive to me by the hour,' he said. 'I was searching for the new, listening for the sound of whatever was happening, and what I found was so close to children's culture that I wanted to communicate with this whole new generation. Children dominate the culture like never before, whether in film, music or art. The intellectual vanguard today might just be under the age of 13. It's frightening, but kind of wild.'[7]

To coincide with the launch of the kids' range and Yoox's fifth anniversary, McLaren organised the release of a 10-inch vinyl mini LP, which featured Wild Strawberries' 'Foxy Lady', a track recorded with the chip musician Bubblyfish and, in recognition of the debt he owed to them for setting him on his latest musical path, two tracks from Jacques Fantino and Thierry Criscione's concept album *Boy Playground*.

The Fashionbeast garments, which were produced in limited runs, sold out, though he and Kim did not revisit the concept with another collection. As online commentators pointed out, consumers of clothing containing references to 8-bit culture were more likely to be in their thirties with children of their own.[8]

However innocent McLaren's intentions for Fashionbeast clothes, they passed under the general media radar, and his reputation as a Svengali and pop-cultural magpie continued to be foregrounded in the substantial British broadsheet profiles he commanded.

One such, by feature writer Ginny Dougary in *The Times*, recounted John Lydon's description of McLaren as 'the most evil man on earth or, according to everyone else, amoral'.

McLaren, now sixty, didn't bother countering this view, and told Dougary that his proudest achievement was

the moment when I was able to imitate my grandmother's imagination. It was what ultimately inspired me to go to art school in the first place and discover a new way of looking at life and then putting it into practice. You see, my grandmother really loved chaos and really loved discomfort. When she thought everybody was uncomfortable that was always most attractive to her because that was when she thought people really revealed themselves. And I always believed in that aspect.

According to McLaren, this meant that he was 'always going to be a loner' and Dougary pressed him on whether he had ever loved anybody. His surprising answer, particularly since he had been with Young Kim for several years, was Vivienne Westwood.

'But I find it hard to look at people as people that you are meant to love,' said McLaren.

I think I have the words 'willing prey' stamped on my forehead because if you don't have strong enough connections to family, you're always looking for connection. You are very open, and so some people get attached to you very quickly and get very possessive of you because you're easily possessed. And then you're also easily able to discard and people get very hurt by that, which is a problem I've found during my life. So it's not that you prostitute yourself, you just don't quite have that sense of belonging. You don't quite have that ability to be loyal to your friends.

Dougary asked McLaren whether he intended to make more of an effort with his son Joe. 'I think that is something that I'm beginning to face,' said McLaren tentatively. 'It concerns me, probably more than it ever has in my entire life and times, with him and without him, and I'm attempting – I think that's the best word to use – to try to help, if it's not too late, to make him feel appreciated. Simple as that, really. I don't think he does for some reason.'

The reason was clear to anyone with even a cursory knowledge of this particular father-and-son relationship, given McLaren's prolonged absences and regular denigration of Corré's mother, but there now appeared at least a willingness to make amends.

McLaren told Dougary that he felt more vulnerable as a result of hitting sixty, but that he had not given up on the precept that had determined his life. 'It is hard to be bad. You do have to work at it,' he exclaimed.

And, yes, my grandmother was right. Who wants to be good? Tony Blair's good, and he's horrible.

Whenever I've not listened to authority, I've always felt much more attractive as a person and I've always felt that the decisions I've made may have been hellish or extremely provocative or confrontational, but ultimately they've been pretty worthwhile.

And so, yes, I prefer to be bad.[9]

The repetition of this line served to undermine McLaren's credibility in establishment quarters. When the Costume Institute of New York's Metropolitan Museum of Art staged a punk-based mega-show *AngloMania: Tradition and Transgression in British Fashion* in the spring of 2006, he wasn't invited while the likes of John Lydon and Vivienne Westwood were feted by the exhibition organisers such as *Vogue* editor

Anna Wintour, despite the fact that the majority of the clothes on display were designed by him and Westwood.

The irony is that the dubious provenance of many of the garments, whose purchase had been personally overseen by Costume Institute curator Andrew Bolton, eventually led to widescale reclassification: in 2014, the designation of thirty items that had been recorded as authentic was changed to 'attributed to' McLaren and Westwood, while two Bondage suits, acquired specifically for *AngloMania*, were 'de-accessioned', since they were determined to be questionable.[10]

In 2006 Malcolm McLaren was asked by the American video artist Jeremy Blake to become the subject of one of his 'cinematic portraits'.

McLaren knew Blake through his partner, the video-games designer Theresa Duncan, who had written the *Artforum* profile of McLaren a couple of years previously.

McLaren was first introduced to Duncan in New York in the late 1990s. 'She was just about to venture off to Hollywood and her agent wanted me to meet her,' recalled McLaren later. 'I found her vivacious, full of herself. Incredibly self-confident, but also innocent about the world she was getting herself into. She had an idea for a movie, a fashion-driven, coming-of-age story called "Alice Underground". The unexpected thing about Theresa, though, was her mind. For all her youth-culture thing, when she spoke she had real curiosity. She was intellectually driven.'[11]

Through the early 2000s, McLaren came to know the golden couple – both striking-looking with wild streaks – when they lived in Hollywood. Eventually, Duncan became frustrated over the obstacles she found placed in her way during the development of a script and she and Blake began to act strangely. Among their claims was that the Church of Scientology was responsible for an array of problems in their personal life because an association with the rock-star Scientologist Beck had gone sour.

'She seemed a bit naïve about Hollywood,' McLaren told *Vanity Fair*, reflecting as much on his own fruitless spells in Los Angeles as Duncan's.

'She went in hoping people would listen to her, but in Hollywood you're the one who has to listen.'[12]

All the while, Blake was making a name for himself with his hallucinatory digital art, the pinnacle of which was arguably the 2002–4 *Winchester* trilogy, about the sinister Californian gothic house built in the late nineteenth century by the heiress to the rifle-manufacturing fortune as a shelter to the ghosts of all those who had perished as a result of her family business.

The seductive, filmic aspects of Blake's work, and the ways in which he blended imagery with soundscapes, impressed McLaren, who was also struck by the qualities summarised by the American critic Deven Golden: 'Watching a video this way ceases to be a scheduled event. Instead, one has the opportunity, the luxury, of absorbing the artwork over time, in different moods, in a variety of circumstances, even in that odd moment out of the corner of your eye. You can enter the work at any point and leave at any point.'[13]

So McLaren was delighted when Blake proposed a portrait to be called *Glitterbest* after McLaren's Sex Pistols-era management company. Intent on exploring 'the originality, flamboyance and pioneering work of a cultural icon', the artist aimed to incorporate a voiceover of McLaren delivering a Duncan-written 'mad stream of consciousness' over the collaged video elements.[14]

According to the American critic Dan Levin, Blake 'soon began to recognize phrases and words that corresponded to imagery and references from Mr McLaren's life growing up in post-war Britain and his time as the Sex Pistols' flamboyant manager, a cheeky, roguish figure who personified the late 1970s. There was also a larger theme among the layers: that of recasting a quintessentially anti-establishment figure as a hero of the British Empire for his wild creative contributions.'[15]

Returned to New York, the couple succumbed to rampant paranoia and in July 2007 the forty-year-old Duncan was found lifeless in their East Village apartment. She had overdosed on prescription drugs and alcohol. A week later, Blake, thirty-five, walked into the Atlantic Ocean at Rockaway Beach; his body was found by a local fisherman five days later.

The *Glitterbest* portrait was intended for exhibition at a Washington, DC gallery in the autumn of 2007 but remains unfinished. Fragments, including still images of McLaren's and Sid Vicious's heads grafted onto nineteenth-century military portraits, were later shown as part of a retrospective show of Blake's work.[16]

In the aftermath of the double tragedy McLaren gratuitously speculated on Blake's sexuality. 'If we're being honest Jeremy was gay,' he told the *Independent*. 'I don't think his relationship with Theresa was all that sexual. She was a mother to him. When I saw them in Hollywood, he was always terribly concerned that people would think he was a fag – he walked around with this hip flask of whisky in his pocket and he was constantly swigging from it, like some kind of cowboy.'[17]

Blake's methods in creating social and historical visual pile ups emulated McLaren's long-term practice across a range of disciplines, but now he began applying them to the film installations that would return him to the formal status of artist in the final years of his life.

Chapter 40

In the spring of 2007, Malcolm McLaren and Jeremy Blake were interviewed together for a news report on British television network ITV. This made passing mention of the work-in-progress *Glitterbest*; the point of the broadcast was to flag McLaren's participation in the latest of the reality shows that dominated Western television in the 2000s.

The production and realisation of this programme, entitled *The Baron*, was to be fraught with problems, not least physical threats to McLaren by a mob of angry villagers as well as the death after filming of one of the leads. But *The Baron* marked the start of a brief and fascinating phase in McLaren's later life. He had delighted in mixing high and low culture ever since his first exhibition at Keith Albarn's Kingly Street gallery in 1967, but during the next year or so he seesawed even more dramatically between pursuing fine art projects (by this time he was serving as a contemporary arts consultant to the posh auction house Phillips de Pury) and simultaneously indulging his obsession with mass media.

The principal attraction was money to fund his artistic endeavours. Paid handsomely for his participations in reality shows, McLaren was also genuinely interested in disrupting the ruling pop-cultural form of the era. And so the allure of showcasing his avant-garde provocations to the widest possible audience proved irresistible.

In many respects, *The Baron* wasn't an auspicious start to this plan. The unfamiliar territory in which the celebrities were placed was the God-fearing Scottish fishing village of Gardenstown in Aberdeenshire. McLaren agreed to compete for the courtesy title of 13th Baron of Troup against the cockney actor/comedian Mike Reid, who had a long-running role in the popular soap *EastEnders*, and anodyne British pop singer Suzanne Shaw.

Each contestant stayed with a family in the village, which had 800 residents and five churches; the avowedly atheist McLaren, uncomfortably, was made to room with a group of Evangelical Christians. The format of the show demanded the winner be voted by locals on the basis of personal encounters and a public 'election' address.

This promised an opportunity to revisit the various manifestos of McLaren's life, not least that of the London mayoral campaign, but, within a few days, McLaren had alienated villagers – none of whom had heard of him – by declaring a 'Sinner's Day, for all to have sex like crazy', and annoyed one fisherman in particular by painting the encircled anarchist 'A' sign on the side of his boat.

This was small beer, but the election address enabled McLaren to provoke the jeering villagers en masse. He opened his speech by describing their home as 'absolutely boring, the worst place I've ever been to in my entire life, I'm sick to death already and I've only been here a few days.'

To growing catcalls and boos, McLaren played up the pantomime aspects of his character by announcing his aim to become 'the wickedest, baddest, most hooligan-ish and sexiest Baron ever. You need a bad Baron to change your culture and your beliefs. I suggest you give over your village to the hedonistic cannabis growers who live on the edges.'

McLaren also proposed the annual construction of a folkloric wicker man on the beach. He suggested the villagers should sit around this at night and 'take lots of drugs and drink yourselves stupid'. At this point Gardenstown harbourmaster Michael Watt leapt to the stage and attempted to manhandle the candidate away from the microphone. Eventually he succeeded, but not before McLaren shouted, 'I'd like to transform Gardenstown into a heathen's paradise,' and finished with the exclamation, 'Don't you know Jesus Christ is a sausage?'

It was this statement that prompted the production company's security to intervene as Watt grabbed McLaren by the neck and swung him around by his anorak. Not that the harbourmaster, the townsfolk, the TV crew or the viewers were to know, but in uttering the blasphemy

McLaren was, in fact, quoting from a stunt by the early twentieth-century German Dadaist prankster Johannes Baader.

The television channel was satisfied that it had suitably sensationalist material, particularly when the Revd Donald Martin, a Church of Scotland minister, confirmed that the locals were 'horrified' by McLaren, but Mike Reid's death by heart attack during post-production delayed the broadcast of the series by a year.[1] Soon after leaving Gardenstown, McLaren gave his opinion of its inhabitants, any affection for the land of his fathers evidently dissipated by the experience. 'You never saw such deformed, awful-looking creatures,' said McLaren. 'It was an absolutely sorrowful place. Never, ever go to Scotland if you can help it.'[2]

Contrast *The Baron* with the project that engaged McLaren on his return to New York.

After he gave a talk on punk and contemporary art at an Art Basel event in the city, McLaren received an invitation from Stefan Brüggemann to participate in a group exhibition the Mexican artist was organising for autumn 2007 at Chelsea's I-20 Gallery.

Brüggemann – who also invited France's Pierre Bismuth, Britain's Turner Prize winner Martin Creed and Greece's Miltos Manetas to participate – called his show *Shallow* and asked the contributors to deliver works that reflected 'speed thinking and the acceleration of ideas reacting within the boundaries of hyper-contemporary culture'.[3]

'The word shallow', often used to describe pop culture, was a useful beginning,' wrote McLaren the following year.

A pubescent experience of outrageous sexual thoughts began to assault my senses, encouraging me to remember and imagine how it was when I first heard a rock 'n' roll record – how it liberated me to feel sexy with everyone and everything, and then have sex with no-one.

No matter how shallow people say pop music is, and in particular its origins (part organised crime, part teenage werewolf), it continues to confound, astound and seduce something deep within all of us. No matter how shallow people say sex is, it continues to occupy and post-occupy everyone's thoughts, forcing us to be irresponsible, childish and everything this society hates, and why not? Let's be shallow, I thought.[4]

McLaren's response to the brief merged sex and pop in a film installation comprising eight portentous works he described as 'musical paintings'. McLaren worked with a film editor on found footage extracted from a variety of 1960s and 1970s porn movies. In keeping with the *Shallow* theme, he focused on segments that were shot before the participants in the films had sex: characters smoking, sipping coffee, lounging on sofas and descending sets of stairs naked.

By slowing the film speed and repeating certain sequences, the anticipation was heightened and a painterly quality was introduced to what had previously been ephemeral visual material. And here at last was a permanent home for the aural collages he had compiled over recent years; McLaren cut the films to such tracks as 'Mexico, Manhattan & Malibu' and Jungk's version of 'Foxy Lady'.

There was a practical reason for McLaren's slo-mo approach, as he explained to his friend, the New York arts writer Glenn O'Brien. 'I couldn't find images that sustained in real time the length of the pop songs that I had already cut up and remade,' said McLaren.

I couldn't find images of people about to have sex that sufficiently interested me for that length of time. But if I slowed the image down, it started to make sense to me. It didn't matter that they didn't move to the groove or to the rhythm. In fact, I was glad for that because I didn't want them to fall into sync.

I more or less worked toward something in the three- to three-and-a-half-minute range of time, and then I just slapped one of these cut-up musical pieces on it that I felt might work. I instinctively went for what, at that second, seemed like marrying the two – the image and the sound.[5]

The films were well received when installed at the I-20 Gallery along-side such companion pieces as Brüggemann's 1997 vinyl text, which read 'From anything to anything in no time', Bismuth's circle-pierced wall installation entitled *Something Less, Something More* and Creed's shallow-planed work on A4 paper.

McLaren's inclusion in the exhibition marked a sea-change in the art-world perspective on him. Although he had personally known many of the young artists who rose to prominence on both sides of the Atlantic in the 1980s and 1990s, the pervading view of McLaren up until this point may be summarised by British art critic Matthew Collings' take: 'Let's face it, he always seems a bit tiresome.'[6]

O'Brien hailed McLaren's contribution to *Shallow* as proof of his artistic status. 'McLaren has been on the leading edge of art since the 70s, but back then, it wasn't so easy for people to understand that managing a rock band, even one that was a total media event – the Sex Pistols – could be art,' wrote O'Brien in *Interview*. 'But now he's come out of the closet and made it official: Malcolm McLaren is an artist.'

McLaren confessed to O'Brien his nervousness about joining the exhibition. 'At first, I really wasn't sure my finished product worked,' he said. 'For the first time in a very, very, very, long time, I was extremely shy about showing any of my work! I finally went down to the gallery to meet the other artists who were installing. I showed one – only one – which was two people watching other people having sex, to gauge the reaction. They liked it. I was very happy.'[7]

The process of constructing the films was painstaking, but McLaren was so encouraged by the I-20 show that he resolved to expand the number in the installation and exhibit it elsewhere.

Meantime, he had established a presence on BBC Radio as a broad-caster, drawing on his life story to front a series of programmes made with London production house Just Radio. Among these was Malcolm McLaren's *Musical Map of London* and his *Musical Map of Los Angeles*, which both won Sony Gold Awards for best UK radio features.

Later, McLaren was to spend several days looking back at his life for a three-hour New Year's Day show for the network's 6 Music channel. In this he not only claimed that he had shouted 'Pierre Cardin!' at the Beatles when he saw them perform in their collarless suits in the early 1960s but that he gave John Lennon his white silk suit in New York in the mid-1970s (this anecdote being based, of course, on Bob Gruen's memory of borrowing McLaren's Let It Rock zoot jacket to attend the Grammys).

Within days of *Shallow* closing at the Chelsea gallery, the high art/low culture pendulum swung the other way and McLaren was on the eastern coast of Australia preparing to join the cast of the latest series of Britain's hit primetime show *I'm a Celebrity . . . Get Me Out of Here*.

The programme-makers recognised that McLaren's reputation and ability to cause a fuss – as seen in his participation in *The Baron* – would boost viewing figures, so offered him £350,000, the show's biggest partic-ipation fee to date (McLaren had initially demanded £500,000).

This was to some extent justified; McLaren was much more well-known than the likes of TV soap star Gemma Atkinson, former boyband member Jason J. Brown and PR supremo (and model for *Absolutely Fabulous*'s Edina) Lynne Franks.

On investigating the challenge that lay ahead during the two-week stay in the sub-tropical forest in Springbrook National Park, McLaren was surprised to find that the areas where the cast would be situated was 'a glorified film set. I was shocked to hear I was never going to be in any danger. The medic told me: "Things are so safe, I would send my own kids in to do the show." There is nothing bad in there. They're hoodwinking the public. Viewers need to wake up to the fact that the celebrities are just a motley crew in ITV's horror movie.'

McLaren's disappointment was genuine; Young Kim has written about his foolhardy intrepidity and willingness to take physical risks. But McLaren had never watched the show so didn't understand what was obvious to most viewers; that the situations were engineered and participant safety secured at all times.

On the day that filming was to begin, McLaren decided that he was not taking part and refused to leave his hotel room, despite the imprecations of cast members such as Lynne Franks, who was filmed hammering on his door and begging him to join the rest of them.

This was to no avail. McLaren left Australia the next day, telling the British press that he understood the programme's popularity 'and all about the pantomime torture camp. I had every intention to appear on the show. But when the trials are tricks to fool the public about a danger that isn't there, it proves this show is nothing more than a circus. In my opinion, it's totally and utterly fixed. This is not a reality show, it's a fake one.'[8]

Yet the experience, for which McLaren was not paid, didn't deter him from joining a special 'celebrity hijack' season of the British version of *Celebrity Big Brother* a couple of months later as he hit his sixty-second birthday.

This was to be McLaren's most successful intervention into the spectacle of reality TV.

The formula for this series dictated that each day a different well-known person acted as 'Big Brother', taking control of the house in which the contestants dwelled and organising tasks, creating new rules and communicating with the housemates in the so-called Diary Room. McLaren was booked by the programme's celebrity producer James Dearlove alongside the likes of comic actors Matt Lucas and Roseanne Barr and chat-show host Joan Rivers.

'Malcolm's name crept onto the list because the producer Phil Edgar-Jones was interested in having someone who would be subversive,' says Dearlove, who arranged for McLaren to fly from New York and appear over two days towards the end of the series, in the hope that he would inject some much-needed dynamism.[9]

Aware that the contestants were as young as eighteen, McLaren drew on his own youth and suggested a wine-tasting session. He also asked for consoles to be distributed among the housemates so that they could play the video game *Guitar Hero*. 'I didn't think much of his plans at the time,' confesses Dearlove. 'They seemed a bit run-of-the-mill.'

This was to underestimate McLaren's willingness to upset the apple-cart. The set-up precluded the 'hijacker' from entering the house, but McLaren would have none of it even though later in his segment there was to be a live broadcast of an eviction of one of the contestants. 'He started talking to them from the booth via the link and then went, "Fuck this, I'm coming in!"' says Dearlove. 'The whole production gallery was looking at me, thinking, "What the fuck?" No one had done this before.'

The TV crew scrambled a camera to follow McLaren onto the set. 'Once he was in he was very difficult to get out,' says Dearlove. 'There was a huge panic because we had the live eviction coming up, so I was sent to deliver the wine to the store room. Every time he came to pick up a bottle I'd be whispering, "Malcolm, you've got to get out of there" and he'd respond, "No! Fuck it! I'm hijacking the house! That's what you got me here for!"'

McLaren ignored the Tannoy requests that he leave and set about blindfolding the contestants and had them sample a variety of French wines in the manner that he was taught in the early 1960s, spittoon and all. He even adopted the role of the general, 'Blueface', who had educated him all those years before at Sandeman's, telling the youths how one burgundy was 'fine because it has a minerality to it' while the sound was muted when he compared another to 'an older woman who has to be treated with care'.

Bored at first, by the end of the session the contestants had been animated by their wine intake and crowded around McLaren, pitching questions at him.

'He was in there for hours, telling the housemates to ignore Big Brother and the rules, to reject the evictions and rebel against authority,' says Dearlove. 'And the *Guitar Hero* music threatened to drown out the eviction announcement.'

Dearlove eventually managed to grab McLaren and usher him from the set before this took place. 'He was nonplussed but could see that I was now in trouble. One of the problems of working in telly is that you regularly have execs shouting at you as if someone is going to die, but of course it's just television. Malcolm thought this was hysterically funny and basically took pity on me.'

With McLaren safely off the premises, having been dispatched to his central London hotel, the Sanderson, Dearlove was told to cancel the booking for next day. 'They said that they couldn't handle Malcolm,' smiles Dearlove, who broke the news to McLaren over breakfast. 'He said, "I suppose you and me have the day off, don't we? Let's spend it together." From then on we just clicked.'

Dearlove, a musician and painter, became part of the circle that enjoyed occasional meals and conversations with McLaren during his frequent visits to London. 'He was always interested in what was going on, and talked to me about his various projects,' says Dearlove.

Among these was 'Diorama', which was coming into focus. By now, McLaren had settled on the timeframe for the musical, which would take place between Christian Dior's introduction of the New Look in 1947 to his death a decade later.

'The house of Christian Dior opened on the coldest day in fifty years in Paris, with people freezing in the salons and watching this display of clothes that really sent everybody back to the dark ages of La Belle Époque,' explained McLaren to Glenn O'Brien.

These hour glass-shaped women, these full skirts, these padded thighs, these false icons. But that ultimately became something embraced by Hollywood to be used as an image to convey the new teenage rock 'n' roll lifestyle. Now how did they do that? How did they take something made by this man – Christian Dior, who was already middle-aged and trying to reinvent his mother's costumes – and make clothing that was almost a symbol of reactionary thinking into a symbol of the outlaw spirit and of rebellion and the youth culture? That idea just fascinated me.

This fascination, said McLaren, lay in the attempts by Paris 'to regain its position as the centre of civilisation, and not knowing how to do it in those post-war austere times. Meanwhile America was knocking at their door, this culture of desires rather than necessity, in the form of products that we never knew could exist before this whole youth culture: rock 'n' roll, blue jeans and icons like Marilyn Monroe.'

As ever, research was central to the project. McLaren read up on Paris after the liberation and tried to concoct a fractured storyline to reflect the cut-up approach of his music.

'If I could trap it inside this house of Christian Dior, from its birth in '47 to Dior's death in '57, that seemed to me something worth really investigating as a musical,' said McLaren, who hoped that the project would reach fruition in a couple of years. 'It has to be radical in its presentation and has to build its own audience,' he said. 'Broadway could start to rev up, because there have been a lot of movies turned into musicals and that has brought a different appetite to Broadway. There are several generations now going to the theatre. When that happens, it means that the door is a little more open.'[10]

By the summer of 2008, McLaren had completed a new, extended version of the film installation shown at Stefan Brüggemann's exhibition. *Shallow 1–21*, as it was now called, was chosen by Art Basel artistic director Cay Sophie Rabinowitz to be exhibited at the art fair alongside works by the Italian Monica Bonvicini and Mexican Pedro Reyes in a new curated section, Art Basel Projects.

McLaren explained that the approach from Rabinowitz propelled him 'to make as big a statement as I could. I thought, I'll show so many that no one will be able to watch them in one continuous moment in time; they wouldn't actually stand in the room that long. People could jump in and jump out. It wasn't narrative-based so it didn't really matter. I decided on 21 because I liked the number.'[11]

A peepshow booth draped in heavy red curtains was constructed for visitors to view McLaren's piece from wooden benches. 'The sound system throbbed and flickered endlessly and the booth was packed until closing time,' said McLaren. 'Many of the Art Basel attendants were soon discovered slouched inside, gazing at the sexual, loud, rockin' foreplay.'[12]

Shallow 1–21 achieved the status of public art when McLaren gave permission to the New York arts group Creative Time to video project the installation on MTV's giant outdoor screen suspended high above Times Square between 44th and 45th Street. The move was welcomed by the musician and performer David Byrne, who told McLaren before the screenings were held over a three-week period, 'I've been getting good and shallow with your videos … the intimations of sex is adolescent, slightly creepy and maybe timid. In Times Square the videos will be surrounded by giant ads for jeans, designer perfumes, and musicals, some of which feature much sexier poses, and are much more in-your-face than your work.'[13]

The new installation was the result of three months' focus in McLaren's studio, during which he produced thirty films from which the final selection was made. 'Every day, I would go down to these awful record stores, and troll around and bring back fifty to sixty CDs,' he explained. 'I'd go through them all and nitpick and cut 'em up and stick them together and bash on some simple groove that I'd grabbed from some piece of software and cut them up again until I thought: "That works, day's ended. I've done one."'

He explained that Brüggemann's title for the I-20 group show had nagged at him: 'Though I didn't choose it originally, the word "Shallow" stuck with me. I thought, well, everybody accuses pop culture of being nothing short of shallow, of having shallow feelings, and in many respects, that's right. But often where something is shallow, there's also something much deeper.'[14]

This went to McLaren's moving image choices. 'I took the shallowest movies, which are these sex movies with charming little preambles, the kind of movies I remember projecting on 8mm in my squats with other art students when we were bored and cold on those winter nights,' he said.

They'd write these shabby little stories, ten-minute intros, just to give the movie some integrity beyond a bonking session. For this project, I watched something like five hundred intros from between 1962 and 1972, because in 1972 or thereabouts, that part of the movie industry changed radically and became just pure bonking. When the earlier movies were made, porn stars didn't really exist, and a lot of those people might have been students, or just ordinary people having fun, or wannabe actors or actresses. There's a fabulous naïveté to them that is very revealing, especially when you slow them down.

To promote the Creative Time project, McLaren participated in an in-conversation with the British curator Mark Beasley hosted by the organisation's board member Peggy Jacobs at a 5th Avenue penthouse. An hour in, recalled Beasley, McLaren had only arrived at the early 1970s and the opening of Let It Rock.

'I'd asked a total of two questions – it didn't matter,' wrote Beasley later. 'McLaren had no need of inquiry or the suggested framing of his life's work; just press play and listen as the days and tales crafted like manifestos became years, and the years and ideas became a movement. For those that knew him, McLaren's real work was his voice, his eloquent turn of a phrase, booming theatrics and potent thoughts infecting all those that came under its spell.'[15]

By the summer of 2008, nearly a year after he had started work on *Shallow*, McLaren was rationalising the piece in terms of his abiding interest in the tensions between karaoke culture and authenticity. 'Today, we're so used to being stuffed with eye candy, with fast food, fast art, fast culture, that to take something really simple and just slow it down is the opposite of how we live,' he said.[16]

Simultaneous to McLaren's immersion in the international art circuit, a decision to endorse a punk fashion book a couple of years previously rebounded on him.

In 2006 McLaren had received a request from a London clothing dealer to provide a foreword to a short-run independently printed coffee-table book about 1970s garments designed with Vivienne Westwood. McLaren was sent jpegs by mail of examples to be included, and supplied an essay for a fee. Among others who contributed texts to the book were the writer Jon Savage, Sex Pistol Glen Matlock, journalist Jonh Ingham and Ted Polhemus, the anthropologist who had featured Sex at an ICA symposium.

Fast forward two years, to the period when he was engrossed by *Shallow 1–21*, and McLaren was approached by executives from New York publisher Rizzoli seeking his approval for a lower-priced commercial version of the book for sale in the US. On finally reviewing the original, McLaren found that a sizeable amount of the clothes featured in the limited edition were not authentic, and, in effect, his essay had lent the publication credibility. In time, he was successful in persuading Rizzoli to drop the project from its schedules, but McLaren was by then provoked into action: for the twenty-two months that remained of his life he was dedicated with great zeal to exposing those who sought to fake his designs.

This was boosted by the fact that, around the time of the Rizzoli affair, McLaren was contacted by British artist Damien Hirst to review a group of thirty or so punk garments he was considering buying. These were purported to be originals, but the majority were extremely suspect.

Alarm bells began to ring and McLaren's investigations turned up the presence of more fakes, which had been circulated by a number of fraudsters not only to leading auction houses and vintage fashion collectors on both sides of the Atlantic, but also prominent museums such as the Met, which had featured many of his designs with Westwood a couple of years previously.

Coincidentally, McLaren was asked to advise detectives from Scotland Yard's Arts and Antiquities Squad. They had arrested individuals for circulating fake artworks by the street artist Banksy, but also found them to be in possession of around a hundred counterfeit Sex and Seditionaries garments.

McLaren launched a public campaign against counterfeiting but failed to gain the support of either Vivienne Westwood or Joe Corré. Undaunted, McLaren decided to assist the police and provided Scotland Yard with a thoroughgoing report on the clothing, confirming that they weren't authentic. He died before the case came to court, and though his written testimony was compelling, McLaren's absence weakened the prosecution. In the event the case was ordered to 'lie on file'. This occurs in Britain when it is not necessary to secure a conviction because other guilty pleas have been entered. The offenders received suspended sentences for circulating tens of thousands of pounds' worth of rogue Banksy artworks.

'The fact is that shirts and t-shirts have been bought from copyists and then attached with newly manufactured Sex & Seditionaries labels in an attempt to make them look authentic and pass them to the unknowing and ill-educated (who sadly include museum curators as well as unwitting fans),' wrote McLaren. 'That is what has prompted me to act in this regard. I suppose this culture needs saving to reclaim its integrity.'[17]

PART X

History Is for Pissing On

Chapter 41

Among the visitors to the *Shallow 1–21* peepshow booth on the first day of Art Basel in 2008 was the German art consultant Bernd Wurlitzer.

'There are no coincidences. That's what I always think when something significant happens in my life,' wrote Wurlitzer, who was 'thrilled' by McLaren's installation. 'After half an hour visitors were asked to leave. The opening was over and the hall was being closed. I had seen and heard *Shallow 15–21*. Such a contemporary work. I was fascinated, but what about *1–15*? The next day my flight went back to Berlin and other appointments did not leave me any time to go back to see the rest. I was sure that this work had to go to Berlin.'[1]

Wurlitzer proposed showing *Shallow 1–21* at the city's ScheiblerMitte gallery the following autumn and McLaren responded by suggesting that the work should form the centrepiece of a group show. McLaren was keen, not least because Wurlitzer was a descendant of the jukebox makers who had dominated 1950s rock 'n' roll. He came up with the exhibition title and theme – *Musical Paintings* – and Wurlitzer commissioned new pieces from thirteen other artists, including three recommended by McLaren from New York: Rodney Graham, Rob Pruitt and Michael Queenland.

All participants made music-connected contributions. For example, four installations by Scotland's Jim Lambie included *Screamadelica*, which was made from duct tape and photo-printed eyes cut from magazines and covered the gallery entrance floor and walls. This had appeared as the cover of an LP by the group Primal Scream, while Damien Hirst's series of disc etchings, suggested by gallerist Aurel Schiebler, were described by McLaren as 'like ruined records'.[2]

The essay he wrote for the pocket-sized *Musical Paintings* catalogue combined many of his preoccupations; not just karaoke and authenticity,

771

but also the opening of Sex, his art school days and the more recent excursions into what he now termed '8-Bit Punk' and 'Rock 'n' Roll Gameboy'.

Peter Culshaw has talked about McLaren's unique ability to view himself and his work dispassionately, and while the claims he made for *Shallow 1–21* in this text could be seen as self-aggrandising, there is truth in his description of the strange aesthetic impact of the installation. 'In linking musical cut-ups to the face of unadulterated sexual encounters (the foreplay before the paid and shallow sexual act) I can't say what happened is what happened,' wrote McLaren, grasping to describe the transformation that occurred when he fused the aural and visual elements. 'Something else took place in this process. The alchemy made possible another meaning far deeper than what existed before. It made for a feeling of slowness. It emotionally connected, made at times, a certain ugliness beautiful and gave the word "shallow" a curious lift.'[3]

Like Bernd Wurlitzer, the British curator David Thorp was taken by *Shallow 1–21* on a visit to Art Basel, making the connection between McLaren's cut-up technique and the deliberately randomised approaches of his hero William Burroughs.

As a result, once *Musical Paintings* was over, the work was shown as part of a group show called *Collision Course* organised by Thorp at one of the most prestigious art addresses in the world, London's Royal Academy of Arts. Thorp understood that one entry point to McLaren's oeuvre was through the prism of radical art practice. 'McLaren consistently applied Situationist approaches to his own musical collages, including *Duck Rock* and *Paris*, which contains echoes of the psychogeographic maps of the city created by Guy Debord in the late 50s and 60s,' wrote Thorp in 2015. 'But it is in *Shallow 1–21* that the manifestation of McLaren's absorption in the cut-up process reaches its apotheosis.'[4]

The late 2000s and the spring and summer of 2009 in particular represented a high point for McLaren. Young Kim and McLaren's residence was by now the atelier of a building in rue Saulnier behind the Folies

Bergère. The space had been the studio of the Dutch painter Kees van Dongen in the early years of the twentieth century.

McLaren later related how he and Kim once received a visit from a curator at the Netherlands Institute of Art History in The Hague, who showed him photographs of Van Dongen in situ. 'I wonder how he lived here,' wrote McLaren a few months later. 'Regardless of the fact that this studio is a marvel of light, it is all but impossible to get a stick of furniture into the space, so narrow are the doors and so tight the stairwell. I had to cut my bed in half and put it back together again so I could sleep sandwiched along the mezzanine. Best is the view: grand, sweeping, romantic, across the rooftops of Paris to the Sacré Coeur.'

McLaren said that he told the curator he found Van Dongen's work banal:

She comments kindly that anyone who has lost the connection with the fundamental in art also lacks sense for the banal. I look at her, amused and curious as to what will come out of her mouth next. She doesn't mean the ability to see that something is banal, she says, but the ability to understand the artistic value of banality. She thanks my girlfriend for iced coffee and explains further, 'A great work of art is the complete banality, and the fault with most banalities is that they are not banal enough.' I am sold.[5]

Happiness at home in Paris and New York coincided with the growing acceptance of McLaren at the highest levels of the academic and commercial wings of the art world; together these provided a balm for the previous decade's misfires and wrangles.

A collaboration with James Jebbia of the world-beating brand Supreme – which took its name from the World's Famous Supreme Team – paid homage to McLaren's standing in the street-style community; hoodies, hats, T-shirts and Vans shoes were decorated with graphics commissioned from Keith Haring and Dondi White for *Duck Rock* and stills from the 'Buffalo Gals' video.

The Keith Haring Estate attempted to cut up rough, sending a complaint to Supreme claiming that it owned the rights to the *Duck Rock* cover, not McLaren. He swiftly put them right, pointing out that he paid for the artist's works and that they formed but one element of the overall design. Similarly, this applied to the Haring artworks that appeared in the Witches collection.

'It was work for hire and [Haring] was well aware that the work would be exploited in such ways as are customary with a fashion company and indeed a record company,' wrote McLaren to the supportive Supreme. 'He was just a kid on the street drawing everywhere, like all graffiti artists in NY at that time. I was one of the first to acknowledge his talent and support him by bringing him to Europe.'[6]

At the other end of the scale, McLaren's performative lecture style was attracting top-flight bookings, including an in-conversation in Monaco at the *Financial Times'* annual symposium on the luxury business.

Here McLaren lined up with such heavy-hitters as LVMH chairman Bernard Arnault, the bosses of Tod's, Burberry, Oscar de la Renta and Jimmy Choo, and *Monocle* editor Tyler Brûlé.

McLaren was recommended by the *FT*'s fashion editor Vanessa Friedman – now chief fashion critic at the *New York Times* – and was asked to give his thoughts on the effects of the credit crunch on luxury goods in an interview with the paper's editor Lionel Barber, who recalls him as being 'garrulous, funny and interesting'.[7]

An opportunity for a more rambunctious setting offered itself when McLaren was booked by the theatrical promoters David Johnson and John Mackay, who had previously presented such big-draw names as author Malcolm Gladwell and activist and documentary-maker Michael Moore, to create a one-man show to road test at the 2009 Edinburgh Festival Fringe and then take around the world.

McLaren proposed a monologue to be part fabulist autobiographical stand-up and part societal critique over dinner with Johnson and Mackay at Piccadilly restaurant the Wolseley.

'Eyeing the crowd surrounding us – Lucian Freud and his daughter

Bella, Alan Rickman and fans, Justin Timberlake and American record producers from my not-so-distant past – I realise fate is playing me a card and decide that is what I will do,' wrote McLaren in a diary written for the *FT*. ' "It's agreed," David says, "but what shall we call it? Confessions of a Rock 'n' Roll Swindler?"

' "No," I say, "History Is For Pissing On." ' [8]

By finessing his speaking style over a number of years, McLaren had aligned himself with a number of other younger visual artists who had also chosen the path identified by McLaren's friend, the US-based British curator Mark Beasley, as 'lecture-as-performance'.

Beasley had been investigating the form since the early 2000s, when he booked the likes of Mark Titchner, Bonnie Camplin and Mark Leckey to give talks in London's Conway Hall, site of much political demagoguery. 'Performance had been "out" for so long that it was a format that could really be messed with, in ways that art-world audiences didn't necessarily understand then,' says Beasley. 'That subcultural sensibility really reinvigorated it. Now it feels commonplace; every artist I've met from the UK in the past decade has a libretto or a text or a spoken word performance ready to go. No bad thing! With the advent of the digital, there's a yearning to be in a room with other bodies, and to hear the source speak unmediated.'

McLaren had told Beasley about the experience of giving talks in Asia in the 1990s when he discovered karaoke culture. 'He'd been signed by an agent who was putting him out in front of two thousand people with a microphone, and he would just go at it,' recalls Beasley.

[McLaren] couldn't believe that anyone would show up for these events, but they did. If you look at the market for these experiences, I think there is some real desire, inter-generationally, for content that isn't mediated by a screen. To hear with one's own ears, to see with one's own eyes.

A long time has passed between Futurism and now, from the birth of modern forms of performance to our present iterations, but I think that eventually performance will be accepted the same way photography has been, as an integral but fluid component of the institution. More and more, we see performances happening in many different kinds of spaces within galleries and museums – not only social or theatrical settings – such that the primary challenge for their presenting institutions has become simply dealing with the flow of people.[9]

There is no doubt that McLaren had been mining this territory for some time, and in *History Is for Pissing On* he created a format that was ribald, theatrical, occasionally uncomfortable but relentlessly provocative. His grandmother would have been proud.

'There were plenty of pithy lines,' wrote reviewer Bruce Dessau. 'The theme of his playful monologue is that history is there to be messed with. More precisely it was a chance to hammer home his life story. The flame-haired anecdotalist is very watchable – half cunning fox, half Mick Hucknall's dad.'[10]

By the time the sold-out show had ended, Johnson and Mackay were fielding enquiries to book McLaren from as far afield as Sydney. Interest had been bolstered by a spat over the content of an extract from the show that McLaren had been due to perform at an event staged during the companion Edinburgh International Book Festival.

McLaren had chosen to relate his time spent at Sandeman's as an apprentice wine taster, with allusions to the sexually charged terms the general known as Blueface used to describe different wines. The shocked hosts of the event, a prim New York storytelling group called Moth, objected to the content and the length of his contribution. Accusing Moth of attempting to censor him, McLaren told *Scotland on Sunday*: 'I will not have my stories pigeonholed by PC New York intellectual toffs.'[11]

As if to declare his egalitarian credentials, McLaren also took part in the judging of 'Live & Unsigned', a talent contest held in the southern coastal city of Portsmouth during the same month as his Edinburgh appearance. In the wake of the popularity of such programming as *Pop*

Idol and *The X Factor*, where else were we to find the person who assembled the line-up of rock music's most controversial group?

In the *FT* diary he aligned his participation with his abiding obsession. 'I am on a mission: I have this undeniable thirst for something authentic,' wrote McLaren. 'I have never been a good judge of anything, not women, not friends. I am feeling submissive sitting here at the back of Portsmouth Guildhall. I've got "willing prey" printed across my forehead; I am an icon of 21st-century unhappiness.'

The task appeared to McLaren to be insurmountable. Some 60 acts had been culled from 10,000 applicants, and were judged on performances held across a day in the city's Guildhall. 'Looking for the authentic here might be like looking for a ruby in a field of tin,' wrote McLaren.

A couple of performers garnered his interest, one a south London teenager named Harry Houseago. 'A strange-looking boy in ill-fitting adult clothes strums away on a guitar. His strings break but he continues regardless,' wrote McLaren. 'The sound is terrible. Sympathy from the emcee allows him a reprieve. His few friends wait in anticipation and horror. Then Harry Houseago reprises his song, a fragile tune distinguished by a lyric that describes his recent love affair with a hospital bed, a place he never wants to leave. Harry Houseago is 16 and I award him full marks. He is a dysfunctional, impossible-to-define, wonderful creature.'[12]

McLaren was firing on all cylinders. Back in New York, arts writer Adrian Dannatt caught up with him 'in fine form at a recent townhouse drinks bash'.[13]

Meanwhile, McLaren and Young Kim took their places as fixtures at New York Fashion Week; he even unwillingly became involved in US *Vogue* editor Anna Wintour's attempt to inject consumer confidence after the financial crash: the Fashion's Night Out promotion, with boutiques in Manhattan staging parties and remaining open until midnight. 'The whole event sounds like something I want to avoid at all costs but I can't,' explained McLaren later.

I am recognised by the Belgian designer Dries Van Noten and his team. The American design duo Proenza Schouler ask me to host a party at the old Pyramid club. Cynthia Rowley's show I've missed already. Thom Browne is on the line and I'm on a deadline. It's 6 p.m. and the city is already swamped by gangs of teenage girls hunting for free champagne, cupcakes, ice-cream, popcorn and candy floss. They are determined to catch a glimpse of a star – be it at Barneys, Bergdorf Goodman's, Saks, or wherever . . . it's a free-for-all in Manhattan tonight.[14]

McLaren's indulgence of the youthful energy of New York's fashion world was tempered by his growing reputation as a serious artist. An edition of *Shallow 1–21* acquired by the art collectors Brook and Pam Smith was loaned to the Pennsylvania Academy of Fine Arts in Philadelphia for exhibition, while a request to also show the installation came from the English arts centre the Baltic in Gateshead.

Meanwhile, McLaren and Young Kim enjoyed the heady whirl of artistic experiences New York offered, within a few days visiting a show by the artists Mike Kelley and Mike Smith in the Sculpture Center, Queens, and then joining Larry Gagosian's party for artists Takashi Murakami and Anselm Reyle at the new Standard Hotel's sybaritic Boom Boom Room.

For some time McLaren had been complaining of feeling unwell and suffered what appeared to be a heavy cold that had lingered all summer. A visit to McLaren's doctor initiated a full health check. The report came back with bad news about his lungs.

According to Kim, the extent of McLaren's illness was not fully real-ised when the symptoms were first noticed. 'Malcolm was freaked out,' she said. 'He called me up from the doctor's office and said, "Young, I have lung cancer, I have lung cancer," but the doctor said, "Oh no, he's perfectly fine, he just has these spots, they're completely benign, you don't have to worry about it." Then, just a few months later, his left lung had filled with fluid.'[15]

In the autumn of 2009, McLaren was diagnosed with mesothelioma, a cancer that develops in the lining that covers the outer surface of some of the body's organs. The most common cause is exposure to asbestos; it is likely that this occurred when he smashed jagged holes in the false ceiling at 430 King's Road during the conversion to Seditionaries more than thirty years previously.

The life expectancy for sufferers is twenty-one months, depending on the stage of the disease and overall health. McLaren had been a cigarette smoker since a young age, though had largely given up over the previous decade.

The condition is incurable, but around 10 per cent of sufferers live up to five years after diagnosis. McLaren and Kim resolved to keep the matter private while they investigated a range of alternative medical solutions.

Always a dedicated worker, McLaren now threw himself even more energetically into the diverse range of projects on his slate; as well as 'Diorama', he had been commissioned to write and present a thirteen-part series for BBC Radio entitled 'The Ruins', and was also repurposing material from the CNAP advertising archive, uncovered by Eugenia Melián two decades before, for another film installation.

Naming the new work *Paris, Capital of the XXIst Century*, McLaren returned to contemplating the city that had enchanted him for most of his life.

Chapter 42

Malcolm McLaren's choice of title for his new installation was a reference to its model, 'Paris, Capital of the 19th Century', the German philosopher and writer Walter Benjamin's uncompleted manuscript summarising his critical studies of the French city.

Benjamin first approached this project in two essays of the same title in the 1930s and later reworked them into text that aimed, in the words of academic David Frisby, to recover the 'prehistory of modernity, one of whose central locations was the Parisian arcades conceived as the threshold of a primal world of fantasy, illusion and phantasmagorias that expressed the dreamworld of capitalism'.[1]

McLaren was aware of the fraught history of the Benjamin manuscript. Leaving it with the writer Georges Bataille before fleeing Paris on the arrival of the Wehrmacht in June 1940, the stateless Jew Benjamin killed himself by morphine poisoning three months later while hiding in a town in Catalonia. The treatise survived the war stored in the Bibliothèque Nationale de France, and was published decades later, first in French in the 1980s and later in English translation in 1999 as *The Arcades Project*.

But McLaren arrived at the title for his project by mistake. He misread the numerals 'XIX' on the German edition of Benjamin's book as 'XXI'. 'What a genius, I thought, to have come up with such an audacious title as that, as far back as the 30s,' said McLaren. 'I simply had to use it!' Later, he realised his error. 'Nevertheless, I left my title intact.'[2]

Rather than the historical shopping passages or their contemporary retail manifestations, McLaren chose as the basis for his new work the CNAP archive, détourning twenty-one adverts to produce an hour-long installation that matched Benjamin's plan to represent 'fantasy, illusion, and phantasmagorias' by juxtaposing the commercials – whether for lavatory paper, spreadable cheese or furniture polish – with found music and his own performative spoken-word pieces.

'I selected those that I definitely could make an intervention with and by doing so, become part of its life,' explained McLaren. 'This started to change the context and began a new narrative, taking the work into the present. To be precise, I thought of simply being a flâneur walking through Paris [and] through its advertising over the last 100 years.'[3]

As the American critic Greil Marcus has pointed out, this was achieved by 'repetition, panning, pastiche, collage, digital manipulation, musical scores both congruent and disruptive, [and] McLaren voice-overs that combine the seductive and the insufferable in a single breath'.[4]

Marcus makes a pertinent point; the artist is much more present in this installation than in *Shallow*. Given what he was going through privately during the compilation of the piece, it is understandable that Paris has an explicitly personal edge.

One sequence used an insurance ad featuring a professional tumbler repeatedly falling down a set of stairs without hurting himself. It's replete with the slapstick humour enjoyed by McLaren but after a while queasiness sets in for the viewer. This is no longer funny; the figure has lost control of his life, doomed to inexorably fall.

Another uses repetition and manipulation to drive a simple advert for the processed cheese Boursin into the void. Starting with the sound of a hunting horn, a man wakes up, shouts the name of the product, leaps out of bed and searches from room to room until he opens the fridge door and finds three packs to the climactic sound of a pipe organ.

When this plays again and again, the exposure of the film stock is heightened each time until it bleaches into total white. 'There are no images,' wrote Greil Marcus. 'The man has been devoured by the commodity – and because without a consumer there can be no commodity, the commodity has devoured itself.'[5]

As he laboured over the film, McLaren was constantly consulting with doctors and undertaking a variety of treatments. But this was but one of a number of projects he was juggling, as McLaren upped his activities to a furious pitch. The *New Yorker*'s Judith Thurman recalled Kim and McLaren being 'full of plans for work and travel, especially work, which is to say, new fusions' when she met them at a party for the Serbian performance artist Marina Abramović's sixty-third birthday in the autumn of 2009.[6]

While the couple remained confident about his prospects of beating cancer, intimations of mortality were evidently setting in.

A few weeks after the diagnosis McLaren was a featured speaker alongside a raft of academics and business executives at a huge digital education symposium held in London.

McLaren was invited to participate by his friend, the event's organiser Graham Brown-Martin. 'We had a conversation about the possibilities offered by digital technology,' says Brown-Martin. 'At that time I had a fairly Utopian view, believing that, because it was accessible to everyone, it would have the effect of levelling the playing field to all of our advantage. Malcolm took the opposite view, that it would have an isolating effect, and do long-term damage to society. He may well have been right. Whatever, it's at that point I said, "Well, come along and tell us about it."'

After confessing that education was not a subject in which he was expert, McLaren opened his speech to audience laughter with a line he favoured towards the end of his life: 'I have been accused of being a charlatan, a con man or, maybe most flatteringly, the culprit responsible for turning British popular culture into nothing more than a cheap marketing gimmick. This is my chance to prove that these accusations are absolutely true.'[7]

The body of the talk touched on by-now familiar ground to McLaren watchers: his art school years, Sex and the Sex Pistols and the celebration of amateurism that had been the keynote of his life and activities.

Before McLaren took the stage, Brown-Martin was approached by a journalist from the august *Times Educational Supplement*. 'He told me I had made a grave mistake by putting this terrible man on,' recalls

Brown-Martin. 'This was based on absolute fucking prejudice, on bullshit he'd probably read in the *Daily Mail*. Malcolm's talk was brilliant. Half a dozen people walked out, which I thought was fantastic. That's just what you want from a conference. The vast majority in the audience – government department staff, educators – declared it the best thing they'd ever heard. He made many salient points, not least that learning from a computer is not the same as the lived experience. It is, as he said, like fucking a rubber doll.'

In comparison with previous talks, though, this was a low-energy performance, with McLaren's tone understandably muted. There was little humour, laughter nor the eccentric *joie de vivre* that marked him out as a singular presence on the lecture circuit.

Paris, Capital of the XXIst Century received its first showing at a group exhibition at the Baltic, the arts centre in a converted flour mill overlooking the Tyne river in Gateshead, north-east England; the Baltic's Godfrey Worsdale had booked *Shallow 1–21* a few months earlier on David Thorp's recommendation.

Taking the stage after the screening, McLaren was on loquacious form during an interview with the British arts writer Michael Bracewell and later could be found amid the hurly-burly of the chaotic after party, genially conversing with attendees.

Press representatives at the Baltic found him 'strangely modest' when asked to assess his place in the history of modern British culture. 'I'm most probably a missing link that a lot of people don't know,' he told one journalist. 'Someone has to tie the loose ends between the sixties and the nineties. That has been left open to me because no one is aware what artists had to face in the seventies.'

McLaren was also sanguine when responding to the charge that his recent work was not as game-changing as the creation and stewardship of the Sex Pistols. 'It's not a question of peaking, it's just very hard to top,' he conceded. 'Everything begins to look very small by comparison – unless you come to terms with the idea that small is beautiful you could be traumatised by that.'[8]

There is no denying McLaren's reflective mood when he and Young Kim undertook a trip the following month first to London for a meeting and then on to Moscow for a screening of *Shallow 1–21*, as conveyed in the third and final diary he produced for the *Financial Times*' weekly 'Life & Arts' section.

'Leaving Paris, I can't help feeling nostalgic: what is it that makes me want to return there as soon as I leave?' asked McLaren.

Was it something the Impressionists picked up on? The silvery light that flickers across their paintings of rain-soaked Parisian streets? As the train draws out of Gare du Nord, the city looks unapologetically melancholy. In the Channel tunnel, the train stops and I find myself thinking not of the recent breakdowns but of the 1940s and my childhood. A time of blackouts and, excitingly, never knowing what is going to happen next.

Yet when I think of scrambling across the bombsites of London I do not recall the same lightness of being as I do when I think of ambling through Paris. Rain brings no mystery to London. Grey skies are grey skies. Just that. No charm, no seduction. It is all about the roofs. The Parisian tin roofs do something magical. London's slate roofs don't do the same job. We arrive at St Pancras: food malls and karaokeville . . . Welcome to London!

McLaren was in town for further discussions on 'The Ruins', which were to comprise his selection from the BBC's sound archives; each of the thirteen programmes was to be built around recordings of personal relevance. For example, he wanted to relate a 1960s speech made by Black Panthers leader Eldridge Cleaver about the revolutionary implications of indulging in 'The Twist' to his co-opting of rock 'n' roll and 1950s style to make radical youth statements in the 1970s. McLaren also hoped to find a recording of the notorious slum landlord Peter Rachman playing with his group Night Sounds Combo, whose performances McLaren had witnessed as a teen habitué of Rachman's Soho club La Discotheque.

Part of the appeal in such fragments lay in their distance from digital life, McLaren informed his BBC producers. 'We have entered an audio-visual age where the new generation's do-it-yourself aesthetic has truly broken the hold that pop culture's industry once had on youth,' McLaren told them.

> We live in a world where everybody is an expert, and those young experts have caused the demise of pop culture. The marriage of sex and pop music – its DNA, so to speak – has been considered over-rated for some time by this generation. Talent shows and a how-to-get-rich-and-famous-for-doing-nothing culture is what counts now. Nobody truly young hangs out any more. Pop music mattered once because it was about just that: hanging out, wishing, wanting, imagining, preparing for sex and more than likely, never getting any . . .'

On the latter point, McLaren found that the nudity in *Shallow 1–21* had been excised before the screening in Moscow. 'It's butchered,' he wrote in his diary. 'I take a philosophical view. I am not surprised. Just saddened.'

Back in Paris in early December, McLaren visited the Montana bar, a reopened 1950s dive on rue Saint-Benoît. Here, regardless of his condition, McLaren indulged his love of dancing, twisting in honour of Eldridge Cleaver to the sounds of 1960s yeh-yeh group Les Chats Sauvages, whose music was featured in *Paris, Capital of the XXIst Century*. 'Out in the cold night air, I immerse myself in the bath of the crowd and window-shop with them for a while. Nowhere else does one find so many tasteless things as in Paris. That is precisely why it is still the place where the inspiration of art lives on.'[9]

But the relentlessness of his lifestyle dictated that, within a few weeks, McLaren had returned to New York for a screening of the final version of *Paris* at the city's Swiss Institute. Manhattan's cultural elite was out in force; among those in attendance were art dealer and curator Jeffrey

Deitch, filmmaker Alexandra Kerry, hotelier Sean MacPherson, top-flight art and design publicist Karla Otto and fashion designers Kai Kühne, Sam Shipley and Jeff Halmos. The event included a repeat of the Baltic in-conversation with Michael Bracewell. Happy to field questions about the *Paris* installation, McLaren remained touchingly hopeful that 'Diorama' would make it to the stage. 'This project has stayed in my heart for a long time,' he told *Paper* magazine's Elizabeth Thompson. 'And as I struggle with it, and will it into production, I believe it will emerge triumphant.'[10]

By now frail, McLaren decided with Kim to inform a select few as to his condition. Among these was his brother Stuart Edwards. One night soon afterwards, Edwards's taxi cab was hailed by George O'Dowd and the club entrepreneur Philip Sallon in London's East End. Edwards told his passengers, who, of course, had both associated with McLaren in their pasts, about McLaren's battle with cancer. In turn, O'Dowd and Sallon felt it their duty to inform Joe Corré, who contacted his father.

The facts of his health were also relayed to McLaren's New York friend James Truman. 'He told me he was sick,' says Truman, who met McLaren at a branch of Le Pain Quotidien where McLaren and Young Kim ate regularly. 'It was an unexpected place for us to meet, as we usually lunched at more boozy places. But Malcolm was now eating clean, and in his typical way, he had studied the tenets of healthful eating and expounded on them at length. Malcolm had an ability to become an expert in anything that interested him – he truly knew more about wine than most professional sommeliers – and had a lavish gift to expound upon it.'

After trying a range of alternative therapies in Paris, London, New York and Switzerland, McLaren returned to the latter where he received treatment at the Paracelsus holistic clinic in St Gallen. Both McLaren and Kim were confident that he would respond well to the multidisciplinary medical attention, but towards the end of the first week of April, on Easter Sunday, McLaren's lungs deteriorated and he was rushed to a clinic at the Cantonal hospital in Bellinzona, the capital of Swiss canton Ticino. The IOSI (Oncological Institute of Italian-speaking Switzerland) is recognised worldwide for excellence in cancer diagnosis, research and therapy; Beatle George Harrison received care there in his final days.

Kim was by now accompanied by Sarah Bolton, McLaren's assistant from the 1990s, and became sufficiently concerned to summon Joe Corré to Bellinzona. He arrived with Ben Westwood, and together and separately the four attended the facility as McLaren slipped into unconsciousness.

Malcolm McLaren succumbed to cancer on 8 April 2010. News of his death reverberated around the world and, as he had predicted, his role as Sex Pistols manager was mentioned in the opening sentences of the obituaries and news reports.

A true artist, Malcolm McLaren was unable to resist processing his experiences, even unto the very end; the final work he completed was not, in fact, *Paris, Capital of the XXIst Century*, but an elegiac soundscape created for a March 2010 womenswear catwalk show staged in Paris by the Belgian fashion designer Dries Van Noten.

This was based in large part on excerpts from the melancholic 'Love Music' (otherwise known as 'Scène d'Amour'), from composer Bernard Herrmann's soundtrack to Alfred Hitchcock's 1958 frightener *Vertigo*, juxtaposed with the bellowed a capella folk chant 'The Building' by 1980s British group the Mekons.

Also in the mix were samples of 1977 crowd chatter recorded at London punk club The Roxy, and the rackety, feedback-drenched 'In Love' by the all-female DIY group the Raincoats. Also incorporated was the wordless yodelling known as the 'Zäuerli', which is local to the St Gallen area where McLaren had received treatment.

Poignantly, in the closing minute of the mix, the Burundi beat, as found by McLaren while attempting to court an assistant in the Centre Pompidou sound library more than three decades and a lifetime away, played out against the climax of Herrmann's composition.

'The juxtaposition of both punk vocal and Hitchcockian theme suddenly makes the material feel completely contemporary,' McLaren announced when the Van Noten show was held.[11]

But in the immediate aftermath of his death the work could be seen not as the incidental backdrop for the selling of garments, however elegant, but for what it was: a powerful autobiographical collage expressing existential anguish and mortal dread.

Epilogue

During his visit to the clinic in Bellinzona, Ben Westwood wore a T-shirt with a proclamation demanding the freedom of the jailed Native American campaigner Leonard Peltier, a cause célèbre of his mother's; he and Joe Corré announced to the world's media that McLaren's final words were a repetition of the slogan 'Free Leonard Peltier'. The unlikelihood of this was confirmed when Young Kim pointed out that she was summoned to attend his bedside without them in McLaren's final moments.

But this disagreement was as nothing to the dispute that exploded when the contents of McLaren's will were revealed. Drafted by a Swiss lawyer, this left everything to Kim, and included a clause specifically excluding McLaren's son Joe.

On first sight, this appeared cruel and divisive. But as Kim explained, the plainness of the language was to ensure that there would be no contesting ownership of the intellectual property rights residing in the artworks, fashion designs, graphics, and musical and film works McLaren created during his lifetime. Among these, of course, were the garments produced with Vivienne Westwood from 1972 to 1984; as enshrined in both the partnership agreement and dissolution document, 50 per cent resided with McLaren, who had been resolute that this should be controlled by Kim.

The will was revealed a few days after the carnival-style funeral for McLaren's interment in Highgate Cemetery, the north London gothic home to such permanent residents as Karl Marx and the English novelist George Eliot. The ceremony, at a deconsecrated church in central London, was arranged by Joe Corré and included children tap-dancing to McLaren's rendition of 'You Need Hands' and a *yoik*, a keening vocal interpretation of the sounds of nature performed by Ánde Somby, a member of the Saami people from northern Norway.

On display, McLaren's coffin was sprayed with the slogan Too Fast to Live Too Young to Die. Meanwhile a low point was reached when a halting address by Westwood was rudely interrupted by incoherent heckling from the one-time manager of The Clash, Bernard Rhodes.

Outside the church, the coffin was carried away to the strains of Sid Vicious's version of 'My Way' while celebrities such as Bob Geldof and Tracey Emin were photographed with the likes of attention-seeking Adam Ant in front of the world's media as shrieking attendees were scooped onto double-decker buses daubed in dayglo colours for a street parade to a party at former stables in Camden Town.

'The media scrum and the way people dressed and behaved at the funeral seemed to define Malcolm's entire life by just the two-and-a-half years of Punk,' says attendee Graham Brown-Martin. 'It was a really strange affair.'

A couple of weeks later Corré launched a legal challenge to the will, on the basis that McLaren had not been of sound mind when he wrote it. In 2012 this was rejected by a court, which awarded Kim the sum of McLaren's estate, valued at $263,113 (£169,750).

'Malcolm wanted to make sure his legacy was protected,' Kim explained in 2013. 'It wasn't Malcolm being a jerk, but he didn't trust Joe's taste. Malcolm loved him as a son, he couldn't help it, although I can't say he liked him as a person. They hadn't seen each other for years. He also understood that I loved him and really cared about him. That's when he began caring about his legacy.'[1]

Corré later confessed that he had felt 'devastated' by his father's codicil. 'My father wasn't a paternal man,' he said in 2015. 'I don't think he was cut out to be a father. He never wanted to be one.'[2]

By the time his appeal had been rejected, Corré had commissioned a large marble headstone for McLaren's grave, complete with inset death mask and a paraphrase of the Harrow lecturer's adage, reading: 'Better a spectacular failure, than a benign success.'

Corré wasn't to know this, but McLaren's wish as expressed to Kim in his final days was for a totem pole rather than a traditional headstone: this would have featured the head of his grandmother Rose among others.

The public wrangling over McLaren's physical legacy overshadowed assessment of his creative influence, which was in fact accurately pinpointed by an acquaintance, the performance art curator Mark Beasley, within two days of his death.

No. 430 King's Road during McLaren's occupancy 'deserves equal billing alongside other rebellious venues for anti-social gathering and encounters with the new, from Gustave Courbet's Pavilion of Realism to Andy Warhol's Factory,' wrote Beasley, who revealed that in his final months McLaren was planning a lecture presentation titled 'Jesus Christ Is a Sausage'. 'It suggested no let-up in his caustic wit,' wrote Beasley. 'A consummate entertainer, no moment spent with Malcolm was anything less than to be presented with glimpses of a possible fantastic future, though as he exaggeratedly put it he was "nooo fortune teller". Wicked devilry has always been the greatest part of the creative spirit, and Malcolm's legacy is the sense of possibility and pleasure of the exuberant dilettante.'[3]

McLaren's partner in the early 1990s, Eugenia Melián, witnessed first-hand the dedication he brought to bear on a variety of projects they generated together in Los Angeles, London and Paris. 'Malcolm was unrelenting in his pursuits, extremely hard-working and focused,' she says. 'He was actually a far cry from the image painted of him as the ditzy airhead running around from pitch to pitch conning everyone and stealing ideas. It was moving to see how much energy and enthusiasm he put into each lead ... everything could be expanded upon, dug into, turned into something else. Malcolm was curious about the world and never stopped reading, going to museums, doing research and listening to music from all over the world. He was avid in his quest for new information and different cultures, so it breaks my heart and makes me very angry that people have that clichéd POV of him: the swindler, the clown, the opportunist. That's so old, boring and uninspired.'

Melián accepts that McLaren's brilliance could be marred by a self-destructive streak. This, she says, was due to a personality trait with which he is not publicly associated but is identified by his most intimate associates: lack of confidence. 'That came from the terrible hurt from his family past, but it meant that he did not abide by the rules,' says Melián. 'He meant no harm, he just knew no better. His terrible childhood also explains a lot. It is petty to focus on the negatives and far more interesting to look at the uniqueness of the man and his mark on the world.'

Another close friend, James Truman, says McLaren's significance in part relies on his repeated circumvention of the gatekeepers of the creative areas he investigated. 'People who propel themselves to the top of any field naturally assume a defensive position, which entails repelling outsiders and engaging accomplices in taking themselves enormously seriously,' says Truman. 'This is especially true in the worlds of art, fashion and academia. That Malcolm had an impact on all of these, that he was able to successfully penetrate each on his own terms, while taking none of them seriously, seems more miracle than damnation.'

And Truman recognises the importance of Paris to McLaren the man and the artist. 'Oddly enough, it was Paris, with all its lingering pomposity, that seemed to understand Malcolm the best, and it was no surprise that he felt at home there,' adds Truman. 'Perhaps it's because the French have such a rich lineage of revolutionaries and brilliant misfits. When I'd go over to Paris for fashion weeks, I'd often invite Malcolm to join me at the shows. He'd never have a ticket, and for some shows, like Galliano or Gaultier or McQueen, there would be hundreds of people outside pleading to be let in. Malcolm would part the crowd and just walk in. The one time security didn't recognise him, he announced, with great ceremonial flair, "Je suis Malcolm McLaren" and simply sauntered past.'

Contrastingly, McLaren's relationship with his home country was rarely comfortable, and in Britain his memory is regarded, if at all seriously, with a great deal of mistrust. James Truman again: 'Malcolm was always a weird, quasi-shamanic figure, who never let on when he was joking and when he was serious, and there's profound purpose to that, but it's also highly unnerving. For the UK in particular, the intention of the media, whether on the left or the right, is to tame and domesticate. Yesterday's rebels become tomorrow's loveable uncles, under the approving rubric "former bad boy". Failing that, they become downgraded to some kind of caricature or tragedy. Malcolm was never part of that, and I don't believe ever would have been, because he saw it and knew to resist it. Put another away, a disrupter once identified is like an outlaw once captured. The show is over.'

Truman misses what he describes as his friend's 'brilliant mind and foresight', and summons a particularly instructive memory for our times.

'A week after 9/11 I was sitting in a downtown restaurant in New York with Malcolm and he started expounding on the rise of Nazism, and how one day soon America would be cheering its own brand of brutal nationalism and turning on "the outsider",' says Truman. 'It took fifteen years but he was quite right. At the time, of course, everyone around us in the restaurant was craning their necks and looking flustered, and I remember wishing that Malcolm would talk quieter. But that was his brilliance. He refused to talk quieter.'

Acknowledgements

I am extremely grateful to Young Kim for allowing me access not only to first-hand materials but also important background and detailing as well as documentation held in the archive of the Malcolm McLaren Estate.

I am also indebted in particular to Barbara Nicola for enabling me to understand more about Peter McLaren, who remained a mysterious figure in his son's life for so long, as well as to Fred Vermorel for his illuminations about McLaren's student years, Eugenia Melián for her insights and exhaustive information regarding the creation of some of McLaren's most distinctive works, and to Alan Moore and Lou Stoppard for their perceptive contributions.

I also owe a debt of gratitude to Eileen Gunn and the Royal Literary Fund for coming to my aid at a crucial time and especially to my brilliant agent Maggie Hanbury: thank you for fighting my corner at every turn.

At Constable, Andreas Campomar has been the epitome of a patient, sympathetic and collaborative editor while Howard Watson provided assured handling of the text. Neal Purvis, Jake Riviera and Nick Vivian receive much appreciation for having set me on the path to realising this book, though it is Caz Facey's care, support, love and guidance that have been crucial every step of the way.

I am also thankful to the following for their assistance, contributions and memories: Keith Albarn, Stephen Alexander, Valerie Allam, Toby Amies, Marc Ascoli, Lionel Barber, Roberta Bayley, Will Birch, Richard Boch, Craig Bromberg, Graham Brown-Martin, Paul Burgess, Richard Cabut, Jamie Camplin, Claire Catterall, Bob Chait, Brian Clarke, Nik Cohn, Martin Cole, Caroline Coon, Diana Crawshaw, Gary Crowley, Peter Culshaw, David Dagley, Steven Daly, Willy Daly, Jean-Charles de Castelbajac, Bruce Dessau, Jeff Dexter, Tony Drayton, Nick Egan, Will

English, Anthony Fawcett, Dominique Fenn, Duggie Fields, Christine Fortune, Stephen Foster, Rebecca Frayn, the late Jim French, Hiroshi Fujiwara, Paul Gardner, Bob Geldof, Yvonne Gold, Leigh Gorman, Michael Gorman, Nat Gozzano, Andrew Greaves, Bob Gruen, Michael Halsband, Andy Harries, Derek Harris, David Harrison, Fayette Hauser, Richard Hell, Michael Holman, Jerry Hopkins, Barney Hoskyns, Imogen Hunt, Jonh Ingham, David Johnson, Lloyd Johnson, Rory Johnston, Emma Jolly, Dylan Jones, Mick Jones, Gert Jonkers, Stewart Joseph, Ben Kelly, Scott King, Robert Kirby, Danny Kleinman, Gene Krell, Malcolm Le Grice, Don Letts, Mark Lewisohn, Andrea Linz, Nick Logan, Frances Lynn, Alasdair McLellan, John Marchant, Mariann Marlowe, David Marsh, Barry Martin, Glen Matlock, David May, John May, Jonathan Meades, Bradley Mendelson, Menno Meyjes, Robin Millar, Jordan Mooney, Trevor Myles, Judy Nylon, Paddy O'Connell, George O'Dowd, Marco Pirroni, Barry Plummer, Ted Polhemus, Mark Pringle, Kieron Pym, the late Michael Rainey, Stephane Raynor, Ben Reardon, Paul Reeves, Bernard Rhodes, Len Richmond, Steve Ridgeway, Michael Roberts, the late Tommy Roberts, Tony Russell, Chris Salewicz, Philip Sallon, Tom Salter, Rat Scabies, Robin Scott, Kate Simon, Paige Simpson, Martine Sitbon, Charlotte Skene Catling, Donald Smith, Graham K. Smith, Neil Spencer, Joe Stevens, Henri Struck, Ian Stuttard, Anna Sui, John Sutherland, Sylvain Sylvain, Julien Temple, Jeremy Thomas, David Thorp, James Truman, Tony Tyler, Ian Tyson, Callum Vass, Kosmo Vinyl, Harriet Vyner, the late Jim Walrod, Ted Walters, John Wardle, Adam Waterfield, Michael Watts, Jon Wealleans, Jane Withers, Simon Withers, Simon Witter, Matthew Worley, Peter York, Marc Zermati and the many others who have offered advice, encouragement and information.

Notes

Unless otherwise indicated, all quotes from Malcolm McLaren are from material in the archive of the Malcolm McLaren Estate, including his autobiographical notes and notes for articles, lectures and radio documentaries, or from interviews and correspondence with the author.

Chapter 1

1 Notes, Peter McLaren, 1998. Unless otherwise indicated all quotes by Peter and Ivy McLaren are from Peter's personal notes.
2 Allison Jean Abra, *On with the Dance: Nation, Culture, and Popular Dancing in Britain, 1918–1945* (University of Michigan, 2009).
3 Laurence Ward, *The London County Council Bomb Damage Maps 1939–45* (reprint, Thames & Hudson, 2015).
4 James Morrison, 'The Boy Scout Who Became the Svengali of Punk', *Independent* (9 November 2003).
5 *The Cardinal and the Corpse*, dir. Chris Petit and Iain Sinclair (Channel 4, 1992).
6 Maurice 'Pip' Goldstein, in Rachel Lichtenstein, *On Brick Lane* (Penguin, 2008).
7 Michael Billington, *Harold Pinter* (Faber & Faber, 2007).
8 All quotes by Barbara Nicola are from an interview with the author, 2015.
9 These were routine, not, as his son Stuart Edwards later speculated, because Peter McLaren was employed by the intelligence services. See Morrison, 'The Boy Scout'.
10 All quotes from Johnny Black are from the transcript for an interview which appeared in *Over 21*, May 1982. http://www.rocksbackpages.com/Library/Article/malcolm-mclaren-2

Chapter 2

1 I have borrowed phrasing here from my brother Michael Gorman's account of our own fractured family life in post-war London in *Broken Pieces: A Library Life 1941–78* (American Library Association, 2011).
2 *Malcolm McLaren: Artful Dodger* (BBC2, 24 April 2010).
3 Black, 1982.

4 Quotes from Rebecca Frayn are from an interview with the author, 2019, and also from her private memoir 'The Horrors of Oxford Street'.
5 *The South Bank Show: Malcolm McLaren*, dir. Andy Harries (LWT, 1984).
6 Dr Mark Duffett, 'As Potentially Explosive as the Contents of My Head or My Underpants: An Interview with Fred Vermorel Part One', Pop Research Links (3 October 2017), http://pop-music-research.blogspot.com/2017/10/as-potentially-explosive-as-contents-of.html.
7 Fred and Judy Vermorel, *Sex Pistols: The Inside Story* (revised edition, Omnibus Press 1987; first edition, *The Sex Pistols*, Universal, 1978).
8 *Malcolm McLaren: Artful Dodger*.
9 London Metropolitan Archives, Tower Hamlets Commissioners of Sewers ratebooks; CLC/B/192/F/001/MS11936/487/970769: The National Archives, PROB11/1459/77: District Surveyors Returns: Tower Hamlets Local History Library and Archives, Building Control file 15942; P07316; LCP00017.
10 Lauren Hutton, 'The Malcolm McLaren I Knew', *Guardian* (12 December 2010).
11 *The South Bank Show: Malcolm McLaren*.
12 Neil Spencer, 'Malcolm McLaren: The Age of Piracy vs The Age of Conservatism', *New Musical Express* (9 August 1980).

Chapter 3

1 Nik Cohn, *Today There Are No Gentlemen* (Weidenfeld & Nicolson, 1971).
2 Penny Reel, 'The Young Mod's Forgotten Story', *New Musical Express* (15 September, 1979).
3 Penny Reel, oral history interview, Hackney Museum, http://museum.hackney.gov.uk/object10198.
4 Jon Wilde, 'An Audience With ... Malcolm McLaren', *Uncut* (September 2006).
5 Clive Sinclair, 'Cabbage Face', *Independent* (5 August 1995).
6 Paul Gorman, *The Look: Adventures in Rock & Pop Fashion* (revised edition, Adelita, 2006; first edition, Sanctuary, 2001).
7 Ibid.
8 Ibid.
9 Malcolm McLaren, 'Never Mind the Bordeaux – Food: Eat, Memory', *New York Times Magazine* (11 March 2007).
10 'All Back to My Place', *Mojo* (February 2001).
11 Black, 1982.
12 'Have Your Say', *BBC News* (9 April 2010), http://www.bbc.co.uk/blogs/haveyoursay/2010/04/your_memories_of_malcolm_mclar.html.
13 McLaren, 'Never Mind the Bordeaux'.
14 Ibid.
15 To John Hind, 1984, reprinted as 'Malcolm McLaren: Why I Gave Up Wine Tasting for Art', *Guardian* (16 March 2014).

16 McLaren, 'Never Mind the Bordeaux'.

17 Hind, 'Malcolm McLaren'.

18 Peter Barnsley, 'The Young Take the Wheel', *Town* (September 1962).

19 McLaren, 'Never Mind the Bordeaux'.

20 Hind, 'Malcolm McLaren'.

Chapter 4

1 Jon Savage, *The England's Dreaming Tapes* (Faber & Faber, 2009).

2 Vermorel, *Sex Pistols* (1987 edition).

3 John Beck and Matthew Cornford, *The Art School & the Culture Shed* (Centre for Useless Splendour, 2014).

4 Simon Frith and Howard Horne, *Art into Pop* (Methuen, 1987).

5 Ian Proctor, 'Fond Memories of a Pioneering Art School', *Get West London* (23 August 2012).

6 Fred Vermorel, *Vivienne Westwood: Fashion, Perversity & the Sixties Laid Bare* (Overlook Press, 1996).

7 Draft of article for *Art Quarterly* (March 2000).

8 Ibid.

9 Ibid.

10 Ibid.

11 Ibid.

12 Vermorel, *Vivienne Westwood*.

13 Ibid.

14 Duffett, 'As Potentially Explosive'.

15 Unless otherwise indicated, quotes from Fred Vermorel are from interviews with the author, 2014–2019.

16 Vermorel, *Vivienne Westwood*.

17 Vermorel, *Sex Pistols* (1987 edition).

18 Vermorel, *Vivienne Westwood*.

19 Fred Vermorel, 'Blowing Up the Bridges So There Is No Way Back', *Eyes for Blowing Up Bridges: Joining the Dots from the Situationist International to Malcolm McLaren* (John Hansard Gallery, 2015).

20 Jon Savage, *England's Dreaming: Sex Pistols & Punk Rock* (Faber & Faber, 1991).

21 Ramos, who died in 2018, lived in the terrace opposite 430 King's Road, where McLaren was to operate his boutiques with Vivienne Westwood from 1971 to 1984.

22 Duffett, 'As Potentially Explosive'.

Chapter 5

1 Jane Mulvagh, *Vivienne Westwood: An Unfashionable Life* (revised edition, HarperCollins, 2003; first edition, HarperCollins, 1998).

2 Savage, *England's Dreaming*.

3 Unless otherwise indicated, quotes from Keith Albarn are from an interview with the author, 2013.

4 Vermorel, *Vivienne Westwood*.

5 Vermorel, *Vivienne Westwood*.

6 Unless otherwise indicated, quotes from Duggie Fields are from interviews with the author, 2016 and 2017.

7 'Match Held Under Stars & Stripes', *The Times* (26 July 1966).

8 Vermorel, 'Blowing Up the Bridges'.

9 Craig Bromberg, *The Wicked Ways of Malcolm McLaren* (Omnibus, 1991; first edition, Harper & Row, 1989).

10 Mulvagh's description in *Vivienne Westwood* of McLaren at this age.

11 Bromberg, *The Wicked Ways* (1991 edition).

Chapter 6

1 Savage, *England's Dreaming*.

2 Mulvagh, *Vivienne Westwood* (2003 edition).

3 Vermorel, *Vivienne Westwood*.

4 Mulvagh, *Vivienne Westwood* (2003 edition).

5 Michael Watts, 'The Rise and Fall of Malcolm McLaren Part One: Tin Pan Alley Meets an Idea Whose Time Has Come', *Melody Maker* (16 June 1979).

6 'I said not to worry, I was on the Pill. Only I was lying,' Westwood quoted in Cole Moreton, 'Never Mind the Bollocks', *Independent* (14 December 1997). According to Fred Vermorel, Westwood told his ex-wife Judy the same thing in the 1970s.

7 Bromberg, *The Wicked Ways* (1991 edition).

8 Mulvagh, *Vivienne Westwood* (2003 edition).

9 Lucy Harrison, *Carnaby Echoes – 26 Kingly Street: Artists' Own Gallery* (2013), https://vimeo.com/70927009.

10 Kenneth Tynan, 'The Arts Lab: A Ramshackle Prototype for the ICA', *Observer* (25 February 1968).

11 Vermorel, 'Blowing Up the Bridges'.

12 Thomas Levin in *On the Passage of a Few People Through a Rather Brief Moment in Time: The Situationist International 1956–1972*, dir. Branka Bogdanov (1989).

13 Ibid.

14 Fred Vermorel, 'At the End, They Even Stole His Death', *GQ* (March 2011).

15 Vermorel, *Vivienne Westwood*.

16 Essay, Croydon College of Art, 1967. Courtesy Malcolm McLaren Estate.

17 'Henry Moore, Bridget Riley and Malcolm McLaren uncovered at Croydon Museum', *Culture 24* (9 October 2009).

18 Notes, Croydon College of Art, 1967. Courtesy Malcolm McLaren Estate.

19 To the author, 2010.

20 Harry Doherty, 'Now Pop for Pure People', *Melody Maker* (5 May 1979).

21 Jamie Reid and Jon Savage, *Up They Rise: The Incomplete Works of Jamie Reid* (Faber & Faber, 1987).

22 Vicki Maguire, *Shamanarchy: The Life & Work of Jamie MacGregor Reid* (Liverpool John Moores University, 2010).

23 For an examination of the protests at the college, see Lisa Tickner, *Hornsey 1968: The Art School Revolution* (Frances Lincoln, 2008).

24 John Mair, 'The Agitators', *Guardian* (10 July 2003).

25 Duffett, 'As Potentially Explosive'.

26 *On the Passage of a Few People*.

27 Doherty, 'Now Pop for Pure People'.

28 Reid and Savage, *Up They Rise*.

29 Luise Neri, 'Malcolm McLaren, Cannibal of looks and Sounds', in Maria Luisa Fria and Stefano Tonchi (eds), *Excess: Fashion and the Underground in the '80s* (Edizioni Charta, 2004).

30 Savage, *The England's Dreaming Tapes*.

31 Bromberg, *The Wicked Ways* (1989 edition).

32 Savage, *The England's Dreaming Tapes*.

Chapter 7

1 I am grateful for the detail here from Fred Vermorel's contemporary correspondence with McLaren.

2 Cresswell was dismissive of youth culture and what he saw as bourgeois pretension and provocation. 'I'm a genuine member of the working class,' he once announced (*New Society*, Vol. 25, 1973). In the late 1980s, as dean of arts at Goldsmiths, Cresswell caused a stir by removing a contentious nude study from view before a visit to the college by Princess Anne. See John A. Walker, *Art & Outrage* (Pluto Press, 1984).

3 In conversation with Paul Taylor, February 1985. Reproduced in Paul Taylor, 'The Impresario of Do-It-Yourself', in *Impresario: Malcolm McLaren & the British New Wave* (New Museum of Contemporary Art/ MIT Press, 1988).

4 *On the Passage of a Few People*.

5 Both of these anecdotes were related to Craig Bromberg for his 1989 book on McLaren. Curiously, Poynter left Goldsmiths for the Royal College of Art in 1967, a year before McLaren's arrival.

6 Vermorel, 'Blowing Up the Bridges'.

7 Ibid.

8 Christopher Hibbert, *King Mob: The Story of Lord George Gordon and the Riots of 1780* (Longmans, Green & Co, 1959). It has previously been claimed the name came from the graffiti 'His Majesty King Mob' left in Newgate Gaol by Gordon rioters, but there is no evidence that it existed, as confirmed by Dave Wise at the Bristol Anarchist Book Fair in 2016. See https://www.brh.org. uk/site/events/dave-wise-and-stuart-wise.

9 Dave Wise, 2016.

10 BCM/King Mob, *Art Schools Are Dead* (October 1968).

11 Vermorel, 'Blowing Up the Bridges'.

12 Letter to Vicki Maguire, 2008.

13 All quotes from Barry Martin are from an interview with the author, 2014.

14 Paul Hoch and Vic Schoenbach, *LSE: The Natives Are Restless. A report on student power in action* (Sheed & Ward, 1969).

15 Sex Pistols bassist Glen Matlock has related that McLaren indicated to him in the 1970s that he was one of the individuals who broke the gates down.

16 Jonathan Green, *Days in the Life: Voices of the English Underground* (Heinemann, 1988).

17 Gabriel Pomerand, Isidore Isou, Georges Poulot and Guy Marester, *La Dictature Lettriste* (June 1946).

18 Katherine Levy, 'Malcolm McLaren: The Long Lost Paintings', *Seven* (16 May 2010).

19 'Goldsmith's 5-day Arts Freak Out Plan', *International Times* (4 July 1969).

20 Email to the author, 2018.

21 Vermorel, *Sex Pistols* (1987 edition).

22 Dave Walton, '1969: Revolution as Person and as Theatre, Revolt Against the Age of Plenty', http://web.onetel.net.uk/~davewalton/archive/local/1969.html.

23 'Free Festival, Free Beer, Free Shambles', *Kentish Mercury* (10 July 1969). See also, http://transpont.blogspot.com/2010/04/malcolm-mclaren-in-new-cross.html.

24 Paul Thompson, comments, http://transpont.blogspot.com/2010/04/malcolm-mclaren-in-new-cross.html.

Chapter 8

1 Taylor, 'The Impresario of Do-It-Yourself'.

2 Bromberg, *The Wicked Ways* (1991 edition).

3 Black, 1982.

4 Stuart Wise, 'Veteran Situationists behind King Mob and Revolt Against Plenty', Bristol Anarchist Book Fair (2016), https://www.brh.org.uk/site/events/dave-wise-and-stuart-wise/.

5 Mulvagh, *Vivienne Westwood* (2003 edition).

6 Ibid.

7 Reid and Savage, *Up They Rise*.

8 Jop van Bennekom and Gert Jonkers, 'Malcolm McLaren', *Fantastic Man* (Spring/Summer 2005).

9 As reported in contemporary journals including the *Bookseller* and the *Herald of Library Science*. See also https://sites.gold.ac.uk/goldsmithshistory/.

10 Unless otherwise indicated, quotes from Tommy Roberts are from interviews with the author, 2000, 2010 and 2011.

11 Paul Gorman, *Mr Freedom: Tommy Roberts – British Design Hero* (Adelita, 2012).

12 Gorman, *The Look* (2006 edition).

13 Quotes from Bob Chait are from an interview with the author, 2016.

14 Cohn, *Today There Are No Gentlemen*.

15 *Melody Maker* (18 September 1971).

16 Chas Hodges, *Chas & Dave: All About Us* (John Blake Publishing, 2013).

17 John Collis, *Gene Vincent and Eddie Cochran: Rock 'n' Roll Revolutionaries* (Penguin, 2011).

18 Vermorel, *Sex Pistols* (1987 edition).

Chapter 9

1 Neri and McLaren, 'Malcolm McLaren'.

2 Interview with the author, 2000.

3 Interview with Steve Jones, *Jonesy's Jukebox*, Indie 103.1 (6 May 2005).

4 Unless otherwise indicated, quotes from Trevor Myles are from interviews with the author, 2005 and 2014.

5 'Paradise Garage: Up the Workers', *Harpers & Queen* (September 1971).

6 All quotes from Bradley Mendelson are from interviews with the author, 2017.

7 William Rothenstein, *Men And Memories: Recollections of William Rothenstein 1872–1900* (Faber & Faber, 1931).

8 John Richardson, *The Chelsea Book: Past and Present* (Historical Publications, 2003).

9 Evelyn Waugh, 'Review, World's End, Pamela Hansford Johnson', *Night And Day* (22 July 1937).

10 Interview with David Mlinaric, Victoria and Albert Museum (February 2006) http://www.vam.ac.uk/content/articles/i/david-mlinaric/.

11 Interview with the author, 2008.

12 Jonathan Aitken, *The Young Meteors* (Secker & Warburg, 1967).

13 From synopsis of interview with Michael Rainey by Bernard Braden, *Now and Then*, Adanac Productions (4 April 1967).

14 Interview with Jane Ormsby-Gore, Victoria and Albert Museum (March 2006), http://www.vam.ac.uk/content/articles/i/jane-ormsby-gore/.

15 Interview with the author, 2011.

16 Ormsby-Gore, 2006.

Chapter 10

1 Gorman, *The Look* (2006 edition).

2 Cohn, *Today There Are No Gentlemen*.

3 Interview with the author, 2000.

4 Iggy Pop, 'The John Peel Lecture', The Lowry, Salford (13 October 2014).

5 Nick Kent, 'Malcolm McLaren: Meet the Colonel Tom Parker of the Blank Generation', *New Musical Express* (27 November 1976).

6 Robert Goldwater and René d'Harnoncourt, *Modern Art in Your Life* (MoMA, 1949).

7 Quotes from Tom Salter are from an interview with the author, 2015.

8 Unless otherwise indicated, quotes from Willy Daly are from an interview with the author, 2011.

9 Vivien Goldsmith, 'Rock – Not So Much a Gimmick, More a Way of Life', *Chelsea News* (February 1972).

10 A London-born Patrick Francis Casey a couple of years older than McLaren died in 1980 at the age of thirty-six. It is not known whether this is the same. McLaren said that any enquiries he had made were met with a dead end.

Chapter 11

1 Goldsmith, 'Rock'.

2 Mike Stax, 'Screaming Lord Sutch: An Interview with a Raving Loony', *Ugly Things*, no. 18 (2000).

3 Unless otherwise indicated, quotes from Gene Krell are from interviews with the author, 2006 and 2013.

4 Gene Krell, *Vivienne Westwood* (Universe Publishing, 1997).

5 Jerry Hopkins, 'Beatle Loathers Return: Britain's Teddy Boys', *Rolling Stone* (2 March 1972).

6 Quotes from Yvonne Gold are from an interview with the author, 2013.

7 Caroline Baker and Harri Peccinotti, 'The Group', *Nova* (February 1972).

8 Valerie Wade and Hans Feurer, 'New Suede Shoes', *Sunday Times Magazine* (14 May 1972).

9 Michael Hellicar, 'Peacocks on Parade', *Daily Mirror* (30 May 1972).

10 Interview with the author, 2000.

11 Transcript of an interview with Malcolm McLaren, imomus.com, (3 August 2002).

12 Dr Chuck Tryon, 'Walter Benjamin, "Paris, Capital of the Nineteenth Century"', 2002, http://homes.lmc.gatech.edu/~ctryon/fwp/benjaminparis.htm.

13 Geoffrey Aquilina Ross, 'The Teds Are Back', Rock 'N' Roll Revival Official Programme, *Evening Standard* Special (5 August 1972).

14 Douglas Gordon, 'Hey ... Hey ... the Rock Machine', *Frendz* (September 1972).

15 Rogan, *Starmakers & Svengalis: A History of British Pop Management* (Queen Anne Press, 1988).

16 Sean O'Hagan, 'His Dark Materials', *Observer* (3 May 2009).

17 O'Hagan, 'His Dark Materials'.

18 Quotes from David Harrison are from an interview with the author, 2018.

19 Jerry Hopkins, 'Fifties Trivia: New Rave in England', *Rolling Stone* (4 January 1973).

Chapter 12

1 Malcolm McLaren, 'Dirty Pretty Things', *Guardian* (28 May 2004).

2 Gorman, *Mr Freedom*.

3 Goldsmith, 'Rock'.

4 Unless otherwise indicated, quotes from Jean-Charles de Castelbajac are from an interview with the author, 2018.

5 Malcolm McLaren, 'A Long Friendship', for 'Timeless', Jean-Charles de Castelbajac (1993).

6 Amanda Knight, 'An introduction to Robert Rauschenberg', *City Lit Blog* (23 February 2017).

7 Quotes from Don Letts are from an interview with the author, 2000.

8 Catherine Tennant, 'Shophound at the World's End', *Vogue* (April 1973).

9 Quotes from Roberta Bayley are from an interview with the author, 2013.

10 Cohn, *Today There Are No Gentlemen*.

11 Quotes from Marco Pirroni are from an interview with the author, 2014.

12 'Those Were the Days My Friend', *Club International* (July 1973).

13 Unless otherwise indicated, quotes from Glen Matlock are from an interview with the author, 2000.

14 Glen Matlock with Pete Silverton, *I Was a Teenage Sex Pistol* (Omnibus Press, 1990).

Chapter 13

1 Sylvain believes the encounter took place in the spring of 1971 as the Dolls were forming. This is impossible; McLaren was a student at Goldsmiths and Westwood was a schoolteacher at that time.

2 Unless otherwise indicated, quotes from Sylvain Sylvain are from an interview with the author, 2016.

3 Nina Antonia, *Too Much Too Soon* (Omnibus, 1998).

4 Malcolm McLaren, 'Dirty Pretty Things', *Guardian* (28 May 2004).

5 Ibid.

6 'Small Talk', *Andy Warhol's Interview* (November 1973).

7 David May, 'Sado Sex for the Seventies', *Gallery International*, vol. 1, no. 4.

8 May, 'Sado Sex'.

9 Interview with the author, 2016.

10 Interview with the author, 2015.

11 Matlock, *I Was A Teenage Sex Pistol*.

12 *Mahler*, Goodtimes Enterprises (1974).

13 'Mahler', *Variety* (31 December 1973).

14 McLaren, 'Dirty Pretty Things'. McLaren occasionally dated the visit by the entire group to a year earlier, November 1972, but Sylvain and others have confirmed that they did not meet McLaren on that occasion.

15 Kasia Charko, 'The New York Dolls Gig, Big Biba Rainbow Room, November 26th 1973' (13 July 2013), https://kasiacharko.wordpress.com/2013/07/13/the-new-york-dolls-gig-big-biba-rainbow-room-november-26th-1973/.

16 Nick Kent, 'New York Dolls: Dead End Kids on the Champs-Elysées', *New Musical Express* (26 January 1974).

17 Ibid.

18 Antonia, *Too Much Too Soon*.

19 'London Belles', *West One* (7 December 1973).

Chapter 14

1 Nick Kent, 'The Politics of Flash', *New Musical Express* (6 April 1974).

2 Notes, shop ledger (March 1974). Courtesy Malcolm McLaren Estate.

3 Nick Kent, 'Farewell Androgyny *n.* hermaphroditism (Gr. *Gyne*, woman)', *New Musical Express* (16 March 1974).

4 Savage, *England's Dreaming*.

5 Steve Jones with Ben Thompson, *Lonely Boy* (Heinemann, 2016).

6 Ibid.

7 Interview with the author, 2011.

8 Doherty, 'Now Pop for Pure People'.

9 Kent, 'The Politics of Flash'.

10 Chrissie Hynde, *Reckless* (Ebury Press, 2015).

11 Savage, *The England's Dreaming Tapes*.

12 Jones, *Lonely Boy*.

13 Matlock, *I Was a Teenage Sex Pistol*.

14 Malcolm McLaren to Roberta Bayley (2 May 1974).

15 McLaren in conversation with Maria Finders, Venice Biennale, 2009.

16 Matlock, *I Was a Teenage Sex Pistol*.

17 Nils Stevenson, *Vacant: A Diary of the Punk Years 1976–79* (Thames & Hudson, 1999).

Chapter 15

1 R. D. Laing, *The Divided Self: An Existential Study in Sanity and Madness* (Penguin, 1960).

2 Withers, 'From Let It Rock to Worlds End: 430 King's Road', in *Impresario: Malcolm McLaren & the British New Wave* (New Museum of Contemporary Art/MIT Press, 1988).

3 Matlock, *I Was a Teenage Sex Pistol*.

4 'Sex', *Curious*, vol. 1, no. 3 (Summer 1975).

5 May, 'Sado Sex'.

6 Malcolm McLaren, 'Introduction', in Malcolm McLaren (ed.), *Musical Paintings* (JRP–Ringier, 2009).

7 Malcolm McLaren, 'Foreword', in Gorman, *The Look* (2001 edition).

8 Bromberg, *The Wicked Ways* (1991 edition).

9 Peter Saville, 'Essay', in Paul Gorman, *Reasons to Be Cheerful: The Life and Work of Barney Bubbles* (Adelita, 2008).

10 Quotes from Bernard Rhodes are from an interview with the author, 2007.

11 In conversation with Maria Finders, Venice Art Biennale, 2009.

12 Tabou & Cie, mysterious French artist who depicted Parisian nightlife and jazz culture.

13 Interview transcript for Will Birch, *Ian Dury: The Definitive Story* (Pan Macmillan, 2010).

Chapter 16

1 Quotes from Bob Gruen are from interviews with the author, 2013 and 2018.

2 Bromberg, *The Wicked Ways* (1989 edition).

3 I am grateful to the website From the Archives for its detailed chronology of New York Dolls performances, particularly those between 17 January and 10 April 1975. See http://www.fromthearchives.com/nyd/chronology.html.

4 Sylvain Sylvain with Dave Thompson, *There's No Bones in Ice Cream: Sylvain Sylvain's Story of the New York Dolls* (Omnibus Press, 2018).

5 McLaren, 'Dirty Pretty Things'.

6 Sylvain, *There's No Bones*.

7 Ibid.

8 Malcolm McLaren interview, imomus.com.

9 Ibid.

10 Richard Hell, *I Dreamed I Was a Very Clean Tramp* (HarperCollins, 2013).

11 Alan Betrock, 'New York Dolls, Little Hippodrome', *Phonograph Record* (April 1975).

12 Nina Antonia, *Johnny Thunders: In Cold Blood* (Cherry Red, 1987).

13 From The Archives (2019).

14 Gillian McCain and Legs McNeil, *Please Kill Me: The Uncensored Oral History of Punk* (Grove Press, 1996).

15 McLaren, 'Dirty Pretty Things'.

16 Antonia, *Johnny Thunders*.

17 Interview with the author, 2015.

18 Hell, *I Dreamed*.

19 McCain and McNeil, *Please Kill Me*.

20 McLaren, 'Dirty Pretty Things'.

Chapter 17

1 Interview with the author, 2009.

2 Mulvagh, *Vivienne Westwood* (2003 edition).

3 Caterine Milinaire and Carol Troy, *Cheap Chic* (Harmony Books, 1975).

4 Ian Kelly and Vivienne Westwood, *Vivienne Westwood* (London: Picador, 2014).

5 Mulvagh, *Vivienne Westwood* (2003 edition).

6 This was a still from the 1913 French silent crime film serial, *Fantômas*.

7 Harriet Vyner, *Groovy Bob: The Life and Times of Robert Fraser* (Faber & Faber, 1999).

8 May, 'Sado Sex'.

9 'Barber's Shop Quintet', *Club International*, vol. 4, no. 5 (May 1975).

10 Angela Neustatter, 'Trail Blaisers', *Guardian* (27 May 1975).

11 As cited in Birch, *Ian Dury*.

12 Stuart Grundy and John Tobler, *The Record Producers* (BBC Books, 1982).

13 McLaren, 'Dirty Pretty Things'.

14 Vermorel, *Sex Pistols* (1978 edition).

15 Interview with the author, 2011.

16 Mark Paytress, *Siouxsie & the Banshees: The Authorised Biography* (Sanctuary, 2003).

17 Unless otherwise indicated, quotes from George O'Dowd are from interviews with the author, 2003–4.

18 McLaren, 'Foreword', in Gorman, *The Look* (2001 edition).

19 Nick Kent, 'Mick Jagger Hits Out at Everything in Sight!', *New Musical Express* (15 October 1977).

20 *The Filth and the Fury*, dir. Julien Temple (Film Four, 2000).

21 Quotes from Ben Kelly are from an interview with the author, 2013.

22 Beverly Lyons, 'Clean-cut Scots Band Bay City Rollers Inspired Sex Pistol Johnny Rotten's Punk Look, *Daily Record* (30 July 2018).

23 Interview with the author, 2015.

24 May, 'Sado Sex'.

25 Credit is due to Tom Vague and Derek Harris, who explored this connection in their book *King Mob Echo: From 1780 Gordon Riots to Situationists, Sex Pistols and Beyond* (Dark Star, 2000).

26 Nicholas de Jongh, 'They Had the T-shirt off His Back', *Guardian* (2 August 1975).

27 'MP Attacks T-shirt Charge', *Guardian* (5 August 1975).

28 'Chelsea Shop Owners Charged with Indecent Display', *Kensington & Chelsea Post* (8 August 1975).

29 'Between the Sheets', *Curious*, vol. 1, no. 4 (Autumn 1975).

30 John Sutherland, 'Introduction', *Offensive Literature: Decensorship in Britain 1960–82* (Junction Books, 1982).

31 Quotes from Ted Polhemus are from an interview with the author, 2014.

32 May, 'Sado Sex'.

Chapter 18

1 Nick Kent, 'The Lost Pistol', *Punk: The Whole Truth*, *Mojo* special edition (May 2005).

2 A reference to Kent's jerky, pharmaceutically enhanced gait. Troy Tempest was

a character in the 1960s puppet series *Stingray*. Matlock, *I Was a Teenage Sex Pistol*.

3 Christopherson, a photographer and founding member of Throbbing Gristle and Psychic TV, did not, as has been reported, design a controversial window display for Sex but did later work with the punk retail outlet Boy.

4 Interview with Steve Jones, *Jonesy's Jukebox*, KLOS (6 May 2005).

Chapter 19

1 Vermorel, *Sex Pistols* (1978 edition).

2 *Jonesy's Jukebox* (6 May 2005). Disclosure: I was in the Roebuck sitting with McLaren, who was an acquaintance of an older brother of mine, the night Lydon first met the rest of the group.

3 John Lydon with Keith and Kent Zimmerman, *Rotten: No Irish, No Blacks, No Dogs* (Hodder & Stoughton, 1993).

4 Ibid.

5 *Jonesy's Jukebox* (6 May 2005).

6 Matlock, *I Was a Teenage Sex Pistol*.

7 *Blood on the Turntable: The Sex Pistols* (BBC Three, September 2004).

8 Interview transcript, in conversation with Peter Culshaw, Covent Garden (January 2004).

9 Michael Watts, 'The Rise and Fall of Malcolm McLaren Part Two: The Four Horsemen of the Apocalypse Go Riding', *Melody Maker* (23 June 1979).

10 *Jonesy's Jukebox* (6 May 2005).

11 Bromberg, *The Wicked Ways* (1989 edition).

12 This had been put in place by Peter Christopherson. Hipgnosis shared an entrance with the Pistols' rehearsal space.

13 The surviving graffiti is one of the reasons the building is now listed as a site of architectural interest. 'Anarchy in the UK: Sex Pistols' Denmark Street Home Given Listed Status', *Daily Telegraph* (22 March 2016).

14 Vermorel, *Vivienne Westwood*.

Chapter 20

1 The phrase is from Meghan Morris, 'Asleep at the Wheel', *New Statesman* (26 June 1987), regarding French philosopher Jean Baudrillard's view on the aggravation of existing states of affairs.

2 Vermorel, 'Blowing Up the Bridges'.

3 *On the Passage of a Few People*.

4 Quotes from Danny Kleinman are from an interview with the author, 2015.

5 Savage, *England's Dreaming*.

6 Lydon, *Rotten*.

7 Matlock, *I Was a Teenage Sex Pistol*.

8 May, 'Sado Sex'.

9 Unless otherwise indicated, quotes from David May are from an interview with the author, 2012.

10 Unless otherwise indicated, quotes from Rory Johnston are from an interview with the author, 2019.

11 Kate Phillips, 'Queen Elizabeth College All Night Christmas Ball', *New Musical Express* (27 December 1975).

12 Quotes from Joe Stevens are from an interview and correspondence with the author, 2012–13.

13 Interview with the author, 2000.

14 Neil Spencer, 'Don't Look Over Your Shoulder But the Sex Pistols Are Coming', *New Musical Express* (21 February 1976).

15 Interview with the author, 2010.

16 Rogan, *Starmakers & Svengalis*.

17 Kent, 'Malcolm McLaren: Meet the Colonel'.

18 Rick Skymanski, 'Would You Buy a Rubber T-shirt from This Man?', *Street Life* (1 May 1976).

19 Unless otherwise indicated, quotes from Len Richmond and David Dagley are from an interview with the author, 2011.

20 Len Richmond, 'Buy Sexual', *Forum* (June 1976).

Chapter 21

1 Unless otherwise indicated, quotes from Julien Temple are from an interview with the author, 2018.

2 I am grateful to collector/Sex Pistols expert Paul Burgess, who owns a notebook of McLaren's from this period.

3 Interview with the author, 2019.

4 Mark Williams, 'Say a Prayer for the Pretenders, *Melody Maker* (17 February 1979).

5 Savage, *England's Dreaming*.

6 Lyndsey Parker, 'Backspin', Yahoo.com (4 April 2017).

7 John Robb, *Punk Rock: An Oral History* (London: Ebury Press, 2006).

8 'Where's Your Equipment?', *100 Club Stories* (Ditto Press, 2018).

9 *On the Passage of a Few People.*

10 Pierre Mikaïloff, *Camion Blanc: Kick Out the Jams Motherfucker! Punk Rock 1969–78* (Camion Blanc, 2012).

11 van Bennekom and Jonkers, *Fantastic Man.*

12 Rogan, *Starmakers & Svengalis*.

13 'Wilde-Hinterhof-Typen *Müll*-Mode', *Bravo* (30 September 1976).

14 Unless otherwise indicated, quotes from James Truman are from interviews with the author, 2018–19.

15 Jon Savage, *Sex Pistols and Punk: Faber Forty-Fives: 1976* (Faber & Faber, 2012).

16 Interview with Peter Gordon (1983) for Irwin Chusid's syndicated college radio show, wfmu.org.

17 Brian Southall, *Sex Pistols: 90 Days at EMI* (Omnibus, 2007).
18 Savage, *Sex Pistols*.
19 McLaren speaking at the 'In the City' conference, Manchester (September 1993).

Chapter 22

1 Ibid.
2 *Jonesy's Jukebox* (6 May 2005).
3 For an examination of McLaren's place in the continuum of British pop music management from the 1950s to the 1980s see Rogan, *Starmakers & Svengalis*.
4 Peter York, 'Them', *Harpers & Queen* (October 1976).
5 Transcript for *Blood on the Turntable*.
6 Blair Jackson, 'Chris Thomas: Three Decades on the Cutting Edge and in the Charts', *Mix* (1 January 1999).
7 Used to communicate the death of the main character Yorick, the blank page was one of a series of unusual typographical features and engravings in Sterne's book.
8 Catherine McDermott, *Street Style: British Design in the 80s* (The Design Council, 1987).
9 Jane Withers, 'From Let It Rock'.
10 Kent, 'Meet the Colonel'.
11 'Young Nation', *Nationwide* (BBC One, 28 November 1976).
12 *Today* (Thames Television, 1 December 1976). The earlier uses of 'fuck' were on BBC broadcasts: critic Kenneth Tynan in 1965 and journalist Peregrine Worsthorne in 1973.
13 Jones, *Lonely Boy*.
14 Matlock, *I Was a Teenage Sex Pistol*.

Chapter 23

1 *The South Bank Show: Malcolm McLaren*.
2 'Pistols Shock Horror!', letters page, *Sounds* (11 December 1976).
3 'In the City' conference.
4 Guy Debord, *The Society of the Spectacle* (unpublished translation, 1990).
5 'In the City' conference.
6 Southall, 'Sex Pistols'.
7 Phil McNeil, 'Spitting in the Eye of the Hurricane', *New Musical Express* (15 January 1977).
8 'These Revolting VIPs! Sex Pistols in Rumpus at Airport', *Evening News* (4 January 1977).
9 Southall, 'Sex Pistols'.
10 Matlock, *I Was a Teenage Sex Pistol*.
11 As largely objective accounts, Richmond's diaries are a valuable record.

Extracts from December 1976 to August 1977 were published in Vermorel, *Sex Pistols*.

12 'Pistols Sign with A&M', *Sounds* (19 March 1977).

13 Bromberg, *The Wicked Ways* (1989 edition).

14 *The South Bank Show: Malcolm McLaren*.

15 Vermorel, *Sex Pistols* (1978 edition)

16 Bromberg, *The Wicked Ways* (1989 edition).

17 'In the City' conference.

18 'Young Businessmen of the Year', *Investors Review and Financial World* (21 December 1977).

19 Duffett, 'As Potentially Explosive'.

20 Interview with the author, 2008.

21 Savage, *England's Dreaming*.

22 Neil Spencer and Kathy Sweeney, '1977: The Queen's Punk Jubilee', *Observer* (29 April 2012).

Chapter 24

1 'Student', *Private Eye* (13 February 1970).

2 *Blood on the Turntable*.

3 Richard Branson, 'The Sex Pistols Thames River Party', virgin.com (12 August 2016), https://www.virgin.com/richard-branson/sex-pistols-thames-river-party.

4 Rory Johnston to Rob Banks, *God Save the Sex Pistols* (2004), http://www.philjens.plus.com/pistols/pistols/rory_johnston_interview.htm.

5 Spencer and Sweeney, '1977'.

6 Paul Gorman, *In Their Own Write: Adventures in the Music Press* (Sanctuary, 2002).

7 Peter Culshaw, 'So I Pitched My Oscar Wilde Film to Spielberg', *Observer* (21 March 2004).

8 Spencer and Sweeney, '1977'.

9 For example: 'I was brought up in the Houses of Parliament under the Traitors and Treasons Act. It was probably the worst, because that discussion alone carried a death penalty if voted against.' 'John Lydon Looks Back on 40 Years of Public Image Ltd', *Rolling Stone* (21 September 2018). Parliamentary record Hansard records only one discussion of the group, when Bruce George, MP for Walsall South, pressed for a code of practice to be introduced at punk venues to tackle crowd violence: https://api.parliament.uk/historic-hansard/commons/1977/jun/14/pop-concerts.

10 Branson, 'The Sex Pistols Thames River Party'.

11 McLaren interviewed by Patrik Schuden at ZKM, Karlsruhe (11 August 2000).

12 Vermorel, 'Blowing Up the Bridges'.

13 McLaren to Charlie Gillett, Capital Radio (29 January 1983).

14 *The South Bank Show: Malcolm McLaren*.

15 Sandy Robertson, 'A Non-Interview with Malcolm McLaren', *Sounds* (18 June 1977).

16 According to author and Sex Pistols authority Jon Savage, it is possible this letter was drafted but not sent.

17 Duffett, 'As Potentially Explosive'.

18 'Russ Meyer', *The Incredibly Strange Film Show*, dir. Andy Harries (Channel 4, 9 September 1988).

19 Roger Ebert, 'McLaren & Meyer & Rotten & Vicious & Me', rogerebert. com (11 April 2010).

20 Ebert, 'McLaren & Meyer'.

21 Jimmy McDonough, *Big Bosoms and Square Jaws: The Biography of Russ Meyer, King of the Sex Films* (Three Rivers Press, 2006).

22 'Who Killed Bambi?', original story by Malcolm McLaren, Roger Ebert, Russ Meyer, Rene Daalder and Rory Johnston, registered with the Writers Guild of America West Inc (8 October 1977).

23 Charles M. Young, 'Rock Is Sick and Living in London', *Rolling Stone* (17 October 1977).

24 Vermorel, *Sex Pistols* (1987 edition).

25 Barry Cain, 'Public Image: Can They Win?', *Record Mirror* (4 November 1978).

26 The literal translation in Benjamin's 'Theses on the Philosophy of History' (1940) is: 'There is no document of civilisation which is not at the same time a document of barbarism.'

27 Nick Kent, 'Never Mind the Sex Pistols, Here Comes the Wrath Of Sid!', *New Musical Express* (17 December 1977).

28 Ebert, 'McLaren & Meyer'.

29 Doherty, 'Now Pop for Pure People'.

30 'Who Killed Bambi?'.

31 To Charlie Gillett (1983).

32 Young, 'Rock Is Sick'.

33 Quotes from Jeremy Thomas are from an interview with the author, 2018.

34 McDonough, *Big Bosoms*.

35 *The Incredibly Strange Film Show*.

36 Note to the author, 2013.

37 Quotes from Ian Stuttard are from an interview with the author, 2017.

38 'Pistols movie is ON again', *Sounds* (19 November 1977).

39 Transcript, *Blood on the Turntable*.

40 *Blood on the Turntable*.

41 J. Tobler, 'Sex Pistols Sid Vicious and Johnny Rotten (1977)', Rock's Backpages Audio: The Sex Pistols, http://www.rocksbackpages.com/Library/ Article/sex-pistols-sid-vicious-and-johnny-rotten-1977.

42 Robert Traini and James Whitaker, 'Sex Pistol and Girl in Drugs Probe', *Sun* (1 December 1977).

43 Kent, 'Never Mind'.

Chapter 25

1 Nicholas de Jongh, 'Rotten Day for Punks', *Guardian* (20 January 1978).

2 Transcript, *Blood on the Turntable*.

3 Interview with the author, 2001.

4 Johnny Rogan, *Starmakers & Svengalis*.

5 Duffett, 'As Potentially Explosive'.

6 From Regehr's affidavit for *Lydon v. Glitterbest and others*, 1979, as published among the addenda to Lydon, *No Irish*.

7 Richard Meltzer, *Vinyl Reckoning, A Whore Just Like the Rest: The Music Writings of Richard Meltzer* (Da Capo, 2000).

8 Savage, *England's Dreaming*.

9 Quotes from Fayette Hauser are from an interview with the author, 2013.

10 Chris Salewicz, 'Malcolm McLaren ... The True Poison!', *The Face* (May 1981).

11 Vermorel, *Sex Pistols* (1978 edition).

12 'In the City' conference.

13 From Lydon's affidavit in *No Irish*.

14 'In the City' conference.

15 Transcript, *Blood on the Turntable*.

16 Doherty, 'Now Pop for Pure People'.

17 'Malcolm McLaren Talks to Slash', *Slash* (July 1978).

18 Transcript, *Blood on the Turntable*.

19 Vermorel, *Sex Pistols* (1987 edition).

20 Westwood later repudiated the design and withdrew it from sale, but her inclusion of the artwork in the licensing of McLaren/Westwood designs to the retailer Boy meant that it was reproduced in the 1980s and is still available online today. Jarman never forgave Westwood. See Derek Jarman, *Smiling in Slow Motion, Diaries 1991–94* (Vintage, 2001).

21 J. Tobler, 'Sid Vicious (1978)', Rock's Backpages Audio: Sid Vicious, http://www.rocksbackpages.com/Library/Article/sid-vicious-1978.

22 In his affidavit in *Lydon v. Glitterbest and others* dated 2 February 1979, van Egmond records that Virgin director Simon Draper informed him in the spring of 1978 that 'Public Image could consider themselves in the region of £200,000 better off on delivery of their first album'.

23 Rogan, *Starmakers & Svengalis*.

24 Vermorel, *Sex Pistols* (1987 edition).

25 Reid and Savage, *Up They Rise*.

26 Ibid.

27 *Jonesy's Jukebox* (6 May 2005).

28 This derived from 'We think it is high time to put an end to the dead time that has dominated this century', in 'Now, The SI!', *Internationale Situationniste*, no. 9 (1964).

29 I am grateful to fashion historian Imogen Hunt; she researched the

elements of the Vive le Rock/Punk Rock Disco design for her 2015 thesis at the London College of Fashion.

30 Dave and Stuart Wise, *The End of Music* (King Mob/BCM, 1978).

31 The Snow White scenario first appeared in an illustration featuring sixty-four Disney characters performing sexual and drug-oriented acts. Drawn by Wally Wood, this was published in a 1967 issue of the satirical US publication *The Realist*.

32 Interview with the author, 2006.

33 Kaori O'Connor and Farrol Kahn (eds), *Fashion Guide 1978* (Hodder & Stoughton, 1978).

34 John Lydon with Andrew Perry, *Anger Is an Energy: My Life Uncensored* (Simon & Schuster, 2015); Nick Levine, 'John Lydon Praises Mick Jagger for Paying Sid Vicious's Murder Charge Lawyers'. *New Musical Express* (9 November 2013), https://www.nme.com/news/music/sex-pistols-12 -1237951.

35 Transcript, *Blood on the Turntable*.

36 Charles Shaar Murray, 'New Barbarians: A Tale of Two Rock 'n' Roll Addicts', *New Musical Express* (26 May 1979).

37 'Malcolm McLaren: "I Don't Mind Being Accused of Being Fagin, in Many Respects I Was"', *GQ* (June 2000).

38 'Another Break for Sid Vicious', *Soho Weekly News* (18 January 1979).

39 *Final 24: Sid Vicious*, dir. Stan Griffin, William Hicklin (Cineflix Productions, 2007).

40 Ibid.

41 Ibid.

42 'The Sound of Breaking Glass', *Melody Maker* (28 October 1978).

43 Transcript, *Blood on the Turntable*.

44 L. Jaffee, 'Sid Vicious on Trial', *Imagine* (1979), http://www.rocksback-pages.com/Library/Article/sid-vicious-on-trial.

45 Transcript, *Blood on the Turntable*.

Chapter 26

1 Watts, 'The Rise and Fall of Malcolm McLaren Part One'.

2 Savage, *England's Dreaming*.

3 *Blood on the Turntable*.

4 Ibid.

5 Eve Zibart, 'Death of a Punk Star', *Washington Post* (3 February 1979).

6 *Final 24: Sid Vicious*.

7 Michael Watts, 'Rotten v. McLaren: No Winner', *Melody Maker* (24 February 1979).

8 Malcolm McLaren letter (15 March 1979). Excerpt published in Taylor, 'The Impresario of Do-It-Yourself'.

9 Watts, 'Rotten v. McLaren'.

10 In a 2009 email to the author, McLaren described Temple as 'untrustworthy'.

11 Bromberg, *The Wicked Ways* (1989 edition).
12 Ibid.
13 Interview with the author, 2015.
14 Watts, 'The Rise and Fall of Malcolm McLaren', both 'Part One and 'Part Two'.
15 John Lahr, *Prick Up Your Ears: The Biography of Joe Orton* (Allen Lane, 1978).
16 From the entry in Orton's diary for Monday 9 January, 1967, later published in John Lahr (ed.), *The Orton Diaries* (Methuen, 1986).
17 Black, 1982.
18 Pat Hackett (ed.), *The Andy Warhol Diaries* (Warner Books, 1989), entry for 23 June 1979.
19 Black, 1982.

Chapter 27

1 Transcript, *Blood on the Turntable*.
2 Neri, 'Malcolm McLaren'.
3 Pete Silverton, 'Sun Gold & Piracy: Malcolm's Vision for the 80s', *Sounds* (26 July 1980).
4 Krystyna Kitsis, 'Malcolm McLaren', *ZG #7: Desire* (1981).
5 *Blood on the Turntable*.
6 Watts, 'The Rise and Fall of Malcolm McLaren Part One'.
7 Neri, 'Malcolm McLaren'.
8 *Malcolm McLaren: Artful Dodger*.
9 John May, 'Rock 'n' Roll $windl£', *New Musical Express* (27 October 1979).
10 Black, 1982.
11 Adam Ant, *Stand & Deliver* (Sidgwick & Jackson, 2006).
12 Black, 1982.
13 Black, 1982.
14 Neri, 'Malcolm McLaren'.
15 Quotes from Andy Harries are from an interview with the author, 2019.
16 Ant, *Stand & Deliver*.
17 Culshaw, 'So I Pitched My Oscar Wilde Film'.
18 John Doran, 'Adam Ant: The British Masters Chapter 6', *Noisey* (22 April 2013).
19 Andy Capper, 'Remembering Malcolm McLaren', *Vice* (9 April 2010).
20 *Malcolm McLaren: Artful Dodger*.
21 Dan Graham, 'Malcolm McLaren and the Making of Annabella', in *Impresario: Malcolm McLaren & the British New Wave* (New Museum of Contemporary Art/MIT Press, 1988).
22 Silverton, 'Sun Gold & Piracy'.
23 Though he also claimed that he was inspired by 'Nipper', the little dog in the EMI retail chain HMV's logo, the phrase came from another of McLaren's Let It Rock-era 78s, the call-and-response 'Bow-Wow-Wow', a 1948 B-side by Deek Watson's second Brown Dots group.

24 Silverton, 'Sun Gold & Piracy'.

25 Reid and Savage, *Up They Rise*.

26 Neri, 'Malcolm McLaren'.

Chapter 28

1 Fred Vermorel, 'McLaren Exposed', *Sounds* (11 April 1981).

2 Peter Gordon, wfmu.org.

3 Reid and Savage, *Up They Rise*.

4 Paul Rambali, 'McWowow', *New Musical Express* (14 February 1981).

5 Salewicz, 'Malcolm McLaren'.

6 As cited in Graham, 'Malcolm McLaren'.

7 Salewicz, 'Malcolm McLaren'.

8 Ibid.

9 Vermorel, *Vivienne Westwood*.

10 Vermorel, *Vivienne Westwood*.

11 'Scandal Continues to Stick to Malcolm McLaren', *Smash Hits* (27 November 1980).

12 Vermorel, 'McLaren Exposed'.

13 Salewicz, 'Malcolm McLaren'.

14 Ibid.

15 *The South Bank Show: Malcolm McLaren*.

16 Salewicz, 'Malcolm McLaren'.

17 Jon Savage, 'Vivienne Westwood', *The Face* (January 1981).

18 Robert O'Byrne, *Style City: How London Became a Fashion Capital* (Frances Lincoln, 2009).

19 Tamsin Blanchard, 'A View from the Front Row', *Guardian* (15 February 2018).

20 'In the City' conference.

21 Mulvagh, *Vivienne Westwood* (1998 edition).

22 Mulvagh, *Vivienne Westwood* (1998 edition).

23 Interview with the author, 2014.

24 Mulvagh, *Vivienne Westwood* (1998 edition).

25 *South Bank Show: Malcolm McLaren*.

26 Graham, 'Malcolm McLaren'.

27 Salewicz, 'Malcolm McLaren'.

28 Unless otherwise indicated, quotes from Nick Egan are from an interview with the author, 2019.

29 Interview for *Malcolm McLaren: Musical Paintings*, ScheiblerMitte, Berlin (November 2008).

30 Luke Bainbridge, 'Naked Cover Stars', *Observer* (23 April 2006).

31 Graham, 'Malcolm McLaren'.

32 Steve Taylor, 'Take the Manet and Run', *The Face* (November 1981).

33 Quotes from Michael Holman are from an interview with the author, 2018.

34 *South Bank Show: Malcolm McLaren.*
35 *Beat This: A Hip-Hop History*, dir. Dick Fontaine (BBC, 1984).

Chapter 29
1 Mulvagh, *Vivienne Westwood* (1998 edition).
2 'The Modern Romantics, Cue', *Vogue* (May 1981).
3 Robert Palmer, 'The Latest British Invasion: The New Tribalism', *New York Times* (25 November 1981).
4 Quotes from Leigh Gorman are from an interview with the author, 2019.
5 'Savage' showcard. Courtesy Malcolm McLaren Estate.
6 Interview with the author, 2014.
7 Black, 1982.
8 Ibid.
9 Gordon, wfmu.org.
10 Kitsis, 'Malcolm McLaren'.
11 Trevor Horn, *Record Collector* (June 2019).
12 Black, 1982.
13 Wolfe used the French term '*nostalgia de la boue*' in a 1970 *New York* article, which appeared in an extended format in the eponymous *Radical Chic & Mau-Mauing the Flak-Catchers* (Bantam Books, 1971).
14 Withers, 'From Let It Rock'.
15 Bromberg, *The Wicked Ways* (1989 edition).
16 Malcolm McLaren, 'Nostalgia of Mud' staging notes (March 1982). Courtesy Malcolm McLaren Estate.
17 Mulvagh, *Vivienne Westwood* (1998 edition).
18 Dave McCullough, 'The Prodigal Bison', *Sounds* (4 December 1982).
19 From a keynote address to New Music Seminar, Sheraton Centre Hotel, New York (19 July 1982).
20 Black, 1982.
21 Ibid.
22 *The South Bank Show: Malcolm McLaren.*
23 Roy Spencer, 'Classic Albums: Malcolm McLaren's *Duck Rock*', *MusicRadar* (15 April 2014).
24 Paul Rambali, 'Malcolm McLaren', *The Face* (June 1983).
25 Unless otherwise indicated, quotes from Tony Russell are from an interview with the author, 2019.
26 Tony Russell, 'Haywire in the Hills', *Old Time Music*, no. 39 (Spring 1984).
27 Trevor Horn, *Red Bull Academy Daily* (31 January 2013).
28 'Double Dutch', *New Yorker* (11 March 1974).
29 Laura Schwartzberg, 'Double Dutch's Forgotten Hip-Hop Origins', *Vice* (31 March 2015).
30 Gordon, wfmu.org.
31 *The South Bank Show: Malcolm McLaren.*

32 Ibid.

33 Marek Kohn and Paul Rambali, 'Intro', *The Face* (April 1983).

34 Rambali, 'Malcolm McLaren'.

35 Horn, *Red Bull Academy Daily*.

36 McCullough, 'The Prodigal Bison'.

37 Rambali, 'Malcolm McLaren'.

38 'Punkature' showcard notes (October 1982). Courtesy Malcolm McLaren Estate.

Chapter 30

1 Michael Watts, 'Malcolm McLaren: Proud Pirate of Punk', *The Times* (27 May 1983).

2 Ibid.

3 Neil Tennant, 'The New Adventures of Malcolm McLaren', *Smash Hits* (6 January 1983).

4 Russell, 'Haywire in the Hills'.

5 Interview with the author, 2019.

6 A recording of McLaren's undated appearance on the Charlie Gillett show is available at https://bootsalesounds.blogspot.com/2013/06/charlie-gillett-malcom-mclaren-re-up.html.

7 Some of the Duck Rockers have survived; as of 2013, Ron West had the original one minus the horns; another is in the hands of a Japanese collector; and one which appeared in a 1980s Dutch TV advert for a yoghurt drink, resides in an American collection.

8 Quotes from Simon Withers are from interviews with the author, 2016 and 2019.

9 Ziggy Oh, 'Interview with Keith Haring', *Crowd Magazine* (March 1984).

10 'Svengali Steps Out', *Time Out* (6 May 1983).

11 Interview with Mark Goodman, *MTV News* (1984).

12 Oh, 'Interview with Keith Haring'.

13 Mulvagh, *Vivienne Westwood* (1998 edition).

14 See Mulvagh, *Vivienne Westwood* (1998 edition), pp. 175–7 for a portrait of Ness.

15 Helen Roberts, 'Style', *The Face* (April 1983).

16 Rambali, 'Malcolm McLaren'.

17 Bromberg, *The Wicked Ways* (1989 edition).

18 'Duck for the Oyster' New York shoot notes (1983). Courtesy Malcolm McLaren Estate.

19 Paolo Hewitt, 'Herbie Rides Again', *New Musical Express* (6 August 1983).

20 Gordon, wfmu.org.

21 David Johnson, 'Intro', *The Face* (December 1983).

22 David Johnson, 'Autumn in Paris', *The Face* (December 1983)

23 Johnson, 'Intro'.

24 David Johnson, 'Worlds End ... the Big Showdown', *Evening Standard* (4 November 1983).

25 Mulvagh, *Vivienne Westwood* (1998 edition).

26 Danny 'Shredder' Weizman, 'Malcolm McLaren: Building Better Bandwagons', *LA Weekly* (22 March 1985).

27 'In the City' conference.

28 Jim Sullivan, 'Malcolm McLaren's New Wave', *Boston Globe* (20 February 1985).

29 Ibid.

30 Ibid.

31 From an interview with Malcolm McLaren, August 1984, torpedothearkblogspot.com (24 April 2015).

32 Glenn O'Brien, 'Mozart, Puccini, Bizet and McLaren', *Artforum* (December 1984).

33 *The South Bank Show: Malcolm McLaren.*

34 Harold Loren, 'Media Artist + Filmmaker: Nick Egan', haroldloren.com (December 2015).

35 O'Brien, 'Mozart'.

36 Mark Leviton, 'Malcolm McLaren: The Great Opera Swindle', *BAM* (June 1985).

37 O'Brien, 'Mozart'.

38 Weizman, 'Malcolm McLaren'.

39 Sullivan, 'Malcolm McLaren's New Wave'.

Chapter 31

1 Dylan Jones, 'Lost in Love', *i-D* (April 1987).

2 Ibid.

3 Bromberg, *The Wicked Ways* (1989 edition).

4 Ibid.

5 Culshaw, 'So I Pitched My Oscar Wilde Film'.

6 Quotes from Menno Meyjes are from an interview with the author, 2019.

7 Bromberg, *The Wicked Ways* (1989 edition).

8 Leviton, 'Malcolm McLaren'.

9 Journalist Ernest Ingersoll in *Scribner's Monthly* as quoted in David M. Friedman, *Wilde in America* (New York: Norton & Company, 2014).

10 Quotes from Paige Simpson are from an interview with the author, 2019.

11 Lauren Hutton, 'The Malcolm McLaren I Knew', *Guardian* (12 December 2010).

12 Jones, 'Lost in Love'.

13 Hutton, 'The Malcolm McLaren I Knew'.

14 Jones, 'Lost in Love'.

15 Anthony Kiedis and Larry Sloman, *Scar Tissue* (New York: Hyperion, 2004).

16 Unless otherwise indicated quotes from Craig Bromberg are from an interview with the author, 2018.

17 From the preface and acknowledgements, *Impresario: Malcolm McLaren & the British New Wave* (New Museum of Contemporary Art/MIT Press, 1988).

18 Jones, 'Lost in Love'.

19 Quotes from Alan Moore are from an interview with the author, 2019.

20 *The Burgess Variations*, episode 2, dir. Nigel Finch (BBC2, November 2002).

21 As recorded in an opening section of Bromberg, *The Wicked Ways* (1989 edition).

22 See, for example: 'Petition to wind up Glitterbest Ltd', No. 006742, Royal Courts of Justice (25 November 1985).

23 Dylan Jones, 'Lydon on Lager', *i-D* (March 1986).

24 Jones, *Lonely Boy*.

25 Savage, *England's Dreaming*.

26 Ibid.

27 Vyner, *Groovy Bob*.

28 Culshaw, 'So I Pitched My Oscar Wilde Film'.

29 Mark Blake, *Bring It on Home: Peter Grant, Led Zeppelin and Beyond* (Constable, 2018).

30 Jones, 'Lost in Love'.

31 Larry Wilson, 'The Godfather of Punk', *Pasadena Weekly* (11 September 1986).

32 Tim Lawrence, *Hold Onto Your Dreams: Arthur Russell and the Downtown Music Scene 1973–92* (Duke University Press, 2009).

33 Mark Lindores, 'Life's a Ball: A Brief History of Voguing', *Mixmag* (10 October 2018).

34 Interview for *Fashion TV*, New York (1989).

35 Peter Culshaw, 'Malcolm McLaren: 1946–2010', *The Arts Desk* (9 April 2010).

Chapter 32

1 Jones, 'Lost in Love'.

2 Ibid.

3 Mulvagh, *Vivienne Westwood* (1998 edition).

4 Kathryn Flett, 'Vivienne Westwood', *The Face* (May 1987).

5 Vermorel, *Sex Pistols* (1987 edition).

6 Dan Graham, *Two-Way Mirror Power: Selected Writings of Dan Graham from His Art* (MIT Press, 2000).

7 Martin Power, *Hot Wired Guitar: The Life of Jeff Beck* (Omnibus, 2012).

8 Tom Hibbert, 'Malcolm McLaren: Pernicious? Moi?', *Q* (August 1989).

9 'Bassist Bootsy Collins Stages His Return', *Los Angeles Times* (22 December 1990).

10 Mike Mettler, 'Sweet Sonic Dream Mixes Are Made of Dave Stewart', *The Sound Barde* (10 February 2016).

11 Richard Stengel, 'And Bad Teeth: Why the British Love LA, Why LA Loves the British', *Spy* (September 1988).

12 *Playbill*, vol. 88, no. 6 (June 1988).

13 Taylor, 'The Impresario of Do-It-Yourself'.

14 Unless otherwise indicated, quotes from Jane Withers are from an interview with the author, 2019.

15 Peter Schjeldahl, 'Impresario: Malcolm McLaren & the British New Wave', *7 Days* (12 October 1988).

16 Michael Gross, 'Pagan's Progress', *New York* (12 September 1988).

17 *Rapido TV* (BBC Two, 10 November 1988)

18 Hibbert, 'Malcolm McLaren'.

19 Jones, 'Lost in Love'.

20 *The Last Resort with Jonathan Ross*, dir. Andy Harries (Channel 4, 17 December 1988).

21 Ginny Dougary, 'Who Wants to Be Good?', *The Times* (9 March 2006).

22 Ibid.

23 Natasha Fraser-Cavassoni, *After Andy: Adventures in Warhol Land* (Blue Rider Press, 2017).

24 Gross, 'Pagan's Progress'.

25 Chi Chi Valenti, 'Nations', *Details* (October 1988).

26 Mark Lindores, 'Life's a Ball', *Mixmag* (10 October 2018).

27 'Waltz Darling Released', *People* (16 October 1989).

Chapter 33

1 Chrissy Iley, 'Lauren Hutton's Life After Death', *Sunday Independent* (9 May 2010).

2 All quotes from Eugenia Melián are from email exchanges with the author, 2019.

3 Dougary, 'Who Wants to Be Good?'.

4 Culshaw, interview transcript (2004).

5 Postcard, Malcolm McLaren to his father (August 1989).

6 Culshaw, interview transcript (2004).

7 Letter, Malcolm McLaren to his father (30 May 1990).

8 Ibid.

9 'In the City' conference.

10 Ibid.

11 Blake, *Bring It on Home.*

12 Van Bennekom and Jonkers, *Fantastic Man.*

13 Culshaw, 'So I Pitched My Oscar Wilde Film'.

14 Eva MacSweeney, 'McLaren's Clarion Call', *Vogue* (June 1994).

Chapter 34

1 John Fairchild, *Chic Savages* (Simon & Schuster, 1989).
2 Mulvagh, *Vivienne Westwood* (1998 edition).
3 MacSweeney, 'McLaren's Clarion Call'.
4 Haidee Findlay-Levin, 'Paris: Malcolm McLaren in conversation with Haidee Findlay-Levin', *Acne Paper*, no. 8 (Summer 2009).
5 As cited by Eugenia Melián, November 2019.
6 Findlay-Levin, 'Paris'.
7 Ibid.
8 Robin Millar, 'In Paris with Malcolm McLaren', in his autobiography 'A Diamond Life' (undated), http://robinmillar.org.uk/autobiography/malcolm-mclaren.
9 MacSweeney, 'McLaren's Clarion Call'.
10 Millar, 'In Paris with Malcolm McLaren'.
11 Ibid.
12 MacSweeney, 'McLaren's Clarion Call'.
13 Jez Butterworth, 'Who Knows Where Plays Come From?', nickhernbooksblog.com (31 October 2013).
14 Quotes from Charlotte Skene Catling are from an interview with the author, 2019.
15 Interview with the author, 2019.
16 Alex Williams, 'More Cash from Chaos', *New York* (17 April 1995).
17 *The New Music* (ABC, 1994).

Chapter 35

1 Mulvagh, *Vivienne Westwood* (1998 edition).
2 'I have kept in storage all patterns all samples and his personal scribbles, approximately 250 pieces, this was his life's work.' Derek Dunbar email to the author (25 June 2013).
3 Culshaw, interview transcript (2004).
4 Unless otherwise indicated, quotes by Peter Culshaw are from interviews with the author, 2018–19.
5 Ben Thompson, 'The Interview: Malcolm McLaren', *Independent* (23 June 1996).
6 Ibid.
7 Andrew Wilson, 'Introduction', *I Groaned with Pain* (Stolper-Wilson, 1996).
8 Video interview, *I Groaned with Pain*, Eagle Gallery (London, 1996).
9 Interview with Ariel Van Straten for *Don't Tell It* (London, 1996).
10 Quotes from Graham Brown-Martin are from an interview with the author, 2016.
11 Malcolm McLaren, 'Elements of Anti-Style', *New Yorker* (22 September 1997).
12 Dougary, 'Who Wants to be Good?'.
13 Quotes from Henri Struck are from an interview with the author, 2019.

14 'The Latest Girl Band Set to Storm the Charts', Reuters (4 March 1998).

Chapter 36

1 van Bennekom and Jonkers, *Fantastic Man*.
2 Malcolm McLaren, 'Selling Jungk', *Punch* (February 1998).
3 Malcolm McLaren, '8-Bit Punk', *Wired* (November 2003).
4 McLaren, 'Selling Jungk'.
5 Kate Spicer, 'The Kate of Kuala Lumpur', *Independent* (16 November 1997).
6 Lisa Verrico, 'Wok 'n' Roll', Lisa Verrico, *Sunday Times Style* (1 February 1998).
7 McLaren, 'Selling Jungk'.
8 Jane Hughes, 'Culture Melt', *Newsweek* (15 December 1997).
9 'The Latest Girl Band', Reuters.
10 TV interview for Reuters (17 February 1998).
11 Alan McGee with Luke Brown, *Creation Stories* (Sidgwick & Jackson, 2013).
12 As quoted in Kwok-kan Tam, *The Englishicized Subject: Postcolonial Writings In Hong Kong, Singapore and Malaysia* (Springer, 2019).
13 Wyn Davies's May 2010 notes on the project are on his YouTube channel, https://www.youtube.com/watch?v=a9xWHQ-RhXE.
14 Katja Neumann, 'Stephen Williams', *Dear Magazin* (25 July 2007).
15 TV interview for Reuters (16 October 1999).
16 Culshaw, 'Malcolm McLaren'.
17 Malcolm McLaren, 'My Vision for London', *New Statesman* (20 December 1999).
18 McGee, *Creation Stories*.
19 McLaren, 'My Vision for London'.
20 Ed Main, 'McLaren's Web of Wonder', *BBC News* (10 February 2000).
21 'Punk Godfather Joins Mayor Race', *BBC News* (17 December 1999).
22 Mark Beasley, 'Malcolm McLaren: Remembering the Unruly Entrepreneur, Artist and Self-styled Godfather of Punk', *Frieze* (12 April 2010).
23 Interview with the author, 2019.
24 Auberon Waugh, 'From the Pulpit', *Literary Review* (December 1999).

Chapter 37

1 Main, 'McLaren's Web of Wonder'.
2 *Open House with Gloria Hunniford* (Channel 5, undated, January 2000).
3 Deeson, 'Malcolm McLaren'.
4 Young Kim, 'Mr Mischief', *Vogue*, Special Edition: Met Gala (2013).
5 van Bennekom and Jonkers, *Fantastic Man*.
6 Glenn O'Brien, 'Malcolm McLaren', *Interview* (24 November 2008).
7 Malcolm McLaren CV, 2000.
8 Deeson, 'Malcolm McLaren'.

9 Geoffrey McNab, 'Malcolm McLaren: Master and Servant', *Independent* (31 May 2002).

10 Lynn Yaeger, 'Radical Party', *Village Voice* (17 October 2000).

11 Christoph Grunenberg and Max Hollein, 'Foreword', *Shopping: A Century of Art and Consumer Culture* (Tate Liverpool/Schirn Kunsthalle Frankfurt, Hatje Cantz Publishers, 2002).

12 Young Kim, 'Mr Mischief'.

13 McLaren, '8-Bit Punk'.

14 McNab, 'Malcolm McLaren'.

15 Ibid.

Chapter 38

1 Emerson Rosenthal, 'On Its 25th Birthday, Game Boy Is Alive and Well in the Art World', *Vice* (21 April 2014).

2 McLaren, '8-Bit Punk'.

3 Gareth Morris, Open letter to Malcolm McLaren (April 2004), http://micro-music.net.

4 Kevin Driscoll and Joshua Diaz, 'Endless Loop: A Brief History of Chiptunes', in Rebecca Carlson (ed.), 'Games as Transformative Works', *Transformative Works and Cultures*, no. 2 (2009).

5 Culshaw, 'So I Pitched My Oscar Wilde Film'.

6 Culshaw, interview transcript (2004).

7 Peter Goff, 'Malcolm in the Middle', *South China Morning Post* (3 October 2003).

8 Culshaw, 'So I Pitched My Oscar Wilde Film'.

9 Ibid.

10 First printed in *New York World* (20 January 1928).

11 Letter from Malcolm McLaren to Mary Butler (26 March 2004).

12 Letter from Claire Wilcox to Les Molloy (27 February 2004).

13 Press release, Office of Malcolm McLaren (31 March 2004).

14 Letter from Claire Wilcox to Malcolm McLaren (19 March 2004).

15 Letter from Malcolm McLaren to Claire Wilcox (18 March 2004).

16 'Westwood's Ex "Written Out of History"', *Daily Telegraph* (5 June 2004).

17 Theresa Duncan, 'Game Boy Music', *Artforum* (May 2004).

18 Van Bennekom and Jonkers, *Fantastic Man*.

19 'Has Anybody Here Seen My Old Friend Martin?', *T Magazine* (13 March 2005).

20 Van Bennekom and Jonkers, *Fantastic Man*.

Chapter 39

1 Ibid.

2 Ibid.

3 'Has Anybody Here Seen My Old Friend Martin?'

4 *Jonesy's Jukebox* (6 May 2005).

5 Adrian Dannatt, 'Philippe Bradshaw: Artist Whose Work Was "Absolutely Mad"' (16 September 2005).

6 'Composer's Complaint Dismissed', *L'Obs* (25 November 2005).

7 Eric Wilson, 'From Punks to Children', *New York Times* (22 December 2005).

8 'A1 Most: Fashionbeast Clothing by Malcolm McLaren' (22 December 2005), https://daddytypes.com/2005/12/22/al-most_fashionbeast_8-bit_clothing_by_malcolm_mclaren.php.

9 Dougary, 'Who Wants to Be Good?'.

10 'Trouble at the Met: Status of Half of the Punk Collection Downgraded But Dubious Designs Continue to Toxify Costume Institute Collection', paulgor-manis.com (2 September 2014).

11 Nancy Jo Sales, 'The Golden Suicides', *Vanity Fair* (January 2008).

12 Ibid.

13 Deven Golden, 'Notes on Jeremy Blake', artcritical.com (February 2004).

14 Sales, 'The Golden Suicides'.

15 Dan Levin, 'After Death, Unfinished Artwork Gets a Life', *New York Times* (29 November 2007).

16 *Wild Choir: Cinematic Portraits by Jeremy Blake*, Corcoran Gallery, Washington, DC (February–March 2008).

17 Charles Darwent, 'Jeremy Blake: Creator of Moving Paintings', *Independent* (9 September 2007).

Chapter 40

1 'Anarchy in Gardenstown: How Sex Pistols Guru Was Thrown Out of a Highland Village', *Scotsman* (7 May 2007).

2 Nigel Farndale, 'Malcolm McLaren: Punk? It Made My Day', *Daily Telegraph* (30 September 2007).

3 Press release, *Shallow*, I-20 Gallery, New York (15 September–27 October 2007).

4 McLaren, 'Introduction', *Musical Paintings*.

5 O'Brien, 'Malcolm McLaren'.

6 Matthew Collings, *Blimey! From Bohemia to Britpop: The London Artworld from Francis Bacon to Damien Hirst* (21 Publishing, 1997).

7 O'Brien, 'Malcolm McLaren'.

8 'Malcolm McLaren Reveals Why He Quit: "I'm a Celeb Is a Fake"', *Daily Mail* (13 November 2007).

9 Quotes from James Dearlove are from an interview with the author, 2018.

10 O'Brien, 'Malcolm McLaren'.

11 Ibid.

12 McLaren, 'Introduction', *Musical Paintings*.

13 'Drink the New Wine: David Byrne & Malcolm McLaren', *Creative Time* (2008).

14 Malcolm McLaren, 'Malcolm McLaren Talks about "Shallow"', *Artforum* (16 July 2008).

15 Beasley, 'Malcolm McLaren'.

16 McLaren, 'Malcolm McLaren Talks about "Shallow"'.

17 'Malcolm McLaren: A Statement', rockpopfashion.com (2 August 2008).

Chapter 41

1 Bernd Wurlitzer in Malcolm McLaren (ed.), *Musical Paintings* (JRP–Ringier, 2009).

2 McLaren, 'Introduction', *Musical Paintings*.

3 Ibid.

4 David Thorp, 'Joining the Dots', *Eyes for Blowing Up Bridges: Joining the Dots from the Situationist International to Malcolm McLaren* (John Hansard Gallery, 2015).

5 'The Diary: Malcolm McLaren', *Financial Times* (1 August 2009).

6 Email, Malcolm McLaren to James Jebbia and Supreme executives (22 September 2009).

7 Email to the author, 2019.

8 'The Diary: Malcolm McLaren' (1 August 2009).

9 Evan Moffitt, 'A Portrait of the Curator as the Young Grebo Rocker', *Garage* (7 September 2017).

10 Bruce Dessau, 'Anarchy-influenced Lecture from Malcolm McLaren', *Evening Standard* (24 August 2009).

11 Hazel Mollison, 'McLaren Reads Riot Act Over Show Censorship', *Scotland on Sunday* (23 August 2009).

12 'The Diary: Malcolm McLaren' (1 August 2009).

13 Adrian Dannatt, 'McLaren and the "Dear Leader"', *Art Newspaper* (September 2009).

14 'The Diary: Malcolm McLaren' (26 September 2009).

15 Emily Dugan, 'Asbestos from His Punk Shop Killed McLaren', *Independent* (11 April 2010).

Chapter 42

1 David Frisby, *Fragments of Modernity: Theories of Modernity in the Work of Simmel, Kracauer and Benjamin* (MIT Press, 1986).

2 Elizabeth Thompson, 'Malcolm McLaren on Paris, Capital of the XXIst Century and his Dior Musical', *Paper* (19 February 2010).

3 Ibid.

4 Greil Marcus, 'Sale of the Century: Malcolm McLaren's Paris, Capital of the XXIst Century', *Artforum* (March 2010).

5 Ibid.

6 'Malcolm McLaren: Synthesizer Of Genius', Judith Thurman, *The New Yorker* (8 April 2008).

7 Malcolm McLaren, 'Never Mind the Bollocks, Here's the Txt Pistols', Barbican Brewery, London (5 October 2009).

8 Jonathan Brown, 'Malcolm McLaren: "I'm Most Probably a Missing Link"', *Independent* (27 November 2009).

9 'The Diary: Malcolm McLaren', *Financial Times* (2 January 2010).

10 Thompson, 'Malcolm McLaren on Paris'.

11 Christine Muhlke, 'Requiem for Malcolm: McLaren's Last Mix', *New York Times* (9 April 2010).

Epilogue

1 'Malcolm McLaren's Girlfriend Opens Up About Will Battle', *Daily Mail* (10 July 2013).

2 Wendy Leigh, 'Why Sex Pistols Manager . . .', *Telegraph*, (27 November 2015).

3 Beasley, 'Malcolm McLaren'.

Index